Madrid

timeout.com/madrid

Published by Time Out Guides Ltd, a wholly owned subsidiary of Time Out Group Ltd.
Time Out and the Time Out logo are trademarks of Time Out Group Ltd.

© Time Out Group Ltd 2007
Previous editions 1995, 1997, 1999, 2000, 2002, 2004

10 9 8 7 6 5 4 3 2 1

This edition first published in Great Britain in 2007 by Ebury Publishing
Ebury Publishing is a division of The Random House Group Ltd,
20 Vauxhall Bridge Road, London SW1V 2SA

Random House Australia Pty Limited 20 Alfred Street, Milsons Point, Sydney, New South Wales 2061, Australia
Random House New Zealand Limited 18 Poland Road, Glenfield, Auckland 10, New Zealand
Random House South Africa (Pty) Limited Isle of Houghton, Corner Boundary
Road & Carse O'Gowrie, Houghton 2198, South Africa

Random House UK Limited Reg. No. 954009

For details of distribution in the Americas, see www.timeout.com

ISBN 10: 1-904978-62-2
ISBN 13: 978190497 8626

A CIP catalogue record for this book is available from the British Library

Printed and bound in Germany by Appl

The Random House Group Limited makes every effort to ensure that the papers used in our books are made from
trees that have been legally sourced from well-managed and credibly certified forests.   Our paper procurement policy
can be found on www.randomhouse.co.uk.

Time Out Guides Limited
Universal House
251 Tottenham Court Road
London W1T 7AB
Tel + 44 (0)20 7813 3000
Fax + 44 (0)20 7813 6001
Email guldes@timeout.com
www.timeout.com

Editorial

Editor Sally Davies
Deputy Editor Simon Cuppock
Copy Editors Ismay Atkins, Phil Harriss
Consultant Editors Harvey Holtom, Simon Hunter
Listings Editor Kristen Bernardi, Alex Phillips
Proofreader Gill Harvey
Indexer James Mitchell

Managing Director Peter Fiennes
Financial Director Gareth Garner
Editorial Director Ruth Jarvis
Deputy Series Editor Dominic Earle
Editorial Manager Holly Pick

Design

Art Director Scott Moore
Art Editor Pinelope Kourmouzoglou
Senior Designer Josephine Spencer
Graphic Designer Henry Elphick
Junior Graphic Designer Kei Ishimaru
Digital Imaging Simon Foster
Ad Make-up Jenni Prichard

Picture Desk

Picture Editor Jael Marschner
Deputy Picture Editor Tracey Kerrigan
Picture Researcher Helen McFarland

Advertising

Sales Director Mark Phillips
International Sales Manager Fred Durman
International Sales Consultant Ross Canadé
International Sales Executive Simon Davies
Advertising Sales (Madrid) InMadrid
Advertising Assistant Kate Staddon

Marketing

Group Marketing Director John Luck
Marketing Manager Yvonne Poon
Sales and Marketing Director North America Lisa Levinson

Production

Group Production Director Mark Lamond
Production Manager Brendan McKeown
Production Coordinator Caroline Bradford

Time Out Group

Chairman Tony Elliott
Financial Director Richard Waterlow
Time Out Magazine Ltd MD David Pepper
Group General Manager/Director Nichola Coulthard
Time Out Communications Ltd MD David Pepper
Time Out International MD Cathy Runciman
Group Art Director John Oakey
Group IT Director Simon Chappell

Contributors

Introduction David Lennard. **History** Nick Rider (*The Family of Charles IV* Clayton Maxwell). **Architecture** Harvey Holtom (*Going spaces* Nick Funnell). **Madrid Today** David Lennard (*Mayor at work* Simon Hunter). **Seeing the Bulls** Robert Elms. **Movida Movies** Rob Stone (*All very Welles* Nick Funnell). **Flamenco** Rob Stone. **Where to Stay** Helen Jones, Danny Wood. **Sightseeing** Harvey Holtom, Sally Davies, Robert Latona (*Weird wheels and wonderful stories* Simon Hunter; *Life and death* Richard Schweid; *Poetry of the absurd, The quick and the dead* Michael Jacobs; *El Salón del Prado* Clayton Maxwell; *A heap of faith* Annie Bennett; *Garden of enlightenment* Nick Rider; *From the Nile to Parque Oeste* Nick Funnell). **Restaurants** Clayton Maxwell, Sally Davies (*Sign language* Simon Hunter). **Tapas** Sally Davies (*Sunday best* Clayton Maxwell). **Cafés & Bars** Sally Davies (*Tertulias* Michael Jacobs; *The grape and the good* Clayton Maxwell). **Shops & Services** Harvey Holtom, Simon Hunter (*Blanket band* Helen Jones). **Festivals & Events** Harvey Holtom (*Burial of the Sardine* Clayton Maxwell). **Children** Andrew Wallace. **Film** Rob Stone. **Galleries** Clayton Maxwell. **Gay & Lesbian** Barry Byrne, Pablo Espinoza, Jimmy Shaw (*Taking Pride* Simon Hunter). **Music** *Classical & Opera* Delaina Haslam; *Rock, Roots & Jazz* Simon Hunter (*Noise in the hood* David Oancia). **Nightlife** Simon Hunter. **Sport & Fitness** Alex Leith (*Splash out* Clayton Maxwell). **Theatre & Dance** Delaina Haslam (*Merely Players* Harvey Holtom). **Trips out of Town** Sally Davies (*View of Toledo* Nadia Feddo, *Spires and tyres* Annie Bennett, *Garden airs* Nick Funnell). **Directory** Nathalie Pédestarres (*Mind your queues and peeing* Simon Hunter). **Additional reviews throughout** Sally Davies, Simon Hunter.

Maps maps@tribalwerks.com.ar. Pages 320 & 334 JS Graphics (john@jsgraphics.co.uk); page 335 courtesy of Renfe; page 336 courtesy of Consorcio de Transportes de Madrid.

Photography by Jon Santa Cruz, except: pages 13, 14, 29, 285 Getty Images; page 15 Topfoto; pages 16, 171 Aisa; page 19 Museo Municipal Madrid/The Bridgeman Art Library; pages 20, 206 Topham Picturepoint; page 24 Sotheby's/akg-images; pages 26, 80, 82, 83, 85 Museo Del Prado; page 46 Image.net; pages 47, 282 Nick Funnell; page 71 Rafael Vargas; page 204 Turespaña; page 281 4Corners Images.

The following images were provided by the featured establishments/artists: pages 81, 208, 260.

The Editor would like to thank Laura Cuenca at the Patronato de Turismo de Madrid, Gema Sese at the Thyssen, Teodoro García at the Reina Sofía, Concha Vela and Charo Lapausa Pintado at the Prado, María Najera, Leticia Saharrea, Pepe García, Montse Planas, Dez Petrie and Charlotte Thomas. Special thanks to John O'Donovan.

Contents

Introduction

Madrid has had a host of identities since men first settled the fortifiable site by the shallow River Manzanares. From Roman waystation and Arab garrison town to the hub of perhaps the most powerful global empire the world has known, and from there to a war-torn wasteland – few other European capitals can claim a past anything like as chequered. Its history is a complex mosaic of peoples and cultures, and its present reflects that complexity.

In the 21st century, the city is re-inventing itself yet again, and exploring Madrid today brings the visitor face to face with all the achievements and dilemmas of '*la transición*': the post-Franco explosion of ideas and expression of newfound freedom. Nowadays the heart of Spain is throbbing to the rhythm of a fresh pacemaker. There are new inhabitants, new infrastructure and new habits, bound together by an enduring sense of historical continuity. The old and the new are bubbling together, mostly harmoniously, and *madrileños* are as interested to see the results as any visitor.

Reminders of the past are everywhere and it's hard to know where to begin: you can't ignore the Prado, Thyssen or Reina Sofía,

housing some of the finest collections of art anywhere in Europe, and Sunday isn't Sunday in Madrid without a visit to the Rastro fleamarket and a leisurely breakfast vermouth in a nearby bar. 'Madrid de Los Austrias', the grand Habsburg-created area east of the Plaza Mayor, breathes the 17th and 18th centuries from every cobble, while the Retiro beckons with its acres of green space and neatly manicured walkways.

But the now clamours for attention as well: the Jean Nouvel-designed extension to the Reina Sofía museum, opened in 2005, is as courageously incongruous as it is successful, and the renovation and pedestrianisation of the network of narrow streets round the Puerta del Sol have made walking through the area infinitely more pleasant. Even Richard Rogers' award-winning new terminal at Barajas airport is worth a shuttle ride when you arrive.

New investment, fresh faces and what seems to be a never-ending economic boom have energised Madrid and its inhabitants. The city continues to relish its substance and renew its form. If you've never been, it's a must. If you knew it before, you'll be astonished at the changes.

ABOUT TIME OUT CITY GUIDES

This is the seventh edition of *Time Out Madrid* one of an expanding series of Time Out guides produced by the people behind the successful listings magazines in London, New York and Chicago. Our guides are all written by resident experts who have striven to provide you with all the most up-to-date information you'll need to explore the city or read up on its background, whether you're a local or a first-time visitor.

THE LIE OF THE LAND

We have divided the city into areas – simplified, for convenience, from the full complexity of Madrid's geography – and the relevant area name is given with each venue listed in this guide (for an overview of the neighourhood names used, see p320). And there is also a series of fully indexed colour street maps, a map of the surrounding countryside and maps of the metro and local train network at the back of the guide, starting on p321. Marked on the street maps are the specific locations of hotels (❶), restaurants (❶), tapas bars (❶) and cafés and bars (❶).

Mail addresses in Spain include a five-digit postcode, which for Madrid always begins 28 and is written before the name of the city (as in 28014 Madrid). We have given these codes for organisations or venues you might need to write to, such as hotels.

ESSENTIAL INFORMATION

For all the practical information you might need for visiting the area – including visa and customs information, details of local transport, a listing of emergency numbers, information on local weather and a selection of useful websites – turn to the Directory at the back of this guide. It begins on page 291.

THE LOWDOWN ON THE LISTINGS

We have tried to make this book as easy to use as possible. Addresses, phone numbers, bus information, opening times and admission prices are all included in the listings. However, businesses can change their arrangements at any time. Before you go out of your way, we'd strongly advise you to phone ahead to check opening times and other particulars. While

every effort and care has been made to ensure the accuracy of the information contained in this guide, the publishers cannot accept responsibility for any errors it may contain.

PRICES AND PAYMENT

We have noted where venues such as shops, hotels, restaurants and theatres accept the following credit cards: American Express (AmEx), Diners Club (DC), MasterCard (MC) and Visa (V). Many will also accept euro travellers' cheques, and/or other cards such as Carte Blanche.

The prices we've listed in this guide should be treated as guidelines, not gospel. If prices vary wildly from those we've quoted, ask whether there's a good reason. If not, go elsewhere. Then please let us know. We aim to give the best and most up-to-date advice, so we want to know if you've been badly treated or overcharged.

Advertisers

We would like to stress that no establishment has been included in this guide because it has advertised in any of our publications and no payment of any kind has influenced any review. The opinions given in this book are those of Time Out writers and entirely independent.

TELEPHONE NUMBERS

It is necessary to dial provincial area codes with all numbers in Spain, even for local calls. Hence all normal Madrid numbers begin 91, whether or not you're callling from outside the city. From abroad you must dial the international code, followed by 34 for Spain, then the 91.

To dial numbers as given in this book from abroad, use your country's exit code (00 in the UK, 011 in the US), followed by the country code for Spain (34), and then the 91.

MAPS

We've included a series of fully indexed colour maps to the centre of the city at the back of this guide – they start on p320 – and, where possible, we've printed a grid reference against all venues that appear on the maps.

LET US KNOW WHAT YOU THINK

We hope you enjoy *Time Out Madrid*, and we'd like to know what you think of it. We welcome tips for places that you consider we should include in future editions and take note of your criticism of our choices. You can email us at guides@timeout.com.

> There is an online version of this book, along with guides to over 100 international cities, at **www.timeout.com**.

Time Out
Travel Guides

Worldwide

All our guides are written by a team of local experts with a unique and stylish insider perspective. We offer essential tips, trusted advice and honest reviews for everything you need to know in the city.

Over 50 destinations available at all good bookshops and at timeout.com/shop

Time Out Guides

In Context

Features

Palacio de Comunicaciones.
See p113.

History

From shanty town to imperial capital in seven easy centuries.

Around 100 years after Madrid had become capital of the Spanish Empire on the whim of Philip II, an attempt was made to construct an ancient past for it, and writers developed the story of its descent from a Roman city called Mantua Carpetana. Though there were Roman towns nearby at Alcalá de Henares (Complutum) and Toledo (Toletum), and Roman villas along the valley of the Manzanares, there is no real evidence that there was ever a local Mantua, or that any of these settlements was the origin of modern Madrid. The story of Mantua Carpetana, however, served to obscure the insignificance of Madrid before Philip II moved his Court here in 1561, and above all the embarrassing fact that it was founded by Muslims: specifically, in about 860, during the reign of Mohammed I, fifth Emir of Córdoba.

ARABIAN SIGHTS

Following their eruption into the Iberian peninsula in 711, the Arab armies did not occupy the inhospitable lands north of the Sierra de Guadarrama, but established a frontier more or less along the old Roman road linking Mérida, Toledo and Saragossa. The original *qasr* (a word absorbed into Spanish as Alcázar) or fortress of Madrid was one of a string of watchtowers built north of this line in the ninth century, as Christian raids into Al-Andalus became more frequent. The rocky crag on which it stood, where the Palacio Real is today, was ideal for the purpose, since it had a view of the main tracks south from the Guadarrama. It also had excellent water, from underground streams within the rock. Madrid's original Arabic name, Mayrit or Magerit, means 'place of many springs'.

Mayrit became more than just a fortress, with an outer citadel, the eastern wall of which ran along the modern C/Factor, and a wider town or *medina* bounded by the Plaza de la Villa and C/Segovia. A section of wall, the Muralla Arabe on Cuesta de la Vega, and the remains currently being excavated next to the Palacio Real are the only remnants of Muslim Madrid visible in the

Ferdinand and Isabella bid Columbus farewell. *See p15.*

modern city. Both citadel and *medina* consisted of a mass of narrow alleys, like the old quarters of North African cities today.

Mayrit was attacked by Christian armies in 932 and 1047, and in the 970s was used by the great minister of Córdoba, Al-Mansur, as a base for his celebrated 100 campaigns against the north. By the 11th century it had a population of around 7,000, among them Abul-Qasim Maslama, mathematician, astronomer, translator of Greek literature and experimenter in magic.

CHRISTIAN CONQUEST
In the 11th century the Caliphate of Córdoba disintegrated into a mass of petty princedoms called *taifas*, and Mayrit became part of the Emirate of Toledo. In 1086 Alfonso VI of Castile was able to take advantage of this situation to conquer Toledo, and with it Madrid. The town's main mosque became the church of Santa María de la Almudena, which would survive until the 19th century. For many years, however, Madrid would remain on the front line. In 1109 it was again besieged, by a Moorish army that camped below the Alcázar in the place ever since known as Campo del Moro (Field of the Moor). A new wall was built, enclosing the area between the Alcázar and Plaza Isabel II, Plaza San Miguel and Plaza Humilladero.

Christian Madrid was a very rural town, and most of the population who worked did so on the land. Madrid did acquire large religious houses, notably the Friary of San Francisco, where the church of San Francisco el Grande still stands, supposedly founded by St Francis of Assisi in 1217. Madrid was still not entirely Christian, however. Many Muslims, known as Mudéjares, had stayed in the conquered areas, retaining their own laws and religion, and were

prized by the Castilian monarchs for their skills as builders and masons, still seen today in the towers of San Nicolás de los Servitas and San Pedro el Viejo. In Madrid they were confined to the area known as the Morería. Medieval Madrid also had a smaller Jewish population, concentrated outside the walls in Lavapiés.

Madrid did finally begin to play more of a role in the affairs of Castile in the 14th century. In 1309 the Cortes or parliament met here for the first time. Medieval Castile did not have a fixed capital, but instead the Court followed the king around the country, and the Cortes met in many different towns at different times. In the 14th and 15th centuries Castile was dogged by a series of social revolts and civil wars, between monarchs, the nobility and rival claimants from the royal family. Against this backdrop Madrid began to gain popularity as a royal residence, a country retreat more than a centre of power.

Political instability did not prevent substantial economic progress in 15th-century Castile, with Madrid becoming a reasonably prosperous trading centre for the first time. Trade outgrew the old market in Plaza de la Villa, and in the 1460s an area east of the 12th-century wall was built up as a ramshackle new market square, the origin of the Plaza Mayor. A new town wall was built, not for defence but so that taxes could be levied on people living in the new parts of the town. Its eastern entrance was a new gate, the Puerta del Sol.

THE CATHOLIC KINGS
The end of the 15th century saw a new era open in Castilian and Spanish history. In 1476 Enrique IV's sister Isabel and her husband Fernando of Aragon succeeded in bringing the civil wars to an end. Their marriage united different Spanish

kingdoms, although each retained its own institutions for another two centuries. Within Castile they established an absolute monarchy and a professional army that enabled them to intervene in the wars of Renaissance Italy. The devout Isabella was one of the instigators of the militant sense of religious mission that marked imperial Spain. Detesting medieval Spain's religious coexistence, she ordered the expulsion of all Jews in 1492 and the forcible conversion of the Mudéjar Muslims in 1502; a reinforced Inquisition policed her measures. Also in 1492 came the conquest of Muslim Granada, winning Ferdinand and Isabella the title 'Most Catholic Kings' from the Pope, and financial support for Columbus's first voyage to America.

Picture this The Majas

In the 18th century, ordinary people in European cities began to look increasingly similar, wearing more or less the same three-cornered hats, breeches and mop-caps. Not so in Madrid, where this was the era of the *majos* and *majas*. A *majo* wore embroidered shirts, a short jacket with a swathe of buttons, a hair-net, and carried a knife. *Majas* wore short, mid-calf skirts with a mass of petticoats, pearl-white stockings, embroidered bodices, an intricately braided hairstyle and a dramatic lace mantilla. They were drawn from trades such as coach-driving, dressmaking, cigarette rolling or market trading and most often from Lavapiés. *Majas* especially were known for their wit, grace and verbal ferocity. In a capital that was still largely a city of servants, but whose servants were renowned for talking back, they deferred to no one.

They were mostly seen in all their finery at fiestas such as the Romería de San Isidro. Goya depicted them often. Also, their cocky elegance led to them being taken up by the upper classes, so that even *grandes dames* like the Duchess of Alba would dress up as *majas*, which is what probably gave rise to the story that Goya's nude and clothed *majas* are portraits of the Duchess herself.

This theory has been discredited by scholars in recent years, but still has many subscribers; the woman depicted does bear a startling resemblance to the Duchess, and the large bow around her waist featured in several of Goya's portraits of her. And, yes, it is possibly true that the Duchess had an affair with the painter, with whom she holed up for several months on one of her country estates after her husband died. It is unlikely, however, that she would allow herself to be painted in such a way, given her standing in society and the certain exposure of the works. Some critics suggest the head was painted on the body later, and this is certainly the visual effect.

What is irrefutable, however, is that Goya was obsessed with Alba, and a more likely explanation for the likeness is simply that he tended to project her image on to an idealised form of female beauty.

Goya's **Clothed Maja** *(below) and* **Nude Maja** *are found at the Prado (see p80).*

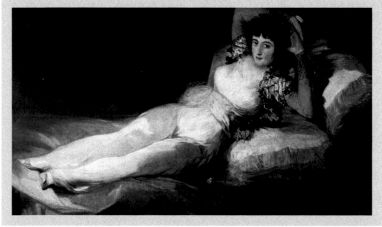

The *pícaro*: illustration from a novel by Francisco de Quevedo. *See p18*.

Madrid retained a degree of royal favour, helped and continued its modest growth, and at the end of the Middle Ages had a population of around 10,000-12,000.

On 11 May 1561 the small-time aristocrats who ran the town of Madrid received a letter from their king, Philip II, warning that he, the entire royal household and all their hundreds of hangers-on would shortly be coming to stay. They immediately set about panic-buying food from surrounding towns, using the money set aside for the fiesta of Corpus Christi, much to the irritation of the local population. No one quite realised, though, that this visit was intended to be a permanent stay.

THE EMPIRE STRIKES OUT

In the previous 50 years the Spanish monarchy had been transformed. Ferdinand and Isabella were succeeded by their grandson Charles of Habsburg (1516-56). Through his father, Philip,

Duke of Burgundy, Charles also inherited Burgundy (the Netherlands and large parts of eastern France) and the Habsburg lands in central Europe, and would in 1519 receive the title Holy Roman Emperor, as Charles V. He would also acquire ever-larger territories in America. Thus Spain became part, and increasingly the centre, of a worldwide empire.

When he first visited Spain in 1517 Charles appointed French speakers to many state posts. This led in 1520 to the revolt of the Comuneros, in which the towns of Castile, Madrid among them, rose up against foreign influence and the encroachment of royal power on their traditional freedoms. However, after this had been suppressed in 1521, Charles came to value Spain – above all Castile – more and more, as the most loyal part of his empire.

Charles and his successors had an immense sense of the greatness of their dynasty and their imperial mission, believing that their vast territories had come to them through providence and that it was their right and duty to defend both them and the Catholic faith. This would involve continual and ever more costly wars, against the French, the Muslim Turks and the northern Protestants. This idea of mission combined perfectly with the crusading, military spirit already imbued in the Castilian Church, army and aristocracy.

Charles V made no attempt to give Castile a capital. However, on his visits to Spain he spent considerable time in Madrid, hunting at El Pardo and giving the town another grand title, Imperial y Coronada (Imperial and Crowned).

CAPITAL IDEA

In 1555 Charles abdicated and the title of Holy Roman Emperor went to his brother Ferdinand, but Spain and Burgundy were passed to Charles's son, Philip II (1556-98). The fundamental figure in Madrid's history, Philip was a deeply pious, shy, austere man. His father had travelled incessantly about his many dominions, and led his armies into battle. Philip, in contrast, ruled his inheritance from behind a desk, as a kind of king-bureaucrat, sometimes dealing with over 400 documents a day. This extraordinary exercise in paperwork naturally required a permanent base.

Moreover, in the 1540s Charles V had introduced Burgundian state ritual into the relatively informal Court of Castile. Every appearance of the monarch followed a set ceremonial order, with a ritual etiquette that became ever more elaborate in succeeding generations as the Habsburgs amplified their idea of their own grandeur. The number of Court attendants mushroomed, making an itinerant Court all the more impractical.

Why Philip chose a town without a cathedral, college or printing press as capital remains unclear. The fact that Madrid was near the centre of the Iberian peninsula probably appealed to him, as he was fascinated by geometry and Renaissance ideas of a king as the 'centre' of the state, but his choice made no economic sense at all, since it gave Spain the only major European capital not on a navigable river. Madrid – which for centuries would normally be referred to in Spain as 'La Corte', the Court, never as a city in its own right, which indeed it wasn't – would be a capital of the monarchy's own creation, a pure expression of royal power.

Having established his ideal capital, Philip did little to build or plan it. He had extended the Alcázar when he was still crown prince, then his attention shifted to El Escorial, where he increasingly spent his time. Royal piety was demonstrated by the endowment of new houses

for religious orders, such as the Descalzas Reales. Philip II founded 17 convents and monasteries in Madrid, Philip III 14 and Philip IV another 17, and they would cover a third of the city until the 19th century. A wider city wall was put up in 1566, and the Puente de Segovia in the 1580s. Philip's favourite architect, Juan de Herrera, planned the rebuilding of the Plaza Mayor, but the only part built during his reign was the Casa de la Panadería in 1590. Philip's idea of a capital seemed more like a collection of royal establishments than a living city.

Reality, however, was more powerful than this rudimentary concept. The establishment of the Court and aristocracy in Madrid – the great centres of consumption and patronage – made it a magnet for people from all over Spain and abroad. The population went from under 20,000 in 1561 to 55,000 in 1584 and close to 85,000 by 1600. Building did not keep up with the influx, and a law decreed that in any house of more than one storey, the upper floor could be requisitioned to house members of the Court. In response, people simply put up houses with only one floor, and much of the new Madrid grew as a mass of shabby, low buildings slapped together out of mud.

This improvised capital did not impress foreign visitors. Lambert Wyts, a Flemish aristocrat who arrived in 1571, said that it was 'the foulest and filthiest town in Spain'. Thick mud made it impossible to ride a horse down the main streets in winter until a few cobbles were put down in the 1580s. There were no drains of any kind, and the streets were full of waste thrown out of the houses every night, producing an 'unbearable stench'.

Madrid had taken on a characteristic that would stay with it to this day – that it was a city of outsiders, in which at least 50 per cent of the population was from somewhere else. Another trait for which Madrid would repeatedly be condemned was that it was a city that consumed but did not produce anything. The trades that did develop in Madrid – shoe-making, carpentry, jewellery-making, fan-making, laceworking – were overwhelmingly oriented to servicing the Court and aristocracy.

The economic frailty of Madrid reflected that of Castile as a whole. The gold and silver of Mexico and Peru seemed to give the Habsburg kings limitless potential wealth. The demands of their wars, however, were immediate, and could only be met by loans from foreign bankers. The result was soaring, uncontrollable debts, which not even American gold could service. Also, the country's political hierarchy had been built on the basis of giving the aristocracy, the *hidalgos* or lesser gentry and the Church immense privileges, including exemption from taxation.

This meant that the ever-increasing war taxes hit precisely and only the few productive sectors of the population. Young men of working age were also continually being drawn off for the army. For a country with the social system of Castile, constant imperialism was nearly suicidal; in time, it would lead to the eradication of the growth that had been visible under Ferdinand and Isabella, and a catastrophic decline in the rural population.

IN DAYS OF GOLD

One aspect of Spain during its 'Golden Century' was its intense Catholic faith. This was also, though, the golden age of the *pícaro*, the chancer, the figure living on his wits, as seen in the many picaresque novels of the period. In a society that valued aristocracy, status and military or state service over productive activity, and in which the real economy was rapidly dwindling, their numbers naturally multiplied.

The mecca for all *pícaros* was Madrid, the one place where ex-soldiers, landless peasants and drifters would be most likely to find a niche, as servants or bodyguards, or by gambling, pimping, thieving or many other means. The great poet and satirist Quevedo wrote a whole book cataloguing the varieties of Madrid's low life and how they acquired cash. Madrid also contained a great many of the very poor, living off the charity provided by the huge number of religious houses in the city.

Pícaros were not only found among the poor. Madrid also drew in thousands at the other end of society, often *hidalgos* with estates run to ruin, who came hoping to attach themselves to some lordly patron and so break into the circles of the Court. For them, maintaining appearances, presenting an image of aristocracy, was everything. In 1620 Madrid acquired its first guidebook, the 'Guide and advice to strangers who come to the Court, in which they are taught to flee the dangers that there are in Court life', by Antonio Liñán y Verdugo, a lawyer from Cuenca. He warned provincials who might have to do business in Madrid that in 'this Babylon', 'of every four things one sees, one cannot believe even two', for everything was just 'fabulous appearances, dreamed-up marvels, fairy-tale treasures, and figures like actors on a stage'.

This volatile mass naturally needed entertainment. One source was the theatre, the focus of the extraordinary literary vitality of the city at this time. There were also fiestas and royal ceremonies, and even foreigners who complained about the mud and the stink were impressed by the variety of luxuries that could be had in Madrid, from Italian lace to fresh fish, brought caked in ice from the Basque coast.

THE COURT ADJOURNS

In 1571 came the greatest success of Philip II's reign with the defeat of the Turkish fleet off Lepanto in Greece. In 1580 he became King of Portugal and appeared to be at the height of his strength. However, suspensions of payment on his debts were becoming frequent, and in the 1560s a rebellion broke out in the Netherlands that would develop into a morass into which Spanish armies and wealth would disappear without trace. His dispute with England – leading to the Armada catastrophe – and interventions in France's religious wars, were as costly.

As the number of unresolved problems mounted, a gnawing frustration spread through Castilian society, and scapegoats were sought. The former Muslims, nominally converted in 1502, were put under increasing pressure and then expelled from Spain in 1609, and the Inquisition – if not the all-pervading force of Protestant caricature – gained great powers to investigate deviations from Catholic orthodoxy.

Philip II died in 1598 at El Escorial, aged 71. His son Philip III (1598-1621) and grandson Philip IV (1621-65) had neither the intelligence, confidence or normally the motivation to carry on with the awesome burden of work he had set as an example. Philip III began the practice of ruling through a favourite or *valido*, in his case the Duke of Lerma. Spain's impoverished state, aggravated by a devastating plague in 1599, was impossible to ignore, and Lerma responded by making peace with England and the Dutch.

He also committed the ultimate injury to Madrid by moving the Court to Valladolid, in 1601. The main stated reason was that this would help revive the economy of northern Castile, although Lerma also stood to benefit personally. He also argued that Madrid, in any case, was so overrun with undesirables that it had become intolerable. The monarchy's purpose-built capital was out of control and it would be best to write it off and start again.

Within a few months Madrid was so deserted 'it appeared as if the Moors or the English had sacked and burnt it'. By 1605 the population had fallen back to just 26,000, little more than before Philip II's arrival in 1561. However, the Valladolid experiment did not work, and it became evident that Madrid had acquired a momentum that was difficult to disregard. In 1606 the Court returned, amid huge rejoicing, and only a year later the population was already back to 70,000.

POMP AND CIRCUMSTANCE

It was after Madrid's definitive establishment as capital, with Philip III's brief declaration *Sólo Madrid es Corte* (Only Madrid is the Court), that more was at last done to give it the look of a grand city. The Plaza Mayor was finally completed in 1619, followed by the Ayuntamiento or city hall and the Buen Retiro palace. The aristocracy, too, began to build palaces around the city once they were assured they would not have to move on again, and Madrid acquired several much more elaborate baroque churches.

The Plaza Mayor was the great arena of Habsburg Madrid. Able to hold a third of the city's population at that time, it was the venue for state ceremonies, bullfights, executions, *autos-da-fé* (the ritual condemnation of heretics), mock battles, circus acts and carnival fiestas, as well as still being a market square. Particularly lavish entertainments were staged in the plaza in 1623 for the Prince of Wales, the future King Charles I, who arrived in Madrid under the alias of 'Tom Smith' in a fruitless attempt to negotiate a marriage with the sister of Philip IV.

Habsburg Madrid functioned rather like a giant theatre, a great backdrop against which the monarchy could display itself to its subjects and to the world. On either side were royal estates, which determined the shape of the city left in the middle and its peculiar north-south pattern of growth. Several times a year royal processions took place, with stops for various ceremonies in the Plaza Mayor and High Masses in various churches. For the occasion, buildings were covered in garlands, and temporary arches erected along the route with extravagant decoration extolling the virtues of the dynasty. As the Spanish monarchy slid towards economic collapse the lavishness of these ceremonies only increased, maintaining an illusion of power and opulence.

Away from this ceremonial route, the Habsburgs built few squares and no grand avenues, and old Madrid continued to develop along the tangled street plan it retains today. Even so, the opulence of the Court – and the poverty outside the capital – still attracted more people into the city, and in about 1630 Madrid reached its maximum size under the Habsburgs, with possibly as many as 170,000 inhabitants. In 1656 it was given its fifth and final wall, roughly surrounding the area now considered 'old Madrid', which would set the limits of the city for the next 200 years.

THE PRICE OF WAR

For many years the centre of all the Court pomp was King Philip IV. Throughout the 1620s and 1630s, while the Court maintained its image of grandeur, his *valido,* the Count-Duke of Olivares, struggled to maintain the Spanish empire against threats on every side. In the 1620s Spain won a series of victories, and for a time it seemed the rot had been stopped. In 1639, though, a Spanish fleet was destroyed by the Dutch, and in 1643 the French crushed the Spanish army at Rocroi in Flanders. Naval defeats made it ever more difficult for Spain to import gold and silver from America. Olivares sought to extend taxation in the non-Castilian dominions of the crown, which led in 1640 to revolts in Portugal and Catalonia. Portugal regained its independence, and the Catalan revolt was only suppressed after a 12-year war.

By mid-century the effects of endless wars on Castile were visible to all, in abandoned villages and social decay. Even Madrid went into decline, so that by 1700 the city's population had fallen back to about 100,000. In the 1660s, the total

Madrid in the 18th century, painted by Lorenzo de Quiros.

Picture this The Family of Charles IV

It is not a pretty picture. Charles IV, King of Spain from 1788-1808, was known as a simple fellow of mushy intellect, and his wife, María Luisa, as a nymphomaniac. The pair, primarily the Queen, took a fancy to the young Manuel Godoy, a royal guard about half her age. They appointed the handsome playboy to chief minister and he promptly became the Queen's lover. Unperturbed by playing the cuckold, Charles turned a blind eye to his wife's wanton ways, and María Luisa, happy with having her cake and eating it, called the relationship – King, Queen, chief minister – 'the earthly trinity'. Godoy was in a good position. A lusty, simple fellow himself, he had his wife, a mistress, and the Queen. The royal couple showered him with gifts and titles, and grandly named him the Prince of Peace. However, the ruling threesome did not sit well with either the commoners or the aristocracy, and the Queen's son, crown prince Ferdinand, was particularly disgusted. A bitter rivalry grew between Ferdinand and Godoy, who was suspected of plotting to rob Ferdinand of the future crown, on top of bedding his mother.

But no one should feel too sorry for Ferdinand. In 1808, Napoleon's troops, on their way to occupy Portugal, decided to stop over in Spain and conquer Castile as well. Ferdinand, however, had entered into secret negotiations with Bonaparte, hoping to overthrow his mother and father. In a plot-line worthy of *Hamlet*, Charles came upon a mysterious note in his prayer book revealing his son's alleged plot against him. Ferdinand was summarily imprisoned for high treason, with his own mother calling him 'a spiked vine of cowardice'.

The 'earthly trinity' was unsettled by these events of familial betrayal and invading Frenchmen. Smelling trouble, they decided to make a run for it, but didn't get far, and Charles eventually abdicated the throne in favour of his plotting son. Ferdinand was to become one of the most malevolent kings in all of Spanish history – he would go on to re-establish the Inquisition and publicly draw and quarter his enemies.

Goya's masterful painting only thinly veils the Shakespearean familial tensions brewing. It is a menacing, unflattering family portrait. The painting has famously been described as that of 'a corner baker and his wife after having won the lottery'. Hemingway called it a 'masterpiece of loathing'. Lascivious María Luisa dominates the canvas, much taller here than in life. She is the figure of control, both in the painting and in the government of Spain. The children at her sides are María Isabel and Francisco de Paula, both of whom were rumoured to be Godoy's children. Poor Charles stands to her left, dwarfed by the presence of his wife; he stares blankly from the canvas, looking like a distracted, rounder version of George Washington. Behind him is his epileptic brother, Don Antonio. Beside Don Antonio is the small face of Doña Carlota, the King's eldest daughter, who was deformed in a hunting accident and inherited the same nymphomania as her mother. On the left side of the painting, hidden in shadows, is the King's senile sister, Doña María Josefa, a dark haggard face in the back. And in front of her, the scheming Ferdinand. Godoy is conspicuous by his absence.

Goya's **The Family of Charles IV** *is found at the Prado (see p80).*

collapse of the Spanish empire seemed an immediate possibility. Castile, the first world power, had been left poorer than many of the countries it had tried to dominate.

END OF THE HABSBURG LINE

In the Court, meanwhile, life became ever more of a baroque melodrama. Of Philip IV's 12 legitimate children by his two wives, only two girls had survived into adulthood – the youngest the Infanta Margarita, the little princess in Velázquez's *Las Meninas*. In 1661, however, when Philip was already prematurely aged, the queen, Mariana of Austria, had a son, conceived, the king wrote to his friend the nun Sister María, 'in the last copulation achieved with Doña Mariana'. Philip IV died in 1665, leaving as regent his widow Mariana.

The new heir, the future King Charles II, was chronically infirm from birth and provided the dynasty with scant consolation. The Habsburgs' marked tendency to ill-health was accentuated by their habit of marrying cousins or nieces. The Habsburg jaw, the growth of which can be followed through family portraits, had in Charles become a real disability. He was unable to eat solid food. Because of this – or, more likely, the endless cures he was subjected to for his many ailments – he suffered uncontrollable diarrhoea, which detracted from the stately dignity of Court ceremonies.

In the meantime, both the economy and the government continued to slide. Concern centred again on the need for an heir, and Charles was married off twice, despite a general belief that he was both impotent and sterile. As it became evident that the throne of the Spanish empire would soon become vacant, the Court was overrun with bizarre intrigues, with different factions and the agents of European powers all waiting on Charles' final demise. In 1695 the French Ambassador reported that the king 'appeared to be decomposing', and could barely walk without assistance. Even so, Charles hung on until the age of 38. In 1700, though, with the pathetic last words, '*Me duele todo*' (It hurts everywhere), he finally died, and the Spanish Habsburg dynasty came to an end.

BOURBON MADRID

Philip V (1700-46), first Bourbon King of Spain, secured his throne in 1714, after the 12-year War of the Spanish Succession. He was the grandson of Louis XIV of France and María Teresa, daughter of Philip IV of Spain. Castile, abandoning its more usual francophobia, gave him complete support. The alternative, Archduke Charles of Austria, was supported by Catalonia and the other Aragonese territories, to whom he had

promised a restoration of their traditional rights. Twice, in 1706 and 1710, Charles' British, Dutch, Portuguese and Catalan army took Madrid, but was unable to hold it.

Once victorious, Philip reformed his new kingdom along the lines laid down by his illustrious grandfather in France. In 1715 the remaining rights of the former Aragonese territories were abolished, so that it is from this date that Spain can formally be said to exist.

A French king brought with him other innovations. Philip V, raised at Versailles, and his Italian second wife Isabella Farnese were not taken with Madrid or its gloomy Habsburg palaces, and so built their own Franco-Italian villa at La Granja. They were not overly upset when the entire Alcázar burnt down in 1734, and a new Palacio Real was commissioned from Italian architects. Philip V and his administrator of Madrid, the Marqués de Vadillo, also sponsored many buildings by a local architect, Pedro de Ribera.

'The amount spent annually on ceremonials was greater than the navy's budget.'

Reform led to economic recuperation and a recovery in Madrid's population. People still came and went, but it also acquired a more stable resident population, with a merchant community and an artisan and working class. Even so, in many ways Madrid had changed little. Its main function was still to serve the Court, whose ceremonies set the calendar. They were as lavish as ever: until the 1770s the amount spent annually by the Crown in Madrid was greater than the entire budget of the Spanish navy.

Fernando VI (1746-59) was a shy but popular king who gave Spain its longest period of peace for over 200 years. Childless, he was succeeded by half-brother Charles III (1759-88). Previously King of Naples for 20 years, he too was less than impressed by Madrid. However, more than any of his predecessors he set about improving the city, becoming known as Madrid's Rey-Alcalde or 'King-Mayor'.

ENLIGHTENMENT STRIKES

Charles was fascinated by Enlightenment ideas of progress, science and the applied use of reason. No democrat, he sought to bring about rational improvement from the top. Reforms were undertaken in the bureaucracy and armed forces, and to improve trade with Spanish America. He challenged the privileges of the religious orders, and expelled the Jesuits from Spain in 1767 for their refusal to co-operate.

In Madrid, Charles first undertook to do something about the mud in winter, suffocating dust in summer and foul smells at all times – which were noted by every visitor to the city. A 1761 decree banned the dumping of waste in the streets, and Charles' Italian engineer-architect Francesco Sabatini began building sewers and street lighting. A string of major buildings was erected, of which the Casa de Correos in Puerta del Sol and the Puerta de Alcalá are the best-known. A later queen of Spain remarked that it sometimes seemed as if all the monuments of Madrid had been built by Charles III.

Charles III's grandest project was the Paseo del Prado (*see p114* **El Salón del Prado**). He sent scientific expeditions to every corner of his empire, and planned to exhibit the fruits of their varied researches in a Museum of Natural Sciences – now the Museo del Prado – and the adjacent Jardín Botánico.

'Italian minister Squillace provoked one of history's first fashion revolts.'

Popular reaction to the king's improvements was mixed, some of them being resented as foreign impositions. A decree of Charles III's Italian minister Squillace provoked one of history's first fashion revolts. In 1766 he banned the traditional long cape and wide-brimmed hat and ordered the use of the international three-cornered hat, arguing that the capes were used by criminals to conceal weapons. In what became known as the Motín de Esquilache (Squillace Riot), a mob marched on the Palacio Real and forced the repeal of the decree.

Reform and improved trade did create a feeling of well-being in late 18th-century Madrid. Nevertheless, Spain was still a very feudal society, and the real economy remained backward and frail. And, in an absolute monarchy, a great deal depended on each monarch. Charles IV (1788-1808), whose rather dozy face was immortalised by Goya (*see p20* **Picture this**), had none of his father's energy or intelligence. Also, he chose as his minister the corrupt Manuel Godoy. After the French Revolution, Spain joined other monarchies in attacking the new regime; in 1795, however, Godoy made peace and then an alliance with France, leading to an unpopular war with Britain. Then, in 1808, when Godoy was vacillating over changing sides once again, he was forestalled by anti-French riots that proclaimed Charles IV's son Fernando as king in his place. Napoleon sent troops to Madrid, assuming this decrepit state would be as easy

to conquer as any other. It was not to be, at least not initially, and the consequences were horrific (*see p26* **Picture this**).

Once victory was his, Napoleon made his brother, Joseph Bonaparte, King of Spain. In Madrid he tried in a well-meaning fashion to make improvements, among them some squares for which the city has since been very grateful, notably the Plaza de Oriente and the Plaza Santa Ana. However, this did nothing to overcome the animosity around him. In 1812 the Duke of Wellington and his army arrived to take the city, in a battle that destroyed much of the Retiro palace. The French were finally driven out of Spain in 1813. As well as the fighting itself, the year 1812 brought with it a catastrophic famine, which in Madrid killed over 30,000 people.

The shock of this upheaval initiated a period of instability that continued until 1874 – in fact, it could be said that the instability only really ended with the death of Franco in 1975. Spain withdrew into its own problems, with one conflict after another between conservatives, reformists, revolutionaries and other factions. Each struggled to impose their model on the state and create a political system that could accommodate, or hold back, the pressures for modernisation and some form of democracy.

In 1812 a Cortes had met in Cádiz and given Spain its first constitution. This assembly also gave the world the term 'liberal'. Yet when Fernando VII (1808-33) returned from French captivity in 1814, his only thought was to cancel the constitution and return to the methods of his ancestors. His absolute rule, though, was incapable of responding to the bankruptcy of the country. The regime was also struggling to hold on to its American colonies, by then in complete rebellion. In 1820 a liberal revolt in the army forced Fernando to reinstate the constitution. He was saved three years later, ironically by a French army, sent to restore monarchical rule. Meanwhile, defeat at Ayacucho in Peru (1824) left Spain with only Cuba, Santo Domingo and Puerto Rico of its former American empire.

In 1830 Fernando VII's wife María Cristina gave birth to a daughter, soon to be Queen Isabel II (1833-68). Previously, the most reactionary sectors of the aristocracy, the Church and other ultra-conservative groups had aligned themselves behind the king's brother Don Carlos. When Fernando died in 1833, Carlos demanded the throne, launching what became known as the Carlist Wars. To defend her daughter's rights, María Cristina, as Regent, had no choice but to look for support from liberals, and so was obliged to promise some form of constitutional rule.

OLD ROMANTICS

For the next 40 years Spanish politics was a see-saw, as conservative and liberal factions vied for power, while the Carlists, off the spectrum for most people in Madrid, occasionally threatened at the gates. Madrid was the great centre for aspiring politicians, and the problems of Spain were discussed endlessly in its salons and new cafés, which multiplied around this time. This was the era of Romanticism, and writers such as the journalist Larra and poet José Espronceda were heavily involved in politics. Similarly, many of the politicians of the day were also writers.

Much of the time, though, these reformers were shepherds in search of a flock, for there were no true political parties. The only way a faction could hope to gain power was with the support of a general with troops at his disposal.

The *pronunciamiento*, or coup, was the main means of changing governments, and soldiers identified with particular sides – Espartero, Serrano and Prim for the progressives, Narváez and O'Donnell (who was a descendant of Irish soldiers) for the conservatives – were the heroes of their followers. Later, many from either side had monuments or streets named after them. The clashes were never decisive, and it was later remarked that Spain had gone through seven decades of agitation without ever experiencing a revolution.

This political instability did not mean that life in Madrid was chaotic. Visitors in the early 1830s found a small, sleepy, shabby city, which seemed sunk in the past. Convents and palaces still occupied nearly half its area. It was around this time that Spain acquired its romantic aura. A growing number of foreigners visited, drawn by Spain's timeless, exotic qualities. One was the French writer Prosper Mérimée, who in 1845 wrote his novel *Carmen*, later put to music by Bizet, who himself never visited Spain at all.

EXPANSION AND TURMOIL

The 1830s, however, also saw the single most important change in Madrid during the 19th century. In 1836 the liberal minister Mendizábal took advantage of the church's sympathy for Carlism to introduce his Desamortización or Disentailment law, which dissolved most of Spain's monasteries. In Madrid, the church lost over 1,000 properties. Most were demolished remarkably quickly, and an enormous area thus became available for sale and new building.

Some urban reformers saw this as an opportunity to build broad, airy avenues, following the always-cited example of Paris. Some major projects were undertaken, the most important being the rebuilding of the Puerta del Sol, in 1854-62. However, most of the local traders who benefited from Desamortización lacked the capital to contemplate grand projects, and built separate blocks without ever challenging the established, disorderly street plan. The districts of old Madrid took on the appearance they have largely kept until today, with great numbers of tenement blocks. They allowed Madrid to grow considerably in population, without going outside its still-standing wall of 1656.

A few factories had appeared in the city, but for the most part the Industrial Revolution was passing Madrid by. Constitutional governments expanded the administration, and the ambitions of the middle class were focused on obtaining official posts rather than on business ventures. Two more major changes arrived in the 1850s. In 1851 Madrid got its first railway, to Aranjuez, followed by a line running to the Mediterranean. Railways would transform Madrid's relationship with the rest of the country, opening up a realistic possibility of it fulfilling an economic function. Equally important was the completion of the Canal de Isabel II, bringing water from the Guadarrama, in 1858. Madrid's water supply, still part-based on Moorish water courses, had been inadequate for years. The canal, inaugurated with a giant spurt of water in Calle San Bernardo, removed a crippling obstruction to the city's growth.

Madrid's population was by this time over 300,000. Steps were finally taken for it to break out of its old walls, and in 1860 a plan by Carlos Maria de Castro was approved for the Ensanche (extension) of Madrid, in an orderly grid pattern to the north and east. However, as with earlier rebuilding, the plan came up against the chronic lack of large-scale local investors. The only major development undertaken quickly was the section of C/Serrano bought up by the flamboyant speculator the Marqués de Salamanca, whose name was given to the whole district. Moreover, even the marqués was unable to sell many of his properties to Madrid's conservative-minded upper classes at a viable price.

Meanwhile, the political situation was deteriorating once again, after a long period of conservative rule that began in 1856. Isabel II had become deeply unpopular, surrounded by an aura of sleaze and scandal. In September 1868, yet another military revolt deposed the government and, this time, the queen as well.

There followed six years of turmoil. The provisional government invited an Italian prince, Amadeo of Savoy, to become king of a truly constitutional monarchy. However, in December 1870 General Prim, strongman of the new regime, was assassinated. Carlist revolts broke out in some parts of the country, while on the left new, more radical groups began to appear. At the end of 1868, a meeting in Madrid

Carlo Bossoli's *A View of the Plaza Mayor* (1860).

addressed by Giuseppe Fanelli, an Italian associate of Bakunin, led to the founding of the first anarchist group in Spain. The Cortes itself was riven by factions, and Amadeo decided to give up the struggle and go back to Italy.

On 12 February 1873 Spain became a republic. Rightist resistance became stronger than ever, while many towns were taken over by left-wing juntas, who declared them autonomous 'cantons', horrifying conservative opinion. To keep control, Republican governments relied increasingly heavily on the army. This proved fatal, and on 3 January 1874 the army commander in Madrid, General Pavía, marched into the Cortes, sent all its members home, and installed a military dictatorship.

THE BOURBONS RETURN

At the end of 1874 the army decided to restore the Bourbon dynasty, in the shape of Alfonso XII (1874-85), the son of Isabel II. The architect of the Restoration regime, however, was a civilian politician, Antonio Cánovas del Castillo. He established the system of *turno pacífico*, or peaceful alternation in power (thus avoiding social tensions), between a Conservative Party, led by himself, and a Liberal Party that was made up of former progressives. The control of these 'dynastic parties' over the political system was made secure by election-rigging and occasional repression.

In the late 1870s the wealthy of Madrid set out on a building boom. They finally overcame their reluctance to leave the old city, and the Salamanca area became the new centre of fashionable life. Most of the district's new apartment blocks had lifts, first seen in Madrid in 1874. In earlier blocks upper floors had been let cheaply, so that rich and poor had

often continued to live side by side. With lifts, however, a top floor could be as desirable as a first, and this kind of class mixing faded.

Government and official bodies, too, undertook a huge round of new building. The Banco de España, the Bolsa and the main railway stations are all creations of the 1880s. Madrid meanwhile acquired a larger professional middle class; it also attracted intellectuals from around the country.

At the same time, Madrid was receiving an influx of poor migrants from rural Spain, with over 200,000 new arrivals between 1874 and 1900. Economic growth was reflected in the appearance of yet more small workshops rather than factories. There were also many with next to no work, and the 1880s saw the beginning of a housing crisis, with the growth of shanty towns around the outskirts of the city.

The established order seemed in little danger in the first decades of the Restoration. The events of 1868-74 had discredited the old Romantic idea of the unity of the people in pursuit of democracy. In 1879 the Spanish Socialist Party, the PSOE, was founded, but for a long time the level of agitation in the capital was very limited.

THE EMPIRE STRIKES BACK

Just before the end of the century, however, the preconceptions on which Spanish political life had been based received a shattering blow. The Restoration regime presented itself as having returned the country to stability and some prestige in the world. However, in the 1890s Spain was involved in colonial wars against nationalists in the Philippines and Cuba. In 1898, the government allowed itself to be manoeuvred into war with the United

States. In a few weeks, almost the entire Spanish navy was sunk, and Spain lost virtually all its remaining overseas territories. Known simply as 'The Disaster', this was a devastating blow to Spain's self-confidence. The regime itself was revealed as decrepit and incompetent, based on a feeble economy. Among intellectuals, the situation sparked off an intense round of self-examination and discussion of Spain's relationship with the very concept of modernity. Politically, it signalled the beginning of the end of the cosy settlement of 1874.

Although the intellectual debates of this time centred on Spain's apparent inability to deal with the modern world, the problems of the regime were not due to the country being backward. Rather, they spiralled out of control because after 1900 the country entered an unprecedented period of change.

CITY WITHOUT LIMITS

Sudden economic expansion was set off by three main factors. One, ironically, was the loss of the colonies, which led to large amounts of capital being brought back to the country. Most important was World War I, which provided unheard-of opportunities for neutral Spain in the supply of goods to the Allied powers. Then, during the worldwide boom of the 1920s, Spain benefited hugely from foreign investment.

Within a few years Spain had one of the fastest rates of urbanisation in the world. The economic upheaval caused by the world war led to runaway inflation, spurring a huge movement into the cities. Madrid did not grow as rapidly as industrial Barcelona, which had become the largest city in the country. Nevertheless, after taking four centuries to reach half a million, it doubled its population again in just 30 years, to just under a million by 1930. Only 37 per cent of its people had been born in the city.

The most visible manifestation of this growth was a still-larger building boom. Bombastic creations such as the Palacio de Comunicaciones were symptomatic of the expansive mood. Most important was the opening of the Gran Vía in 1910, a project that had first been discussed no less than 25 years previously, which would transform the heart of the old city with a new grand thoroughfare for entertainment, business and banking.

Another fundamental innovation was electricity. The city's trams were electrified in 1898, and the first metro line, between Sol and Cuatro Caminos, opened in 1919. Electricity allowed Madrid, far from any other source of power, finally to experience an industrial take-off in the years after 1910. It was still far behind

Barcelona as an industrial city, but was much more important as a base for major banks. Larger companies and new industries brought with them more aggressive styles of working, and a more industrial working class. Many lived in shabby slum districts in the outskirts, or 'misery-villes' of shanties that mushroomed around the city. At the same time, expansion in banking and office work was also reflected in the large number of white-collar workers.

Madrid was also, more than ever, the mecca for intellectuals and professionals from right across the country. This was the background to the enormous vigour of the city's intellectual life at this time, the so-called 'Silver Age' of Spanish literature. From writers of 1898 such as Antonio Machado and Baroja to the famous poets of the 1927 generation, Rafael Alberti and García Lorca, the city welcomed an extraordinary succession of literary talent, not to mention painters, historians and scientists. From the 1910s onward, Madrid's cafés were full of talk, forums for discussion multiplied, and any number of newspapers and magazines were published. The sheer range of activity was remarkable.

In politics, this urban expansion made it impossible for the 'dynastic parties' to control elections in the way they were able to do in small towns and rural areas. In 1910, a Republican-Socialist coalition won elections in Madrid for the first time. Tensions came to a head in 1917, with a general strike throughout the country. In the following years the main focus of conflict was Barcelona, where virtual urban guerrilla warfare broke out between the anarchist workers' union, the CNT, and employers and the state. In 1923 the Captain-General of Barcelona, General Primo de Rivera, suspended the constitution and declared himself Dictator, under King Alfonso XIII.

In Madrid, this was first greeted with relative indifference. However, by his action Primo de Rivera had discredited the king and the old dynastic parties, without putting anything in their place. A widespread movement against the monarchy developed in the '20s, based in a sentiment that a society that felt increasingly mature should not have a ramshackle, discredited government imposed upon it.

In 1930 Primo de Rivera resigned, exhausted. The king appointed another soldier, General Berenguer, as prime minister. In an attempt to move back towards some form of constitutional rule, the government decided to hold local elections on 12 April 1931. They were not expected to be a referendum on the monarchy. However, when the results came in it was seen that republican candidates had won sweeping majorities in all of Spain's cities.

THE SECOND REPUBLIC

On 14 April 1931, as the results of the local elections became clear, the streets of Spain's cities filled with people. In Madrid, a jubilant mass converged on the Puerta del Sol. It was these exultant crowds in the streets that drove the king to abdicate and spurred republican politicians into action, for they had never expected their opportunity to arrive so soon.

The second Spanish Republic arrived amid huge optimism, expressing the frustrated hopes of decades. Among the many schemes of its first government, a Republican-Socialist coalition, was a project for Madrid, the Gran Madrid or 'Greater Madrid' plan, intended to integrate the sprawling new areas around the city's edge. A key part of it was the extension of the Castellana, then blocked by a racecourse above C/Joaquín Costa. The racecourse was demolished, and the Castellana was allowed to snake endlessly northward, forming one of the modern city's most distinctive features. Also completed under the Republic was the last section of the Gran Vía, from Callao to Plaza de España, site of Madrid's best art deco architecture.

Possibilities of further change and renovation, however, were to be entangled in the accelerating social crisis that overtook the Republic around this time. The new regime aroused expectations that would have been difficult to live up to at the best of times. Instead, its arrival coincided with the onset of the worldwide depression of the 1930s. Moreover, Spain's own – partly unreal – 1920s boom had exceeded the real capacity of the country's economy. Activity slowed down, and unemployment spread.

At the same time, labour agitation and republican legislation brought wage increases for those in work. This caused panic among

Picture this The Third of May

Nearly 200 years old, this remains one of the world's most modern paintings. It marked a complete transformation in the portrayal of war. Previously, with very few exceptions, war paintings had presented war as noble contest, glorifying heroic deeds and celebrating kings and commanders – a prime example hangs nearby in the Prado, Velázquez' *Las Lanzas*. In Goya's war images, in contrast – whether the *Tres de Mayo* or the *Desastres de la Guerra* – there is no glory, only misery, brutality and chaos. Death, mutilation and casual savagery are more prominent than victories. There are no generals or famous heroes, only faces in the crowd. There is heroism – again anonymous – but it seems wild, desperate, ultimately futile. It is this searingly honest, unblinking sense of the truth and horror of violence that makes the *Tres de Mayo* so permanently contemporary.

many employers, who became easy fodder for a belligerent, resurgent right. Levels of tension were even more intense in the country-side, where agrarian reform was bogged down by conservative opposition.

THE POLARISATION OF POLITICS

As frustration grew among workers, calls for the end of republican compromise in a second, social, revolution increased, especially from the anarchist CNT and the Communist Party. Even the Socialist Party was radicalised. On the right, similarly, the loudest voices – such as the fascist Falange, founded in 1933 by José Antonio Primo de Rivera, son of the former dictator – demanded authoritarian rule as the only means of preserving social order. The vogue for extremism was fed by the mood of the times, in which Nazism, Italian Fascism and Soviet Communism appeared as the most dynamic international models.

In 1933 the coalition between Socialists and liberal republicans broke up. With the left split, elections were won by conservative republicans backed by the CEDA, a parliamentary but authoritarian right-wing party. Reform came to a halt. In October 1934 the CEDA demanded to have ministers in the government, and a general strike was called in response. It was strongest in the mining region of Asturias, where it was savagely suppressed by a rising general called Francisco Franco.

Left-wing parties were subjected to a wave of repression that radicalised their supporters still further. In new elections in February 1936, however, the left, united once again in the Frente Popular (Popular Front), were victorious. In Madrid the Front won 54 per cent of the vote.

A liberal-republican government returned to power, with Manuel Azaña as president. By this time, however, the level of polarisation and of

The events portrayed were very real. On 2 May 1808 Madrid awoke to learn that Napoleon had kidnapped the Spanish royal family, and that French troops were taking over the country. The French expected little resistance beyond skirmishes and some manageable grumbling. Instead, uncoordinated Spanish army units and, above all, the people of Madrid fought the invaders street by street, using knives or their bare hands. In the Puerta del Sol, the crowds hurled themselves against the Mamelukes, the Arab mercenaries Napoleon had acquired during his 1798 invasion of Egypt. As the day wore on, the French gradually won control of Madrid, and in the early morning of 3 May – enraged that they had had to fight so hard against a mere street mob, rather than real soldiers – they set out to teach the city a lesson. Captured 'insurgents' were disposed of in mass executions on the hill of Príncipe Pío, which is now at the southern end of the Parque del Oeste.

Goya painted his *Dos de Mayo*, of the struggle in the Puerta del Sol, and *Tres de Mayo* in 1814, just after the French had been driven out of Spain. How much personal observation went into them is an unanswered question. Goya was in Madrid during those days, and one of his gardeners later claimed the artist had watched the executions through a telescope. However, this is impossible to confirm.

With its pared-down style foreshadowing 20th-century expressionism, the *Tres de Mayo* is the first truly modern image of war. Its resonances do not end there. The French were genuinely surprised and absolutely infuriated by the resistance they met in Spain. Napoleon's empire regarded itself as carrying a systematised version of the glorious French Revolution around Europe: in return for their obedience, countries like Spain that had been ruled by backward monarchies were offered the joys of rational Enlightenment administration, new roads, education – in short, progress. Goya himself, as a liberal, had been suspected of being an *afrancesado*, a French sympathiser, but he found himself disgusted by the brutality with which the French imposed their power. And most ordinary Spaniards opposed the invasion almost instinctively. The *Dos de Mayo* and *Tres de Mayo* capture all the mad, savage chaos of a mass uprising and, in the *Tres*, its terrible consequences. As has often been pointed out, the insurgents about to be executed have individual faces and expressions, whether defiant, terrified or lost in despair. The French soldiers form a faceless, uniformed line. As such, they can be understood as representing every anonymous power that has tried to impose its own idea of progress at gunpoint.

Goya's **The Third of May 1808 in Madrid** *is found at the Prado (see p80).*

sheer hatred in the country was moving out of control. Right-wing politicians called almost openly for the army to save the country. The military had already laid their plans for a coup.

REVOLUTION AND WAR

On 18 July 1936 the generals made their move, with risings all over Spain, while German and Italian aircraft ferried Franco's colonial army from Spanish Morocco to Andalucia. In Madrid, troops failed to seize the city and barricaded themselves inside the Montaña barracks, the site of which is now in the Parque del Oeste.

The coup was the spark for an explosion of tension. The workers' parties demanded arms. On 20 July, as news came that the army had been defeated in Barcelona and many other cities, the Montaña was stormed and its defenders massacred, despite the efforts of political leaders to prevent it.

With the right apparently defeated, Madrid underwent a revolution. Among left-wing militants the mood was ecstatic: factories, schools, the transport system and other public services were all taken over, and, although the government remained in place, it had little effective power. Ad-hoc militias and patrols were the only power on the streets, and, amid the paranoia and hatred that were the other side of revolutionary excitement, summary executions of suspected rightists were common.

Meanwhile, the war still had to be fought. Franco's regular troops were advancing from Seville preceded by stories of reprisals more terrible than anything done by the 'red terror' in Madrid. The militias seemed powerless to stop them. Defeat for the Republic seemed inevitable. German planes bombed the city. On 6 November, as Franco's advance guard arrived, the government left for Valencia, a move widely seen as desertion.

CITY UNDER SIEGE

Without a government, however, a new resolve was seen in the city. In the southern suburbs the troops were resisted street by street. Women, children and the elderly joined in building trenches and barricades, and comparisons were immediately drawn with 2 May 1808. On 9 November the first foreign volunteers, the International Brigades, arrived, doing wonders for morale. Madrid had become the front line of international democracy. After savage fighting Franco halted the frontal assault on Madrid in November 1936.

Madrid saw little more direct fighting. From the Casa de Campo, where the remains of trenches and bunkers still exist today, the army settled in to a siege. Attempts to push them back north and south of Madrid were

unsuccessful. The city was regularly bombed, and bombarded by artillery, who took their sights from the Gran Vía, 'Howitzer Avenue'.

People adapted to the situation. You could go to war by tram, and combatants were taken their lunch on the line along the Gran Vía. Right-wingers were scarcely harassed after the first few months. The siege, however, ground down the spirit of November 1936. Shortages were acute; particularly terrible was the severe winter of 1937-8, when doors and furniture were burnt for fuel. The powerful role established by the Communists, won through the Republic's dependence on the Soviet Union as its only source of arms, alienated many who were not Party supporters.

General Franco, meanwhile, was advancing on other fronts. During 1937 his forces overran the Basque Country and Asturias, and in March 1938 they reached the Mediterranean near Castellón. In January 1939 they conquered Catalonia. In Madrid, fighting broke out behind Republican lines between the Communists, committed to fighting to the end, and groups who wanted to negotiate a settlement with Franco. Those in favour of negotiation won, but Franco had no intention of compromising. On 28 March 1939 the Nationalist army entered the Spanish capital.

THE LONG DICTATORSHIP

Madrid emerged from the Civil War physically and psychologically battered. Throughout the city, hundreds of buildings stood in ruins. Buildings, however, could be rebuilt fairly quickly; healing the damage done to the city's spirit would take decades.

The Madrid of the 1940s was the sombre antithesis of the expansive city of ten years previously, or its current outgoing, vivacious self. A great many *madrileños* had lost someone close to them, to bombs, bullets, firing squads or prison camps. The black market rather than art and literature dominated café conversation, and the figures of earlier years were mostly in exile, or keeping indoors.

The existence of 'two Spains' (right–left, traditional–liberal, rich–poor) was all too apparent. As the victors marched in, they wasted no time in rounding up members (or just suspected sympathisers) of 'enemy' groups, anarchists, Communists, union members and liberals. Some were turned in by neighbours, creating a sordid atmosphere of bitterness and distrust. During the early '40s, while the rest of the world was wrapped up in World War II, thousands were executed in Spain. Others paid the price of defeat by serving as forced labour on fascist landmarks such as the Valle de los Caídos, Franco's victory monument and tomb.

Madrid's loyalty to the Republic almost led to it losing its capital status, as voices were raised calling for a more 'loyal' city to represent the country. Tradition and financial interests bore more weight, however, and the capital stayed put. The Falange, official party of the regime, produced extravagant plans to turn Madrid into a Spanish version of Imperial Rome, but a lack of funding and galloping inflation scotched most of these nouveau-Imperialist notions. The economy was in a desperate state, and Spain went through a period of extreme hardship, the *años del hambre* ('hunger years'); many remember not having eaten properly for ten years after 1936. This poverty also led to the phenomenon that would most shape the face of Madrid in the post-war decades: massive immigration from Spain's rural provinces.

Madrid has grown faster than any other European capital this century. A 'big village' of just over half a million at the turn of the century, and 950,000 in 1930, it passed the three million mark by 1970.

Until the 1950s, migrants arriving in Madrid found few real opportunities for work, in an economy that was internationally isolated and excluded from Marshall Aid and the other reconstruction packages of post-war Europe. After 1945 many in Spain and abroad assumed that the Franco regime would shortly go the way of its former friends in Germany and Italy.

Who's brave enough to stop clapping? **General Francisco Franco**.

Most European countries continued to shun the regime, at least in public, but in 1953, as the Cold War intensified, Franco was saved by the US government's 'our son-of-a-bitch' policy in choosing allies. A co-operation treaty gave the regime renewed credibility and cash in exchange for air and sea bases on Spanish soil, and later President Eisenhower flew in to shake the dictator's hand.

For those not devoted to the regime, life under Franco was often a matter of keeping one's head down and getting on with things. Football and other forms of escapism played an enormous part in people's lives.

The national Stabilisation Plan of 1959 gave the fundamental push to Madrid's development, and brought Spain definitively back into the Western fold. The plan revolutionised the country's economy, and especially that of the Madrid region. In the 1960s, tourism began to pump money into Spain, and Madrid trebled in size to become an industrial powerhouse. Quiet tree-lined boulevards were widened to make way for cars, and elegant Castellana palaces were replaced by glass-sheathed monoliths. Madrid took on much more of the look, and feel, of a big city.

LIFE AFTER FRANCO

The 1960s also saw the revival of opposition to the regime in the shape of labour unrest, student protests, and the rise of the Basque organisation ETA. The oil crisis of 1973 coincided with the assassination by ETA of Franco's prime minister, Admiral Carrero Blanco, when a bomb planted beneath a Madrid street launched his car right over a five-storey building. The regime, already challenged by political opposition, now had to deal with rising unemployment, inflation and a moribund Franco. The transition to democracy had begun.

Franco died in November 1975, closing a parenthesis of nearly 40 years in Spanish history. A new age, uncertain but exciting, dawned. In July 1976 King Juan Carlos, chosen by Franco to succeed him, named a former Falange bureaucrat, Adolfo Suárez, as prime minister. Nobody, however, knew quite what was going to happen.

To widespread surprise, Suárez initiated a comprehensive programme of political reform. Clandestine opposition leaders surfaced, parties were legalised and famous exiles began coming home. The first democratic elections since 1936 were held in June 1977, and a constitution was approved in late 1978. Suárez' centrist UCD (Centre-Democratic Union) won the national elections, but local elections in Madrid in 1979 were won by the Socialists, led by Enrique Tierno Galván as Mayor.

The 'other' Spain, however, had not disappeared. In fact, it was starting to feel nervous. Hard-core Francoists were horrified at the thought of Socialists and/or Communists coming to power. Significantly, many of the 'old guard' still held influential positions in the armed forces, and were not inclined to give them up easily.

On 23 February 1981 democrats' worst nightmares appeared to come true when a Civil Guard colonel called Tejero burst into the Cortes with a squad of men, firing his pistol into the air. Tanks were in the streets in Valencia, and there was uncertainty everywhere. In Madrid, however, troops stayed in their barracks. A little after midnight, King Juan Carlos appeared on TV and assured the country that the army had sworn him its allegiance and that the coup attempt would fail. The next day, people poured on to the streets to demonstrate support for freedom and democracy.

The wolf had shown his teeth, but they were not as sharp as had been feared. Moreover, the coup attempt significantly helped to win Felipe González and the socialist PSOE their landslide victory in the elections of November 1982.

SOCIAL REVOLUTION, CITY RENOVATIONS

The late 1970s and early '80s saw the arrival of democracy and free speech, the loosening of drug laws and the breakdown of old sexual conventions. Long-repressed creative impulses were released. The compulsorily staid Madrid of earlier years gave way to an anything-goes, vivacious city: an explosion of art, counter-culture and nightlife, creativity and frivolity known as the Movida – very roughly translatable as 'Shift' or 'Movement'.

The Socialists used their control of Madrid's Ayuntamiento – led by the fondly remembered Tierno Galván – to renovate the city's weak infrastructure, with long-overdue facelifts in squares and parks. Mayor Tierno also provided unprecedented support for various progressive causes and for the arts, launching a whole string of new festivals.

If Tierno Galván's local administration was happy to be regarded as godfather to the Movida, the national government of Felipe González was still more eager to be seen as leaders of a reborn country. Decades of isolation ended with Spain's entry into the EU in 1986. This had a near-immediate effect on the economy, and in the late '80s the country was the fastest-growing member of the EU. The González governments achieved major improvements in some areas – among them health and the transport system – but also frustrated the expectations of many of their supporters, often giving the impression they believed modernisation would solve all Spain's problems more or less by itself.

The apotheosis of the country's transition was the 'Year of Spain' in 1992, with the Barcelona Olympics, Expo '92 in Seville and, with a somewhat lower profile, Madrid's year as Cultural Capital of Europe. Afterwards, a different mood became apparent. Spain's pre-'92 boom had postponed the effects of the international downturn at the end of the '80s, but it hit Madrid with a vengeance in 1993. Breakneck growth had created its own problems, and land speculation sent property prices spiralling. The Socialists, who were in any case inseparable from the boom, began to be dragged down by a staggering stream of revelations of corruption.

Disenchantment with the Socialists and a newly cautious mood that followed the brash overconfidence of the boom years were major factors behind the rise of the re-formed right of the Partido Popular (PP). Even before Spain's great year, in 1991, the PSOE had lost control of the Madrid city administration to the PP.

THE POPULAR VOTE

The 1990s in Spain were markedly different in feel and content from the preceding decade. Led by the deliberately bland José María Aznar, the Partido Popular ably connected with the groundswell of discontent provoked by the later years of Socialist administrations. In the 1993 election Felipe González, long the great survivor of Spanish politics, lost his overall majority, but staggered on for another three years by means of a pact with Catalan nationalists. Next time, however, in 1996, the winners were the PP, even though they too still had to rely on pacts with minority parties to be able to form a sustainable government. The PSOE was sent into opposition for the first time in 14 years.

In Madrid the PP had already made its mark on local life. Having rallied voters by denouncing the sleaze and corruption that overwhelmed the PSOE, and the Socialists' irresponsible – as many saw it – spending of taxpayers' money, the PP felt it had a clear mandate to cut back and balance the books. In Madrid, this meant cuts in budgets for arts festivals, a tightening up on licences for new bars and clubs and a general attack on the supposed excesses of the nightlife scene.

Despite harsh criticism for its perceived philistine approach to culture, its decidedly un-liberal stance on issues such as immigration or gay rights or its Francoist origins, the PP managed an absolute majority in the 2000 general elections thanks mainly to its practical,

managerial approach to the economy and the disarray of the opposition. Its second term in office was a different story, with the 2002 general strike, closely followed by the sinking of the *Prestige*, Spain's worst-ever ecological disaster. Aznar's flirtation with Bush and Blair led to Spain participating, albeit in a small way, in the Iraq war, against the wishes of 94 per cent of the Spanish people.

'Spain participated in the Iraq war, against the wishes of 94 per cent of the population.'

The 11 March bombings, and the subsequent media manipulation, were the last straw. The Socialists, under the mild-mannered José Luis Zapatero, had been carefully rebuilding and were now seen as a preferable, honest and decent alternative. On taking power Zapatero's government immediately brought the Spanish troops back from Iraq and since then has embarked cautiously but firmly on a programme of modernisation of political structures and society. Steps have been taken to redefine the nature of relationships between the autonomous regions and the Spanish state; gay marriages have been legalised and a law to provide help for families with income-less dependants has been promulgated. Importantly, and controversially from the PP's standpoint, the first steps have been taken along what promises to be a long and rocky road to peace in the Basque Country. In March 2006 ETA declared a 'permanent ceasefire' but later claimed responsibility for a bomb that exploded at Barajas airport, killing two, in December 2006. At the time of writing the repercussions for the peace process and, with it, Zapatero's government, were still unclear.

In Madrid itself, the PP still controls both city and region, under Alberto Ruiz-Gallardón and Esperanza Aguirre respectively. Though belonging to the same party, they represent radically different styles and their mutual aversion is no secret. They have managed to show a united front – albeit somewhat frostily – namely during the failed campaign to secure the 2012 Olympics and at recent unveilings of new public works, but they will need to bury their differences in the longer term if Gallardón is returned to City Hall after the May 2007 municipal elections. Both city and region will then have to face the multiple challenges of Madrid's unbridled growth, the regeneration of the centre, immigration, rising crime and the attempt to get the 2016 games.

Key events

c860 AD Madrid founded during the reign of Emir Mohammed I of Córdoba.
1085-6 Alfonso VI of Castile conquers Toledo and Madrid.
1109 Madrid besieged by Moorish army.
1212 Battle of Navas de Tolosa: decisive defeat of Muslims in Spain.
1309 First Cortes (parliament) held in Madrid.
1476 Isabella becomes unchallenged Queen of Castile after battle of Toro.
1492 Conquest of Granada; expulsion of Jews from Spain; discovery of America.
1520-1 Madrid joins Comuneros revolt.
1547 Birth of Cervantes in Alcalá de Henares.
1561 Philip II moves the Court to Madrid from Toledo.
1563-84 Building of El Escorial.
1566 Beginning of Dutch Revolt.
1574 First permanent theatre opened in Madrid, the Corral de la Pacheca.
1588 Defeat of the Armada against England.
1599-1600 Plague and famine in Castile.
1601-6 Court moved to Valladolid.
1605, 1615 *Don Quixote* published.
1609 Expulsion of former Muslims from Spain.
1617-9 Completion of Plaza Mayor.
1632-40 Buen Retiro palace built.
1640 Revolts in Portugal and Catalonia.
1643 Battle of Rocroi: Spanish army in Flanders decisively defeated by the French.
1665 Philip IV is succeeded by Charles II, aged four.
1700 Charles II dies without an heir.
1702-14 War of the Spanish Succession: Philip V, first Bourbon King of Spain.
1715 Decree of Nova Planta; Spain created as one state.
1734 Alcázar of Madrid destroyed by fire.
1761 Charles III bans waste dumping in Madrid streets.
1778 Goya moves to Madrid from Aragon.
1808-12 Madrid under French occupation.
1812 Cortes in Cádiz agrees first Spanish constitution; disastrous famine in Madrid.
1814 Fernando VII abrogates constitution.
1810-24 The Latin American Wars of Independence.
1820 Military coup begins three years of liberal rule.
1823 French army restores Fernando VII to full power.
1833 Carlist Wars begin on death of Fernando VII; constitutional government established in Madrid, with limited powers.

1836 Main decree on Disentailment of Monasteries; University of Alcalá de Henares moved to Madrid.
1851 Railway line to Aranjuez inaugurated.
1858 The Canal de Isabel II water system is inaugurated.
1868 Revolution overthrows Isabel II.
1871 Amadeo of Savoy becomes king of Spain. First trams in Madrid, drawn by mules.
1873 Amadeo abdicates; Republic declared.
1874 January: The Republic becomes a military dictatorship after a coup. December: Alfonso XII is declared King.
1879 Spanish Socialist Party (PSOE) founded.
1898 Spanish-American War: a disaster for Spain. Madrid's tramlines electrified.
1910 Building of Gran Vía initiated.
1917 General strike in the whole of Spain.
1919 First Madrid metro line opened.
1923 Primo de Rivera establishes dictatorship.
1930 Fall of Primo de Rivera.
1931 Proclamation of Second Republic.
1934 General Strike against the entry of right-wing ministers into government; the strike is bloodily suppressed in Asturias by General Franco.
1936 February: elections won by Popular Front. July: military uprising against left-wing government. November: Francoist forces launch assault on Madrid.
1939 1 April: Franco declares war over.
1946-50 UN imposes sanctions on Spain.
1953 Co-operation treaty with USA.
1959 Stabilisation Plan opens up the Spanish economy.
1961 First violent attack by Basque nationalists of ETA.
1970 Juan Carlos declared as General Franco's successor.
1975 20 November: Death of Franco.
1977 15 June: Spain's first democratic general election.
1979 April: Enrique Tierno Galván elected Socialist Mayor of Madrid.
1982 Socialists win national elections.
1986 1 January: Spain joins the EEC.
1991 Popular Party (PP) takes over Madrid city council.
1992 Madrid becomes European City of Culture. Barcelona hosts the Olympics; Seville hosts Expo '92.
1996 Partido Popular win national elections.
2004 Socialists win the general election three days after March 11 terrorist attacks kill 192.

Architecture

A city of imperial glories and modern inventiveness.

Madrid's past, turbulent and grand in equal measure, is barely apparent from the city's architecture. The city walls stayed up until the 1860s – longer than in most European cities – meaning that Madrid was forced to build on top of itself, replacing existing constructions at such a rate that by the late 19th century it was a surprisingly modern city.

Its history is, however, reflected in a highly individual, eccentric mixture of architectural styles. To a greater or lesser degree traces of most of Madrid's past epochs and their influences – Moorish, Flemish, Italian, French and American – are to be found. A truly *madrileño* architectural identity is elusive, but the city can claim one, typically unusual, style as its own – neo-Mudéjar (*see p34* **Very Moorish**). Madrid also has many totally unique monuments.

IN THE BEGINNING

The first town wall was built by the Moors, and a segment of it (known as the **Muralla Arabe**) can be found on Cuesta de la Vega, near the Almudena cathedral. Remains of the original Muslim fortress are also now being excavated next to the Palacio Real. For centuries after their 're-conquest', Madrid and most of Castile continued to have large populations of Muslims living under Christian rule, the Mudéjares. The Castilian monarchs were greatly in thrall to their superior building skills, especially in bricklaying and tiling, and throughout the Middle Ages many of the country's most important buildings incorporated techniques and styles that had originated in Muslim Andalucia. Hallmarks of the Mudéjar style are Moorish arches and intricate geometric patterns in brickwork, as seen on the 12th-century tower of Madrid's oldest surviving church, **San Nicolás de las Servitas**, built by Arab craftsmen (the body of the church was later rebuilt). Madrid's other Mudéjar tower, on **San Pedro el Viejo**, was built 200 years later. Other medieval buildings in Madrid, such as the 15th-century **Torre de los Lujanes** in Plaza de la Villa, were much plainer in style, reflecting the town's humble status before 1561.

CAPITAL GAINS

Capital status, briefly in 1561 and definitively from 1606, utterly transformed Madrid and its architecture. As royal seat, 'the Court', the tastes of successive rulers were especially important.

Philip II's favourite architect, Juan de Herrera, was the first to leave a stamp on the city. He and his royal master had little idea of urban planning, but their major constructions – the **Puente de Segovia** (1584), the first stages of the Plaza Mayor, the widening of Calles Atocha, Segovia and Mayor – gave Madrid a shape that lasts to this day.

El Escorial (*see p268*), designed by Herrera and the older architect Juan Bautista de Toledo, firmly established the 'Herreran' or 'Court' style – austere, rigid and typically employing grey slate for rooftops and the ubiquitous pointed turrets – that became near-obligatory for major

Very Moorish

Around 1870 an architectural style emerged in Madrid that the city can claim as its very own, neo-Mudéjar. It would turn up in all kinds of structures, but the first example of the style was the new bullring commissioned to replace the plain 18th-century one that stood near the Puerta de Alcalá. In the revivalist atmosphere of the 19th century, architects Ricardo Rodríguez Ayuso and Lorenzo Alvarez Capra decided not to look to Gothic or Egyptian traditions for inspiration, but searched instead for something to revive that was closer to home. They opted for the styles and superb bricklaying techniques that had been employed by the Muslim Mudéjar master builders of medieval Castile.

Neo-Mudéjar uniquely incorporated Moorish horseshoe arches, interlaced brickwork and arabesque tiling, together with a modern use of glass and cast iron. The 1870s bullring no longer stands, but the style became near-obligatory for *plazas de toros* throughout Spain, and Madrid's next ring at **Las Ventas** (*pictured*), completed in 1934, sports many neo-Mudéjar features. The style was extended to many other buildings. Perhaps the best in Madrid is the **Escuelas Aguirre**, also by Ayuso and Alvarez Capra, at the intersection of Calles Alcalá and O'Donnell on the north side of the Retiro park. Its outstanding feature is a slim minaret-style tower, with a glass and iron lookout-gallery on top. Another splendid Arab-inspired tower is the giant spire of the **Santa Cruz** church at the top of C/Atocha (No.6, by Plaza Benavente), built in 1899-1902.

Other impressive neo-Mudéjar structures scattered around Madrid include the former water tower that is now the **Sala del Canal de Isabel II** exhibition space, and the Castellana

façade of the **ABC Serrano** shopping mall (*see p182*). In La Latina there is the giant **Iglesia de la Paloma** church, which serves at the focal point of one of Madrid's most historic *fiestas* (*see p208*); the building was completed in 1911 by Álvarez Capra with neo-Gothic elements in its twin-towered frontage. The style was also used for more everyday buildings, as in the block of flats at C/Barquillo 21 in Chueca, which displays a remarkable façade that combines diamond-pattern brickwork and neo-Moorish plaster details, complemented by some elaborate iron-work balconies.

buildings in Madrid until the end of the
Habsburg era in 1700, despite changes in
fashion elsewhere in Europe. Now a symbol
of the 'Madrid of the Austrias', it is also known
as Castilian baroque, but few of its features are
especially 'Castilian': the slate pinnacles came
from Flanders, which appealed to the Flemish-
born Charles V and his son Philip.

Herrera's chief disciple, Juan Gómez de Mora,
modified his master's legacy with a lighter and
less monolithic style. He oversaw the completion
of the **Plaza Mayor** in 1619 – his original plan
is still recognisable in the slate spires, high-
pitched roofs and dormer windows – and the
1630 **Casa de la Villa**, the City Hall. Gómez
was also structurally innovative, as seen in the
massive cellars and housing blocks along Cava
San Miguel, which back on to and complete the
Plaza Mayor. Due to the abrupt drop in the level
of the land, he was obliged to build up to eight
storeys high for these blocks to meet the rest
of the square, making them Madrid's tallest
buildings until the 20th century. However,
he fell out of favour with Philip IV's minister
the Count-Duke of Olivares; in 1636, accused
of stealing a Titian from the royal collection,
Gómez was promptly dispatched to design
drainage ditches in Murcia.

His great rival in Madrid was Gian Battista
Crescenzi, an Italian who adopted the 'Court
style' – with some Italian flourishes – to please
his Spanish masters. Both architects probably
worked, at different times, on the **Palacio de
Santa Cruz** near the Plaza Mayor, built in
1629-43, nowadays the Foreign Ministry. It
shows clear Italian baroque influences, with a
façade much more richly shaped than anything
Herrera would have tried. Crescenzi, with Gómez'
former assistant Alonso Carbonell, also undertook
the largest single building scheme of Habsburg
Madrid, the **Palacio del Buen Retiro** (*see
p118*), parts of which survive still.

Though the Habsburgs commissioned much
that was noble and even palatial, 17th-century
visitors to Madrid still saw haphazard growth,
chaos and dirt rather than a city fit to be capital
of the first worldwide empire. Much building
was unimpressive owing to the increasingly
rickety economy, which meant bricks and
mortar were favoured over expensive stone.

BOURBON RENEWAL

The expiry of the Spanish Habsburgs with King
Charles II in 1700 was followed by war, and the
arrival of the Bourbons, under Philip V. The
new dynasty endeavoured to embellish and
dignify Madrid. The Bourbons were French,
and Philip V's second wife, Isabella Farnese,
was Italian, and these two influences would
long predominate in the dynasty's architectural

tastes. Nevertheless, Philip V's administrator in
Madrid, the Marqués de Vadillo, commissioned
a local architect, Pedro de Ribera, for many
projects, among them the 1722 Hospice, now
the **Museo Municipal**, the **Cuartel Conde
Duque** barracks, now the Centro Cultural
Conde Duque, the **Puente de Toledo** and
many churches. Ribera's buildings, while still
following the Herreran tradition, feature
exuberant baroque façades centred on
elaborately carved entrance porticoes, which
lend a touch of fantasy absent in Habsburg
Madrid. Many Ribera entrances still survive
on buildings that have since been rebuilt, as
in the 1734 Palace of the Dukes of Santoña at
C/Huertas 3, now occupied by the Cámara de
Comercio. In churches such as **San José** on
C/Alcalá, Ribera gave Madrid's religious
architecture a delicately ornate style.

The influence of French and Italian architects
was more apparent elsewhere in 18th-century
Madrid. After the old grey-spired **Alcázar**
burnt down in 1734 Philip V commissioned
a new **Palacio Real** from a group of mainly
Italian architects led by Filippo Juvarra and
Giambattista Sacchetti. Responsible for many
projects was Charles III's 'chief engineer',
Francesco Sabatini. The great exponents
of the sober, 'pure' neo-classicism of the
later years of Charles III's reign, however,
were Spaniards: Ventura Rodríguez, who
had also worked on the Palacio Real, and
Juan de Villanueva, architect of the **Museo
del Prado** and the **Observatorio**. Like the
greatest project of the king's reign, the **Paseo
del Prado** – of which these buildings were
part – they clearly reflect Enlightenment
ideals of architecture and urban planning.

RISE AND SPRAWL

Joseph Bonaparte's brief reign (1808-13) saw
the first demolition of monasteries and convents,
to be replaced by squares such as Plaza Santa
Ana. Generally, though, the first half of the
19th century brought architectural stagnation
to Madrid. After the great clearance of
monasteries began in the 1830s, many of
the buildings that replaced them were simple
apartment and tenement blocks, such as the
corralas (*see p105*). Public buildings of this
time, such as the 1840s **Cortes** or the **Teatro
Real** (*see p233*), were often conservative and
neo-classical in style.

Greater changes came to Madrid after 1860,
with the demolition of the walls and Carlos
María de Castro's plan for the city's extension
or '*ensanche*' (*see p110*). Areas covered by the
plan are easy to spot on a map by their grid
street pattern. Chief among them is the Barrio
de Salamanca, still the most self-consciously

Late baroque detailing on the 'new' **Palacio Real** – completed in 1764. *See p35.*

grand *barrio* of the *ensanche*. Its wealthiest residents built in an eclectic mix of styles (French Second Empire was very popular); some of their opulent mansions still stand on Calles Velázquez and Serrano. Other *ensanche* districts – Chamberí, Argüelles, Delicias – show rational urban layout, wide thoroughfares and regular-sized blocks.

Public buildings of the first years of the Bourbon Restoration were as eclectic as Salamanca mansions. Madrid's own revivalist style, neo-Mudéjar, was used for official buildings, bullrings, churches, homes and factories. This style, initiated by architects Ricardo Rodríguez Ayuso and Lorenzo Álvarez Capra around 1870, incorporated Moorish arches, arabesque tiling and interlaced brickwork with modern use of glass and iron. One outstanding example is the **Escuelas Aguirre**, complete with minaret tower and glass and iron lookout gallery, at the intersection of Calles Alcalá and O'Donnell, across from the Retiro. Also worth a look are the 1911 **Iglesia de la Paloma**, in La Latina, and the block of flats at C/Barquillo 21, in Chueca. In contrast, one of the most extraordinary constructions of the time, Ricardo Velázquez' **Ministerio de Agricultura** in Atocha, is a remarkable combination of Castilian brickwork and extravagant, French Beaux Arts-style sculpted decoration. This was also the great

period of cast-iron architecture in Madrid, with fine structures such as the city markets and the **Estación de Atocha**.

Art nouveau (called '*modernismo*' in Spain), so characteristic of early 20th-century Barcelona, aroused little interest in Madrid, but there are some examples. The **Sociedad General de Autores** (1902), by Jose Grasés Riera, is the best known (it looks like an iced cake), but the **Casa Pérez Villamil** at Plaza Matute 6, off C/Huertas, is also impressive.

CUTTING A SWATHE

As the *ensanche* progressed and Madrid's economy boomed from the 1900s to the 1920s, the city's architects looked for inspiration forwards and backwards in time, and both inside and outside Spain. The **Gran Vía** (*see p98*), a slightly weird monument to cosmopolitanism, was born of this thinking.

An all-modern thoroughfare through Madrid's old centre, the Gran Vía destroyed 14 old streets, becoming grander and more eccentric as it progressed. Writer Francisco Umbral claims it recalls New York or Chicago, but its first building of any standing, the 1905 **Edificio Metrópolis**, shows French inspiration. No.24 is neo-Renaissance, the 1930s **Palacio de la Música** cinema (No.35) has distinctly baroque touches, and the 1929 **Telefónica** building (on the corner of C/Fuencarral) is a New York

Going spaces

In February 2006 one of the largest buildings in Europe opened its doors to the public a few miles from Madrid's city centre. At more than a million square metres the new airport terminal at Barajas is the biggest on the planet.

The project was completed by a consortium of the Richard Rogers Partnership (RRP), Spanish practice Estudio Lamela, and engineering firms TPS (UK) and Initec. Inspired by ideas that emerged out of RRP's work on London Heathrow's still-to-be-completed Terminal 5, it's an impressive piece of work that has already bagged 2006's prestigious RIBA (Royal Institute of British Architecture) Stirling Prize for architecture. If you touch down at either of Terminal 4's two rod-shaped buildings, you'll immediately be knocked out by their giddying kilometre-long spaces. One structure, the main terminal, has room for nearly 40 aircraft; the other, a satellite building two kilometres away and reached by a fun automated underground railway, has space for 26. The simple 'kit of parts' design, consisting of a series of repeating 18-metre by 9-metre modules, was quick to erect and allows for easy expansion.

Unifying the spaces are the distinctive, undulating Chinese bamboo-insulated roofs that form a brown sea of wooden waves stretching as far as you can see. These roofs are supported by central 'trees', each coloured to create a graduated rainbow effect down the uniform halls. They stretch out over the edge of the buildings' glass façades, sheltering them from the hot sun – part of a passive environmental system that also includes low-energy ventilation.

Natural light is a key feature, flooding in through the glass walls and rooftop oval skylights and penetrating down to all six levels – three above ground

and transparent; three below ground and concrete – through deep 'canyons'. These canyons divide the main terminal lengthways into three clear sections to aid orientation for passengers: one for check-in, one for security and one for boarding.

With its environmental sensitivity and simple palette of materials (which also includes natural stone floors), T4 emphasises clarity and tranquillity, aiming to soothe the stresses and strains of travel. Yet despite this, the structure's sheer size – it can take nearly half an hour to get from security to some satellite terminal gates – can turn a dash for a last call into a nerve-wracking endurance test.

The new terminal has proved a huge success, but its high profile also means it has attracted the worst kind of attention. At 9am on Saturday 30 December 2006, a bomb in a Renault Trafic van ripped through one of the integrated car parks, destroying more than half of it and, despite telephone warnings, killing two people. The blast also caused damage to the main terminal building across the forecourt. Basque separatist group ETA claimed responsibility, breaking a nine-month ceasefire. Services got back to normal pretty quickly, but this was a regrettable end to the first year of Madrid's elegant new gateway to the world.

skyscraper in miniature. The 1930 apartment block at Gran Vía 60 is a classic of *madrileño* cosmopolitanism, by Carlos Fernández Shaw, who in 1927 also built a futuristic petrol station where C/Alberto Aguilera meets Vallehermoso. Also working at this time was the very original Antonio Palacios, main architect of the **Palacio de Comunicaciones** (1904-18) – a remarkable hotchpotch of Spanish, American and Viennese art nouveau influences – and the more subtle **Círculo de Bellas Artes**.

During its brief existence the Spanish Republic further encouraged rationalist, rather self-consciously modern architecture, as in the earliest parts of the **Nuevos Ministerios**. Art deco architecture was in vogue, in office blocks like the **Capitol** building on Gran Vía (corner of C/Jacometrezo) or the curious model housing district of **El Viso**, with some of the most unusual domestic architecture in Madrid.

Civil war and the arrival of the Franco regime brought much destruction, and had an immediate impact in architecture. Falangist architectural thinking was dominated by nostalgia for a glorious past, and so Madrid acquired monster constructions that looked straight back to imperial Spain's Golden Age, combined with ideas from German and Italian Fascist architecture. The results were often grandiose, bombastic and, probably unwittingly, kitsch. The foremost example is the **Ministerio del Aire**, at the top of C/Princesa. Originally planned on a German model, on completion it resembled a pastiche Escorial, Herreran pinnacles and all, hence its nickname, the 'Monasterio del Aire'. In Plaza de España is the manically colossal **Edificio España**, the work of brothers Joaquín and José María Otamendi, completed in 1953. Conceived along American lines to be a 'small city' in one huge block, with shops, offices, a hotel and apartments, the building acquired all sorts of neo-Herreran decorative touches outside, ending up as a Castilian baroque skyscraper. The affluent Barrio de Salamanca also contains a good many retro constructions from the era, above all huge churches such as the 1952 **San Francisco de Borja** at the corner of Calles Serrano and Diego de León, vast in scale and ambition, and based on 17th-century Jesuit baroque churches in Madrid, Toledo and Rome.

By the 1950s the regime's ideological enthusiasms were fading, although it still sought to impress. Built with no pretence at neo-baroque or anything similar is the tacky 32-floor 1957 **Torre de Madrid** on Plaza de España, reminiscent of Latin American constructions of the same era. These years, though, also saw the beginnings of real modernity in Madrid, most notably with Francisco Cabrero and Rafael Aburto's Casa Sindical at Paseo del Prado 18-20, built in 1948-9 for the Francoist labour unions and now the Health Ministry. This was a forerunner of much later rationalist architecture in the city.

Until the 1960s the floundering Spanish economy still limited the scope for building. When the economy did improve, Madrid opened up to international influences, but much of its newest buildings were dreary apartment blocks, built for a rapidly growing population.

BACK TO THE FUTURE

As Spanish society and the economy opened up with the rebirth of democracy in the late 1970s, one effect of Francoist retro-obsessions was that Spanish architects – and the public – felt little inclination to look back with nostalgia or add neo-classical fronts to new buildings, and welcomed modernity with gusto. The most influential contemporary architects in Madrid have been Alejandro de la Sota and Francisco Sáenz de Oíza, both active since the 1950s, and Sáenz's gifted and original protégé Rafael Moneo.

An important factor in building during the 1980s was the Socialist takeover of the city council, in 1979, and the government in 1982. Mayor Tierno Galván's Ayuntamiento was committed to the regeneration of public spaces, and so facilitated the emergence of one of the characteristic features of modern Madrid – daringly imaginative 'grand revamps' of long-decrepit historic buildings. An outstanding example is the **Estación de Atocha**, a run-down, filthy 1880s cast-iron railway terminal that revamp specialist Rafael Moneo transformed into a spectacular multi-purpose space. The **Reina Sofía** and **Thyssen** museums – also by Moneo – were similarly rebuilt, and the Centro Cultural Conde Duque was created out of Ribera's 1720s barracks, making effective use even of cracks in the old façade.

Outside the public domain the most vigorous contributions to Madrid since the 1980s have been the skyscrapers that line the upper Paseo de la Castellana, by the **AZCA** area, such as the **Catalana Occidente** insurance company building (No.50), the superb white 1988 **Torre Picasso** by Minoru Yamasaki, and the spectacular leaning towers of the **Puerta de Europa** at Plaza Castilla. With Madrid's expansion much recent building has been on the city's edge, such as the **Feria de Madrid** complex (*see p297*), a corporate showcase, Manuel Delgado and Fernando Vasco's **Estadio de la Comunidad de Madrid**, a dramatic structure in the form of a tilted oval plate, and most recently, the Richard Rogers' neon extravaganza that is Barajas airport's new terminal (*see p37* **Going spaces**).

Madrid Today

Bigger, brighter and brasher than before.

The terrorist attacks of 11 March 2004 on Madrid's commuter rail network changed many things, both in the city and in Spain as a whole. Three days later, José Maria Aznar's right-wing PP (Partido Popular) government, which had been expecting a relatively easy election victory, was rudely swept from office, victim of the voters' anger at its deceitful and inept reaction to the outrage. A new PSOE (Partido Socialista Obrero Español: socialist) administration was catapulted unexpectedly into power and, once the dust had settled, began to whittle away industriously at every aspect of the old regime that it could conveniently reach. The city licked its wounds and began to heal.

In the first three years of its mandate, José Luis Rodríguez Zapatero's government has reversed official attitudes to immigration, legalised gay marriage, taken steps to curb the influence of the Church in education, and redrawn the relationship between the centre and the regions, most notably in Catalonia. It has tinkered with the tax laws, started to improve the inadequate safety net of the Spanish welfare state, and until the unexpected Barajas airport bombing in December 2006 had

been making moves towards a viable peace process in the Basque country. As for foreign policy, the government has attempted to reinsert Spain into the heart of Europe and to become a serious player in the quest for peace in the Middle East. The saturnine Prime Minister appears a driven man, intent on being remembered as the leader of a great reforming administration. Meanwhile, the PP, as defeated parties do, has retreated into its core constituency, and politics has become sharply confrontational. Some cautious commentators have pointed out that historically, Spain has a poor track record of coping with entrenched and polarised attitudes, but not much attention is currently being paid to these folk.

The heady days following the election are long gone, and the grind of day-to-day politics has returned, with Madrid finding itself in a privileged but awkward position. It is the first city of a nation that seems to be redefining itself as a quasi-federal state, and as such retains its status, despite fears that the new Catalan statute favours the old rival, Barcelona, at Madrid's expense. Spain's strong economic growth, among the highest in the EU, is being driven by the capital, and the renewal of the historic tension between the centre and the periphery has revitalised the city's attitude to itself and to the rest of the country. The decade-long housing boom goes on and on, although interest rate rises and financial scandals have slowed it somewhat. At the turn of the millennium, City Hall and the province of Madrid, both controlled by the PP, embarked on a massive and fiendishly expensive infrastructure regeneration programme, originally tied to the city's bid to host the 2012 Olympics. This has left large parts of the capital in what seems like a permanent state of reconstruction (*see p41* **Mayor at work**). Whatever the pros and cons of these projects, they have helped drive unemployment down to historic lows and generated a feeling of optimism (albeit heavily laced with exasperated grumbling).

The 2007 local election results will shape what happens in Madrid over the next few years. Another PP win will mean the electorate have bitten the bullet and decided that the eventual benefits promised by Alberto Ruiz Gallardón's grandiose urban renewal dream outweigh their current despair at the state of the city. They may be in for a surprise. The idea of a congestion charge, London style, is being trailed, and if introduced will elicit howls of pain and rage from almost everyone.

A tax on the right to sit in gridlocked traffic while pumping more contaminants into the already semi-opaque air will be regarded as a deadly threat to civil liberties. On the other hand, if the previously unknown Miguel Sebastián steals a surprise victory, and becomes Madrid's first Socialist mayor for nearly two decades, the challenges facing his inexperienced new administration will be daunting. He will have a mandate to deal with the disruption caused by the rebuilding, and the €6 billion (and rising) of public debt that has been incurred, and will have to decide which projects can be axed and which are so far gone that completion is inevitable. Behind any immediate policy changes though, and providing the yardsticks by which either victor will be judged, lurk the problems of affordable housing for the young and for immigrants – both currently priced out of the market – and the channelling of money out of public works and back into the community. And if the housing bubble bursts, as it must eventually, then all bets are off.

THE CHANGING FACES OF MADRID

Walk down any street in Madrid today and listen. Spanish is being spoken, of course, but the accents that you'll hear are not all from Spain; the lilting tones of South America and the mangled grammar of other immigrants are everywhere. You'll hear Romanian, Polish, and every other European language, not to mention Chinese, Arabic, and a medley of African tongues. Suddenly, Madrid seems as multicultural as London, and to many *madrileños* this has come as a profound and unwelcome shock.

Poll after poll has identified immigration as Spaniards' in general, and *madrileños*' in particular, number one concern. This is hardly surprising: the almost daily images of exhausted sub-Saharan men, women and children being eased out of their ramshackle craft and laid in rows, living or dead, on the beaches of the Canary Islands, are a depressing reminder that Spain is on the front line of the refugee exodus from Africa. The fact is, however, that the bulk of immigration is through Barajas airport or over the Pyrenees. From a level of less than two per cent in 1996, the capital's foreign-born population now stands at a whopping 15 per cent, the highest in the country. The 'visibility threshold' has long been breached, and attitudes are hardening.

Nationally, the government is making determined efforts to square the circle, as is the city administration. A campaign commitment to orderly and legal immigration resulted in a partial amnesty for illegal immigrants who

Mayor at work

Since Alberto Ruíz Gallardón left the position of Regional President and stepped up as Mayor of Madrid in 2003, his public appearances have fallen into a familiar pattern. Each week, he travels to some area of the city plagued by diggers, cranes and cement mixers, inspects the work in progress, and thanks the nearby residents and business people for their understanding and patience. This mayor is intent on modernising Madrid.

On average, there have been 70 major construction projects under way at the same time in Madrid over the past few years: some at a minor level, like the pedestrianisation of Huertas, and some on such a scale – like the mammoth job of sending the M30 ring road underground and into tunnels – you'd be forgiven for thinking the city was emerging from some kind of Blitzkrieg.

The M30 project has caused most controversy, and certainly most disruption. Gallardón has, or will have, spent some €3.5 billion on the road. Whether it will be a success is yet to be seen, considering that, as we go to press, only one stretch of the tunnels has been opened. What is certain, though, is that the project has been the curse of commuters and taxi drivers for two whole years.

Truth be told, when it comes to modernisation, the mayor may well have a point. Unlike Barcelona and Seville, cities that were revamped for the Olympics and the Expo respectively, Madrid has never had an excuse for a bit of cement-based cosmetic surgery. It was, according to Gallardón, at risk of getting left behind by other European capitals such as London and Paris. Of course, the Madrid bid for the 2012 Olympics was a great motivator for the works, and the city's failure to win the bid was a major setback for the mayor. But within no time, Gallardón announced that Madrid would be back in the running for the 2016 Games.

Whatever the promised benefits of the works and the Games, for ordinary *madrileños* the endless construction has been massively disruptive. Many have had to endure a daily obstacle course on their walk to the office, as they negotiate piles of sand and bricks and two-metre-deep holes in the pavement. In addition, the landscape has been blighted with green plastic fencing. When the mayor opened the C/Montera as a newly pedestrianised street, there was one chunk of it yet to be converted into a paved zone. The reason? It was still being dug up to make way for the new Chamartín-Atocha rail link. Even the completed works have yet more works to be wrought upon them.

Nevertheless, some of the completed projects have been highly popular. The pedestrianisation of Huertas, for example, banished the traffic and added gold-leaf lettering to the pavement in the 'literary neighbourhood'. And the complete refitting of the square at Tirso de Molina saw a run-down area banished of its winos and junkies, to be replaced by playgrounds, fountains and a permanent flower market. Top marks to the mayor for those two.

But the real test for the popularity of the mayor's projects will come at the elections in May 2007: the month when, funnily enough, all of the work is due to be completed. Only then will *madrileños* get to judge whether the disruption and bother of all that construction has been worth it – or whether Gallardón is, as many commentators have called him, a pharaoh, desperate to leave his imprint on the city during his time in office. Whatever the case, once Sol is clear of those dreaded green screens, expect to see a roaring trade in 'I survived the roadworks' T-shirts.

registered and found employment, and official reports and working papers all stress that the high level of economic growth is a direct result of immigration and the incorporation of immigrants into the workforce. Certainly, most bars and restaurants in the city appear to be staffed by South Americans, and their kitchens by sub-Saharan Africans and Filipinos; the construction industry is heavily Andean and east European, and cleaners and home-helps are almost uniformly of immigrant origin. But while a low-wage, grey economy in the service sector may be a key motor of economic growth, the trickle-down effect is, so far, absent, with job security zero and exploitation rife.

The upside of the phenomenon is an explosion of small businesses, corner shops, specialist food outlets and restaurants, which has transformed the city. Five years ago, good Chinese or Indian food was hard to come by, and expensive when you found it. Now, *madrileños* can experiment with the pleasures of non-Spanish cuisine at affordable prices, and the choices are increasing every day. Korean, Lebanese, Uruguayan, Japanese, Thai… they're all available now.

The inner-city heart of immigrant settlement, Lavapiés, is a world community in miniature. To the surprise of many who predicted disaster and confrontation, the cross-fertilisation of cultures has created a vibrant and fascinating, if sometimes frustrated, neighbourhood. Compared to the sullen mood of the last months of the Aznar government, the city is buzzing.

SMOKING THEM OUT?

The other eye- and nose-catching change is in the attitude to tobacco. As was the case in Ireland and Italy, the new anti-smoking laws – which among other things require bars and restaurants over 100sq m to have separate, contained non-smoking areas – have been accepted with surprising placidity. Now, every shop and office building has its outdoor ashtrays in place for addicted employees, and larger bars and restaurants have (mostly) complied with the new regulations. The regional government of Madrid, however, chose to challenge some of the new law's provisions in the courts, with the result that many smaller establishments remain in a smoky limbo. A high proportion of them have no areas for non-smokers. Clubs and late-night venues are also protesting the ban on economic grounds. It is too soon to say what the verdict of the appeal court will be, but at least it's now possible to eat and drink in comfort.

NEW TIMES, NEW MOODS

Plus ça change, plus c'est la même chose.
If the 1980s was a time to party amid the experimentalism and excesses of the post-Franco Movida, then the 1990s saw many of the Movida generation settle down to a job and a mortgage. After the scandals associated with the Socialists under Felipe González, many voters identified the PP with the grown-up business of making money. But what goes around comes around, and the PP soon became seen as the party of self-interest and arrogance and not listening to the people. Now the grandchildren of the Movida, left-wing and postmodern, are looking for fun, and mostly, they're finding it.

There's a generation gap at work in people's perception of 'happening Madrid'. To anyone over 30 the scene was better ten years ago than now, but to visitors and the new cohorts of youth, the sparkle of Madrid at night is still irresistible. Maybe this is something that happens to all generations in all cities at all times, but the tensions and changes of the past three years have conspired to make the phenomenon more noticeable here. The fun-zones of the city have become more defined, though the division owes as much to attitude as age, and nowhere is exclusionary. Teenagers and Generation Xers party in Moncloa and Argüelles; older twentysomethings cluster in the bars around Alonso Martínez; the over-30s opt for La Latina. Huertas is for everybody. Unfortunately, the price of partying has soared, with drinks costing up to 50 per cent more than they did three years ago, though they're still cheap compared to other European capitals.

The range of activities available has widened over recent years: not merely restaurant choice, but stimuli for all the senses. High culture and low amusement are still crammed together cheek by jowl, and somehow manage to mingle without too much friction. Madrid is small compared to other European capitals, sitting compactly around its own core. It has never aspired to be Euro-hip in the way that Barcelona has. This is not a self-regarding city where style and appearance are all, and the important thing has always been to be out and about with friends, afloat in the crowded good humour of the streets.

This guide sometimes bemoans Madrid's loss of innocence, but innocence is always ephemeral. March 2004 was a political watershed, turning the country back towards Europe after the Atlanticism of the Aznar government, but it also restarted Madrid's love affair with itself. The city is more expensive, populous, anonymous and competitive than it was even five years ago, but it's still Madrid. Internationalism is fine, but the local heartbeat is strong and the old lady is kicking up her heels again. To *madrileños* nothing is more interesting than Madrid.

Plaza de Toros de Las Ventas. *See p44.*

Seeing the Bulls

Robert Elms puts the case for the 'fiesta nacional'.

For many visitors to Spain the bullfight is a barbaric anachronism, a preening blood sport that is dying out in this modern land. Well, they're right about it being bloody: this is not a fun day out for the squeamish. But they're wrong on every other count. First off, it isn't a sport. The essence of sport is an even contest where the end result is unpredictable. The events in the arena are not a competition, and the end result is always the same – the bulls will die. The harsh reality is that you are watching the ritual slaughter of six animals for sheer entertainment. Closest perhaps to opera, and reviewed in the culture section of most newspapers, this is a theatrical performance, a tragedy, involving a truly wild animal and men in *trajes de luces*, 'suits of lights'. Of course it isn't fair; it isn't supposed to be.

And it certainly isn't dying out. Over the last few years the number of events held throughout Spain – and the number of people attending them – has been rising to record levels. Television has taken the top stars of the ring to new heights and the leading matadors are among the highest-paid performers in the world. That young boy in tight trousers might well be earning €120,000 (£80,000) a day for his murderous work. Therefore a great ticket for an important fight can set you back a good deal of money, if, that is, you can get your hands on one at all. On the big days in the big rings, every seat is sold and the atmosphere at this highly social event is electric, with the whole city seemingly hanging on every pass.

And it isn't really a bullfight either – that's a clumsy English mistranslation of *la corrida*, the bull-running. Any man foolish enough to fight a wild bull would die in seconds. The Iberian fighting bull is arguably the most dangerous animal in the world and the idea is to control it and then dance with it before dispatching it; to create a fleeting but sometimes profound beauty out of the act of slaughter. To the Spanish this is a celebration of death, which in other countries is hidden away, as countless animals die in ignominy in abattoirs. The bull, which has lived a minimum of four years of absolutely natural existence, on the finest pasture Spain

Where and how

The 25,000-capacity Las Ventas bullring holds *corridas* every Sunday from March to October, as well as on various public holidays and festivals. The traditional starting time is 7pm, though some kick off as early as 5pm.

Tickets for Sunday bullfights can be obtained at the *taquillas* (ticket windows) near the main entrance of the bullring or online at the official website (see details below). Prices vary greatly. As a rule of thumb the nearer the seat is to the arena, the pricier the ticket. Any equivalent ticket is cheaper in *sol* (in the sun) than in *sombra* (in the shade). Thus a front row seat in *sombra* for a *corrida de toros* will cost you €115.50, while a seat in the gallery in *sol* for the same fight only costs €3.80. Prices are halved for *novilladas* (fights with young bulls and young matadors).

If you can't get a ticket at the *taquillas*, there are plenty of authorised agents in Madrid, though they charge 20 per cent commission. Try La Taurina (C/Pasaje Matheu s/n, 91 522 92 16) or Localidades Galicia (Plaza del Carmen 1, 91 531 27 32). There is also an independent online booking service, www.ticketstoros.com, with pages in English. Tickets can then be collected at the TEYCI kiosk, just a few metres from the main *taquilla*, an hour before the *corrida* begins. You'll need to show your passport, or confirmation email if you booked online.

Plaza de Toros de Las Ventas

C/Alcalá 237 (91 726 35 70/www.las-ventas.com). Metro Ventas. **Open** Box office Mar-Oct 10am-2pm, 5-8pm Fri, Sat; from 10am on fight days. Closed Nov-Feb. **Tickets** €2-€115.50. **Credit** MC, V.

LAS FERIAS

The best time to watch a top-quality *corrida* is during the Feria de San Isidro. For 20 consecutive evenings from mid May to early June, bullfights are held at 7pm, including *novilladas*, *rejones* (on horseback) and *Goyescas* (in period costume). It is, however, difficult to get tickets for what is the highlight of the season for bullfighting aficionados. Most tickets for the San Isidro are snapped up way in advance by season-ticket holders. Any that are unclaimed are put on sale five days before the corresponding fight; by law 1,000 tickets for each fight must be put up for sale at 10am of the day of the fight, though huge queues form for these. San Isidro is preceded by the Feria de la Comunidad, which has a number of *novilladas* and a major fight on 2 May. Fights are also held daily during the Feria de Otoño, beginning in late September.

THE CULTURE

A good introduction to bullfighting is Ernest Hemingway's often brilliant account of this most Spanish of spectacles, *Death in the Afternoon*. You can find reviews and forthcoming line-ups in the local press and in weekly magazines such as *6 Toros 6* and *Aplausos*. You can mix with aficionados before and after fights, in bars and restaurants near Las Ventas such as Los Timbales (C/Alcalá 227); Donde Leo and El Albero, both at C/Pedro Heredia 22; or Taberna de Sierra on C/Villafranca 11. In May, before San Isidro, you can inspect the bulls, which are on public display in the Casa del Campo near Batán metro. The bulls can also be seen at Las Ventas on the morning of each fight.

OUTSIDE MADRID

Many towns within easy reach of Madrid stage *corridas* on some Sundays during the season and on their annual saint's day. Many also hold bull fairs, with daily bullfights, during their annual fiestas. These small-town fairs often include an *encierro*, in which young bulls are run through the streets first thing in the morning, as in Pamplona's San Fermín. But be warned: bull-running requires a deal of acquired skill, and untrained tourists should be aware that joining in is extremely dangerous. Several have died doing so.

The first bullfights of the year take place in freezing February in **Valdemorillo**, to the north-west of Madrid. **Aranjuez** holds important bullfighting *ferias* on 30 May and in early September. But August is the cruellest month for the bulls: **Chinchón** has *novilladas* in its historic Plaza Mayor, and a smaller event takes place in **Manzanares el Real**. The most spectacular *encierro* close to Madrid is in **San Sebastián de los Reyes**, while the most prestigious fair is the one in **Colmenar Viejo**; both in late August. **Toledo** holds a bullfight on Corpus Christi day.

There is more information on these towns in the **Trips Out of Town** chapter (*see pp266-289*). For dates and details of transport, *see p308* **Tourist information**.

can provide, then gets his chance for a day of destiny and maybe even glory in the sun. 'We are going to see the bulls,' they say.

At heart, the Spanish attitude to the *corrida* comes from a profoundly different view of nature. In Britain, for example, a temperate country, long urbanised and industrialised, nature is a distant green and fluffy thing that has to be protected. In Spain, a land still tied to agriculture, where the sun is too hot and the soil too poor, nature is a powerful, noble adversary, which has to be respected but dominated. And the fighting bull is its greatest champion. Day after day Spain sends her young men (and the occasional woman) out on to the sand (*arena* simply means sand) to enact this elaborate metaphor of man's continuing struggle with nature, to prove that beauty can still be summoned from the beast.

If this all sounds preposterously poetic, that's because it is. Artists and writers as diverse as Picasso and Hemingway, Orson Welles and García Márquez have been attracted to the bloody arenas, because at best the bullfight is a profound lyrical and visceral exploration of the meaning of both death and life. Lorca, the great Andalucían poet, so enamoured of the bulls, called *la corrida* 'the last serious thing'. And the Spanish certainly take it seriously.

But that doesn't mean that if you go and see one it will be any good. Even the superstar matadors don't come with a guarantee, and what they are attempting is a difficult and dangerous business with a genuinely wild and unpredictable animal. The ideal is that the various prescribed stages of this highly technical ritual are played out fluently and smoothly, all grace and style. The bull should be brave and noble, and the men controlled and artistic. The emotional high point should be the *faena*, when the matador is in the ring alone with the bull and the true dance of death occurs. This is where man and animal become almost as one as they pass each other time and again, closer and closer, in a heart-stopping blur of crimson and gold. Then the moment of truth arrives and the great beast should be felled with a single blow from the sword. That's how it should be.

But of course it isn't always, and what is supposed to be elegant and honest can end up brutal and clumsy, unworthy of the poetry and the art. Sometimes the bulls are flawed and weak, other times the matadors cowardly and sloppy. There are tricks, too, to fool all but the most ardent eye, and horns can be shaved to reduce the danger. This is a serious business and it can be a dodgy one.

But then, one blazing afternoon under an unforgiving southern sun, all the fates will fall into place. A bull, fierce and swift and handsome, will come racing out into a packed *plaza*, hear the crowd gasp, and see the matador straighten. He will charge and charge and the men will work with valour and honour to make sure that his death, and therefore his life, is a memorable one. The extraordinary emotion transmitted from the matador, the man in the gleaming gold, charged with the terrible task of dealing death, will infect the crowd. As he connects and cavorts with the bull, *olés* soft and long will start to emerge, a collective exhalation, as a single man takes the primeval power of this beautiful adversary and slows it to a dream with a few sublime swishes of his cape. Then, finally, in frozen silence he will leap over the horns, his sword straight to the heart and his place in the annals assured.

On such, all too rare, days, the dreadful danger and the awesome artistry will touch every soul present. I've seen grown men sob on such days. I've seen and felt and known why Spain still clings to this ancient and terrible entertainment, as the very soul of its identity, *la fiesta nacional*. If you dare to see for yourself, you may possibly witness such a rare and wondrous afternoon.

Bullfighting memorabilia.

Movida Movies

Lights, camera… ¡*acción*!

The seasonal skies of Madrid that enthralled Goya and Velázquez have been a similar gift to film-makers. Many foreign epics of the 1960s were made in the studios on the city's outskirts, including Anthony Mann's *El Cid* (1961) and *The Fall of the Roman Empire* (1964), Nicholas Ray's *King of Kings* (1961) and *55 Days at Peking* (1963), and David Lean's *Dr Zhivago* (1965). Recent internationally made films to have employed the city and environs include Milos Forman's *Goya's Ghosts* (2006) and Paul Greengrass's *The Bourne Ultimatum* (2007), the concluding episode of the Euro-tripping, amnesiac spy tale.

But although Madrid makes the top rank alongside such cinematic cities as New York, Paris and Tokyo, it is best understood by Spanish film-makers, who have captured the skies, architecture and contrasts in several classic and modern masterpieces. The creative force of Spanish cinema was especially intense during the Movida, the cultural, sexual and chemical free-for-all that followed Spain's transition to democracy in the 1970s and early '80s – immortalised in Pedro Almodóvar's earliest films.

The Movida took its name from a Spanish phrase meaning 'to have a business thing happening', which also doubled as slang for 'a drug transaction'. It was partly an ad hoc translation of British punk that assumed a similarly neo-patriotic stance by assimilating traditional Spanish values into its bizarre new get-up. Unlike British punk, however, the Movida was not so much a working-class movement as a drug-fuelled middle-class pretence of bohemian rebellion against the imbalanced society of the recent past.

Perhaps the most crucial venue of the Movida's cinematic manifestation was the Alphaville (C/Martin de los Heros 14), which has recently changed its name to Golem. This still-thriving cinema opened in 1977 (when Spain's transition to peaceful democracy and public liberty was assured), and immediately established its revolutionary credentials with a week-long festival of Cuban films. Early screenings also included such underground favourites as Andy Warhol's *Flesh* (1968) – shown to sensorially enhanced audiences – as well as the most transgressive Spanish films of the period like Iván Zulueta's *Arrebato*

(*Rapture*, 1980). *Arrebato* is a fevered collage of horror clichés seen through the paranoid perspective of its semi-autobiographical protagonist, a director who battles his own warped psyche by filming himself while asleep.

The former Alphaville continued to feature politically charged cinema, especially of the contemporary German kind. Wim Wenders' *The American Friend* (1977) still holds the record for the longest continuous run, at an impressive 67 weeks. This pales, however, alongside the ten years of late-night screenings enjoyed by Almodóvar's *Laberinto de pasiones* (*Labyrinth of Passion*, 1982), which was (perhaps only coincidentally) partly produced by the cinema's manager.

Laberinto de pasiones is a melodramatic, absurdist farce about a nymphomaniac called Sexilia (Cecilia Roth), a gay Islamic terrorist named Sadec (Antonio Banderas) and the son of the exiled Shah of Iran (Imanol Arias). Gobsmacked by the film's outrageousness,

All very Welles

Rivalled only by Hemingway in his Hispanophilia, Orson Welles was no stranger to Madrid – drawn by history, sanctuary and a love of bulls. Welles had decamped from Hollywood to Europe at the end of the 1940s. His first significant sojourn in Madrid was in 1954 to direct *Confidential Report* (aka *Mr Arkadin*), a near rerun of *Citizen Kane* about an amnesiac millionaire (Welles) who hires a smuggler to uncover his shady past. Welles shot the film at Madrid's Sevilla Films Studios (now a giant supermarket), apparently 'borrowing' items from the lobby of his hotel, the Castellana Hilton, to dress the sets of the under-funded production. For Arkadin's Spanish castle Welles used the fairytale Alcázar in Segovia, whose striking Roman aqueduct also served as a backdrop.

Back in town, Welles would hang out in spots like Viva Madrid (C/Manuel Fernández y González 7, Santa Ana, 91 429 36 40), Casa Labra (C/Tetuán 12, Sol, 91 531 00 81) and Museo Chicote (Gran Vía 12, 91 532 67 37, www.museo-chicote.com), where the likes of Ava Gardner, Grace Kelly and Frank Sinatra also passed through. He indulged his love of bullfighting at the Las Ventas ring, pitching up there in summer 1955 to film an episode of his six-part ITV series, *Around the World with Orson Welles*.

Quixotic old Spain captivated Welles, so much so he spent from 1955 to his death in 1985 struggling to film Cervantes' novel – in Spain and elsewhere. Significant chunks of this unfinished masterpiece now reside in the Filmoteca Española in Lavapiés. Spain's palpable sense of the past (and Spanish funding) led Welles to film his Shakespeare reworking *Chimes at Midnight* here (1964-65), employing the medieval architecture around Madrid, including the turreted walls of Avila to recreate 15th-century 'Merrie England'. The film's spectacular battle scenes were shot in Madrid's Casa de Campo park.

Another *Chimes...* location was the medieval town of Chinchón, south-west of Madrid, where in autumn 1967 Welles also filmed the Isak Dinesen story *The Immortal Story*. With a few strategically placed Chinese banners and suitably attired extras, Chinchón's rickety houses effectively doubled for 19th-century Macao. It's said that at one point during filming, Welles tumbled backwards into a fountain, immediately clambering out again, ignoring the laughter, to call for a retake. In the 1960s, Welles sought solace from his professional disappointments here. He rented a house on C/Toledillo and enjoyed the town's *anís* each morning with the locals, as well as finding time to autograph one of the wine vats at Mesón Cuevas del Vino (*pictured*). Rumour has it he wanted to be buried in Chinchón (his ashes were ultimately scattered on bullfighter Antonio Ordoñez's ranch in Ronda, Andalucía).

Things weren't always so peaceful, however. In August 1970 a wing of the villa he owned in Madrid's Aravaca quarter burnt down, destroying precious scripts, films and personal treasures, including the only print of his first, pre-*Kane* film *Too Much Johnson*. It's depressing to think of the lost wonders, but they also add to the myths – the myths that brought Welles here, that he constructed about himself and that others continue to construct.

most international critics failed to notice the romanticism and compassion that Almodóvar clearly felt for those who had so recently been marginalised from Spanish society.

As well as in film, the Movida was documented in the magazine *La Luna*, in Francisco Umbral's long-running column in the *El País* newspaper, and in TV programmes. There were also alternative music and variety shows presented by Paloma Chamorro and Almodóvar's earliest (and recently reconciled) muse, the actress Carmen Maura.

Maura starred with the punk diva Alaska in *Pepi, Luci, Bom y otras chicas del montón* (*Pepi, Luci, Bom and Other Girls Like Mom*, 1980), which was two years in the making on a £20,000 budget raised by Almodóvar from his friends. In this scatological melodrama of female solidarity, Pepi (Maura) and Bom (Alaska) seek to liberate the masochistic Luci (Eva Siva) from her marriage to a policeman who respects her too much to beat her. Luci becomes a groupie for a band of degenerates, which provokes her jealous husband into beating her senseless, thereby resulting in a happy ending. The perverse yet romantic logic of the film was a faithful reflection of its time and audience, many of whom featured in the scenes set in the legendary Rock-Ola nightclub (a cavernous dive, both garish and grimy, crammed with glam rockers, punk rockers and simply off their rockers) and other venues of the Movida, such as the Alphaville, which hosted the première in October 1980.

Almodóvar's humour became gradually darker in his later films, when disillusionment with democracy and the fall-out from the drug-fuelled and sex-motivated excesses of the Movida soiled the carefree mood. By *¡Átame!* (*Tie Me Up! Tie Me Down!*, 1989) the director was seeking to reconcile his wayward characters with the more conventional elements of Spain, such as the family unit and fidelity, because the human cost of the Movida in terms of drug abuse and AIDS by then so apparent. Drugs had been the main spur to the fantasy nightlife, but by *¿Qué he hecho yo para merecer esto?* (*What Have I Done to Deserve This?*, 1984) the drug-dealing son of glue-sniffing housewife Gloria (Carmen Maura) is warning her not to graduate to hard drugs and in *¡Átame!*, although the psychopathic Ricky (Antonio Banderas) kidnaps ex-junkie porn star Marina (Victoria Abril), he shows great concern for her returning need. Indeed, a prime motor of the plot of *Todo sobre mi madre* (*All About My Mother*, 1999) is the effort of the female collective to rescue one of their ilk from her addiction, and there is clearly something desperately retrospective about the wish-fulfilment ending of this film, which culminates in the miraculous birth of a child whose immune system holds a cure for AIDS.

Sadly, the Rock-Ola nightclub (C/Padre Xifré 5), which featured in *Laberinto de pasiones*, is now a supermarket. Several of the most iconic venues of the Movida have also gone, such as the Carolina discotheque (C/Bravo Murillo 202), which became a clothes shop. Nevertheless, the Alphaville (now the Golem) and the clubs El Penta (C/Palma 4), La Vía Láctea (C/Velarde 18) and El Sol (C/Jardines 3) remain, with the latter recently hosting a reunion concert by the leading groups of the period.

La Bobia bar on the edge of the Rastro (C/San Millán 3), where the opening sequence of *Laberinto* was filmed, is still standing, but now home to a rather dull café. A leisurely walking tour could start from here, after which you could move on up to the Plaza Mayor, where Otto and Ana so narrowly miss each other in Julio Medem's *Los amantes del Círculo Polar* (*Lovers of the Arctic Circle*, 1998), and on to the Plaza de España, where Sofia and Jota collide in Medem's *La ardilla roja* (*Red Squirrel*, 1993). From here, you can either head up the raucous Gran Vía, so miraculously deserted in Alejandro Amenábar's *Abre los ojos* (*Open Your Eyes*, 1997), or head into the sidestreets surrounding the Ópera district, where Matías meets his cousin Violeta in Fernando Trueba's *Ópera prima* (*First Effort*, 1980). Either route should get you to Callao in time for an *aperitivo* beneath the hoarding of the FNAC superstore (C/Preciados 28), which hosted the advertising for Leo's novel in Almodóvar's *La flor de mi secreto* (*The Flower of My Secret*, 1995), before a stroll to the Sevilla metro station where Antonio, the rogue ETA terrorist, shoots a cop in Imanol Uribe's *Días contados* (*Running Out of Time*, 1994). Enjoy lunch in one of the bars on the Plaza de Colón, close to the María Guerrero Theatre (C/Tamayo y Baus 4) where Becky (Marisa Paredes) performed 'Piensa en mí' in Almodóvar's *Tacones lejanos* (*High Heels*, 1991). Then consider an afternoon spent shopping in the chic barrio of Chueca, where Almodóvar filmed *La ley del deseo* (*Law of Desire*, 1987) or the bustling Tetuán, where he set much of *Volver* (2006).

Whatever less truthful guide books might have you believe, the Movida is now long gone, being uniquely of its time and therefore rightly defunct. You can still go from bar to bar in Madrid, check out a gig at El Sol, catch something avant-garde at Alphaville, and pretend along with many avid tourists and nostalgic Spaniards that the Movida is still happening. But resist the pretence – Almodóvar turns 60 in 2009 and, like him, this extraordinary period in Madrid's cultural history is best revisited through his films.

Corral de la Pacheca. *See p52.*

Flamenco

A taste of the south.

The Gypsy *cantaor*, the singer of flamenco *cante jondo*, or 'deep song', is the voice of his race and the keeper of its myths. Although flamenco is commonly perceived and exploited as a joyful and colourful form of song and dance, it is really about suffering and anguish. Its origins lie in the language and traditions of the Andalucian Gypsies, whose beliefs and fears are expressed in a performance style that employs a complex mythology to recount the suffering of their ancient exile, the history of their marginalisation, and the existential anguish that results.

Members of a lowly Indian caste once attached themselves to Arabian armies moving west into North Africa, serving them as blacksmiths, cooks and entertainers. They moved on through Egypt, from where they took their name ('E-gypti-an'), before arriving in southern Spain. The first organised group of Gypsies reached Spain in 1462 pretending to be pilgrims to the Catholic faith, and were consequently afforded protection and provisions by the Spanish nobility. By the end of the 15th century, these nomads had outstayed their welcome. Racism was stirred up by clerical propaganda that accused Gypsies of witchcraft and cannibalism, and in 1499 the kingdoms of Castile and Aragon ordered Gypsies to settle within 60 days or be banished.

Persecution intensified under Charles V, when Gypsies were hunted and enslaved in the galleys. In 1619 all Gypsies were sentenced to death if they refused to settle, inter-marry and live like good Christians. This enforced sedentariness resulted in concentrated settlements in Andalucía, when a national rout of Gypsies in July 1749 caused them to flee towards the south and led to an inevitable deterioration in living conditions in the overburdened areas of Seville, Granada and Cadiz. The brutality of this measure had the desired effect and by 1763 conditions were peaceful enough for Carlos III to declare an amnesty for Gypsies with the objective of transforming them into useful citizens. Fortunately, Andalucía, with its warm climate and fertile earth, was much to their liking and they prospered by smithery, fortune-telling and musicianship. This last skill was especially appreciated by the Catholic church, which employed Gypsies to perform at religious festivals and ceremonies.

Gypsies maintained cordial working relationships with the local populace while preserving their customs, language, song, dance and oral traditions in the privacy of their own homes. On the foundations of Indian traditions of performance, Gypsy musicians, singers and dancers constructed a style that overwhelmed traditional folksong. By the mid 19th century, professionals were performing for public audiences on the stages of *cafés cantantes* (theatre-bars) and *tablaos* (restaurants with a stage). During the Franco years there was an effort to disenfranchise the Gypsies from a song and dance that had become identified with Spanish culture, but when flamenco and folksong proved inseparable, this policy was adapted to claim that flamenco had been indigenous to Spain all along.

Post-dictatorship, authentic flamenco underwent a revival thanks to the growing clusters of migrant Gypsy camps on the outskirts of Madrid and the emergence of such figures as the legendary *cantaor* Camarón de la Isla and the guitarist Paco de Lucía. A pop-rock type of flamenco became ubiquitous, but at the other extreme from the wine-bar muzak of the Gypsy Kings and the kitsch spectacles of Joaquín Cortés there are plenty of innovative and exciting performers. Today's flamenco fan can keep up to date with what's happening by visiting the specialist shop El Flamenco Vive (C/Conde de Lemos 7, www.elflamencovive. com) near the Palacio Real, or by looking at www.flamenco-world.com.

CD-wise, for traditional *cante* there is nobody better than Camarón de la Isla (try *Camarón: Antología*, 1996) but since his death in 1992 the more contemporary Enrique Morente (*Lorca*, 1998) has become the reigning *cantaor*. For an equivalent female voice, try the traditional Carmen Linares (*Carmen Linares en antología*, 1996), the decidedly Moorish Estrella Morente (*Mi cante y un poema*, 2001) or the infectious rhythms of Niña Pastori (*Eres Luz*, 1998). For an innovative fusion of flamenco with Cuban rhythms, try Bebo & Cigala (*Lágrimas negras*, 2003) and for the ancient Arabic sounds of *flamenco andalusí* choose Lole y Manuel (*Nuevo Día: Lo mejor de Lole y Manuel*, 1994), who are so hip they feature on the soundtrack to Quentin Tarantino's *Kill Bill Vol. 2*.

VENUES

Time was that theatres such as the Teatro Real and Teatro Pavón were the equivalent of Carnegie Hall for flamenco artists. Nowadays the big stars play for big money to bigger audiences in concert halls and even stadiums, but you can still see unknowns imitating the legends and trying out new trends in pursuit of *duende*, the somewhat malevolent spirit-guide that is said to possess the greatest performers.

The most authentic flamenco inhabits a closed world and is proud of it; but if you know where to go and are lucky on the night you might be granted a peek. Madrid's original *cafés cantantes* are long gone but visitors can still catch a feel by crawling the bars around the district of Huertas and the Plaza Santa Ana, where a lucky dip of extravagantly nicknamed performers can sometimes yield a future star. These shows are mostly spontaneous so don't expect them to be advertised. The best way to see flamenco is to bar-hop in streets that live and breathe it, such as C/Echegaray. Rule of thumb: the more the punters look like the performers, the more chance there is that you're in the right place.

Where people are most likely to see Spanish dance, though, is at a *tablao*, of which there are several in Madrid; below is a selection of those with more genuine performances. As well as the show, you can dine or just drink; both are appallingly expensive, but if you stay till closing time you may get your money's worth of flamenco dance and music. The fun really starts around midnight, when most tourists go off to bed and the major artists appear; until then you may just get the kitsch jollity of the *cuadro de la casa* (the house musicians and dancers). Flamenco purists are notoriously snobbish about what's on offer in Madrid, but even they are thrilled by the performances at **Casa Patas**, where guitarists are skilled, dancers ooze power and grace, and singers are as they should be – bloody terrifying.

Also, as well as watching a Spanish dance show, you can join in, by heading to a *sala rociera* or Andaluz dance club for a bout of *sevillanas* and the odd rumba. For some prior preparation, many schools offer classes in popular Spanish dances (*see p263*).

FESTIVALS

A great way of experiencing flamenco dance is as part of the city festivals in honour of **San Isidro** (*see p205*) and the summer's **Veranos de la Villa** (*see p207*), while the **Festival Flamenco Cajamadrid** is held in February and March in the **Teatro Albéniz** (C/Príncipe 25, Huertas & Santa Ana, 91 360 14 80), and **Madrid en Danza** runs May-June and features many of the best flamenco dancers.

Al Andalús

C/Capitán Haya 19, Chamartín (91 556 14 39). Metro Cuzco. **Open** 10pm-6am Mon-Sat. **Performances** 10.30pm, 11pm, 1.30am. **Admission** €18. **Credit** AmEx, DC, MC, V.
With *sala rociera* decor of the most kitsch kind, this place offers a raucous live show, but the best part of all is watching the mainly middle-aged public throw themselves into *sevillanas* till dawn. The admission price includes one drink.

Clap your hands say yeah

Audiences who sit in respectful silence and applaud politely at the end of a performance of flamenco *cante* (song) and *toque* (guitar) might actually be insulting the performers. That's because audience participation – *jaleo* – is an essential part of authentic flamenco, and no truly great performance is ever given or witnessed without it. So this is no time to be shy: give as good as you get and you'll get as good as you give.

Watch and listen to how the guitarist bullies the *cantaor*, the singer of flamenco 'deep song', into giving their utmost. The guitarist plucks around the first murmurings of the *cantaor* until he hears the right tone being struck by his partner's voice, whereupon his sudden *rasgueo* (strum) alerts the *cantaor* to the fact that this is the direction to be taken. When you hear these single *rasgueos*, you'll know the performance is warming up. Listen closely to the guitarist and the experts around you in the audience. They'll start to goad the singer with phrases such as '*Ezo e*' ('*Eso es*' – 'That's it'), '*Vamos ya*' ('Let's go') and '*Anda ya, chiquillo*' ('Go with it, man'). Any *cantaor* worth his salt will respond by digging deeper.

A rhythmic rapping will begin, soft at first as these complicit torturers tap their palms flat against table-tops. Gradually you'll become aware of their rings and bracelets rapping on the wood and the sound will become sharper.

Some will turn their fingers in, forming fists that will punch up the rhythm. When the tattoo is solid and inescapable, the guitarist shows the way to go by tearing off on his own before returning quietly for the *cantaor*, who should by now be humming in time with the rhythm, nodding his head, eyes closed, tapping a foot and summoning up the true voice of deep song as if it were a mix of phlegm and bile, which it is. The audience pushes him to the edge with the calls and rapping and if he needs an extra shove the clapping (*palmas*) will start, leaving him no place to turn. Now wait. Wait for it.

The sound you'll hear is that of a man falling into the abyss of human existence and landing in a spiritual wasteland that is floating in an indifferent cosmos. If he's any good, that is. Growls, howls and a great range of guttural vocalisations of pain and despair are the true language of the authentic *cante* and the words are not so important as the tone of the performance. How many times will the guitarist scoop up the *cantaor* and make him fall again? How cruel will the audience be in forcing the martyrised *cantaor* to face the pain of their shared existential suffering? It depends on the night and the skill of the performer, for whom alcohol is not just a vice but an anaesthetic. Bruised knuckles, teary eyes and a headache? OK, now you can applaud.

Almonte

C/Juan Bravo 35, Salamanca (91 563 25 04). Metro Diego de León. **Open** 11pm-6am daily. **Admission** minimum consumption 1 drink. **Credit** AmEx, MC, V. **Map** p325 N6.
This 'flamenco disco' attracts a much younger crowd than Al Andalús. Beautiful youths flaunt it freestyle before *sevillanas* prompt a free-for-all. The evening is for dancing, the night is to be seen dancing. Try to work your way downstairs, where the most attention-grabbing dancing can be admired and – go on – attempted.

El Arco de Cuchilleros

C/Cuchilleros 7 (91 364 02 63). Metro Sol. **Open** 9pm-3am Tue-Sun. **Performances** 10.30pm-2am. **Admission** (incl 1 drink) €18 Tue, Wed; €10 Thur-Sun. **Credit** AmEx, DC, MC, V. **Map** p327 F12.
An expensive tourist trap that provides a pre-packaged thrill for the undemanding. The generic flamenco show (with live singers and guitarists on Tuesday and Wednesday) alternates with the weekend spectacle of *rocieros*: groups of frilly,

folklore-drenched performers, whose song and dance originate in the pilgrimage to the Virgen del Rocío in Huelva.

Café de Chinitas

C/Torija 7, Sol & Gran Vía (91 559 51 35/91 547 15 02/www.chinitas.com). Metro Santo Domingo. **Open** 8.30pm-late Mon-Sat. **Performances** from 10.15pm. **Admission** (incl dinner) €60 or/up; (incl drinks) €31. **Credit** AmEx, DC, MC, V. **Map** p327 F11.
An indulgent evening's entertainment for those who like to play at being 19th-century aristocrats – and don't mind paying 21st-century prices. At least this self-styled 'Cathedral of Flamenco' makes an effort, with sumptuous decor that contributes to the experience. The food and floorshow are expensive, yes, but at least it means the owners can afford to pay top euro for flamenco stars, who may not break a sweat but will still send you reeling into the night.

Candela

C/Olmo 2, Lavapiés (91 467 33 82). Metro Antón Martín. **Open** 11pm-5.30am Mon-Thur, Sun; 10pm-6am Fri, Sat. **No credit cards. Map** p328 H13.

An ideal place to soak up atmosphere, though performances are impromptu and only take place downstairs and after hours. Still, this in-the-know watering hole for professional musicians and amateurs is welcoming to knowledgeable and respectful aficionados.

Las Carboneras

Plaza del Conde de Miranda 1, Los Austrias (91 542 86 77/www.tablaolascarboneras.com). Metro Sol. **Open** 8.30pm-midnight Mon-Sat. **Performances** 9pm Mon-Thur; 8.30pm, 9-11pm Fri, Sat. **Admission** (incl 1 drink) €22. **Credit** AmEx, MC, V. **Map** p327 F12.
Packed with tourists, this bar-restaurant still offers value for money, with an energetic, passionate show performed by enthusiastic dancers. The set menus comprise typical fare, and diners are exempt from the admission charge. Highly polished flamenco for that inauthentic but unashamedly fun night out.

Casa Patas

C/Cañizares 10, Lavapiés (91 369 04 96/www.casa patas.com). Metro Antón Martín. **Open** 1.30-4.30pm, 8pm-2am Mon-Thur; 1.30-4.30pm, 7.30pm-2am Fri, Sat. **Performances** 10.30pm Mon-Thur; 9pm, midnight Fri, Sat. **Admission** (incl 1 drink) €26 Mon-Thur; €31 Fri, Sat. **Credit** AmEx, DC, MC, V. **Map** p327 H14.
This is a plush and somewhat pricey place to savour traditional or nuevo flamenco. Recent topliners have included Chaquetón, Remedios Amaya and Niña Pastori. A highly prized venue with a reputation to maintain, Casa Patas is deservedly proud of its standing and treats its loyal, knowledgeable and sometimes intimidating audience with mutual respect. Feast on traditional rabo de toro (bull's tail) for that authentic edge. The same owners have a bar, Pata Chico, alongside, for pre-flamenco drinks. Occasionally the artists will head there for a drink after the show.

Corral de la Morería

C/Morería 17, Los Austrias (91 365 84 46/www. corraldelamoreria.com). Metro La Latina. **Open** 9pm-2am daily. **Performances** from 10.30pm.

Admission (incl dinner) €75 and up; (incl drinks) €35. **Credit** AmEx, DC, MC, V. **Map** p327 E13.
More serious and exacting than Las Carboneras, this long-standing *tablao* sports seemingly authentic Arab decor and an atmosphere to match. A relaxed mix of tourists, fans (Hemingway, Che Guevara and Picasso have all paid a visit) and professionals enjoy a solid, expensive and sometimes exhilarating show.

Corral de la Pacheca

C/Juan Ramón Jiménez 26, North of centre (91 353 01 00/www.corraldelapacheca.com). Metro Cuzco. **Open** 9pm-midnight daily. **Performance** 10.30pm. **Admission** €32 (incl 1 drink). **Credit** AmEx, MC, V.
This grand centre of popular and traditional flamenco boasts a history of star performers and even starrier punters. Built on the site of a 17th-century theatre, it began life as a *tablao* but grew into an imposing venue with a large auditorium and stage. **Photo** *p49.*

La Soleá

C/Cava Baja 34, Los Austrias (91 366 05 34). Metro La Latina. **Open** 10pm-6am Tue-Sat. **Credit** MC, V. **Map** p327 F13.
This small but amiable bar in the centre of Madrid boasts a constant babble of flamenco aficionados and a roster of performers that alternate with spontaneous (and variable) songs from the clientele. Great fun on a good night, but it can also be surprisingly dull. Watch out, too, for the occasional rough element.

Torres Bermejas

C/Mesonero Romanos 11 (91 532 33 22/www. torresbermejas.com). Metro Callao. **Open** 8.30pm-2am daily. **Performance** 9.30pm. **Admission** (incl dinner) €70; (incl drink) €32. **Credit** AmEx, DC, MC, V. **Map** p327 H11.
Modelled somewhat kitschly on the Alhambra, this bar plays hosts to authentic Gypsy flamenco and a faithful in-crowd, managing to absorb the tour parties without spoiling the mood. The paella and the Rioja veal are, like the flamenco, rich and satisfying.

Casa Patas.

Where to Stay

Hotel de las Letras. *See p59.*

Where to Stay

The boutique has landed.

Hostal Oriente *(see p57)*; cleanliness and comfort at a bargain price.

For a compact city, Madrid has an unusually large number of hotels. In fact, so many new properties have opened in the past few years that there are concerns that there are too many, in the centre at least. For visitors, of course, this can only be a good thing. Intense competition means higher standards of accommodation and service, even in the lower-priced places. In particular, the difference between budget and mid-range hotels is becoming increasingly marginal, with the newer *hostales* now offering en suite bathrooms in most rooms. And, across all price brackets, staff are friendlier and keener to help than ever before. Fans of boutique hotels, meanwhile, will be pleased to hear that the concept has finally made it to Madrid.

STARS, PRICES AND DISCOUNTS

Star ratings are somewhat arbitrary in Spain, and the difference between four- and five-star hotels can be hard to spot. Mid-range hotels have not been the city's strong point, but this is beginning to change thanks to chains such as **Room Mate** and **High Tech Hotels**.

In this chapter we have arranged hotels and *hostales* by area and price category, according to the cost of a standard double room. Hotels charging over €300 are categorised as 'luxury'; those costing between €150 and €300 are classed as 'expensive'; 'mid-range' is between €60 and €150; 'budget' is less than €60.

Breakfast is not included unless otherwise stated. In addition, in all but the cheapest hotels, plenty of cut-price offers are to be had at weekends and over the summer. In fact, nabbing a luxury hotel at a knock-down price is probably easier in Madrid than in most other European cities, especially if you book early. Check websites or call direct for details.

Note that a *hostal*, also known as *pensión*, is closer in meaning to 'guesthouse' than 'hostel'. Not all *hostales* have someone on the door 24 hours a day, so check how to get back in at night. These places, often full of dark corridors and odd decor, tend to be efficient family-run affairs, and while some owners speak English, any effort on your part to attempt a few words of Spanish will be well received.

It's also worth noting that many *hostales* and *pensiones* are located up several flights of stairs in old buildings with no lift. If this is likely to be a problem, check before you book.

BOOKING A ROOM

If you arrive in Madrid without accommodation, try one of the following agencies:

Brújula

Estación de Atocha (91 539 11 73). Metro Atocha. **Open** 8am-10pm daily. **Map** p329 L15/16.
Estación de Chamartín (91 315 78 94). Metro Chamartín. **Open** 7.15am-2pm daily.

Hotel de las Letras. *See p59.*

A private agency (the name means 'compass') based in Atocha and Chamartín railway stations, Brújula can reserve rooms in any price category. You must leave a payment as a guarantee for the reservation and you will also be charged a €2.50 booking fee.

Viajes Aira

Terminals 1, 2 & 4, Barajas Airport (91 305 42 24/fax 91 305 84 19/www.viajesaira.com). **Open** 7am-midnight daily.

Viajes Aira has three hotel reservation desks in the arrivals area of Barajas airport. It mainly deals with hotels of three stars and above, although it does have some *hostales* on its books. There is no booking fee.

Los Austrias & La Latina

See also p72 **Hostal Madrid**, an apart-hotel with single and double rooms to rent.

Expensive

Hotel Palacio San Martín

Plaza de San Martín 5, 28013 (91 701 50 00/www.intur.com). Metro Ópera or Sol. **Rates** €119-€184 single; €119-€229 double; €300 suite. **Credit** AmEx, DC, MC, V. **Map** p327 G11 ➊

This hotel, housed in a 19th-century former palace on a quiet but very central little square, was converted into a hotel in 2001. Its comforts are old-school, and thankfully it has maintained much of its former glory, with period façade, high stucco ceilings, wood panelling and an attractive central courtyard. A stunning rooftop terrace restaurant looks out over the surrounding area, while a huge presidential suite, also on the rooftop, comes complete with jacuzzi – and more of those views.

Business centre. Gym. Internet (wireless). Restaurant. Room service. TV (pay movies).

Mid-range

Room Mate Mario

C/Campomanes 4, 28013 (91 548 85 48/www.room-matehotels.com). Metro Ópera. **Rates** (incl breakfast) €85.60-€149.80 single; €96.30-€160.50 double; €123-05-€192.60 suite. **Credit** AmEx, DC, MC, V. **Map** p327 F11 ❷

The first in a new chain of stylish, mid-range hotels. Especially popular among a design-appreciative public (for which, often, read 'gay'), Room Mate Mario oozes affordable chic, from the ergonomic white plastic chairs in the black-tiled lobby to the smart chequered grey and white bathrooms. The staff (black-shirted, naturally) are as welcoming and easy on the eye as the spacious rooms, and the location on an elegant Ópera side street is unbeatable. *Business centre. Disabled-adapted room. No smoking rooms (10). Internet (wireless, free shared terminal). Telephone. TV.*
Other locations: Room Mate Alicia C/Prado 2, Santa Ana (91 389 60 95); **Room Mate Laura** Trav. de Trujillos 3, Sol & Gran Vía (91 701 16 70).

Petit Palace Arenal

C/Arenal 16, 28013 (91 564 43 55/www.hthoteles. com). Metro Sol. **Rates** €96.30-€214 single/double. **Credit** AmEx, DC, MC, V. **Map** p327 F11 ❸

Fans of chintz should steer well clear, but the new and excellent-value High Tech chain of hotels is perfect for techno fiends on a budget. The Arenal's compact but sleekly designed rooms have flat-screen TVs and free ADSL connection, and more expensive rooms come equipped with a PC (also with free net access) and an exercise bike. Four of the superior rooms have showers fitted with solarium, sauna and radio. *Business centre. Disabled rooms (1). Internet (highspeed). No-smoking floors (5). TV.*
Other locations: Posada del Peine C/Postas 17, Sol (91 523 81 51); **Tres Cruces** C/Tres Cruces 6, Sol & Gran Via (91 522 33 27); **Puerta del Sol** C/Arenal 4, Sol (91 521 05 42), and throughout the city.

Budget

Hostal Oriente

C/Arenal 23, 4 izq, 28013 (91 548 03 14/fax 91 547 84 53). Metro Ópera. **Rates** €37 single; €57 double; €75 triple. **Credit** DC, MC, V. **Map** p327 F11 ❹

Right on the doorstep of the opera house, and just a short walk from Sol, the comfortable Oriente is in an excellent location. The 19 rooms all have compact bathrooms, TVs and air-conditioning, and the friendly staff are a further draw. **Photo** *p55. TV.*

Hostal Riesco

C/Correo 2, 3°, 28012 (91 522 26 92). Metro Sol. **Rates** €38 single; €49 double. **No credit cards.** **Map** p327 G11 ❺

This *hostal* feels more like a hotel, with its dark wood lobby, stucco ceilings and chintzy curtains. All rooms come with en suite bathrooms, and several

have balconies bedecked with flowers. The location is hard to beat – it's rare to find such good-value accommodation so close to Sol and the Plaza Mayor.

Sol & Gran Vía

Expensive

Hotel Emperador

Gran Vía 53, 28013 (91 547 28 00/www.emperador hotel.com). Metro Santo Domingo. **Rates** €192.60 single; €241.85 double; €353.10-€560 suite. **Credit** AmEx, DC, MC, V. **Map** p323 F10 ❻

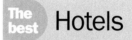

Hotels

For getting a feel of Old Madrid
Generations of travellers have turned to **Residencia Sud-Americana** (*see p64*) or, at the other end of the scale, the **Hotel Orfila** (*see p69*) for its intimate, old-world atmosphere.

For getting a feel of New Madrid
It doesn't get any hipper than the **Hotel Urban** (*see p60*), the **Hotel de las Letras** (*see p59*), or the **ME Madrid Reina Victoria** (*see p60*).

For taking a dip
Swim in style in the rooftop pool at the **Hotel Emperador** (*see p57*). The bar alongside will keep your liquid levels high.

For both business and pleasure
The **Hotel Eurobuilding** (*see p70*) and **Hotel Puerta América** (*see p71*) are packed with business facilities, but have much to occupy leisure travellers.

For making an entrance
The **Hotel Wellington** (*see p67*), with its elegant chandeliers and frescoes, will take your breath away.

For celeb-spotting
Try the **ME Madrid Reina Victoria** (*see p60*) for celluloid stars, the **Ritz** (*see p65*) for anyone who's on a promotion tour, and the **Hotel Santo Mauro** (*see p69*) for those searching for secrecy.

For unusual decor
The **Hotel Villa Real** (*see p60*) for a Roman mosaic in your bedroom, or the **Hotel Puerta América** (*see p71*) for a room designed by the world's finest architects.

While the traffic speeds by on the Gran Via outside, the Emperador has to deal with its own constant flow of student groups and tourists. The hotel is well located for visiting the city's major sights and has a wonderful rooftop swimming pool (which is also open to non-residents for a fee). Rooms are conservatively decorated, and the bathrooms that have been renovated are a huge improvement on the old brown 1970s-style suites.
Bar. Business centre. Disabled-adapted rooms (9). Gym. No-smoking floors (3). Internet (wireless). Parking (€22.47 per day). Room service. Pool (outdoor). TV (satellite).

Hotel de las Letras
Gran Via 11, 28013 (91 523 79 80/www.hotel delasletras.com). Metro Gran Via. **Rates** €149.80-€256.80 single/double. Credit AmEx, DC, MC, V. **Map** p324 H11 ❼
The new Hotel de las Letras laughs in the face of the current hotel vogue for teak and slate, and plumps instead for bold paintwork in red, orange and purples, with literary quotations strewn across its walls. It does this with remarkable aplomb, thanks to stylish furniture and well-designed rooms. Bathrooms are huge, with stacks of fluffy towels and luxury toiletries, and even standard rooms come with balconies. Downstairs is a comfortable spa and gym, along with a small library with free internet access. The ground floor bar hums with bright young things day and night, but the hotel's hip credentials play second fiddle to sheer comfort. A gem. **Photo** *p56.*
Bar. Disabled-adapted room. No-smoking floor. Internet (wireless). Restaurant. Spa. Room Service. TV (satellite).

Hotel Santo Domingo
Plaza de Santo Domingo 13, 28013 (91 547 98 00/www.hotelsantodomingo.com). Metro Santo Domingo. **Rates** €128.40-€156.20 single; €176.55-€185.10 double. **Credit** AmEx, DC, MC, V. **Map** p323 F11 ❽
Courteous staff welcome guests to this well-located hotel. Rooms are individually decorated in elegant pastel colours and, despite the location, they're surprisingly quiet (especially those facing C/Isabel la Católica). Serious portraits stare down from their frames in the lobby and corridors, keeping the mix of tourist and business clientele company. Comfortable, central and just that little bit cheesy, it's a combination that works.
Bar. Disabled-adapted room. Internet (wireless). Parking (€18 per day). Restaurant. Room service. TV (satellite).

Tryp Ambassador
Cuesta de Santo Domingo 5-7, 28013 (91 541 67 00/www.trypambassador.solmelia.com). Metro Santo Domingo. **Rates** €154-€191.55 single; €175-€210.10 double; €245.50-€406.60 suite. **Credit** AmEx, DC, MC, V. **Map** p323 F11 ❾
Located in a former palace, the Ambassador manages to retain a vaguely baronial air despite being part of a chain. Suits of armour stand guard in the corridors, while plush upholstery adorns the public spaces and the large, light-filled atrium. The fact that the decent-sized rooms haven't been renovated recently only adds to the charm – think '70s-style bathroom suites and squeaky French windows. Breakfast is expensive (€17) but abundant and good.
Bar. Business centre. Internet (wireless). Restaurant. Room service. TV (satellite).

Mid-range

Hotel Arosa
C/Salud 21, 28013 (91 532 16 00/www.best western.es/arosa.html). Metro Gran Via. **Rates** €68.50-€109.15 single; €90-€159.50 double. **Credit** AmEx, DC, MC, V. **Map** p323 H11 ❿
This friendly, well-equipped and good-value 134-room hotel is situated right in the heart of the action. The spacious, air-conditioned rooms all come with clean, modern, wooden furnishings and bright marble bathrooms, and some of the more expensive doubles have a private seating area looking out on to the busy Gran Via. The public areas include a kitschy fake leopard-skin reception, and a restaurant and bar that Almodóvar would be proud of.
Bar. Internet (wireless). Parking (€15 per day). Room service. TV (pay movies).

Hotel Carlos V
C/Maestro Victoria 5, 28013 (91 531 41 00/www. bestwestern.es/hotelcarlosv.html). Metro Sol. **Rates** €101 single; €133 double. **Credit** AmEx, DC, MC, V. **Map** p323 G11 ⓫
The corporate feel is avoided in this Best Western hotel with homely touches, from the motley but charming crew running reception and the *trompe l'oeil* lift door, to the tapestries in the corridors and the botanical prints in the colourful and elegant breakfast room. The rooms on the top floor are the nicest, and some have their own large, Astroturfed terraces (though you pay a bit extra for this).
Bar. Internet (wireless). Room service. TV (satellite).

Budget

Hostal Andorra
Gran Via 33, 7º, 28013 (91 532 31 16/www. hostalandorra.com). Metro Gran Via. **Rates** €45 single; €60 double. **Credit** AmEx, DC, MC, V. **Map** p323 G11 ⓬
Brightly painted rooms, floral bedspreads and comfortable leather recliners confirm the homely atmosphere of this centrally located *hostal*. While the roar of the Gran Via's traffic is unforgiving, the interior is calm, with cleanliness and facilities that belie the rates. Every room has satellite TV, and the bathrooms, while compact, are clean and modern.
TV.

Hostal Triana
C/Salud 13, 1º, 28013 (91 532 68 12/www.hostal triana.com). Metro Gran Via. **Rates** €39 single; €50 double; €68 triple. **Credit** MC, V. **Map** p323 H11 ⓭

A popular and efficiently run business, this traditional good-value 40-room *hostal* has been open for more than four decades, and attracts guests of all ages. Rooms are sparklingly clean with modern en suite bathrooms. It's worth booking early. *Disabled-adapted room. TV.*

Huertas & Santa Ana

Luxury

Hotel Urban

Carrera de San Jeronimo 34, 28014 (91 787 77 70/ www.derbyhotels.com). Metro Sevilla or Sol. **Rates** €192.60-€352.45 single/double. **Credit** AmEx, DC, MC, V. **Map** p328 I11 ⓮
The Derby chain (see also the Hotel Villa Real, below) is owned by Catalan archaeologist Jordi Clos, and ancient figurines and artworks are found throughout the rooms, common areas and in the Egyptian museum in the basement. This cultural treasure trove is a perfect counterpoint to the painfully hip surroundings – a glass and steel atrium, rooms sexily designed with teak and leather and what must be the coolest doormen in the city. Other pluses include extremely friendly staff and a much needed plunge pool on the roof. **Photo** *p61.*
Bar. No-smoking floor. Internet (high-speed, pre-pay wireless). Pool (outdoor). Restaurant. Room service. TV (satellite).

Hotel Villa Real

Plaza de las Cortes 10, 28014 (91 420 37 67/ www.derbyhotels.es). Metro Banco de España. **Rates** €203.30-€373.45 single; €246.10-€416.25 double; €543 junior suite; €627.05 duplex. **Credit** AmEx, DC, MC, V. **Map** p328 I12 ⓯

The Villa Real – as the name suggests – reflects owner Jordi Clos's interest in Roman archaeology. The guest rooms are elegant, with marble bathrooms boasting large picture windows, and many have panels of Roman mosaics. Most double rooms have split-level sitting areas, some duplex suites come with their own jacuzzi and the luxury suites have private terraces.
Bar. Business centre. Internet (wireless). No-smoking floor (1). Parking (€21.40 per day). Restaurant. Room service. TV (satellite).

ME Madrid Reina Victoria

Plaza Santa Ana 14, 28012 (91 701 60 00/ www.mebymelia.com). Metro Sevilla or Sol. **Rates** €203.30-€321 single/double. **Credit** AmEx, DC, MC, V. **Map** p328 H12 ⓰
Although plans to turn this into Europe's first Hard Rock hotel didn't quite come off, the Melia chain has appropriated the lovely old Hotel Reina Victoria to showcase its new 'ME' brand. These, we are told, are 'experience-based personality hotels'. Whatever that means, and despite smallish rooms, the end result is supremely comfortable, with luxury bedlinen, Aveda toiletries and lots to keep gadget-fiends happy, not only with plasma screens, CD and DVD players, but even iPod adapters (ask at reception for a pre-set iPod if you left yours at home). **Photo** *p64.*
Bar. Business centre. Disabled-adapted rooms (4). Gym. No-smoking floors (5). Internet (wireless). Parking (€32.48 per day). Restaurant. Room service. TV (pay movies, satellite).

Westin Palace

Plaza de las Cortes 7, 28014 (91 360 80 00/www. palacemadrid.com). Metro Banco de España. **Rates** €249-€470 single/double; €589-€3,579 suite. **Credit** AmEx, DC, MC, V. **Map** p328 I12 ⓱

What's where

Though Madrid is pretty small for a capital city, its accommodation is spread over a wide area, so it's a good to have an idea of what you want before you book.

Sol and **Gran Vía** are the best areas for mid-range accommodation right in the thick of things, and, though pretty touristy, are home to a clutch of decent bars and restaurants. Heading north of here, **Malasaña** has a choice of good budget *pensiones*, particularly along C/Palma. Bordering Malasaña to the east, **Chueca** is home to some great one-off properties. Both areas, especially Malasaña, boast a real neighbourhood vibe.

South of Chueca, lively **Huertas** and **Santa Ana** are both great areas for cheap *pensiones* and, increasingly, boutique hotels. On the edge of here, the Paseo del Prado provides

a variety of budget accommodation right on the doorstep of the Big Three art museums. Upmarket areas include **Retiro** and **Los Austrias**. Though located across town from each other (Retiro is between the Prado and the Retiro park in the east, Los Austrias is adjacent to the Royal Palace to the west), both are home to Madrid's old money, and both are peaceful – though bars and restaurants can be expensive.

Just north of the Parque del Retiro, around the chic shopping street C/Serrano, is **Salamanca**. If you feel at home among the smart, wealthy set, you'll blend in well here. Business travellers should head for **Chamberí**, to the north of the centre, and, further north, to **Chamartín**, both of which are convenient for transport to the airport.

The chic and sleek **Hotel Urban** (*see p60*).

One of the most famous hotels in Madrid, the Palace successfully combines old-world elegance with cutting-edge facilities. The lounge areas and stunning atrium have an air of sumptuousness, and the latter features opera performances once a month. The hotel's reasonably priced, comfortable bars and restaurants are popular with visiting celebs and politicians from the parliament buildings across the road, and, luckily for non-residents, they're open to all. The hotel is brought into the 21st century with a fully equipped fitness centre, sauna and solarium.
Bar. Business centre. Disabled-adapted room. Gym. Internet (wireless). No-smoking floor. Parking (€25 per day). Restaurant. Room service. TV (satellite).

Expensive

Hotel Lope de Vega

C/Lope de Vega 40, 28014 (91 360 00 11/www.hotel greenlopedevega.com). Metro Antón Martin. **Rates** €114.50-€152 single; €120-€194.75 double; €170.15-€245 triple; €184-€248 suite. **Credit** AmEx, DC, MC, V. **Map** p328 J12/13 ⑬
A stone's throw from the Prado, this anonymous-looking hotel is a shrine, of sorts, to one of Spain's most celebrated playwrights. The rooms are done up in standard-issue mid-range decor, but are a good size, comfortable and many have large balconies. Posted outside each one is information about Lope

de Vega, and the corridors are lined with pictures of his productions. Other nice touches on the landings include books about the great man himself and other literary giants, along with bowls of fruit.
Bar. No-smoking floors (5). Internet (high-speed). Parking (€18 per day). Room service. TV (pay movies).

Mid-range

Hostal Persal

Plaza del Ángel 12, 28012 (91 369 46 43/www. hostalpersal.com). Metro Sol or Antón Martín. **Rates** (incl breakfast) €53.50-€74.90 single; €80.25-€101.65 double; €112.35-€128.40 triple; €139.10-€150.70 quad. **Credit** AmEx, MC, V. **Map** p328 H12 ⑲
The Persal's rooms don't quite live up to the first impressions given by the glass front and swish lobby, but thankfully they're modern, spotlessly clean and more than functional (it's well worth paying the extra for a nicer one on the upper floors). If you're travelling as a family or a group, the hard-working staff are especially welcoming and helpful.
Bar. TV (satellite).

Hotel Asturias

C/Sevilla 2, 28014 (91 429 66 76/www.chh.com). Metro Sevilla. **Rates** (incl breakfast) €53-€80 single; €80-€111 double. **Credit** AmEx, MC, V. **Map** p328 H11 ⑳

"LA LATINA RECUPERA SU MUSA"

Restaurante
Cafe y
Cocktail Bar

Costanilla de San Andrés, 12 (Pza de la Paja)
Tfno: 91 354 02 55

Within spitting distance of Sol, this bustling 19th-century hotel is nothing to write home about from the outside. Inside, though, the 170 rooms are bright and spacious, decorated in simple whites and creams, with carpets and furnishings that blend well with the wooden floors and fittings. Some have views over the gorgeous Teatro Reina Victoria, but ask for an interior room if noise bothers you.
Bar. Restaurant. TV (satellite).

Hotel Mora

Paseo del Prado 32, 28014 (91 420 05 64/www.hotel mora.com). Metro Atocha. **Rates** €57 single; €75 double. **Credit** AmEx, DC, MC, V. **Map** p328 J13 ㉑
If you like marble, you'll love the Mora's foyer, with its caramel-coloured columns and chandeliers. The rooms are functional but comfortable, and some have views over the tree-lined Paseo del Prado. Not surprisingly, given the location and price, it can be hard to get a room, so try to book early.
Bar. TV.

Hotel El Prado

C/Prado 11, 28014 (91 369 02 34/fax 91 429 28 29/www.pradohotel.com). Metro Antón Martín. **Rates** €83.46-€107 single; €128.40 double; €167.99 suite. **Credit** AmEx, DC, MC, V. **Map** p328 H/I12 ㉒
The sister hotel to the Lope de Vega (*see p61*), the Prado too has an anonymous look from the outside, but the rooms are prettily furnished, this time with a wine theme. Curtains and upholstery are adorned with vine patterns and the downstairs lounge is filled with books, videos and magazines about viticulture. There are bowls of fruit to munch on in the public areas and free internet access in the lounge.
No-smoking rooms (40). Internet (shared free terminals (2), wireless). TV (satellite).

Hotel Santander

C/Echegaray 1, 28014 (91 429 95 51/www.hotel santandermadrid.com). Metro Sevilla or Sol. **Rates** €80-€90 double. **Credit** MC, V. **Map** p328 H11 ㉓
The Santander's glamorous, gilded entranceway makes for a foyer with character, and if you can get over the rather offputting list of house rules (no visitors after midnight, no noise after 11pm, for example) you'll enjoy your stay. The rooms are elegant, kitted out with decent furniture and wooden floors. Some are more like suites, with small seating areas where you can have breakfast – room 105 is particularly bright and spacious.
TV.

Budget

Hostal Alaska

C/Espoz y Mina 7, 4°, 28012 (91 521 18 45/www.hostalalaska.com). Metro Sol. **Rates** €38 single; €50 double; €60 triple. **Credit** MC, V. **Map** p327 H12 ㉔
Exceptionally large rooms for this price range, decorated with splashes of bright blue, give this comfortable, colourful *hostal* a bit of a beachside feel.

The atmosphere is homely and laid-back, and guests have use of a fridge and washing machine. The five doubles and one single all come with bathrooms, and many have balconies. It's on the fourth floor but a lift has now been installed.
TV.

Hostal Armesto

C/San Agustín 6, 1°, 28014 (91 429 90 31). Metro Antón Martín. **Rates** €45 single; €50 double. **Credit** MC, V. **Map** p328 I12 ㉕
This great-value six-room *hostal* in the centre of Huertas is run by a friendly husband and wife team. Rooms are spotless and all of them have their own small bathroom with shower; some boast views over the garden of the San Agustín palace next door. The Armesto is a particularly good choice for art lovers on a tight budget, being well situated for the famous art museum triumvirate.
TV.

Hostal Astoria

Carrera de San Jerónimo 30-32, 2°, 28014 (91 429 11 88/www.hostalastoria.com). Metro Sevilla or Sol. **Rates** €53.50 single; €69.55 double. **Credit** AmEx, DC, MC, V. **Map** p328 H11 ㉖
Managed by (mostly) friendly staff, the Astoria is a good choice if you want to be centrally located, with basic facilities at a very good price. All 26 rooms are relatively spacious and have en suite bathrooms, but try to get the biggest available, and one preferably facing away from the street.
TV.

Hostal Casanova

C/Lope de Vega 8, 1°, 28014 (91 429 56 91). Metro Antón Martín. **Rates** €30 single; €40 double; €51 triple. **Credit** MC, V. **Map** p328 I12 ㉗
Run by a friendly family and in a quiet street just off newly pedestrianised C/Huertas, this *hostal* is especially good value for those travelling in threes. Rooms are basic but bright, some with bathrooms, and all with air-conditioning.

Hostal Delvi

Plaza Santa Ana 15, 3° dcha, 28012 (91 522 59 98/www.hostaldelvi.com). Metro Sevilla or Sol. **Rates** €25 single; €38 double. **Credit** MC, V. **Map** p328 I12 ㉘
Located on lively Plaza Santa Ana and in a delightfully eccentric building, the Casa de Guadalajara, the Delvi is ideal for backpackers. An entrance hall decorated with ceramics of winged cherubs leads you past the Guadalajara Club, then up to the third floor (there's no lift) where an elderly couple run this good-value *hostal*. Rooms are basic, but some have showers and a toilet, and others boast views of the square.

Hostal Horizonte

C/Atocha 28, 2° B, 28012 (91 369 09 96/www.hostalhorizonte.com). Metro Antón Martín. **Rates** €25-€38 single; €38-€72 double. **Credit** MC, V. **Map** p327 H13 ㉙

One of the oldest *pensiones* in Madrid, the Horizonte has stayed in the same friendly family throughout its 65-year history. The manager is the young and helpful Julio César, a font of knowledge about the history and cultural life of the city. Rooms are colourfully decorated, clean and comfy, and the welcoming atmosphere is unbeatable. **Photo** *p67*.

Hostal Martín

C/Atocha 43, 1˚ izq, 28012 (91 429 95 79/www. hostalmartin.com). Metro Antón Martín. **Rates** €39 single; €48 double; €60 triple. **Credit** AmEx, DC, MC, V. **Map** p328 H13 ③

This very friendly, first-floor *hostal* has a pleasantly rough-and-tumble family feel about it. The 26 high-ceilinged air-conditioned rooms all come with an en suite bathroom and decent shower. The helpful couple who run it speak various languages between them and can book you into other hotels if you're moving on to other parts of the country. The hearty breakfast includes plenty of fresh fruit and very good coffee.
TV (satellite).

Hostal-Residencia La Coruña

Paseo del Prado 12, 3˚, 28014 (91 429 25 43/ www.hcoruna.com). Metro Banco de España. Closed Aug. **Rates** €25 single; €38 double. **No credit cards. Map** p328 J12 ③

Well located for art lovers, this welcoming family-run *hostal* is basic but functional. The six bedrooms are clean, with high ceilings, chandeliers and plain furniture. All have washbasins, and two bathrooms are shared among guests.
TV.

Residencia Sud-Americana

Paseo del Prado 12, 6˚, 28014 (91 429 25 64). Metro Banco de España. **Rates** €30 single; €35-€50 double. **Credit** MC, V. **Map** p328 J12 ③

This place has a real feel of Old Madrid, with mini Goya reproductions lining the creaky, wooden-floored hallway. Whitewashed walls, high ceilings and dark wooden furniture give the rooms a centuries-old atmosphere and some have lovely views over the tree tops of the Paseo del Prado. One bathroom is shared between eight rooms, but all have their own washbasin. You'll find it very difficult to find this sort of old-world elegance elsewhere at such a cheap price, particularly if you're after a single room. There is also a dorm room, sleeping up to six people, for €18 each.

Hostal San Antonio

C/León 13, 2˚, 28014 (tel/fax 91 429 51 37). Metro Antón Martín. **Rates** €30 single; €45 double; €65 triple. **No credit cards. Map** p328 I12 ③

A clean, quiet and cool modern *hostal,* tranquil by day, buzzing on weekend nights. Rooms are comfortable and generously sized for the price, and all come with air-conditioning and en suite toilet and shower room. Most look out on to a busy street, so it can get quite noisy at night.
TV.

Lavapiés

Budget

Hostal Apolo

C/Juanelo 24, 28012 (tel/fax 91 360 08 00). Metro Tirso de Molina. **Rates** (incl breakfast) €52 single/ double. **Credit** MC, V. **Map** p327 G13 ③

This is the best of the few hotel options in the lively and multicultural Lavapiés area. The new owner is eager to please and proud of his establishment. Rooms are rather functional but clean and good value, and all have en suite bathrooms.
Bar. TV.

ME Madrid Reina Victoria. *See p60.*

Chueca

Expensive

Petit Palace Ducal

*C/Hortaleza 3, 28004 (91 521 10 43/www.ht
hoteles.com). Metro Gran Vía.* **Rates** €112.55-€171
single/double; €155-185 triple; €230 quadruple.
Credit AmEx, DC, MC, V. **Map** p324 H11 ⬤
Part of the High Tech chain, the Petit Palace Ducal
is one of the city's few boutique hotels, and blends
seamlessly into its hyper-cool Chueca surroundings.
Staff are young and friendly, and the striking red
and black design eye-catching. All rooms have free
high-speed internet access, and so-called High Tech
rooms also come with flat-screen PCs, exercise bikes
and sauna or hydromassage shower. The Ducal is
also practical in its provision of family rooms, with
bunk beds for those travelling *en familia*. Given all
this, the prices are extremely reasonable, and it's
even worth spending that little bit extra for a sixth-
floor room with small terrace.
*Bar. Business centre. No-smoking floors (5).
Internet (wireless). TV (satellite).*

Budget

Hostal Benamar

*C/San Mateo 20, 2˚ 3D, 28004 (91 308 00 92).
Metro Alonso Martínez or Tribunal.* **Rates** €39.60
single; €52.45-€58.85 double; €68.50 triple. **Credit**
MC, V. **Map** p324 I9 ⬤
Well situated between Chueca and Alonso Martínez,
this *hostal* can be divided into two different parts.
The friendly owners promote the recently renovated
section, which has marble floors, modern en suite
bathrooms and computers in every room. The other
section is older but clean, with shared bathrooms
and cheaper rates.
Internet (highspeed). TV.

Hostal Residencia Santa Bárbara

*Plaza de Santa Bárbara 4, 3˚, 28004 (91 446
93 08/fax 91 446 23 45). Metro Alonso Martínez.*
Rates €45 single; €56-€66 double. **Credit** MC,
V. **Map** p324 I8 ⬤
This well-connected *hostal* provides friendly service
in a secure building. The rooms are basic but they
are also clean and every one has walk-in shower
facilities. The friendly Italian owner and the staff all
speak good English.
TV.

Malasaña & Conde Duque

Mid-range

Hostal Sil/Hostal Serranos

*C/Fuencarral 95, 2˚, 28004 (91 448 89 72/
www.silserranos.com). Metro Bilbao.* **Rates**
€51 single; €69 double; €90 triple. **Credit** MC,
V. **Map** p323 H8 ⬤

Clean and smartly decorated, these *hostales* are well
located for night-time revelling – indeed, rooms looking out on to C/Fuencarral will bear witness to the
madrileño enthusiasm for partying well into the
early hours. Although interior rooms are a little
darker, the noise is minimal and the price slightly
lower. All rooms have air-conditioning, small bathrooms and digital TV, and the properties are run by
a fun couple and their English-speaking children.
Internet (high-speed). TV (satellite).

Hotel Alexandra

*C/San Bernardo 29-31, 20015 (91 542 04 00/
www.halexandra.com). Metro Noviciado.* **Rates**
€79 single; €100 double; €128 triple. **Credit**
AmEx, DC, MC, V. **Map** p323 F10 ⬤
A few minutes' walk from the Gran Vía and the
metro, the Alexandra is well located for sightseeing.
All rooms are clean and pretty quiet, but you can
request an interior room to avoid the traffic noise
from C/San Bernardo. Although the hotel is slightly anonymous in its style, the staff are friendly and
the area and prices just that little bit less touristy
than if you cross the Gran Vía towards Sol.
No-smoking rooms (21). TV.

Salamanca & the Retiro

Luxury

AC Palacio del Retiro

*Alfonso XII 14, 28014 (91 523 74 60/www.ac-
hotels.com). Metro Banco de España or Retiro.* **Rates**
€107-€238 single; €238-€337 double.
Credit AmEx, DC, MC, V. **Map** p328 K11 ⬤
With their palette of greys and browns, the rooms
can seem a little dour and masculine after the frothy
extravagances of the belle-epoque building in which
they are housed. The hotel is beautifully located near
the park and Prado, however, and the staff eager to
please. Amenities are good – rooms feature plasma-
screen TVs and CD players – as is breakfast (as one
would expect for €27). **Photos** *pp68-69.*
*Bar. Disabled-adapted rooms (2). No-smoking floors
(3). Internet (wireless). Restaurant. Spa. Room
Service. TV (satellite).*

Hotel Ritz

*Plaza de la Lealtad 5, 28014 (91 701 67 67/
www.ritzmadrid.com). Metro Banco de España.*
Rates €545.70-€652.70 single/double; 1,064.65 junior
suite; €2,354-€3,584.50 suite; €4,975.50 royal suite.
Credit AmEx, DC, MC, V. **Map** p328 J12 ⬤
Madrid's Ritz was built in 1910, thanks to a personal intervention by King Alfonso XIII, who had been
embarrassed at the time of his wedding to Princess
Victoria four years earlier because his guests could
not find a hotel that was up to scratch. When the
hotel first opened, the handful of bathrooms, one
telephone per floor and lift were considered the
height of luxury, and it soon attracted politicians,
royalty and writers. Today the 167 rooms maintain
some of the original belle-époque style, though the

Clean water. It's the most basic human necessity. Yet one third of all poverty related deaths are caused by drinking dirty water. Saying *I'm in* means you're part of a growing movement that's fighting the injustice of poverty. Your £8 a month can help bring safe water to some of the world's poorest people. We can do this. We *can* end poverty. Are you in?

shouldn't everyone get clean water? I don't think that's too much to ask for

Let's end poverty together.
Text 'WATER' and your name to 87099 to give £8 a month.

Standard text rates apply. Registered charity No.202918

oxfam.org.uk

I'm in

Oxfam

Sarite Morales, Greenwich

Sleep like a prince and pay like a pauper at the **Hostal Horizonte**. *See p63.*

swirly carpets and occasionally shabby fittings are incongruous in such a setting. And, for the price, it has fairly minimal fitness facilities (and no pool). In terms of today's clientele, the Ritz has shaken off its slightly stuffy image and now welcomes celebs it once shunned; however, guests must still adhere to a strict dress code in the restaurant.

Bar. Business centre. Disabled-adapted room. Gym. Internet (high-speed, wireless). No-smoking floors (2). Restaurant. Room service. TV (satellite).

Hotel Villa Magna

Paseo de la Castellana 22, 28046 (91 587 12 34/ www.madrid.hyatt.com). Metro Rubén Darío. **Rates** €294-€530 single/double; €615-€851 suite; €3,504-€3,740 presidential suite. **Credit** AmEx, DC, MC, V. **Map** p324 K7/8 ⓜ

Although it's a modern, rather nondescript building from the outside, the lavishly entitled Villa Magna, a Park Hyatt Hotel, more than lives up to its reputation – and tariffs – on the inside. The huge lobby, full of jewellery displays, international businessmen and polite staff, leads to two excellent restaurants and a champagne bar, whose lunch menu is surprisingly reasonably priced. The 164 rooms and 18 suites, looking out over the busy Paseo de la Castellana or the exclusive C/Serrano, have good facilities and, like the rest of the hotel, are spacious and elegantly decorated. There's also a top-notch gym, if leisure is part of your agenda.

Bar. Business centre. Disabled-adapted rooms (10). Gym. Internet (wireless). No-smoking floors (7). Restaurant. Room service. TV (satellite).

Hotel Wellington

C/Velázquez 8, 28001 (91 575 44 00/www.hotel-wellington.com). Metro Retiro. **Rates** €187.25-€321 single; €187.25-€428 double; €428-€642 suite. **Credit** AmEx, DC, MC, V. **Map** p325 M10 ⓜ

More than half a century after it opened, the Wellington is still extremely graceful, with chandeliers, marble and murals, and groups of guests in formal eveningwear milling around the lobby. Polite staff are on hand to cater to guests' every need. The hotel is just a stone's throw from the city's most expensive shopping area, Salamanca, and has a summer pool with terrace – ideal for relaxing on after all that retail therapy. Rooms vary in size and are decorated in a conservative but classic style, and the hotel's main restaurant, Goizeko, serves Basque dishes in elegant surroundings.

Bar. Business centre. Internet (wireless). No-smoking floors (4). Parking (€20 per day). Restaurant. Room service. Pool (outdoor). TV (satellite).

Expensive

Hotel Alcalá

C/Alcalá 66, 28009 (91 435 10 60/www.nh-hoteles. com). Metro Príncipe de Vergara. **Rates** €123.05-159.45 single; €130.54-€178.70 double. **Credit** AmEx, DC, MC, V. **Map** p325 M/N10 ⓜ

Even though the chain status of this hotel gives it uniformity and a certain anonymity, the NH Alcalá offers modern accommodation with good facilities and professional staff. Not surprisingly, its location (right near the Retiro) and style (rooms with contemporary decor and good sound-proofing) make it a popular choice. The restaurant serves Basque food, while an early-riser breakfast caters to business travellers on a tight schedule.

Bar. Internet (wireless). No-smoking floors (5). Parking (€21.40 per day). Restaurant. Room service. TV (pay movies, satellite).

Hotel Meliá Galgos

C/Claudio Coello 139, 28006 (91 562 66 00/www. solmelia.com). Metro Rubén Darío. **Rates** €124.15-€278.20 single/double; €240.25-€460.10 suite. **Credit** AmEx, DC, MC, V. **Map** p325 L6 ⓜ

This large, glitzy and bustling hotel is part of the Sol Meliá group. It's located in the heart of the business district, so it comes as no surprise that there

are 11 conference rooms – but is also popular with the well-heeled leisure set. The 'Servicio Real' floor offers a separate reception, a free bar, yet more mod cons in the rooms and secretaries for hire, and even the standard rooms are large and comfortable – if somewhat dated in decor. The gym comes complete with sauna and whirlpools, while the breakfast spread is spectacular.

Bar. Business centre. Gym. No-smoking rooms (120). Internet access (high-speed). Restaurant. Room service. TV (pay movies, satellite).

Mid-range

Hostal-Residencia Don Diego

C/Velázquez 45, 28001 (91 435 07 60/www. hostaldondiego.com). Metro Velázquez. **Rates** €69 single; €96 double; €128 triple. **Credit** AmEx, DC, MC, V. **Map** p325 M8

The Don Diego lies above a row of upmarket private apartments on one of Madrid's most exclusive streets. Rooms are plain but clean and good value, and, because of the location, the *hostal* is popular with the business crowd and those attending trade shows at the IFEMA.

No-smoking rooms (37). TV (satellite).

Budget

Hostal Arco Iris

C/O'Donnell 27, 6 dcha, 28009 (91 575 50 15/www. hostalarcoiris.com). Metro O'Donnell. **Rates** €38-€45 single; €48-€55 double. **Credit** AmEx, DC, MC, V. **Map** p325 O10

Although it's a little more expensive than most *hostales*, the Rainbow's colour schemes make a refreshing change when compared with the dark corridors of the other budget accommodation in the city centre. Rooms are modern and bright, with clean

bathrooms, and the friendly staff are happy to add extra beds to make triples or twins. Stays of two nights or more receive a discount. Well worth a look. *Internet access (wireless). TV.*

Argüelles

Expensive

Hotel Husa Princesa

C/Princesa 40, 28008 (91 542 21 00/www.hotelhusa princesa.com). Metro Ventura Rodríguez. **Rates** €200.10 single; €235.50 double; €534-€754 suite. **Credit** AmEx, DC, MC, V. **Map** p322 D8

Beyond the Plaza de España and the hustle and bustle of Gran Vía lies the Husa Princesa, decorated with large reproductions of Goya and Velázquez classics in each room. Two floors are known as 'club class', providing extra amenities such as a pillow menu, butler service and mid-morning snacks. The hotel's gym and large sports complex are impressive, incorporating an indoor pool, saunas, steam baths and 150 exercise machines, plus a beauty treatment area. The hotel is a favourite of airline staff, who can often be seen sunning themselves on the outdoor terrace tapas bar and café. Offers include weekend breaks with flamenco show included and a flat rate on all rooms booked on the internet.

Bar. Business centre. Gym. No-smoking floors (6). Parking (€25.30 per day). Restaurant. Room service. Swimming pool (indoor). TV (pay movies, satellite).

Mid-range

Hotel Tirol

C/Marqués de Urquijo 4, 28008 (91 548 19 00/ www.t3tirol.com). Metro Argüelles. **Rates** €85.60-€138.40 single/double; €140-€160.50 triple; €175 suite. **Credit** AmEx, MC, V. **Map** p322 D7

AC Palacio de Retiro. *See p65.*

Situated within easy reach of the Parque del Oeste, the Tirol is well located for those wishing to discover the greener side of Madrid. The hotel recently became part of the T3 chain, and while some rooms have been renovated, with modern decor, others have yet to be revamped, a fact reflected in their lower price.
Business centre. TV (satellite).

Chamberí

Luxury

Hotel Hesperia Madrid
Paseo de la Castellana 57, 28046 (91 210 88 00/www.hesperia-madrid.com). Metro Gregorio Marañón. **Rates** €363.80-€411.95 single; €417.30-€470.80 double; €470.80-€4,705. suite. **Credit** AmEx, DC, MC, V. **Map** p321 K5 ⑩
Part of a Catalan chain, Hesperia Madrid is what you'd call 'contemporary luxury'. The dimly lit entrance gives way to white and cream surroundings, while plants lend a necessary splash of colour. In contrast, guest rooms feature dark wood and strong tones. Interior rooms have larger bathrooms, though guests wanting a jacuzzi and terrace will have to move up to the Executive and Presidential levels. The Catalan restaurant, Santceloni, directed by Michelin-starred chef Santi Santamaría, is among the best in the city.
Bar. Business centre. Garden. Internet access (wireless). No-smoking floors (5). Parking (€23.54 per day). Restaurant. Room service. TV (satellite).

Hotel Orfila
C/Orfila 6, 28010 (91 702 77 70/www.hotelorfila. com). Metro Alonso Martínez or Colón. **Rates** €278.20-€331.70 single; €331.70-€406.60 double; €422.65-€545.70 suite. **Credit** AmEx, DC, MC, V. **Map** p324 J8 ㊿

This small mansion in a tranquil residential area has been transformed into a quietly elegant five-star hotel. Built in the 1880s as a private home for an artistic family, the Orfila also contained a theatre and a literary salon during the 1920s. Thankfully, the hotel has held on to its 19th-century decor, not to mention its façade, carriage entrance and dramatic main stairway. The bedrooms are wonderfully quiet – once installed it's hard to believe you're in the middle of a bustling city – and one of the four suites is intimately tucked away in the attic. The elegant restaurant looks on to the lovely garden patio, and guests take tea in the lobby in the afternoon.
Bar. No smoking rooms. Internet access (wireless). Parking (€21.40 per day). Restaurant. Room service. TV.

Hotel Santo Mauro
C/Zurbano 36, 28010 (91 319 69 00/www.achotel santomauro.com). Metro Rubén Darío. **Rates** €290 single; €337.05 double; €511.45 suite. **Credit** AmEx, DC, MC, V. **Map** p324 J7 ㊾
Famous in recent times as the Beckhams' first residence in Madrid, this exquisite hotel is discreetly hidden away in the embassy-lined streets that separate the Castellana from busy C/Santa Engracia. Out of sight behind tall walls and trees, the elegant and peaceful entrance prepares guests for the experience to come. The 51 rooms, housed in two parts of what was the residence of the Duke of Santo Mauro, are luxuriously decorated, and boast king-size beds and floor-to-ceiling picture windows hung with opulent silk drapes. The old palace library has been converted into a high-class restaurant and former ballrooms are now conference rooms opening on to an immaculately kept garden. **Photo** *p70.*
Bar. Business centre. Disabled adapted room. Gym. Internet (wireless). No-smoking rooms (35). Parking (€20.90 per day). Restaurant. Room service. Pool (indoor). TV (satellite).

Favoured hideaway of the stars, the **Hotel Santo Mauro**. *See p69.*

InterContinental Madrid

Paseo de la Castellana 49, 28046 (91 700 73 00/fax 91 319 58 53/www.madrid.intercontinental.com). Metro Gregorio Marañón. **Rates** €481.50-€561.75 single/double; €1,123.50-€2,247 suite; €4,280 presidential suite. **Credit** AmEx, DC, MC, V. **Map** p321 K6 ⑤

The InterContinental is a long-standing Madrid favourite. The elegant decor in the lobby extends to the rooms, most of which overlook the Paseo de la Castellana. The hotel appeals to a wide-ranging clientele, being well located for the business districts but also offering special packages for fans visiting the Bernabéu football stadium. In terms of eating and drinking options, the modern Bar 49 is perfect for a cocktail or two before dinner, the El Jardin restaurant serves French cuisine outdoors during the summer months, and the café serves light meals overlooking the lovely garden.

Bar. Business centre. Disabled-adapted rooms (4). Gym. No-smoking floors (5). Internet (wireless). Parking (€32.10 per day). Restaurants. Room service. TV (satellite).

Expensive

Gran Hotel Conde Duque

Plaza Conde del Valle Suchil 5, 28015 (91 447 70 00/fax 91 448 35 69/www.hotelcondeduque.es). Metro San Bernardo. **Rates** €88.80-€148.75 single; €111.30-€358.45 double. **Credit** AmEx, DC, MC, V. **Map** p323 F7 ㊹

A quiet, out-of-the-way hotel with front rooms facing a leafy pretty plaza. Rooms are tastefully kitted out with yellow and green upholstery, while the belle-époque salon downstairs serves afternoon tea. Beds are king-size and one room, 315, has a waterbed. Previous guests have included Celia Cruz

and Marcel Marceau, and Pedro Almodóvar has been spotted in the bar. Guests can use the gym on the other side of the square. Special rates, inclusive of breakfast, occasionally apply at weekends. Check the website for details.

Bar. Business centre. Gym. Internet access (high-speed). No-smoking floors (5). Parking (€15.30 per day). Restaurant. Room service. TV (pay movies, satellite).

Hotel Zurbano

C/Zurbano 79-81, 28003 (91 441 45 00/www.nh-hoteles.com). Metro Gregorio Marañón. **Rates** €95-€164 single; €100-€199 double; €153-€302 suite. **Credit** AmEx, DC, MC, V. **Map** p321 J5 ㊺

Part of the NH chain, the Zurbano is split between two buildings. Rooms are immaculate (if a little bland) and incredibly well soundproofed, given the location right near the chaotic C/José Abascal and its never-ending traffic jams. The size of the rooms varies according to the building (the one furthest up on the street tends to have the biggest bedrooms). For travellers needing to be near the northern business district or within easy reach of Barajas airport, the location couldn't be better.

Bar. Business centre. Disabled-adapted room. Internet access (wireless). No-smoking floor. Parking (€16.05 per day). Restaurant. Room service. TV (pay movies, satellite).

Expensive

Hotel Eurobuilding

C/Padre Damián 23, 28036, Chamartín (91 353 73 00/www.nhhoteleurobuilding.com). Metro Cuzco. **Rates** €161-€264 single/double; €417-€539 suite. **Credit** AmEx, DC, MC, V.

The very name conjures up images of blandness, but this hotel is set in an appealing residential area. Yes, it's a twin-tower giant, with 459 rooms, but for sports fans and business travellers the location is hard to beat, right near the Palacio de Congresos and Real Madrid's Estadio Bernabéu. The hotel offers a range of services including a spa and beauty salon. Apartment-size suites are available for long stays. *Bar. Business services. Disabled-adapted rooms. Gym. Internet (wireless). No-smoking floors (2). Restaurant. Room service. Spa. TV (satellite).*

Hotel Puerta América

Avda America 41, 28002, East of centre (91 744 54 00/www.puertamerica.com) Metro Cartagena. **Rates** €181.90-€235.40 single/double. **Credit** AmEx, DC, MC, V.

The Puerta América will not be to all tastes, least of all, probably, those of the business travellers attracted by its proximity to the airport, but is a wonderland for design buffs. Each of its 12 floors and public spaces is designed by an all-star cast of architects, taking in Norman Foster, Richard Gluckman, Marc Jewson and Ron Arad. Guests can select the floor of their choice on arrival, but most popular tend to be Zaha Hadid's rooms (which appear to be sculpted from snowdrifts) or Arata Isozaki's studies in Japanese minimalism. The building itself (along with the pool and gym) was designed by Jean Nouvel. *Bars (2). Disabled-adapted rooms (8). Gym. No-smoking floors (2). Internet (wireless). Pool (indoor). Restaurant. Spa. Room service. TV (satellite).*

Mid-range

Hotel Don Pío

Avda Pío XII 25, 28016, Chamartín (91 353 07 80/www.hoteldonpio.com). Metro Pío XII. **Rates** €84-€145 single; €110-€160 single/double. **Credit** AmEx, MC, V.

Quite a way from the centre but right opposite Pío XII metro and Chamartín railway station, and just 15 minutes from the airport, this hotel offers good facilities for the price. The lobby is decorated with dark wooden panelling and antique furniture, while the 41 spacious rooms, arranged round a glass-roofed atrium, are clean, bright and spacious. The marble bathrooms feature hydromassage baths – handy if you've walked back to the hotel after a day's sightseeing. Rates are even better at weekends. *Business centre. Disabled-adapted room. No-smoking floors (2). Internet (wireless). Parking (€10.70 per day). Restaurant. Room service. TV (satellite).*

Aparthotels

Aparthotels are generally made up of self-catering suites or small apartments, usually with kitchen facilities (sometimes basic), reception and maid service. They offer reduced weekly, monthly or longer-term rates, so are handy if you're staying in town for a while.

Hotel Puerta América.

Where to Stay

Aparto-hotel Rosales

C/Marqués de Urquijo 23, Argüelles, 28008 (91 542 03 51/fax 91 559 78 70/www.aprosales.com). Metro Argüelles. **Rates** €69.55-€155.15 single; €96.30-€274.35 double; €128.40-€272.85 apartments. **Credit** AmEx, DC, MC, V. **Map** p322 C7 ⑤⑥

Halfway between a conventional hotel and apart-hotel, the Rosales provides accommodation ranging from spacious and comfortably furnished bedsitters to suites. All boast kitchens and marble-clad bathrooms, and larger rooms also have a lounge. Other facilities include a coffee shop and a decent restaurant. Perfectly located for the Parque del Oeste. *Internet (wireless). Parking (€16.24 per day). Restaurant. Room service. TV (satellite).*

Hostal Madrid

C/Esparteros 6, 2°, Los Austrias, 28012 (91 522 00 60/www.hostal-madrid.info). Metro Sol. **Rates** €50 single; €70 double; €100-€145 apartments. **Credit** MC, V. **Map** p327 G12 ⑤⑦

The rooms at this friendly and centrally located *hostal* are basic, their white and yellow paintwork a little on the dilapidated side and the bathrooms somewhat cramped. The spacious self-catering apartments are a better bet if there are more than two of you. Each has one or two bedrooms, a kitchen and washing facilities, and three have terraces with views over the city. All have similar facilities but prices vary according to size. Note that discounts are available on stays of more than a week. *Internet (wireless). TV.*

NH Suites Prisma

C/Santa Engracia 120, Chamberí, 28003 (91 441 93 77/www.nh-hoteles.com). Metro Ríos Rosas. **Rates** €83.46-€161.60 suite apartments. **Credit** AmEx, DC, MC, V.

This hybrid aparthotel consists of 103 huge suites that are perfect for long stays – especially if you need to work. All have an office area, sitting room, basic kitchenette and bathroom, and all are decorated in the NH chain standard colours. Close by is one of Madrid's most popular public pools, the Canal de Isabel II (*see p258*), which also has tennis courts. *Bar. Internet (wireless). Restaurant. Room service. TV (pay movies, satellite).*

Youth hostels

Much of Madrid's youth hostel accommodation is situated outside the city centre, within easy reach of the mountains – great if you're into walking or skiing. A list of council-owned youth hostels in and around the city can be found on the website www.munimadrid.es (go to 'Tourist Information' then 'Find Accommodation', then 'Rural Lodgings').

Albergue San Fermín

Avda de los Fueros 36, South of centre, 28041 (91 792 08 97/www.san-fermin.org). Metro San Fermín/bus 23 from Plaza Mayor. **Rates**

(incl breakfast) €13 per person; €10 under-26s. €30 double. *Locker* €2. *Towel* €2. **Credit** AmEx, DC, MC, V.

Part of a local regeneration project for the San Fermín area to the south of the centre, this hostel is great value. The modern building houses clean and bright dorms as well as computer facilities, a TV room and a hall for cultural events. It is non-smoking throughout.

Barbieri International Hostel

C/Barbieri 15, Chueca, 28004 (91 531 02 58/www.barbierihostel.com). Metro Chueca or Gran Vía. **Rates** (incl breakfast) €17-€19.50 per person. *Daytime use incl storage & facilities* €5. *Locker* €1. **Credit** MC, V. **Map** p324 I10 ⑤⑧

Right in the middle of Chueca, this hotel is popular with budget travellers of all nationalities. The double rooms and dorms for three or seven people are basic but clean, and there are kitchen facilities, a TV room with DVD player and a book exchange service. Staff are very friendly and the atmosphere relaxed, and because the reception area is manned 24 hours a day there's no curfew.

Campsites

There's a fair sprinkling of campsites all around the Madrid region and towards the Guadarrama and Gredos mountains. Most are open year-round. A full list of local sites is available from tourist offices.

Camping El Escorial

Ctra de Guadarrama a El Escorial, km 3.5, 28280 (91 890 24 12/www.campingelescorial.com). Bus 664 from Moncloa. **Rates** €5.35 per person, per car, per tent. *Electricity* €3.75. **No credit cards.**

This luxury campsite, located in the foothills of the Sierra de Guadarrama around 45 minutes from Madrid, is set in 40 hectares (99 acres) of grounds lined with oak trees. There are wooden chalets (€55-€155) that accommodate five people and have heating for winter stays, as well as pitches for caravans, tents and motorhomes. Facilities are ample – in addition to four swimming pools and various sports courts (football, basketball, tennis and more), there are two discos, a restaurant, café-bar, launderette and supermarket, plus organised activities for children. Not far from the skiing resort of Navacerrada and a short drive from El Escorial, this is a good base for discovering the province.

Camping Osuna

Avda de Logroño s/n, Northern suburbs, 28042 (91 741 05 10/fax 91 320 63 65). Metro Canillejas. **Rates** €6.20 per person, tent or car; €6 bike; €9.85 caravan. *Electricity* €4.70. **No credit cards.**

This is the closest campsite to central Madrid, and the only one within reasonable distance of a metro station. Services include a supermarket, laundry facilities, a restaurant and a bar with a summer terrace that features live entertainment in the evenings.

Sightseeing

The Retiro. *See p117.*

Museo Thyssen-Bornemisza

Permanent Collection & Carmen Thyssen-Bornemisza Collection

One of the more complete collections of Western painting from the 13th to the 20th Century. A thousand works of art by masters such as Duccio, Van Eyck, Memling, Holbein, Carpaccio, Dürer, Raphael, Caravaggio, Titian, Rubens, Rembrandt, Ruysdael, Tiepolo, Canaletto, Watteau, Friedrich, Homer, Corot, Sargent, Manet, Sisley, Renoir, Degas, Van Gogh, Gauguin, Cézanne, Picasso, Braque, Léger, Mondrian, Miró, Pollock, Rothko, Kandinsky, Hopper, Rauschenberg, Lichtenstein.

www.museothyssen.org

Paseo del Prado, 8   28014 Madrid   Foto © Adrian Tyler

Introduction

Where's where in Madrid, from *kilómetro cero* to the outer limits.

Seen from the air, or on a map, two of Madrid's main features immediately stand out. One is the immensely long **Paseo de la Castellana**, a north-south arterial avenue that slices Madrid in two and links the old city with its newer northern business districts. Either side of the Castellana the street layout is a rational, grid-iron pattern. The second feature is the cramped old city with its narrow streets centred on the **Puerta del Sol**. This is literally the centre of the city, in that all street numbers in Madrid count outwards from Sol, and it contains *kilómetro cero* (marked by a pavement plaque) from which distances to the rest of Spain are measured. Much of old Madrid converges on this square. The Habsburg city (Los Austrias), including **Plaza Mayor**, the heart of Golden Age Madrid, lies south-west along C/Mayor. **Plaza Santa Ana** and **Huertas** are to the south-east. Running east from Sol is C/Alcalá, which connects the square with the **Plaza de Cibeles**, the junction with the Castellana that leads to modern Madrid. Just north of Sol the historical but buzzing areas of **Malasaña** and **Chueca** border on the Gran Vía.

One appealing aspect of Madrid is its compact, easily negotiable size. The **Prado**, the **Thyssen** and the **Reina Sofía** sit along the Paseo del Prado in what is known as the 'Golden Triangle' of art, with most other historic attractions close by, falling between Glorieta de Bilbao and the Puerta de Toledo and Atocha (from north to south), and between the Palacio Real and Plaza de Cibeles (from west to east). A car would be a hindrance in old Madrid and, although public transport is good, walking is often the easiest (and quickest) option. A map is useful but not indispensable: even visitors wandering with no specific destination in mind are easily orientated by the changing flavours of the neighbourhoods.

Although small, central Madrid does have well-defined *barrios* whose borders are often easy-to-spot main arteries. There is a problem of nomenclature since, within any given *barrio*, locals may consider a cluster of streets to have a special feel and so give it a name of its own, so different people may refer to the same area by different names. Exactly what constitutes a *barrio*'s particular character can be elusive,

Sightseeing

Don't miss **Madrid**

Have an art attack
Wear comfortable trainers and take plenty of energy bars to get around Madrid's three art palaces, the **Prado** (*see p80*), the **Thyssen** (*see p83*) and the **Reina Sofía** (*see p69*).

Have a row
Messing about in boats is easily done at the leafy, shaded **Retiro** (*see p117*), or the vast and verdant **Casa de Campo** (*see p123*).

Get high
A ride on the **Teleférico de Madrid** cable car (*see p123*) or a trip up the communications tower, the **Faro de Madrid** (*see p125*), gives spectacular views.

Purple haze
Pollution, ironically, makes for incredible magenta sunsets. Take them in either from a *terraza* at **Las Vistillas** (*see p91*) or the **Paseo del Pintor Rosales** (*see p123*).

Nun better
The **Real Monasterio de las Descalzas Reales** (*see p98*) has a collection of sumptuous art, the **Convento de la Encarnación** (*see p97*) an eerie display of saintly remains. But the biscuits from the **Convento de las Carboneras** (*see p104* **Walk through**) are simply divine.

Fair and square
With nippers in tow, check out the **Parque de Atracciones** funfair (*see p210*), and then let them loose in the playground in the stunning **Plaza de Oriente** (*see p93*) while you recover on the sidelines with a stiff drink.

The royal oui
Hello! readers can visit the otherwise unremarkable **cathedral** (*see p93*) to see where Felipe and Letizia said 'I do', and then the many-splendoured **Palacio Real** next door (*see p94*), where the wedding banquet was held.

Plaza de Oriente. *See p93.*

involving myriad details that only locals fully appreciate. Residents often use the name of the nearest metro station for convenience. The area division we use throughout this guide simplifies Madrid's intricate geography, for convenience and comprehensibility.

TICKETS AND TIMES

Spanish national museums give discounts for students, and admission is free to everyone under 18 or over 65 (bring ID). Many museums are free on Sundays (when they can get very crowded) or, for EU citizens, Wednesdays; some smaller museums are always free.

Most museums are shut on Mondays, with the exception of the Reina Sofía, which closes on a Tuesday. Many of the national museums offer volunteer guides free of charge, but they rarely speak English. To have a personal English-speaking guide you usually have to pay. Only the major museums have catalogues in English; similarly, most exhibits are labelled exclusively in Spanish.

Tours

Bus tours

Descubre Madrid (*below*) also runs bus tours.

Madrid Vision

91 779 18 88/www.madridvision.es. **Tours** *21 Dec-20 Mar* 10am-7pm daily. *21 Mar-20 June* 10am-9pm daily. *21 June-20 Sept* 9.30am-midnight daily. *21 Sept-20 Dec* 10am-9pm daily. **Tickets** €15.30; €8.40 6-16s; free under-6s. **No credit cards.**
Three circular routes – Historical, Modern and Monumental Madrid – cover the major sights in the centre, Salamanca and the Retiro. Good places to board include Sol, Gran Vía and the Plaza de España, but the tickets (bought on board) enable you to hop on and off all day. A reasonable commentary is available in various languages, via headphones.

Coach tours

The following two companies offer city tours featuring bullfights, flamenco and so on. More expensive tickets usually include dinner and a show. They also provide the same time-worn menu of tours of the towns around Madrid (Toledo, Segovia, El Escorial and so on), as well as trips to the Warner Bros Park in San Martín de la Vega. Phone for further details, including departure times and prices.

Juliá Travel

Gran Vía 68 (91 559 96 05/www.juliatravel.com). Metro Santo Domingo. **Open** 8am-8pm Mon-Sat. **Credit** MC, V. **Map** p323 G10.

Trapsatur

C/San Bernardo 5, Malasaña (91 541 63 20/ www.trapsatur.com). Metro Santo Domingo. **Open** booking department 9am-1.30pm, 4-7.30pm Mon-Fri; excursions in & around Madrid 8am-8pm daily. **Credit** MC, V. **Map** p323 F10.

Walking tours

Carpetania Madrid

C/Jesús del Valle 11, 4 dcha, Malasaña (91 531 40 18/www.carpetaniamadrid.com). Metro Noviciado. **Open** 9am-9pm daily. **Tours** €5-€7. **Credit** AmEx, DC, MC, V. **Map** p323 G9.
All the guides here are art history specialists. As well as some well-thought-out routes around the city – based on literary themes, parks and gardens and so on – there are expert guided tours available for all exhibitions, temporary and permanent.

Descubre Madrid

C/Mayor 69, Los Austrias (91 588 29 06/7). Metro Sol. **Open** 9.30am-8.30pm Mon-Fri. **Tickets** *On foot* €2.50-€7. *By bus* (Sept-May only) €6.10; €4.65 concs. **Credit** AmEx, DC, MC, V. **Map** p327 G11.
With over 100 different itineraries (by bus and on foot), this service, run by the tourist board, offers the

opportunity to get up close to all aspects of the city, focussing on architecture, literature, history and individual *barrios*. Some tours include sights that are otherwise hard to get into. Walking tours depart from the tourist office in the Plaza Mayor (*see p308*), though you're advised to book beforehand at the tourist board central office at the above address to guarantee a place. Let them know in advance if you want an English-speaking guide.

Descubremadrid.com

If you prefer to see the city independently, this website (not connected with Descubre Madrid, above) has a large number of routes. By day, they cover literary, medieval and art themes; at night there are different ones. All come complete with maps, history and suggested refuelling stops; they are written in English and Spanish and can be printed out.

Madrid Card

Information 91 588 29 00/www.madridcard.com. **Prices** 1 day €38; 2 days €48, €44 if bought online; 3 days €58, €53 if bought online. Available from tourist offices (*see p308*), from Chamartín and Atocha stations and from many travel agencies.

Available for periods of one, two or three days, the Madrid card offers free admission to up to 40 of the city's main museums, discounts on the Madrid Vision tour bus (*see p76*), as well as at many shops, restaurants, clubs, theatres and so on. Information about associated establishments comes in a detailed guide, with map. The only hitch is that the card is quite expensive, so it is only really suitable for those with bags of energy.

Weird wheels and wonderful stories

While walking tours can be a great way to get the feel of a city, you're limited by the amount of pavement pounding you can do in a day. Enter **Madsegs** (www.madsegs.com, mobile 659 824 499; *pictured*), who provide you with a two-wheeled way to see Madrid that also gives you a chance to try the people mover that's so easy to use only George W could fall off. Your tour guide is Antony, a Scot who walked away with first prize for his Segway skills at the first international Segfest, so you're in safe hands. The tours take you right across the city, with Antony imparting historical facts of the sights you see along the way. The €60 per person fee includes the three-hour route, safety instruction on the Segway, a drink in a bar and a CD of photos snapped on the tour itself.

Should you lack a mad uncle who knows his history, you can always rent a surrogate at **Wellington Society** (mobile 609 143 203, www.wellsoc.org), a history-cum-bar-hopping tour of the city brought to you by the eccentric Stephen Drake-Jones. The president of the society is none other than the eighth Duke of Wellington, although he is sadly absent from the tours. Tours focus on history and wine – if these don't rock your boat, as Drake-Jones puts it, 'Don't bother coming' – and seamlessly combine historical tales with plenty of stops in top tapas bars and other *madrileño* eateries. They attract a mixture of locals and tourists from all over the world. Large groups can book in advance and, if you fancy it, Drake-Jones will even take you on an out-of-town trip to places such as Segovia, Ávila or Toledo.

Run by husband-and-wife team Carlos (from Spain) and Jennifer (from the US), **Letango** (C/Gobernador 11, 1º dcha, mobile 661 752 458, www.letango.com) tailors its tours to each group, taking in Spanish culture, cuisine and historical anecdotes. They'll take you anywhere from a pastry shop to an old hangout for once-exiled politicians, and chances are they'll be able to answer all of your questions. As well as showing you round Madrid, they can also arrange tours to other cities, arranging everything from the accommodation to car hire.

Sightseeing

The Paseo del Arte

Three of the best – the very best – the world of art can offer.

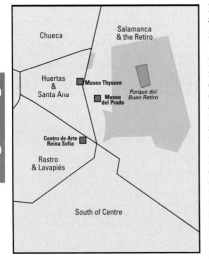

In the **Prado**, the **Thyssen** and the **Reina Sofía**, Madrid has three art palaces that are quite simply world class. You'll find them dotted along the Paseo del Prado, in what has increasingly, and slightly facetiously, come to be known as the 'Golden Triangle'. This formidable trio of museums has made Madrid the world's capital of art for many people in the know, and with the changes afoot at the time of writing, this label is only set to stick more firmly.

The big three are getting bigger. Starting in the mid 1990s, the Prado, Reina Sofía and Thyssen each conceived expansion plans that have been slowly hatched and nurtured and are now finally beginning to take real shape. By the time they will have finally been completed, the government will have spent, it is reckoned, something like €150 million (and counting), the largest public investment in the history of the three museums. The initiative takes advantage of the proximity of the three art collections, barely ten minutes' walk from one another. Together they will form what is known as the 'Paseo del Arte', much in the manner of Berlin's 'Museum Island', London's 'Museum District' or Washington's 'Museums on the Mall'. The axis that unites them all, the

Paseo del Prado, is also to be remodelled by a team of architects under the leadership of Álvaro Siza, the Portuguese winner of the Wolf Prize back in 2001.

First past the post was the Thyssen-Bornemisza Museum , which unveiled its new wing back in June 2004. The extension comprises 16 new exhibition rooms, a new café-restaurant and offices in two buildings adjacent to the Palacio de Villahermosa, making the museum L-shaped. The project represents an impressive expansion of 50 per cent on the museum's original space.

Second in the race was the Reina Sofía. French architect Jean Nouvel was in control of the project, which includes a three-building extension and gives the museum a second façade, which faces to the south-west. As well as the massive amounts of additional space, the way the three constructions are laid out has provided this crowded part of Madrid with a brand new public square. The new constructions, light and 'dematerialised' with glass playing a major role, are united under a massive zinc roof, which contrasts radically with the massive, opaque solidity of the Sabatini building. The building dedicated to temporary shows opened in 2004, followed in September 2005 by the library and auditorium.

Last but not least is the Prado, whose plan is perhaps the most ambitious. It is certainly the most controversial and most subject to delays. With no large backyard and only one annexe (the Casón del Buen Retiro – the ballroom of the Palacio del Buen Retiro, which once stood on this site), the Prado can only expand by taking over nearby sites. Behind the museum is the San Jerónimo church, whose adjoining cloisters, a national heritage site, were earmarked for the construction of a large building for temporary shows, with Rafael Moneo at the helm. His cube-shaped building, not to mention its location on the site of the cloisters, has caused a furore (but is scheduled to open in summer 2007), as has the takeover of another of the parts of the Palacio del Buen Retiro still standing. Until recently, this, the former ballroom, housed the Military Museum (which, in turn, has been moved to Toledo). Realistic expectations are that the work will be completed towards the end of the first decade. Final budget? Nobody's even prepared to guess.

Sightseeing

The Prado. *See p80.*

From the Prado, *see p81.*

TICKETS

A joint ticket, the Paseo del Arte, gives entry to the Prado, the Reina Sofía and the Thyssen-Bornemisza for €14.40. It is available from the ticket desks at all three museums; after visiting one you can visit the other two at any time in the same calendar year. Each museum also has its own 'friends' tickets, giving unlimited entry for a year, which are more expensive and more widely publicised. A better deal is the €36.06 annual museum ticket, available from any state-run museum, which gives unlimited entry to all the main museums (except the Thyssen).

The Prado

Housed in a gigantic neo-classical building begun by Juan de Villanueva for King Charles III in 1785, the Prado is Madrid's best-known attraction. Charles originally wanted to establish a museum of natural sciences, reflecting one of his chief interests, but by the time it opened, in 1819, this plan had changed: the Prado was a public art museum – one of the world's first – displaying the royal art collection. Spain's 'non-king', Joseph Bonaparte, had first proposed the idea and it was taken up by the restored King Fernando VII, who took on board the demands of the Real Academia de Bellas Artes and those of his second wife, María Isabel de Braganza, considered the museum's true founder.

The Prado is currently undergoing a highly ambitious expansion programme that involves several phases and that almost certainly has a few years left to run. The remodelling of the Casón del Buen Retiro, an annexe opposite the Retiro park, is due to be completed late in 2007 (but is subject to endless delays); this building will then house the works of Luca Giordano, to complement his stunning mural on the domed ceiling. Behind the main museum, on the site of the the San Jerónimo cloisters, the new and highly controversial cube-shaped edifice designed by Rafael Moneo should be unveiled in the summer of 2007.

As for the collection itself, the core is still the royal holdings, so it reflects royal tastes and political alliances from the 15th to the 17th centuries: court painters Diego de Velázquez and Francisco de Goya are well represented. Political ties with France, Italy and the southern, Catholic Netherlands also assure the presence of works by Titian, Rubens and Hieronymous Bosch, among others. The collection did have some gaps, mainly owing to Spain's hostilities with England, Holland and other Protestant states and the Spanish monarchs' unfamiliarity with artists pre-dating the High Renaissance, but recent acquisitions have evened things out somewhat.

Spanish monarchs had begun collecting long before, and by the 1500s Queen Isabella already had a substantial collection of works by Flemish artists. During the reigns of Emperor Charles V (1516-56) and Philip II (1556-98), Italian and Flemish works continued to dominate. Titian was a favourite of both kings, and the eclectic Philip II also purchased several works by Bosch, among them the enigmatic, slightly surreal triptych *Garden of Earthly Delights*, which he had hanging on his bedroom wall in El Escorial. The white face beneath a hat in the 'Hell' panel is widely believed to be the artist himself. *See also p82* **Life and death**.

Philip IV (1621-65) is seen as the greatest of the Habsburg art collectors, and the leading connoisseur of his day. Flemish influence was still very strong, and the king was a major patron of Rubens. The latter was contemptuous of Spanish painters until he saw the work of the young Velázquez, who would serve Philip IV as court painter for nearly 40 years (1623-60). Velázquez also supervised the acquisition of other works for Philip IV, adding nearly 2,000 paintings by Renaissance and 17th-century masters.

Spain's first Bourbon King, Philip V (1700-46), brought with him one of the museum's most extraordinary possessions, displayed in the basement: the Tesoro del Delfín ('Treasures of the Grand Dauphin'). The Dauphin, eldest son of Louis XIV of France and father of Philip V of Spain, accumulated a massive art collection, part of which was left to Philip. The 'Treasure' is mostly 16th- and 17th-century Italian *objets d'art*, such as rock-crystal vases studded with semi-precious stones and with gold and silver trims.

The last monarch to add significantly to the royal collection was Charles IV (1788-1808), the employer of Goya, possibly the least respectful court painter who ever lived (for Goya's portrait of Charles IV's family, *see p20* **Picture this**). Following Charles's death, the collection would be supplemented by later purchases and works seized from religious houses following their dissolution in the 1830s.

HIGHLIGHTS

With such a concentration of masterpieces, it is impossible to do the Prado justice in a single visit. The free maps provided at the entrances, available in English, will help guide the visitor to the must-sees. The ground floor contains earlier painting and sculpture; stunning Spanish Romanesque murals and Gothic altarpieces; works from the Italian Renaissance (masterpieces by Botticelli, Titian, Caravaggio and Rafael, whose *Portrait of a Cardinal* is pictured on p80); 15th-century Flemish painting, with the world's greatest collection of Hieronymus Bosch; plus El Greco, and German paintings such as Dürer's extraordinary 1498 *Self-Portrait*. Also on this floor you'll find the classical and Renaissance sculpture, and the vault that currently houses the Tesoro del Delfin, until its eventual transfer to the Palacio del Buen Retiro.

Entering via the Puerta Alta de Goya, you reach the first, and what is considered the 'principal', floor. Here you encounter French and Italian 16th-and 17th-century painting, with works by Poussin, Claude Lorrain and Artemisia Gentileschi, among others, followed, on the left, by several rooms of Flemish works (Rubens, Breughel, van Dyck). Stretching ahead on the right is a long gallery with Spanish paintings of the same period, featuring Murillo, Ribera and Zurbarán (his *Saint Casilda* is featured on p85). This leads to one of the Prado's greatest attractions: the Velázquez Rooms.

In the great hall in the centre of this floor are Velázquez's massive state portraits of Philip IV and his court, with their air of melancholic grandeur, and his wonderful *Surrender of Breda* (known in Spanish as *Las Lanzas*), which are all due to move to the Palacio del Buen Retiro at some point. Pride of place, though, is taken by *Las Meninas*, often described as the greatest painting in the world, because of its complex interplay of perspectives and realities. Velázquez inserted himself at the left of the picture, supposedly painting a portrait of the king and queen, who appear bizarrely in a 'mirror' at the end of the room, but in whose place stands every viewer, watched forever by Velázquez, the little Infanta Margarita and other figures in the painting. Different but equally impressive are the artist's extraordinary *Los Borrachos* ('The Drunkards') and the portraits of the royal dwarves.

The rooms devoted to Goya, are at the south end of the first floor and on the floor above. Every stage of his career is superbly represented, from cynical portraits of the aristocracy to the *Majas* (*see p15* **Picture this**). An important recent addition to the collection is his portrait of the *Marquesa de Chinchón*. There are also his tremendous images of war, such as the masterpiece *The Third of May* (*see p26* **Picture this**), depicting the executions carried

From the Thyssen, *see p84.*

Life and death

In Room 56 of the Prado are two of the greatest paintings ever done of the Last Judgement: Pieter Breughel the Elder's *The Triumph of Death*, painted in 1562, and *The Garden of Earthly Delights*, the triptych by Hieronymus Bosch (El Bosco to the Spanish), thought to have been completed around 1501. It is one of the greatest canvases of all times, a painting that spans centuries at a leap.

The Triumph of Death is no lightweight effort either, and even if Breughel had not also been Flemish and an unabashed admirer of Bosch's painting, it would still be a good choice to put near *Earthly Delights*. It is smaller, a single canvas, but imagined in hallucinatory detail that is every bit a counterweight to the Bosch. In it, hundreds of skeletons herd the living into a huge rectangular box, a coffin big enough to hold all the quick in the world and turn them into dead. The humans are terrified, helpless, shoved, pushed and prodded along by skeletons. There is a huge bony horse and astride it is a skeletal general in death's army, huge scythe in one hand, reaping as he tramples through the waves of terrified human beings. A dog feeds on a dead woman's body. The horizon is high on the painting, the whole shocking scene in the foreground fades into dark spectral colours punctuated by pockets of leaping flames, gleaming brimstone in the crepuscular light.

out by French troops in Madrid in 1808. Even more fascinating than these are the *Pinturas Negras* or 'Black Paintings', the turbulent pictures executed by Goya in his final years. Witchcraft, violence and historical drama combine in an astonishing array of monstrous images, many originally painted on the walls of his home, the Quinta del Sordo, between 1819 and 1823. On the second floor there are his earlier, lighter, portraits and the carefree tapestry cartoons he designed for the royal palaces. Here too are European paintings from the 18th century. A couple of rooms also contain works by the German neo-classical master Mengs, the Italian Tiepolo and the French painter Watteau.

Museo del Prado

Paseo del Prado s/n, Retiro (91 330 28 00/91 330 29 00/www.museoprado.es). Metro Atocha or Banco de España. **Open** 9am-8pm Tue-Sun. **Admission** €6; €3 concessions; free under-18s, over-65s. Free to all Sun. *Paseo del Arte ticket* €14.40. **Credit** (shop only) AmEx, DC, MC, V. **Map** p328 J12/13. **Photos** *p79.*

On the facing wall is Bosch's triptych, two metres high, the centre panel twice the width of the wings, which fold in over it. Painted on the back of the wings, so as to form another scene when they are covering the centre panel, is the third day of creation as described in Genesis: the globe of Earth a wet twilight fog of greys and blues, spectral, uninhabited. Waiting, with the animal world yet to come. This is a part of the painting that is much less known than the main triptych, which depicts our peopled world in its implacable fullness and flesh, its joys and sufferings, all in amazingly modern detail.

The left panel shows the Garden of Eden in its innocence, but even here all is not peace and light, as beasts swallow other beasts, hinting at the savage brute world on which ours is built. In the centre panel is the antediluvian world of the senses – the world as we know it, a variety of human pleasure as modern as television or Hollywood's latest scandal. Sensual romps we have no trouble recognising as our own. The pleasures of the flesh in trysts, threesomes, group gropes, everyone indulging. Beside it, in the last panel, hell itself, Judgement Day, when the former revellers are tied and tortured by ghouls and animals: miserable, dominated, impaled, ensnared and enslaved, their cities burning in the implacable darkness of the last days.

The Garden of Earthly Delights is full of the most modern of physical forms, from a round earth to airships. The power of its images is undimmed across the centuries, and its images still resonate to this day.

The Thyssen

When the Thyssen-Bornemisza Museum opened in 1992, Madrid added the second point to its 'Golden Triangle'. The private collection of the late Baron Hans-Heinrich Thyssen-Bornemisza is widely considered the most important in the world. Consisting of 775 paintings, it came to Madrid on loan, but in 1993 a purchase agreement was signed with the Spanish state. The Baron's decision to sell was doubtlessly influenced both by his wife, Carmen 'Tita' Cervera, a former Miss Spain, and by the offer to house the collection in the then-empty Palacio de Villahermosa, an early 19th-century edifice that was superbly reconverted by architect Rafael Moneo at fantastic cost. Thanks to this revamp, involving terracotta-pink walls, marble floors and skylights, it is possible to view the works with near-perfect illumination. In 2004, the museum unveiled its new wing, in which some 200 paintings and sculptures from Carmen Cervera's own collection are on display.

Sightseeing

The collection was started by the Baron's father in the 1920s but was dispersed among his heirs after he died in 1947. The Baron bought back the paintings from his relatives and then extended the collection, buying up first Old Masters and then more contemporary works during the 1960s. The Baron's own home in Lugano, Switzerland, only had space to exhibit around 300 works, leading him to look for a larger home for the collection, most of which may now be seen in Madrid, though some paintings are housed in the MNAC museum in Barcelona.

THE COLLECTION

Following the collection in chronological order gives you a lesson in Western art history. Beginning on the second floor, you'll find 13th-century works, notably by the early Italians, such as Duccio di Buoninsegna's *Christ and the Samaritan Woman*. You finish the tour on the ground floor, where Roy Lichtenstein's *Woman in Bath* is on show (**photo** *p81*), or in the basement café, where Renato Guttuso's 1976 *Caffè Greco* hangs. Along the way, you'll have seen examples of all the major schools. The collection partly complements the Prado and Reina Sofía's collections with substantial holdings of 17th-century Dutch painting, Impressionism, German Expressionism, Russian constructivism, geometric abstraction and Pop Art.

The Thyssen's detractors say the collection is a ragbag, catch-all gathering of every kind of style, put together with neither a sense of discrimination nor an eye for quality. However, one of the Thyssen's great attractions is that, while it is extraordinarily broad in scope, it is also recognisably a personal collection that reflects a distinctly individual taste, as seen in the wonderful room dedicated to early portraits, with works by Antonello da

Messina and Hans Memling. Equally quirky is the section on early North American painting, including a *Presumed Portrait of George Washington's Cook* by Gilbert Stuart and works by American artists who are rarely seen in Europe, among them Thomas Cole, Frederick Remington and Winslow Homer.

The Thyssen also has its share of real masterpieces. Among the Old Masters, the works of Duccio, van Eyck and Petrus Christus stand out. The museum's most famous painting, however, is the great Florentine master Domenico Ghirlandaio's idealised *Portrait of Giovanna Tornabuoni* (1488), in the Portrait Room. Two rooms further on is Vittore Carpaccio's allegorical *Young Knight in a Landscape* (1510), another gem. From among the masters of the Flemish School is the sublime *Annunciation* diptych by van Eyck, which is more like a three-dimensional sculptural relief than a painting. The Thyssen is particularly strong in the German Renaissance, with many works by Cranach the Elder, a remarkable series of portraits by different artists and Albrecht Dürer's *Jesus Among the Doctors*, which portrays an idealised, almost effeminate Christ pressed upon by diabolical doctors.

From the later 16th century and baroque there are superb paintings, such as Titian's *Saint Jerome in the Wilderness*, Mattia Preti's unsettling *A Concert* and Caravaggio's magnificent *Saint Catherine of Alexandria* (**photo** *p81*). There are also representative works by El Greco, Rubens, Guercino, Tintoretto and Jusepe Ribera, and a Bernini marble, *Saint Sebastian*.

The first floor, below, begins with several rooms of 17th-century Dutch pictures – arguably the least interesting section of the Thyssen – followed by the most varied part of the museum, with such pieces

Museo Thyssen-Bornemisza.

as a sombre *Easter Morning* by Caspar David Friedrich; a Goya portrait of his friend, *Asensio Juliá*; a great selection of Impressionists (Monet, Manet, Renoir, Cézanne, Degas dancers, two beautiful and little-known van Goghs); and even Constable's 1824 *The Lock* – although not jumbled together, but carefully ordered and arranged. The collection is generally strong in German art of all kinds, with several rooms of Expressionists and powerful works by Emil Nolde, Ernst Ludwig Kirchner, Otto Dix, Max Beckmann and Blue Rider group artists Franz Marc and Kandinsky.

Also present, on the ground floor, are some more familiar modern masters – Braque, Mondrian, Klee, Max Ernst and Picasso (in the shape of his 1911 *Man with a Clarinet*), among others. The last few rooms focus on the USA, with a fabulous Georgia O'Keeffe, *New York with Moon*, plus *Hotel Room* by Edward Hopper and Robert Rauschenberg's 1963 *Express*. *Large Interior, Paddington* by Lucian Freud, an early David Hockney, *In Memoriam Cecchino Bracci*, and Ronald Kitaj's *The Greek from Smyrna* are also on display.

THE CARMEN THYSSEN-BORNEMISZA COLLECTION

This extension opened in 2004 and incorporates two adjoining buildings: Nos.19 (the Palacio de Goyeneche) and 21 of the C/Marqués de Cubas. The new space exhibits some 220 works of the 300 belonging to the private collection of 'Tita' Cervera, which she has ceded to the Spanish state for an 11-year period (though three were already up and the collection's future remains uncertain). In addition there is a huge area for temporary shows and the library, restoration workshops and cafeteria have all been enlarged.

Access is from Room 18 on the second floor, which leads straight into rooms with early Italian and Flemish works by the likes of Luca Giordano, Jan Breughel and van Dyck, outstanding among which is the latter's *Christ on the Cross*. Moving on you will enter a well-illuminated gallery that contains views and landscapes by Canaletto, Constable, Corot, Guardi and van Gogh. In the next room are 18th-century French and Italian painting and beyond that is the exhibition 'Naturalism and the Rural World', a selection of 19th-century paintings from North America. Room H contains the works of the early Impressionists, among them Degas, Pisarro, Monet, Renoir and Sisley. Downstairs on the first floor you'll find work by North American Impressionists and other artists from the period of late Impressionism. Two rooms are given over to Gauguin (the displays include his *Mata Mua* and *Coming and Going, Martinique*) and other post-Impressionists. From then on, you move into German Expressionists, Fauvists and the early 20th-century avant-garde movements. In addition, there is a Rodin Room, where one of the Baroness's four sculptures by the French artist is on show; the others are spread throughout the first floor.

From the Prado, *see p81*.

Museo Thyssen-Bornemisza

Palacio de Villahermosa, Paseo del Prado 8, Huertas & Santa Ana (91 420 39 44/www.museothyssen.org). Metro Banco de España. **Open** *Sept-mid July* 10am-7pm Tue-Sun. *Mid July-Aug* 10am-11pm daily. **Admission** €6; €4 concessions; free over-65s & under-12s. *Paseo del Arte ticket* €14.40 *Temporary exhibitions* €5; €4 concessions. **Credit** AmEx, DC, MC, V. **Map** p328 J12. **Photo** *p84*.

The Reina Sofía

Occupying an immense, slab-sided building, the Reina Sofía boasts an impressive façade with glass and steel lift-shafts, designed by British architect Ian Ritchie. Now, though, the museum has just as impressive a rear, in the form of three buildings, principally built of glass and steel, arranged around a courtyard and all covered by a triangular, zinc-and-aluminium roof, the work of French architect Jean Nouvel. This ambitious extension project adds almost 30,000 sq m to the already vast art space in the patio to the south-west of the main edifice. It includes temporary exhibition spaces.

The Reina Sofía's great jewel is unquestionably *Guernica*, Picasso's impassioned denunciation of war and fascism, a painting that commemorates the destruction in 1937 of the Basque town of Guernica by German bombers that flew in support of the Francoist forces in the Spanish Civil War. Certain art historians, sometimes encouraged by Picasso

Sightseeing

himself, have seen it more in formal terms, as a reflection on the history of western painting using elements from the work of the Old Masters. Picasso refused to allow the painting to be exhibited in Spain under the Franco regime, and it was only in 1981 that it was finally brought to Spain from the Museum of Modern Art in New York. *Guernica* has been in the Reina Sofía since 1992, when it was transferred from the Cason del Buen Retiro amid great controversy. The artist had intended the painting to be housed in the Prado – of which the Casón is at least an annexe – and his family bitterly opposed the change of location. There is no question that the acquisition of *Guernica* hugely boosted the prestige of the Reina Sofía, but the conflictive saga of the painting's final resting place has continued: Bilbao, capital of the Basque province of Vizcaya, which contains the town of Guernica, has staked a claim on the picture for its Guggenheim Museum. However, since the painting belongs to the Spanish state, any such move is very unlikely.

The rest of the Reina Sofía's permanent collection, which came mainly from the old Museo Español de Arte Contemporáneo in Moncloa, has been much criticised. For many, the museum's claim to be an international centre for contemporary art is frankly fallacious. At best, it is pointed out, it is a reasonable collection of Spanish contemporary art, with some thin coverage of non-Spanish artists. It certainly contains works by practically all the major Spanish artists of the 20th century – Picasso, Dalí, Miró, Julio González, Tàpies, Alfonso Ponce de León and Antonio Saura are all present – but even here the representation of individual artists is often patchy, with few major works.

In response, an active acquisitions policy adopted in the early 1990s has sought to fill some gaps in the range of Spanish art and to add works by major foreign artists. Pieces by Donald Judd, Anish Kapoor, Bruce Nauman, Tony Cragg, Ellsworth Kelly and Julian Schnabel were all added, along with Picasso's 1928 Figura. However, the acquisitions budget has been very tight in recent years, especially in the context of the museum's expansion scheme and that of the Prado, but has allowed for the addition of works by Miró, Gris, André Breton, Man Ray, Joaquín Torres García and others.

The director, Ana Martínez de Aguilar, has faced a very tough challenge, given the museum's new dimensions, and the art world will be watching her every move. The experts believe that the museum should bring 'grand' international temporary shows, practically non-existent over the last few years; review and improve the permanent collection; and define a clear acquisitions policy. The possibilities are immense, as are the chances of failure.

THE COLLECTION

The permanent collection is currently on the second and fourth floors of the Sabatini building and temporary exhibitions have until now been presented on the ground and third floors. However, the opening of the extension will mean changes in this layout in the near future. The third floor will provide additional space and allow the museum to exhibit a wider selection of pieces from the permanent collection, some of which have only ever been on show temporarily, in rotation. The ground floor will continue to be used for temporary shows and also features Espacio Uno, a space for cutting-edge installations and new multimedia work.

As things stand, the second floor begins with a selection of works that look at the origins of Modernism in Spanish art, haphazardly placing together artistic currents from different parts of Spain – Basque painters such as Zuloaga, Regoyos and Echevarría, Catalan Modernists such as Rusiñol, Nonell and Casas – even though they have relatively little in common. Next is the first Avant-Garde Room, with pieces by the Uruguayan Joaquín Torres García and other artists who worked in Spain, such as Picabia and the Delaunays, followed by a room dedicated to Juan Gris. Then comes the major draw for most visitors: the Picasso Rooms, divided into pre- and post-Civil War, with *Guernica* in the centre.

Miró, Julio González and Dalí have rooms of their own. Paintings by the latter include *The Great Masturbator* and *The Enigma of Hitler*. Several of the works by Miró are from his later life, the 1970s. After a room on international Surrealism (Ernst, Magritte), there follows one on Luis Buñuel; the final displays on this floor look at Spanish art of the 1930s, taking you to the end of the Civil War (1939).

The fourth floor runs from Spain's post-war years up to the present day, starting with figurative art and the beginnings of abstraction in Spain, taking in Tàpies, Mompó, Oteiza, Palazuelo and Equipo 57. For international context, there are also works by Bacon, Henry Moore and Lucio Fontana, alongside Saura and Chillida. Later rooms feature Pop Art, figurative work by Arroyo and Minimalism, with pieces by Ellsworth Kelly, Dan Flavin and Barnett Newman. Overall, though, the collection of non-Spanish art remains very limited.

The Reina Sofía serves as a venue for many other activities. It runs the Palacio de Cristal and Palacio de Velázquez exhibition halls (in the Retiro), which are used to present dynamic shows of sculpture and installations. It's also home to Madrid's principal contemporary music centre, the Centro para la Difusión de la Música Contemporánea (*see p233*). This is soon to move into the extension, where there will be a 500-seat auditorium and another for 200. The museum also has exceptional book, music, art and video libraries, and a superior book and souvenir shop.

Museo Nacional Centro de Arte Reina Sofía

C/Santa Isabel 52, Lavapiés (91 467 50 62/ http://museoreinasofia.mcu.es). Metro Atocha. **Open** 10am-9pm Mon, Wed-Sat; 10am-2.30pm Sun. **Admission** €6; €3 students; free under-18s, over-65s. Free to all 2.30-9pm Sat & all Sun. *Paseo del Arte ticket* €14.40. **Credit** (shop only) AmEx, DC, MC, V. **Map** p328 J14/15.

Museo Nacional Centro
de Arte Reina Sofía.

The Old City

Where medieval alleys meet Habsburg and Bourbon splendour.

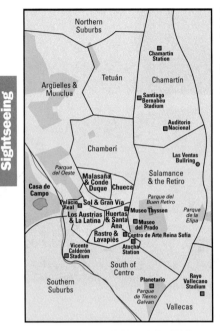

Northern
Suburbs

Chamartín
Station

Tetuán

Chamartín

Argüelles &
Moncloa

Santiago
Bernabéu
Stadium

Auditorio
Nacional

Chamberí

Las Ventas
Bullring

Parque
del Oeste

Malasaña
& Conde
Duque

Chueca

Salamance
& the Retiro

Casa de
Campo

Parque del
Buen Retiro

Palacio
Real

Sol & Gran Vía

Museo Thyssen

Los Austrias
& La Latina

Huertas
& Santa
Ana

Museo
del Prado

Parque
de la
Elipa

Rastro &
Lavapiés

Centro de Arte Reina Sofía

Vicente
Calderón
Stadium

Atocha
Station

South of
Centre

Southern
Suburbs

Planetario

Rayo
Vallecano
Stadium

Parque
de Tierno
Galván

Vallecas

South of Gran Vía

Los Austrias

The oldest part of the city, site of the Muslim town and of most of medieval Madrid, falls between **Plaza de la Cebada**, **Plaza Mayor** and the **Palacio Real**. Even though most of the streets still follow their original medieval lines, this may not be immediately apparent today. Like several other parts of the Old City, this area has been smartened up recently, and is now home to a slew of wine bars and expensive restaurants. Tucked away in side streets are the 12th-century **San Nicolás de los Servitas** (*see p94*) and the city's other Mudéjar tower, the 14th-century **San Pedro el Viejo** (*see p93*). If you continue down C/Segovia beneath the viaduct, you pass a forlorn fragment of the ninth-century **Muralla Árabe** (Arab wall), the only substantial relic of Madrid's Muslim founders.

The area around it, known as the **Parque Emir Mohammed I**, is occasionally used as a venue in summer arts festivals.

Back into town, along C/Mayor is the **Plaza de la Villa** (*see p93*), Madrid's oldest square and home to the city hall, the **Casa de la Villa**. In pre-Habsburg times the square was also the preferred place of residences for the elite; one such residence, the **Torre de los Lujanes**, can still be seen there. Along with the **Casa de Cisneros**, also on the square, the buildings make up a compendium of the history of the city from provincial town to the imperial capital it was to become.

Despite its ancient beginnings, the area has come to be known as the 'Madrid de los Austrias', after the Habsburgs, although in truth Philip II and his dynasty can scarcely claim responsibility for much of it. The greatest monument they *did* build, however, stands at the area's core: the **Plaza Mayor**, archetypal creation of Castilian baroque (a style also known as 'Herreran', after its key architect). On the south side of the plaza there is a **tourist office** (*see p308*) at the corner of C/Toledo, on which stand the twin baroque towers of **San Isidro** (*see p91*), perhaps Madrid's most important historic church. Continue down here to reach **La Latina** and the **Rastro** flea market.

Back in the plaza, the **Arco de los Cuchilleros** (Knifemakers' Arch) runs from the south-west corner via a spectacular bank of steps leading down through C/Cuchilleros to the **Plaza de la Puerta Cerrada**, decorated with some engaging 1970s murals. From here the **C/Cava Baja**, home to many of the most celebrated *mesones*, temples to Madrid's traditional cuisine, runs south.

To the south-east of the square, at the **Plaza de la Provincia**, is another major work in the Herreran style: the squatly proportioned **Palacio de Santa Cruz**, which was the work of several architects between 1629 and 1643. Despite its grand appearance, the palace was originally the court prison, with a dungeon so deep that prisoners had to rub their rags with lard and set them alight to stop themselves from going blind. These days the building has a somewhat more dignified role as the Foreign Ministry. In former times executions often took place in the Plaza de la Cebada, just a tumbril ride away.

Home to Madrid's most traditional restaurants, the **C/Cava Baja**. *See p88.*

A heap of faith

If you are female and single, you might want to make a discreet pilgrimage to the Ermita de San Antonio de la Florida (Paseo de la Florida) if you happen to be in Madrid on 13 June. This is Anthony of Padua's feast day, a saint whose many attributes supposedly include the ability to rustle up boyfriends out of thin air – for Madrid girls at least. The tradition was perhaps started by young seamstresses, as the custom is to turn up at the church with a handful of pins. The girls queue up to drop the pins in the font, then stick thcir hand into the water. The test is whether the pins stick to their hand. If so, love is just around the corner. It's got to be worth a go.

The Iglesia de San Antón on C/Hortaleza, on the other hand is dedicated to Saint Anthony of Egypt, who, like Saint Francis, had quite a way with animals. On 17 January the people of Madrid commemorate this by bringing not only their pets, but also farm animals to the church to be blessed. This causes something of a livestock bottleneck in the narrow, busy C/Hortaleza, as dogs, cats, rabbits, goats, donkeys and pigs wait to enter the church. Not far away, at the Iglesia de Santa Pascual on the Paseo de Recoletos, you might catch sight of a famous face slinking in or out. The church contains a figure of Saint Clare, who in recent times has been appointed the patron saint of television. Actors, actresses and stars of reality TV pop in to ask her to help them get the role that will finally make them a household name.

On 27 July, expect to see a very long queue of people if you are in the vicinity of the Convento de la Encarnación (*see p97*). The reliquary of this 17th-century convent contains a phial of blood purportedly belonging to Pantaleón, the doctor saint. On his feast day, the dubious contents of the phial miraculously liquefy, which augurs great things for those who witness the event. Yet more expectant queuing goes on every Friday outside the Iglesia de Jesús de Medinaceli (*photo below*) on Plaza de Jesús. Inside the church is a statue of Jesus of Nazareth that had fallen into the hands of the Moors and was retrieved against all odds by Trinitarian monks in the 17th century. Kissing the foot of the statue is believed to be very auspicious. In fact, after announcing their engagement in 2003, one of the first things Prince Felipe and his wife-to-be Letizia did was turn up at the church to do just that.

They got married in the Catedral de la Almudena, named after a wooden figure now to be found in the crypt. When the Moors arrived in Madrid, they displaced the Visigoths, who before fleeing hid the statue in the wall of their fortress, along with two burning candles. A few centuries later, when the Christians regained power, the hiding place was discovered – and guess what? Those candles were still flickering away. This happy event has led to a public holiday on 9 November, something that has kept Almudena's as everybody's favourite saint, with no further miracles required.

For centuries C/Mayor was Madrid's main thoroughfare. The cross-streets between Mayor and Arenal offer an odd mixture of bookbinders, picture-framers and Galician restaurants. The western end of C/Mayor, near the **Palacio Real**, has several old palaces and runs out west into C/Bailén, connected southwards to a splendid 1930s concrete **viaduct** that offers views of the sierra and the Casa de Campo. The viaduct's notoriety as a suicide point has led the city authorities to place giant glass panels all along it, giving it a very strange look and feel – without doing much to deter the jumpers. At the southern end of the viaduct are the hill and park of **Las Vistillas**. The park has more great views and is often used for neighbourhood events, concerts and dances during fiestas and in summer. Beyond the park are the river and the elegant arches of the **Puente de Segovia**, a bridge commissioned by Philip II from Juan de Herrera and completed in 1584 to make it easier for the king to get to El Escorial.

Iglesia-Catedral de San Isidro (La Colegiata)

C/Toledo 37 (91 369 20 37). Metro La Latina or Tirso de Molina. **Open** *Sept-July* 7.30am-1pm, 6.30-8.30pm Mon-Sat; 9am-2pm, 5.30-8.30pm Sun. *Aug* 7.30am-8.30pm Mon-Sat; 8.30am-1.30pm, 7.15-8.30pm Sun. **Map** 327 G13.

C/Cava Baja. *See p88.*

Still popularly known as La Colegiata, this massive church, built in 1622-33 once formed part of an important Jesuit college attended by many of the Golden Age playwrights. The high-baroque design by Pedro Sánchez was inspired by the quintessential church of the Jesuits, the Gesù in Rome; the façade was completed by Francisco Bautista in 1664. In 1768, after Charles III expelled the Jesuits from Spain, the church was separated from the college, dedicated to San Isidro and altered by Ventura Rodríguez to house the remains of the saint and his wife, which had been brought here from the Capilla de San Isidro (*see p93*). La Colegiata was the city's provisional cathedral for nearly a century, between 1885 and 1993, when the Catedral de la Almudena (*see p93*) was finally finished and inaugurated.

Museo de San Isidro

Plaza de San Andrés 2 (91 366 74 15/www.munimadrid.es/museosanisidro). Metro La Latina. **Open** *Sept-July* 9.30am-8pm Tue-Fri; 10am-2pm Sat, Sun. *Aug* 9.30am-3pm Tue-Fri; 10am-2pm Sat, Sun. **Admission** free. **Map** p327 F13.

Dedicated to the city's patron saint, the well-digger and labourer San Isidro, this museum sits on the spot where he supposedly lived and performed one of his most famous miracles: when his son, Illán, fell into a well, Isidro made the water rise and thus was able to rescue the unfortunate lad. The well – or *a* well, anyway – is preserved inside the house, as is the chapel built in 1663 on the spot where Isidro allegedly died. According to legend, he was originally buried here too. This is, then, a museum that deals in legends as much as in solid artefacts, and the current material on show is a little limited. More interesting are the finds from local archaeological digs, formerly kept in the Museo Municipal and now in the basement here. They include items from lower-Palaeolithic settlements in the area, as well as artefacts from the Roman villas along the Manzanares, from the Muslim era.

Plaza Mayor

Metro Sol. **Map** p327 G12.

The Plaza Mayor began life in the 15th century as a humble market square, then known as the Plaza del Arrabal ('Square outside the Walls'). In the 1560s, after Madrid was made capital of Spain by Philip II, architect Juan de Herrera drew up plans for it to be completely rebuilt, but the only part constructed immediately was the Casa de la Panadería ('the Bakery'). Finished under the direction of Diego Sillero in 1590, it is typical of the Herreran style, with grey slate roofs, spiky pinnacles and two towers which dominate the sqare. In the early 1990s, in a move unlikely to be contemplated in most countries, this historic edifice was decorated with colourful psychedelic murals. The rest of the plaza was built by Juan Gómez de Mora for Philip III and completed in 1619 although large sections were destroyed by fire in 1790 and had to be rebuilt. Bullfights, carnivals and all the great ceremonies of imperial Madrid were held here. At its centre is statue from 1616 of Philip III on horseback by Giambologna and Pietro Tacca, which stood originally in the Casa de Campo and was moved here in the 19th century.

San Pedro el Viejo. *See p93.*

The square is still an important hub, with most Madrid-wide celebrations, such as the Veranos de la Villa or San Isidro festivals, centred here and a traditional Christmas fair in December. Best enjoyed on quiet weekday mornings, Plaza Mayor has plenty of pavement cafés from which to contemplate its graceful architecture. On Sunday mornings the plaza bustles with a stamp and coin market.

Plaza de la Villa

Metro Ópera or Sol. **Map** p327 F12.

Madrid's oldest square, home to the city's main market place in Muslim and early medieval times, contains three noteworthy buildings. Dominant is the Casa de la Villa, or City Hall, designed in Castilian-baroque style by Juan Gómez de Mora in 1630, although not completed until 1695. The façade was also altered by Juan de Villanueva in the 1780s. It contrasts nicely with the Casa de Cisneros, which was built as a palace by a relative of the great Cardinal Cisneros in 1537. Restored in 1910, it now also houses municipal offices. Opposite the Casa de la Villa is the simple Torre de los Lujanes, from the 1460s, where one of Madrid's aristocratic families once resided. It is believed that King Francis I of France was kept prisoner in the tower by Charles V after his capture at the Battle of Pavia in 1525.

San Andrés, Capilla del Obispo & Capilla de San Isidro

Plaza de San Andrés 1 (91 365 48 71). Metro La Latina. **Open** 8am-1pm, 6-8pm Mon-Thur, Sat; 6-8pm Fri. Open for services only Sun. **Map** p327 E13.

The large church of San Andrés dates from the 16th century, but was badly damaged in the Civil War in 1936 and later rebuilt in a relatively simple style. Attached to it, though (but with separate entrances), are two of Madrid's most historic early church buildings. The Capilla del Obispo (Bishop's Chapel, 1520-35), with its entrance on Plaza de la Paja, is the best-preserved Gothic building in the city. It contains finely carved tombs and a 1550 altarpiece by Francisco Giralte. It remains closed for restoration with the date of reopening as yet undisclosed. Further towards Plaza de los Carros is the Capilla de San Isidro, built in 1642-69 by Pedro de la Torre to house the remains of the saint, which were later transferred to the Iglesia-Catedral de San Isidro.

San Pedro el Viejo

Costanilla de San Pedro (91 365 12 84). Metro La Latina. **Open** 6-8pm daily (phone to check). **Map** p327 F13.

This impressive Mudéjar brick tower dates from the 14th century, although the rest of the church dates from much later, having been rebuilt in the 17th century. **Photo** *p92*.

Ópera

The area between Plaza Mayor and the **Palacio Real** (*see p94*) is named after the **Teatro Real** opera house at its centre. As well as containing some of the city's most important buildings (the **cathedral** among them), this is one of the most elegant areas of Madrid. A tunnel whisks traffic under the stunning **Plaza de Oriente**, so named because it sits east of the palace, making it one of the most pleasant spots for a coffee. Curiously, Madrid owes this stately square, which seems to complement the Palacio Real ideally, not to the Bourbon monarchs but to Spain's 'non-king', Joseph Bonaparte, who initiated the clearing of the area during his brief reign (1808-13). After his departure it was largely neglected before being laid out in formal style in 1844. During the dictatorship, devotees from all over the country stormed the square for a glimpse of Franco, who addressed his rallies from the palace balcony.

At the square's centre is a fine equestrian statue of King Philip IV that once stood in the courtyard of the Palacio del Buen Retiro. It was made in the 1640s by the Italian sculptor Pietro Tacca, who – on the insistence of the Count-Duke of Olivares – was required to create the first-ever monumental bronze statue featuring a rearing horse, rather than one with four feet on the ground. This remarkable feat was achieved with engineering assistance from Galileo.

On the esplanade between the cathedral and palace, archaeological excavations are under way to unearth the remains of the original Muslim fortress and of the foundations of Philip II's Alcázar, covered over by the building of the later Palacio Real. Some of the discoveries, including impressive Moorish arches, is open to public view. Behind the palace, the delightful **Campo del Moro** gardens run down towards the Manzanares and the Paseo de la Florida.

Campo del Moro

Paseo de la Virgen del Puerto (91 454 88 00). Metro Príncipe Pío. **Open** Oct-Mar 10am-6pm daily. *Apr-Sept* 10am-8pm daily. **Map** p322 C/D11.

This vast garden was named after a Muslim leader in the Middle Ages, Ali Ben Yusut, who attempted to capture the fortress that is now the Palacio Real. Unfortunately, it is only accessible from the Paseo de la Virgen del Puerto side, requiring a fairly long walk down Cuesta de San Vicente or Cuesta de la Vega. As a reward, however, you will see two fine monumental fountains. Nearest the palace is *Los Tritones*, originally made in 1657 for the palace in Aranjuez (*see p284*); the other is *Las Conchas*, designed in the 18th century by Ventura Rodríguez. Both were moved here in the 1890s.

Catedral de la Almudena

C/Bailén 10 (91 542 22 00). Metro Ópera. **Open** 10am-2pm, 5-9pm daily. **Map** p326 D12.

This is not Spain's most impressive cathedral, and it's something of a miracle that it exists at all. For centuries, Church and State could not agree on whether Madrid should have a cathedral; once they did, it took 110 years to complete it. In 1883 work began on a neo-Gothic design by the Marqués de Cubas, but this scheme went off course after only the crypt was completed. Another architect, Fernando Chueca Goitia, took over in 1944, and introduced a neo-classical style. Although the cathedral has failed to win much affection over the years, it was finally finished in 1993 and visited by the Pope. The site once contained the church of Santa María de la Almudena, formerly the main mosque of Muslim Madrid (the name comes from the Arabic *al mudin*, 'the mill') until it was knocked down by liberal reformers in 1870. One of its more interesting pieces is the 13th-century polychromatic funerary chest of San Isidro. **Photos** *p95*.

Palacio Real (Palacio de Oriente)

Plaza de Oriente, C/Bailén (91 454 88 00). Metro Ópera. **Open** *Oct-Mar* 9.30am-5pm Mon-Sat; 9am-2pm Sun. *Apr-Sept* 9am-6pm Mon-Sat; 9am-3pm Sun. **Admission** €9 with guided tour; €8 without; €3.50 concessions. Free to EU citizens Wed. **Credit** AmEx, DC, MC, V. **Map** p327 E11.

Commissioned by Philip V after the earlier Alcázar was lost to a fire in 1734, the Royal Palace is rarely used by the royal family, and many of its 3,000 rooms are open to view. The architects principally responsible for the final design, which reflects the taste of the Spanish Bourbons, were Italian – Giambattista Sacchetti and Francesco Sabatini – with contributions by the Spaniard Ventura Rodríguez. Filippo Juvarra, Philip V's first choice, had planned a palace four times as large, but after his death the project became a little less ambitious. Completed in 1764, the late-baroque palace is built almost entirely of granite and white Colmenar stone, and, surrounded as it is by majestic gardens, contributes greatly to the splendour of the city.

Inside you must keep to a fixed route, but are free to set your own pace rather than follow a tour. The entrance into the palace is awe-inspiring: you pass up a truly vast main staircase and then through the main state rooms, the Hall of Halbardiers and Hall of Columns, all with soaring ceilings and frescoes by Corrado Giaquinto and Giambattista Tiepolo. In the grand Throne Room there are some fine 17th-century sculptures commissioned by Velázquez, which were saved from the earlier Alcázar. Other highlights are the extravagantly ornate private apartments of the palace's first resident, Charles III, again decorated by Italians. Particularly striking are the Gasparini Room, the king's dressing room, covered in mosaics and rococo stuccoes by Mattia Gasparini; and the Porcelain Room, its walls covered entirely in porcelain reliefs. A later addition is another giant: the State Dining Room, redesigned for King Alfonso XII in 1880 and still used for official banquets. There are also imposing collections of tapestries, table porcelain, gold and silver plates and finally clocks, a particular passion of the little-admired King Charles IV.

One of the real highlights is the Real Armería (Royal Armoury), reached via a separate entrance off the palace courtyard, with a superb collection of ceremonial armour, much of it actually worn by Charles V and other Habsburgs. Look out too for the suits of armour worn by El Cid and his horse – impressively displayed on life-size statues. On the other side of the courtyard the Real Farmacia, the Royal Pharmacy, is also worth a visit. One of the oldest in Europe, it was wholly dedicated to attending to the many ailments of Spain's crowned heads over several centuries. In years to come, an opportunity to view the excavations of the older Alcázar and Muslim fortress beneath the palace will also form part of the visit. The palace is closed to the public when official receptions or ceremonies are due, so it's a good idea to check before visiting. On the first Wednesday of each month the Royal Guard stages a ceremonial Changing of the Guard in the courtyard, at noon.

There are tours of the Palace throughout the day, but frequency depends on the volume of visitors.

San Nicolás de los Servitas

Plaza San Nicolás (91 559 40 64). Metro Ópera. **Open** 8.30am-1.30pm Mon; 9-9.30am, 6.30-8.30pm Tue-Sat; 10am-2pm, 6.30-8.30pm Sun. **Map** p327 E12.

The oldest surviving church in Madrid stands just a few minutes from Plaza de Oriente. Its 12th-century tower is one of two Mudéjar towers (see also *p93* San Pedro el Viejo), built by Muslim craftsmen living under Christian rule, in the city. Most of the rest of the church was rebuilt later, during the 15th and 16th centuries.

La Latina

La Latina, the area below Plaza de la Cebada, takes its name from the nickname of Beatriz Galindo, teacher of Latin and confidante to Queen Isabella. At the end of the 15th century she paid for a hospital to be built on the square that bears her name. Its site is now occupied by the **Teatro La Latina**, a stronghold of traditional Spanish entertainment. The district is relatively quiet except during its grand fiestas, around the time of **La Paloma** in August (*see p208*).

Basílica de San Francisco el Grande

Plaza de San Francisco (91 365 38 00). Metro La Latina. **Open** *Oct-June* 11am-12.30pm, 4-6.30pm Tue-Sat. *July-Sept* 11am-12.30pm, 5-7.30pm Tue-Sat. Last admission half hr before closing. **Admission** (guided tour only) €3; €2 concessions. **Map** p326 D14.

This huge, multi-tiered church between Puerta de Toledo and the Palacio Real is difficult to miss. A monastery on the site, reputedly founded by Saint Francis of Assisi, was knocked down in 1760; in its place, between 1761 and 1784 Francisco Cabezas and later Francesco Sabatini built this neo-classical

The **Catedral de la Almudena** and around. *See p93.*

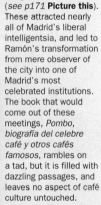

Poetry of the absurd

Few writers have been as central to the life and culture of Madrid as Ramón Gómez de la Serna, one of the most original and influential Spanish authors of the 20th century. Born in 1891 in the old Habsburg heart of Madrid, he trained initially as a lawyer, but never practised. When only 19, while standing on the balcony of his home at C/Puebla 11, he claimed to have had the inspiration for the near untranslatable literary form for which he would best be remembered: *greguerías*.

'Humour + metaphor = *greguerías*', was how Ramón himself defined these brief poetic statements in which words, ideas and objects are brought together in almost stream-of-consciousness fashion ('It is only in botanical gardens that trees carry visiting cards'). These 'attempts to define the indefinable, to capture the fugitive', as La Serna explained them on another occasion, had a significant influence on the Spanish surrealist movement, and on avant-garde literature generally, in Europe and Latin America.

La Serna's love of the absurd and ephemeral, and his ability to uncover the poetical and the extraordinary in the outwardly unremarkable, made him the ideal commentator on Madrid, a city he described as 'the most difficult capital in the world to understand'. He wrote more than 100 books, a great many of which are dedicated to his native city, beginning in 1914 with his first mature work, *El Rastro*. This near 350-page study of Madrid's flea market, a place whose diversity of objects echoes his prose style, with an occasionally indigestible medley of aphorisms and random observations.

As a writer on Madrid, La Serna was matched in his copiousness only by the early 19th-century scholar Ramón Mesonero Romanos; but the Madrid author with whom he felt the closest empathy was the latter's charismatic contemporary Mariano José de Larra, who likewise combined a passionate obsession with the city with a hatred of its middle-class conventions. An empty seat was always kept for the ghost of Larra in the celebrated Saturday night gatherings that La Serna began organising at the Café Pombo (*see p171* **Picture this**). These attracted nearly all of Madrid's liberal intelligentsia, and led to Ramón's transformation from mere observer of the city into one of Madrid's most celebrated institutions. The book that would come out of these meetings, *Pombo, biografía del celebre café y otros cafés famosos*, rambles on a tad, but it is filled with dazzling passages, and leaves no aspect of café culture untouched.

Exiled to Buenos Aires at the start of the Civil War, La Serna lived there until his death in 1963, his writings profoundly impacting Argentine author Jorge Luís Borges. Although the memory of Madrid never left him, he only returned once and was bitterly disappointed. Later his corpse was brought over to Madrid's Sacramental de San Justo, and his Buenos Aires study has been reassembled in Madrid's **Museo Municipal** (*see p106*; *pictured*), alongside that of Mesonero Romanos. The uncluttered simplicity of the latter's study contrasts with La Serna's fantastical anarchy, mesmerising with such details as convex mirrors, a stuffed leopard, flying swans on the walls and revolving mirror balls worthy of a suburban disco.

church. Most challenging was the construction of the spectacular dome, with a diameter of 33m (108ft). The dome has recently been restored, but work on the rest of the basilica is expected to go on for several more years, so expect some parts to be covered with scaffolding. Inside there is an early Goya, *The Sermon of San Bernardino of Siena* (1781), and several frescoes by other artists.

Sol

The **Puerta del Sol** represents the very heart of Madrid, both because it contains kilómetro cero (the mark from which distances from the city are measured) and for its time-honoured role as chief meeting place. Famously, through the centuries people have come to Sol to find out what's going on. Until the 1830s the block between C/Correo and C/Esparteros was occupied by the monastery of San Felipe el Real, the steps and cloister of which were, in Habsburg Madrid, one of the recognised *mentideros* – literally 'pits of lies', or gossip-mills – where people came to pick up on the latest news, anecdotes or scurrilous rumours. In a city with no newspapers – but where who was in or out of favour was of primary importance – *mentideros* were a major social institution, and rare was the day when at least one of the great figures of Spanish literature, such as Cervantes, Lope or Quevedo, did not pass by here. The steps of San Felipe were also overlooked by one of the largest brothels of the era, another attraction for men about town. On a more respectable note, the Café Pombo, home to legendary *tertulias* (*see p171* **Picture this**), stood on the corner of C/Carretas. It is still Madrid's most popular meeting point, particularly the spot by the monument with the symbols of Madrid (a bear and a *madroño* or strawberry tree) at the junction with C/Carmen.

Under the Habsburgs the Puerta del Sol, the main, easternmost gate (*puerta*) of 15th-century Madrid, was surrounded by churches and monasteries. It was rebuilt in its present form in 1854-62. The square's most important building is the **Casa de Correos**, built in 1766 by Jaime Marquet as a post office for Charles III. Today it houses the regional government, the Comunidad de Madrid, but in the Franco era it had much grimmer connotations, as the Interior Ministry and police headquarters. It was altered significantly in 1866, when the large clock tower was added; this is now the building's best-known feature, since it's the clock the whole country sees on New Year's Eve, when revellers crowd into the square to eat their lucky grapes, one for each stroke of midnight. In the 1990s the tower developed a precarious incline due to rot in its timbers, but

it was rebuilt and unveiled once again in 1998. Sol is also where Napoleon's Egyptian cavalry, the Mamelukes, charged down on the *madrileño* crowd on 2 May 1808, as portrayed in one of Goya's most famous paintings.

Sol has been in a despair-inducing state of late, bristling with JCBs and ringed with iron fencing, while the tunnel linking Atocha and Chamartín stations is excavated. Optimistic estimates place the completion date in 2008.

Tucked in the middle of the area between Sol, Arenal, C/Alcalá and Gran Vía is the **Real Monasterio de las Descalzas Reales**, bursting with artworks and a deliciously unexpected oasis amid the traffic and bustle of Sol. At the west side of the area, just above the Plaza de Oriente, is the peaceful and little visited **Convento de la Encarnación**, also worth a look. Just north of that, occupying the site of another convent, is the old 19th-century **Palacio del Senado** (Senate), now made redundant by its back-to-back counterpart in granite and smoked glass by Santiago Goyarre.

Running almost alongside C/Preciados up to Gran Vía is newly pedestrianised but still shabby C/Montera, lined with cheap, dated shops and the main area for street prostitution in the city centre. At the top, parallel with Gran Vía, is C/Caballero de Gracia, with a 19th-century oratory that lays on special Masses for the working girls, many of them Latin American, who operate along the street. While seedy, this area is not generally dangerous, and is heavily policed. Care should be taken walking around late at night, however, especially if you're on your own.

Convento de la Encarnación

Plaza de la Encarnación 1 (91 547 05 10/ information 91 454 88 00). Metro Ópera or Santo Domingo. **Open** 10.30am-12.30pm, 4-5.30pm Tue-Thur, Sat; 10.30am-12.30pm Fri; 11am-1.30pm Sun. **Admission** €3.60; €2 concessions. Free to EU citizens Wed. **Map** p323 E11.

Before the Alcázar burned down, this understated convent was its treasury, connected by a concealed passageway. In 1611 it was inaugurated as a monastery by Philip III and his wife Margaret of Austria, and rebuilt to a design by Gómez de Mora. However, much of the original building, including the church, was damaged by fire in 1734 and rebuilt in a classical-baroque style in the 1760s by Ventura Rodríguez. It still contains a community of around 20 nuns, but most of the building is open to the public. Although not as lavishly endowed as the Descalzas Reales, it contains a great many pieces of 17th-century religious art, the most impressive of which is Jusepe Ribera's shimmering chiaroscuro portrait of John the Baptist. The Encarnación's most famous and memorable room, however, is the *reliquiario* (relics room). In its glass casements are displayed some 1,500 saintly remains, bone fragments and former possessions of saints and martyrs, in extravagantly bejewelled copper, bronze, glass, gold and silver reliquaries. Its prize possession is what purports to be the solidified blood of San Pantaleón, kept inside a glass orb. The blood reportedly liquefies each year from midnight on the eve of his feast day, 27 July (*see p90* **Heap of faith**). Note that visits are by guided tour only, and tours leave 30 minutes after the first person signs up; so there's little point turning up as it opens.

Real Monasterio de las Descalzas Reales

Plaza de las Descalzas 3 (information 91 454 88 00). Metro Callao or Sol. **Open** 10.30am-12.30pm, 4-5.30pm Tue-Thur, Sat; 10.30am-12.30pm Fri; 11am-1.30pm Sun. **Admission** €5; €2.40 concessions. Free to EU citizens Wed. **Map** p327 G11.

The convent of the Descalzas Reales ('Royal Barefoot Nuns') is the most complete 16th-century building in Madrid and still houses a cloistered community. It was originally built as a palace for Alonso Gutiérrez, treasurer of Charles V, but was converted into a convent in 1556-64 by Antonio Sillero and Juan Bautista de Toledo after Philip II's widowed sister Joanna of Austria decided to become a nun. Founded with royal patronage, the Descalzas became the preferred destination of the many widows, younger daughters and other women of the royal family and high aristocracy of Spain who entered religious orders. Hence it also acquired an extraordinary collection of works of art – paintings, sculptures, tapestries and *objets d'art* – given as bequests by the novices' families. Equally lavish is

the baroque decoration of the building itself, belying its sternly austere façade, with a grand painted staircase, frescoed ceilings and 32 chapels, only some of which can be visited.

The largest non-Spanish contingents in its art collection are Italian, with Titian, Bernardino Luini, Angelo Nardi and Sebastiano del Piombo, and Flemish, with Breughel (an *Adoration of the Magi*), Joos Van Cleve and Rubens. The Descalzas is also an exceptional showcase of Spanish baroque religious art, with works by Gaspar Becerra, Zurbarán, Claudio Coello and even a tiny painting attributed to Goya. In addition, as you walk around you can catch glimpses of the nuns' courtyard vegetable garden, which has remained virtually unchanged since the convent was built, and is closed to the public. The monastery was seen by very few until the 1980s, when it was restored and partially opened as a museum. It can be visited only with official tours, which leave every 20 minutes and last around 50 minutes. Frustratingly, the guides rarely speak English, there is no printed information about the convent, and the paintings are not labelled. It is still an enjoyable place to visit, though, for the sheer sumptuousness of its artworks and fittings.

Gran Vía

The **Plaza de España**, at the western end of the Gran Vía, is dominated by Franco's bombastic architecture. It is flanked by two classic buildings of the type sponsored by the regime when out to impress: the '50s-modern **Torre Madrid** (1957) and the enormous **Edificio España** of 1948-53. The three

Plaza de España.

Walk through Literary Madrid

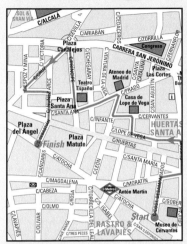

Duration: 30mins

The cafés, theatres and churches around Plaza Santa Ana were the centre of literary life during Spain's 16th- and 17th-century Golden Age.

Begin at the junction of C/Atocha with Costanilla de los Desamparados.

C/Atocha 87 was once the printing press where the first edition of *Don Quixote* was published. This is now the **Museo Cervantino**. See the bronze bas-relief of a scene from the book and, above it, the head of Cervantes.

Walk up Desamparados and turn right down C/Moratín.

At the **Plazuela de San Juan** is a plaque celebrating poet and playwright Leandro Moratín, born here in 1760.

Turn left up C/Jesús and left again on C/Lope de Vega.

The church ahead of the junction, on the right, is the **Iglesia de Jesús de Medinaceli**, famously a 17th-century centre of rumour and gossip, especially when attended by the great actresses of the time. Up on C/Lope de Vega, on the left, is the **Convento de las Trinitarias**, where Cervantes was originally buried (his remains have since disappeared). On the anniversary of his death, a mass is held for him and the other great Spanish writers.

Turn right up C/Quevedo.

On the right-hand corner is a plaque marking the house where 17th-century rivals Francisco de Quevedo and Luis de Góngora lived.

Quevedo, a satirist, made mincemeat of the hapless and terminally ill poet Góngora in an exchange of verse. He also triumphed posthumously, when the council renamed the street after him, omitting to mention Góngora on the plaque. At the end of the street, on C/Cervantes 11, is the **Casa-Museo de Lope de Vega** (*see p102*), where Lope de Vega lived and died. No.2 on this street was built on the site of Cervantes' old house.

Turn left, and right down C/León to C/Prado.

At No.21 is the Ateneo library, with an impressive marble staircase, walls lined with portraits of Spain's greatest figures and delightfully antiquated rooms. Back up C/Prado, you arrive at the Plaza Santa Ana, home to the **Teatro Español** (*see p262*) and bars such as the **Cervecería Alemana** (*see p170*), where writers such as the playwright Ramón del Valle-Inclán and, later, Ernest Hemingway were regulars. The theatre itself sits on the site of one of the great open-air *corral* theatres of the Golden Age.

Facing the theatre, turn left up C/Príncipe.

This street was home to many of the favoured literary haunts of the day, but the only one that remains is **Las Cuevas de Sésamo** at No.7 (*see p246*), worth a visit for the quotes painted on the walls and the printed history they will give anyone who's interested.

At Plaza Canalejas turn left down C/Cruz.

C/Victoria on the left has a plaque marking the site of the writers' and politicians' meeting point and subject of Benito Pérez Galdos' eponymous novel, **La Fontana de Oro**. The Irish bar built on the site shares the name but little else. Further up C/Cruz is a mural depicting a reflection of the street, and asking 'Where has the theatre gone? Or is the street the theatre?' The theatre in question is the **Corral de la Cruz**, another open-air theatre that stood on the site.

Turn left down C/Álvarez Gato, right through the square and down C/San Sebastián.

What is now a florist in the yard on the corner with C/Huertas used to be the graveyard for the adjacent **Iglesia de San Sebastián**; the ancient olive tree remains as a symbol of all the literary luminaries buried there. Opposite is a plaque showing the site of the **Fonda de San Sebastián** – favoured hangout of the 18th-century writers. Further down, in the church itself, are plaques celebrating the writers baptised, married or buried here.

statues in the middle – of Cervantes, Don Quixote and Sancho Panza – are by Teodoro Anasagasti and Mateo Inurria, from 1928. The square around them is big, noisy and not a particularly relaxing place to sit.

The Gran Vía itself was created in 1910 by slicing through the Old City so that traffic could easily reach Cibeles from C/Princesa. Intended to be a broad modern boulevard, it got grander still when World War I made neutral Madrid a clearing house for international money. With the economy booming, developers and architects set out to embrace modernity as hard as they could to show that, if you wanted something impressive, they could provide it. In the following decades, each generation added its own stamp and the result is certainly eclectic.

Heading down the Gran Vía, the area north and east of Sol was originally the city's financial district, hence the number of grand edifices owned by banks and insurance companies. Its other great avenue is **C/Alcalá**, which follows the centuries-old main route into Madrid from the east. In the 18th century, when it was lined by aristocratic palaces, it was described as the grandest street in Europe. It is still pretty impressive today, with a wonderful variety of 19th- to early 20th-century buildings,

from the dignified 1882 **Banesto** building (corner of C/Sevilla) to the cautiously modernist **Círculo de Bellas Artes** (*see below*). There are also fine older constructions along the street, such as the austere neo-classical Finance Ministry, built as the **Aduana**, or customs administration, by Francesco Sabatini in 1761-9, and, alongside it, the **Real Academia de Bellas Artes de San Fernando** (*see below*). At the point where Alcalá and Gran Vía meet, stands Pedro de Ribera's exuberantly baroque church of **San José** (1730-42), with a plaque inside to commemorate the fact that Simón Bolívar was married here in 1802.

Círculo de Bellas Artes

C/Alcalá 42 & C/Marqués de Casa Riera 2 (91 360 54 00). Metro Banco de España. **Open** *Café* 9am-midnight Mon-Thur; 9am-3am Fri, Sat. *Exhibitions* 11am-2pm Mon, Sun; 11am-2pm, 5-8pm Tue-Sat. **Admission** €1. Free 2-4pm Mon-Sat. **Map** p328 I11. The Círculo de Bellas Artes occupies a superb building, designed by Antonio Palacios and completed in 1926. It is a key player in every aspect of the Madrid arts scene: as well as a beautifully airy main floor café, with a gracious pavement terrace, the Círculo offers a plethora of classes, exhibitions, lectures and concerts in its theatre and concert hall, as well as an annual masked ball for carnival.

Museo de la Real Academia de Bellas Artes de San Fernando

C/Alcalá 13 (91 524 08 64/Calcografía Nacional 91 524 08 83). Metro Sevilla or Sol. **Open** 10am-2pm Mon, Sat, Sun; 9am-7pm Tue-Fri. *Calcografía Nacional* 9-2.30pm Mon-Fri. *Temporary exhibitions* 10am-2pm, 5-8pm Tue-Fri; 10am-2pm Sat, Sun. **Admission** €3; €1.50 students; free under-18s, over-65s. Free to all Wed. *Calcografía Nacional* free. **No credit cards. Map** p327 H11.

This undervisited museum is in fact one of Madrid's most important and oldest permanent artistic institutions (it was founded in 1794). The eclectic collection is partly made up of works of varying quality donated by aspiring members in order to gain admission to the academy. The museum's greatest possessions, though, are its 13 works by Goya, an important figure in the early years of the Academia. They include two major self-portraits; a portrait of his friend, the playwright Moratín; a portrait of Charles IV's hated minister Godoy; and the *Burial of the Sardine* (*see p206* **Picture this**), a carnival scene that foreshadows his later, darker works. Another of the academy's most prized possessions is the Italian mannerist Giuseppe Arcimboldo's *Spring*, a playful, surrealistic portrait of a man made up entirely of flowers. It was one of a series on the four seasons painted for Ferdinand I of Austria in 1563: *Summer* and *Winter* are still in Vienna, but the whereabouts of *Autumn* is unknown. There are also important portraits by Velázquez and Rubens, and several paintings by Zurbarán. Among the later works, the best known are some Picasso engravings and a Juan Gris; the most surprising are the colourful fantasies of Múñoz Degrain and the De Chirico-esque work of Julio Romero de Torres. Look out too for Leandro Bassano's superb *La Riva degli Schiavoni*.

The academy also has a valuable collection of plans and drawings, including those of Prado architect Juan de Villanueva, and rare books. In the same building is the Calcografía Nacional, a similarly priceless collection and archive of engraving and fine printing, which has many of the original plates for the great etching series of Goya.

Huertas & Santa Ana

Spain has more bars and restaurants per capita than anywhere in the world, and you can get the impression that most of Madrid's are crowded into the wedge-shaped swathe of streets between Alcalá and C/Atocha. Oddly enough, this clearly defined area has an identity problem, for the authorities can never agree on a name; however, if anyone suggests a pub crawl down Huertas, or a jar in Santa Ana, it will always bring you – and several thousand others on any weekend – to the right place.

This was once the haunt of Madrid's Golden Age literary set (*see p99* **Walk through**), which explains the district's fussy alternative name of Barrio de las Letras ('The District of Letters'). Here were the theatres that provided them with a living, along with whorehouses and low dives for entertainment. It is still the city's most distinctive theatre district. Close by, but not too close, lived the nobles who might have tossed a couple of ducats their way if they buttered them up in a sonnet. Otherwise there were feuds, libellous exchanges and duels to fall back on. A recent tidying up of the area has brought about pedestrianisation of much of Huertas's street, and literary quotes inlaid in bronze underfoot.

Lope de Vega's charming old house, the **Casa-Museo Lope de Vega** (*see p102*), with its tiny garden, is on the street named after his enemy, Miguel Cervantes, the author of *Don Quixote*. Cervantes lived around the corner on C/León, but was buried in the enclosed convent of the **Trinitarias Descalzas** (the 'Barefoot Trinitarians') on C/Lope de Vega, which seems deliberately confusing. Coming upon the massively plain, slab-like brick walls of the Trinitarias amid the Huertas bars is a great surprise, and gives a vivid impression of what old Madrid must have looked like before the great clear-out of religious houses in the 1830s, of which this is a rare survivor.

Círculo de Bellas Artes. See p100.

Sightseeing

Palacio Longoria. *See p107.*

A reverential nod is in order to the wonderful **Ateneo** library on C/Prado, the literary and philosophical club that became a cultural institution and has been a major centre of discussion and thought at many times in its history, most notably in the years leading up to the Republic of 1931 (*see p25*). In the old days, Ateneo members could also find any number of cafés nearby with a suitably literary atmosphere.

The **Carrera de San Jerónimo** borders the north of the district. Once part of the Ceremonial Route of the Habsburg and Bourbon monarchs, today it is one of the centres of official Madrid. On one side is the **Congreso de los Diputados**, Spain's parliament building, while opposite is the **Westin Palace** hotel (*see p60*), where politicians go to mingle and relax. Further up the hill is **Lhardy**, the classic Franco-Spanish restaurant founded in 1839 (*see p144*). North of San Jerónimo, behind the Congreso, is the grand 1856 **Teatro de la Zarzuela**, the city's most characterfully distinguished music theatre.

To the south of the Carrera de San Jerónimo several streets run back towards Huertas proper. On C/Echegaray is **Los Gabrieles**, until recently a much-loved bar sheathed in perhaps the world's most photographed wall-to-wall tiles. Depending on the progress of the building's conversion into luxury apartments, you may still catch a glance. Yet another beautifully tiled bar, **Viva Madrid** (*see p173*),

lies just around the corner on C/Manuel Fernández y González, while the nearby **Villa Rosa** on C/Nuñez de Arce also has an impressive tiled exterior.

Last, but in no way least, there is the core of the district, **Plaza Santa Ana**. Like Plaza de Oriente, this popular square was bequeathed to Madrid by poor, unappreciated Joseph Bonaparte, who tore down yet another convent to do so. Somebody should thank him: lined by some of the city's most popular bars and pavement terraces, Santa Ana has long been one of Madrid's favourite places for hanging out for an entire afternoon or three. On the eastern side of the plaza is the distinguished **Teatro Español**, on a site that has been a theatre continuously since 1583 when the Corral del Príncipe opened its doors to the *mosqueteros*, a heckling mob whose reactions were so violent, they sometimes forced terrified playwrights to change plots mid-play.

Casa-Museo Lope de Vega

C/Cervantes 11 (91 429 92 16). Metro Antón Martín. **Open** 9.30am-2pm Tue-Fri; 10am-2pm Sat. Closed Aug. **Admission** €2; €1 students, over-65s. Free to all Sat. **No credit cards. Map** p328 I12.
Spain's most prolific playwright and poet, Félix Lope de Vega Carpio (1562-1635) spent the last 25 years of his life in this simple, tranquil three-storey house. Oddly enough, the street in which it stands is now named after his arch rival Cervantes (who, confusingly, is buried in a convent on the nearby

C/Lope de Vega). The house and charming garden – remarkable survivors from the Golden Age – are the most interesting things to see. The furniture and ornaments, are approximations to Lope de Vega's household inventory rather than being the originals. However, even the garden, where Lope would sit after a day's writing, contains the same fruit trees and plants he detailed in his journals. The house can be visited with guided tours. Some guides speak English; call in advance to check.

Colección Permanente del Instituto de Crédito Oficial (ICO)

C/Zorrilla 3 (91 420 12 42/www.ico.es). Metro Banco de España. **Open** 11am-8pm Tue-Sat; 10am-2pm Sun. **Admission** free. **Map** p328 I11.
This small museum is run by the ICO, a state credit bank. Its collection has three main parts: most important among them is Picasso's *Suite Vollard* series, a milestone in 20th-century prints, dating from 1927 to 1937. There is also a fine selection of modern Spanish sculpture and some international painting from the 1980s.

Congreso de los Diputados (Las Cortes)

Plaza de las Cortes (91 390 65 25/6). Metro Banco de España or Sevilla. **Open** *Guided tours* 10.30am-12.30pm Sat. Closed Aug. **Admission** free. **Map** p328 I12.
Spain's parliament, the Cortes, was built in 1843-50 by Narciso Pascual y Colomer on the site of a recently demolished monastery, which has led to no end of problems, as the plot is too cramped to accommodate the legislators' ancillary offices. A classical portico gives it a suitably dignified air, but the building is best distinguished by the handsome 1860 bronze lions that guard its entrance. Tourists are welcome on the popular free Saturday guided tours. Given demand, it's best to phone ahead; groups of more than 15 can also book to visit on weekdays.

Lavapiés

South of Sol and the Plaza Mayor is the area traditionally considered the home of Madrid's *castizos*. *Castizos* are something like London's East End cockneys: rough-diamond chirpy types straight out of a Spanish *My Fair Lady*. Many of them materialise round here in best bib and tucker – cloth caps for the men; long, frilly dresses for the ladies – for the city's summer festivals. Since the end of the '90s, however, Lavapiés has taken on a new characteristic: as a big recipient of non-Spanish immigration – from China, Pakistan, North and West Africa – it is becoming the city's most multicultural neighbourhood.

These districts have always been the kind of place where newcomers to the city could find a niche. Historically they were known as the *barrios bajos*, in the double sense of low-lying and full of low life – the closer to the river, the shabbier the surroundings. In imperial Madrid, most of the food brought to the city came in through the **Puerta de Toledo** (*see p106*), and many of the tasks that the upper classes wanted neither to see nor smell, such as

Walk through Royal Madrid

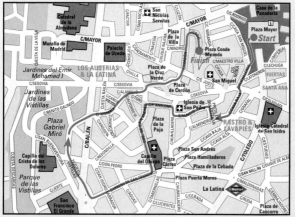

of note to survive 19th-century reconstruction are **San Andrés** church and the **Capillas del Obispo** and **San Isidro**.

Walk up the Costanilla de San Andrés.

On the other side of San Andrés there is what appears to be one rambling square. However, different sections of the square are traditionally known by different names. As well as the **Plaza de la Cebada** (Barley Square), once the site for public executions, and the **Plaza de San Andrés**, there is the **Plaza de la Puerta de Moros** (Moors' Gate) – site of the gateway to the Muslim quarter, or Morería, under Christian rule.

From there turn right down Carrera de San Francisco.

The cavernous dome of **San Francisco el Grande** at the end is seen in several of Goya's skylines.

Right of the church, continue along Travesía de las Vistillas to C/Moreria, which winds back over C/Bailén to Plaza de la Morería.

The knot of streets between here and **Plaza de la Paja** and **Puerta de Moros** formed the Morería, to which Madrid's community of Mudéjar Muslims were confined for four centuries. The little **Plaza de la Morería** was the site of the mosque and the Aljama, the Muslim community courts.

From there follow C/Alamillo to C/Segovia. Cross over it, and head up through C/Conde, left at C/Cordón to the Plaza de la Villa.

This little alley leads round into the **Plaza de la Villa**, with the city hall. It began life as the Arab souk, and continued to be main square until the creation of the Plaza Mayor.

Turn right down C/Codo (Elbow Street) to Plaza Conde de Miranda.

Stop off at the 17th-century **Convento de las Carboneras**, where nuns sell own-baked biscuits through a grille in the wall (*see p194*).

Duration: 45mins

The 16th-century exteriors that once fronted Madrid's interconnecting squares – Paja, Plaza de la Cruz Verde, Plaza de los Carros – were mostly replaced in the 1800s. Nevertheless, these intimate plazas and most of the winding streets of the district of Los Austrias still follow their original Arab and medieval courses, and a walk around these alleys can still be evocative of the Habsburg city, and the medieval town before it.

From Plaza Mayor, walk down the steps under Arco de Cuchilleros in the SW corner.

Walking down C/Cuchilleros, named after the knifemakers who long ago plied their trade here, look out for the 18th-century **El Sobrino de Botín** (*see p139*) on the left, allegedly the oldest restaurant in the world. Continue across the Puerta Cerrada into C/Cava Baja, and you will be walking along the line of the 12th-century wall, now lined with restaurants specialising in traditional *madrileño* cuisine.

Cut right up C/Almendro, and take the first right down the narrow Pretíl de Santisteban.

At the end is the pretty C/Nuncio, now home to several wine bars. Turn left, and on the Costanilla de San Pedro is the dusty 17th-century church of **San Pedro el Viejo**, with its 14th-century minaret-like Mudéjar tower.

Carry on past San Pedro, left down C/Príncipe de Anglona, and veer left to Plaza de la Paja.

'Straw Square' was the medieval grain and fodder market, and probably marked the most southern point of the Arab wall. Buildings to slaughtering and tanning, were concentrated here. Consequently, these districts became home to Madrid's first native working class. In the 18th century the *majos* and *majas* from these streets were admired by the intelligentsia for their caustic wit (for Goya's portraits of them, *see p15* **Picture this**), perhaps sowing the seed for the *castizo* tradition.

On the eastern edge of La Latina is the **Rastro**, Madrid's time-honoured Sunday flea market. It runs all the way down Ribera de Curtidores to the Ronda de Toledo from **Plaza Cascorro**, with its monument honouring a young soldier raised in a nearby orphanage, who volunteered for a suicide mission in Cuba in the 1890s. A true cultural phenomenon, the Rastro is also a district with a strong identity, moulded by centuries of acting as an emporium for goods of all kinds. The market is a social experience more than a shopping destination, but look out for the pickpockets. For more on the Rastro, *see p196*.

If, on the other hand, instead of trying to make your way down the Rastro, you head from Plaza Cascorro slightly eastwards down **C/Embajadores**, you will enter Lavapiés proper. Because of the rapid changes in the area, Lavapiés is sometimes portrayed, in local conversations and the press, as an urban crisis zone to be avoided. This is one of the areas with a high incidence of petty crime, commonly associated with gangs of North African boys living on the streets, who have especially bad relations with the local Chinese shopkeepers. However, these images have a tendency to get out of proportion: there are places in Lavapiés it's probably best to steer clear of (the small square halfway down Mesón de Paredes, by C/Cabestreros, is the most obvious example), but it would be a shame if this led anyone to avoid the whole neighbourhood, for this web of sloping, winding streets remains one of the most characterful parts of Old Madrid.

Plaza Tirso de Molina, with its statue of the Golden Age dramatist whose name it bears, is the main crossroads between these *barrios bajos* and the city centre proper. It has recently been cleaned up and is home to a permanent, fragrant flower market, among other things. From here C/Mesón de Paredes, which is one of the two main arteries of historic Lavapiés (the other is C/Embajadores), winds off down the hill. Along Mesón de Paredes today there are still some of Madrid's most historic *tabernas*, but they stand next to shops selling tropical fruit, Moroccan tea houses, halal butchers, African fabric stores and any number of Chinese-owned wholesale stores selling discount jewellery and T-shirts.

Also on Mesón de Paredes, near the bottom by C/Sombrerete, is **La Corrala**, the city's best surviving example of an 1880s courtyard tenement, predictably garnished with freshly washed sheets and underwear billowing from the balconies. After the demolition of Madrid's monasteries in the mid 19th century, many streets in these districts were rebuilt with these distinctive, open-balconied tenements. *Corralas* always faced an inner patio, multiplying noise and lack of privacy, factors of urban life that have luckily rarely bothered Spaniards. The *corrala* has become a characteristic of Madrid life; this one, restored in the 1980s, is used in summer as a setting for a season of *zarzuela* comic operas. A later *corrala*, not easily visible from the street, is at C/Embajadores 60. At the bottom of this area is a dynamic new exhibition space and cultural centre, **La Casa Encendida** (*see below*).

The **Plaza de Lavapiés** is believed to have been the centre of Madrid's medieval Jewish community, expelled, like all others in her dominions, by the pious Queen Isabella in 1492. Today the recently renovated square has several good cafés and restaurants, as well as the new **Teatro Valle-Inclán** (*see p262*). The narrow, very steep streets between the plaza and C/Atocha are more tranquil than those around Mesón de Paredes, and, with boxes of geraniums on virtually every balcony, often strikingly pretty. Despite all the changes in the area, these closely packed streets of old apartments, shops and workshops still convey the essence of a distinctive urban way of life. At the top of the area by C/Atocha is the **Filmoteca Española** film theatre, in the old Cine Doré (*see p216*).

Running away from the south-east corner of the Plaza de Lavapiés is **C/Argumosa**, known as the 'Costa Argumosa', with shops, restaurants and outdoor-terrace bars that make a popular summer alternative to the more expensive and hectic places further into town. Argumosa leads towards Atocha and the **Centro de Arte Reina Sofía**, the opening of which has led to the appearance nearby of attractive one-off shops and galleries. Close by, filling a big stretch of C/Santa Isabel, is the 17th-century **Convento de Santa Isabel**, sponsored, l ike the Encarnación, by Margaret of Austria, wife of Philip III, and one of the largest religious houses to escape the liberals' axe in the 1830s.

La Casa Encendida

Ronda de Valencia 2 (91 506 38 75/www.lacasa encendida.com). Metro Embajadores. **Open** 10am-10pm daily. **Admission** free. **Map** p328 H15.
This exciting new multidisciplinary centre in a large neo-Mudéjar building was conceived as a space for cultural interchange. Spread over four floors, the

Sightseeing

'Burning House' is directed by José Guirao, former director of the Reina Sofía. It offers exhibitions principally by emerging artists working in all genres, but also features cutting-edge performance art and music (including short seasons of video artists) and activities for kids. The centre also includes a fair-trade shop, a library and classrooms for courses in, above all, IT and languages.

Puerta de Toledo

Glorieta de la Puerta de Toledo. Metro Puerta de Toledo. **Map** p327 E15.
Slightly swallowed up in the traffic at the meeting point of the Old City and the roads in from the south-west, this neo-classical gate was one of the monuments commissioned by Napoleon's brother Joseph in his brief span as King of Spain. After his departure it was rejigged to honour the delegates from the Cortes in Cádiz, and then King Fernando VII.

North of Gran Vía

Chueca

The neighbourhood of Chueca, bounded by the Gran Vía, C/Fuencarral and the Paseo de Recoletos, has been through several transformations. In the 18th century C/Hortaleza was the site of the Recogida, a refuge for 'public sinners', where women could be confined for soliciting on the street or merely on the say-so of a male family member. Release was only possible through marriage or a lifetime tour of duty in a convent. In the 19th century Chueca became a more respectable, affluent district, but by the 1970s and early '80s it had turned into a shabby, declining area. Since then, though, it has undergone a spectacular revival, due, above all, to it having become the gay centre of Madrid.

The epicentre of the scene is **Plaza de Chueca**; its terraces are packed with buzzing crowds on hot summer nights, and the only limitation on the scene could be whether the plaza can actually hold any more people. On the back of the gay scene, many more restaurants, trendy shops, cafés and clubs have opened up, and Fuencarral, the borderline between Chueca and Malasaña, is now the heart of Madrid's club-fashion scene. Many gay venues have acquired a fashionable crossover status among the hip non-gay crowd (to the extent that some gays now find some Chueca clubs too 'diluted'). Whatever, Chueca has established itself as a booming free zone for socialising of all kinds, gay and heterosexual.

The north side of the district, above C/Fernando VI, is not really Chueca proper and is often known as **Alonso Martínez**, after the

metro station. It's not so much part of 'gay Chueca' either, although it too has many new restaurants and bars. Instead, it's one of the foremost preserves of Madrid's teen scene. Streets such as Fernando VI or C/Campamor and Plaza Santa Bárbara are lined with bars and clubs catering to a young crowd, and on weekend nights the roads are packed too, with noisy (but safe) crowds of kids. Just west of here are the city's history museum, the **Museo Municipal**, and the **Museo Romántico** (for both, *see below*), closed until 2008.

Towards Recoletos, Chueca also becomes more commercial and more upmarket by day. C/Barquillo is full of hi-fi shops, while C/Almirante and its cross-street C/Conde de Xiquena are important fashion shopping zones. Off Almirante in C/Tamayo y Baus is one of Madrid's most important theatres, the **Teatro María Guerrero**.

This area is also part of official Madrid, with the giant **Palacio de Justicia** on C/Bárbara de Braganza. It was formerly the Convento de las Salesas, built in 1750-58 under the patronage of Queen Bárbara, wife of Fernando VI. It has housed law courts since 1870. Its refined classical baroque contrasts nicely with the art nouveau of the **Palacio Longoria**, a few streets away. To the south of Chueca, towards C/Alcalá, there is an isolated relic of Philip II's Madrid, the **Plaza del Rey** and venerable 1580s **Casa de las Siete Chimeneas**, originally designed by Juan de Herrera, architect of El Escorial.

Museo Municipal

C/Fuencarral 78 (91 588 86 72/www.muni madrid.es/museomunicipal). Metro Tribunal. **Open** *Sept-July* 9.30am-8pm Tue-Fri; 10am-2pm Sat, Sun. *Aug* 9.30am-2.30pm Tue-Fri; 10am-2pm Sat, Sun. **Admission** free. **Map** p324 H9.
Until the end of 2007 at the earliest, only part of this museum is open, owing to thorough renovation work. The building itself boasts an exuberantly ornate entrance by Pedro de Ribera, one of the finest examples of baroque architecture in Madrid, and worth seeing in itself. In the part that is open there is an exhibition, 'Madrid Ciudad', that comprises the best of the museum's collections of artefacts dating from Habsburg times through to the 19th century. For pre-Habsburg Madrid, visit the Museo de San Isidro (*see p91*).

Museo Romántico

C/San Mateo 13 (91 445 64 02/www.mec.es). Metro Tribunal. **Closed for renovation. Map** p324 H9.
Closed until 2008, the Romántico contains a charming collection of furniture, paintings, ornaments, early pianos and other pieces that evoke the Romantic period of 19th-century Spain. Phone the above number or check the website for details of when it will reopen.

Sightseeing

Sociedad General de Autores (Palacio Longoria)

C/Fernando VI, 4 (91 349 95 50). Metro Alonso Martínez. **Map** *p324 I8.*

Given the extraordinary output of Catalan *modernista* architects such as Gaudí in Barcelona in the early 20th century, it is remarkable, to non-Spaniards at least, that there is not a single example of their work in Madrid. The only thing at all like it is this building in Chueca, designed by José Grasés Riera in 1902 as a residence for banker Javier González Longoria. The voluptuous façade looks as if it was formed out of wet sand, moulded by an expert in giant cake decoration. It was once thought that Catalan architecture influenced Grasés, but Héctor Guimard and French art nouveau seem to have been a more direct inspiration. It is now owned by the Spanish writers' and artists' association. **Photo** *p102.*

Malasaña & Conde Duque

By day the neighbourhood of Malasaña, between C/Fuencarral and San Bernardo, still has a quiet neighbourhood feel, with grannies watering their geraniums on wrought-iron balconies and idiosyncratic corner shops. By night, though, this has long been an epicentre of Madrid's bar culture. It's nothing like as trendy or as adventurous as Chueca, though; rather, Malasaña is still associated with laid-back cafés, rock bars and cheap, grungy, studenty socialising, at least until the tentacles of Old City gentrification really take hold.

On 2 May 1808 this area was the centre of resistance to the French. The name of the district comes from a 17-year-old seamstress heroine, Manuela Malasaña, who was shot by the invaders for carrying concealed weapons (her scissors) or ammunition to the Spanish troops – there are various versions of her exploits. The name of the main square, **Plaza Dos de Mayo**, also recalls that day. Where the square is today was then the Monteleón artillery barracks, from where the artillery captains Daoiz and Velarde galvanised the resistance of the people. The last remaining part of the barracks, a gate, stands in the square with a monument to the two men.

Sightseeing

Centro Cultural Conde Duque. *See p109.*

Walk through Working Madrid

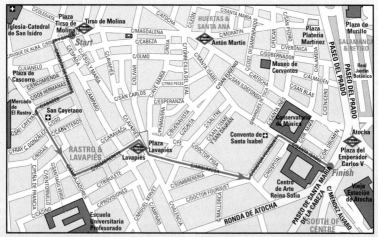

Duration: 30mins

Tatty, atmospheric Lavapiés shows Madrid's past, present and future. Once the Jewish quarter, long the main working-class area and still home to a large gypsy community, Lavapiés is now the most racially mixed neighbourhood in the city. It has acquired an often exaggeratedly bad reputation, but it's generally safe by day.

Begin at Plaza Tirso de Molina.
At its eastern end is the **Teatro Nuevo Apolo**, part art deco and part neo-Mudéjar. On the south side of the plaza is the present headquarters of the CNT anarchist workers' union, a reflection of Lavapiés' long-term association with left-wing politics.

Turn down C/Mesón de Paredes.
The street is named after the long-gone inn of Señor Paredes, inventor of the *emparedado*, a type of sandwich. For refreshment today, there is the historic **Taberna de Antonio Sánchez** at No.13 (*see p162*). Mesón de Paredes once boasted all manner of shops, but nowadays these are mostly Chinese-run *venta al mayor* (wholesale) clothes shops.

Turn right down C/Abades and left on C/Embajadores.
'Ambassadors Street' was so named because all Madrid's foreign embassies were moved here during a 17th-century outbreak of the plague. Just by the corner of C/Oso, amid the urban disorder, there is the baroque church of **San Cayetano**, built by a variety of architects, including Ribera and Churriguera, between 1678 and 1761. Despite the many hands involved in its construction, its façade is one of the most finely worked in Madrid. Opposite, a plaque signals the house of the great 18th-century architect Pedro de Ribera.

Turn left at C/Sombrerete.
'Little Hat Street' was named after the hat in which a Portuguese monk, Miguel dos Santos, was paraded through the streets before being hanged in the 16th century. He had been accused of acting as accomplice to a pastry chef, Gabriel de Espinosa, who claimed to be the missing heir to the Portuguese throne. After the hanging, the hat was left on a muck heap in this street. Where the street opens out to become the **Plaza Agustín Lara** are the ruins of the 18th-century church and school of the **Escuelas Pías de San Fernando**, destroyed in the Civil War. Facing the ruins across from C/Mesón de Paredes is Madrid's most famous *corrala* tenement block (*see p105*).

Continue to Plaza de Lavapiés.
A former stamping ground for the *majos* and *majas* (*see p15* **Picture this**), and once the centre of the Jewish area, the Plaza has a scruffy appeal. From here runs tree-lined **C/Argumosa**, with its Indian restaurants and pavement cafés.

At the far end, go left into C/Doctor Fourquet.
Home to several art galleries, this street also leads to C/Santa Isabel and the **Reina Sofía**.

The area gained a tough reputation in the 1980s, when used needles and broken bottles used to litter the *plaza* and sidestreets in the mornings, but urban renovation schemes have been very successful, and the neighbourhood feels a lot safer to walk around at night. It is now one of the centres of the San Isidro festivals in May (*see p205*), hosting nightly concerts, fairs and outdoor parties.

The streets between Fuencarral and San Bernardo abound with great cafés, bars and restaurants. There are also indications – such as the broad-arched doorways for carriages – that the 19th-century well-to-do once lived here. One of the most rewarding streets is **C/San Vicente Ferrer**, with jewellery shops and a delightful 1920s tile display advertising the long-defunct pharmacy Laboratorios Juanse. Other old ceramic signs on the **C/San Andrés** feature a little boy signalling that his chamber pot is full, and a dramatic, reclining vamp. C/La Palma and C/Divino Pastor, with craft and jewellery shops, are equally worth a stroll. To the north is Glorieta de Bilbao, site of one of Madrid's best traditional cafés, the **Café Comercial** (*see p175*).

The atmosphere gets more lively as you approach the streets near Fuencarral that lead down to the Gran Vía, such as **Corredera Baja de San Pablo**. This is an area of cheap restaurants, wholesale produce dealers in white aprons, shops selling nothing but light bulbs and working-class people who have known each other all their lives. Recent additions are club-style fashion shops, especially towards or on C/Fuencarral. At the corner of the Corredera Baja and C/Ballesta there is an unusual brick church, built by Philip III for his Portuguese subjects in Madrid. Later it was set aside for German Catholic émigrés, and is still known as **San Antonio de los Alemanes**. It is rarely open to visitors. Just a block away along C/Pez, often unnoticed amid the shops, bars and theatres that surround it, is the slab-walled convent of **San Plácido**, another of Madrid's surviving religious houses. Down where C/Fuencarral meets Gran Vía is the **Fundación Telefónica** exhibition space.

The area west of C/San Bernardo is most commonly known as **Conde Duque**, after its finest monument, the **Centro Cultural Conde Duque**, which occupies the giant barracks (*cuartel*) built in 1717-54 by Pedro de Ribera for King Philip V's royal guard. It was wonderfully renovated by the Tierno Galván city council in the 1980s as an arts centre (*see below*). Nearby is the **Museo Municipal de Arte Contemporáneo** (*see below*), and slightly hidden next to it is one of Madrid's least-seen treasures, the **Palacio de Liria**.

Centro Cultural Conde Duque

C/Conde Duque 11 (91 588 58 34/www.muni madrid.es). Metro Noviciado or Ventura Rodríguez. **Open** 10am-9pm Tue-Sat; 11am-2.30pm Sun. **Admission** free. **Map** p323 F8.

Housed in a former barracks, built in the 18th century for Philip V's guard by Pedro de Ribera, the magnificently restored Conde Duque is a multipurpose cultural centre. Around a dozen shows, both artistic and historical, are held annually in the two exhibition spaces and the two vast patios. Open-air concerts in summer bring in a range of performers. Also housed here are the city's newspaper and video libraries, as well as the Museo Municipal de Arte Contemporáneo (*see below*), which opened in 2001.

Fundación Telefónica

C/Fuencarral 3 (91 531 29 70/www.fundacion. telefonica.com/arte_tecnologia). Metro Gran Vía. **Open** 10am-2pm, 5-8pm Tue-Fri; 10am-2pm Sat, Sun. Closed Aug. **Admission** free. **Map** p323 H11.

Run by Telefónica, the national telephone company, this foundation functions on several levels. The Museo de las Telecomunicaciones is a permanent exhibition illustrating the history of telecommunications. Another large space is used to display selections from its permanent collection of Spanish art, including various works by Eduardo Chillida, Luis Fernández, Miró, Picasso and Tàpies and it also has a permanent show based around post-Civil War Spanish artists of the so-called Madrid and Paris schools, the latter in exile. Temporary exhibitions feature both the arts and technology.

Museo Municipal de Arte Contemporáneo

C/Conde Duque 9 (91 588 58 61). Metro Noviciado. **Open** 10am-2pm, 5.30-9pm Tue-Sat; 10.30am-2.30pm Sun. **Admission** free. **Map** p323 F8.

The council's contemporary art collection covers painting and graphic work, along with sculpture, photography and drawing. The first floor relates works and artists of different generations and media to show the plurality of Madrid's art scene. Highlights include work by Eduardo Arroyo, Ouka Lele, Eduardo Urculo, Jorge Oteiza and Eva Lootz.

Palacio de Liria

C/Princesa 20 (91 547 53 02/fax 91 541 03 77). Metro Ventura Rodríguez. **Open** *Guided tours* 10am, 11am, noon Fri. Booking essential. Closed July-Oct. **Admission** free. **Map** p323 E8.

This sober, neo-classical palace, completed in 1783 and refurbished in the 1910s by Edwin Lutyens, is still very much the private property of Spain's premier aristocrat, the Duchess of Alba. The extraordinary collection includes work by Rembrandt, Palma Vecchio, Titian and Rubens, and one of the most important Goyas in private hands: his portrait of an earlier Duchess of Alba in red and white. The problem is, the current duchess has no need to open her palace to public view. Space on the Friday guided tours has to be requested several weeks in advance.

Salamanca & the Retiro

From Prada to Prado.

Salamanca is an area best known for its designer shopping and the futuristic architecture along its Paseo de la Castellana, but the area is also home to some of the city's most fascinating small museums. South of here the Retiro is a verdant oasis of entirely old-fashioned delights: a boating lake, puppet shows and old men playing dominoes under the plane trees. Linking the two areas are wide boulevards, adorned with handsome statues, inspiring fountains and three of the greatest museums in the world.

Salamanca

In the mid 19th century, as it became evident that Spanish cities needed to expand beyond their old walls, attempts were made to ensure that this happened in an orderly way. Madrid and Barcelona had plans approved for *ensanches* ('extensions'). Carlos María de Castro's 1860 plan for Madrid envisaged the expansion of the city north and east in a regular grid pattern, with restrictions on building height and public open spaces at regular intervals within each block to ensure a healthy, harmonious landscape. The problem, however, was that for a good while few members of Madrid's middle classes seemed to have the money or motivation to invest in such a scheme, and they preferred to stay within the cramped, noisy Old City. That Madrid's *ensanche* got off the ground at all was due to a banker, politician and speculator notorious for his dubious business practices, the Marqués de Salamanca.

The marquis had previously built his own vast residence, now the **Banco Hipotecario**, on Paseo de Recoletos in 1846-50. He spent one of the several fortunes he made and lost in his lifetime building a first line of rectangular blocks along C/Serrano, from C/Goya up to Ramón de la Cruz. However, his ambitions overstretched his resources, the apartments proved expensive for local buyers, and he went terminally bankrupt in 1867. Nevertheless, it is to the rogue Marqués, not the old Castilian university town, that Madrid's smartest *barrio* owes its name.

It was only after the Restoration of 1874 that Madrid's wealthier citizens really began to appreciate the benefits of wider streets and residences with more class than the musty old neighbourhoods could supply. Once the idea caught on, the exodus proceeded apace, and the core of Salamanca was built up by 1900. The wealthiest families of all built individual palaces along the lower stretch of the Paseo de la Castellana, in a wild variety of styles – French imperial, Italian Renaissance, neo-Mudéjar. The block on C/Juan Bravo between Calles Lagasca and Velázquez contains a magnificent example: the neo-baroque palace of the **Marqueses de Amboage**, now the Italian Embassy. From the C/Velázquez side it's possible to see the extraordinarily lush gardens. Other mansions are scattered around the district, tucked in between apartment blocks. Those who could not quite afford their own mansion moved into giant apartments in the streets behind. The area has been the centre of conservative, affluent Madrid ever since.

Salamanca is a busy area, with streets that often boom with traffic, and so the best time to explore it is Saturday morning, when the shops are open but traffic has slackened. Streets such as Calles Jorge Juan, Ortega y Gasset, Goya and Juan Bravo yield top designers, art galleries and dealers in wines, silver or superior leather goods. Salamanca also has its own social scene, based around C/Juan Bravo, with shiny, smart bars and discos. Towards the east end of C/Goya there is a slightly more affordable shopping area; on the very eastern flank of Salamanca is Madrid's bullring, **Las Ventas**; and south of here is the numismatic **Museo Casa de la Moneda** (*for both, see p112*).

Art buffs are advised to head for the marble tower with sculpture garden at C/Castelló 77, base for the **Fundación Juan March**'s first-rate collection of modern art, which also hosts great contemporary art shows and free classical concerts (*see below*). For private art galleries, C/Claudio Coello, parallel to C/Serrano, is the city's most elegant centre. At the north end of Serrano is the eclectic **Museo Lázaro Galdiano** (*see p112*).

The blocks of Serrano, Claudio Coello and Lagasca below C/Ortega y Gasset are the oldest part of Salamanca, the first section built up by

the Marqués in the 1860s. Streets here are narrower, traffic less intense and shops closer together, making the area more amenable for strolling, browsing and snacking. There are charming buildings with intriguing details – such as the glass-galleried block on the corner of Claudio Coello and C/Ayala. The block between Claudio Coello and Lagasca on C/Ayala also contains the **Mercado de la Paz**, Salamanca's excellent market.

Fundación La Caixa

C/Serrano 60 (91 426 02 02/www.obrasocial. lacaixa.es). Metro Serrano. **Open** 11am-8pm Mon, Wed-Sat; 11am-2.30pm Sun. **Admission** free. **Map** p325 L7.

Run by La Caixa, a Catalan savings bank, this space has rightly won praise for the quality of its exhibitions. Over the last few years shows have featured art and artefacts of the Nubian people, the Greek artist Nikos Navridis and never-before-seen photographs by the Catalan intellectual and US resident Josep Alemany.

Fundación Juan March

C/Castelló 77 (91 435 42 40/www.march.es). Metro Núñez de Balboa. **Open** *Mid Sept-mid June* 11am-8pm Mon-Sat; 10am-2pm Sun. *Mid June-July, first 2wks Sept* 10am-2.30pm daily. Closed Aug. **Admission** free. **Map** p325 N6.

This cultural foundation, set up by the wealthy financier Juan March in 1955, is one of the most important in Europe. Each year, a couple of major exhibitions are held here, and a decent selection

The **Palacio de Comunicaciones** – part post office, part wedding cake. *See p113.*

Museo de Esculturas al Aire Libre.
See p117.

of the foundation's 1,300 works of contemporary Spanish art is also on permanent display. Free concerts, held at noon, are also worth checking out.

Museo Arqueológico Nacional

C/Serrano 13 (91 577 79 12/www.man.es). Metro Serrano. **Open** 9.30am-8pm Tue-Sat; 9.30am-3pm Sun. **Admission** €3.01; €1.50 students; free under-18s, over-65s. Free to all 2.30-8.30pm Sat & all Sun. **No credit cards. Map** p324 K10.

One of Madrid's oldest museums, dating back to 1867, this shares the same building as the Biblioteca Nacional and Museo del Libro. It traces the evolution of human cultures, from prehistoric times up to the 15th century, and the collection of artefacts includes finds from the Iberian, Celtic, Greek, Egyptian, Punic, Roman, Paleochristian, Visigothic and Muslim cultures. Remarkably, the great majority of pieces came from excavations carried out within Spain, illustrating the extraordinary continuity and diversity of human settlement in the Iberian peninsula. To tour the whole museum in chronological order, begin in the basement, which holds palaeontological material such as skulls, tombs and a mammoth's tusks, still attached to its skull. Some of the most interesting relics are from the area around Madrid itself, such as the many 4,000-year-old neolithic bell-shaped pottery bowls. The first floor holds the museum's most famous possession, the *Dama de Elche*, the intricate stone bust of an Iberian priestess, believed to date from 500BC. Further up, the usual definition of archaeology is stretched to include interesting exhibitions on post-

Roman Visigothic and Muslim Spain, with wonderful ceramics and fine metalwork from Moorish Andalucia. After that there is a whole series of rooms dedicated to pieces from the Middle Ages and later eras. In the garden, steps lead underground to a reproduction of the renowned Altamira prehistoric cave paintings in Cantabria.

Museo Casa de la Moneda

C/Dr Esquerdo 36 (91 566 66 66/www.fnmt.es/ museo). Metro O'Donnell. **Open** *Sept-July* 10am-5pm Tue-Fri; 10am-2pm Sat, Sun. *Aug* 10am-2pm Mon-Fri. **Admission** free.

This museum for enthusiasts of philately and numismatics boasts a huge collection, dating from the 18th century, that is among the most important in the world. The history of coins is represented in chronological order, and complemented by various displays of seals, bank notes, engravings, rare books and medals, plus around 10,000 sketches and drawings from Spain, Italy and Flanders, ranging from the 16th to 18th century. Recent acquisitions include the die in which the last peseta coins were cast and examples of the last print-run of 10,000 peseta notes.

Museo Lázaro Galdiano

C/Serrano 122 (91 561 60 84/www.flg.es). Metro Gregorio Marañón. **Open** 10am-4.30pm Mon, Wed-Sun. **Admission** €4; €3 concessions. Free to all Wed. **No credit cards. Map** p321 L6.

This unjustifiably little-known museum holds the extraordinarily eclectic collection of 15,000 paintings and *objets d'art*, covering 24 centuries, that was accumulated over 70 years by the financier and bibliophile José Lázaro Galdiano (1862-1947). Its holdings include paintings by Goya and Bosch, an important collection of work from the Dutch and English schools, and some wonderful Renaissance ornamental metalwork. The four-storey mansion and its gardens are a sight in themselves.

Plaza de Toros de Las Ventas

C/Alcalá 237 (91 356 22 00/museum 91 725 18 57). Metro Ventas. **Open** (Museum) *Nov-Feb* 9.30am-2.30pm Mon-Fri. *Mar-Oct* 9.30am-2.30pm Tue-Fri; 10am-1pm Sun. **Admission** (Museum) free.
More than 22,000 spectators can catch a bullfight in this, Spain's largest arena, completed in 1929. Like most early 20th-century bullrings, it is in neo-Mudéjar style, with often playful use of ceramic tiling. Around it there is ample open space to accommodate the crowds and food vendors, so it's easy to get a good look at the exterior. It's not necessary to go to a *corrida* to see the ring from within. When the bulls are back on the ranch, concerts are often held here, and alongside the ring there is the small Museo Taurino. The museum holds sculptures and portraits of famous matadors, as well as *trajes de luces* (suits of lights), including the pink-and-gold outfit worn by the legendary Manolete on the afternoon of his death in the ring in 1947 (alongside the blood-transfusion equipment that was used in attempts to save him). Among the 18th-century paintings is a portrait of *torero* Joaquín Rodriguez Costillares, once thought to be by Goya but now labelled as anonymous.

Plaza de Cibeles

Midway between the Puerta del Sol and the Retiro park, this four-way intersection and its statue and fountain signify Madrid to Spaniards as much as the Eiffel Tower or the Empire State Building identify their particular cities. It is surrounded by some of the capital's most prominent buildings: the **Palacio de Comunicaciones** (*see below*) which houses the city's main post office, the **Banco de España** (*see below*), the **Palacio Buenavista** (now the Army headquarters) and the **Palacio de Linares**, which houses the **Casa de América** (*see p114*). The Ventura Rodríguez statue in the middle is of Cybele, the Roman goddess of fertility and symbol of natural abundance, on a chariot drawn by lions. The goddess and the fountain around her have traditionally been the gathering point for victorious Real Madrid fans (Atlético supporters soak themselves in the fountain of Neptune, by the Thyssen museum) and the place where wins by the Spanish national football team have been celebrated.

Banco de España

Plaza de Cibeles. Metro Banco de España. **Map** p324 J11.

This grandiose pile was designed in 1882 by Eduardo Adaro and Severiano Sáinz de la Lastra to house the Bank of Spain. The eclectic style was most influenced by French Second Empire designs, with a few Viennese touches. The decorative arched window and elaborate clock above the main entrance are best appreciated from a distance.

Palacio de Comunicaciones

Plaza de Cibeles (91 396 27 33). Metro Banco de España. **Open** 8.30am-9.30pm Mon-Fri; 8.30am-2pm Sat. **Map** p324 J11.
Newcomers to Madrid find it hard to believe that this extraordinary construction, dwarfing the Plaza de Cibeles and regularly compared to a sandcastle or a wedding cake, could be just a post office (though there are rumours that this could be set to change if the city council has its way). It was designed in 1904 by Antonio Palacios and Joaquín Otamendi. Completed in 1918, it is the best example of the extravagant style favoured by Madrid's elite at its most expansive. The design was influenced by Viennese art nouveau, but it also features many traditional Spanish touches, with a grand entrance (complete with oversized revolving door), a Hollywood film-set staircase, soaring ceilings, stunning columns and grand marble floors. **Photo** *p111*.

Paseo de Recoletos

While other cities have rivers cutting through them as navigational points of reference, Madrid has two great avenues: the Gran Via and its continuation, C/Alcalá, running east–west, and the **Paseo de la Castellana** – which becomes the **Paseo de Recoletos** and the **Paseo del Prado** as it runs north–south. The leg that runs north of Cibeles, Paseo de Recoletos, was mostly added in the 1830s and '40s. The Palacio de Linares, now the **Casa de América** (*see p114*), is perhaps the best preserved of the palaces built by wealthy families after the Restoration. The curiously grand marble palace a little further north on the right, which is now the **Banco Hipotecario**, was once the residence of the Marqués de Salamanca, 19th-century Madrid's huckster-in-chief (*see p110*). It famously had the first flushing toilets in Madrid, an amenity the marquis later offered to residents in his new housing developments.

At the north end of Recoletos, on the right, stands the huge building housing the **Biblioteca Nacional** and, behind it, the **Museo Arqueológico Nacional** (*see p112*). The most ambitious project of the reign of Isabel II, the building was commissioned in 1865, but only completed in 1892. It overlooks the **Plaza de Colón**, where, at Columbus's feet, a cascading wall of water, beautifully cooling in summer, conceals the entrance to

El Salón del Prado

Thanks to Charles III's untiring efforts in the 18th century, the Paseo del Prado was to become the social heart of the city. Charles's idea was for this to become a centre of learning, with the main research institutions for arts and sciences, all open to the public, based here. He had it adorned with statues and fountains, and the whole area became known as the Salón del Prado. Early photos show women strolling with parasols while men in black bowlers hold ardent discussions. The 19th-century writer Richard Ford effused: 'The Prado, a truly Spanish thing and scene, is unique; and as there is nothing like it in Europe, and oh, wonder! no English on it, fascinates all who passes the Pyrenees.'

Oh, wonder! In time, however, thanks to the invention of the combustion engine, the Paseo del Prado was to become less of a promenade and more of a motorway, with cars speeding through red lights and tour buses blocking the view of the famous fountains. The current mayor's 'Plan Especial Prado-Recoletos', however, seeks to remedy this. The team behind the project, headed by award-winning Portuguese architect Álvaro Siza, intends to reclaim the Paseo for pedestrians. By the time it is finished, in 2012 or thereabouts, a broad expanse of walkable promenade will link the big three museums to Atocha train station with minimal interference from passing traffic.

The Plan Especial will restore other elements of the Prado and Recoletos area to their mid 19th-century glory. The towering statue of Christopher Columbus in the Plaza de Colón will be transferred back to its original spot in the centre of the adjacent roundabout. (The story goes that the pointing finger of the Columbus statue was intended to point towards the Dominican Republic, his first settlement, but an error in calculations means that he is currently pointing towards Greenland. Here's another chance to get it right.) The team will remove the modernist fountain façade of the Centro Cultural de la Villa, expand and rejuvenate areas of the Retiro park and the Botanical Gardens, and build a 'hill of sciences' on the south side of the Retiro to house new museums, a science centre and an 18th-century observatory.

Pedestrianisation is the most contentious and potentially disruptive element of the Plan: 12 lanes of traffic will be cut to six, four of which will be reserved for public transport. Madrid's car-crazy populace will have to adjust, using parallel streets and the M-30 loop. Carlos De Riaño, one of the head architects behind the Plan, explains matter-of-factly: 'It must be this way. Pedestrianisation is happening throughout Europe; people cannot drive so much in historical centres.'

The timing could not be better. At the time of its completion, all three of Madrid's star museums – the Museo del Prado (*see p83*),

the **Centro Cultural de la Villa** arts centre (*see below*). Controversial plans recently drawn up for the area include moving Columbus to the centre of the roundabout, losing the famous waterfall and instead enclosing the entrance to the Centro Cultural in an enormous glass 'egg'.

Casa de América

Palacio de Linares, Paseo de Recoletos 2 (91 595 48 00/www.casamerica.es). Metro Banco de España. **Open** 11am-8pm Mon-Sat; 11am-3pm Sun. **Admission** free. **Map** p324 J11.

Housed in the 1872 Palacio de Linares, the Casa de América showcases Latin American art, both by established figures and emerging talents. It also has the important role of promoting cultural contacts between Spain and the Continent. As well as this, there are film seasons, music, theatre and talks given by leading writers, film directors, playwrights and political figures. There are also print and video libraries, a good bookshop and a terrace with arts events in summer.

Centro Cultural de la Villa

Jardines del Descubrimiento, Plaza de Colón (91 480 03 00/www.munimadrid.es). Metro Colón. **Open** 10am-9pm Tue-Sat; 10am-7pm Sun. **Admission** free. **Map** p324 K9.

Behind the deafening but refreshing water cascade in Plaza Colón, below the Columbus monument, is the city council's only purpose-built cultural centre. On offer is a mixed bag of theatre, puppets, opera and *zarzuelas* in the summer, as well as art exhibitions, usually featuring important Hispanic artists.

Museo del Biblioteca Nacional

Biblioteca Nacional, Paseo de Recoletos 20 (91 580 77 72). Metro Colón. **Open** 10am-8pm Tue-Sat; 10am-1pm Sun. **Admission** free. **Map** p324 K9/10.

With over three million volumes, Spain's national library has been called the 'Prado of paper'. Among the wealth of printed matter there is every work published in Spain since 1716, Greek papyri, Arab, Hebrew and Greek manuscripts, Nebrija's first Spanish grammar, bibles, and drawings by Goya, the Museo Nacional Centro de Arte Reina Sofía (*see p86*), and the Museo Thyssen-Bornemisza (*see p88*) – will have finished their high-profile expansions. The banking empire La Caixa will have installed a modern new community arts building just north of the Reina Sofía, masterminded by the famous architecture duo Herzog and De Meuron. In the not-too-distant future, strollers will be able to amble freely between Madrid's best museums, fountains and extraordinary new architecture, and the Prado 'salon' will be returned to its 19th-century self – Madrid's best place to see and be seen.

Sightseeing

Velázquez, Rembrandt and many others. Given the precious and fragile nature of the texts, access was limited to scholars, but in 1996 the administration opened this museum to allow the public a glimpse of the library's riches. The displays are conceived as interactive, steering visitors through bibliographical history via multimedia applications including laser shows, videos and holographs.

Paseo de Castellana

Sights along the Castellana are listed here from bottom to top, south to north. The metro system partly avoids the avenue, but the 27 bus runs up and down the whole stretch, covering the Paseo del Prado, Recoletos and the Castellana.

In 1860, when he designed Madrid's 'extension', Carlos Maria de Castro took the significant decision, since the Paseo del Prado and Recoletos were already there, to continue along the same route with the main avenue of the new district. Thus the Castellana was born. Until the Republic of 1931 demolished Madrid's old racetrack, the avenue reached only as far as C/Joaquín Costa. Today it snakes away freely northwards, through thickets of office blocks. It also contains, near the junction with C/Juan Bravo (location of the **Museo de Esculturas al Aire Libre**, *see p117*), Madrid's 'beach' of upmarket terrace bars, at the height of fashion in the mid 1990s and still thronged with *pijos* (something like Sloanes). To the east is the Salamanca district, the heart of affluent Madrid, and the city's most upscale shopping area.

In the 1970s and '80s banks and insurance companies vied with each other to commission in-vogue architects to create corporate showcases along the upper Castellana; see the **Bankinter** building at No.29 and **Bankunión** at No.46. Beyond the latter, the **Museo de Ciencias Naturales** (*see p117*) is set back from the road on a grassy hill; further still, on

Puerta de Europa. *See p117.*

the left, is the Kafkaesque grey bulk of the enormous **Nuevos Ministerios** government complex. Begun in 1932, it contains many government ministries, and is one of the largest projects bequeathed by the Spanish Republic to Madrid. It was designed by a team led by Secundino Zuazo, chief architect of the Gran Madrid plan (*see p26*), in a monolithic '30s rationalist style; then, after the victory of General Franco, the same architect added to the still-unfinished building some curving, traditionalist details more to the taste of the new regime. Inside it has a park-like garden, open to the public.

Beyond that, a huge branch of the Corte Inglés signals your arrival at the **AZCA** complex. The Asociación Zona Comercial A, known to some as 'Little Manhattan', is a glitzy skyscraper development first projected during the Franco regime's industrial heyday in the '60s, but it gained extra vigour in democratic Spain's 1980s boom to become a symbol of Madrid yuppiedom. At its centre is the **Plaza Picasso** – a small park, and amid the office blocks are a chic shopping mall, restaurants and other facilities to make it a self-contained 'workers' city'. At its north end is the **Torre Picasso**, designed by Japanese architect Minoru Yamasaki (also responsible for New York's World Trade Center) in 1988 and, at 157m (515ft), Madrid's tallest building. Beyond it is the circular **Torre Europa**.

A little further up again, opposite each other, are the **Real Madrid** stadium, Estadio Bernabéu (*see p255*), and the **Palacio de Congresos** conference centre. By this time, the view up the Paseo de la Castellana is dominated by the two leaning towers officially known as the **Puerta de Europa** at Plaza Castilla. These remarkable smoked-glass blocks, leaning in at 15° off the perpendicular, are perhaps the greatest monument to Spain's 1980s boom. They were begun with finance from the Kuwait Investment Office (so that the towers are more often called the **Torres KIO**) and left unfinished for years after a financial scandal in 1992. With their rather phallic fountain in the middle, they have now joined the landmarks of modern Madrid.

Museo de Ciencias Naturales

C/José Gutiérrez Abascal 2 (91 411 13 28/www. mncn.csic.es). Metro Gregorio Marañón. **Open** *Sept-June* 10am-6pm Tue-Fri; 10am-8pm Sat; 10am-2.30pm Sun. *July, Aug* 10am-6pm Tue-Fri; 10am-3pm Sat; 10am-2.30pm Sun. **Admission** €3; €2.40 concessions. **No credit cards**.

The Natural Science Museum occupies two spaces in a huge building overlooking a sloping garden on the Castellana. Much of the north wing is given over to temporary exhibitions: generally a couple of

small-scale ones are held annually and a larger, more ambitious one, lasting about a year, is organised every 18 months. They tend to be hands-on, interactive and fun for kids. Permanently in this wing is 'Mediterranean Nature and Civilisation', a large exhibition of Mediterranean flora and fauna, illustrating the region's biodiversity. The smaller space to the south contains a simpler, more old-fashioned presentation of fossils, dinosaurs and geological exhibits. A replica of a diplodocus dominates the two-floor space, surrounded by real skeletons of a glyptodont (giant armadillo) and other extinct animals. The most distinguished skeleton here, though, is that of the *Megatherium americanum*, a bear-like creature from the pleistocene period unearthed in Luján, Argentina, in 1788.

Museo de Esculturas al Aire Libre

Paseo de la Castellana 41. Metro Rubén Darío. **Map** p325 L6.

An unconventional museum, this '70s space at the junction of the Castellana with C/Juan Bravo was the brainchild of engineers José Antonio Fernández Ordóñez and Julio Martínez Calzón. Designing a bridge across the avenue, they thought the space underneath would be a good art venue, and sculptor Eusebio Sempere convinced fellow artists to donate their work. All the major names in late 20th-century Spanish sculpture are represented – including Pablo Serrano, Miró, Chillida – and much of their work is spectacular, especially the dynamic stainless-steel *Mon per a infants* ('A world for children') by Andreu Alfaro and the spectacular cascade by Sempere that forms a centrepiece. **Photos** *p112.*

The Retiro & around

The most attractive section of Madrid's north–south avenue, and the one that most new arrivals in Madrid first become familiar with, is the oldest: the **Paseo del Prado**, from Atocha up to Plaza de Cibeles. Once an open space between the city wall and the Retiro (*prado* means 'meadow'), it was given its present form in 1775-82, from a design chiefly by José de Hermosilla; it was the most important of Charles III's attempts to give his shabby capital the kind of urbane dignity he had seen in Paris and Italy. The king intended it to be a grand avenue lined by centres of learning and science. Originally called Salón del Prado, the form of the main section, from Cibeles to Plaza Cánovas del Castillo, was modelled on Piazza Navona in Rome, with three fountains by Ventura Rodríguez: **Cibeles** at the most northerly point, **Neptune** to the south and a smaller figure of **Apollo** in the middle. The southern stretch of the Paseo, tapering down to Atocha, has another statue, the *Four Seasons*, in front of the Museo del Prado. In the 19th century the Paseo del Prado was the great promenade of Madrid.

Virtually the entire population, rich and poor, took a turn along it each evening, to see and be seen, pick up on the latest city gossip, make assignations and show off new clothes.

Despite the traffic, the tree-lined boulevard still has many attractions today, most notably Madrid's 'big three' great art museums (*see also pp78-87*, **Paseo del Arte**). As well as Charles III's creations, such as the **Jardín Botánico** (*see p120*) and the **Museo del Prado** itself, there are, at the very bottom, the **Centro de Arte Reina Sofía** and Atocha station (*see p120*). On the south side of the Botanical Gardens there are the rows of second-hand bookstalls of the **Cuesta de Moyano**. Further up, by the statue of Neptune, there is the **Museo Thyssen**, almost opposite such important elements in local life as the **Bolsa** and the **Hotel Ritz**. To the left, looking up, streets lead off into Huertas and the Old City, while to the right is the tranquil district of the Retiro.

When Philip II ruled Madrid, this whole area was just open country, apart from the church of **San Jerónimo** (*see p120*) and a few other royal properties. In the 1630s it was made into gardens – unprecedented in size for the era, at nearly 122 hectares (300 acres) – that became part of the **Palacio del Buen Retiro**, built by the Conde Duque de Olivares for Philip IV to impress the world. Gardeners were brought in from across Europe to create the park and its lake, and to ensure that it would feature shade and flowers throughout a Madrid summer. Charles III first opened sections of the park to the public in 1767, but it was only after the fall of Isabel II in 1868 that the gardens became entirely free to the public. After it became a park, the Retiro acquired most of its many statues, particularly the giant 1902 monument to King Alfonso XII presiding over the lake.

Since it was made open to all, the Retiro has found a very special place in the hearts and habits of the people of Madrid. On a Sunday morning stroll, especially before lunch, you will see multigenerational families watching puppet shows, dog-owners and their hounds, children playing on climbing frames, vendors hawking everything from *barquillos* (traditional wafers) to etchings, palm and tarot readers, buskers from around the world, couples on the lake in hired boats, kids playing football, elderly men in leisurely games of *petanca* (boules), cyclists, runners, and a good many bench-sitters who want nothing more than to read the paper. During the week it's much emptier, and it's easier to take a look at some of the 15,000 trees, the rose garden and the park's fine exhibition spaces: the **Palacio de Cristal** (*see p122*), **Palacio de Velázquez** (*see p122*) and the

Casa de Vacas (*see p120*). Built in the 19th century, they were extensively renovated during the 1980s.

At the southern end of the park is the **Observatorio Astronómico** (*see p120*), a fine neo-classical building. However, the greatest curiosity of the park is Madrid's monument to Lucifer, in the moment of his fall from heaven. Known as the **Angel Caído** (Fallen Angel), this bizarrely unique statue on the avenue south of the Palacio de Cristal is thought to be the only monument to the devil in the world.

After the death of Philip IV in 1665, little use was made of the Retiro, although the palace gained a new lease of life when the Alcázar burned down in 1734, as it became the primary royal residence in Madrid until the Palacio Real was completed in 1764. However, in 1808 Napoleon's troops made it a barracks, and when the British army arrived in 1812 to fight over Madrid, much of it was destroyed.

On the north side of the park, forming a bridge between it and Salamanca, is the grand **Puerta de Alcalá** (*see p122*), still imposing despite being surrounded by the hectic traffic of the Plaza de la Independencia. The districts around and south of the Retiro are in some ways similar to Salamanca, but less emphatically affluent and more mixed. The knot of elegant streets between the park and the Paseo del Prado make up Madrid's most concentrated museum district, with, as well as the **Museo del Prado** itself, the **Museo Naval** (*see p120*), the **Bolsa de Comercio de Madrid** (*see below*) and the **Museo Nacional de Artes Decorativas** (*see p120*).

Just southwest of the park, right on Glorieta de Atocha, is one of the area's biggest but least-known sights: the magnificently grandiose 1880s **Ministry of Agriculture**, by Ricardo Velázquez, the same architect who designed the delicate exhibition halls inside the Retiro itself. A few blocks east from here along the (traffic-ridden) Paseo Reina Cristina, a turn right down C/Julián Gayarre leads to the **Real Fábrica de Tapices**. On Julián Gayarre there is also the much rebuilt **Basílica de Atocha** and the odd, often deserted, **Panteón de Hombres Ilustres**, containing the elaborate tombs of Spanish politicians of the 19th century.

Bolsa de Comercio de Madrid

Plaza de la Lealtad 1 (91 589 22 64). Metro Banco de España. **Open** *Exhibition space* noon Mon-Fri. **Admission** free. **Map** p328 J11.

In the same plaza as the Hotel Ritz, Madrid's stock exchange is a landmark as well as a business centre. Enrique María Repullés won the competition to design it in 1884, with a neo-classical style chosen to reflect that of the nearby Prado. The building has

The quick and the dead

The Spanish philosopher Miguel de Unamuno famously wrote that the dead in Spain were never allowed to rest. The truth of this observation will become apparent to anyone who wonders what has happened to the tombs of famous Spaniards who have died in Madrid. Remarkably, the remains of none of the city's outstanding Golden Age figures, including Cervantes, Lope de Vega and Calderón de la Barca, have survived, though there was a brief moment of excitement in 1999 following the discovery of bones wrongly believed to be those of Velázquez and his wife.

Even those Spaniards wealthy enough in the past to have paid for *sepultura perpetua* (others still have their bodies automatically removed from their tombs after ten years) have not been guaranteed a tranquil posthumous life. The expansion or destruction of churches have led to constant transferences of corpses, during the course of which a high proportion of these have been mislaid or misidentified.

In view of this unfortunate situation a decision was finally taken in 1869 to create what Spain so obviously lacked – a national pantheon for its heroes. The domed late 18th-century Basílica de San Francisco was set aside for this purpose, and on 19 June, the remains of Calderón and other famous Spaniards were taken to the church in a triumphant procession involving cannon-fire and horse squadrons. But barely had the corpses had time to recover from their journey than the parishes from where they had come began to reclaim them. In the case of Calderón, the body would be moved several more times before disappearing altogether.

The fiasco of San Francisco did not put an end to the idea of a Spanish pantheon. In the 1890s, next to the then ruined 16th-century Basílica and Monastery of Atocha, the Panteón de Hombres Ilustres (*photo right*) was built. However, this too proved a failure, and most of the illustrious corpses for whom it was intended were taken away, leaving just the remains of largely forgotten politicians. Today it's one of Madrid's least visited sites, but nonetheless worth a look for its inappropriately Italianate architecture, and its splendidly elaborate tombs by Benlliure and other fashionable Spanish sculptors of the period.

While the Panteón de Hombres Ilustres is centrally located, visitors with a love of cemeteries will find themselves travelling to some of the city's poorest outlying districts.

The largest of the city's cemeteries is that of the Almudena, out to the east (metro García Noblejas), the terrifying scale of which, not to mention the dusty, grim surroundings, gives it a compelling morbid appeal. Across the road is the comparatively intimate Civic Cemetery. Tidied up in the early 1990s following the burial here of the Communist leader Dolores Ibarruri ('La Pasionaria'), this contains the tombs of hundreds of opponents to Franco and the Catholic Church. At the end of the Civil War numerous Republican prisoners were shot here and thrown into a mass grave.

But the most absorbing of Madrid's cemeteries is the Sacramental de San Justo, attached to the cemetery of the Hermitage of San Isidro (bus 17) out west. In a state of poignant neglect, this overgrown, cypress-shaded wasteland is the resting place of some of the more distinguished writers of 19th- and 20th-century Spain, from the romantic Madrid poet Mariano José de Larra to prolific writer and man-about-town Ramón Gómez de la Serna. Luis Buñuel was greatly drawn to this cemetery; his memory of coming across the hair of a woman protruding from a cracked grave here was used by him in his film The Phantom of Liberty.

two distinct areas: one is the trading area; the other, open to the public, houses an exhibition on the market's history. Visitors are admitted at noon only; phone to arrange a visit.

Centro Cultural Casa de Vacas

Parque del Retiro (91 409 58 19). Metro Retiro. **Open** 11am-2pm, 5-9pm Mon-Fri; 11am-9pm Sat. Times may vary. **Admission** free. **Map** p329 L11.
This exhibition space in the Retiro, close to the boating lake, is run by the local council and offers shows on a variety of subjects, ranging from children's books to wildlife photography and even footwear through the ages.

Estación de Atocha

Glorieta del Emperador Carlos V. Metro Atocha. **Map** p328 K15.
Madrid's classic wrought-iron and glass main rail station was built in 1888-92, to a design by Alberto del Palacio. It remained much the same, gathering a coating of soot, until the 1980s, when Rafael Moneo – he of the Museo Thyssen – gave it a complete renovation in preparation for Spain's golden year of 1992. Entirely new sections were added for the AVE high-speed train to Andalucía and the *cercanías* local rail network, and an indoor tropical garden installed, in an imaginative blend of old and new.

Jardín Botánico

Plaza de Murillo 2 (91 420 30 17/www.rjb.csic.es). Metro Atocha. **Open** Oct-Feb 10am-6pm daily. *Mar* 10am-7pm. *Apr, Sept* 10am-8pm daily. *May-Aug* 10am-9pm daily. **Admission** €2. Free under-10s. **No credit cards. Map** p328 K13/14.
Madrid's luscious botanical gardens were created for Charles III by Juan de Villanueva and the botanist Gómez Ortega in 1781. They are right alongside the Paseo del Prado, just south of the Prado museum, but inside this deep-green glade, with over 30,000 plants from around the world, it's easy to feel that city life has been put on hold. A sign at the entrance asks that you treat the gardens as if they were a museum, but don't feel bad about getting comfortable with a book for a while; it is one of the best spots in Madrid to do so.

Museo de Antropología y Etnología

C/Alfonso XII 68 (91 539 59 95/www.mn antropologia.mcu.es). Metro Atocha. **Open** 10am-8pm Tue-Sat; 10am-3pm Sun. **Admission** €2.40; €1.20 students; free under-18s, over-65s. Free to all 2.30-7.30pm Sat & all Sun. **No credit cards. Map** p328 K15.
This three-storey building between the Retiro and Atocha station houses several levels, each devoted to a specific region or country. The first level has an extensive collection from the Philippines (a former Spanish colony), dominated by a 6m (20ft) dugout canoe. Among the bizarre highlights are a 19th-century Philippine helmet made from a spiky blowfish, shrunken human heads from Peru and the skeleton of Don Agustín Luengo y Capilla, an Extremaduran who was 2.25m (7ft 4in) tall. Even more enticing is

a shrivelled tobacco leaf-skinned mummy, said to have once been in Charles III's royal library. Both are in the annexe to the first level.

Museo Nacional de Artes Decorativas

C/Montalbán 12 (91 532 64 99/www.mec.es). Metro Banco de España. **Open** 9.30am-3pm Tue-Sat; 10am-3pm Sun. **Admission** €2.40; €1.20 students; free under-18s, over-65s. Free to all Sun. **No credit cards. Map** p328 K11.
The Decorative Arts Museum houses more than 15,000 *objets d'art*, furniture and tapestries from all over Spain, plus many from China. One of the most prized rooms is the fifth-floor tiled kitchen, painstakingly transferred from an 18th-century Valencian palace, whose 1,604 painted tiles depict a domestic scene, with a huddle of servants making hot chocolate. Also of great interest is the second floor, where the Spanish baroque pieces are concentrated, among them ceramics from Talavera and Teruel, textiles, gold and silver work and jewellery cases from the Tesoro del Delfín (Treasure of the Grand Dauphin), the rest of which is in the Prado. Elsewhere are 19th-century dolls' houses, antique fans, an ornate 16th-century four-poster bedstead and a Sèvres jug given to Queen Isabel II by Napoleon III.

Museo Naval

Paseo del Prado 5 (91 532 87 89/www.museo navalmadrid.com). Metro Banco de España. **Open** 10am-2pm Tue-Sun. Closed Aug. **Admission** free. **Map** p328 J11.
Madrid's naval museum contains examples of the booty accumulated by Columbus and other early mariners during Spain's period of maritime expansion and an array of navigational instruments, muskets, guns and naval war paintings. Glass displays enclose primitive weapons, some of which, like the swords lined with sharks' teeth from the Gilbert Islands, promise greater damage than their Western counterparts. The most impressive room is dominated by a huge mural-map that traces the routes taken by Spain's intrepid explorers; in front of it are two equally impressive 17th-century giant globes. This same room also holds the museum's most valuable possession: the first known map of the Americas by a European – a parchment paper drawing by royal cartographer Juan de la Cosa believed to have been made for Ferdinand and Isabella in 1500. Worth a look also is the room occupied by items salvaged in 1991-3 from the *Nao San Diego*, which sank in the China Seas in 1600.

Observatorio Astronómico

C/Alfonso XII 3 (91 527 01 07/www.oan.es). Metro Atocha. **Open** *Guided tours* 11am Fri. **Admission** free. **Map** p329 L15.
One of Charles III's scientific institutions, the Observatorio was completed after his death in 1790. Beautifully proportioned, it is Madrid's finest neoclassical building, designed by Juan de Villanueva. It still contains a working telescope, which can only

Real Fábrica de Tapices. *See p122.*

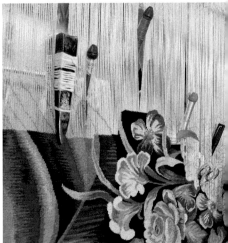

The Retiro. *See p118.*

be seen by prior request. One room is also open to the public, but only on Fridays at the time of writing, while the building undergoes renovation.

Palacio de Cristal

Parque del Retiro (91 574 66 14). Metro Retiro. **Open** *Oct-Apr* 10am-6pm Mon, Wed-Sat; 10am-4pm Sun. *May-Sept* 11am-8pm Mon, Wed-Sat; 11am-6pm Sun. **Admission** free. **Map** p329 M13.
This 1880s glass and wrought-iron construction, an outpost of the Reina Sofía, is a lovely, luminous space for viewing art. Shows here often involve large-scale installations, sculpture or pieces conceived specifically for the space.

Palacio de Velázquez

Parque del Retiro (91 573 62 45). Metro Retiro. **Open** *Oct-Apr* 10am-6pm Mon, Wed-Sat; 10am-4pm Sun. *May-Sept* 11am-8pm Mon, Wed-Sat; 11am-6pm Sun. **Admission** free. **Map** p329 M12.
Built by Ricardo Velázquez for a mining exhibition in 1883, this pretty brick and tile building amid the trees of the Retiro is topped by large iron and glass vaults. Another Reina Sofía annexe, its galleries are wonderfully airy, and host very good temporary shows, including a recent one by Julian Schnabel. Contemporary dance has also featured recently.

Puerta de Alcalá

Plaza de la Independencia. Metro Retiro. **Map** p324 K11.
A short distance along C/Alcalá from Cibeles, in the middle of another traffic junction, stands one of the most impressive monuments built for King Charles III, a massive neo-classical gate designed by his favourite Italian architect Francesco Sabatini to provide a grand entrance to the city. It was built

between 1769 and 1778, using granite and stone from Colmenar. Possible to miss in daytime traffic, it is unavoidably impressive at night.

Real Fábrica de Tapices

C/Fuenterrabía 2 (91 434 05 50/www.real fabricadetapices.com). Metro Menéndez Pelayo. **Open** *Guided tours only* 10am-2pm Mon-Fri (last tour approx 1pm). Closed Aug. **Admission** €3; €2 under-7s. **No credit cards**. **Map** p329 M15.
Goya created some of his freshest images as designs for Madrid's royal tapestry factory, founded in 1721. Originally it was in Chueca, but has been here since 1889. The hand-working skills and techniques used haven't changed, and are evident from the intricate, painstaking work carried out in its two sections – the carpet room and the tapestry room. Goya designs are a mainstay of the work that's done here today (the factory also maintains carpets for royal palaces and the Ritz as well as undertaking work for private clients). Guided tours are normally in Spanish, but if you call in advance an English-speaking guide can usually be arranged. **Photos** *p121.*

San Jerónimo el Real

C/Moreto 4 (91 420 30 78). Metro Banco de España. **Open** *Oct-June* 10am-1.30pm, 5-8.30pm daily. *July-Sept* 10am-1pm, 6-8.30pm daily. **Map** p328 K12.
Founded in 1464 and rebuilt for Queen Isabella in 1503, this church near the Retiro was particularly favoured by the Spanish monarchs, and used for state ceremonies. Most of the original building was destroyed during the Napoleonic Wars, and the present church is largely a reconstruction that was undertaken between 1848 and 1883. The cloisters at the side of the church are being taken over for use as galleries by the Prado (*see p83).*

Other Districts

Madrid's suburbs offer a wealth attractions from quirky museums, relaxing gardens and amusement parks… to an authentic Egyptian temple.

Sightseeing

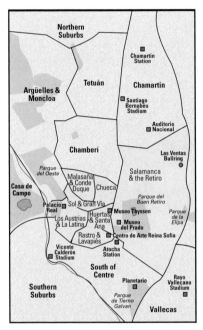

City walls and building restrictions over the centuries have meant that even Madrid's furthest-flung attractions are in a concentrated area, within easy reach of the city centre.

North & west

Casa de Campo

Once a royal hunting estate, the verdant, sprawling parkland of the **Casa de Campo**, to the west of the city, was only opened to the public under the Republic in 1931. Five years later it became a key site for Franco's forces in the Civil War battle for Madrid, its high ground being used to shell the city centre and the university. Remains of trenches still exist.

Today the Casa is home to the **Parque de Atracciones** funfair and the **Zoo** (for both, *see p210*), as well as, near Lago metro, **swimming pools** (*see p257*) and **tennis courts** (*see p258*),

and a large boating lake. The cafés that ring the lake make a fine place for an outdoor lunch, and cyclists should note that most of the park's roads are closed to cars on Sunday mornings.

Once you stray away from the criss-crossing roads much of the park is surprisingly wild, and it's possible to have a real country walk through its woods and gullies. A favourite way to visit is via the **Teleférico** cable car (*see below*) from the **Parque del Oeste** (*see p124*), which runs over the trees almost to the middle of the Casa, where there are viewpoints, an (undistinguished) bar-restaurant and picnic spots.

Couples seeking seclusion favour the Casa de Campo, both by day and night, and the area by the Teleférico has been a gay cruising spot, although police have been cracking down on this. In contrast, one new feature of the modern Casa is that Madrid's city authorities seem near set on turning the roads from Lago metro to the Zoo into a semi-official prostitution zone, with the aim of moving prostitution from the city centre. Consequently, by night, and often by day, there are female and transvestite prostitutes along these roads, displaying their assets pretty outrageously to cruising drivers, and leaving some pretty unpleasant debris behind them. One very Spanish aspect of this is that many of the other users of the park, by day at least, don't let this bother them, but carry on lunching, cycling or whatever, regardless.

Teleférico de Madrid

Paseo del Pintor Rosales (91 541 74 50). Metro Argüelles. **Open** *Apr-Sept* noon-8.30pm Mon-Fri; noon-9pm Sat, Sun. *Oct-Mar* noon-7pm Mon-Fri; noon-7.30pm Sat, Sun. **Tickets** (return) €4.20; €3.30 concessions. Free under-3s. **Map** p322 B8.
An extraordinary 2.5km (1.5-mile) trip over the Casa de Campo and Parque del Oeste in a cable car. The views of the Palacio Real, Río Manzanares, city skyline and park are breathtaking. There are even some interesting close-ups of the park's seedier goings-on.

Argüelles & Moncloa

West of Conde Duque lie the districts known as Argüelles and Moncloa. **Argüelles**, properly speaking, is the grid of streets between Plaza de España, C/Princesa, Plaza de Moncloa and Paseo del Pintor Rosales. The Paseo is known for its *terrazas* – open-air bars that are ideal for

Parque del Oeste.

taking the air on summer evenings. The Paseo sits above the **Parque del Oeste**, which, designed by Cecilio Rodríguez in the 1900s, is one of Madrid's most attractive spaces. The park was completely relaid after forming part of the front line in the Civil War. **La Rosaleda**, the rose garden, is beautiful in spring. The Montaña del Principe Pío, at its southern end, is one of the city's highest points, with great views of the Palacio Real and the incongruous **Templo de Debod** (*see p129* **From the Nile to Parque Oeste**), an Egyptian temple that was presented to Spain in 1968. This was the site of the Montaña barracks, the Nationalists' main stronghold at the start of the Civil War, before it was demolished and the hill incorporated into the park. Below the Teleférico stop a path leads to the **Ermita de San Antonio de la Florida**, with its Goya frescoes (*see below*), and beyond that, the river. The fountain below the Teleférico used to preside over the roundabout at Príncipe Pío station, but was moved to the park in 1994. In its place by the station there is now the **Puerta de San Vicente** – an entirely new, quite convincing reconstruction of the 18th-century gate that once stood on this side of the city. On Sundays Madrid's Andean community takes over the Parque del Oeste, organising volleyball tournaments and picnics; after dark, the area around the fountain, like the Casa de Campo, becomes a prostitution zone.

In the southern corner of the district, just off Plaza de España, is the **Museo Cerralbo** (*see p125*). In the opposite, northern corner, unmissable at the end of C/Princesa, stands one of the biggest, most significant creations of the Franco regime, the **Ministerio del Aire** or Air Ministry, built in the 1950s, in kitsch-Castilian baroque style and popularly known as the 'Monasterio del Aire', thanks to its resemblance to El Escorial.

Alongside the Ministry is the Plaza de Moncloa, Moncloa metro station and the departure points for many bus services to towns north and west of Madrid. There is also Franco's fake-Roman triumphal arch, built to commemorate victory in the Civil War. To the north of the plaza, in the **Moncloa** district lies the sprawling campus of the Universidad Complutense, the **Ciudad Universitaria**. Consequently, the streets just to the south and east have plenty of student bars. Within the university, specific attractions, are the **Museo de América** (*see below*) and the **Faro de Madrid** observation tower, and beyond that the new **Museo del Traje** (*see p126*).

Ermita de San Antonio de la Florida

Glorieta de San Antonio de la Florida 5 (91 542 07 22). **Metro Príncipe Pío.** **Open** 10am-2pm, 4-8pm Tue-Fri; 10am-2pm Sat, Sun. **Admission** free. **Map** p322 B9.

This plain neo-classical chapel was completed by Felipe Fontana for Charles IV in 1798. Quite out of the way, north of Príncipe Pío station on the Paseo de la Florida, it is famous as the burial place of Goya, and for the unique, and recently restored, frescoes of the miracles of St Anthony, incorporating scenes of Madrid life, which he painted here in 1798. In contrast to the rather staid exterior, the colour and use of light in Goya's images are stunning. Featuring a rare mix of elements, including his unique, simultaneously ethereal and sensual 'angels', they are among his best and most complex works. On the other side of the road into the park is a near-identical second chapel, built in the 1920s to allow the original building to be left as a museum. There are free guided tours of the Ermita, in Spanish and English, at 11am and noon on Saturdays.

Faro de Madrid

Avda de los Reyes Católicos (91 544 81 04). Metro Moncloa. **Open** 10am-1.45pm, 5-8.45pm Tue-Sun. **Admission** €1; 50¢ concessions.
This radio and communications tower, at 92m (302ft), provides one of the best views of the whole of the city and the sierras in the distance. Diagrams along the floor point out highlights of the city, though with age they're becoming increasingly difficult to decipher. The best bit, though, is the stomach-lurching ride up in the glass lift.

Museo de América

Avda de los Reyes Católicos 6 (91 543 94 37/http:// museodeamerica.mcu.es). Metro Moncloa. **Open** 9.30am-3pm Tue-Sat; 10am-3pm Sun. **Admission** €3.01; €1.50 concessions. Free Sun. **No credit cards.**
This museum comprises the finest collection of pre-Columbian American art and artefacts in Europe, a combination of articles brought back at the time of the Conquest and during the centuries of Spanish rule over Central and South America, plus later acquisitions generally donated by Latin American governments. The collection includes near-matchless treasures: there is the *Madrid Codex*, one of only four surviving Mayan illustrated glyph manuscripts in the world; the *Tudela Codex* and illustrated manuscripts from central Mexico, which depict the Spanish Conquest; superb carvings from the Mayan city of Palenque, sent back to Charles III by the first-ever modern survey expedition to a pre-Hispanic American ruin in 1787; and the Gold of the Quimbayas, a series of exquisite gold figures from the Quimbaya culture of Colombia, which were presented to Spain by the Colombian government. All the main pre-Columbian cultures are represented – further highlights include Aztec obsidian masks from Mexico, Inca stone sculptures and funeral offerings from Peru, and finely modelled, comical and sometimes highly sexual figurines from the Chibcha culture of Colombia. There are also exhibits from the Spanish colonial period, such as the *Entry of the Viceroy Morcillo into Potosí* (1716) by the early Bolivian painter Melchor Pérez Holguín, a series of paintings showing in obsessive detail the range of racial mixes possible in colonial Mexico, and a collection of gold and other objects from the galleons *Atocha* and *Margarita*, sunk off Florida in the 18th century and only recovered in 1988.

The collection is arranged not by countries and cultures, but thematically, so that rooms are dedicated to topics such as 'the family', 'communication' and so on, with artefacts from every period and country alongside each other. Without some knowledge of the many pre-Columbian cultures this can be confusing and uninformative. Frustrating, then, but it's still a superb, intriguing collection, and temporary shows are usually interesting.

Museo Cerralbo

C/Ventura Rodríguez 17, Argüelles (91 588 29 00/ 91 713 04 44/www.museocerralbo.mcu.es). Metro Plaza de España. **Open** 9.30am-3pm Tue-Sat; 10am-3pm Sun. **Admission** €2.40; €1.20 concessions. Free to all Wed & Sun. **No credit cards. Map** p323 E10.
Laid out in a sumptuous late 19th-century mansion in Argüelles is the incredible private collection of artworks and artefacts assembled by Enrique de Aguilera y Gamboa, the 17th Marqués de Cerralbo. A man of letters, reactionary politician and traveller who fanatically collected pieces everywhere he went, he bequeathed his collection to the state with the stipulation that it should be displayed exactly how he had arranged it himself. Thus the contents are

Ermita de San Antonio de la Florida. *See p124.*

Garden of Enlightenment

Just to the north of the A-2 motorway, now surrounded by Madrid's eastern sprawl, there is a jewel of a romantic fantasy garden, a remarkably preserved monument to 18th-century taste, the **Capricho de la Alameda de Osuna**. Within its 14 hectares is an artificial river leading between lakes, woods, rose gardens, mock temples and a whole range of cool, surprising corners. The gardens were begun in the 1780s for the Duke and Duchess of Osuna, the most cultivated couple among the Spanish aristocracy of their day, enthusiastic promoters of the ideas and enquiring spirit of the Enlightenment and great patrons of the artists, writers and musicians of their day. The Capricho was their country estate, and under the direction of the Duchess became a special combination of salon and pleasure garden. In the 1790s an invitation to spend a day there was the hottest ticket in Madrid, for both the aristocracy and the intelligentsia.

The Capricho has been called 'the essence of a feminine garden', and its design closely reflected the Duchess's personal taste. Her main architect was Jean-Baptiste Mulot, a French gardener who had previously worked for Marie-Antoinette, although much of the Capricho is in the English style, with simulated natural landscapes between smaller formal gardens. An Italian theatre designer, Angelo Maria Borghini, was brought in to construct many of the Capricho's fanciful buildings. Wandering visitors were to be surprised and delighted by a succession of different ambiences: from secluded alcoves to broad vistas; from the tranquillity of boat rides on the lakes out to tiny artificial islands to sampling the simple life at the Casa de la Vieja, a mock peasants' cottage. Also waiting to be discovered were replica Greek and Egyptian temples, a ballroom, an open-air theatre and the Abejero and even an ornate beehive in the shape of a classical temple. Within the Capricho the Osunas' aristocratic friends, men and women, could mingle with artists and intellectuals and talk freely, whether of gossip or great ideas, in an atmosphere that was very different from the paralysing etiquette of the royal court. New poems were read, and operas and music performed: Haydn was a favourite composer. This liberal informality encouraged by the Duchess – already deeply suspect for her 'French' ideas – also soon led to unstoppable rumours that far more illicit activities were going on among the Capricho's intimate arbours than just chat.

The Duke and Duchess of Osuna were also among the first important patrons of Goya, and their support played a major part in winning him acceptance among high society. Among the several paintings that Goya produced for the Osunas' house at El Capricho were two oddities, the *Aquelarre* ('Witches' Sabbath') and *Escena de Brujas* ('Witchcraft Scene') – both now in the Museo Lázaro Galdiano – precursors of his later macabre, sensual paintings, which could indicate a more decadent taste in the Duke

laid out in a crowded manner, with paintings in three levels up the walls, and few items labelled. Among the many paintings, though, there are El Greco's *The Ecstasy of St Francis of Assisi* – the real highlight – and works by Zurbarán, Alonso Cano and other Spanish masters. The upstairs area contains an astonishing collection of European and Japanese armour, weapons, watches, pipes, leather-bound books, clocks and other curiosities. The mansion itself is of interest; virtually intact, it gives a good idea of how the aristocracy lived in the Restoration period – look out especially for the lavish ballroom.

Museo del Traje (Museum of Clothing)
Avda Juan de Herrera 2 (91 550 47 00/www. museodeltraje.mcu.es). Metro Moncloa. **Open** 9.30am-7pm Tue-Sat; 10am-3pm Sun. **Admission** €3; €1.50 concessions. Free to all 2.30-7pm Sat & all Sun. **No credit cards**.

This museum is a must for those interested in any aspect of clothing. The collections comprise over 160,000 garments covering six centuries of Spanish fashion, though there are some much older items, among them fragments of Coptic cloth and Hispano-Muslim pieces. The permanent exhibition shows up to 600 items at any one time, rotating them frequently both to protect them and to allow returning visitors to appreciate the breadth and diversity of the collection. It is arranged chronologically, in 14 spaces, among which are two outstanding monographic rooms, one covering regional costume, the other containing pieces by Mariano Fortuny y Madrazo, son of the painter, whose creations were worn by the likes of Isadora Duncan. Other rooms cover costume from the Enlightenment and the *castizo* (Madrid's working classes); early 19th-century French influences; Romanticism; *belle époque*, the avant-garde, post-Civil War fashion and the modern and Duchess alongside their more celebrated Enlightenment rationalism. The Capricho is also famous as the place where Goya, then aged 40, met the 23-year-old Duchess of Alba, in 1786, and so where his obsession with her began. Scandalous and impulsive, known for breaking whichever social conventions suited her, dressing as a Madrid *maja* or street girl and having a string of male escorts from aristocrats to bullfighters, the Duchess of Alba was nevertheless a good friend of the high-minded Duchess of Osuna, and a frequent visitor to El Capricho.

The gardens were badly knocked about by Napoleon's troops – who also shot the head gardener, the French émigré Pierre Prévost – but were later reclaimed by the Duchess of Osuna, who lived on there until her death, aged 82, in 1834. El Capricho then suffered decades of decay and occasional destruction – during the Civil War – before it became the property of the city of Madrid, in the 1970s.

Capricho de la Alameda de Osuna

Paseo de la Alameda de Osuna (information 010). Metro El Capricho. **Open** *Oct-Mar* 9am-6.30pm Sat, Sun. *Apr-Sept* 9am-9pm Sat, Sun.

era. A room is dedicated to the great couturier Balenciaga and another to Spanish haute couture. Visitors can learn about how clothes are made in 'didactic areas' and a further exhibition space shows temporary displays, the first showcasing a century of *Vogue* photography. Facilities include a reading/internet room, bookshop, and café-restaurant

Templo de Debod

Montaña del Príncipe Pío (91 366 74 15). Metro Plaza de España or Ventura Rodríguez. **Open** 10am-2pm, 4-6pm Tue-Fri; 10am-2pm Sat, Sun. **Admission** free. **Map** p322 D9.
This Egyptian structure, which sits on the outskirts of the Parque del Oeste, dates back 2,200 years and is dedicated to the gods Amun and Isis. It was sent, block by block, by the Egyptian government in 1968 in thanks for Spain's help in preserving monuments threatened by the Aswan Dam. *See also p129* **From the Nile to Parque Oeste**.

Chamberí

Directly north of Malasaña is the *barrio* of Chamberí, one of the first working-class districts outside the walls to be built up in the second half of the 19th century. Consequently, and generably justifiably, it has become one of the few areas outside the old city considered to have genuine *castizo* character. A pleasant place to while away an evening in this area is the circular **Plaza de Olavide**, ringed with pavement cafés. Just to the east of here is the charming **Museo Sorolla**. On the north side of Chamberí is Madrid's main water supply, the Canal de Isabel II. On C/Santa Engracia, a neo-Mudéjar water tower has been converted into a unique photography gallery, the **Sala del Canal de Isabel II** (*see p128*).

Sightseeing

Museo Sorolla.

Museo Sorolla

Paseo del General Martínez Campos 37 (91 310 15 84/www.emcu.es/nmuseos/sorolla). Metro Gregorio Marañón or Iglesia. **Open** 9.30am-3pm Tue, Thur, Fri; 9.30am-6pm Wed; 10am-3pm Sat, Sun. **Admission** €2.40; €1.20 concessions. Free to all Sun. **No credit cards. Map** p321 J6.

Often considered a neo-Impressionist, Valencia-born Joaquín Sorolla was really an exponent of 'luminism', the celebration of light. He was renowned for his iridescent, sun-drenched paintings, including portraits and family scenes at the beach and in gardens. Sorolla's leisured themes and greetings-card-esque (and indeed they are often used as such), aesthetic are easy to dismiss, but most find his luminous world at least a little seductive. This delightful little museum, housed in the mansion built for the artist in 1910 to spend his latter years, has been recently restored and boasts 250 works. The works are exhibited on the main floor, in his former studio areas. The salon, dining room and breakfast room are furnished in their original state with the artist's eclectic decorative influence in evidence. The garden, Moorish-inspired but with an Italianate pergola, is a delightful, peaceful oasis of calm, seemingly miles away from the roaring traffic outside.

Sala del Canal de Isabel II

C/Santa Engracia 125 (91 545 10 00). Metro Ríos Rosas. **Open** 11am-2pm, 5-8.30pm Tue-Sat; 11am-2pm Sun. **Admission** free.

This water tower, built in elaborate neo-Mudéjar style in 1907-11 is considered a gem of Madrid's industrial architecture. It is now home to a stylish exhibition space that specialises in photography, ranging in quality from good to world-class.

Tetuán & Chamartín

North of Chamberí is **Tetuán**, a modern, working area centred on C/Bravo Murillo, and, to the east, **Chamartín**, which contains the major business area of modern Madrid. The main point of interest for visitors is the local market, the **Mercado de Maravillas**, at C/Bravo Murillo 122, just north of Cuatro Caminos – it's the largest market in the city. On Sunday mornings, too, a 'Rastro' gets going on C/Marqués de Viana. Also well worth a visit is the **Museo Tiflológico** just north of here. A museum designed especially for blind and partially sighted visitors it by no means excludes other visitors; in fact it's hands-on approach is particularly suitable for those with children in their group.

Across the Castellana, north-east of Nuevos Ministerios, is **El Viso**, an anomaly in high-rise Madrid. It was developed in the 1920s as a model community on garden-city lines, on the fringes of the city at that time, and some of its individual houses are museum-worthy examples of art deco. Unsurprisingly, the district has retained its desirable (and expensive) status. At the southern tip of this area is the incongruously political cultural centre, the **Residencia de Estudiantes**. Further east again is **La Prosperidad**, also once a model housing development, although most of its early buildings have been replaced by modern blocks. Within it is the **Auditorio Nacional de Música** (*see p232*).

From the Nile to Parque Oeste

For two millennia the ancient Egyptian Templo de Debod stood on the banks of the River Nile in Lower Nubia, southern Egypt. Then in 1968, the Egyptian government dismantled the structure brick by brick, shipped it across the Med and reassembled it on the Montaña del Príncipe Pío, at the southern tip of Parque Oeste – as thanks for Spain's help in saving Abu Simbel's temples from immersion in Lake Nasser (the artificial lake created by the building of the Aswan High Dam).

There, unassumingly, the temple remains. Visitors are free to step inside its cool, sometimes disorientingly dark interior and explore the ancient stone corridors and chambers; adventurous types will enjoy getting down on their hands and knees to crawl through some of the smaller passageways. Audiovisual presentations and relics help conjure up a sense of the past. Upstairs, a diorama shows the temple's original location: near the first cataract of the Nile and close to a key religious centre dedicated to Isis (goddess of magic and wife and sister of Osiris), on the island of Philae.

First built as a temple to Isis and Amun, the principal god of the Egyptian and Meroitic (Kushite) religions, construction took place between 200BC and 180BC at the instigation of Adikhalamani, king of the Meroitic people. The Meroites occupied what is now southern Egypt and northern Sudan from 800BC to AD350. Reliefs on the temple's wall record Adikhalamani worshipping and making offerings to Amun, Isis and other gods. Later, pharaohs of the Ptolemaic dynasty (305-30BC) and Roman rulers, including Augustus, Tiberius, and perhaps Hadrian, added futher chapels, an entrance hall, stairs, a terrace, a processional way and a landing quay.

In ancient times it was believed that the gods physically lived in the temple, so only the pharaoh and his priests could enter. Every day in the main chapel at sunrise, the priest would begin the important dawn ritual of cleaning, decorating and making offerings to the statues of Amun and Isis. He would offer meat, beer and other foodstuffs, then finally, to Amun, a statue of Maat, personification of the concepts of Egyptian order and justice. The priest would then exit, carefully cleaning away all traces of his activity, including his own footprints. Such ceremonies – others were performed at midday and dusk, and at specific times of the year – continued in the Templo de Debod into the sixth century AD, when it was abandoned after Byzantine emperor Justinian ordered the closure of the centre on Philae (an event generally taken to mark the end of ancient Egypt).

Today, a thousand miles from home, Templo de Debod remains one of the few ancient Egyptian architectural works that can be seen in its entirety outside Egypt – and it's the only one in Spain.

El Pardo. *See p131.*

Museo Tiflológico

C/La Coruña 18 (91 589 42 00/www.museo.once.es).
Metro Estrecho. **Open** 10am-2pm, 5-8pm Tue-Fri;
10am-2pm Sat. Closed Aug. **Admission** free.
Owned and run by ONCE, the organisation for blind
and partially sighted people, this special museum
presents exhibitions of work by visually-impaired
artists (the name comes from the Greek *tiflos*, sight-
less). Work here is intended to be touched, and is
generally sculptural, three-dimensional, rich in texture and highly tactile. As well as temporary shows
the museum has a large permanent collection of
instruments devised to help the blind over the years,
and a series of scale models of monuments from
Spain and around the world.

La Residencia de Estudiantes

C/Pinar 21-23 (91 563 64 11/www.residencia.
csic.es). Metro Gregorio Marañón. **Open** (during
exhibitions, phone to check) 10am-8pm Mon-Sat;
10am-3pm Sun. **Admission** free.
From its foundation in 1910 until the war in 1936,
The Residencia de Estudiantes was the most vibrant
cultural centre in Madrid, and a powerful innovative
force in the whole country. Though it was a students'
residence – García Lorca, Buñuel and Dalí all stayed
there in the early days – 'La Resi' also organised
visits to Madrid by leading artists and scientists of
the day and was active in the propagation of avant-
garde ideas from outside Spain. The Civil War and
subsequent regime severely stifled intellectual freedom and the Residencia languished until the late
1980s, when it was resurrected as a private foundation sponsored by Spain's official scientific research
council. Once again a centre of excellence, it hosts
talks by major international figures, plus conferences and exhibitions, recitals, films and concerts.

The northern suburbs

The northern and western *extrarradio* offers a
radical contrast to the south. The thing to do for
those with the necessary cash in Madrid has been
to adopt the Anglo-Saxon way of life and move
out of city flats into house-and-garden districts
like **Puerta de Hierro**, north of the Casa de
Campo. Named after the 1753 iron gate to the
royal hunting reserve of El Pardo, its posh homes
are no match for **La Moraleja**, off the Burgos
road, an enclave for executives and diplomats.
    The growing districts to the east are not
nearly so lush. The area along the A-2 motorway
towards the airport is intended to be Madrid's
major commercial development zone, with the
Feria de Madrid trade fair complex and the
Parque Juan Carlos I, which lies between
the airport and the Feria de Madrid centre. Oddly
enough, the area already contains, swallowed up
in the urban spread, one of Spain's most appealing
and neglected 18th-century gardens, the **Capricho
de la Alameda de Osuna** (*see p126* **Garden
of Enlightenment**).

Parque Juan Carlos I

Avda de Logroño & Avda de los Andes.
Metro Campo de las Naciones.
This huge park, Madrid's newest green (and brown)
space, lies between the airport and the Feria de
Madrid trade fair centre. With time it should become
one of the city's more attractive spaces, but it has
taken a while for the trees to grow to provide shade.
That said, the park's current draws include a series
of different gardens within a circle of olive trees, an
artificial river and other water features.

El Pardo

Around ten miles (15 kilometres) to the north-
west of the city lies a vast expanse of parkland.
Here is the main residence of the Spanish royal
family, the **Palacio de la Zarzuela**, but the
reason most people will venture up here is for
the peculiar sensation of nosing around in the
house where General Franco lived and worked
for the 35 years up to his death in 1975, the
Real Palacio de El Pardo, situated in the
peaceful 18th-century town of El Pardo. Today
the place serves mainly to host foreign dignitaries
and heads of state, most notably in recent years
during the 2004 wedding of the heir to the
throne, Prince Felipe.
    The hills and woodlands are also worth
a visit, however, being remarkably unspoilt
thanks to those long protected years of dictatorial
and regal status, and they contain an amazingly
rich wildlife. Not surprisingly, game features on
many restaurant menus in the town.

Real Palacio de El Pardo

C/Manuel Alonso (91 376 15 00/www.patrimonio
nacional.es). Bus 601 from Moncloa. **Open** *Apr-Sept*
10.30am-5.45pm Mon-Sat; 9.30am-1.30pm Sun. *Oct-*
Mar 10.30am-4.45pm Mon-Sat; 10am-1.30pm Sat.
Admission €5; €2.50 concessions. Wed free to EU
citizens. **No credit cards.**
In 1405 Henry III constructed a hunting lodge here,
but the first monarch to take a really serious interest in El Pardo's excellent deer and game hunting
estate was Charles I of Spain (Charles V of the Holy
Roman Empire), who built a sizeable palace here. His
successor, Philip II, added many important works
of art but most of these were lost in a fire in 1604,
and after various architectural changes the building
was finally reconstructed on Charles III's orders by
18th-century architect Francesco Sabatini; superb
murals by Bayeu and Maella were added at this
time. The current furnishings, paintings and tapestries were added during the 19th and 20th centuries.
    In addition to its main role today as a diplomatic
rendezvous, the palace is partially open to the public and there are tours of its ornate and gaudy interior with its ornamental frescoes, gilt mouldings and
some fine tapestries, many of which were woven in
the Real Fábrica de Tapices to Goya designs. There's
an ornate theatre, built for Charles IV's Italian wife

Sightseeing

María Luisa of Parma, where censorious film fan Franco used to view films with his cronies before deciding on their suitability for the great unwashed, but in truth the only rooms of real fascination are the Generalísimo's bedroom, dressing room and '70s bathroom – decorated to his own specifications.

Outside you can wander in the palace's attractive gardens or explore or picnic in at least part of the magnificent surrounding parkland known as Monte de Pardo – even though much of this is still closed to the public. Other nearby highlights include the Convento de los Capuchinos (Ctra del Cristo, 91 376 08 00, open 9am-1pm, 4.30-8pm daily), famed for Gregorio Fernández's wooden baroque sculpture of Christ; the Quinta del Pardo, a small 18th-century summer house, and the single-storey Casita del Príncipe, built in 1785 by Juan de Villanueva and noted for its lavish lounges, though both have been closed to the public for some years. **Photos** *p130*.

South

South of centre

The barrios of southern **Embajadores** – namely **Delicias**, **Arganzuela** and **Legazpi** – occupy a triangular chunk of land just south of the old city, bordered by the Manzanares river, the M-30 motorway and the rail lines from Atocha. Low rents attract a fair number of resident foreigners. Conventional attractions are few – the **Museo del Ferrocarril** (*see below*) and the **Parque Tierno Galván**, with the **IMAX Madrid** and **Planetario de Madrid** (for both, *see p210*) – but the area contains the **Estación Sur** bus station, and two symbols of Madrid, the **Atlético Madrid** stadium and, alongside it, the Mahou brewery. Beyond that is the river, and the **Puente de Toledo**, which was built by Pedro de Ribera for Philip V in 1718-32.

Just south of the river is the **Parque de San Isidro**, containing a charming 18th-century hermitage dedicated to the city's patron saint. The hermitage is the traditional focus of the Romería (Procession) de San Isidro. The park still fills with life and crowds during the **San Isidro** fiestas every May (*see p205*). At other times it's very tranquil; the view from the hill of San Isidro is familiar as one painted many times by Goya, and is still recognisable, despite the tower blocks.

Museo del Ferrocarril

Paseo de las Delicias 61 (91 506 83 33/www.museo delferrocarril.org). Metro Delicias. **Open** 10am-3pm Tue-Sun. Closed Aug. **Admission** €3.50; €2 concessions. Free to all Sat. **No credit cards**.
Housed in the elegant but disused Delicias station, with ironwork by Gustave Eiffel, Madrid's railway museum has an evocative collection of models, old locomotives, railway equipment and memorabilia. There is also a room dedicated to clocks, including the one that marked time when Spain's first ever train chugged from Barcelona to Mataró. You can climb on the trains, have a drink in an old restaurant car or watch film footage of Spanish railways. This great museum for kids offers occasional theatre performances, a bring-and-buy market for model train enthusiasts, and more. It is located about 100 yards off the main road, behind the national railway offices.

Vallecas

Vallecas, beyond the M-30 south-east of the city, was already an industrial suburb in the 1930s, and manages to remain one of the areas of Madrid with a firm sense of its own identity. It doesn't lay much claim to being traditionally *castizo*, however, even though many of its residents originally came here as overspill from the city centre. Rather, the name 'Vallecas' in Madrid immediately brings to mind the post-Civil War, post-1950s working class.

Vallecas is known for a strong sense of neighbourly solidarity. The area has its own football team, **Rayo Vallecano**, which is forever struggling to keep up with its money-laden neighbours. Car stickers proclaim 'Independence for Vallecas' (spelt 'Vallekas' by hipper natives, who have their own punky sense of cool). It also has a pleasant tree-lined main drag, more than enough to mark it out from the other areas around it. There have been problem districts not far away, such as **Entrevías**, home to some of Madrid's largest Gypsy communities.

Outer limits

Southern suburbs

Carabanchel, **Leganés**, **Getafe**, **Móstoles** and **Alcorcón** form the southern industrial belt of Madrid, virtually all of it built up since the 1960s. Areas still within the city, such as **Orcasitas**, blend into the towns of the *extrarradio*, the outskirts, and concrete flyovers and tower blocks make up the urban landscape.

These areas are now better connected thanks to the extension of the metro system, and central city dwellers occasionally come down here for entertainment: **Alcorcón** holds a flamenco festival, and **Fuenlabrada** has a clutch of teen-macro-discos. The popularity of hard rock in these suburbs is also attested to by Calle AC/DC in Leganés, inaugurated by the rock legends themselves in 2000. On the street is a converted bullring that has become one of the most important music venues in Madrid, **La Cubierta de Leganés** (*see p237*).

Eat, Drink, Shop

Features

Memento. *See p155.*

Restaurants

Molecular gastronomy takes its place alongside the suckling pig.

Not so long ago, it used to be that even dishes from Asturias were thought exotic here in the capital. However, the times they are a changin' and, thanks in part to immigration, these days *madrileños* have become Spain's unlikely flag-bearers for culinary globalisation. Mexican, of course, has always been around, and Asian, particularly, has become de rigueur. But add to this list the overwhelming popularity of Italian, French, Cuban, Middle Eastern, Thai and Japanese restaurants in town and wonder at the future of the paella.

Among the many pluses of these international newcomers, three advantages stick out: style, spice and vegetables. Where the dining scene used to be all red-checked tablecloths or old-style elegance, now those who fancy the chic and minimal have a place to go and look glam. And if your taste buds are inclined to more nuances of spice, the hottest of chilli peppers or eye-watering wasabi, you can rest easy. Then, the good news for vegetarians is that the options are no longer limited to tortilla, or green beans with the ham picked out. The multitude of new Asian restaurants always has vegetarian options, as do, increasingly, the Italian, Middle Eastern and other foreign eateries. So rejoice in the glories of diversification and eat your veggie fill.

That said, this city remains a bastion of unreconstructed Spanish cuisine and what has often been described as 'brown food'. The famous *cocido madrileño* – a stew of various bits of meat, offal and vegetables served up in three courses – is still eaten religiously, particularly at weekends. The down-home *casas de comida* (eating houses) are packed daily with regulars who are perfectly happy with a plain *ensalada mixta* followed by a greasy pork chop and the ubiquitous *flan* for dessert. Even the young and cool are faithful to the less expensive classic *mesones* (old-style taverns), while the most upscale traditional places still require you to join a waiting list.

For *lo más típico*, head for the area around Los Austrias and La Latina, particularly along C/Cava Baja, leading south from the Plaza Mayor – a veritable pilgrim's way to the most traditional *madrileño* cuisine. If you're not up for lentils and roast lamb, head over to Chueca, where you'll find hipper, stylish restaurants (many of which offer great value at lunchtime)

and a plethora of international eateries. Round these parts, one restaurant closes as another opens, but many have stood the test of time. The most upmarket restaurants, on the other hand, can be found in the Salamanca area, and particularly in the expensive business hotels around the Paseo de la Castellana.

TIMING

Rule number one for visitors to Madrid: don't go out too early. *Madrileños* rarely eat lunch before 2pm, although go after 4pm and you may find people sweeping up around you. Probably due to a combination of substantial

The best Restaurants

To spend it like Beckham
La Broche (*see p156*); **Santceloni** (*see p156*); **La Terraza** (*see p141*).

For dinner and a show
La Favorita (*see p155*); **Gula Gula** (*see p141*); **Laydown** (*see p155*).

For dinner à deux
La Sinfonia Italiana (*see p152*); **Come Prima** (*see p147*).

For no-frills Asian
Baisakhi (*see p148*); **Kawara** (*see p142*); **Adrish** (*see p152*).

For blood 'n' guts
La Botillería de Maxi (*see p137*); **Freiduría de Gallinejas** (*see p147*).

For minimalist chic
La Broche (*see p156*); **Nodo** (*see p154*).

For the catch of the day
Ribeira Do Miño (*see p150*); **Xentes** (*see p140*).

After the match of the day
Summa (*see p156*); **Asador Donostiarra** (*see p154*).

Best for Sunday brunch
Home (*see p153*); **Olsen** (*see p147*); **Le Petit Bistrot** (*see p147*).

Eat, Drink, Shop

lunches and the heat, dinner is usually eaten late as well – around 10pm, and even later in the summer. It's advisable to book a table in most places for Friday and Saturday night, and at other times if you're in a big group. Many restaurants close on Sunday evening and all of Monday. August is livelier than it used to be, but most restaurants still close for at least two weeks. Where possible, we've indicated this, but it's best to ring and check.

By law, restaurants are obliged to declare on the menu if VAT (IVA) is included and if there's a cover charge. In practice, however, they almost never do, and there almost always is (strictly speaking cover charges are illegal, but are often disguised as a charge for bread). There's no set rule for tipping, but leaving a couple of euros or so is the norm.

MENU DEL DIA

Opinions differ over whether the *menú del día* was introduced to attract tourists or to feed hungry workers who can't get home at lunchtime. Either way, it can be a great way to eat cheaply and well, and all but the swankiest restaurants are obliged to offer one. It usually consists of a starter, main course and dessert, bread and some occasionally dubious wine. Dishes cost much less than they would do à la carte (although portions tend to be smaller) and the *menú del día* also provides a chance to sample some of the more upmarket places on a budget. Standard Spanish restaurants tend to offer typical *comida casera* (home cooking), and many international restaurants will follow suit, rather than offer anything that would be available à la carte, so don't expect fireworks.

Sign language

It's a nerve-racking choice. S or C? A-ha, you say, S must be *señor*! The men's room! Well, no. S is in fact '*señora*', and C, '*caballero*', meaning gentleman. But what if you see C and D? Who is the D? That would be '*dama*', meaning 'lady'. It's not always so simple. Many bars and restaurants in Madrid seem to have spent hours dreaming up original ways to designate their lavatory doors.

Stromboli (*see p175*), for example, has abridged the words *chicos* (boys) and *chicas*

(girls), labelling the doors simply 'OS' and 'AS'. That one has even the natives scratching their heads (or should that be scratching their 'ads'?). In cases such as these, it's important to know that words ending in O are male, and words ending in A are female. Take **La Viuda Blanca** (*see p139*), meaning 'the white widow'. There you are either a *viuda* or *viudo* (widower). In **Alqamara** on C/Espíritu Santo it's useful to know that the bar is run by lesbians, hence '*Vosotros*' (meaning 'you', masculine plural), and '*Nosotras*' (meaning 'us', feminine plural).

Then there are those that opt for pictures or symbols. Much simpler, you'd think – well, no. Take **Jellyfish Café** on C/Pelayo. There, a fish tail means men's, a jellyfish means women's. Or then there's **Olsen** (*see p147*), where the Nordic theme extends to the lavs, with a wooden stag representing the gents' and an antlerless deer for the ladies'. **La Soberbia** on C/Espoz y Mina keeps it nice and Spanish with a small version of roadside Osborne sherry bulls for the men. Easy. The ladies' version is exactly the same as the men's, just painted with a Friesian pattern and with a pink udder attached.

Then there's the really obvious. At **Matador** on C/Cruz you will see a graphic pencil drawing of a staggeringly ugly pair of male and female genitals. But however confusing these pictorial or textual signs may be, they're still infinitely preferable to the labelling chosen by **La Ida** (*see p177*), where the absence of anything written on either door makes for an entertaining toilet roulette.

Casa Lucio.

Los Austrias & La Latina

La Botillería de Maxi

C/Cava Alta 4 (91 365 12 49/www.labotilleriade
maxi.com). Metro La Latina. **Open** 1-4pm, 8.30pm-
midnight Tue-Sat; 12.30-6pm Sun. Closed last 2wks
Aug. **Main courses** €7-€10. **Set lunch** €9 Tue-Fri.
No credit cards. Map p327 F13 ❶
Fashionably scruffy young waiting staff and blaring flamenco in a no-frills classic setting make for
an unpretentious blend of old and new. This is the
place for an offal first-timer – the callos a la
madrileña (tripe in a spicy sauce) are acknowledged
as the best in town. For less accustomed stomachs,
there are enticing options too: mojama (wind-dried
tuna), fish pie and all manner of inventive things
made with manchego cheese.

La Camarilla

C/Cava Baja 21 (91 354 02 07/www.lacamarilla
restaurante.com). Metro La Latina. **Open** 1-4pm,
9pm-midnight Mon, Tue, Thur-Sun. **Main courses**
€17-€19.50. **Set lunch** €10.90 Mon, Tue, Thur. **No
credit cards. Map** p327 F13 ❷
Of the many traditional restaurants on this stretch
of road, La Camarilla offers the most innovative versions of Spanish home cooking: gazpacho with
mango, revuelto (scrambled egg) with mushrooms
and parmesan, and various tasty cod dishes. The
setting is reminiscent of a genteel 1930s hotel and
the staff incredibly friendly. Creative tapas and a
hearty menú del día are served in a relaxed front
room and luxurious gourmet meals in an adjoining
formal dining room.

Casa Ciriaco

C/Mayor 84 (91 548 06 20). Metro Ópera or Sol.
Open 1-4pm, 8.30pm-midnight Mon, Tue, Thur-Sun.
Closed Aug. **Main courses** €14.50-€20.50. **Set
lunch** €20 Mon, Tue, Thur, Fri. **Credit** DC, MC,
V. **Map** p327 E12 ❸
Pick your way down the side of the open kitchen to
a deep dining room hung with pictures of visiting
royals and grateful celebrities, along with rather
grimmer photos of the 1906 bombing of Alfonso

XIII's wedding procession – which happened right
outside the door. Undamaged, and still going strong,
Casa Ciriaco was a meeting place for the intelligentsia in pre-Civil War days, and although it no
longer attracts too many thinkers, the Castilian fare
is a taste of days gone by. Cochinillo (suckling pig)
is the speciality, along with partridge and butter
beans, when in season. Waiters are as old-school as
you'd expect, but very friendly.

Casa Lucio

C/Cava Baja 35 (91 365 32 52/www.casalucio.es).
Metro La Latina. **Open** 1-4pm, 9pm-midnight
Mon-Fri, Sun; 9pm-midnight Sat. Closed Aug.
Main courses €18-€25. **Credit** AmEx, DC,
MC, V. **Map** p327 F13 ❹
A restaurant unsurpassed by any other in Madrid
for its famous patrons: King Juan Carlos, Bill Clinton
and Penélope Cruz among them. This is the place of
historical rendezvous, where Aznar and Bush's
wives did lunch back when alliances were in the
making. It also knows how to cook up one cracking
solomillo (beef). The key to Lucio's glory is the use
of a coal-fired oven and the best olive oil. Another
star dish is a starter of lightly fried eggs laid on top
of a bed of crisp, thinly cut chips. Be sure to ask for
a table on the first floor.

Casa Marta

C/Santa Clara 10 (91 548 28 25/www.restaurante
casamarta.com). Metro Ópera. **Open** 1.30-4pm Mon;
1.30-4pm, 9pm-midnight Tue-Sat. Closed Aug. **Main
courses** €9-€14. **Set lunch** €10 Mon-Fri. **Credit**
AmEx, DC, MC, V. **Map** p327 F11 ❺
Every Saturday, according to the novel, Don Quixote
ate duelos y quebrantos (scrambled eggs, ham, bacon,
chorizo and brains) and you can still try them at
Casa Marta – although they usually leave out the
brains these days. A quaint old place, it's been a
favourite since the beginning of the 20th century,
when opera-goers and singers would stop in for a
tipple after performances. The satisfying platos de
cuchara ('spoon food') – warming bowls of cocido,
beans and lentils – are another star turn that always
pulls in the crowds.

Julián de Tolosa

C/Cava Baja 18 (91 365 82 10). Metro La Latina.
Open 1.30-4pm, 9pm-midnight Mon-Sat; 1.30-4pm
Sun. **Main courses** €20-€30. **Credit** AmEx, DC,
MC, V. **Map** p327 F13 **6**
Probably the most modern in the *barrio*, this upscale
Basque restaurant is all smooth wood, glass and
brick, housed in a 19th-century building. With a very
limited, simple menu, the main attraction here is the
grilled steak (*chuletón de buey*), a contender for the
city's best. Try the idiazábal cheese, a speciality
from the little Basque town of the same name. The
maître d' will steer you through an excellent selection of more than 100 wines.

La Musa Latina

*Costanilla San Andrés 12 (91 354 02 55/www.
lamusalatina.com). Metro La Latina.* **Open** 2-5pm,
8.30pm-midnight Mon-Thur, Sun; 2-5pm, 8.30pm-
1am Fri, Sat. **Main courses** €7.50-€12. **Set
lunch** €7.50-€10 Mon-Fri. **Credit** MC, DC, V.
Map p327 E13 **7**
After an enforced closure thanks to some overzeal-
ous licence-enforcing by the council, La Musa Latina
is open once more. The menu has lost a few
favourites, such as the selection of tapas, but there's
still plenty here to enjoy. The mixed grill and the
roasted vegetables make a great combination, plus
there are plenty of indulgent desserts to choose from
– go for the chocolate brownie. Waiters are super-
cool but friendly, and the diners are a mixture of the
well-heeled and the clubby crowd. Given the choice
between this and the sister restaurant in Malasaña,
go for this one – it's roomier.

El Sobrino de Botín

*C/Cuchilleros 17 (91 366 42 17/91 366 30 26/www.
botin.es). Metro Sol.* **Open** 1-4pm, 8pm-midnight
daily. **Main courses** €10-€22. **Set meal** €34.80.
Credit AmEx, DC, MC, V. **Map** p327 F12 **8**
The world's oldest restaurant (with a signed Norris
McWhirter certificate to prove it) is still coming up
with the goods after nearly 300 years. For all its popularity as a tourist destination, its nooks and cran-
nies add up to an atmospheric – if cramped – dining
spot. Botín turns out great roasts, including that old
Spanish favourite: *cochinillo* (suckling pig). The
cordero (lamb) is also superb, as are the *almejas*
(clams) *Botín*. And, yes, seeing as you asked,
Hemingway did come here.

La Taberna del Alabardero

*C/Felipe V 6 (91 541 51 92/www.grupolezama.es).
Metro Ópera.* **Open** 1-4pm, 9pm-midnight daily.
Main courses €18-€25. **Set lunch** €32.10 daily.
Credit AmEx, DC, MC, V. **Map** p327 F11 **9**
Father Lezama first started up his traditional tavern in 1974, when he put underprivileged boys to
work as waiters in this converted 16th-century townhouse. With a quiet *terraza* on the street that runs
along the north side of the Teatro Real, it is still one
of the most popular post-theatre dining spots, serving traditional tapas at the bar and Basque cuisine
in the restaurant at the back. Lezama is no longer a

priest but a very prosperous restaurateur – he has
opened six more restaurants throughout Spain and
one in Washington, DC. Some of those original boys
are now shareholders in the Alabardero Company.

Taberna Salamanca

*C/Cava Baja 31 (91 366 31 10/mobile 605 181
862). Metro La Latina.* **Open** 8.30pm-midnight
Tue, Wed; 1-4pm, 8.30pm-midnight Thur; 1-4pm,
8.30pm-1am Fri, Sat; 1-6pm Sun. Closed mid July-
mid Aug. **Main courses** €9-€15. **Set lunch** €9.50
Tue-Sun. **No credit cards. Map** p327 F13 **10**
On a street crammed with high-priced eateries, this
is where the cool, young, and more frugal set comes
to eat. There are three lunch *menús* to choose from,
offering the usual Spanish pickings – the *croquetas*,
courgette tortilla and endives with roquefort cheese
are all pretty dependable. The staff are friendly and
young, with a tendency to whack up the stereo.

El Viajero

*Plaza de la Cebada 11 (91 366 90 64). Metro
La Latina.* **Open** 1.30-4pm, 9pm-12.30am Tue-Sat;
2-4.30pm Sun. Closed 3wks Jan & last 3wks Aug.
Main courses €9-€12. **Set lunch** €11.50 Tue-Fri.
Credit AmEx, DC, MC, V. **Map** p327 F13 **11**
La Latina scenesters in sideburns and retro couture
still flock to this three-storey bar/restaurant famous
for its rooftop *terraza*. The food, a mixed array of
Mediterranean dishes and barbecued meats, is delicious, if a little overpriced. The carpaccios are melt-
in-the-mouth and the pastas, particularly the *taglioni
marinera*, drip with flavour. Discriminating carni-
vores love El Viajero for the high-quality, hormone-
free Argentine meat, while sweet-tooths rejoice over
the scrumptious tiramisu. **Photo** *p140.*

La Viuda Blanca

C/Campomanes 6 (91 548 75 29). Metro Ópera.
Open 1.30-4.30pm, 9.30pm-midnight Mon-Sat; 1.30-
4.30pm Sun. Closed 2wks Aug. **Main courses** €14-
€18. **Set lunch** €11.50 Mon-Fri. **Credit** AmEx, DC,
MC, V. **Map** p327 F11 **12**
Once you're past the hulking doorman and your eyes
have adjusted to the dazzling glamour, this trendoid
club-restaurant is surprisingly welcoming. The waiters are divine and disarmingly friendly, and the food
(particularly the set lunch) is excellent value. Lamb
stew with cardamom and mashed new potatoes
deserve a special mention, as does the turbot chop
suey with lemon butter. At night a DJ takes to the
decks, while the daytime charms include a sunny,
plant-filled atrium.

Viuda de Vacas

C/Cava Alta 23 (91 366 58 47). Metro La Latina.
Open 1.30-4.30pm, 9pm-midnight Mon-Wed, Fri,
Sat; 1.30-4.30pm Sun. Closed 1st 2wks Sept. **Main
courses** €9-€16. **Credit** MC, V. **Map** p327 F13 **13**
Walking through the old red linen curtains that
frame the entrance of Viuda de Vacas is rather
like entering a Spanish movie set; in fact, Pedro
Almodóvar has filmed here on several occasions,
and just admiring the chipped tile and refectory

Eat, Drink, Shop

Firm favourite of the in crowd, **El Viajero**. *See p139.*

table interior, you can see why. This classic in good Castilian home cooking has been in the Canova family for three generations; it was established long ago by the feisty grandmother (the widow of Señor Vacas, hence the restaurant's odd bovine name). Favourite dishes include the stuffed courgettes and the baked hake or sea bream. At the time of writing there was talk of an imminent refurbishment. More's the pity, some might say.

Xentes

C/Humilladero 13 (91 366 42 66). Metro La Latina. **Open** 12.30pm-midnight Tue-Sat; 12.30pm-5pm Sun. Closed Aug. **Main courses** €8-€25. **Credit** AmEx, DC, MC, V. **Map** p327 F14

With the TV blaring and some half-hearted nautical decor, this is a rather strange setting for some of the best seafood in Madrid. But the Galician patrons at the bar happily scarf oysters and beer, and the diners in the back are just as delighted with their *pulpo a gallega* (octopus with paprika) and *arroz con bogavantes* (lobster paella). Sample the Galician *tetilla* cheese and wash it down with the lovely light Albariño house wine.

International

Emma y Júlia

C/Cava Baja 19 (91 366 10 23). Metro La Latina. **Open** 9pm-midnight Tue; 2-4pm, 9pm-midnight Wed-Thur; 2-4pm, 9pm-1am Fri, Sat. Closed July. **Main courses** €9.50-€13. **Credit** AmEx, DC, MC, V. **Map** p327 F13

Smack in the middle of a street known as the epicentre of stout *cocido*-type cuisine is this incongruous and popular Italian eaterie – a sound alternative when a big salad and pizza are in order. The staff are friendly, the environment laid-back, and the food solid. The breaded artichokes are divine and the house red is good and cheap. It's often wise to reserve in advance.

Marechiaro

C/Conde de Lemos 3 (91 547 00 42). Metro Ópera. **Open** 9pm-midnight Mon; 2-4pm, 9pm-midnight Tue-Sat. Closed 2wks Aug. **Main courses** €10-€15. **Credit** AmEx, DC, MC, V. **Map** p327 F11

You know a pizzeria is worth its salt when it attracts this many Italians. Two Neapolitans are behind this modest little place that offers some of the best pizzas in the city. Cooked in wood-fired ovens, they have thin, flavourful crusts and fresh ingredients. Pastas are good too, but they definitely play second fiddle. Decor is pungent-orange walls sporting a mix of Venetian masks and old photos of Maradona.

Vegetarian

El Estragón

Costanilla de San Andrés 10 (91 365 89 82). Metro La Latina. **Open** 1.30-4pm, 8.30-11.30pm daily. **Main courses** €11-€13.50. **Set lunch** €10 Mon-Fri. **Credit** AmEx, DC, MC, V. **Map** p327 E13

El Estragón's underlying concept appears to be 'vegetarian food for meat-eaters', and thus there is no shortage of soya 'meatballs', 'hamburgers' and so on. Where this place really excels, however, is in its straightforward vegetarian dishes, such as a fabulous towering heap of *risotto verde* containing every green vegetable you can think of, topped with stringy emmental. It is also a delightful place to sit and dream, with its terracotta tiles, perky blue-and-white gingham and view over Plaza de la Paja. Should contemplation pale, there is free net access.

Sol & Gran Vía

La Bola Taberna

C/Bola 5 (91 547 69 30). Metro Ópera or Santo Domingo. **Open** 1-4pm, 8.30-11.30pm Mon-Sat; 1-4pm Sun. Closed Aug. **Main courses** €12-€13. **Set meal** €24. **Credit** MC, V. **Map** p323 F11

Eat, Drink, Shop

Holding court on a quiet backstreet, this dignified, classic Madrid restaurant is considered by many to be the home of *cocido*, the huge and hearty stew beloved of *madrileños* and a test for the biggest of appetites. La Bola is still run by the same family that founded it in the 19th century, and the *cocido* (which is only served at lunchtime) is still cooked traditionally in earthenware pots on a wood fire. Unfortunately, this impressive pedigree has led to a certain complacency, verging on the arrogant, in some of the waiting staff.

Don Paco

C/Caballero de Gracia 36 (91 531 44 80). Metro Gran Vía. **Open** 1.30-4.30pm Mon, Sat. 1.30-4.30pm, 8.30-11.30pm Tue-Fri. Closed Aug. **Main courses** €10.50-€12. **Set lunch** €30 Mon-Sat. **Set dinner** €35 Tue-Fri. **Credit** MC, V. **Map** p324 I11 **⓳**

Don Paco, now in his 80s, is a former bullfighter from Jérez, and the Andalucian matador in him is charmingly apparent in his 45-year-old restaurant. With photos of famous visitors (the King and his parents were regulars, and Bob Hope ate here too) and Andalucian memorabilia covering the walls, it oozes southern style. *Tinto de verano* ('summer wine' cut with lemonade) on tap, ample sherry options… who needs Seville? Dishes can be variable, and this is more about atmosphere.

La Gloria de Montero

C/Caballero de Gracia 10 (91 521 67 01). Metro Gran Vía. **Open** 1.15-4pm, 8.30-11.45pm Mon-Sat. **Main courses** €6-€9.50. **Credit** AmEx, MC, V. **Map** p324 H11 **⓴**

The philosophy behind this wildly popular chain of restaurants involves swish, elegant surroundings, a sophisticated menu and dirt-cheap pricing. And yes, it's all that. What are less palatable are the dour, inexperienced waitresses and the production-line cooking. This doesn't matter so much with starters like rocket and feta salad, or puddings like fruit carpaccio with soured yoghurt, and strawberry tiramisu with cocoa ice-cream, but it does begin to grate when your steak (wine reduction, wild mushrooms) has been spot-cooked in a microwave. **Other locations**: **Bazaar** C/Libertad 21, Chueca (91 523 15 05); **La Finca de Susana** C/Arlaban 4, Huertas & Santa Ana (91 429 76 78).

Gula Gula

Gran Vía 1 (91 522 87 64/www.gulagula.net). Metro Banco de España or Sevilla. **Open** 1-4.30pm, 9.30-11.30pm daily. **Lunch buffet** €7-€10.50. **Dinner buffet** €17.50-€23.40. **Credit** AmEx, DC, MC, V. **Map** p324 H11 **㉑**

Prepare yourself for muscled waiters in scant clothing, singing drag queens and bawdy humour – this is Gula Gula (Greedy Greedy). It's all about the show, darling, less about the food, but even that isn't half-bad. Most people skip the hot dishes (though they have shown some moments of inspiration lately) and stick to the all-you-can-eat salad buffet, which is fair to middling. But what's truly inspiring here are the tiny leather shorts worn by the waiters.

Suite

C/Virgen de los Peligros 4 (91 521 40 31/www.suitecafeclub.com). Metro Sevilla. **Open** 1.30-5pm, 9.30pm-3.30am Mon-Fri; 9.30pm-4.30am Sat. **Main courses** €10-€15. **Set lunch** €11. **Set dinner** €30. **Credit cards** AmEx, DC, MC, V. **Map** p328 H11 **㉒**

With a bar-lounge-restaurant downstairs and a housey dancefloor upstairs, Suite is the 'eat, drink and dance' hybrid for nights when you feel like staying in one place. Located in an anonymous office building near Puerta del Sol, this is sleek 1970s retro: Austin Powers meets Ibiza (back when it was good). The food is as stylish as the cool young *madrileños* who eat here – opt for the salmon marinated in coffee or the grilled duck magret.

La Terraza del Casino

C/Alcalá 15 (91 532 12 75/www.casinodemadrid.es). Metro Sevilla. **Open** 1.30-4.30pm, 9-11.30pm Mon-Fri; 9-11.30pm Sat. Closed Aug. **Main courses** €30-€33. **Credit** AmEx, V. **Map** p328 H11 **㉓**

The very staid environs of this gentlemen's club dining room (wear a tie) provide the unlikely setting for a restaurant inspired and partly overseen by superchef and molecular gastronomist Ferran Adrià. Diners, for the most part, look utterly nonplussed by dishes such as 'Dragon Oil' – balls of texturised olive oil partly frozen in clouds of liquid nitrogen at the table, into which the diner bites, emitting smoke from the nose. These theatrical culinary events and the beauty of dishes such as the tiny filo 'ice-cream cone' of trout roe, quail's yolk and wasabi do not detract, however, from the flavours, which are out of this world. *See also p145* **Ringing in the new**.

International

Caripén

Plaza de la Marina Española 4 (91 541 11 77). Metro Santo Domingo. **Open** 9pm-3am Mon-Sat. Closed Aug. **Main courses** €12-€35. **Credit** DC, MC, V. **Map** p323 E11 **㉔**

At first glance, this French bistro seems a wee bit run down, but nonetheless it's all class – in a campy, Broadway kind of way. Behind the dangling blue Christmas-tree lights are tables occupied by singing, dancing, canoodling patrons having a very good time, oblivious to the excellent skate in black butter or crêpe with salmon and caviar. The merry atmosphere owes a lot to the staff, particularly Juanjo, who floats through the restaurant spreading his charm like a host(ess) well versed in the art of entertainment. The late opening hours are another bonus.

Delfos

Cuesta de Santo Domingo 14 (91 548 37 64). Metro Santo Domingo. **Open** 1.30-4.30pm, 8pm-12.30am Tue-Sat; 1.30-4.30pm Sun. **Main courses** €10-€18. **Set lunch** €9.95 Tue-Fri. **Credit** AmEx, DC, MC, V. **Map** p323 F11 **㉕**

Delfos is here to prove that Greek food is not all kebabs and salads. In taverna-style surroundings, with just-on-the-right-side-of-tack Greek details –

Eat, Drink, Shop

statues and strings of blue-and-white flags – friendly waiters serve up an unexpected variety of dishes. A good start is the *pikilia megali*, a platter of garlicky Greek olives, rich fried feta cheese, refreshing tsatsiki, lemony taramasalata, stuffed vine leaves and more. The moussaka and lamb with nut and honey are also scrumptious. If you dare, try the retsina.

Kawara

C/Aduana 23 (91 532 89 03). Metro Sol. **Open** 1.30-4pm, 8.30-11.30pm Mon-Sat. **Main courses** €8-€14. **Set lunch** €12.50 Mon-Fri. **Credit** MC, V. **Map** p328 H11 ㉖

If you prefer your Japanese food without the monochrome designer minimalist look that usually accompanies it, then this is your place. Hidden on a backstreet behind the Puerta del Sol, Kawara is a sashimi in the rough. Trust the tell-tale sign of authenticity (the patrons silently reading Japanese newspapers over their soup) and order the reasonably priced sushi tray: it comes with miso, followed by eight pieces of sushi and a large maki roll. Apart from that, there is a wide range of sashimi, noodle and meat dishes. Ask for tea, which will be replenished throughout your meal by Akiko, the sweet lady who runs the place.

Menu glossary

Eat, Drink, Shop

Basics

Primer plato (**entrante**) first course; **segundo plato** second or main course; **postre** dessert; **plato combinado** quick, one-course meal, with several ingredients served on the same plate; **aceite y vinagre** oil and vinegar; **agua** water (**con gas/sin gas** fizzy/still); **pan** bread; **vino** wine (**tinto** red, **blanco** white, **rosado** rosé); **cerveza** beer; **la cuenta** the bill; **servicio incluído** service included; **propina** tip.

Cooking styles & techniques

Adobado marinated; **al ajillo** with olive oil and garlic; **al chilindrón** (usually chicken or lamb) cooked in a spicy tomato, pepper, ham, onion and garlic sauce; **a la marinera** (fish or shellfish) cooked with garlic, onions and white wine; **a la parilla** charcoal-grilled; **al pil-pil** (Basque) flash-fried in sizzling oil and garlic; **a la plancha** grilled directly on a hot metal plate; **al vapor** steamed; **asado** (**al horno de leña**) roast (in a wood oven); **crudo** raw; **en salsa** in a sauce or gravy; **escabechado**, **en escabeche** marinated in vinegar with bay leaves and garlic; **estofado** braised; **frito** fried; **guisado** stewed; **hervido** boiled; **(en) pepitoria** casserole dish, usually of chicken or game, with egg, wine and almonds; **relleno** stuffed.

Huevos (eggs)

Huevos fritos fried eggs (sometimes served with chorizo); **revuelto** scrambled eggs; **tortilla asturiana** omelette with tomato, tuna and onion; **tortilla francesa** plain omelette; **tortilla de patatas** Spanish potato omelette.

Sopas y potajes (soups & stews)

Caldo (**gallego**) broth of pork and greens; **fabada** rich Asturian stew of beans, chorizo and *morcilla* (black blood sausage); **gazpacho** cold soup, usually of tomatoes, red pepper and cucumber; **purrusalda** (Basque) soup of salt cod, leeks and potatoes; **sopa de ajo** garlic soup; **sopa castellana** garlic soup with poached egg and chickpeas; **sopa de fideos** noodle soup.

Pescado y mariscos (fish & shellfish)

Almejas clams; **atún**, **bonito** tuna; **bacalao** salt cod; **besugo** sea bream; **bogavante** lobster; **caballa** mackerel; **calamares** squid; **camarones** small shrimps; **cangrejo**, **buey de mar** crab; **cangrejo de río** freshwater crayfish; **dorada** gilthead bream; **gambas** prawns; **kokotxas** (Basque) hake cheeks; **langosta** spiny lobster; **langostinos** langoustines; **lubina** sea bass; **mejillones** mussels; **mero** grouper; **merluza** hake; **ostras** oysters; **pescadilla** whiting; **pescaditos** whitebait; **pulpo** octopus; **rape** monkfish; **rodaballo** turbot; **salmonete** red mullet; **sardinas** sardines; **sepia** cuttlefish; **trucha** trout; **ventresca de bonito** tuna fillet; **vieiras** scallops.

Pasta Nostra Pizza Nostra

Carrera de San Jerónimo 32 (91 360 08 27).
Metro Sevilla. **Open** 1.30-4.30pm, 8.30pm-midnight
Mon-Thur, Sun; 1.30-4.30pm, 8.30pm-1am Fri, Sat.
Main courses €11.50-€13.50. **Credit** AmEx, MC,
V. **Map** p328 I11 **㉗**
Who said you couldn't get great 'za in Madrid?
Pizzas at this unassuming Italian ristorante could
convince even the most discriminating of patrons.
Try the house special: the eponymous Pizza Nostra,
an insanely tasty mix of bresaola, rocket, mozzarella
and corn that keeps the locals coming back weekly.
The crust is light and the cheese not too heavy, so
even though the pizzas are the size of tractor tyres,
they can be gobbled easily by one person. There are
also ample pasta and salad choices.
Other locations: C/Jovellanos 5, Huertas & Santa
Ana (91 532 11 00); C/Fuencarral 116, Chamberí (91
593 01 13).

Taj

*C/Marqués de Cubas 6 (91 531 50 59). Metro Banco
de España.* **Open** 1-4pm, 8.30-11.30pm Mon-Thur;
1-4pm, 8.30pm-midnight Fri-Sun. **Main courses**
€7.50-€13.75. **Set lunch** €11.50 Mon-Fri. **Credit**
AmEx, DC, MC, V. **Map** p328 I11 **㉘**

Carne, aves, caza y embutidos (meat, poultry, game & charcuterie)

Bistec steak; **buey, vacuno** (cuts **solomillo, entrecot**) beef; **butifarra** Catalan sausage; **callos** tripe; **capón** capon; **cerdo** pork, pig; **chorizo** spicy sausage, served cooked or cold; **choto** kid; **chuletas, chuletones, chuletillas** chops; **cochinillo** roast suckling pig; **cocido** traditional stew of Madrid; **codillo** knuckle (normally ham); **codornices** quails; **conejo** rabbit; **cordero** lamb; **costillas** ribs; **estofado de ternera** veal stew; **faisán** pheasant; **gallina** chicken; **hígado** liver; **jabalí** wild boar; **jamón ibérico** cured ham from Iberian pigs; **jamón serrano** cured ham; **jamón york** cooked ham; **lacón** gammon ham; **lechazo, cordero lechal** milk-fed baby lamb; **liebre** hare; **lomo (de cerdo)** loin of pork; **morcilla** black blood sausage; **pato** duck; **pavo** turkey; **perdiz** partridge; **pollo** chicken; **riñones** kidneys; **salchichas** frying sausages; **sesos** brains; **ternera** veal (in Spain it is slaughtered later than most veal, so is closer to beef).

Arroz y legumbres (rice & pulses)

Alubias, judías white beans; **arroz a banda** rice cooked in shellfish stock; **arroz negro** black rice cooked in squid ink; **fideuà** seafood dish similar to a paella, but made with noodles instead of rice; **fríjoles** red kidney beans; **garbanzos** chickpeas; **judiones** large haricot beans; **lentejas** lentils; **pochas (caparrones)** new-season kidney beans.

Verduras (vegetables)

Acelgas Swiss chard; **alcachofas** artichokes; **berenjena** aubergine/eggplant; **calabacines** courgettes/zucchini; **cebolla** onion; **champiñones** mushrooms; **col** cabbage; **ensalada mixta** basic salad of iceberg lettuce, tomato and onion; **ensalada verde** green salad, without tomato; **espárragos** asparagus; **espinacas** spinach; **grelos** turnip leaves; **guisantes** peas; **habas** broad beans; **judías verdes** green beans; **lechuga** lettuce; **menestra** braised mixed vegetables; **patatas fritas** chips; **pepino** cucumber; **pimientos** sweet peppers; **pimientos de piquillo** slightly hot red peppers; **pisto** mixture of cooked vegetables, similar to ratatouille; **setas** forest mushrooms; **tomate** tomato; **zanahoria** carrot.

Fruta (fruit)

Arándanos cranberries or blackcurrants; **cerezas** cherries; **ciruelas** plums; **fresas** strawberries; **higos** figs; **macedonia** fruit salad; **manzana** apple; **melocotón** peach; **melón** melon; **moras** blackberries; **naranja** orange; **pera** pear; **piña** pineapple; **plátano** banana; **sandía** watermelon; **uvas** grapes.

Postres (desserts)

Arroz con leche rice pudding; **bizcocho** sponge cake; **brazo de gitano** swiss roll; **cuajada** junket (served with honey); **flan** crème caramel; **helado** ice-cream; **leche frita** custard fried in breadcrumbs; **membrillo** quince jelly (often served with cheese); **tarta** cake; **tarta de Santiago** sponge-like almond cake; **torrijas** sweet bread fritters.

Quesos (cheeses)

Burgos, villalón, requesón white, cottage-like cheeses, often eaten as dessert; **cabrales** strong blue Asturian goat's cheese; **idiazábal** Basque sheep's milk cheese; **mahón** mild cow's milk cheese from Menorca; **manchego** (**tierno, añejo, semi, seco**) hard sheep's-milk cheese (young, mature, semi-soft, dry); **tetilla** soft cow's milk cheese; **torta del casar** tangy sheep's milk cheese from Extremadura.

Eat, Drink, Shop

Olsen's subterranean vodka bar. *See p147.*

Everything about Taj promises serious curry – from the jingly-jangly muzak to the fanned linen napkins and plastic flowers. The menu includes all the usuals, but the *degustación* of samosa, pakora, tandoori chicken, lamb curry, pilau and naan is a good bet. Try to get the curries *picante* (hot), though the waiters may decide that that can't be what you really mean and give you *medio* anyway. Desserts are a bit limited and the decor slightly naff, which is curiously reassuring.

Huertas & Santa Ana

El Cenador del Prado

C/Prado 4 (91 429 15 61). Metro Antón Martín.
Open 1.30-4pm, 9pm-midnight Mon-Fri; 9pm-midnight Sat; 1.30-4pm Sun. **Main courses** €12.50-€17.75. **Set meal** €22.50 Mon-Thur; lunch Fri, Sat. **Credit** AmEx, DC, MC, V. **Map** p328 H12 **㉙**
Don't let the design extravagance – fuschia walls, explosive murals of fruit and gilt mirrors – distract you from the Herranz brothers' culinary talents: tasty Spanish cuisine with imaginative twists. Several decadent *menús de degustación*, one for vegetarians, offer good value. The *patatas a la importancia* (fried in garlic, parsley and clam sauce) are superlative, and the wine list is good and well priced. Don't miss desserts; try the pear with wine sauce and blue-cheese ice-cream. Dishes are artistically prepared and some are veritable sculptures.

Champagneria Gala

C/Moratín 22 (91 429 25 62/www.paellas-gala.com). Metro Antón Martín. **Open** 1-3.30pm, 9-11.30pm Mon-Thur; 1.30-4pm, 9pm-midnight Fri-Sun. **Main courses** €13. **No credit cards. Map** p328 I13 **㉚**
This garden atrium, dripping in ivy and gaudy chandeliers, is a festive place to stick your fork in one of 28 varieties of paella. But it's the *porrón* – a long-spouted jug from which you pour a stream of wine down your throat – that makes this really fun: everyone must try their turn at this subtle art. The Champagneria Gala has ever so slightly become a victim of its own success, however, and the quality of the food has diminished in recent years as the number of tourists has grown – there have been numerous tales of over-salty paella and under-friendly service.

La Cueva de Gata

C/Moratín 19 (91 360 09 43). Metro Antón Martín. **Open** 11.30am-4.30pm, 7.30pm-midnight Mon-Sat. Closed 2wks Aug. **Main courses** €11.50-€20. **Set lunch** €12. **Credit** AmEx, DC, MC, V. **Map** p328 I13 **㉛**
Buttercup-yellow walls and tablecloths set off a constantly changing selection of bright oil paintings (all for sale), while downstairs there's a cave-like basement with a handful of tables that might be better for groups. Eating à la carte is still good value, but the set lunch has gone up a notch in price, though is still reasonable – it might include celery and apple soup to start, chicken with capers and cherry tomatoes, and a baked apple to finish. Other nice touches include the jug of iced water automatically placed on the table, soft Brazilian jazz and gentle lighting.

Lhardy

Carrera de San Jerónimo 8 (91 521 33 85/ www.lhardy.com). Metro Sol. **Open** 1-3.30pm, 8.30-11pm Mon-Sat; 1-3.30pm Sun. Closed Aug. **Main courses** €24-€40. **Credit** AmEx, DC, MC, V. **Map** p327 H11 **㉜**
This landmark restaurant, which opened in 1839, is credited with having introduced French haute cuisine into the culinary wilderness of Madrid. Founder Emile Lhardy is said to have been enticed to the city by none other than *Carmen* author Prosper Mérimée, who told him there was no decent restaurant in the Spanish capital. These days it's rated as much for its history and belle-époque decor as for the (expensive) food. The menu is as Frenchified as ever, although there's also a very refined *cocido*, good game and *callos* (tripe), in addition to an excellent, if pricey, wine list.

La Vaca Verónica

C/Moratín 38 (91 429 78 27/www.lavaca veronica.es). Metro Antón Martín. **Open** 2-4pm, 9pm-midnight Mon-Fri, Sun; 9pm-midnight Sat. **Main courses** €15.50-€18. **Set lunch** €15 Mon-Fri. **Credit** AmEx, DC, MC, V. **Map** p328 J13 **㉝**
With canary-yellow walls, puffed-up banquettes, bright paintings and a certain Gallic charm, Veronica the Cow is a whimsical reprieve from the

Ringing in the new

When Jake and Brett are about to part ways in Madrid, at the end of Hemingway's *The Sun Also Rises*, what do they do? Go eat suckling pig and drink three bottles of Rioja at the world's oldest restaurant, **El Sobrino de Botín** (*see p139*), more commonly known as Botín. Back in the late 19th century, when King Alfonso XII's sister needed a break from the palace, she would wander over to **La Bola Taberna** (*see p140*) to get a bowl full of her favourite dish – a gutsy *cocido madrileño*. Every Saturday Don Quixote would tuck into a plate of *duelos y quebrantes* – a mess of scrambled eggs, ham, chorizo, brains and tripe – at **Casa Marta** (*see p137*).

Cocido, suckling pig and offal. This is Madrid's culinary history and, happily, her culinary present. The pig and Rioja at Botín are still great, despite the crowds of tourists and the demise of Lady Brett and Jake. The *cocido* is still eaten regularly at La Bola, though the Infanta has long gone. And Antonio Roiloa, the owner of Casa Marta, is still proud to serve Quixote's Saturday dish, though he often takes the brains out to appease more delicate tastebuds. These heavy dishes are as much Madrid as the Prado and Plaza Mayor.

So what does Madrid's ardent traditionalism mean for *nueva cocina*, the new wave of experimental cooking blowing over this way from the Catalan coast? Spearheaded by Catalan culinary legend Ferran Adrià, *nueva cocina* is renowned for its fantastical repertoire of edible foams, air and hot jellies, improbable pairings of flavour, and twists of texture and temperature. Can this surrealist revolution of food as we know it make any sense in a city in which the hearty stew reigns supreme?

Paco Roncero, a *madrileño* and one of Spain's finest chefs, thinks so. Roncero, the man behind the Michelin-starred **La Terraza del Casino** (*see p141*), finds himself in the challenging position of ambassador for *nueva cocina* in the capital. Adrià actually oversees the restaurant, with himself and Roncero working in tandem to concoct whimsical creations like a 'lollipop' parmesan wafer, and barnacles in aspic with tea.

Things were slow to take off and Madrid was reluctant to embrace these Catalan culinary imports. But Roncero is seeing an attitude shift: *madrileños* are showing

curiosity, he says, and they come to the restaurant already knowing about the famous foams and strange textures and wanting to journey through the *menú de degustación* – an array of the team's best inventions.

One of Roncero's specialities lies in reinventing the traditional dishes. Take his *croquetas de jamón* (ham croquettes) – quivering globes of exquisitely tasty liquified ham, coated in fine breadcrumbs, that explode in the mouth. *Madrileños* love them. They're not so much croquettes as the essence of them, in much the same way that Miró isn't exactly painting a bird, but its essence. The *cocido*, however, remains untouched: he explains, speaking with quiet reverence, that it is one dish he is not quite ready to take on. 'That one is still too difficult,' he says, 'but maybe in the future.'

'We must always have respect for our traditional cooking,' insists Roncero. 'Leaving it behind is like leaving behind a part of who we are. But that doesn't mean we can't have fun with new things.

bustling streets of Huertas. Attracting business types and hipsters alike, it's a fine choice for a quality *menú del día*. Pesto pasta, the abundant 'cow's tray' of chorizo, *morcilla* (black blood sausage) and other meats, and various salads are just some of the tasty options on offer.

International

Come Prima

C/Echegaray 27 (91 420 30 42). Metro Antón Martín. **Open** 9pm-midnight Mon; 1.30-4pm, 9pm-midnight Tue-Sat. Closed 2wks Aug. **Main courses** €12-€17. **Set lunch** €15 Tue-Fri. **Credit** AmEx, DC, MC, V. **Map** p328 H12 ③④

The toothsome risottos and own-made pastas here are a godsend for Italian gastronomes. Don't miss the risotto with mushrooms, parmesan and white-truffle oil, or the perfectly executed pasta with lobster. Since it opened a few years ago, Come Prima has brought in a classy crew of Spaniards (including, rumour has it, Prince Felipe), who pack the place out every night, even on a Monday. With white curtains and tablecloths, green wood-panelled walls and Italian opera posters, you could almost be in the Tuscan countryside.

Pizzeria Cervantes

C/León 8 (91 420 12 98). Metro Antón Martín. **Open** 1.30-4.30pm, 8.30-12.30pm Mon-Thur, Sun; 8.30pm-12.30am Tue; 1.30-4.30pm, 8.30pm-1.30am Fri, Sat. Closed 2wks July. **Main courses** €8.50-€10. **Set lunch** €10 Mon-Fri. **Credit** AmEx, DC, MC, V. **Map** p328 I12 ③⑤

This unassuming little hideaway doesn't shut down the kitchen during the day, so when most restaurants are sweeping the streets, you can take refuge in its tasty pizzas and pastas (the Chicana pizza with jalapeños is especially loved by fans of spicy hot food). Despite the name, this place exceeds the definition of pizzeria, with a long list of salads, crêpes, risottos and standard fare such as roast beef and *solomillo*. The neighbourhood regulars are fans of the cheap breakfast deal and love to linger over *café con leche* and the papers.

Olsen

C/Prado 15 (91 429 36 59/www.olsenmadrid.com). Metro Antón Martín or Sevilla. **Open** 1-4pm, 8pm-midnight Mon-Thur, Sun; 8pm-12.30am Fri, Sat. **Main courses** €14-€17. **Set lunch** €10 or €15 Mon-Fri. **Credit** AmEx, MC, DC, V. Map p328 I12 ③⑥

A hugely successful new Scandinavian-flavoured restaurant and basement vodka bar, all moulded beech and curiously hip snow scenes, and serving some of the freshest food ideas around. Especially good are the hot corn blinis served with dishes of caviar, sour cream, smoked salmon and shredded wild trout, while the selection of Nordic canapés paired with shots of various vodkas comes a close second. Bread is also excellent, and comes in the shape of five types of own-made bagel, speared like quoits on a pin. **Photo** *p144*.

Le Petit Bistrot

Plaza Matute 5 (91 429 62 65/www.lepetitbistrot. net). Metro Antón Martín. **Open** 1.15-3.45pm, 9.15-11.45pm Tue-Sat; 11.30-2.30pm Sun. **Main courses** €14-€20. **Set lunch** €12.50 Mon-Fri; €16.50 Sat, Sun. **Credit** AmEx, MC, V. **Map** p328 H12/13 ③⑦

A cosy little corner of traditional France, with bare-bricked walls, yellow paintwork and a roll-call of dishes that verges on the parodic: deep-fried brie; garlicky snails, cod brandade, coquilles St Jacques, Châteaubriand and so on. The Gallic desserts do not disappoint either, and this may the only place to get decent tarte tatin or profiteroles in the city. On Sundays the vibe is a lazy one, for a protracted brunch involving Viennese pastries, eggs, hot chocolate and *Le Monde*.

Other locations: C/Ponzano 60, Chamberí (91 399 04 51).

Vegetarian

Artemisa

C/Ventura de la Vega 4 (91 429 50 92). Metro Sevilla. **Open** 1.30-4pm, 9pm-midnight daily. **Main courses** €7.50-€20. **Set lunch** €10.50 Mon-Fri. **Credit** AmEx, DC, MC, V. **Map** p328 H/I12 ③⑧

With the nondescript decor so typical of Madrid's vegetarian restaurants, Artemisa might seem no different from the rest. But the salads are bigger and more creative, and the soy burgers have more flavour. The satisfying *menú de degustación* lets you try it all: veggie paella, *croquetas*, aubergine salad and more. They also have a few non-veggie options: try the chicken Armagnac made with organic free-range chicken – absolutely scrumptious.

Other locations: C/Tres Cruces 4, Sol & Gran Vía (91 521 87 21).

Lavapiés

Casa Lastra Sidrería

C/Olivar 3 (91 369 08 37/www.casalastra.com). Metro Antón Martín. **Open** 1.30-4pm, 8pm-midnight Mon, Tue, Thur-Sat; 1.30-4pm Sun. Closed July. **Main courses** €12-€17.50. **Set lunch** €12.50 Mon-Fri. **Credit** AmEx, DC, MC, V. **Map** p327 H13 ③⑨

Asturian food is now gaining international acclaim, but the regulars at Casa Lastra have known how good it is for a long time. Always packed with happy locals munching *cabrales* (a strong Asturian blue cheese) and *pote asturiano* (a stew with cabbage, haricot beans, black pudding, chorizo and potato) at the bar, or dining on *perdiz* (partridge) and *merluza a la sidra* (hake in cider) at the back, this is the place to come to sample good home cooking – and, of course, wash it down with a glass of traditional still cider.

Freiduría de Gallinejas

C/Embajadores 84 (91 517 59 33). Metro Embajadores. **Open** 11am-11pm Mon-Sat. Closed 3wks Aug. **Main courses** €6-€7. **No credit cards.** Map p327 H16 ④⓪

Eat, Drink, Shop

Still going strong after a century, this is the best place in the city for deep-fried lamb intestines and other tasty titbits. Not for faint stomachs, this offal institution offers superbly prepared testicles, glands and stomach linings, all accompanied by strong red wine. Worth checking out just for the lively scene and for a taste of Old Madrid's innard circle.

Restaurante Soidemersol

C/Argumosa 9 (91 539 73 71). Metro Atocha or Lavapiés. **Open** 1-5pm, 8pm-midnight Tue-Sun. **Main courses** €5-€10. **Set lunch** €8 Mon-Thur, €10 Fri-Sun. **Credit** AmEx, DC, MC, V. **Map** p328 H14 **⑪**

Also confusingly known as El Económico and Los Remedios (turn it backwards to see why), the Soidemersol is something of an institution. In recent years, the premises have had a bit of a facelift, but it retains a friendly neighbourhood feel, along with the wooden furniture and original tiling. Try the seafood risotto, calf's liver and onions, or beef ragoût with vegetables. There are tables outside in summer.

Tutti-Plen

C/Buenavista 18 (91 467 46 90). Metro Antón Martín. **Open** 1.30-4pm, 8.30pm-midnight Tue-Sat; 1.30-4.30pm Sun. **Main courses** €5.50-€8. **Set menu** €8. **Credit** AmEx, DC, MC, V. **Map** p328 I14 **⑫**

Tutti-Plen's menu says: 'This isn't fast food; take your time and enjoy the atmosphere.' And it's best to heed this comment – dishes can take a while to arrive. When this funky restaurant opened a few years back, its 'so-laid-back-we're-horizontal'

Café Oliver. *See p149.*

approach promised to make it a short-term venture, but it has proved a hit with the arty Lavapiés crowd. The very reasonably priced menu includes several vast salads and excellent crêpes, as well as the more upmarket salmon tartare and *lomo de buey* (steak), followed by wicked puddings.

International

Baisakhi

C/Lavapiés 42 (91 521 80 31). Metro Lavapiés. **Open** 12.30pm-4pm, 8pm-midnight daily. **Main courses** €7-€9. **Credit** MC, V. **Map** p328 H14 **⑬**

For good-value Indian food, Baisakhi is probably the best bet along what has become Madrid's answer to Brick Lane. The waiters all speak English, and the dishes on the menu include the old favourites, helpfully named in English. If you like a bit of poke in your curry, then be sure to ask for a spicier version of your chosen dish, as Spaniards don't generally like their food hot. This is the perfect place for a summer's evening, as the terrace is infinitely preferable to the slightly shabby interior.

Shapla

C/Lavapiés 42 (91 528 15 99). Metro Lavapiés. **Open** 10am-1.30am daily. Closed Sept. **Main courses** €5-€7. **Set meal** €7.25. **Credit** MC, V. **Map** p328 H14 **⑭**

The restaurant formerly known as Casa Juanito decided to change its name. Pity – the contrast of bog-standard Spanish caff on the outside and the almost exclusively male clientele from India and Pakistan somehow added to its charm. And even though they've attempted to upscale (witness the arrival of the ubiquitous pink tablecloth), this is still the greasy spoon of Indian eating in Madrid. Expect the usual suspects, many of them veggie – at really low prices.

Chueca

El 26 de Libertad

C/Libertad 26 (91 522 25 22). Metro Chueca. **Open** 1-4pm Mon; 1-4pm, 8pm-midnight Tue-Thur; 1-4pm, 9pm-1am Fri, Sat. **Main courses** €9.40-€16.80. **Set lunch** €10-€13 Mon-Sat. **Credit** MC, V. **Map** p324 I10 **⑮**

With its deep colours and lavishly set tables, El 26 de Libertad is over-the-top elegance bordering on the camp. But not too fine to be fun, and a favourite in the *barrio* – the bar is often brimming with *caña* drinkers. The food is Spanish, but with a creative edge in the *morcilla* (black pudding), cannelloni and anchovies filled with spinach and pine nuts, for example, and food presentation is as lavish as the decor. At lunchtime only a simple *menú* is available, so book for dinner to put them through their paces.

El Armario

C/San Bartolomé 7 (91 532 83 77/www. elarmariorestaurante.com). Metro Chueca or Gran Vía. **Open** 1.30-4pm, 9pm-midnight daily.

A taste of old Havana at **Zara**. *See p152.*

Closed 3wks July. **Set lunch** €10 Mon-Sat; €12 Sun. **Set dinner** €30. **Credit** AmEx, DC, MC, V. **Map** p324 I10 ⊕

Aptly named 'The Closet', this restaurant in the heart of Chueca makes up for its diminutive size with generous portions. This is Mediterranean food with an edge; soups and salads are above the norm. The *menú del día* is a find, and might include cream of spinach soup to start, followed by some oriental chicken and a pud. It's always packed, so get there before the crowds, especially for lunch. Charming service is a real plus when eating at close quarters.

El Bierzo

C/Barbieri 16 (91 531 91 10). Metro Chueca. **Open** 1-4pm, 8-11.30pm Mon-Sat. **Main courses** €6-€9.50. **Set lunch** €9, €11, €12.50 Mon-Fri; **Set dinner** €17.90. Closed Aug. **Credit** MC, V. **Map** p324 I10 ⊕

El Bierzo is one of the best of Madrid's long-established *casas de comida* – honest, dependable neighbourhood joints where you can get a good *menú del día* at a reasonable price. It buzzes, particularly during lunch, with a loyal crowd feasting on simple dishes: roast chicken, seven types of tortilla and excellent *setas al ajillo* (wild mushrooms fried in garlic). Just a chat with the friendly owner, Miguel, is worth coming here for.

El Bogavante del Almirante

C/Almirante 11 (91 532 18 50). Metro Banco de España or Chueca. **Open** 2-4pm, 9pm-midnight Mon-Sat; 2-4pm Sun. Closed 2wks Aug. **Main course** €18-€20. **Credit** AmEx, DC, MC, V. **Map** p324 J10 ⊕

Almirante wins the award for most fanciful set design. Nestled in a cave-like basement, a ponderous lobster claw hangs from the ceiling, while black outlines of sea creatures swirl across shrimp-pink walls. The staff, clad in black, add to the scene, which feels more Manhattan than Madrid. Seafood is their forte. The fish specials are always excellent, but the *arroz con bogavante* (lobster paella) takes the prize. Almirante and its lobster have been attracting an international set since opening in 2000.

Café Oliver

C/Almirante 12 (91 521 73 79/www.cafeoliver.com). Metro Colón. **Open** 1.30-4pm, 9pm-midnight Mon-Thur; 1.30-4pm, 9pm-1am Fri, Sat; 11.30am-4pm Sun. **Main courses** €12-€15. **Set lunch** €13.90. **Credit** AmEx, DC, MC, V. **Map** p324 J10 ⊕

Still an in spot for the international crowd, Café Oliver runs the gamut of French, Spanish, Italian and Moroccan without falling into the dreaded (con)fusion trap. Highlights include the *bomba de chocolate*, definitely a candidate for top all-time pudding. The plush red velvet banquettes and large windows looking out on the street make Café Oliver an ideal place for Chueca people-watching. Ideal on a Sunday for American brunch: pancakes, eggs benedict, waffles, coffee and newspapers. The downstairs cocktail bar is cool and loungy, with DJs playing soul, R&B and house. **Photo** *p148.*

Casa Manolo

C/Orellana 17 (91 308 73 78). Metro Alonso Martínez. **Open** 1-4pm Mon-Thur; 10am-4pm, 9pm-midnight Fri, Sat. Closed Aug. **Main courses** €10-€17. **Set lunch** €13.50. **Credit** MC, V. **Map** p324 J9 ⊕

One of the best sources of *cocina casera*, or home cooking, in Madrid, Casa Manolo has an endearing, homely atmosphere, enhanced by the black-and-white photo of the owner's grandmother and aunt presiding over the restaurant. But even though it's all about tradition, this place prepares creative mouthwatering salads that put the usual *ensalada mixta* to shame – the aubergine with tomato and goat's cheese, for example, must be one of the best in the city. And then there's lentil soup, *cocido* and other hearty stews, all supremely well prepared.

Extremadura

C/Libertad 13 (91 531 82 22). Metro Chueca. **Open** 1-4pm Mon; 1-4pm, 9pm-midnight Tue-Sun. **Main courses** €12-€14. **Credit** DC, MC, V. **Map** p324 I11 🔟
With festive live piano accompaniment, this is the spot to try out specialities from one of Spain's least-known regions, Extremadura. It's both classy and country – beautifully set tables with enormous glasses (for the excellent wines) combine with painting and pottery from the region. The food is marked by Extremadura's former days of austerity, with game that could be hunted on the dry plains. The trademark dish, *migas*, is a mix of breadcrumbs, chorizo and peppers that shepherds concocted to make use of old bread. Try the *torta del casar*, a soft, pungent regional cheese.

Los Jiménez

C/Barbieri 14 (91 521 11 86). Metro Chueca. **Open** 12.30-4pm, 9pm-midnight Tue-Sat; 12.30-4pm Sun. Closed Aug. **Main courses** €9-€12. **Set lunch** €8.60. **Credit** MC, V. **Map** p324 I10 🔟
Refreshingly unpretentious, Los Jiménez was serving no-frills food long before Chueca became the gay capital of Spain. Ghastly fluorescent lights overhead, the smell of frying and a menu board that spans the wall behind the bar – basically, it's a good old-fashioned greasy spoon. Popular with old-time locals, new kids and anyone with an appreciation for good value, who come here for all the Andalucian staples: oxtail stew, tripe, *cocido* and generous, if basic, salads.

Madrilia

C/Clavel 6 (91 523 92 75). Metro Gran Vía. **Open** noon-4pm, 9pm-midnight Mon-Thur, Sun; noon-4pm, 9pm-1am Fri, Sat. **Main courses** €12-€15. **Set lunch** €13.40 Mon-Fri. **Credit** AmEx, DC, MC, V. **Map** p324 H11 🔟
Swanky, stylish, but not ridiculously expensive, this is an enclave for business-lunch types and design-conscious locals from the gay community. Madrilia cooks up fresh and fashionable Italian food – a short list of antipasti, pasta and the odd meat or fish dish. Some waiters appear to have been chosen for cheekbones rather than experience, so you may find yourself occasionally ignored.

Momo

C/Libertad 8 (91 532 73 48). Metro Chueca or Gran Vía. **Open** 1-4pm, 9pm-midnight Mon-Sat. **Main courses** €9.50-€13. **Set lunch** €9.90. **Set dinner** €12 Mon-Fri; €15 Sat. **Credit** AmEx, DC, MC, V. **Map** p324 I11 🔟

Momo claims to offer *cocina creativa* – an apt description, considering that their most popular dishes are fried manchego cheese and *mocos de chocolate* (literally, 'chocolate bogies'). The orange-walled decor is *creativo*, too, although it borders on arty hotchpotch. The reasonable menu at both lunch and dinner brings in a steady flow of fans, generally young and casual, but it can be a bit hit-or-miss – the battered fish is best avoided, but stuffed aubergines are better, and puddings generally reliable.

La Mordida

C/Belén 13 (91 308 20 89/www.lamordida.com). Metro Chueca. **Open** 1.30-5pm, 8.30pm-1am daily. **Main courses** €10-50. **Credit** AmEx, DC, MC, V. **Map** p324 I9 🔟
Joaquín Sabina, the gravelly voiced Madrid musician and legend, does restaurants, too, but who'd have expected it to be Mexican food? And such good authentic Mexican food too, straight from the heart of Tenochtitlan. Usually full to bursting with high-spirited tequila drinkers, this is the place to embrace *mole*, the Mexican chocolate sauce that often scares the uninitiated away. The *pavo* (turkey) *con mole* melts in your mouth and the *cochinita pibil* (pork tacos with spicy chilli sauce) is equally exquisite. See which local celebs or Sabina song references you can identify on the wall's wildly painted murals.
Other locations: C/Fuentes 3, Los Austrias (91 559 11 36); Trva del Conde 4, Los Austrias (91 547 30 03).

El Puchero

C/Larra 13 (91 445 05 77). Metro Bilbao or Tribunal. **Open** 2-4pm, 9pm-midnight Mon-Sat. Closed Aug. **Main courses** €12-€19. **Credit** AmEx, DC, MC, V. **Map** p324 H8 🔟
Excitingly for El Puchero, red gingham is making a comeback after 30 years in the cold. Here it had never gone away – in tablecloths, cushions, lamp-shades and curtains. Almost unchanged too is the range of tasty country classics – from *civet de liebre* (hare stew) to *criadillas* (don't ask) – and some excellent seafood. It's a good idea to reserve at lunchtime, when the matronly waitresses are rushed off their feet with the demands of local office workers.
Other locations: C/Padre Damián 37, Chamberí (91 345 62 98).

Ribeira Do Miño

C/Santa Brígida 1 (91 521 98 54/www.maris queriaribeiradomino.com). Metro Tribunal. **Open** 1-4pm, 8-11.30pm Tue-Sun. Closed 2wks Jan & all Aug. **Main courses** €11-€17.50. **No credit cards. Map** p324 H9 🔟
Galician in origin, this one's for seafood lovers. Heaped platters of prawns, crab, goose-necked barnacles, lobster and other sea creatures make it the ideal place to roll up your sleeves and get cracking shells. Other typical *gallego* dishes that add a little heat to the fun are pancakes doused in *orujo* (a fiery spirit made from grapes) and set aflame, and the *queimada* – a bowl of *orujo* set on fire and then cooled with black coffee. No reservations are allowed, so grab a ticket and wait.

Salvador

C/Barbieri 12 (91 521 45 24). Metro Chueca.
Open 1.30-4pm, 9-11.30pm Mon-Sat. Closed Aug.
Main courses €15-€18. **Set lunch** €20 Mon-Fri.
Credit AmEx, DC, MC, V. **Map** p324 I10 ⑤⑧
Every inch of this old classic is crammed with bull-fighting memorabilia. You'll find good traditional fare – lentil soup, *revueltos* (concoctions with scrambled egg, often with seafood or asparagus), *solomillo* (beef) with french fries – but the real treat is the atmosphere. The formal but friendly waiters will patiently answer questions about the decor, and some of the patrons look like they may have been bullfighters themselves… many, many years ago.

Tienda de Vinos (El Comunista)

C/Augusto Figueroa 35 (91 521 70 12). Metro Chueca. **Open** 1-4.30pm, 9pm-midnight Mon-Sat. Closed mid Aug-mid Sept. **Main courses** €5-€8. **No credit cards. Map** p324 I10 ⑤⑨
This restaurant's popular name comes from its role as a lefty meeting point years ago, under Franco (but Tienda de Vinos is all you'll see above the door). It's one of the city's real classics and a visit is essential, and no one makes any grand claims about its unchanging and unchallenging menu. To start, there are soups: gazpacho, lentil or own-made broth, followed by liver and onions, lamb cutlets, kidneys in sherry and plenty of fish. Service is known for being deadpan, but if you're lucky, you'll get one of the two charming great-grandsons of the original owner.

International

Al-Jayma

C/Barbieri 1 (91 523 11 42). Metro Chueca or Gran Vía. **Open** 1.30-4pm, 9pm-midnight Mon-Fri; 1.30-4.30pm, 9pm-12.30am Sat, Sun. **Main courses** €3.90-€7.80. **Credit** AmEx, DC, MC, V. **Map** p324 I11 ⑥⓪
With its Berber rugs and intricate tiling, Al-Jayma is a microcosm of Morocco within Madrid. Sit back on the floor cushions to nibble on houmous and falafel, share one of their sumptuous tagines (try the lamb with dates), dig into a mountain of couscous or feast on the vegetarian options. There are also tables, of course, for longer-limbed folk. Carafes of the house wine are cheap but good, and the mint teas are typically sweet. The shock comes with the bill and how little you pay for good food and atmosphere.

La Dame Noire

C/Pérez Galdós 3 (91 531 04 76/www.ladame noire.com). Metro Chueca or Tribunal. **Open** 9pm-midnight Mon-Thur, Sun; 9pm-2am Fri, Sat. **Main courses** €11-€14. **Credit** AmEx, DC, MC, V. **Map** p324 H10 ⑥①
Welcome to Moulin Rouge, a culinary brothel of baroque kitsch. With a colour scheme of shocking reds, blues and golds, and a fine collection of crystal and china, candles and cherubs, this restaurant is divinely ornate. Amid the decadence, you pay reasonable prices for sumptuous French classics: fried

camembert, a green salad with warm goat's cheese, pork tenderloin or veal brochette. If you're lucky, Jean-Luc, one of the owners, may wear his trousers that match the embossed wallpaper. They are looking to move, however, so keep an eye on the website.

Indochine

C/Barquillo 10 (91 524 03 17). Metro Banco de España. **Open** 1.30-4pm, 9pm-midnight daily. **Main courses** €9.75-€13. **Set lunch** €12.90. **Credit** AmEx, DC, MC, V. **Map** p324 J11 ⑥②
Yet another of the pan-Asian restaurants to hit Madrid. Yes, it's Asian fusion with modern design, but Indochine is more relaxed and less style-conscious than the rest. It's best for a lunchtime *menú del día*: enjoy piquant sweet and sour soup followed by some decent pad thai and then – the most interesting part – green-tea ice-cream with caramelised walnuts on top (trust us, it's good). If you're going à la carte, the Peking duck is a safe bet. Ask for a table in the front, near the tall windows looking out on C/Hortaleza; the back rooms are a bit on the dreary side.

Lia

C/Reina 25 (91 522 34 83). Metro Gran Vía. **Open** 1.30-4.30pm, 9-11.30pm Mon-Thur; 1.30-4.30pm, 9pm-midnight Fri; 9pm-midnight Sat. Closed Aug. **Main courses** €10-€13. **Set lunch** €9. **Credit** AmEx, DC, MC, V. **Map** p324 I11 ⑥③
An attractive mix of laid-back Santo Domingo and cool New York, this Dominican oasis is a friendly place to wash down solid Caribbean fare with cold Presidentes (the national beer of the Dominican Republic). Tour the island with the *menú de degustación*; or, if you want to keep the tab low, order from the menu and drink domestic beers. Try the yucca appetiser followed by *pollo guisado* – totally toothsome. Lia, the restaurant's namesake, owner and an actress from New York, is as gracious as her restaurant. Frequented by a smart, arty crowd.

La Panza es Primero

C/Libertad 33 (91 521 76 40). **Open** 1.30pm-1am daily. **Main courses** €7.50-€9.50. **Set lunch** €9.50. **Credit** AmEx, DC, MC, V. **Map** p324 I10 ⑥④
Aflame with colour and funky Mexicana (indigenous art, skeletons and so on), The Belly Comes First is a Mexican *cantina* that has conquered Madrid with its nachos con guacamole. The most original item on the menu is the *pollo cabreado*, a chicken dish made with cabrales cheese from Asturias (hence the name) and *chipotle* sauce with smoked jalapeño peppers. There's no skimping on the spices, either – the chilli pepper symbols next to certain dishes on the menu indicate the heat factor.
Other locations: C/Campoamor 2, Chueca (91 319 82 15); C/Segovia 17, Los Austrias (91 364 12 28).

La Piazzetta de Chueca

Plaza Chueca 8 (91 523 83 22). Metro Chueca. **Open** 1-4pm, 8-11.30pm Mon-Thur, Sun; 1-4pm, 8pm-12.30am Fri, Sat. **Main courses** €8-€10.50. **Set lunch** €14 Mon-Thur. **Credit** DC, MC, V. **Map** p324 I10 ⑥⑤

Eat, Drink, Shop

Plaza Chueca has plenty of bars, but only one great restaurant, and this is it. It's fairly small inside La Piazzetta, but the place is attractively decked out in warm beige tones, with plenty of natural light streaming in from the square. The menu boasts tasty but simple Italian cuisine, with starters such as grilled vegetables or buffalo mozzarella with tomato, and great pasta main courses such as spaghetti in tomato sauce with anchovies, white wine and garlic. The tiramisu is a must, or try the *zuppa inglese*. It's especially perfect for summer evenings, when you can dine on the terrace.
Other locations: Boccondivino C/Castelló 81, Salamanca (91 575 79 47).

La Sinfonia Italiana

C/Fernando el Santo 25 (91 308 12 96). Metro Alonso Martínez. **Open** 2-4pm, 9.30pm-midnight Mon-Sat. **Main courses** €12-€22. **Credit** MC, V. **Map** p324 K8

With only eight tables, this little gem is *prima terra* for Italian food in Madrid. Exceptionally cosy and romantic, no detail is neglected, from the pre-meal prosecco, through the own-made pastas, to the heavenly tiramisu. The staff are consummately Italian – sincere, engaging, attractive and experts in the very serious matter of eating and drinking (the Italian wine list is fabulous). An ideal spot for an intimate evening.

Zara

C/Infantas 5 (91 532 20 74). Metro Chueca or Gran Vía. **Open** 1-4pm, 8-11.30pm Mon-Fri. Closed Aug. **Main courses** €9-€12. **Set menus** €20-€25. **Credit** AmEx, DC, MC, V. **Map** p324 H10/11

It's easy to walk right past these wooden doors and miss the little Havana with red-chequered tablecloths that lies within. Inés, the owner, left her home city over 30 years ago, but brought the best Cuban recipes with her – try the 'Typically Tropical' dishes like *ropa vieja* (literally, 'old clothes', but actually shredded beef), black beans and rice with pork, and minced beef with fried bananas. Daiquiris are the drink of the house – lime, banana, strawberry… whatever fruit is in season – and their killer recipe is a closely guarded secret. Good Cuban food, low prices: you may have to wait in line. **Photo** *p149.*

Malasaña & Conde Duque

International

Adrish

C/San Bernardino 1 (91 542 94 98/www.restaurante adrish.com). Metro Noviciado or Plaza de España. **Open** 1-4pm, 8.30pm-midnight Mon-Thur, Sun; 1-4pm, 8.30pm-1am Fri, Sat. **Main courses** €8-€12. **Set meal** €23, €29. **Credit** AmEx, DC, MC, V. **Map** p323 F9

The looks of the place may be a tad dreary, but you'll forget all about the mauve tablecloths once you taste the tandoori chicken with almonds (aka chicken chap). Adrish was one of the first restaurants to

Memento. *See p155.*

appear on the global restaurant street that is C/San Bernardino, and although it rarely seems full, it has survived with dignity. The large tandoori oven and charcoal grill produce some tasty dishes and a variety of naan breads, even if the spiciness has dropped to a level acceptable to local palates. Vegetarians will no doubt be happy to see the thali of assorted curries with roti and rice.

Bufalino

C/Puebla 9 (91 521 80 31). Metro Gran Vía or Tribunal. **Open** 1pm-4pm, 8pm-midnight Mon-Sat. **Main courses** €8.50-€12. **Set lunch** €9.50 Mon-Sat. **Credit** MC, DC, V. **Map** p323 H10

Run by an Italian and Argentine couple, Bufalino takes the cuisines of their respective countries and fuses them together, offering up a fine selection of fresh pastas made on site every day, along with panini and polenta. The restaurant gets packed out at around 11pm as its regulars pop by for a few drinks, and as such, the noise levels in the small space go through the roof. The service always comes with a big smile, and a recent refurbishment has added a little sparkle.

Gumbo

C/Pez 15 (91 532 63 61). Metro Noviciado. **Open** 2-4pm, 9pm-midnight Tue-Sat; 2-4pm Sun. Closed 2wks Aug. **Main courses** €9.50-€12. **Set lunch** €9.50. **Credit** MC, V. **Map** p323 G10

Bona fide N'Awlins chef Matthew Scott has some good Creole spices simmering in his gumbo pot. In a simple locale tastefully decorated (nice poster of *Gone With the Wind*), you can sample scrumptious New Orleans classics: fried green tomatoes, seafood gumbo, black steak. For festive group dinners, ask Matthew to bring out a parade of tapas-like dishes to share. And only a fool would resist the desserts: the pecan and the peanut butter pie are unforgettable. The *menú del día* is pretty well handled too.

Home

C/Espíritu Santo 12 (91 522 97 28/www.home burgerbar.com). Metro Tribunal. **Open** 1.30-4pm, 8.30pm-midnight Tue-Sat; 1-4pm, 8.30-11pm Sun. **Credit** AmEx, MC, V. **Map** p323 H9 **71**
If you associate burger bars with junk food, then think again. Home is the brainchild of a French Canadian restaurateur, who has created a carefully thought-out menu using 100% organic produce. The attention to detail is fantastic, from the diner-style

décor complete with cheesy table lamps to the menus, which come printed on American supermarket paper bags. The clientele is a curious mix of the asymmetrical haircut crew from the neighbourhood and office workers popping in for lunch. Downsides include service with a scowl, and the fact that you normally need to reserve.

Siam

C/San Bernardino 6 (91 559 83 15). Metro Noviciado or Plaza de España. **Open** 1-4.30pm, 8pm-midnight daily. **Main courses** €9.90-€11.50. **Set lunch** €9.50. **Credit** AmEx, DC, MC, V. **Map** p323 F9 **72**

Quick fixes

It's a phenomenon often noted by visitors that Madrid lacks the sandwich bars found on every corner of most European capitals. The Spanish have always been appalled by the idea of lunch as refuelling, let alone – horror of horrors – eating at one's desk. No, lunch here is a leisurely affair, and it can be hard to contact anyone between the hours of 1.30 and 4.30pm. With this in mind, the recent appetite for the innovative and the fast has taken everyone by surprise.

Stand on the corner of C/Libertad and C/San Marcos in Chueca to get

the picture. On one corner is **Diurno**, the café/takeaway/video rental hotspot (*see p223*), a wild success in the neighbourhood. On the opposite corner is the **Dosa Grill** (C/Libertad 17, 91 360 47 50, www.dosa. biz), an airy little café to grab a quick and delicious dosa, also getting rave reviews. Nearby is **The Wok** (C/San Marcos 31-33, 91 531 69 79) where *madrileños* in need of a quick plate of noodles spill out of the door.

No place better typifies the phenomenon than famed Catalan chef Ferran Adrià's venture into quality fast food, the abominably named **Fast Good** (*see p156*). The idea is to make fast food good food, and the rules are simple: use fresh, high-quality ingredients, aim for a few easy hot options like *panini* and burgers (all prepared with a gourmet flourish), ditch the animal fat in favour of olive oil, and

chuck in a handful of extravagances like lychee and red peach juice for good measure. Make it fast and easy, create a colourful modern atmosphere amid Madrid's ever-busy office nexus, and wait and see what happens.

So far, so fast. Fast Good's success is undeniable, and it's packed with eager diners every night of the week. But this is far from the American franchises peddling mystery meat across the globe. This is a Spanish-originated endeavour providing swift good meals that fall somewhere between fast food and the *menú del día*. Plus, it's been branded with the Adrià stamp, an almost guaranteed seal of success (although we could live without the plastic cups and cutlery).

So does Madrid's current love affair with the speedy suggest that the days of the long Spanish lunch are numbered? Never in a million *menús del día*.

Eat, Drink, Shop

Texan David Haynes has poured his heart and the experience of years spent in Thailand into this restaurant, and the investment has paid off with a loyal and enthusiastic clientele. Authenticity is his thing (please don't ask for bread) and he imports vegetables and spices that he can't get hold of in the city. Try the spicy Thai green curry, or just ask him to recommend a menu. There is also a fabulous range of cocktails and special teas. While you eat, listen to David switch between French, Spanish, Texan and Thai as he serves.
Other locations: Bangkok C/Arenal 15, Sol & Gran Via (91 559 16 96).

Toma

C/Conde Duque 14 (91 547 49 96). Metro Noviciado or Plaza de España. **Open** 9pm-12.30am Tue-Sat. **Main courses** €10-€18. Closed 1wk end Dec, 1wk Jan. **Credit** MC, V. **Map** p323 F9 ⓰
A tiny restaurant with cherry-red walls and an informal feel, Toma has quickly become a real favourite of the neighbourhood. Its homely, laid-back atmosphere can make the prices seem rather high, especially if you end up having to sit at the bar, but the food is commensurately good. From duck magret with pak choi to tuna tartare with lemon and soy, or rack of lamb with honey and mustard, the preparation is equally assured, and the results often divine. If it's available, finish with the creamy cappuccino cheesecake.

Vegetarian

La Isla del Tesoro

C/Manuela Malasaña 3 (91 593 14 40). Metro Bilbao or San Bernardo. **Open** 1.30-5pm, 9pm-1am daily. **Main courses** €8.80-€10.50. **Set lunch** €9.50. **Credit** AmEx, DC, MC, V. **Map** p323 H8 ⓮
One of Madrid's few vegetarian eateries not stuck in a circa-1978 gastronomic time warp, La Isla del Tesoro (Treasure Island) is often declared hands-down the best veggie restaurant in Madrid. Matching the international collectibles decor, dishes come from across the globe: try the famous couscous seitan or the *buen rollito* (fresh pasta stuffed with spinach, apple, leek, cheese and nuts). The *menú del día* features dishes from a different nation – from Pakistan to Mexico – each day. Friday, for example, is Morocco day, with good couscous.

Salamanca & the Retiro

La Brasserie de Lista

C/Serrano 110 (91 411 08 67). Metro Núñez de Balboa. **Open** 1-4pm, 9pm-midnight Mon-Thur; 1-4pm, 9pm-12.30am Fri, Sat; 1.30-4.30pm, 9pm-midnight Sun. **Main courses** €12-€17. **Set lunch** €12.30, €18.20. **Set dinner** €34.50. **Credit** AmEx, DC, MC, V. **Map** p325 L6 ⓰
A throwback from the obsession with French cuisine that gripped Spain after the dictatorship, this brasserie could be one of hundreds in Paris, all wood

panelling and parlour palms. On the menu: Caesar salad, onion soup with emmental, sirloin steak with pepper sauce and hamburgers. Other, less predictable, dishes include a succulent duck magret with lime and *membrillo* (quince jelly) purée. The set menu is excellent, or there is a bar at the front where you can just enjoy some tapas.

Casa Portal

C/Doctor Castelo 26 (91 574 20 26/www.casa-portal.com). Metro Goya. **Open** 1.30-4.30pm, 8.30-11pm Mon-Sat. Closed Aug. **Main courses** €16.50-€19.90. **Credit** AmEx, MC, V. **Map** p325 O11 ⓰
Casa Portal specialises in all things traditional from Asturias, hence the mountain of cheeses in the window and the cider being poured from a great height. Apart from cider, this spot has been serving *fabada* (an Asturian bean stew with chorizo), tortilla, fish and shellfish for more than 50 years. Choose between the sawdust-strewn bar at the front and the dining room behind.

International

Nodo

C/Velázquez 150 (91 564 40 44/www.restaurante nodo.es). Metro República Argentina. **Open** 1-4pm, 9pm-midnight daily. **Main courses** €11-€15. **Credit** AmEx, MC, V. **Map** p321 M3 ⓰
With minimalist decor and food to match, Nodo keeps the famous and the fashionable coming back for more. Style aside, some say it's the best sushi in town. Chef Albert Chicote's beef carpaccio with foie gras and coriander coulis typifies the menu, a successful blend of Japanese and Mediterranean. The sashimi and the tuna tataki with garlic get high marks; the service scores lower, but that might be a part of the minimalist serving ethic.

Other districts

A Casiña

Avda del Ángel, Casa de Campo (91 526 34 25/ www.acasina.com). Metro Lago. **Open** 1.30-4pm, 8.30-11.30pm Mon-Sat; 1.30-4.30pm Sun. **Main courses** €12-€22. **Credit** AmEx, DC, MC, V.
A Casiña is one of several restaurants specialising in regional cuisine – in this case Galician – in the Casa de Campo. The restaurant is a reconstruction of a *pazo*, a Galician manor house, and really comes into its own in summer, with tables outside in the garden. Expensive but top-quality fish, shellfish and beef are the highlights, along with favourites from the region, such as *caldo gallego*, a broth made with pork, potatoes and cabbage. There is also a tapas bar, for a cheaper seafood experience.

Asador Donostiarra

C/Infanta Mercedes 79, Tetuán (91 579 08 71/ www.asadordonostiarra.com). Metro Tetuán. **Open** 1-4pm, 9pm-midnight Mon-Sat; 1-4pm Sun. **Main courses** €23.50-€31.75. **Credit** AmEx, DC, MC, V.

If you love meat and you love Real Madrid, you may want to splurge on a night out at the once-preferred *asador* (steakhouse) of David Beckham and the rest of the team, located near the Bernabéu stadium. The celeb crowd is as legendary as the *solomillo*, and they often give away signed photos and other goodies from the team. Dissenting voices say that all the press has had an adverse effect, and the run-of-the-mill salad, steak and potato offerings are not commensurate with the hefty prices; others still claim it's the best *asador* in Madrid, even now El Becks has disappeared over the pond.

Casa Mingo

Paseo de la Florida 34, Casa de Campo (91 547 79 18). Metro Príncipe Pío. **Open** 11am-midnight daily. **Main course** €4-€6. **No credit cards.** **Map** p322 B9 ⑦

A vast and noisy Asturian cider house, open since 1888. This is a great opportunity to rub elbows with *madrileños* really enjoying themselves at one of the long wooden tables. The restaurant does only three things: roast chicken, salad and cider. Turn up before the city gets hungry (around 1.30pm) if you

Santceloni. *See p156.*

want a terrace seat, or take out a chicken and a bottle of cider and head for the River Manzanares for a picnic. At other times, expect to queue.

La Favorita

C/Covarrubias 25, Chamberí (91 448 38 10/ www.restaurante-lafavorita.com). Metro Alonso Martínez or Bilbao. **Open** 2-4pm, 9pm-midnight Mon-Fri; 9pm-midnight Sat. **Main courses** €18-€21. **Set lunch** €25. **Credit** AmEx, DC, MC, V. **Map** p324 I7 ⑦

Opera fanatic Javier Otero converted this charming 1920s mansion into a restaurant and filled it with singing waiters – conservatoire students or artists just starting out on their careers. It's a surprisingly fun way to eat delicious Navarran food: the soprano hits a high note, you savour the *solomillo* with thistles and artichokes, and the whole experience elicits goosebumps. Javier's troupe is so good, in fact, that it is regularly invited to perform at festivals. And the food, made using fresh ingredients from Navarra, hits another high note. Reservations are essential.

Laydown

Plaza Mostenses 9, Chamberí (91 548 79 37/www. laydown.es). Metro Plaza de España or Noviciado. **Open** noon-5pm Sun. 9.30pm-midnight daily. **Set lunch** €18 Sun. **Set dinner** €30. **Credit** AmEx, DC, MC, V. **Map** p323 F10 ⑳

The clue is in the name: at Laydown the table and the tablecloth have been eschewed in favour of pristine white sheets atop long rows of comfy mattresses. Dinner is a set meal – choose from two starters, such as swordfish carpaccio or gnocchi with gorgonzola, and then from three mains, which might include steak cooked in sherry or hake medallions with prawns in a curry sauce. Live music or theatre happens most nights, and then once dinner is over, it's DJ time, as everyone clambers out of bed to bust a few grooves.

Memento

C/Caracas 1, Chamberí (91 448 99 58/www. restaurantememento.com). Metro Bilbao. **Open** 1.30-4.30pm, 8.30pm-midnight Tue-Sat. **Main courses** €18.50-€24. **Set lunch** €18.50 Tue-Fri. **Credit** AmEx, MC, DC, V. **Map** p324 I7 ㉛

With American chef Karen Bell at the helm, Memento offers superb Californian cuisine (though admittedly at Hollywood prices). Highlights include the steamed mussels or the foie gras to start, or the dorado with langoustine ravioli and coconut and curry sauce as a main. A fantastic array of desserts is another bonus, along with a whisky menu. **Photo** *p152.*

El Olivo

C/General Gallegos 1, Chamartín (91 359 15 35/359 03 52). Metro Cuzco. **Open** 1-4pm Mon; 1-4pm, 9pm-midnight Tue-Sat. Closed last 2wks Aug. **Main courses** €27-€31. **Credit** AmEx, DC, MC, V.

Frequented by an over-50 crowd and decorated in a sombre olive-green, this old-school Mediterranean restaurant still ranks high with more discriminating gastronomes. Olive oil is the keystone: the kindly, very formal waiters wheel a cart of bottles over to the table for you to sample with bread; only the best is used for cooking, and there is even olive oil ice-cream (surprisingly good, since you ask). Specialities include the lobster and herb salad, the *solomillo* with foie, and a fine tarte tatin.

Santceloni

Hotel Hesperia Madrid, Paseo de la Castellana 57 (91 210 88 41/www.restaurantesantceloni. com). Metro Gregorio Marañón. **Open** 2-4pm, 9-11pm Mon-Fri; 9-11pm Sat. Closed Aug. **Main courses** €36.50-€48. **Credit** AmEx, DC, MC, V. **Map** p321 K5 ⑥

Named after the village where the famed Barcelona restaurateur Santi Santamaria was born, and run by his protégé Oscar Velasco, the Santceloni was anointed with its first Michelin star after less than a year. Santamaria's success derives from using only the best of local ingredients. Try the poached egg with caviar and cauliflower, or one of Santamaria's trademark dishes: ravioli of sliced raw prawn with a filling of ceps. The tasting menu changes daily depending on available ingredients and will set you back a pretty penny, but it's a chance to relish the talents of one of Spain's celebrity chefs. **Photo** *p155.*

Tatana

C/Galileo 12, Chamberí (91 447 86 69). Metro San Bernardo. **Open** 1-5pm, 9pm-1am daily. **Main courses** €12-€22. **Set lunch** €10. **Credit** MC, V. **Map** p323 F7 ⑥

Descend down some steps to this great little Argentine-run restaurant where loungy sounds wash over a jumble of wooden tables, deep colours and smiling waiters. The home country is very evident on the menu, with lots of pasta (you select your type, then choose a sauce from a separate list) and untranslatable Argentine cuts of beef (*entraña*, *bife de lomo*). The lunchtime menu is a good one – decent salads to start, then roast chicken, perhaps, or stir-fried vegetables with prawns.

International

La Broche

Hotel Miguel Ángel, C/Miguel Ángel 29, Chamberí (91 399 34 37/www.labroche.com). Metro Rubén Darío. **Open** 2-4.30pm, 9-11.30pm Mon-Fri. Closed Aug. **Main courses** €30-€35. **Credit** AmEx, DC, MC, V. **Map** p321 K5 ⑥

Gleaming white on white and with hostesses wearing headsets, this is still one of Madrid's most modern restaurants, even after several years. Ferran Adrià's disciple Sergi Arola works with a *nueva cocina* vocabulary of edible foams and gels and unlikely combinations such as scallop carpaccio with green-apple purée. For all the quirkiness, it tastes pretty sublime too – good enough, in fact, to earn La Broche two Michelin stars. Don't be thrown off by its location in the staid Hotel Miguel Ángel – once inside, you are on another culinary planet.

El Comité

Plaza de San Amaro 8, Chamartín (91 571 87 11). Metro Santiago Bernabéu. **Open** 1.30-4pm, 9pm-midnight Mon-Fri; 9pm-midnight Sat. **Main courses** €14-€24. **Credit** AmEx, DC, MC, V.

Yes, it's out of the way and has the feel of an elite club, but this somehow enhances the appeal. A French restaurant offering exceptionally good food at a price, El Comité also offers the chance to see Madrid's discreetly elegant top people at play. Great starters include Harry's Bar carpaccio and a tempura of langoustines; a main-course highlight is the steak tartare. A classic.

Fast Good

C/Padre Damián 23, Chamartín (91 343 06 55/ www.fast-good.com). Metro Cuzco. **Open** noon-midnight daily. **Main courses** €5-€8.50. **Credit** AmEx, DC, MC, V.

This is the first installation in what is bound to be a trend – it's fast food à la Ferran Adrià, still the hottest chef in Spain and originator of the *nueva cocina* movement. In a colour-crazy, super-designed deli you can pick out innovative salads like the foie with green beans or panini with brie and spinach. The crowning glory, however, is the Fast Good hamburger – a superlative specimen. Everything is made fresh and light – even the fries are cooked in olive oil. So far it's been a big success, despite the clunky name.

Sudestada

C/Modesto Lafuente 64, Chamberí (91 533 41 54). Metro Nuevos Ministerios. **Open** noon-4pm, 9pm-midnight Mon-Sat. **Main courses** €16-€20. **Credit** MC, V.

Run by young Argentines with a passion for Asian food, Sudestada is the new Madrid branch of a Buenos Aires favourite. In its short life it has already received a hugely respected Spanish restaurant award, and is packed out every night. Given the authentic spiciness of its curries – from all over South-east Asia – this gives the lie to the idea that Spanish diners prefer their food bland. Less *picante* options include Vietnamese rolls and dim sum from Singapore. Reservations are all but essential, especially at weekends.

Summa

C/Profesor Waksman 5, Chamartín (91 457 32 27/ www.restaurantesumma.com). Metro Cuzco. **Open** 2-4pm, 9pm-midnight Mon-Fri; 9pm-midnight Sat. **Main courses** €11.50-€13.40. **Set lunch** €18.70. **Credit** AmEx, MC, V.

Giant photos of a birch forest cover the windows and one wall, and in the middle is a traditional sushi bar with little boats floating round a stream from which you can pluck whatever you fancy. The menu incorporates the house Summa roll of salmon, avocado and crab and a great matzuzaki roll of tuna, plaice, squid, salmon, avocado and cheese in nori seaweed, and is fused with things Mediterranean. The all-you-can-eat lunch buffet takes some beating.

Tapas

Take your pick from cleverly constructed canapés and traditional titbits.

Cheerful but incomprehensible – service at **La Torre del Oro**. *See p159.*

In their more fanciful moments, Spaniards will describe them as 'the world on a plate'. They will tell you that the eating of tapas is proof of the country's gregarious nature, its need to share and the importance it places on spending time in good company. Thanks to the tapa, it is possible to spend the whole night in a bar without requiring help to get home. This is the point so often missed by those outside the country, those who reproduce them for dinner parties or nibble them in expensive restaurants in London. For the Spanish, it's not about what you eat, it's about *how* you eat.

An accidental invention, tapas originated in Andalucia and were originally pieces of ham or chorizo that were placed on top of the plate, or slice of bread, used to cover a glass of wine and keep out the dust and flies. The word *tapa*, in fact, means 'lid'. The idea became widely established during the 19th century, with the principal objective of making the customer thirsty in order to sell more drinks. The tapas boom really occurred, however, in the 1940s after the Civil War, when many of Madrid's existing bars first appeared.

Tapas vary from region to region, and examples of most are available in Madrid. Galician bars highlight octopus, prawns and seafood, traditionally with white Ribeiro wine, served in little ceramic bowls. In Extremaduran bars you will always find *migas* (crumbs), fried and mixed with chorizo. Asturian bars specialise in cider (*sidra*), theatrically poured from above the head to separate out sediment, accompanied by blood sausage, *morcilla*, or blue *cabrales* cheese. Andalucian bars offer cold dry *fino* sherry with *mojama* (dry-cured tuna) or sardines. Madrid's own specialities are *patatas bravas*, offal (particularly *callos*, tripe), and snails in a hot sauce.

Tapas have become more sophisticated and thus more expensive in recent times, and an evening's *tapeo* can cost more than a full meal in a restaurant. Don't be afraid to dispose of the debris (olive stones, prawn shells and screwed-up paper napkins) by dropping them on the floor, except in the more upmarket places where you should copy what the locals are doing; and remember that a lot of tapas are designed to be eaten with the fingers.

Sunday's best

In Madrid Sunday feels like Friday. Preparing for Monday – laundry, homework, doing the bills – is not given much thought; such tasks can wait until a schoolnight. *Madrileños* like to squeeze the most out of their weekends, hence the Sunday post-Rastro drinking tradition in the *barrio* of La Latina, local merrymaking at its best. On sunny days, the squares and terrazas of La Latina (Plaza de la Paja, Plaza de San Andrés, Plaza del Humilladero) brim with hedonism. Sassy girls lounge on church steps; hipsters with hefty sideburns loll in cafés, *caña* in hand; blue-rinsed matriarchs sit on park benches feeding the pigeons. On rainy days, the best bars in the area burst with smoking, drinking, talking *madrileños*. This giddy atmosphere has a distinctly bohemian feel; neighbourhood drunks, artists, actors, *políticos*, grandmas, the occasional juggler and an impressive number of dogs all turn out to take part.

The essence of the Sunday tradition is vermouth, and the whole ritual, tapas and all, occasionally known as '*haciendo el vermut*' – 'doing vermouth'. Served with ice and a slice of lemon or orange, it's more refreshing with a spritz of soda water – ask for it '*con sifón*'. It's not the dry vermouth familiar to Martini-lovers, but a sweet red vermouth, often best when served from the tap (*grifo*), although the popular **El Bonano** (Plaza de Humilladero 4, 91 366 68 86) serves a delicious bottled variety called Vermut del Pueblo from Catalonia. Ironically, the best vermouths are from around Barcelona, but the Catalans have never shared *madrileños'* affection for the drink. La Latina drinkers claim the prime vermouth hour is 1pm; as one bartender explained, 'I don't know why, but for *madrileños*, it's a religion.'

Vermouth is made from dry white wine blended with an infusion of herbs, flowers, fruit peel, seeds and plants. It's quite sweet and fortified with brandy, giving it a high alcohol content and making it quick to elevate the spirits (essential after a late Saturday night). In Madrid restaurants, it is often the aperitif of choice before the big Sunday lunch.

Originally founded in 1870, the much-loved **Casa Antonio** (C/Latoneros 10, 91 366 63 36), which faces out on to the Plaza de la Puerta Cerrada, is one of the oldest *vermut* bars in Madrid. Hipper places to try it are **La Carpanta** (C/Almendro 22, 91 366 57 83) and the nearby **La Corolla** (C/Almendro 10, 91 364 52 32). Often frequented by three golden labradors, the best pavement tables for a Sunday vermouth are at **Café del Nuncio** (*pictured*; C/Nuncio 12, 91 366 08 53).

Los Austrias & La Latina

El Almendro 13

C/Almendro 13 (91 365 42 52). Metro La Latina.
Open 1-4pm, 7.30pm-12.30am Mon-Thur, Sun; 1-
5pm, 1-5pm, 8pm-1am Fri, Sat. **No credit cards.**
Map p327 F13 ❶

A sleepy, traditional bar during the week, it hots up
at weekends, and drinkers often drift on to the pavements. A peculiar speciality is the *rosca*, a sort of
oversized, filled bagel. These are invariably accompanied by a glass of the house *manzanilla*.

As de los Vinos – La
Casa de las Torrijas

C/Paz 4 (91 532 14 73). Metro Sol. **Open** 10am-4pm,
6-10pm Mon-Thur; 9.30am-4pm, 6-11pm Fri, Sat.
Closed Aug. **No credit cards. Map** p327 G12 ❷

A charmingly old unkempt bar, tiled and mirrored,
with table-tops constructed from old enamel adverts.
Since 1907, it has served little more than *torrijas* –
bread soaked in wine and spices, coated in sugar and
deep-fried – and house wine. There is a handful of
other, simple, tapas, however, and a basic set lunch.

Bodegas Ricla

C/Cuchilleros 6 (91 365 20 69). Metro Ópera.
Open 11.30am-3.30pm, 7pm-midnight Mon, Wed,
Thur; 11.30am-3.30pm, 7pm-1am Fri; 12.30-4pm,
7pm-1am Sat; 12.30-5pm Sun. **No credit cards.**
Map p327 F12 ❸

A tiny, bright and friendly mother-and-son operation, Bodegas Ricla does a great line in garlicky
boquerones and an incongruous one in soft rock.
Cheap but good wine and sherry are available by the
litre, poured from tall clay urns, or there is vermouth
on tap. Also worth trying are the *cecina* (thin slices
of cured venison) and cabrales cheese in cider.

Juana la Loca

*Plaza Puerta de Moros 4 (91 364 05 25). Metro
La Latina.* **Open** 8pm-12.30am Mon; 1-5.30pm,
8pm-2.30am Tue-Fri; 1pm-2am Sat, Sun. **No
credit cards. Map** p327 E13 ❹

Where the hip go to *tapear*. It's kind of pricey, but
offers undeniably creative cooking; a miniature portion of ostrich, plum and crispy bacon, or foie gras
with caramelised apple. Other tasty options might
include salmon with dill, avocado and fresh cheese
or a giant prawn and wild mushroom vol-au-vent.

Matritum

C/Cava Alta 17 (91 365 82 37). Metro La Latina.
Open 8.30pm-12.30am daily. **Credit** DC, MC, V.
Map p327 F13 ❺

Its name is Latin for Madrid, but Matritum has a
great selection of tapas and wine from other regions
of Spain, most notably Catalonia. Try *gambas all cre-
mat* (prawns with burnt garlic) or fabulous canapés
such as *cabrales* cheese with apple compôte or
sobrasada – a spicy, spreadable, Mallorcan sausage.
The wine list, too, is dominated by Catalan labels,
with many notably good bottles from the Penedes.

La Taberna de Cien Vinos

C/Nuncio 17 (91 365 47 04). Metro La Latina.
Open 1-3.45pm, 8-11.45pm Tue-Sun. **No credit
cards. Map** p327 F13 ❻

The 'Taberna' is a bit misleading, as there's nothing
particularly old-fashioned here, but the 'Cien Vinos'
('100 wines') is spot on. Mainly Spanish, there are
also a good few from France and a handful from the
rest of the world. There are upmarket tapas (try bole-
tus with scamorza) to go with them.

Taberna Según Emma

C/Conde de Miranda 4 (91 559 08 97). Metro Ópera.
Open 1.30-4pm, 8pm-1am Mon, Wed, Thur, Sun;
1.30-4pm, 8pm-1.30am Fri, Sat. **Credit** AmEx, DC,
MC, V. **Map** p327 F12 ❼

Step down into a small, lively space with lime-green
walls and wooden tables – run by thirtysomethings
for thirtysomethings. It used to be an Asturian bar and
cheeses from the region and favourites such as clams
with haricot beans remain, alongside newer tapas.

La Taberna del Zapatero

*C/Almendro 22 (91 365 37 57/www.tabernadel
zapatero). Metro La Latina.* **Open** 8pm-midnight
Mon-Thur; 1-4.30pm, 8pm-12.30am Fri, Sat; 1.30-
4pm, 7.30-11.30pm Sun. **No credit cards. Map**
p327 F13 ❽

Occupying the shop of an old shoemaker (*zapatero*),
this is now a boisterous and smoky tapas bar. Old
cobblers' tools are dotted about the place, and the
excellent canapés are known as *suelas*, 'soles'. Fill
your boots with asparagus with brie or cod brandade.

El Tempranillo

C/Cava Baja 38 (91 364 15 32). Metro La Latina.
Open 1-3.45pm, 8pm-midnight daily. Closed Aug.
Credit V. **Map** p327 F13 ❾

Never less than rowdy, decorated in bullring ochre
and bare brick, with flamenco on the sound system,
El Tempranillo offers an impressive range of labels
from nearly every wine-producing region in Spain.
The tapas are addictive too: try the wild mushrooms
in scrambled egg or the sweetbreads.

La Torre del Oro

Plaza Mayor 26 (91 366 50 16). Metro Sol. **Open**
11am-2am daily. **Credit** AmEx, DC, MC, V. **Map**
p327 F12 ❿

It's smack on the Plaza Mayor, so don't expect any
bargains, especially if you sit out in the square, but
this Andalucian bar is the real deal, with bullfighting memorabilia and incomprehensible waiters. If
you can understand and make yourself understood,
ask for prawns or whitebait (*pescaítos*), and accompany them with a cold, dry *fino*. **Photo** *p157.*

Sol & Gran Vía

Las Bravas

*Pasaje Matheu 5, off C/Victoria (91 521 51 41).
Metro Sol.* **Open** 12.30-4pm, 7pm-midnight Mon-
Thur, Sun; 12.30-4pm, 7.30pm-12.30am Fri, Sat.
No credit cards. Map p327 H12 ⓫

Eat, Drink, Shop

Decorated in the luminous orange that characterises its mass-produced sauce, Las Bravas still merits a mention for having, allegedly, invented the *pata-ta brava*. These days, you'll do better elsewhere, unless you're attracted to supermarket lighting. **Other locations**: throughout the Sol area.

Casa Labra

C/Tetuán 12 (91 531 00 81). Metro Sol. **Open** 9.30am-3.30pm daily. **Credit** AmEx, DC, MC, V. **Map** p327 G11 ⑫
Famously the birthplace of the Spanish Socialist Party back in 1879, this legendary bar, with its brown 1950s paintwork and luggage racks, is worth a visit for its history alone. The speciality of the house is the cod *croquetas* served up by dour white-jacketed waiters.

El Escarpín

C/Hileras 17 (91 559 99 57). Metro Ópera or Sol. **Open** 9am-midnight daily. **Credit** AmEx, DC, MC, V. **Map** p327 F11 ⑬
So vast that you'll always find a seat, this Asturian cider bar has the look – bare bricks and long wooden tables – to go with the regional tapas. Natural cider (*sidra*) should be your first request, followed by *lacón* (gammon), *fabada asturiana* (a stew of beans and pork) or chorizo. In cider, naturally.

Huertas & Santa Ana

Alhambra

C/Victoria 9 (91 521 07 08/www.tabernaalhambra. es). Metro Sol. **Open** 10am-2am Mon-Thur, Sun; 10am-3.30am Fri, Sat. **No credit cards**. **Map** p327 H12 ⑭
Named after Granada's magical palace and done up in suitably Andaluz-Moorish style, this is a pretty and peaceful spot during the day, serving basic tapas along with oxtail stew and gazpacho, and a simple set lunch. It's a different place at night, though; awash with Spanish pop, techno and hormones.

Casa Alberto

C/Huertas 18 (91 429 93 56). Metro Antón Martín. **Open** *Sept-June* noon-12.30am Tue-Sat; noon-4pm Sun. *July, Aug* noon-5.30pm, 8pm-1.30am Mon-Sat. **Credit** AmEx, DC, MC, V. **Map** p328 H12 ⑮
One of the city's most evocative old *tabernas*, hung with oil paintings and presided over by a septuagenarian. It still has its old zinc bar complete with running water trough to keep the wine cool and a draught beer head with five founts. Try lambs' trotters, garlicky prawns, chorizo in cider or oxtail stew as tapas, or as more substantial dishes in the restaurant at the back.

Cervecería la Moderna

Plaza Santa Ana 12 (91 420 15 82). Metro Sol. **Open** 11.30-2.30am daily. **Credit** DC, MC, V. **Map** p328 H12 ⑯
Cervecería la Moderna is a large bar-restaurant, which is mercifully untouristed given its location on the Plaza Santa Ana. A varied but consistently good

range of tapas includes hare pâté with whisky; Mexican tacos with beef, cheese and mustard sauce; swordfish and smoked tuna.

La Dolores

Plaza de Jesús 4 (91 429 22 43). Metro Antón Martín. **Open** 11am-1am Mon-Thur, Sun; 11am-2am Fri, Sat. **No credit cards**. **Map** p328 I12 ⑰
Another Madrid classic, with wonderful tiling outside and rows of dusty beer steins inside, La Dolores has been serving ice-cold frothy beer since the 1920s. There's a short list of tapas, which are good if a bit overpriced. Specialities are smoked fish, anchovies and *mojama* (wind-dried tuna). **Photos** *p161.*

La Fábrica

C/Jesús 2 (91 369 06 71). Metro Antón Martín. **Open** 11am-1am Mon-Thur, Sun; 11am-2am Fri, Sat. **No credit cards**. **Map** p328 I12 ⑱
There are long, long lists of the canapés on offer, but most are on display. Try the *matrimonio* (anchovies preserved and fresh, the perfect combination); the theme continues with *divorcio* (anchovies and mussels; no kind of match); or the *orgía* (all three). Ahem.

Los Gatos

C/Jesús 2 (91 429 30 67). Metro Antón Martin or Sevilla. **Open** noon-1am Mon-Thur, Sun; noon-2am Fri, Sat. **No credit cards**. **Map** p328 I13 ⑲
With their reputation for staying out all night, *madrileños* are popularly known as '*los gatos*' (the cats) and there's nowhere better than here to begin a night prowling the tiles. The bar is hung with all manner of paraphernalia from gramophones to choirboy mannequins – here you can get a selection of tasty canapés, and a good frothy beer.

Lhardy

Carrera de San Jerónimo 8 (91 522 22 07/http:// lhardy.com). Metro Sol. **Open** 9.30am-3pm, 5-9.30pm Mon-Sat; 9.30am-3pm Sun. **Credit** AmEx, DC, MC, V. **Map** p327 H11 ⑳
A quiet and refined place, famous for its anchovy or chorizo vol-au-vents, its superb and dainty cakes, and, above all, its two silver samovars from which diners can help themselves to consommé or water. There are also ham or chicken croquettes, and barquetas de riñones – pastry boats with kidneys. **Photos** *p164.*

La Platería

C/Moratín 49 (91 429 17 22). Metro Antón Martín. **Open** 7.30am-1am Mon-Fri; 9.30am-1am Sat, Sun. **Credit** MC, V. **Map** p328 J13 ㉑
Everything from the smoked salmon and red peppers to *caldo gallego*, grilled asparagus or baked potatoes with eggs and garlic, is available in half portions, so this is a perfect place for a quick snack 'twixt the big three museums. The bar is rather cramped, but there are tables outside.

Taberna de Conspiradores

C/Moratín 33 (91 369 4741). Metro Antón Martín. **Open** 1pm-1am Mon-Thur, Sun; 1pm-2am Fri, Sat. **Credit** AmEx, MC, V. **Map** p328 I13 ㉒

The food, wine and liqueurs on offer here are all from from Extremadura, unusually. The speciality is *migas* – fried breadcrumbs baked with sausage, garlic and pancetta – and a dense venison stew. The small space is lined with black and white photographs from the Magnum greats, and occasionally hosts world music or flamenco gigs.

La Tapería

Plaza Platería de Martínez 1 (91 429 40 94). Metro Antón Martín. **Open** 9am-1am Mon-Thur, Sun; 9am-1.30am Fri, Sat. **Credit** AmEx, DC, MC, V. **Map** p328 J13 ㉓
The decor has a bit of a modern, corporate look, but it's nice enough, and the tapas can be very good. Look out for duck liver with apple, sherry and goat's cheese, brie millefeuille with Iberian ham and the mushroom tartlet. The baked new potatoes dipped in a spicy sauce are good to share.

Vinoteca Barbechera

C/Príncipe 27 (91 555 07 54/www.vinoteca-barbechera.com). Metro Antón Martín or Sevilla. **Open** 11am-midnight Mon-Thur, Sun; 11am-1-30am Fri, Sat. **Credit** AmEx, MC, V. **Map** p328 H12 ㉔
It looks a lot grander than it is, which is not to say that the tapas aren't good, just that the bill is a pleasant surprise in these rather lofty surroundings. *Pinchos* include smoked salmon with cream cheese, cabrales with quince jelly and goose liver with apple. **Other locations:** C/Gravina 6, Chueca (91 523 9816); C/Hermosilla 103, Salamanca (91 575 5664).

Rastro & Lavapiés

Café Melo's

C/Ave María 44 (91 527 50 54). Metro Lavapiés. **Open** 9pm-2am Tue-Sat. Closed Aug. **No credit cards. Map** p328 H14 ㉕
It's got all the aesthetic charm of a kebab shop, but this bright little bar is something of a classic. It's famous for its *zapatillas* – huge, open sandwiches (the word, like ciabatta, means 'slipper') with a variety of toppings. A big favourite for late-night munchies with the bohemian element of the *barrio*.

Los Caracoles

Plaza de Cascorro 18 (91 365 94 39). Metro La Latina. **Open** 10.30am-3.30pm, 7-10.30pm Tue-Sat; 10.30am-4pm Sun. **No credit cards. Map** p327 F14 ㉖
Again, this is no looker, but it's a popular post-Rastro stop. Its specialities include the eponymous snails in spicy sauce, knuckle of ham, and *zarajo*, the lamb's intestines wrapped round sticks without which your Madrid trip would not be complete.

La Casa de las Tostas

C/Argumosa 29 (91 527 08 42). Metro Lavapiés. **Open** noon-4pm, 7.30pm-1am Mon-Thur, Sun; 7.30pm-2am Fri, Sat. **No credit cards. Map** p328 I15 ㉗
Welcome to the House of Toast. Toast with scrambled eggs, prawns and wild mushrooms; toast with salmon in white vermouth; toast with gammon and

La Dolores. *See p160.*

Eat, Drink, Shop

Tapas glossary

There are three basic sizes of tapa portion: a *pincho* (more or less a mouthful), a *tapa* (a saucerful or so) and a *ración* (a small plateful). Some bars offer *media raciones* (a half-*ración*). If there's something you like the look of that isn't identifiable on the menu or the list behind the bar, just point to it. Bread (*pan*) normally comes automatically, but if not, just ask. Most often, you let a tapas bill mount up and pay when you've finished, not when you order; it's usually about 25 per cent more expensive if you sit at a table rather than eat at the bar.

For more food terminology, *see p142*.

Basics

Bocadillo sandwich in a roll or part of a French loaf; **cazuelita** small hot casserole; **montados** canapé-style mixed tapas, often a slice of bread with a topping; **pincho/pinchito** small titbit on a toothpick, or mouthful-sized *tapa*; **pulga/pulguita** small filled roll; **ración** a portion (small plateful); **tabla** platter (of cheese, cold meats); **tosta** slice of toast with topping; **una de gambas, chorizo**… one portion of prawns, chorizo…; **por unidad** per item.

Carne, aves y embutidos (meat, poultry & charcuterie)

Albóndigas meat balls; **alitas de pollo** chicken wings; **callos** tripe; **cecina** dry-cured beef; **chistorra** Navarrese sausage with paprika; **chorizo** spicy sausage, eaten cooked or cold; **criadillas** bulls' testicles; **flamenquines** ham and pork rolls in breadcrumbs; **longaniza**, **fuet** mild but chewy, often herby, salami-type sausages; **mollejas** sweetbreads; **morcilla** a black, blood sausage; **oreja (de cerdo)** pig's ear; **pincho moruno** grilled meat brochette; **riñones al Jerez** kidneys cooked in sherry; **salchichón** a large, fatty, soft, salami-type sausage; **San Jacobo** fried ham and cheese escalope; **sobrassada** soft Mallorcan paprika sausage; **torrezno** grilled pork crackling; **zarajo** grilled sheep's intestine on a stick.

Pescado y mariscos (fish & shellfish)

Ahumados smoked fish; **almejas** clams; **anchoas** salted conserved anchovies; **anguilas** eels; **angulas** elvers; **berberechos** cockles; **bienmesabe** marinated fried fish; **boquerones**

---

melted cheese; toast with anchovies and roquefort; toast with cod pâté. And most importantly, toast with wine, many available by the glass.

Casa Granada

C/Doctor Cortezo 17 (91 369 35 96/reservations 91 420 08 25). Metro Tirso de Molina. **Open** noon-midnight Mon-Sat; 11am-8pm Sun. **Credit** AmEx, DC, MC, V. **Map** p327 G/H13 ㉘
A very ordinary bar serving very ordinary food, which has an extraordinary view. To get in, ring the buzzer on street level, and then ride the lift all the way up to the sixth floor – in summer you'll have to fight tooth and nail for a seat on the terrace.

Los Hermanos

C/Rodas 28 (91 468 33 13). Metro Tirso de Molina. **Open** 7am-11pm Mon-Fri; 7am-5pm Sun. Closed Aug. **Credit** MC, V. **Map** p327 G14 ㉙
Just off the main drag of the Rastro is this bar with a strong neighbourhood feel, generous complimentary tapas, a huge range of *raciones* or a great range of *bocadillos*, including a hangover-busting bacon and egg. On Sundays there's a €10 *menú del día* for the market crowd, available in a quieter side room.

El Sur

C/Torrecilla del Leal 12 (91 527 83 40). Metro Antón Martín. **Open** 8pm-midnight Tue-Thur; 1-5pm, 8pm-1am Fri-Sun. **Credit** MC, V. **Map** p328 H13 ㉚

Named after Victor Erice's seminal film, decorated with cinematic posters and popular with long-haired soulful types returning from the nearby Filmoteca. Juan, the friendly and efficient owner, offers an interesting selection of *raciones*: try *ropa vieja* (shredded beef, Cuban style) with thinly sliced, fried potatoes or 'Arabian' lentils.

La Taberna de Antonio Sánchez

C/Mesón de Paredes 13 (91 539 78 26). Metro Tirso de Molina. **Open** noon-5pm, 8pm-midnight Mon-Sat; noon-4pm Sun. **Credit** MC, V. **Map** p327 G13 ㉛
Little changes at this historic bar, from the zinc bar to the bull's head on the wall. Its various owners have all been involved in bullfighting, and *tertulias* of critics, *toreros* and aficionados are still held here. It's local and friendly, with superior tapas (the best is the scrumptious salad you get free with a drink).

El Tío Vinagre

C/San Carlos 6 (no phone). Metro Lavapiés or Tirso de Molina. **Open** 6pm-2am Mon-Thur; 6pm-2.30am Fri, Sat; noon-1am Sun. **No credit cards. Map** p327 H14 ㉜
Under new ownership, and a notch hipper, 'Uncle Vinegar' has wines from around the country, board games and a few tapas: *empanadas*, gazpacho, goat's cheese salad and cured venison. The wooden panelling and marble bar have been enhanced with modern touches, Mojitos foremost among them.

en vinagre/fritos pickled fresh anchovies; **calamares a la romana** squid rings fried in batter; **calamares en su tinta** squid cooked in their ink; **carabineiros** large red ocean prawns; **centollo** spider crab; **chanquetes** tiny fish, served deep fried; **chipirones en su tinta** small Atlantic squid in their ink; **chopito** small cuttlefish; **cigalas** crayfish; **croqueta de bacalao** salt cod croquette; **fritura de pescado** flash-fried fish; **gambas al ajillo** prawns fried with garlic; **gambas en gabardina** prawns deep-fried in batter; **huevas** fish roe; **mojama** dried and salted tuna fish; **navajas** razor clams; **nécora** swimming crab; **percebes** goose-neck barnacles; **pulpo a feira/a la gallega** octopus with paprika and olive oil; **quisquillas** shrimps; **salpicón** cold chopped salad, often with some shellfish; **sepia** large squid; **soldaditos de pavía** strips of salt cod, fried in light batter; **tigres** mussels cooked with a spicy tomato and béchamel sauce; **zamburiñas** small scallops.

Vegetales (vegetable tapas)

Aceitunas, olivas (adobados, rellenos) olives (pickled, stuffed); **almendras saladas**

salted almonds; **pan con tomate** bread rubbed with fresh tomato and olive oil; **patatas bravas** deep-fried potatoes with hot pepper sauce; **perdiz de huerta** lettuce hearts; **pimientos de Padrón** fried, and occasionally hot small green peppers; **queso en aceite** cheese marinated in olive oil; **setas** wild mushrooms.

Other tapas

Caracoles snails; **croquetas** potato croquettes (which may be made with chicken, ham, tuna, and so on); **empanada** flat pies, usually made with a tuna filling; **empanadilla** small fried pasties, usually with a tomato and tuna filling; **ensaladilla rusa** potato salad with onions, red peppers, usually tuna and other ingredients in mayonnaise, now a completely Spanish dish that's still called a Russian salad; **huevos rellenos** stuffed cold hard-boiled eggs; **migas (con huevo frito)** fried bread-crumbs (with fried egg); **pisto manchego** ratatouille with meat (usually ham) and egg; **revuelto** scrambled eggs.

Chueca

La Bardemcilla

C/Augusto Figueroa 47 (91 521 42 56/www.la bardemcilla.com). Metro Chueca. **Open** noon-5pm, 8pm-2am Mon-Fri; 8pm-2am Sat. **Credit** AmEx, MC, V. **Map** p324 I10 ③③

A fun, mellow place, owned by the royal family of Spanish cinema, the Bardems. There are filmic references everywhere, from the doll's house set from *Before Night Falls* to the names of the tapas. *Jamón, Jamón* is *croquetas* (geddit?); *Victor o Victoria* is *gazpacho* or consommé, depending on the season.
Other locations: Corazon Loco, C/Almendro 22, Los Austrias (91 366 57 83).

El Bocaíto

C/Libertad 6 (91 532 12 19). Metro Chueca. **Open** 1-4pm, 8-30pm-midnight Mon-Fri; 8.30pm-midnight Sat. Closed Aug. **Credit** DC, MC, V. **Map** p324 I11 ③④

Film-set traditional, from the bullfight posters and Andalucian ceramics to the old-school tapas and unsmiling, white-jacketed waiters. If you're famous, though, they'll grin for the camera, just as they did with Pedro, Hugh and, goddammit, Mark Knopfler.

El Tigre

C/Infantas 30 (91 532 00 72). Metro Banco de España or Chueca. **Open** 10.30am-1.30am daily. **Credit** V. **Map** p324 I11 ③⑤

If you can actually make it through the door, order a beer or a cider and marvel at the hefty tapas that come with it – patatas bravas, *jamón serrano*, tortilla… it's all free, and each plate varies (and gets bigger) with each round. The bar itself is incredibly noisy, very smoky and always absolutely rammed. But it does disprove the theory that there's no such thing as a free lunch.

Malasaña & Conde Duque

Albur

C/Manuela Malasaña 15 (91 594 27 33). Metro Bilbao. **Open** 1.30-4.30pm, 8.30pm-midnight Mon-Thur; 1.30pm-1am Fri, Sat. **Credit** MC, V. **Map** p323 H8 ③⑥

The speciality is *revueltos* (scrambled egg) with prawns, wild mushrooms and so on, but there's also good ham, chorizo, black pudding, and a variety of wines to accompany them. Generally a quiet place, with soothing buttercup-yellow walls, it gets quite lively later on with a young Malasaña crowd.

Casa do Compañeiro

C/San Vicente Ferrer 44 (91 521 57 02). Metro Noviciado. **Open** 1.30pm-2am daily. **No credit cards. Map** p323 G9 ③⑦

A tiny jewel among tapas bars, with wonderful tiling inside and out. The tapas are mainly from Galicia, with lots of octopus, gammon, pig's ear and, of

Eat, Drink, Shop

course, *caldo gallego*, the typical broth made with cabbage and pork. A glass of crisp, dry *fino* makes the perfect accompaniment.

La Casta

C/Cristo 1 (91 547 77 40). Metro Noviciado.
Open 1-4pm, 7pm-1am daily. **No credit cards.**
Map p323 F8
A cool and relaxing tapas bar with gently revolving ceiling fans and terracotta floors. Tapas include smoked cod, trout and salmon, or there are wooden *tablas* spread with cheese or ham. More unusually, there is Leffe and Guinness on tap. C/Cristo is pedestrianised and there are tables outside, but expect to be assailed by a mixed bag of buskers.

Conache

Plaza de San Ildefonso, C/Santa Barbara 11 (91 522 95 00). Metro Tribunal. **Open** 10am-1am Mon-Thur; 10am-2am Sat; 11-6pm Sun. **Credit** AmEx, MC, V.
Map p323 H9
The Conache look is casually hip, even though the bright lighting and fruit machines keep scenesters at bay. The food, however, is absolutely where it's at. Try stir-fried vegetables with prawns, little rolls of venison and apple, or spinach and brie with figs, and be sure to finish with the sublime cheese mousse with fruits of the forest.

La Fortuna

Plaza de los Mostenses 3 (91 547 30 98). Metro Plaza de España. **Open** 11.30am-midnight Mon-Thur; 11.30am-1am Fri, Sat. Closed 3wks Aug.
Credit MC, V. **Map** p323 F10
It's been around, off and on, since 1800, though renovations have erased all the evidence but a very early photograph. A local favourite is the breakfast of fried egg, bacon and chips, but a decent range of tapas is available all day. Other specialities are *migas*, clams in sherry, and *salmorejo* (a thicker gazpacho).

El Maño

C/Palma 64 (91 521 50 57). Metro Noviciado. **Open** 7.30pm-12.30am Mon-Thur; 12.30-3.30pm, 7.30pm-12.30am Fri-Sun. **No credit cards.** **Map** p323 F8
A relaxed place, with french windows opening on to the street in summer, marble-topped tables, faded yellow paintwork and art deco touches. A good selection of wine is chalked up on the walls, some of it poured from ancient barrels, and there are tortillas served with *pisto*, ragu or squid, brochettes of chicken and lamb and a small selection of canapés.

La Taberna de la Copla

C/Jesús del Valle 1 (91 522 44 22). Metro Tribunal. **Open** 1-4pm, 8pm-1.30am Tue-Sat, 1-4pm Sun. **No credit cards.** **Map** p323 G9/10
Copla is a form of Spanish ballad, as sung by those depicted here in the dozens of crumbling photos. Tapas are named for famous *coplas* – Juanita Reina is ham with tomato; Principe Gitano is tuna with peppers, and a range of tortillas includes La Zarzamora (plain); Ojos Verdes (with ham), and Cinco Farolas (with tuna).

La Taberna de Corps

Plaza Guardia de Corps 1 (91 547 53 27). Metro Ventura Rodríguez. **Open** 1.30pm-1am Mon-Sat; 1.30-5pm Sun. **No credit cards.** **Map** p323 F8
The *surtido* (mixed plate) of canapés and excellent selection of wines aside, the main attraction here (and it sure isn't the dour staff) is the location on a quiet leafy *plaza*. Grab a Rioja or a draught *vermut* and settle down with the papers.

Lhardy. *See p160.*

Taberna 9
C/San Andrés 9 (no phone). Metro Tribunal.
Open *Sept-June* 7.30pm-1am Tue-Thur, Sun; 7.30pm-2.30am Fri, Sat. *July, Aug* 8.30pm-2am Tue-Thur, Sun, 8pm-2.30am Fri, Sat. **No credit cards. Map** p323 G9 ㊹
Fun, funky and very much of its neighbourhood, with a young crowd. Taberna 9 has a straightforward list of canapés, including a good scrambled egg with chorizo, and serves house wine by the very cheap *chato* – a small glass.

La Tabernilla del Gato Amadeus
C/Cristo 2 (91 541 41 12). Metro Noviciado. **Open** 1pm-1am daily. **No credit cards. Map** p323 F8 ㊺
Named after a late, great, Persian cat, this is a tiny, welcoming bar, whose *croquetas* are legendary. The other favourite is the *patatas con mojo picón* (baked new potatoes with a spicy sauce). Although there's not much seating inside (the sister bar nearby is bigger), in summer there are tables outside.
Other locations: C/Limón 32, Malasaña & Conde Duque (91 542 54 23).

Salamanca & the Retiro

Cervecería Santa Bárbara
C/Goya 70 (91 575 00 52). Metro Goya. **Open** 8am-midnight daily. **Credit** MC, V. **Map** p325 O9 ㊻
The prawns are the thing here, consumed in rosy platefuls by the uptown shoppers crowded round the horseshoe-shaped bar. Always full, with a loyal clientele, it is one of the city's meeting places, with a good selection of beers, and tables outside.

Estay
C/Hermosilla 46 (91 578 04 70/www.estayrestaurante.com). Metro Velázquez. **Open** 8am-1am Mon-Sat. **Credit** AmEx, DC, MC, V. **Map** p325 M9 ㊼
Estay's bright, air-conditioned interior, usually filled with baying young mothers heavily laden with shopping bags, does not immediately suggest gastronomic promise. Stick with the place, however, and you'll enjoy scrumptious and sophisticated tapas and cheap wines by the glass.

Hevia
C/Serrano 118 (91 561 46 87/www.heviamadrid.com). Metro Gregorio Marañón. **Open** 9am-1am Mon-Sat. Closed Aug. **Credit** AmEx, DC, MC, V. **Map** p321 L6 ㊽
A quiet, well-heeled crowd frequents this smart bar. Tapas are correspondingly sophisticated – foie gras, caviar, crab and duck liver pâté – and correspondingly pricey. During the summer the tables outside can prove irresistible.

José Luis
C/Serrano 89 (91 563 09 58/www.joseluis.es). Metro Núñez de Balboa. **Open** 9am-1am Mon-Sat; noon-1am Sun. **Credit** AmEx, DC, MC, V. **Map** p321 L6 ㊾
Probably one of the most famous tapas bars in Madrid, and accordingly name-checked in a song by the Catalan folk singer Serrat, the food here is little changed since the 1950s and of a high standard. If your appetite is up to it, try the *brascada* (sirloin with ham and onions); otherwise there are delicate little canapés of smoked salmon tartare, melted brie and similar treats.

North & west

Argüelles

Alhuzena
C/Martín de los Heros 72 (91 544 30 18). Metro Argüelles. **Open** *Sept-June* 8pm-2am Mon-Thur, 8pm-3am Fri, Sat. *July* 8pm-3am Mon-Sat. Closed Aug. **Credit** DC, MC, V. **Map** p322 C7 (50)
A quirky basement bar, kicking to the strains of flamenco and best described as rustic technicolour, with its wooden painted furniture and Gaudiesque mosaic bar. Wine is served in little *chatos*, and the tapas are outstanding: artichokes filled with jamón ibérico, mozzarella with tomato and pesto and crêpes with spinach and ricotta among them.

Chamberí

Another area with a tapas round of its own – Calles Cardenal Cisneros and Hartzenbush are lined with cheapish bars.

Bodegas la Ardosa
C/Santa Engracia 70 (91 446 58 94). Metro Iglesia. **Open** 9.30am-3.30pm, 7-11pm daily. Closed mid July to end Aug. **No credit cards.**
A tiny local bar with a lovely old tiled exterior (confusingly marked No.58) and walls lined with bottles of wine. There are especially good *patatas bravas* and fried pigs' ears, as well as sardines, an array of wonderful shellfish and good beer.

La Nueva
C/Arapiles 7 (91 447 95 92). Metro Quevedo. **Open** 11am-midnight Mon-Sat. Closed Aug. **Credit** DC, MC, V. **Map** p323 G6 (51)
A gorgeous old bar, La Nueva was recently taken over and scrubbed up, losing a little of its character along the way. The new ownership has added a Russian theme, with oysters, champagne, and a vodka and Beluga caviar tasting for €195.50 a head. Meanwhile, back on Planet Earth, there are prawns, or tripe with chickpeas.

Taberna los Madriles
C/José Abascal 26 (91 593 06 26/www.losmadriles.com). Metro Alonso Cano. **Open** 11am-12.30am Mon-Fri; 11am-4pm, 7pm-12.30am Sat. **No credit cards.**
The speciality of this diminutive bar is the *pincho Los Madriles*, with red pepper and anchovies. Also worth trying are the tuna and prawn *pinchos*, the fried potatoes and the *callos*. Decorated with hundreds of black and white photos of its regulars as kids, this old-style bar can get a bit cramped, but has tables outside in summer.

Cafés & Bars

A nation of barkeepers.

The outrageous claims abound: Madrid has over 100,000 bars (about one per 100 residents); the Calle Alcalá has more bars than Belgium; the city has more bars per square metre than anywhere else in Europe. The amazing thing is that they're probably all true. *Madrileños*, even by normal Spanish standards, are a very sociable bunch who place a lot of importance on eating and drinking in company. Consequently the first coffee of the day tends to be drunk in a bar on the way to work, and the second (often accompanied by a glass of wine) will happen around 10.30 or so when groups of office workers head out for breakfast.

In bars in Spain it is customary to pay at the end, although different rules apply in touristy places or on outdoor terraces. To get a waiter's attention try a firm, but questioning, *'oiga'* (literally, 'hear me', a perfectly polite way of attracting someone's attention). Once you've got him/her, ask *'¿Me pones un…?'* ('Could you bring me a…?'). Tipping is discretionary. Change is usually returned in a small dish, and people generally leave just a few coins, regardless of the amount spent. In most bars, you can throw olive stones on the floor, along with toothpicks, paper napkins and so on, but watch what the locals are doing.

COFFEE AND TEA

A *café con leche* is a largish, milky coffee, which can be also served in a glass (*vaso*); ask for a *taza grande* if you want it even bigger. An espresso is a *café solo*; the same with a dash of milk is *un cortado*, while *un americano* is diluted with twice the normal amount of water. With a shot of alcohol, a *solo* becomes a *carajillo*. A true *carajillo* is made with coffee, sugar, some coffee beans and brandy, which is then set alight on top so that the mixture gets mulled a little; a *carajillo* can also be just a *solo* with a shot of *coñac*, and you can equally ask for a *carajillo de whisky, de ron* (rum), *de Bailey's* (pronounced 'bye-lees'), *de anís* or anything else you fancy. Decaffeinated coffee is *descafeinado*, and you will normally be asked if you want it from a sachet (*de sobre*), or the machine (*de máquina*). In summer a great alternative is *café con hielo* – iced coffee.

Tea in bars is usually awful, and unless you specifically request otherwise will often come as a glass of hot milk with a teabag on the side. Very popular, however, are herbal teas

Café de Oriente. *See p168.*

(*infusiones*), such as *menta* (mint) or *manzanilla* (camomile) and nowadays, if the cloud of globalisation has a silver lining, it is that there are a few more cafés around that have some awareness of what decent tea might be.

BEER

Draught beer (*de barril*) is served in *cañas*, a small measure that varies but is less than half a pint, *tubos* in a tall thin glass, or as *dobles* (a little bigger). Some places even serve *pintas* (pints), often in a *jarra*, a large heavy glass with a handle. Bottled beer usually comes in *tercios*, a third of a litre, or in *botellines*, a quarter of a litre. Spain produces some good-quality beers. In Madrid, the favourite is the local Mahou, with two basic varieties – green label Mahou Clásica and the stronger red label Cinco Estrellas. San Miguel is less common, while Andalucian favourite Cruzcampo is growing in popularity. A darker Mahou beer (*negra*) is also available. Shandy is *clara*, and is made with bitter lemon. Imported beers are now common, too, but nearly always cost more.

WINES, SPIRITS AND OTHER DRINKS

All bars have a sturdy cheap red (*tinto*) on offer, and usually a white (*blanco*) and a rosé (*rosado*). Madrid's traditional summer drink is *tinto de verano* (red in a tall glass over ice, with a slice of lemon and topped up with lemonade). Most bars listed here will have at least one decent Rioja and probably a cava, but truly good wines are normally only found in the new-style *tabernas* that take pride in their lists.

Sherry is *jerez*. The type virtually always drunk in Spain is dry *fino*, served very cold. A good fuller-bodied variety is *palo cortado*. Sweet sherries have traditionally been only for export. Red vermouth (*vermut*) with soda is another Madrid tradition, usually as an aperitif, and has recently come back into fashion a little. For a powerful after-dinner drink, try Galician *orujo*, a fiery spirit similar to grappa, that normally comes plain (*blanco*) or con hierbas, in a luminous green colour. Other *digestivos* include *patxarán*, a fruity aniseed-flavoured liqueur from Navarra, and the more Castilian *anís*, the best of which hails from Chinchón and is available dry (*seco*) or sweet (*dulce*).

NON-ALCOHOLIC DRINKS

Low- and alcohol-free beers (Laiker, Buckler, Kaliber) have an important niche in the market; other favourites for non-alcohol drinkers are the Campari-like but booze-free Bitter Kas, and plain tonic (*una tónica*) with ice and lemon. Fresh orange juice, *zumo de naranja*, is often available. Trinaranjus is the best-known bottled juice brand; favourite flavours are orange (*naranja*), pineapple (*piña*) and peach (*melocotón*). *Mosto* is grape juice, served in small glasses, sometimes with ice and a slice. A great and unappreciated Spanish speciality, though, are its traditional summer refreshers: most unusual is *horchata*, a milky drink made with tiger nuts. It has to be drunk fresh, from a specialised shop, as it curdles once made. The same places also offer *granizados* – crushed ice with fresh lemon, orange or coffee. Mineral water (*agua mineral*) can be ordered anywhere, either sparkling (*con gas*) or still (*sin gas*).

Many entries in the **Nightlife** and **Tapas** chapters are also good all-rounders, acting as cafés or bars for at least part of the day.

The best Places

For a pint of Guinness

La Ardosa, the first and still the best (*see p175*), or the Irish bars: **The James Joyce** (*see p179*) or **Finnegan's** (*see p174*).

For a cool tiled interior

La Palmera (*see p178*) for less is more or **Viva Madrid** (*see p173*) for the totally tiled experience.

To watch the world go by

Sit by the windows at either **Café Comercial** (*see p175*), or try **La Mallorquina** (*see p170*).

For seeing and being seen

The **Bellas Artes** (*see p151*) is much loved by the arty crowd, while **Isolée** (*see p174*) is a tad hipper.

For summer nights

Delic (*see p169*), although getting a table can be tricky; or spread out at the **Café El Moderno** (*see p177*).

For meeting fellow visitors

Viva Madrid (*see p173*) certainly has its share of *guiris*, or try a pavement table at the **Cervecería Santa Ana** (*see p170*).

Los Austrias & La Latina

Café del Nuncio

C/Nuncio 12 & C/Segovia 9 (91 366 08 53). *Metro La Latina.* **Open** noon-2am Mon-Thur; noon-3am Fri, Sat; noon-1am Sun. **No credit cards.** Map p327 F13 ❶
Split into two halves at either end of the narrow Escalinata del Nuncio, the Café del Nuncio has lovely cool, dark interiors with gently rotating ceiling fans and soft classical music. The real charm, however, lies in the terrace outside on the stepped slope dividing the two spaces; this is one of the most picturesque streets in the old city.

Café de Oriente

Plaza de Oriente 2 (91 541 39 74). Metro Ópera. **Open** 8.30am-1.30am Mon-Thur, Sun; 8.30am-2.30am Fri, Sat. **Credit** AmEx, DC, MC, V. Map p327 E11 ❷
The *belle époque* interior is entirely fake yet entirely convincing, making this one of the most peaceful and elegant spots to flick through the newspapers or recover from the exertions of the Palacio Real opposite. Despite its location, with tables outside on the stunning Plaza de Oriente, the café seems to be as popular with locals as tourists, who are perhaps put off by its air of grandeur. **Photo** *p167*.

Café del Real

Plaza de Isabel II (91 547 21 24). Metro Ópera. **Open** 9am-1am Mon-Thur, Sun; 10am-2.30am Fri, Sat. **No credit cards.** Map p327 F11 ❸

Delic.

This likeable, cramped café with a lovely façade is good for coffee and cake (chocolate or carrot), though prices are a tad high. Head upstairs to a low-beamed room with red leather chairs and old opera posters, overlooking the *plaza*. The café was a particular haunt of intellectuals, artists and actors in the '80s, but it's popular with a wider crowd these days.

Chocolatería San Ginés

Pasadizo de San Ginés 5 (91 365 65 46).
Metro Ópera or Sol. **Open** 9.30am-7am daily.
No credit cards. Map p327 G11 ❹
Serving chocolate and *churros* (deep-fried batter sticks) to the city night and day since 1894, this veritable institution has had to introduce a ticketing system – pay before you order – to deal with the 5am queues of exhausted clubbers and chipper old ladies. The lighting is a bit much if you fall into the former category, but there are at least tables outside.

De 1911

Plazuela de San Ginés 5, corner C/Coloreros
(91 366 35 19). Metro Ópera or Sol. **Open**
6pm-1.30am Mon-Thur; 6pm-3am Fri, Sat.
No credit cards. Map p327 G11 ❺
Despite the address, De 1911 actually sits on the tiny pedestrian street C/Coloreros, on which it has tables. It is indeed from 1911, but is a curious mix of *belle époque* and neon, Greek statuary and Coca-Cola signs. There's Guinness on tap, strong cocktails and some good tapas: try chorizo in cider or a ham, cheese and tomato brochette.

Delic

Costanilla de San Andrés 14 (91 364 54 50).
Metro La Latina. **Open** 8pm-1.30am Mon; 11am-1am Tue-Thur; 11am-2.15am Fri, Sat; 11am-midnight Sun. Closed last 2wks Aug. **No credit cards.**
Map p327 E13 ❻
A perennial favourite with seemingly everybody; from those looking for a peaceful morning coffee on the leafy Plaza de la Paja to those meeting up for a few bolstering cocktails before a big night out. A globe-trotting menu includes tabouleh, Japanese dumplings and filled ciabatta, and the Chilean chocolate cake is utterly irresistible.

La Fontanilla

Plaza Puerta Cerrada 13 (91 366 27 49). Metro
La Latina. **Open** 11am-2am daily. **Credit** DC,
MC, V. **Map** p327 F12 ❼
La Fontanilla claims to be not the biggest or the best or the oldest, but the smallest Irish pub in Madrid. There's no disputing this singular claim, but it does manage to cram in a couple of wooden tables alongside wide hatches opening on to the street. The myriad beers racked up the walls are sadly not for sale, but there's Murphy's and Guinness, at least, along with some incongruous canapés to nibble at.

Rey de los Vinos

C/Bailén 19 (91 559 53 32). Metro Ópera. **Open**
10am-1am, Mon, Tue, Thur-Sun. Closed mid Feb-mid
Mar. **Credit** MC, V at table. No credit cards at bar.
Map p327 E12 ❽

Kept much as it has been for the last century – very simple, but spacious and light inside with a wide counter and mirrored walls – the King of Wines serves good canapés, and is a great place for a drink after visiting the cathedral. Prices are quite high, especially if you sit outdoors.

Taberna Gerardo
C/Calatrava 21 (91 221 96 60). Metro Puerta de Toledo. **Open** noon-4pm, 8pm-midnight Mon-Sat; noon-5pm Sun. **No credit cards. Map** p327 E14 **❾**
A lively and unpretentious wine bar, Taberna Gerardo is an essential part of the neighbourhood, offering excellent sausage, ham and seafood tapas, as well as a particularly good selection of cheeses.

El Ventorillo
C/Bailén 14 (91 366 35 78). Metro Ópera. **Open** 10am-midnight daily. **No credit cards. Map** p327 E13 **❿**
Just down from the Palacio Real, this terraza offers the finest sunsets in Madrid, with a magnificent location looking out over the Casa del Campo and all the way to the Guadarrama. Not cheap, however.

Sol & Gran Vía

Café del Círculo de Bellas Artes
C/Alcalá 42 (91 521 69 42). Metro Banco de España. **Open** 9am-1am Mon-Thur; 9am-3am Fri, Sat; noon-1am Sun. **Admission** €1; free 2-4pm. **Credit** DC, MC, V. **Map** p328 I11 **⓫**
A quintessential point of reference in the city's café society, the Bellas Artes is utterly elegant. Under new ownership, it is now free to enter at lunchtime for the *menú del día*. Otherwise take a seat amid the columns and female nudes and frown over *El País* with coffee and a croissant to fit right in.

La Mallorquina
Puerta del Sol 8 (91 521 12 01). Metro Sol. **Open** 9am-9.15pm daily. Closed mid July-Aug. **No credit cards. Map** p327 G11 **⓬**
While the bakery downstairs supplies box after ribbon-tied box of flaky *ensaïmada* pastries, croissants and *napolitanas* to what seems like half of Madrid, the upstairs *salón* crackles with the animated chat of *madrileña* blue-rinses and savvier tourists. Windows overlooking the Puerta del Sol make this an unbeatable central spot for breakfast.

Museo Chicote
Gran Vía 12 (91 532 67 37/www.museo-chicote. com). Metro Gran Vía. **Open** 8am-3am Mon-Sat. **Credit** AmEx, DC, MC, V. **Map** p324 I11 **⓭**
Its art deco interior is starting to look a bit shabby around the edges, but Chicote is still the doyen of Madrid cocktail bars. This was famously where Hemingway and other international press hacks would spend their days sheltering from the artillery shells flying down the Gran Vía during the Civil War. Grace Kelly and Ava Gardner, along with just about every Spanish writer, actor or artist of the last 60 years have passed through too. **Photo** *p172.*

Huertas & Santa Ana

Café del Español
C/Príncipe 25 (91 420 43 05). Metro Antón Martín or Sol. **Open** noon-1am Mon-Wed, Sun; noon-2am Thur; noon-3am Fri, Sat. **Credit** V. **Map** p328 H12 **⓮**
Terribly elegant, with columns, green-glass chandeliers and red-velvet banquettes, this quiet café is modelled on its neighbour, the Teatro Español. It's popular for a slice of tarte tatin or a *bocatín* (little sandwich), though is let down by its coffee.

Casa Pueblo
C/León 3 (91 429 05 15). Metro Antón Martín. **Open** 5pm-2.30am daily. **Admission** free. **Credit** AmEx, MC, V. **Map** p328 I12 **⓯**
A handsome, old-fashioned jazz bar hung with antique clocks and black and white photos, Casa Pueblo is popular with a slightly older crowd that knows its whisky. Occasional live music includes jazz and tango (on a Wednesday).

Cervecería Alemana
Plaza Santa Ana 6 (91 429 70 33). Metro Sol. **Open** 11.30am-12.30am Mon, Wed, Thur, Sun; 11.30am-2am Fri, Sat. **Credit** DC, MC, V. **Map** p328 H12 **⓰**
Famous for being Ernest Hemingway's daily haunt (his table, should you be wondering, is the one in the near right-hand corner). The decor is fin-de-siècle German bierkeller, with dusty old paintings and dark wood. The tapas can be uninspired and the waiters are unfailingly gruff, but for many this will be an essential stop.

Cervecería Santa Ana
Plaza Santa Ana 10 (91 429 43 56). Metro Antón Martín or Sol. **Open** 11am-1.30am Mon-Thur, Sun; 11am-2.30am Fri, Sat. **No credit cards. Map** p328 H12 **⓱**
Another on this strip of beerhouses (the most exotic brew on offer here is Guinness), this one was never frequented by Hemingway and is consequently cheaper. Two entrances lead into two different spaces; one with seating and one without, and there are tables outside. Good for a light lunch, with decent salads and a range of *pulgas* (small rolls).

Dos Gardenias
C/Santa María 13 (627 003 571). Metro Antón Martín. **Open** *Sept-May* 8pm-3am Tue-Sun. *June-Aug* 10pm-3am Tue-Sun. **No credit cards. Map** p328 I13 **⓲**
There's no sign on the door – just look out for this mellow little space painted in warm yellow, orange and blue and the emanating chilled-out vibes, soft flamenco and Brazilian jazz. Kick back on a velvet sofa with the house speciality: a Mojito made with brown sugar and Angostura bitters.

Fookar
C/Fúcar 1 (91 420 04 64). Metro Antón Martín. **Open** 9.30am-4pm, 7.30pm-2am Mon-Thur; 9.30am-4pm, 7.30pm-3am Fri, Sat; 4pm-1.30am Sun. **No credit cards. Map** p328 I/J13 **⓳**

Picture this Tertulias

The intellectual life of Spain once revolved around the ephemeral institution known as the *tertulia*. Originating in the humanist salons of 16th-century Seville, the *tertulia* is a gathering of people united by a common interest, which can range from mathematics to gastronomy, but has traditionally been literature. And Spain being a country where people tend to go out rather than meet in each other's houses, these gatherings have invariably been held in bars and cafés.

The rise of the *tertulia* in Madrid, as depicted in many paintings of the time, coincided with the city's emergence in the early 19th century as the centre of a café life rivalling that of Paris and Vienna. Café life has always flourished at times of great political repression, the café being a place whose proverbial smoky gloom has provided a suitably furtive retreat for dissidents. During the grey, autocratic rule of Spain's Ferdinand VII, the *tertulia* became an expression of political and cultural freedom.

Tertulias took place in many of the cafés that by the 1830s had almost entirely encircled the Puerta del Sol. But the most influential of these gatherings was the one associated with a tiny, rat-infested basement café next to the neo-classical Teatro Español (the present bland reconstruction bears little resemblance to the original establishment). The place was officially called the Café del Príncipe, but everyone came to know it as the 'Parnasillo' or 'Little Parnassus', on account of its attracting all the fashionable writers of the day. Among these were the much revered satirical essayist Mariano José de Larra and the writer Ramón de Mesonero Romanos, who famously wrote that in 'this miserable little room' they succeeded in shaking the very foundations of Spanish life and culture.

With the evolution towards the end of the 19th century of Madrid's idiosyncratically late eating and drinking hours, *tertulias* proliferated as never before, reaching their apogee in the 1920s under the guidance of a writer sometimes referred to as 'the second of the Ramones', Ramón Gómez de la Serna. Every Saturday night, from around 10pm until dawn, a *tertulia*, presided over by Gómez de la Serna, was held in what was soon dubbed 'The Sacred Crypt of the Pombo', a now vanished café off the Puerta del Sol. The solemnity of these celebrated meetings was captured in a sombre painting by José Gutiérrez Solana (*pictured*). La Serna is pictured standing, in the centre. These gatherings were also slightly ridiculed by the film-maker Luis Buñuel, who later described how 'we used to arrive, greet each other, and order a drink – usually coffee, and a lot of water – until a meandering conversation began about the latest literary publications or political upheavals.'

Most liberal and avant-garde associates of the Pombo went into exile after the Civil War, thus radically diminishing the cultural life of the capital. Subsequently many of the cafés in the centre of Madrid were succeeded by the HQs of large banks, and many more suffered the humiliation of being transformed into Formica-lined, American-style cafeterias.

La Tertulia del Café Pombo, *by José Gutiérrez Solana, is found at the Reina Sofía (see p85).*

Eat, Drink, Shop

Museo Chicote.
See p170.

A gleefully eccentric little café, with whitewashed brick walls enlivened with splashes of colour – collaged mannequins, installations with plastic fruit and net tutus as lightshades – and where even the loos are kooky. Downtempo and bossa nova set the daytime tone, when regulars drop in to use the free internet access while sipping coffee, but things do tend to liven up at night.

Naturbier

Plaza Santa Ana 9 (91 429 39 18). Metro Antón Martín or Sol. **Open** 11am-1am Mon-Thur, Sun; 11am-2am Fri, Sat. **Credit** MC, V. **Map** p328 H12 ⓴
The least exciting-looking of all the beer cellars lining this side of the Plaza Santa Ana, Naturbier's big draw is its own-made organic beer – in fact it's the only place in Madrid to brew its own. The tapas are also worth checking out, despite the pricing, which is somewhat creative.

Prado 4

C/Prado 4 (91 429 33 61). Metro Antón Martín. **Open** 8am-midnight Mon-Wed; 8am-2.30am Thur-Sat; noon-midnight Sun. Closed 2wks mid Aug. **Credit** AmEx, DC, MC, V. **Map** p328 H12 ㉑
Under new ownership but with the same air of hauteur, Prado 4 emulates, with no little success, one of the grand cafés of the Habsburg empire. It was actually created in the 1980s, but its velvet drapes and marble-topped tables are already looking suitably worn. A planned 2007 refurb may change all that.

Reporter

C/Fúcar 6 (91 429 39 22). Metro Antón Martín. **Open** noon-5pm Mon; noon-2am Tue-Thur, Sun; 7pm-3am Fri, Sat. **No credit cards. Map** p328 I13 ㉒
The piña coladas here are said to be the best in town, but otherwise there are good fruit juices and (during the day, at least) a little garden in this stylish

Huertas cocktail-café, with jazz played at a soothingly low volume and occasional photo exhibitions. It also serves tapas and light meals in the afternoon.

Salón de Té Sherazade

C/Santa María 16 (91 369 24 74). Metro Antón Martín. **Open** 5pm-3am Mon-Thur, Sun; 5pm-4am Fri, Sat. **No credit cards. Map** p328 I13 ㉓
Filled with kilims, hookah pipes, cushions and bronze lanterns, this Moroccan seraglio calls itself a tea room, but effectively functions as one of the most atmospheric chillout bars of the city. The small room downstairs, particularly, is strewn with supine twentysomethings finding inner peace.

Sol y Sombra

C/Echegaray, 18 (91 542 81 93). Metro Sevilla or Sol. **Open** 10pm-5.30am daily. **Credit** V. **Map** p328 H12 ㉔
A curious fusion of neon lighting and taurine decor (the name refers to the seats at a bullfight), which just about comes off. It's certainly very popular with the mix of thirtysomething minor celebs and their well-heeled friends. Live acts feature every night from Wednesday to Sunday, with a mix of Spanish cheese, flamenco-chill and lounge on offer. A sniffy door policy discourages scruffy trainers.

La Venencia

C/Echegaray 7 (91 429 73 13). Metro Sevilla or Sol. **Open** 1-3.30pm, 7.30pm-1.30am daily. **No credit cards. Map** p328 H12 ㉕
Totally unreconstructed, La Venencia is gloriously shabby, with old, peeling sherry posters, barrels behind the bar and walls burnished gold by decades of tobacco smoke. It serves only sherry (locals will order a crisp, dry *fino* or *manzanilla*, leaving the sweet stuff to the occasional tourist that stumbles in here), along with manchego cheese, *cecina* (air-dried beef) and chorizo by way of tapas. Orders are still chalked up on the bar, and an enamel sign asks customers not to spit on the floor.

Viva Madrid

C/Manuel Fernández y González 7 (91 429 36 40). Metro Sevilla or Sol. **Open** 1pm-2am Mon-Thur, Sun; 1pm-3am Fri, Sat. **No credit cards. Map** p328 H12 ㉖
This tiled bar has become a tourist destination in its own right. It is beautiful, with vaulted ceilings and evocative decor, but tends to get rammed with young foreigners looking to pull, or at least get plastered – you either love it or loathe it. Anyone over 21 will best appreciate it in the afternoon.

Yesterday

C/Huertas 10 (no phone). Metro Sevilla or Sol. **Open** 8.30pm-2.30am Mon, Wed, Thur, Sun; 9pm-3.30am Fri, Sat. **No credit cards. Map** p328 H12 ㉗
Back in the '70s this was one of the first bars to open in an area that's now awash with them. On a heaving Saturday it's an oasis; lively but not rammed, with no pretensions, no DJs and no cocktails – just a cosy, antique-filled bar with good music and friendly Spanish-American owners.

Rastro & Lavapiés

El Eucalipto

C/Argumosa 4 (mobile 629 334 998). Metro Lavapiés. **Open** 5pm-2am Mon-Sat; 1pm-2am Sun. **No credit cards. Map** p328 H14 ㉘
Totally tropical, with a beach bar look and pictures of Cuban singers around the walls, El Eucalipto is all about fruit. There are long lists of juices; *batidos* (milkshakes and smoothies); lime, strawberry, mango, raspberry and banana daiquiris; caipirinhas, piña coladas and more.

La Heladería

C/Argumosa 7 (91 528 80 09). Metro Lavapiés. **Open** 10am-midnight Mon-Thur, Sun; 10am-1am Fri, Sat. Closed Nov-Mar. **No credit cards. Map** p328 H14 ㉙
Peruvian owner Yoli is unfailingly charming, and happy to let you try her excellent ice-creams before you buy – blackberry (*mora*) and lemon come recommended. Try the *blanco y negro*, a delicious café frappé with ice-cream, or one of her milkshakes.

Montes

C/Lavapiés 40 (91 527 00 64). Metro Lavapiés. **Open** noon-3.30pm, 8pm-midnight Tue-Thur; noon-3.30pm, 8pm-1.30am Fri, Sat; noon-5pm Sun. Closed Aug. **No credit cards. Map** p327 H14 ㉚
Ignore the inauspicious exterior and raucous crowd spilling on to the street, and inside you'll find a wide variety of excellent wines, backed up by top-notch tapas. The bar is owned by genial Don César, who is something of a gourmet. Bottles of wines are stacked up above the bar with his handwritten comments attached to each one.

Nuevo Café Barbieri

C/Ave María 45 (91 527 36 58). Metro Lavapiés. **Open** 3pm-2am Mon-Thur, Sun; 3pm-2.30am Fri, Sat. **No credit cards. Map** p328 H14 ㉛
An airy and peaceful space with high ceilings and a dusty elegance, its marble-topped tables slightly chipped and its red-velvet banquettes a little worn. A favourite haunt of journos and wannabe travel writers, Barbieri has plenty of newspapers and magazines, but its ordinary coffee comes at a premium and the service lacks much verve.

Oliveros

C/San Millán 4 (91 354 62 52/www.taberna oliveros.com). Metro La Latina. **Open** 1-5pm, 8pm-12.30am Tue-Sat; noon-6pm Sun. Closed mid Aug-mid Sept. **Credit** MC, V. **Map** p327 F13 ㉜
Oliveros is the genuine article, and although it was closed for years, it has been miraculously preserved in its original mid 19th-century bare-bricked state, complete with tiles and zinc bar. Opening hours can be somewhat erratic, however.

Taberna de Tirso de Molina

Plaza de Tirso de Molina 9 (91 429 17 56). Metro Tirso de Molina. **Open** 8am-2am daily. **Credit** MC, V. **Map** p327 G13 ㉝

Eat, Drink, Shop

It has a good stab at looking traditional with tiles, nautically uniformed waiters and exposed brickwork, but this *taberna* is in fact quite new. There are plenty of tables where you can eat a decent breakfast on the way to the Rastro, or a very generous set lunch for €8.25. Tapas are available all day, along with heftier dishes such as the towering *parillada de marisco* (seafood platter).

Vinícola Mentridana

C/San Eugenio 9 (91 527 87 60). Metro Antón Martín. **Open** 1pm-1am Mon-Thur, Sun; 1pm-2am Fri, Sat. **No credit cards. Map** p328 I14 ❸

Frequented by the bohemian hip element of the Lavapiés, this cool wine bar, with tall windows open on to the street, is gently evocative of the old *bodega* it used to be. An impressive list of well-priced wines by the glass is complemented by tasty canapés, along with mulled wine and *caldo* (broth) in winter, or gazpacho and *granizado* in summer.

Chueca

Ángel Sierra

C/Gravina 11 (91 531 01 26). Metro Chueca. **Open** 12.30pm-2.30am Mon-Sat; 12.30pm-2am Sun. **No credit cards. Map** p324 I10 ❸

This battered old bar with its tiled walls, zinc bar top, overflowing sink and glasses stacked on wooden slats has become the Chueca meeting-place *par excellence*, thanks to its position overlooking the main square. A newer room to the back of the bar, however, has a faux pub look enhanced with amplified MOR radio and a rule that only doubles and pints are served after midnight.

El Bandido Doblemente Armado

C/Apodaca 3 (91 522 10 51). Metro Bilbao. **Open** noon-midnight Mon-Wed; noon-2am Thur, Fri; 4pm-2am Sat. Closed 1wk mid Aug. **Credit** AmEx, DC, MC, V. **Map** p323 H8 ❸

An assured and attractively designed café-bookshop, equally at ease providing afternoon sandwiches, evening poetry readings or late-night cocktails. It's spaciously laid out, and also has friendly staff who are knowledgeable on the latest literary trends in Spain.

Bar Cock

C/Reina 16 (91 532 28 26). Metro Gran Vía. **Open** *Sept-June* 7pm-3am daily. *July, Aug* 9pm-4am Mon-Sat. **Credit** AmEx, DC, MC, V. **Map** p324 I11 ❸

A former brothel, Bar Cock is pricey and very stagey, furnished in what Spaniards think to be the style of an 'English pub' (red-velvet curtains, embossed leather armchairs and a fake half-timbered effect), it still continues to attract those who like to think of themselves as being in the know. As a result it can get extremely crowded.

Café Antik

C/Hortaleza 4 (no phone). Metro Gran Vía. **Open** 5pm-2am Mon-Thur; 5pm-3am Fri-Sun. **No credit cards. Map** p324 H11 ❸

Featuring cosy, mismatched-on-purpose furniture and bold-coloured walls, this small haunt would be unremarkable if not for one thing – silence. Just a stone's throw from the bustling Gran Vía, thirty-somethings (including the occasional TV presenter) sip fancy coffees and cocktails until the wee hours, content to hear themselves think.

Del Diego

C/Reina 12 (91 522 75 44). Metro Gran Vía. **Open** *Sept-July* 7pm-3am Mon-Thur; 7pm-3.30am Fri, Sat. Closed Aug. **Credit** AmEx, MC, V. **Map** p324 H11 ❸

Not to all tastes, with an unchanging, late 1980s, steel-and-blonde-wood *Wall Street* vibe, Del Diego is nevertheless deservedly renowned for its consummately smooth barmen and superb cocktails. Pull up a stool and try a zingy mint julep del Diego to kickstart a night's wheeling and dealing.

Finnegan's

Plaza de las Salesas 9 (91 310 05 21). Metro Alonso Martínez. **Open** 11am-2am Mon-Fri; 1pm-2am Sat, Sun. **Credit** DC, MC, V. **Map** p324 J9/10 ❸

One for rugby fans, Finnegan's has its own team, the Madrid Lions, and a talent for sniffing out every conceivable match to show on its large screens. In lean sporting times the void is filled with pub quizzes and DJs (mostly rock) at weekends. Pints of Beamish, Newky Brown and John Smith's complement burgers and other pub grub.

Isolée

C/Infantas, 19 (91 524 12 98/www.isolee.com). Metro Banco de España. **Open** 10am-10pm Mon-Wed; 10am-9pm Thur-Sat; 3.30pm-10.30pm Sun. **Credit** AmEx, DC, MC, V. **Map** p324 I11 ❸

The tendrils of cool emanating from Chueca are creeping ever further, as evinced by Isolée, a multi-faceted café, CD, clothes and kitchenware shop. The café is a little pricey, but serves decent sushi and bagels. Mostly, though, it's a place for the hip to sip espressos and make use of the Wi-Fi.

Olivera

C/Santo Tomé 8 (no phone). Metro Chueca. **Open** 9pm-2am Mon-Thur; 9pm-3am Fri, Sat. **No credit cards. Map** p324 J10 ❸

A relaxed lounge bar, presided over by a portrait of the owner's mother, Yugoslav film star Olivera Markovic. The musical mood is nu jazz and funk, and the mismatched armchairs and sofas make it an easy place to end up staying all night. Increasingly, though, it's become a stop-off on the pre-club round.

Stop Madrid

C/Hortaleza 11 (91 521 88 87). Metro Chueca or Gran Vía. **Open** noon-1am Mon-Wed; noon-3am Thur-Sun. **Credit** MC, V. **Map** p324 H11 ❸

When it opened in 1929, this was the first ham and charcuterie shop in Madrid. It's undergone a few changes since then, but many of the original fittings have been retained, and great pride is taken in sourcing the best ingredients for tapas. Of the 50-strong wine list, all are available by the glass. **Photo** *p175*.

Stop Madrid. *See p174.*

Stromboli Café

C/Hortaleza 96 (91 319 46 28). Metro Alonso Martínez or Chueca. **Open** 6.30pm-3am Mon-Thur, Sun; 6.30pm-3.30am Fri, Sat. **Credit** MC, V. **Map** p324 I9 **44**

Slick design (zebra-print stools and glitter balls) and piles of style mags cater to a young and cooler-than-thou crowd. With downtempo and chillout hotting up with the arrival of the DJ at midnight, Stromboli functions principally as an opportunity for some low-key strutting and a warm-up for the night ahead.

Zanzíbar

C/Regueros 9 (91 319 90 64). Metro Alonso Martínez. **Open** *Sept-July* 8pm-2am Tue-Thur, Sun; 8pm-3.30am Fri, Sat. *Aug* 8pm-2am Thur; 8pm-3.30am Fri, Sat. **No credit cards. Map** p324 I9 **45**

Good causes and ethnic chic combine to create a cute and colourful hangout for right-on revellers. On a small stage at the back there are frequent appearances by bossa nova bands, singer-songwriters and storytellers; at other times soft flamenco and reggae tickle the speakers. A few bar snacks are available, along with fair-trade coffee.

Malasaña & Conde Duque

La Ardosa

C/Colón 13 (91 521 49 79). Metro Tribunal. **Open** 11.30am-1.30am Mon-Thur, Sun; 11.30am-2.30am Fri, Sat. **No credit cards. Map** p323 H9/10 **46**

Having an affair? Then simply duck under the counter to find the most intimate bar-room you could wish for. Out front, meanwhile, this is a lovely old tiled *taberna* lined with dusty bottles, old black and white lithographs and beer posters. A range of canapés has just been added, and the speciality of the house is its draught beer – Bombardier, Budvar and, especially, Guinness.

Bar El 2 De

C/Velarde 24 (91 445 88 39). Metro Tribunal. **Open** *Sept-June* 1pm-2am Mon-Wed, Sun; 1pm-3am Thur-Sat. *July, Aug* 6pm-2am Mon-Wed, Sat; 1pm-3am Thur, Fri. **No credit cards. Map** p323 H8 **47**

This is the emblematic Malasaña hang-out, packed at weekends and drowsily mellow in the afternoons, with a tiled bar and engraved mirrors, nicotine-stained walls and lazily circling ceiling fans. To drink there's vermouth, lager and Beamish on tap, plus plenty of bottled beers and a small range of wines, served (if you dare) in *porrones*, long-spouted drinking jars.

Café Comercial

Glorieta de Bilbao 7 (91 521 56 55). Metro Bilbao. **Open** 7.30am-1am Mon-Thur; 7.30am-2am Fri; 8.30am-2am Sat; 9am-1am Sun. **No credit cards. Map** p323 H8 **48**

Still the classic Madrid bar, with its original battered brown leather seats, revolving doors and marbled walls. A nod to the modern age comes in the shape

The grape and the good

Madrid is an oenophile's playground, with none of the solemnity and hefty price-tags attached to wine-drinking elsewhere. Everyone drinks it here, from builders to nuns. It so pervades daily life, in fact, that the Spanish Ministry of Agriculture categorises wine as food rather than an alcoholic beverage.

Wine-lovers around the globe have now caught on to the fact that Spanish labels are the best value for your euro. *Wine Spectator* and American wine tsar Robert Parker claim it is one of the hottest regions in Europe. The sad fact remains, however, that a lot of bars are happy to serve plonk. To taste the good stuff, get thee to a wine bar. Madrid has a number of cosy little *enotecas* where you can settle in at the bar and try different tasty wines by the glass. **La Cruzada** (C/Amnistía 8, 91 548 01 31), for example, offers a delectable selection of reasonably priced *vinos*. King Alfonso XII reportedly used to frequent this bar when he needed to escape the nearby royal palace for a clandestine tipple. Check out the lovely carvings of bare-breasted women on the bar, dating back to 1827. Other reliable spots for quality wines include **La Taberna de Cien Vinos** (*see p159*), **González** (*see p195*), **Entrevinos** (C/Ferraz 36, 91 548 31 14), **Vinoteca Barbechera** (*see p161*) and **Vinitis** (C/Ventura de la Vega, 15, 91 420 40 90).

An entertaining way to dive into Spanish wine is to attend one of Madrid's many wine-tasting classes, known as *cursos de cata*. **Simply Spain Tours** (91 474 32 93 or mobile 652 66 58 65, www.simplyspaintoursmadrid. com) arranges casual wine and tapas tours of Madrid, or a three-hour course taught by a professional sommelier (followed by gourmet tapas) gets you happily swirling, sniffing and sipping good wine. **La Carte des Vins** (C/Postas 26, 91 354 63 40, www.lacarte desvins.com) is the Madrid outpost of a French franchise, which offers weekly wine-tasting courses in English and Spanish. These include the 'Cata Express', a 90-minute introduction, costing €15, as well as personalised tastings.

AtSpain (91 547 50 91, www.atspain. com), an online shop for Spanish gifts and gourmet products, also arranges fun English wine and tapas classes with sommeliers from Madrid's best wine stores. You might also pay a visit to the Torres Bodega's **Centro Cultural del Vino** (C/Martires Concepcionistas 19, 91 401 77 62), which offers professional wine classes covering everything from soil types to food pairing, over the course of two nights. The city's best wine shops, **Reserva y Cata**, **Lavinia** and **Bodegas Santa Cecilia** (for all, *see p197*), also offer regular *cursos de cata* in Spanish.

of the internet terminals upstairs, where American gap-year students write home about the old men playing chess alongside them.

Café Isadora

C/Divino Pastor 14 (91 445 71 54). Metro Bilbao. **Open** 4pm-2am Mon-Thur, Sun; 4pm-2.30am Fri, Sat. **No credit cards. Map** p323 G8 ④
An elegant shrine to Isadora Duncan, with a chequered floor, marble-topped tables and an eerie collection of prints of 'that scarf', alongside frequently changing exhibitions. Along with a range of *patxaráns*, many of them own-made, is a list of 'aguas'; cocktails made with cava. *Agua de Valencia* is the original and best, featuring orange juice, gin, Cointreau and vodka.

Café Manuela

C/San Vicente Ferrer 29 (91 531 70 37). Metro Tribunal. **Open** *Oct-May* 6pm-2am Mon; 4pm-2am Tue-Thur; 4pm-2.30am Fri, Sat. *June-Sept* 6pm-2.30am. **Credit** MC, V. **Map** p323 H9 ⑤
Stacked to the rafters with board games, Café Manuela has been a hive of activity since the Movida days. Its handsome art nouveau decor and conveniently nicotine-coloured walls are still the backdrop to occasional live music and other performances, but otherwise it's a great place to reacquaint yourself with Cluedo and Mastermind.

Café El Moderno

Plaza de las Comendadoras 1 (91 531 62 77). Metro Noviciado. **Open** *Sept-July* 3pm-1.30am Mon-Thur, Sun; 3pm-2.30am Fri, Sat. *Aug* 5.30pm-1.30am Mon-Thur, Sun; 5.30pm-2.30am Fri, Sat. **No credit cards. Map** p323 F8 ⑤
El Moderno's art deco look is entirely fake, but none the worse for it, and, along with its large terrace, attracts a mixture of local characters and curious tourists. The specialities are teas, milkshakes and hot chocolates, with an impressive 30 varieties of each. Fans of *Sex and Lucia* will recognise the building as Lorenzo's apartment block. Café Comendadoras, under the same ownership and with similar fare, is located right next door, same address (91 532 11 32).

Café de Ruiz

C/Ruiz 11 (91 446 12 32). Metro Bilbao. **Open** 2.30pm-1.30am Mon-Thur, Sun; 2.30pm-2.30am Fri, Sat. **Credit** MC, V. **Map** p323 G8 ⑤
A quiet favourite with the smarter denizens of the neighbourhood, Café de Ruiz is an elegant place, with comfortable sofas and dramatic flower arrangements. A big draw is its own-made ice-cream and other tempting sweet treats, such as hot chocolate with *churros*, milkshakes, lemon tart and cheesecake.

Cafeina

C/Pez 18 (91 522 03 31). Metro Noviciado. **Open** 3pm-2am Mon-Thur; 3pm-3am Fri, Sat. **Credit** AmEx, DC, MC, V. **Map** p323 G9 ⑤
By day dogs chase kids through table legs while their parents chat over mugs of herbal tea. By night the hip hop and jazz DJs attract a different crowd,

young and animated, who mill around the bar clutching killer G&Ts, or smooch on the sofas in the cosy bare-bricked basement. The big night here is Wednesday, for DJ'd flamenco.

Café Rustika

C/Limón 11 (91 542 91 30/www.rustikacafe.es). *Metro Noviciado.* **Open** 5pm-midnight Tue-Thur, Sun; 5pm-2.30am Fri, Sat. **Credit** AmEx, DC, MC, V. **Map** p323 F9 ⑤
Whimsical interiors, funky lo-fi music and lots of hanging lanterns make this one of the most relaxing cafés in a neighbourhood full of them. New ownership brings a randomly international menu with dishes from couscous to chop suey to chocolate cake and a wide selection of teas.

Casa Camacho

C/San Andrés 4 (91 531 35 98). Metro Tribunal. **Open** noon-2am Mon-Thur, Sun; noon-2.30am Fri, Sat. Closed mid Aug-mid Sept. **No credit cards. Map** p323 G/H9 ⑤
A rough diamond, the diminutive Casa Camacho has changed little since it opened in 1928, except for the addition of a fruit machine and a TV – both in constant use. Pre-war dust coats the bottles and plastic flowers on display and the floor is a sea of toothpicks and cigarette ends, but for a slice of real neighbourhood life it can't be beat.

La Granja de Said

C/San Andrés 11 (91 532 87 93). Metro Tribunal. **Open** 1-4pm, 9pm-midnight daily. **Credit** AmEx, DC, MC, V. **Map** p323 G8/9 ⑤
An inviting Moroccan tea house that has all the trimmings: copper lanterns, wall-hangings, Moorish tiling and atmospheric lighting. It's popular with a young and studenty crowd, who linger long over speciality teas – try Taj Mahal (with cinnamon, orange and rose petals) or Oriente Express (green tea with apple, cloves and orange) – plus different types of couscous, salads and tajines.

La Ida

C/Colón 11 (91 522 91 07). Metro Tribunal. **Open** 1pm-2am daily. Closed Aug. **No credit cards. Map** p323 H9/10 ⑤
La Movida meets *Friends* in this cramped but jolly little café, where everybody knows everybody else. This is where the painfully cool neo-punks from the nearby Mercado Fuencarral come to let their guard down, tucking into courgette tart and canapés at the scrubbed pine tables amid perky green walls. Sundays are especially mellow: the perfect set for The One Where They All Got Tattoos. **Photo** *p179.*

Lola Loba

C/Palma 38 (91 522 96 16). Metro Noviciado. **Open** noon-2am Mon-Sat. **No credit cards. Map** p323 G8/9 ⑤
Named after a *copla* singer who ran away from her abusive American millionaire husband and opened this bar. In 1872 he found her and murdered her, and 'tis said her ghost still prowls within the red-brick

walls. What is not known is whether she approves of the jazz, funk and house, or the fab *tostas*, slathered in mozzarella, tomato and basil; caramelised onion with brie, or smoked salmon with camembert.

La Palmera

C/Palma 67 (630 884 470). Metro Noviciado. **Open** 8pm-2am Mon-Thur; 8pm-2.30am Fri, Sat. **No credit cards. Map** p323 F8 🟡
The tiles in this tiny, crowded bar date back to its opening at the beginning of the last century, and have featured in various magazines. For years it lay in terminal decline, until it was bought in the late 1990s by a long-term regular. It almost exclusively serves vermouth and beer to a crowd that, for some reason, includes a loyal German following.

El Parnasillo

C/San Andrés 33 (91 447 00 79). Metro Bilbao. **Open** 2.30pm-3am Mon-Thur, Sun; 2.30pm-3.30am Fri, Sat. **No credit cards. Map** p323 H8 🟡
Long frequented by writers, artists, journalists and intellectuals, the art nouveau El Parnasillo was very much at the centre of Madrid's cultural renewal in the '70s and '80s, to the extent that it was bombed by a far-right group. It's unlikely to excite the same emotion these days, but is still an evocative place for a cocktail, sarnie or *pa tumaca* (bread rubbed with tomato) topped with cheese, ham or smoked salmon.

Pepe Botella

C/San Andrés 12 (91 522 43 09). Metro Tribunal. **Open** *Sept-July* 10am-2am Mon-Thur; 11am-3am Fri, Sat; 11am-2am Sun. *Aug* 3pm-2am Mon-Thur, Sun; 3pm-3am Fri, Sat. **No credit cards. Map** p323 H8 🟡
A cineaste's delight, the colourful Pepe Botella is decked out with film posters and frequented by the likes of director Alejandro Amenábar and actor Eduardo Noriega. For all that, it's wonderfully unpretentious, and attracts an intelligent bunch of mainly thirty- and fortysomethings, who engage in lively debate while smoking for Spain.

El Pez Gordo

C/Pez 6 (91 522 32 08). Metro Callao or Noviciado. **Open** 8pm-2am daily. Closed Sundays in Aug. **No credit cards. Map** p323 G10 🟡
Popular with audiences and actors from the nearby Teatro Alfil, the Fat Fish buzzes at night and is fabulously mellow during the day. The main attraction (aside from the photos of the owner's hideous bulldog) comes in the shape of the creative tapas. Try fried plantain with guacamole, goose confit with red fruit compôte, or the *patatas Pez Gordo* with alioli, anchovies and hot peppers.

Subiendo al Sur

C/Ponciano 5 (91 548 11 47). Metro Noviciado or Plaza de España. **Open** *Sept-July* noon-4pm, 8pm-midnight Tue-Sat; 1-4pm Mon. *Aug* 8pm-2am Tue-Sat. **No credit cards. Map** p323 F9 🟡
Easily missed, this co-operative-run fair trade café and shop is an absolute gem. All profits go to good causes, with products such as Mecca Cola (20% to

Palestinian kids) given top billing. The charming co-owners take turns in the kitchen, each lending ideas from their home country to the daily-changing menu, so chicken in peanut sauce from Equatorial Guinea sits alongside Senegalese *bobotie* and Mexican chicken *mole*. Highly recommended.

Underblue Coctelería

C/Minas 1 (no phone) Metro Noviciado. **Open** 3pm-2am Mon-Sat. Closed 15 Jul-15 Aug. **No credit cards. Map** p323 G9 🟡
A shabby chic lounge bar, serving tisanes and milkshakes by day (when the stylish bar staff outnumber the customers) and cocktails by night. A cavernous basement is cool in every sense, its dimly lit hidden corners furnished with junk shop armchairs and glass-topped coffee tables covered in style mags. Prices are a little higher than the surroundings would suggest.

Salamanca & the Retiro

Balmoral

C/Hermosilla 10 (91 431 41 33). Metro Serrano. **Open** noon-midnight Mon-Sat. **Credit** AmEx, DC, MC, V. **Map** p325 L9 🟡
A very surreal place, probably unique in Spain as drinking experiences go. If Balmoral Castle had a cocktail bar, it would look something like this, with stags' heads and skulls, stuffed grouse, leather banquettes and oil paintings, and deep armchairs gathered round a fireplace. Along with the cocktails, there is a small but decent selection of whiskies.

El Botánico

C/Ruiz de Alarcón 27 (91 420 23 42). Metro Banco de España. **Open** 8.30am-midnight daily. **Credit** AmEx, DC, MC, V. **Map** p328 K13 🟡
Confusingly, this quiet bar-restaurant actually sits on C/Espalter, just around the corner, and overlooking the botanical gardens. Tucked away from the tourist drag, it's very quiet considering its proximity to the Prado, and has a peaceful, shaded terrace. It's a good spot for breakfast, and there are tapas later in the day.

Café Gijón

Paseo de Recoletos 21 (91 521 54 25). Metro Banco de España. **Open** 7.30am-1.30am daily. **Credit** AmEx, DC, MC, V. **Map** p324 J10 🟡
Still charming after all these years, this is Madrid's definitive literary café, open since 1888. It still holds poetry *tertulias* on Monday nights, and publishes a magazine filled with doodles and thoughts from visiting writers. A pianist tinkles the ivories to a packed terrace in summer, while in winter it's heaving inside. Look out for the aged Alfonso, who has been selling cigarettes, matches and lottery tickets, just inside the entrance, for over 30 years.

Castellana 8

Paseo de la Castellana 8 (91 578 34 87). Metro Colón. **Open** 11.30am-2.30am daily. **Credit** AmEx, MC, V. **Map** p324 K8 🟡

La Ida. *See p177.*

See p177.

Known as Jazzanova until recently, Castellana 8 remains a supremely smooth bar-restaurant-club, its black walls softened by clever uplighting, orange velvet cushions and a mellow soundtrack of jazz and blues. Brunch on Sundays is dished up with cocktails and live music, though not, sadly, on the terrace outside, which is limited to drinking only. The upmarket location and older clientele mean predictably higher prices.

Gelati e Frullati

Avda Felipe II 8 (91 577 09 52). Metro Goya. **Open** *Oct-May* 9am-11.30pm daily. *June-Sept* 7.30am-midnight daily. **No credit cards. Map** p325 O10 ⓭
Under Italian, ownership, this fabulous *gelateria* serves the best ice-cream in the city and probably the whole of Spain. Twelve flavours (which rotate daily) are created in a back room, as are fresh panini, focaccia and sublime tiramisu, which complements the excellent Italian coffee. Enthusiastic staff will guide you through, insisting that you try the ambrosial vanilla, the zingy *zabaglione*, and in winter the *helado de panettone*.

The James Joyce

C/Alcalá 59 (91 575 49 01/www.jamesjoycemadrid. com). Metro Banco de España. **Open** 11am-2am Mon-Thur, Sun; 11am-2.30am Fri, Sat. **Credit** AmEx, DC, MC, V. **Map** p324 K11 ⓰
Previously known as Kitty O'Shea's, this is the Madrid outpost of what is now a global chain of Oirish theme pubs. With both Guinness and Murphy's on tap, pub grub, chatty staff and plenty

of rugby and Premier League matches showing on two big screens and three TVs, it's all much as you'd expect. Of more interest, perhaps, is that the pub sits on the site of the historic Café Lion, a haunt of post-Civil War literati.

El Pavellón del Espejo

Paseo de Recoletos 31 (91 319 11 22). Metro Colón. **Open** 8am-1am Mon-Thur; 8am-3am Fri; 10.30am-3am Sat, Sun. **Credit** AmEx, DC, MC, V. **Map** p324 K9/10 ⓱
Not nearly as historic as the neighbouring Gijón, although it may look it: when it opened in 1978, 'the Mirror' ('*el Espejo*') set out to be the art nouveau bar Madrid never had, with positively Parisian 1900s decor. Its terrace bar out on the Paseo de Recoletos occupies a splendid glass pavilion reminiscent of a giant Tiffany lamp. Fashionable and comfortable, it has excellent tapas at reasonable prices.

Argüelles

Bruin

Paseo del Pintor Rosales 48 (91 541 59 21). Metro Argüelles. **Open** 11am-11pm Tue-Thur, Sun; 11am-2am Fri, Sat. **No credit cards. Map** p322 C8 ⓲
A wonderfully old-fashioned ice-cream parlour, with a terrace overlooking the Parque del Oeste. In contrast to its 1950s feel, some of its 40 own-made flavours are decidedly modern: try olive oil, tomato, idiazábal cheese, tomato or sherry. Diabetics get a look-in, too, with the sugar-free varieties.

Eat, Drink, Shop

Monasterio de San Lorenzo de El Escorial

MADRID
LAS ROZAS VILLAGE

BURBERRY CAMPER
CH CAROLINA HERRERA
CK JEANS DIESEL
FARRUTX HACKETT
HUGO BOSS
LA PERLA LOEWE
PUMA SAMSONITE
TIMBERLAND
VERSACE
VILLEROY&BOCH
and many more

MADRID
LAS ROZAS ❀ VILLAGE
OUTLET SHOPPING

Las Rozas Village offers a universe of 95 outlet stores of top designer brands at prices reduced up to 60% all year round, the best walk through fashion in the most exclusive Outlet Shopping Village in Madrid.

Aranjuez

OPEN 7 DAYS A WEEK ALL YEAR ROUND. Consult our website or phone for transport facilities and opening hours information. Regular bus 625 / 628 from Moncloa bus station.

Present this page at Village Reception and for one day, you can enjoy and additional 10% discount over outlet prices in 9 of your favorite brands.* Valid until 31.12.07. Not valid on products that are on promotion.

www.LasRozasVillage.com

© Las Rozas Village 2007

Shops & Services

Buy buy, baby, buy buy.

The high streets of Madrid have undeniably taken on the identikit look of most European capitals, albeit with Spanish chains – Zara, Mango, System Action – proliferating, but get off those main thoroughfares and what strikes you is the curious mix of the traditional and the new. Here the chains and international franchises rub shoulders with museum-piece, family-run businesses and ancient shops dedicated to just one product, espadrilles maybe, or Spanish ceramics.

Madrid is not a large city, and its main shopping areas break down into several distinctive zones, all conveniently within walking distance – or a short metro ride – of each other. Between Sol and Gran Vía are **C/Preciados** and **C/Carmen**, always bustling with shoppers, and boasting a mix of chains and smaller stores selling cheap and mid-price clothes, shoes and accessories. Several branches of El Corte Inglés are to be found in this area. **Gran Vía** itself is given over to the flagship stores of many a household name – H&M, Zara and the Nike Store, to name but three. After battling through the crowds of dawdling shoppers, the tranquil area of **Los Austrias** comes as a welcome respite, given over to musical instrument stores, bohemian gift shops and treasure troves of decorative items. If you're all about labels, then **Salamanca** is the place to be, in particular C/Serrano, where on the same block you will find Loewe, Yves St Laurent and La Perla, as well as smaller designer boutiques throughout the area. **Chueca** is undoubtedly the hippest area in town, in particular C/Fuencarral. Thanks to that epicentre of cool, the shopping mall El Mercado de Fuencarral, the neighbourhood is becoming Madrid's Soho, with names such as Levi's, Puma and Diesel coexisting with the one-off shops that have helped make the street such a hotbed for Madrid's fashion-conscious youth. Just west of here, the area around C/Conde Duque has seen some cool and interesting boutiques spring up in recent years. The city's fleamarket, the **Rastro**, is an obligatory visit, but more for the atmosphere than the goods – you will almost certainly walk away empty-handed.

OPENING HOURS

Opening times are changing, as is the traditional August break. While smaller stores will still close for two or three hours at lunch and stay shut on Saturday afternoons, some mid-size and nearly all large outlets will remain open all day. If you have yet to get used to a two o'clock lunch and can face the heat in the summer, head to the bigger stores in the afternoon and you will miss the crowds. Pressure from large retailers brought about a relaxation of the laws on Sunday opening too, all amid much grumbling from small businesses, who find it very hard to compete

The best Shops

Anthurium
The trendiest, most stylish florist in town. *See p194.*

El Apartamento
Retro furniture, fittings and homewares from this little locale in Malasaña. *See p184.*

Desigual
Quality clubwear from this shop that pulsates with house music. *See p191.*

La Duquesita
The loveliest little period-piece cake shop . The cakes are good too. *See p194.*

Fotocasión
A treasure trove of new and second-hand cameras and accessories. *See p200.*

Joaquín Berao
Solid silver jewellery in chunky, flowing designs. Pricey but not overly so. *See p192.*

Lavinia
A new approach to wine shops: big and bright and bursting with bottles. *See p197.*

Mamblona
Hand-made textiles from Spain and abroad – excellent for gift ideas. *See p189.*

The Deli Room
Choice cuts by Spanish designers in supermarket-chic surroundings. *See p190.*

Up Beat Discos
Soul, jazz and reggae discs are the reason for visiting this '60s-feel shop. *See p198.*

Eat, Drink, Shop

with such timetables. As a result, large retailers can – and do – open every first Sunday of the month. A further bonus on these Sundays is the closure of Gran Vía to private transport. As revenue from tourists becomes more vital to the shopkeepers of Madrid, August is no longer a month where the city closes down.

SALES AND TAX REFUNDS

Sales are usually on through January and February, and then July and August. The rate of IVA, or VAT, is 16 per cent. For non-EU residents, you can claim refund cheques for purchases over the value of €90.15. You can then reclaim the VAT at the Global Refund Office in Barajas airport. Look out for the Tax Free sticker in the window of participating outlets.

One-stop shops

El Corte Inglés

C/Preciados 1-4, Sol & Gran Vía (all branches 901 122 122/Tel-entradas ticket phoneline 902 40 02 22/ www.elcorteingles.com). Metro Sol. **Open** 10am-10pm Mon-Sat; 11am-9pm 1st Sun of mth except Aug. **Credit** AmEx, DC, MC, V. **Map** p327 G11.
Spain's biggest retail concern has blown all the rest of the competition out of the water. El Corte Inglés is the solution when all else fails for some, but the first choice for many. You can get practically everything you need, be it clothes, household goods, books or multimedia products, and the store also offers a range of services from cutting keys to booking tickets. Most outlets also have well-stocked, if expensive, supermarkets. Information points staffed by multilingual employees are a plus as is the post-sale, money-back guarantee. This branch specialises in music and computers, the branch opposite in books, the one on the Paseo de la Castellana has large sports, computer and toy departments and C/Serrano is mostly given over to fashion, jewellery and cosmetics.
Other locations: throughout the city.

FNAC

C/Preciados 28, Sol & Gran Vía (91 595 61 00/ 91 595 62 00/www.fnac.es). Metro Callao. **Open** 10am-9.30pm Mon-Sat; noon-9.30pm Sun, public hols. **Credit** AmEx, MC, V. **Map** p323 G11.
The French giant offers a huge range of CDs, DVDs, videos and books plus computer hardware and software, all at competitive prices and under one roof. Among the CDs there are good world music and flamenco sections, and the helpful staff can look up titles on the database. There is a reasonable English-language book section, with recent paperbacks as well as classics. On the second floor is a room to sit and read while listening to music. Downstairs there's a ticket booking service, a café and paper shop with a good range of foreign press and magazines, and the FNAC Forum, which hosts readings and film and record launches.

After hours

Three names dominate after-hours shopping in Madrid. The most ubiquitous, and open 24 hours a day, is **Sprint** (7/11 re-branded), which sells prepared food, hot and cold drinks, plus press and magazines. **OpenCor** and **Vip's** have shorter hours (8am-2am and 9am-3am respectively), but have a greater selection of goods, including supermarket products, fresh food, CDs, DVDs, books and gifts. In Vip's, Spanish and English-language press is sold, and you can get films processed. After-hours shops are not allowed to sell alcohol after 10pm (9pm on Sundays). All have branches throughout town, but below are the most central.

OpenCor

C/Fuencarral 118, Chamberí (91 591 38 96). Metro Bilbao. **Open** 8am-2am daily. **Credit** AmEx, DC, MC, V. **Map** p323 H7.

Sprint

C/Arenal 28, Los Austrias (no phone). Metro Ópera. **Open** 24hrs daily. **No credit cards. Map** p327 F11.

Vip's

Gran Vía 43 (91 559 66 21). Metro Callao or Santo Domingo. **Open** 9am-3am daily. **Credit** AmEx, DC, MC, V. **Map** p323 G11.

Shopping centres

ABC Serrano

C/Serrano 61 & Paseo de la Castellana 34, Salamanca (91 577 50 31/www.abcserrano.com). Metro Rubén Darío. **Open** 10am-9pm Mon-Sat; noon-8pm 1st Sun of mth. **Map** p325 L6/7.
Occupying the building that once housed the ABC newspaper, this upmarket and well located shopping mall has eight floors. Four of them are dedicated to fashion, designer and high street, sportswear, jewellery, crafts and hi-fi. There are three restaurants on the upper floors, a café on the ground floor and a lively summer *terraza* on the fourth, plus a gym at the top.

Centro Comercial La Vaguada (Madrid 2)

Avda Monforte de Lemos 36, Barrio del Pilar (information 91 730 10 00/www.lavaguada.com). Metro Barrio del Pilar. **Open** 10am-10pm Mon-Sat; 11.30am-10pm 1st Sun of month. *Leisure area only* 10am-2.30am daily.
Madrid's first giant mall, and still the largest in the city, La Vaguada has around 350 outlets. There's a branch of El Corte Inglés (*see above*), and the upper floor is given over to leisure, with cinemas and a bowling alley. A bit of a trek, but the metro line is fast.

Centro Comercial Príncipe Pío

Paseo de la Florida s/n, Moncloa (91 758 00 40/ www.ccprincipepio.com). Metro Príncipe Pío. **Open** 10am-10pm Mon-Sat; 11am-10pm Sun. **Map** p322 C11.

Eat, Drink, Shop

El Rastro. *See p196.*

A welcome addition to one of the city's main transport hubs. Built into the shell of the old train station, the mall manages to pack in a deceptively large amount of shops and eateries – from the Body Shop and H&M to a Vip's restaurant and the obligatory Starbucks. This being a recently completed development, there is of course wi-fi, well-regulated air-con and heating, and a breastfeeding room. A huge multiplex cinema is tacked on the side, although you'll only find films dubbed into Spanish.

El Jardín de Serrano

*C/Goya 6-8, Salamanca (91 577 00 12/www. jardinserrano.es). Metro Serrano. **Open** 9.30am-9.30pm Mon-Sat. **Map** p325 L9.*
This mall may be small but it's a gem, with designer boutiques, expensive shoe shops and a classy café.

Las Tiendas de Serrano

*C/Serrano 88, Salamanca (no phone). Metro Rubén Darío. **Open** 10.30am-2.30pm, 5-8.30pm Mon-Sat (shops may vary). **Map** p325 L7.*
Another small shopping mall, dominated by shops selling upmarket designer fashion, party clothes and accessories, mainly for women.

Antiques

If you want antiques, head to the **Rastro** (*see p196*). On the main drag, C/Ribera de Curtidores, are several arcades where you'll find everything from old junk to authentic antiques. The adjoining streets, such as C/Mira el Río Alta and C/Carnero, are more downmarket and can yield real bargains.

Elsewhere, there are a handful of antique shops in the C/Prado and, over in Salamanca, on and around C/Claudio Coello, are lots of upmarket, specialist dealers.

El Apartamento
C/Ruiz 11, Malasaña (91 445 77 68/www.el apartamento.biz). Metro Bilbao. **Open** 11.30am-2pm, 5.30-8.30pm Tue-Sat. **Credit** MC, V. **Map** p323 G8.
Named after the Billy Wilder movie, this shop specialises in furniture and household items from the '50s, '60s and '70s. Expect lovely tumblers, Formica coffee tables, rolls of wallpaper and plenty more.

Fábrica de Trallas
C/Carnero 21, La Latina (no phone). Metro La Latina. **Open** 10am-1pm Mon-Fri; 10am-2pm Sat. Closed last 2wks Aug. **No credit cards. Map** p327 F14.
Old radios, gramophones and phones, many in Bakelite, are sold at this shop, where serious collectors may find that long sought-after piece.

Galerías Piquer
C/Ribera de Curtidores 29, Rastro (no phone/ www.dai.es/piquer). Metro Puerta de Toledo. **Open** 10.30am-2pm, 5-8pm Mon-Fri; 10.30am-2pm Sat, Sun. **Credit** varies. **Map** p327 G15.
The antique shops in this Rastro arcade stock pieces for punters who don't want to have to brush the dust off their purchases. Opening times may vary.

Tiempos Modernos
C/Arrieta 17, Los Austrias & La Latina (91 542 85 94/www.tiempos-modernos.com). Metro Ópera. **Open** 11am-2pm, 5-8.30pm Mon-Fri; 11am-2pm Sat. Closed Aug. **Credit** AmEx, DC, MC, V. **Map** p323 E11.
Tiempos Modernos deals in modern Spanish painting and hosts temporary shows and exhibitions

of photography and artwork. The main line of business, though, is the great range of '40s, '50s and '60s furniture.

El Transformista
C/Mirá el Río Baja 18, Rastro & Lavapiés (91 539 88 33). Metro Puerta de Toledo. **Open** 11am-2pm Tue-Sun. **No credit cards. Map** p327 F15.
Original '50s and '60s furniture and collectibles are up for grabs at this shop. Almodóvar is rumoured to source items for his movies here.

Books

Fnac (*see p182*) has an excellent general selection. A traditional centre of the book trade is **Calle de los Libreros** ('Booksellers' Street') off Gran Vía, with many specialist bookshops.

La Casa del Libro
Gran Vía 29 (91 521 66 57/www.casadellibro.com). Metro Gran Vía. **Open** 9.30am-9.30pm Mon-Sat; 11am-9pm Sun. **Credit** AmEx, DC, MC, V. **Map** p323 H11.
Madrid's most comprehensive bookshop by far, La Casa del Libro covers just about every subject imaginable in Spanish, but also has good sections of literature, reference and teaching material in English and other languages.

Librería de Mujeres
C/San Cristóbal 17, Los Austrias (91 521 70 43). Metro Sol. **Open** *Oct-June* 10am-2pm, 5-8pm Mon-Fri; 10am-2pm Sat. *July-Sept* 10am-2pm, 5-8pm Mon-Fri. **Credit** MC, V. **Map** p327 G12.
Madrid's best women's bookshop goes by the motto '*Los libros no muerden, tampoco el feminismo*' – 'Books don't bite, neither does feminism'.

Tiempos Modernos.

La Tienda de Madrid

Mercado Puerta de Toledo, 5th floor, Ronda de Toledo 1, Lavapiés (91 364 16 82). Metro Puerta de Toledo. **Open** 10.30am-9pm Tue-Sat; 10.30am-2.30pm Sun. **No credit cards.** **Map** p327 E/F15.

Temporarily rehoused in the Mercado de Toledo market, the Museo Municipal's bookshop offers a wealth of written materials, mainly in Spanish, covering all aspects of the city's history and culture, some of them beautiful coffee-table editions.

Children

Mar de Letras

C/Santiago 18, Los Austrias (91 541 71 09). Metro Ópera. **Open** 10.30am-2pm, 5-8.30pm Mon-Fri; 10.30am-2.30pm Sat. Closed 1wk Aug. **Credit** DC, MC, V. **Map** p327 F11/12.

Mar de Letras is a well-stocked bookshop specialising in kids' editions. Look out too for the English titles, regular English storytelling evenings and educational toys.

English-language books

Booksellers

C/Fernández de la Hoz 40, Chamberí (91 442 79 59). Metro Iglesia. **Open** 9.30am-2pm, 5-8pm Mon-Fri; 10am-2pm Sat. **Credit** AmEx, DC, MC, V. **Map** p324 J6.

Madrid's best English-language bookshop sells a wide selection of literature, videos and DVDs, as well as materials for TEFLers. The branch below also has a children's book section.
Other locations: Plaza de Olavide 10, Chamberí (91 702 79 44).

Hartley's Good Bookshop

C/Padilla 74, Salamanca (91 401 90 77). Metro Diego de León or Lista. **Open** 11am-8pm Mon-Sat. **Credit** AmEx, MC, V. **Map** p325 O7.

A new and friendly English bookshop, struggling somewhat in an area not known for its expat population. Around half the stock is second-hand, kept downstairs in the basement, and there are books for kids as well as DVDs.

J&J Books & Coffee

C/Espíritu Santo 47, Malasaña (91 521 85 76/ www.jandjbooksandcoffee.net). Metro Noviciado. **Open** 11am-11pm Mon-Thur; 11am-2am Fri, Sat; 4-10pm Sun. **Credit** AmEx, DC, MC, V. **Map** p323 G9.

J&J is at once a relaxing little café (at ground-floor level) and a well-stocked second-hand bookshop (in the basement). Activities held here include open-mic sessions and quizzes, and staff can source books that aren't in stock. Storytelling for children takes place on the second Saturday of the month. **Photo** *p187.*

Pasajes

C/Génova 3, Chueca (91 310 12 45/www.pasajes libros.com). Metro Alonso Martínez. **Open** 10am-8pm Mon-Fri; 10am-2pm Sat. **Credit** MC, V. **Map** p324 J8.

This linguists' treasure trove sells a great range of fiction and non-fiction, language-learning materials, maps, audio books and videos. Most things are in English, French, German and Spanish.

Petra's International Bookshop

C/Campomanes 13, Sol & Gran Vía (91 541 72 91). Metro Ópera or Santo Domingo. **Open** Sept-June 11am-9pm Mon-Sat. *July, Aug* 11am-2.30pm, 5-10pm Mon-Sat. **No credit cards.** **Map** p327 F11.

A great range of second-hand books in English and other languages is on offer in this laid-back little shop. Here you can offload excess books or trade them for others. Sadly, Petra the cat, who gave the shop its name, has now passed on.

Second-hand & rare

Most bookshops dealing in rare and antique books are around the **C/Huertas** area. A great place for cheap second-hand books is the **Cuesta de Moyano**, on C/Claudio Moyano, by the Jardín Botánico (map p328 J11). It has a line of kiosks selling second-hand books, from rare editions to remainders. Some are open all week, but Sunday mornings are busiest. The stalls have been temporarily moved to the Paseo del Prado while the stretch is pedestrianised, but should be back in place by May 2007.

Librería San Ginés

Pasadizo de San Ginés 2, Sol (91 366 46 86). Metro Ópera or Sol. **Open** 11am-8pm Mon-Fri; 11am-2.30pm Sat. **Credit** MC, V. **Map** p327 G11.

This Old Curiosity Shop-type place, in an atmospheric passageway, sells everything from scruffy English paperbacks to antique editions.

Eat, Drink, Shop

Travel & maps

Desnivel

Plaza Matute 6, Santa Ana (91 429 97 40/902 24 88 48/www.libreriadesnivel.com). Metro Antón Martín. **Open** 10am-2pm, 4.30-8pm Sat. **Credit** AmEx, MC, V. **Map** p328 H13.
This excellent travel and adventure bookshop sells a wide range of maps and books covering Spain and other countries. Desnivel's own publications include walking and climbing guides, and the shop also has information on organised walks, hikes and so on.

La Tienda Verde

C/Maudes 23 & 38, Chamberí (91 534 32 57/www. tiendaverde.org). Metro Cuatro Caminos. **Open** 10am-2pm, 5-8.30pm Mon-Sat. **Credit** AmEx, DC, MC, V.
Madrid's original and best shop for travel books and maps, the 'Green Shop' now occupies two premises on the same street. At No.23 you will find tourist and nature guides, while No.38 sells maps and specialised mountaineering books.

Children

Clothes

As well as smaller boutiques, larger chains also do affordable, cool clothes for kids, among them **Zara** (*see p191*) and **H&M** (*see p190*).

Max Kinder

C/Carretas 8, Los Austrias (91 521 69 47). Metro Sol. **Open** 10am-8.30pm Mon-Sat. **Credit** MC, V. **Map** p327 H11.

This shop is the junior version of Max Moda, across the street, and does a reasonable range of basic clothes for children from three months to 16 years.

Oilily

C/Hermosilla 16, Salamanca (91 577 56 39/www. oilily-world.com). Metro Serrano. **Open** *Sept-mid July* 10am-8.30pm Mon-Sat. *Mid July, Aug* 10am-2pm, 5-8.30pm Mon-Fri; 10am-2pm Sat. **Credit** AmEx, MC, V. **Map** p325 L9.
The to-die-for togs from this French firm will guarantee that your offspring stand out from the crowd. About as far from traditional Spanish childrenswear as it's possible to imagine.

Step

C/Almirante 28, Chueca (91 522 69 21). Metro Chueca. **Open** 10.30am-2pm; 5-8.30pm Mon-Sat. **Credit** AmEx, DC, MC, V. **Map** p324 J10.
Drop-dead designer shoes by names like Moschino and Kenzo for mini fashpack members.

Toys

Don Juego

C/Alcalá 113, Salamanca (91 435 37 24/www. donjuego.es). Metro Príncipe de Vergara. **Open** *Sept-July* 10am-2pm, 5-8.30pm Mon-Sat. *Aug* 10am-2pm Mon-Sat. **Credit** MC, V. **Map** p329 M10.
This shop specialises in board games for both kids and adults – as well as mah-jong, solitaire, Chinese chequers and chess, it specialises in Go.

Imaginarium

C/Núñez de Balboa 52, Salamanca (91 577 33 55/www.imaginarium.es). Metro Núñez de

Settle down with **J&J Books & Coffee**. *See p185.*

Blanket band

A common sight in Madrid is people running with sheets in their hands, especially around the areas of Sol, Atocha and Bravo Murillo. They're not taking part in the capital's version of the running of the bulls, but rather they are '*los top manta*' ('the blanket-tops'), who sell their pirated CDs and DVDs laid out on squares of material. Once a policeman is spotted, strings tied to the corners of the material are hastily pulled and off they sprint.

Europe's biggest and most successful pirates operate in Spain and the Spanish music industry loses an estimated €150 million in annual record sales through pirating. Whereas an original CD costs up to €20, pirated copies are sold at €3 a pop. The most popular albums are measured by their presence on the sheets: you will find anything from Madonna to the latest Latin sensation, all in plastic pockets with a photocopied cover of the original album as an identifier. Through police operations and anti-pirate campaigns by the General Society of Authors and Writers more arrests have been made and more pirated CDs confiscated in Madrid than in any other Spanish city.

The copies are made with the latest software in flats around the centre of the city, and then sold mainly by African, Latin American and Eastern European immigrants, most of whom are operating without residence permits or visas. Madrid's mayor, Alberto Ruíz Gallardon, has declared that pirating is an act of 'murder against creation' and police and musicians are up in arms about the blanket sensation.

Not content with just challenging the music industry, however, the pirates have in recent years brought in copied DVDs, with some films on the blankets before they even hit the movie screens. Costing less than a cinema ticket, pirated blockbusters, classics and independent movies all feature in the *manta* charts, either copied from DVD releases in the US or filmed inside the cinema.

The other face of pirating that you may meet on a night out in Madrid is that of the *mochilero* (backpacker), usually a Chinese or Indian immigrant, selling copied CDs or DVDs in bars. Surprisingly, you will see some *madrileños* buying from them. Regardless of whether or not they're alcohol-induced impulse buys, these purchases are a growing problem for the industries whose work is being copied, while, on the other hand, the city's escalating immigrant population continues to see the *manta* as a much-needed source of income. The choice is yours.

Balboa or Velázquez. **Open** 10am-9pm Mon-Sat. **Credit** AmEx, DC, MC, V. **Map** p325 M8.
Imaginarium is a standard solution when looking for challenging toys with imagination. Expect to find puppet theatres, modelling materials and shape-recognition, number and alphabet-learning games. **Other locations**: throughout the city.

Sanatorio de Muñecos

C/Preciados 19, Sol (91 521 04 47). Metro Sol. **Open** 10am-2pm, 5-8pm Mon-Fri. **Credit** AmEx, DC, MC, V. **Map** p323 G11.
The 'dolls' hospital' does indeed mend dolls, but also functions as the oldest toy shop in Madrid, full of parents gazing nostalgically at the old-school model cars, teddy bears and so on.

Cleaning & laundry

Self-service *lavanderías* (launderettes) are rather thin on the ground in Madrid: in most there will be an attendant.

Lavandería Automática

C/Don Felipe 4, Malasaña (91 523 32 45). Metro Tribunal. **Open** 10am-9pm daily. **No credit cards.** **Map** p323 H9.

Lavandería Donoso Cortés

C/Donoso Cortés 17, Chamberí (91 446 96 90). Metro Quevedo or Canal. **Open** *Sept-July* 9am-2pm, 3.30-8pm Mon-Sat. *Aug* 9am-2.30pm Mon-Sat. **No credit cards.**

OndaBlu
C/León 3, Huertas (91 369 50 71). Metro Antón Martín. **Open** 9.30am-9pm Mon-Fri; 10.30am-6pm Sat, Sun daily. **No credit cards**. **Map** p328 I12. Also has internet connection.

Crafts & gifts

Antigua Casa Talavera
C/Isabel la Católica 2, Sol & Gran Vía (91 547 34 17). Metro Santo Domingo. **Open** 10am-1.30pm, 5-8pm Mon-Fri; 10am-1.30pm Sat. **Credit** AmEx, MC, V. **Map** p323 F11.
This long-standing family business specialises in traditional blue and white Spanish ceramics. Every available space is crammed with hand-painted designs all sourced from small Spanish producers. The charming owner speaks good English.

Piedra de Luna
C/Príncipe 14, Santa Ana (91 521 63 73). Metro Sevilla. **Open** 10am-2.30pm, 5-10pm Mon-Sat. **Credit** DC, MC, V. **Map** p328 H12.
A treasure trove of good-quality craftwork from around the world. Tuareg kilims, Moroccan ceramics and Indian silver jewellery and painted wooden furniture all feature.

Popland
C/Manuela Malasaña 24, Malasaña (91 446 38 95/www.popland.es). Metro Bilbao. **Open** 11am-8.30pm Mon-Sat. **Credit** DC, MC, V. **Map** p323 G8.
For times when only a Jesus action figure will do, Popland saves the day. The shop is packed with all things pop-culture and plastic, but also film posters, shower curtains and T-shirts. There's also a good range of greetings cards – quite a rarity in Madrid.

Design & household

BD Madrid
C/Villanueva 5, Salamanca (91 435 06 27/www.bd madrid.com). Metro Serrano. **Open** 9.30am-1.30pm, 4.30-8pm Mon-Fri; 10am-1.30pm Sat. Closed Aug. **Credit** AmEx, DC, MC, V. **Map** p325 L10.
BD carries a stunning selection of contemporary furniture designs from Spanish and international names, many with a retro feel. The company is now producing its own pieces, including a kitchen range. Hefty price tags, but worth a visit if only to peruse.

Expresión Negra
C/Piamonte 15, Chueca (91 319 95 27). Metro Chueca. **Open** 11am-2.30pm, 5-8.30pm Mon-Sat. **Credit** AmEx, DC, MC, V. **Map** p324 J10.
Expresión Negra is a great place to indulge in a spot of retail therapy and help the environment at the same time. As well as breathing new life into recycled objects – briefcases, lamps and other objects made out of used Coke cans, sardine tins and so on – the shop also puts a different spin on African handicrafts, with brightly coloured throws, textiles and some unusual metalwork.

Mamblona
C/Regueros 2, Chueca (91 310 41 95). Metro Chueca. **Open** 5-8pm Mon; 11am-2pm, 5-8.30pm Tue-Sat. Closed Aug. **Credit** AmEx, MC, V. **Map** p324 I9.
A charming shop that carries a range of mostly handmade textiles – cushions, homeware and fashion accessories. Products are sourced from India, the UK and Finland; a few are Spanish-made.

PlazAarte
Costanilla de los Capuchinos 5, Chueca (91 522 85 93/www.plazaarte.com). Metro Chueca. **Open** Sept-July 11.30am-2pm, 5-9pm Mon-Sat. *Aug* 6-9.30pm Mon-Sat. **Credit** AmEx, DC, MC, V. **Map** p324 H10.
This is a trendy, Swedish-owned shop/gallery that specialises in contemporary items for the home by up-and-coming national and international designers.

Víctimas de Celuloide
C/Santiago 4, Los Austrias (91 547 61 35/www.victimasdeceluloide.com). Metro Ópera. **Open** 11am-2.30pm, 5.30pm-9.30pm Mon-Sat. **Credit** AmEx, DC, MC, V. **Map** p327 F12.
'Because we are all victims of celluloid,' says the proprietor of this shop selling interior design pieces with a twist, mainly from Nordic suppliers. A pop art influence is noticeable in the selection.

Vinçon
C/Castelló 18, Salamanca (91 578 05 20/www.vincon.com). Metro Velázquez. **Open** 10am-8.30pm Mon-Sat. **Credit** AmEx, MC, V. **Map** p325 M10.
The Madrid outpost of the classic Barcelona design store occupies a former 1920s silver factory. It has everything for the cred-seeking homeowner – furniture, home and garden accessories and attractive gift ideas, often at surprisingly low prices.

Fashion

Boutiques

Exotic-Delitto e Castigo
C/Villanueva 20, Salamanca (91 431 89 33/www.delittoecastigo.com). Metro Retiro or Serrano. **Open** 11am-2.30pm, 5-9pm Mon-Sat. **Credit** AmEx, DC, MC, V. **Map** p325 L10.
This chic establishment is one of the trendiest of its kind in Madrid, carrying smart-casual eveningwear from D&G, Lacroix, Gaultier and Valentino. The C/Villanueva branch holds more sporty/casual lines.

HAND
C/Hortaleza 26, Chueca (91 521 51 52/www.hand-haveaniceday.com). Metro Chueca. **Open** 11am-2.30pm, 5-9pm Mon-Sat. **Credit** AmEx, DC, MC, V. **Map** p324 H10.
HAND stands for for Have a Nice Day, and is run by two discerning Frenchmen. An interesting boutique, it mixes French labels with bits and pieces brought back from their travels in India.

Lotta

C/Hernán Cortés 9, Chueca (91 523 25 05). Metro Chueca or Tribunal. **Open** *Sept-July* 11am-2pm, 5-9pm Mon-Sat. *Aug* 6-10pm Mon-Sat. **Credit** MC, V. **Map** p324 H10.

The Swedish proprietor of Lotta set up her first vintage clothing store in the Rastro in 1992. Now this shop carries vintage clothing from the '50s to the '80s and also stocks colourful dresses designed by the owner herself, using materials from Scandinavia.

The Deli Room

C/Santa Bárbara 4, Malasaña (91 521 19 83). Metro Tribunal or Gran Vía. **Open** 11am-2pm, 5-9pm Mon-Fri; 11am-3pm, 5-9pm Sat. **Credit** MC, V. **Map** p323 H9.

The Deli Room serves up choice cuts from Spanish designers, all presented in stainless-steel deli counters complete with weighing scales and supermarket lighting. It may sound weird but it works.

Designers

For famous Spanish leather specialist **Loewe**, *see p194.*

Adolfo Domínguez

C/Ortega y Gasset 4, Salamanca (91 576 00 84/www.adolfodominguez.com). Metro Núñez de Balboa. **Open** 10.15am-8.30pm Mon-Sat. **Credit** AmEx, DC, MC, V. **Map** p325 L7.

Simple, classical clothing from the well-known Galician designer. Suits are well cut and long-lasting, while accessories and shoes are also big draws. **Other locations**: throughout the city.

Agatha Ruiz de la Prada

C/Serrano 27, Salamanca (91 319 05 01/www.agatha ruizdelaprada.com). Metro Serrano. **Open** *Sept-June* 10am-8.30pm Mon-Sat. *Aug* 10am-2pm, 5-8.30pm Mon-Sat. **Credit** AmEx, MC, V. **Map** p325 L8.

Loud and colourful designs distinguish this designer's work, many emblazoned with her trademark hearts and flowers. The childrenswear range is hugely popular, as is the homeware.

Amaya Arzuaga

C/Lagasca 50, Salamanca (91 426 28 15/www.amayaarzuaga.com). Metro Serrano. **Open** *Sept-June* 10.30am-8.30pm Mon-Sat. *Aug* 10.30am-2pm, 5-8.30pm Mon-Fri; 10am-2pm Sat. **Credit** AmEx, DC, MC, V. **Map** p325 L9.

One of the few Spanish designers with an international presence. Not for everyday wear, but there are some great outfits to be discovered, with a hard-edged punky look. The knitwear is also excellent.

Custo

C/Fuencarral 29, Chueca (91 360 46 36/www.custo-barcelona.com). Metro Gran Vía or Chueca. **Open** 10am-9pm Mon-Sat. **Credit** AmEx, DC, MC, V. **Map** p324 H10.

This Catalan designer is famous for his funky patterned T-shirts, but has expanded the range to include creative and flattering dresses, skirts and coats. Custo sells in boutiques around the world, but is also rapidly expanding its own network of shops, with a new branch on C/Mayor.

Other locations: C/Mayor 37, Los Austrias (91 354 00 99).

Purificación García

C/Serrano 28, Salamanca (91 435 80 13/www.purificaciongarcia.es). Metro Serrano. **Open** 10am-8.30pm Mon-Sat. **Credit** AmEx, DC, MC, V. **Map** p325 L9.

Purificación García is where Madrid's older but elegant woman heads when she wants something smart for the office. Well cut and using natural materials, the clothes are very well priced for the quality.

Other locations: C/Serrano 92, Salamanca (91 576 72 76).

Sybilla

Callejón de Jorge Juan 12, Salamanca (91 578 13 22/www.sybilla.es). Metro Retiro or Serrano. **Open** 10.30am-8.30pm Mon-Sat. Closed 2wks Aug. **Credit** AmEx, DC, MC, V. **Map** p325 L10.

As well as her usual eye-catching outfits for actresses attending the Goyas (the Spanish equivalent of the Oscars), Sybilla also stocks a new range, Jocomomola, aimed at the younger crowd.

High-street fashion

H&M

C/Gran Vía 32 (901 120 084/www.hm.com). Metro Gran Vía. **Open** 10am-9pm Mon-Sat. **Credit** AmEx, DC, MC, V. **Map** p323 H11.

The flagship Madrid branch of the Swedish chain. While the clothes may lack quality, the rock-bottom prices do much to compensate. Don't miss the massive underwear floor and bargain beauty and hair accessories.

Other locations: throughout the city.

Mango

C/Fuencarral 70, Chueca (91 523 04 12/www.mango.es). Metro Bilbao. **Open** 10am-9pm Mon-Sat. **Credit** AmEx, MC, V. **Map** p323 H9.

This Barcelona-based chain can claim responsibility for dressing the majority of young women in Spain. Like Zara, Mango focuses on fresh designs aimed squarely at fashion-conscious teens and working women. This branch has an outlet on the second floor with last season's collection at bargain prices.

Other locations: throughout the city.

Top Shop

Puerta del Sol 6, Sol (91 532 58 92/www.topshop.co.uk). Metro Sol. **Open** 10am-9pm Mon-Sat. **Credit** AmEx, DC, MC, V. **Map** p327 H11.

A three-floor store of the British chain slap-bang in the middle of Sol, plying its trademark mix of high fashion and good-value basics. Beware, though, the stock is a lot more limited than in the UK.

Zara

*C/Princesa 45, Argüelles & Moncloa (91 541 09 02/
www.zara.es). Metro Argüelles.* **Open** 10am-8.30pm
Mon-Sat. **Credit** AmEx, DC, MC, V. **Map** p322 D8.
The Galician giant of the fashion world continues
to dominate both the domestic and international
markets. The key to its popularity lies in its ability
(and speed) in taking the latest catwalk looks from
the major designers and churning out reasonable
quality near-replicas at popular prices.
Other locations: throughout the city.

Street & clubwear

Desigual

*C/Fuencarral 36, Chueca (902 13 81 38/www.desigual.
com). Metro Tribunal or Gran Via.* **Open** 10am-9pm
Mon-Sat. **Credit** AmEx, MC, V. **Map** p323 H10.
Desigual has become a real hit with the club-kids,
and it's easy to see why: gorgeous shop assistants,
pumping house music and affordable, quality club
and streetwear for men and women.

Flip

*C/Mayor 19, Los Austrias (91 366 44 72/www.
flipmadrid.com). Metro Sol.* **Open** 10.30am-9pm
Mon-Sat. **Credit** AmEx, MC, V. **Map** p327 G11/12.
Well-chosen stock from the likes of g-sus, Miss
Sixty, Kangol and Black Flys, all presided over by
über-hip and highly pierced, highly tattooed staff.

Gas

*C/Fuencarral 16, Malasaña (91 701 05 01/www.
gasjeans.com). Metro Gran Via.* **Open** 10am-9pm
Mon-Fri; 10am-10pm Sat. **Credit** MC, V.
Map p324 H10.
'Keep it simple' is the Gas motto and it certainly
does, with collections of crisp cotton and linen
separates, but mainly denim.

Lanikai

*C/Alberto Aguilera 1, Malasaña (91 591 34 13/
www.lanikai.es). Metro San Bernardo.* **Open** *Sept-
July* 10.30am-9pm Mon-Sat. *Aug* 10.30am-2.30pm.
Credit AmEx, MC, V. **Map** p323 G7.
This three-storey emporium has all the essentials for
the keen snowboarder, surfer and skateboarder, or
anyone looking for streetwear by the likes of Etnies,
Carhartt, Diesel and Stylelab.

Miss Sixty

*C/Mesonero Romanos 2, Sol (91 521 50 28). Metro
Callao.* **Open** 10am-8pm Mon-Sat. **Credit** AmEx,
DC, MC, V. **Map** p323 G11.
An oasis of cool in Madrid's most crowded shopping area, the French denim designer's sleek three-
storey outlet furnishes its clientele with everything
a (skinny) girl could want.

Pepita is Dead

*C/Doctor Fourquet 10, Lavapiés (91 528 87 88/
www.pepitaisdead.com). Metro Atocha.* **Open** 11am-
2pm, 5-8.30pm Mon-Sat. Closed 3wks Aug. **Credit**
AmEx, DC, MC, V. **Map** p328 I14.

Along with Lotta, Pepita is Dead is the only shop in
Madrid to specialise in vintage clothing. These items
– mens-, womens- and childrenswear, plus accessories – are all unworn originals, carefully chosen
from the '60s to the '80s.

Snapo

*C/Espíritu Santo 5, Malasaña (91 532 12 23). Metro
Noviciado or Tribunal.* **Open** 11am-2pm, 5-9pm Mon-
Sat. **Credit** AmEx, DC, MC, V. **Map** p323 H9.
Snapo stocks streetwear with attitude, most of it
from its own label, Fucking Bastardz Inc. Designs
are funny and cheeky. The collection is mainly T-
shirts, plus some bags, caps and womenswear.

Sportivo

*C/Conde Duque 20, Malasaña (91 542 56 61).
Metro San Bernardo.* **Open** 10am-9pm Mon-Sat.
Credit AmEx, MC, V. **Map** p323 F8.
With a great range of menswear labels, including
Cantskate, Burro, Levi's Red and Vintage, New
York Industries, YMC and Duffer of St George,
Sportivo is an unmissable stop. The staff are
extremely helpful.

Fashion accessories

Lingerie & underwear

¡Oh, qué luna!

*C/Ayala 32, Salamanca (91 431 37 25). Metro
Serrano.* **Open** 10am-2pm, 5-8.30pm Mon-Fri;
11am-2pm, 5-8.30pm Sat. **Credit** AmEx, DC, MC, V.
Map p325 L8.
Glam, sexy lingerie, negligées and dressing gowns.
It also does a line in bedlinen and swimwear.

Oysho

*C/Fuencarral 124, Chamberí (91 448 83 55/
www.oysho.com). Metro Bilbao.* **Open** 10am-8.30pm,
Mon-Sat. **Credit** AmEx, DC, MC, V. **Map** p323 H7.
Part of the retail group that also includes Zara, Pull
& Bear and Often, Oysho specialises in sexy but
inexpensive underwear designs for younger women.
Other locations: Madrid 2-La Vaguada, C/Monforte
de Lemos 39 (91 730 04 41).

Women's Secret

*C/Velázquez 48, Salamanca (91 578 14 53/
http://womensecret.com). Metro Velázquez.* **Open**
Sept-June 10am-8.30pm Mon-Sat. *July, Aug* 10am-
2pm, 5-8.30pm Mon-Sat. **Credit** AmEx, DC, MC, V.
Map p325 M8.
Quality underwear at very competitive prices, plus
swimwear and skincare products.

Jewellery & accessories

Concha García

*C/Goya 38, Salamanca (91 435 49 36). Metro
Goya.* **Open** 10.30am-8.30pm Mon-Fri; 10.30am-
2.30pm, 5-8.30pm Sat. **Credit** AmEx, DC, MC, V.
Map p325 N9.

Eat, Drink, Shop

Camper.

Concha García's two shops-cum-galleries are important showcases for contemporary and ethnic jewellery design, both national and international.

Joaquín Berao

C/Claudio Coello 35, Salamanca (91 577 28 28). Metro Serrano. **Open** *Sept-July* 10am-2pm, 5-8.30pm Mon-Sat. *Aug* 10am-2pm, 5-8.30pm Mon-Fri; 10am-2pm Sat. **Credit** AmEx, DC, MC, V. **Map** p325 L9.

Chunky, twisted and contorted, but also fluidly elegant, Joaquín Berao's solid silver bracelets, necklaces, earrings and chokers are increasingly the choice of those in the know.

Piamonte

C/Piamonte 16, Chueca (91 523 07 66). Metro Chueca. **Open** 10.30am-8.30pm Mon-Sat. **Credit** AmEx, DC, MC, V. **Map** p324 J10.

Highly desirable bags in all shapes, sizes and fabrics, from denim to super-soft leather. **Other locations**: C/Lagasca 28, Salamanca (91 575 55 20); C/Marqués de Monasterio 5, Chueca (91 308 40 62); C/Villanueva 16, Salamanca (91 435 37 47).

Scooter

Callejón de Jorge Juan 12, Salamanca (91 576 47 49). Metro Serrano. **Open** 10am-8pm Mon-Fri; 11am-2.30pm, 5-8pm Sat. **Credit** DC, MC, V. **Map** p325 L10.

Accessories are the focus of this French store, with funky, chunky jewellery, Anya Hindmarch bags and gorgeous flip flops by Dorotea. The clothes – a mix of funky and ethnic – are worth a look too.

Shoes & leather

Spain is a major producer of footwear, with the Valencia and Alicante areas dominated by shoe factories. As a result, Madrid is a haven for the confirmed shoe addict. The street to head for is Augusto Figueroa, in the heart of Chueca. Here you'll find a street packed with factory '*muestrarios*' (selling samples) such as Vime or Caligae.

Antigua Casa Crespo

C/Divino Pastor 29, Malasaña & Conde Duque (91 521 56 54). Metro Bilbao. **Open** *Sept-July* 10am-1.30pm, 5-8.30pm Mon-Fri. *Aug* 10am-1.30pm, 5-8.30pm Mon-Fri; 10am-1.30pm Sat. Closed last 2wks Aug. **No credit cards. Map** p323 G8.

This perfectly preserved old-fashioned store is dedicated to espadrilles of all sizes and colours.

Camper

C/Serrano 24, Salamanca (91 578 25 60/www. camper.com). Metro Serrano. **Open** 9.30am-8.30pm Mon-Sat. **Credit** AmEx, DC, MC, V. **Map** p325 L10.

Branches of the Mallorcan family firm continue to spring up all over the city. At this one, two large plinths display the entire men's and women's collection – brightly coloured, fun shoes and sandals. **Other locations**: throughout the city.

Street of same

Up until Madrid's promotion to capital status in 1561, and the construction of the Plaza Mayor, guilds of tradespeople and artisans had tended to cluster together in certain streets or quarters. A brief glance at a map of the higgledy-piggledy street layout in the environs of the Plaza Mayor shows this clearly: many streets are named after the guilds, *gremios*, that were concentrated in the immediate vicinity.

A little north of the Plaza Mayor, just across the Calle Mayor, is the Plaza de Herredores, 'Blacksmiths' Square', and running from there to Calle Arenal is the Calle de las Hileras, or 'Spinners' Street'. Parallel to this is Calle Bordadores, 'Embroiderers' Street', whose artisans presumably bought their supplies of *hilo*, thread, one street over. Also serving the textile trade were the *coloreros*, purveyors of dyes, who were established in the tiny street of the same name just a few yards away. To the west of Plaza Mayor is the Calle Sal, thus named because salt was sold from the royal deposits there. A few yards away is the minuscule Calle Botoneras, where buttons were sold, and close by is the Calle de los Esparteros, where mats were manufactured from esparto grass, still used nowadays to make espadrilles. To the south of the square is the Calle Latoneros, where the brassmongers traded. This street feeds into the Calle de los Cuchilleros, 'Knifemakers' Street', where Plaza Mayor butchers bought their cleavers. A little further south, what is nowadays the main drag of the Rastro, the Ribera de Curtidores, 'Tanners' Alley', was close to the city's slaughterhouse. The name 'Rastro' very possibly has its origin in the blood-stained trail, or *rastro*, left by the slaughtered animals.

As the centuries went by and Madrid expanded, these trades slowly disappeared or moved out and other commercial establishments sprang up. During the 19th and 20th centuries other shopping thoroughfares became associated with vendors of certain types of product, even though the street names now had nothing to do with the wares on sale. Right up until the advent of the PC, if you wanted to buy a typewriter you headed for Calles Hortaleza and Hernán Cortés (a couple of shops selling Remington portables are still there). If you needed anything orthopaedic you went to the Calle Carretas, where there are still a couple of establishments selling these items. Books – both new and second-hand – you found in the Calle de los Libreros and the Cuesta de Moyano, as you still do today. The Calles de la Paz and Postas have long had a tradition of shops dealing in religious artefacts and the Plaza de Pontejos still has several haberdashers and remnants shops.

More recently, specialised streets have started to deal in modern goods. Take a walk along the Calle Barquillo in Chueca, you will notice that an abundance of shops there sell hi-fi equipment, hence the nickname Calle del Sonido ('Sound Street'). From here runs the Calle Almirante, which since the '80s has been colonised by a number of designer fashion shops, earning it the moniker of 'Calle de la Moda', a title for which C/Claudio Coello in the Salamanca neighbourhood would now contend. More fashion, of the street- and clubwear variety, is concentrated along the C/Fuencarral, riding the Mercado de Fuencarral wave of the last few years. They may not be tinsmiths or button sellers any more, but many of Madrid's retailers still seem happier having their direct competitors just across the street.

Excrupulus Net

C/Almirante 7, Chueca (91 521 72 44). Metro
Chueca. **Open** Sept-June 11am-2pm, 5-8.30pm
Sat. July, Aug 11am-2pm, 5.30-8.30pm Mon-Fri.
Credit AmEx, DC, MC, V. **Map** p324 J10.
A trio of women are behind this shoe shop, which
brings together unique designs from Catalan and
Mallorcan shoe designers, including Muxart.

Farrutx

C/Serrano 7, Salamanca (91 577 09 24/www.
farrutx.com). Metro Serrano. **Open** Sept-June 10am-
2pm, 5-8.30pm Mon-Fri; 10.30am-2pm, 5-8.30pm Sat.
July, Aug 10.30am-2pm, 5.30-8.30pm Mon-Sat.
Credit AmEx, DC, MC, V. **Map** p324 K10.
Innovative and sharply elegant leather designs
from this popular Mallorcan company, with bags
and shoes too.
Other locations: throughout the city.

Loewe

C/Serrano 26 & 34, Salamanca (91 577 60 56/
www.loewe.es). Metro Serrano. **Open** 10am-8.30pm
Mon-Sat. **Credit** AmEx, DC, MC, V. **Map** p325 L8/9.
The world-famous, elite Spanish leather goods company, selling bags, shoes, cases and a small range
of clothes. Prices are very high.
Other locations: throughout the city.

Nuevos Guerrilleros

Puerta del Sol 5, Sol (91 521 27 08/www.nuevos
guerrilleros.com). Metro Sol. **Open** 10am-8.30pm
Mon-Sat. **Credit** AmEx, MC, V. **Map** p327 H11.
A bargain-basement store with a giant stock of
cheap and cheerful men's and women's shoes, with
occasionally wacky designs.

Repairers

All markets and most streets have a shoe
repairer – look out for rápido or reparación
de calzados signs.

Costura

C/Príncipe 22, Santa Ana (91 522 88 24).
Metro Antón Martín. **Open** 10am-1.30pm,
5-8pm Mon-Fri; 10am-1.30pm Sat. Closed Aug.
Credit V. **Map** p328 H12.
This small shop has a fairly grim selection of shiny
party dresses for the older lady but also has an excellent repair service for any type of clothing.

Florists

For a full list of Madrid florists, see
www.floristerias.org.es.

Anthurium

C/Pelayo 19, Chueca (91 522 69 29/www.anthur
flor.com). Metro Chueca. **Open** 10am-2pm, 5-9pm
Mon-Fri; 10.30am-2pm Sat. **No credit cards**.
Map p324 I10.
The owners of this trendy florist's will put together
an arresting arrangement with a little notice.

Floristas Lola de Castro

C/Huertas 2, Huertas (91 154 59 03). Metro
Antón Martín. **Open** 10am-2pm, 5-8pm Mon-Fri;
10am-2pm Sat. **Credit** AmEx, DC, MC, V. **Map**
p328 H12.
A century-old business (though under new ownership), selling a full range of cut flowers (including
pretty arrangements) as well as potted plants.

Food & drink

Chocolates, cakes & sweets

Antigua Pastelería del Pozo

C/Pozo 8, Santa Ana (91 522 38 94). Metro Sol.
Open 9.30am-2pm, 5-8pm Tue-Sat; 9am-2pm Sun.
Closed last 2wks July, Aug, 1st wk Sept. **No credit
cards**. **Map** p327 H12.
With the same decor and counter as when it opened
in 1830, this lovely old pastelería is a true period
piece, with cakes that live up to its design.

Cacao Sampaka

C/Orellana 4, Huertas (91 319 58 40). Metro
Alonso Martínez. **Open** 10am-9.30pm Mon-Sat;
11am-9.30pm. Closed 2wks Aug. **Credit** AmEx,
MC, V. **Map** p324 J9.
Hand-made choccies arrayed in dazzling displays
and for sale singly or in themed boxes, such as
'Spices of the Americas' or 'Flowers and herbs'.
There are also chocolate jams, chocolate sauces and
chocolate ice-creams and a café on hand to sample
its delights over a cup of coffee. **Photo** p195.

Convento de las Carboneras

Plaza Conde de Miranda 3, Los Austrias (91 548
37 01). Metro Sol. **Open** 9.30am-1pm, 4.30-6pm
Mon-Sat. **No credit cards**. **Map** p327 F12.
The Carboneras nuns make a selection of speciality
cakes and biscuits including mantecados, yemas and
almond biscuits. As this is a closed convent you buy
them through a grille.

La Duquesita

C/Fernando VI 2, Chueca (91 308 02 31). Metro
Alonso Martínez. **Open** 9.30am-2.30pm, 5-9pm
Tue-Sat; 9.30am-3pm, 5-9pm Sun. Closed Aug.
Credit MC, V. **Map** p324 I9.
This traditional pastelería, dating from 1914, has
featured in lots of period-piece movies. Gorgeous
chocolates and cakes are up for grabs, along with
turrón in the run-up to Christmas.

La Mallorquina

Puerta del Sol 8, Sol & Gran Vía (91 521 12 01).
Metro Sol. **Open** 9am-9.15pm daily. Closed mid July,
Aug. **No credit cards**. **Map** p327 G11.
Always bustling with people, La Mallorquina occupies a prime location right on the Puerta del Sol.
Downstairs, the pastry shop sells great cakes and
savouries, all baked on the premises. The upstairs
café has a pre-war feel and a team of old-school
waiters in attendance.

El Riojano

*C/Mayor 10, Los Austrias (91 366 44 82). Metro
Sol.* **Open** *Sept-July* 10am-2pm, 5-9pm daily. Closed
Aug. **Credit** MC, V. **Map** p327 G11.
El Riojano has been in business since 1885, selling
irresistible cakes, pastries, meringues and seasonal
goodies. All are made in the traditional way, with
meringues a particular speciality. Enjoy one with a
coffee in the café out back.

Delicacies

Magerit, stand No.20/21 in La Cebada
market (*see p196*), is an excellent place to buy
cheese. For olives of all varieties, **F Illanas**,
stalls 33-44, in the Mercado de Chamberí,
C/Alonso Cano 10 (91 446 95 89), is a good
bet. Several branches of **El Corte Inglés**
(*see p182*), and most **OpenCor** outlets (*see
p182*) have luxury food sections called El
Club del Gourmet.

La Boulette

*Stands 63-68, Mercado de La Paz, C/Ayala 28,
Salamanca (91 431 77 25). Metro Serrano.* **Open**
9am-2.30pm, 5-8pm Mon-Fri; 9am-2.30pm Sat.
Credit MC, V. **Map** p325 L8.
La Boulette probably has the largest selection of
cheeses in Madrid and possibly the country, with
over 400 varieties, both Spanish and imported, on
sale. The range of goods in the charcuterie section
is similarly impressive.

González

*C/León 12, Huertas & Santa Ana (91 429 56 18).
Metro Antón Martín.* **Open** 9am-midnight Tue-
Thur, 9am-1am Fri, Sat. Closed July. **Credit** AmEx,
DC, MC, V. **Map** p328 I12.
Once a local grocer's, González is now a smart
deli with a fine range of cheeses, charcuterie,
preserves, fruit and nuts, olive oils and plenty more
besides. The back room is now a pleasant, well-
stocked wine bar.

Hespen & Suárez
Mercado Contemporáneo

*C/Barceló 15, Chueca (91 445 39 03/www.hespen
ysuarez.com). Metro Alonso Martínez or Tribunal.*
Open 8.30am-10pm Mon-Fri; 10am-10pm Sat, Sun.
Credit AmEx, MC, V. **Map** p324 H8.
This smart deli offers flavours from around the
world in the form of raw ingredients and dried
goods, plus prepared dishes to take away.

Mantequerías Bravo

*C/Ayala 24, Salamanca (91 576 02 93). Metro
Serrano.* **Open** 9.30am-2.30pm, 5.30-8.30pm Mon-Fri;
9.30am-2.30pm Sat. Closed Aug. **Credit** AmEx, DC,
MC, V. **Map** p325 L8.
A marvellous selection of foodstuffs is on sale in this
Salamanca shop, including meats and cheeses,
wines and spirits and coffees and teas. Homesick
Brits will be pleased with imports such as English
mustard and cream crackers.
Other locations: Paseo General Martinez Campos
23, Chamberi (91 448 09 18).

Eat, Drink, Shop

Cacao Sampaka: a marvellous confection. *See p194.*

La Moderna Apicultura

C/Doctor Esquerdo 47, Salamanca (91 574 52 40).
Metro O'Donnell. **Open** 9.30am-1.30pm, 4.30-8pm
Mon-Fri; 9.30am-1.30pm Sat. **No credit cards.**
Honey is the theme running through this shop, with
no less than 20 varieties, plus chocolate and jam.

Museo del Jamón

Carrera de San Jerónimo 6, Huertas & Santa
Ana (91 521 03 46/www.museodeljamon.es).
Metro Sol. **Open** 9am-midnight daily. **Credit**
MC, V. **Map** p327 H11.
Dotted around town, the various branches of the
'Ham Museum' are a sight to behold, with dozens of
hams dangling from the ceiling. Sample their wares
at the bar or in their restaurants.
Other locations: throughout the city.

Patrimonio Comunal Olivarero

C/Mejía Lequerica 1, Chueca (91 308 05 05/
www.pco.es). Metro Alonso Martínez. **Open** 10am-
2pm, 5-8pm Mon-Fri; 10am-2pm Sat. Closed Aug.
Credit MC, V. **Map** p324 I9.
Olive oil from every region of Spain that produces
the stuff is on sale at Patrimonio Comunal Olivarero.
Quantities go from two-litre bottles to five-litre cans,
and some make lovely gifts.

Health & herbs

NaturaSí

C/Doctor Fleming 1, Chamartín (91 458 32 54/
www.naturasi.it). Metro Santiago Bernabéu.
Open 10am-8.30pm Mon-Sat. **Credit** AmEx,
DC, MC, V.
This 'natural' supermarket sells a huge range of ecological and natural foodstuffs, among them fresh
fruit and veg, cheese and herbal products.

Salud Mediterranea

Paseo Santa María de la Cabeza 3, Atocha (91 527
89 29). Metro Atocha. **Open** 10am-8pm Mon-Fri;
10am-2pm Sat. **No credit cards. Map** p328 J15.
The huge selection of organic and macrobiotic
products at this shop includes hard-to-find
Japanese items and pollen from the bees in the
Sierra de Madrid.
Other locations: C/Ortega y Gasset 77, Salamanca
(91 309 53 90).

Markets

Madrid's markets are a noisy, colourful way
to get close to the locals – and to stock up on
cheap food. They offer a vast range of fruit
and veg, meat, wet fish, cheese, charcuterie
and offal. Spaniards do queue (although it
may not look like it) – just ask *'¿Quién es el*
último/la última?' ('Who's last in the queue?')
before joining. All the following markets
are open from around 9am-2pm and 5-8pm
(15 May-15 Sept until 8.30pm) during the
week, and 9am-2pm on Saturdays.

Anton Martín

C/Santa Isabel 5, Lavapiés (91 369 06 20).
Metro Antón Martín. **Map** p328 I13.

La Cebada

Plaza de la Cebada s/n, La Latina (91 365 91 76).
Metro La Latina. **Map** p327 F13.

Chamartín

C/Bolivia 9, Chamartín (91 457 53 50/http://mercado
dechamartin.com). Metro Colombia.
In an upmarket neighbourhood with many affluent
foreign residents, and produce to match.

Chamberí

C/Alonso Cano, 10, Chamberí (no phone).
Metro Iglesia.
Big, with lots of variety. The fruit and veg stalls in
the middle are among the best in town.

Maravillas

C/Bravo Murillo 122, Tetuán (no phone).
Metro Alvarado.
Madrid's biggest market, and the best for fish.

Los Mostenses

Plaza de Los Mostenses, Malasaña (no phone).
Metro Plaza de España. **Map** p323 F10.
A huge market with an international feel: Chinese
and Mexican products are much in evidence.

La Paz

C/Ayala 28, Salamanca (91 435 07 43). Metro
Serrano. **Map** p325 L8.
A very upmarket market, with a dazzling range of
quality products. It's worth a visit just for the
gourmet cheese stall La Boulette.

El Rastro

C/Ribera de Curtidores, between Plaza de Cascorro &
Ronda de Toledo (no phone). Metro La Latina. **Open**
dawn-approx 2pm Sun. **Map** p327 G14.
The city's most famous market dates back nearly
five centuries. Stalls set up from 7am, with the hard-
core bargain-hunters arriving soon afterwards. In
truth, there are few real deals to be had these days,
but in among the tat are Moroccan stalls selling
lovely leather bags (though be sure to haggle hard),
and antiques stalls and shops that are worth a trawl
(*see also p183-84*). In any case, it's still a quintessential stop on the tourist shopping map, but do
keep an eye on your bag. **Photos** *p183.*

San Miguel

Plaza de San Miguel, Los Austrias (91 548 12 14).
Metro Sol. **Map** p327 F12.
This pretty market has a restored 19th-century
wrought-iron façade. There's a good selection of
produce, and a bustling café in the middle.

Supermarkets

Hypermarkets are mostly to be found on the
main roads around the edge of the city, and are
mainly accessible only by car. If you're mobile

and need to stock up, look for ads for Alcampo, Continente or Pryca. Many branches of **El Corte Inglés** (*see p182*) also have (pricey) supermarkets. For information on Sunday opening, *see p181*. In town, apart from the chains listed below, look out for branches of **Día**, which has a no-frills approach to retailing, and **Lidl**, with reasonable-quality products at unbeatable prices.

Caprabo

Lagasca 51, Salamanca (91 431 77 11/www. caprabo.es). Metro Serrano. **Open** *Sept-July* 9am-9pm Mon-Sat. *Aug* 9am-2.30pm, 5-9pm Mon Sat. **Credit** MC, V. **Map** p325 L8.
Other locations: throughout the city.

Carrefour Express

C/Valencia 2, Lavapiés (91 467 42 08/www. carrefour.es) Metro Lavapiés. **Open** 9am-9.30pm daily. **Credit** MC, V. **Map** p328 H14.
Other locations: throughout the city.

Sabeco

C/Bravo Murillo 16, Chamberí (91 447 37 71). Metro Quevedo. **Open** 9.30am-9pm Mon-Sat. **Credit** MC, V. **Map** p323 G6.
Other locations: throughout the city.

Wine & drink

Bodegas Santa Cecilia

C/Blasco de Garay 72-74, Chamberí (91 445 52 83/ www.santacecilia.es). Metro Islas Filipinas. **Open** 10am-9pm Mon-Sat. **Credit** AmEx, DC, MC, V. **Map** p323 E6.
This *bodega*, occupying two almost-adjacent locales, stocks a vast array of wines, beers and spirits – over 4,000 in total. They're mainly Spanish, while beers and spirits come from all over. The gourmet shop, No.72, hosts frequent tasting sessions.
Other locations: C/Bravo Murillo 50, Cuatro Caminos (91 442 35 32).

Lavinia

C/José Ortega y Gasset 16, Salamanca (91 426 06 04/www.lavinia.es). Metro Nuñez de Balboa. **Open** 10am-9pm Mon-Sat. **Credit** AmEx, DC, MC, V. **Map** p325 M7.
No oenophile should miss visiting Lavinia, which claims to be Europe's largest wine shop. In stark contrast to many of Madrid's dusty old *bodegas*, it's bright, airy and spacious, and staff are knowledgeable and helpful.

Mariano Madrueño

C/Postigo de San Martín 3, Sol & Gran Vía (91 521 19 55/www.dongourmet.com). Metro Callao. **Open** 10am-2pm, 5.30-8.30pm Mon-Fri; 11am-2.30pm, 5.30-8.30pm Sat. Closed 2wks Aug. **Credit** MC, V. **Map** p327 G11.
This classic old *bodega*, dating back to 1895, has a charming interior, with wrought-iron columns and carved wooden shelves. As for the booze on sale, the

selection is enormous, with wines and spirits, plus the *bodega*'s own (lethal) coffee and orange liqueurs.

Reserva y Cata

C/Conde de Xiquena 13, Chueca (91 319 04 01/ www.reservaycata.com). Metro Chueca. **Open** 11am-2.30pm, 5-9pm Mon-Fri; 11am-2.30pm Sat. **Credit** AmEx, DC, MC, V. **Map** p324 J10.
This shop is crammed full of wines from Spain and abroad, all displayed with helpful information and often at prices lower than in the supermarkets. Tasting sessions and courses are also offered.

Hair & beauty

Cosmetics & perfumes

Make Up Store

C/Fuencarral 124, Chamberí (91 593 99 54). Metro Bilbao. **Open** 10am-9pm Mon-Sat. **Credit** MC, V. **Map** p323 H7.
This chain has everything from eyeshadows in every colour to funky make-up bags. Staff are friendly.

Sephora

C/Alberto Aguilera 62, Conde Duque (91 550 20 50/www.sephora.com). Metro Argüelles. **Open** 10am-9.30pm Mon-Sat. **Credit** AmEx, MC, DC, V. **Map** p323 E7.
This popular Parisian cosmetics and perfume chain offers an A to Z of brands, including its own line.
Other locations: Puerta del Sol 3, Sol (91 523 71 71).

Hairdressers

Jofer

C/Galileo 56, Chamberí (91 447 51 60). Metro Quevedo. **Open** 8am-10pm Mon-Sat. **Credit** AmEx, DC, MC, V. **Map** p323 F6.
A good bet if you just want a quick trim or blow-dry. Prices vary but are generally reasonable, and at most branches you don't need an appointment. Waxing, tanning and other services are also on offer.
Other locations: throughout the city.

Juan, ¡por Diós!

C/Pérez Galdós 3, Chueca (91 523 36 49/www. juanpordios.com). Metro Chueca or Gran Vía. **Open** 10am-8.30pm Mon-Sat. **Credit** AmEx, DC, MC, V. **Map** p324 H10.
Currently the place to get your hair cut in Madrid's trendiest quarter, this innovative place also stocks international style magazines, CDs and even a wi-fi connection. **Photo** *p200*.

Massages

Masajes a 1,000

C/Carranza 6, Malasaña (91 447 47 77/ www.masajesa1000.com). Metro Bilbao. **Open** 8am-midnight daily. **Credit** AmEx, MC, V. **Map** p323 G7/8.

Eat, Drink, Shop

That's Masajes for €6 to you and me. While it tries to come up with a new and catchy euro-based name, Masajes a 1,000 (pesetas) continues to rub, knead, pluck and tweeze its way through its loyal clientele. Tanning, waxing and pedicures are also offered, all for various numbers of €6 vouchers.
Other locations: throughout the city.

Sana Sana
C/General Martínez Campos 40, Chamberi (91 310 54 24). Metro Rubén Dario. **Open** *Sept-July* 10am-10pm Mon-Fri; 10am-4pm Sat. *Aug* 11am-7pm Mon-Fri. **Credit** AmEx, DC, MC, V. **Map** p324 J6.
An instant massage chain that offers a ten-minute workover for the harassed exec using specially designed chairs. It also offers shiatsu, sports and anti-stress massage, and beauty treatments. No booking is necessary for the short massage.
Other locations: C/Eloy Gonzalo 13, Chamberi (91 446 28 76).

Spas

See also p257 **Splash out.**

Agua y Bien
C/Martínez Villergas 16, Northern suburbs (91 403 31 73/www.aguaybien.es). Metro Barrio de la Concepción. **Open** 10am-10pm Mon-Fri; 10am-3pm Sat, Sun. **Credit** AmEx, MC, V.
A small but extremely friendly spa, with staff who work hard to put you at your ease. A favourite is the 'thermal circuit', which offers an hour and a quarter's worth of showers, spa treatments, jacuzzi and massage. Staff are distinctly unstarchy.

Chi Spa
C/Conde de Aranda 6, Salamanca (91 578 13 40/ www.thechispa.com). Metro Retiro. **Open** 10am-9pm Mon-Fri; 10am-6pm Sat. **Credit** AmEx, DC, MC, V. **Map** p325 L10.
A sleek, sophisticated space run by the British group David Lloyd. Chi has separate areas for men and women offering specialised body and relaxation treatments, massages with essential oils and spices, hydrotherapy and aromatherapy.

Tattoos & body piercing

Factory Tattoo
C/Montera 24, Sol & Gran Via (91 521 44 69). Metro Gran Via or Sol. **Open** 10am-10pm Mon-Sat. **Credit** AmEx, DC, MC, V. **Map** p327 H11.
Factory is the most popular of the city's tattoo parlours, its seedy location no doubt adding to its allure. If your pain threshold is low, it's worth a visit just to see – and wince at – photos of piercings past.

Music

For wannabe DJs, **C/La Palma** and the surrounding streets are the place to be, with all genres of dance music covered in a plethora of

record shops. Head to **FNAC** (*see p182*) for the best selection of DVDs and music CDs; El Corte Inglés has an ineffective classification system and sprawling layout.

AMA Records
Mercado Fuencarral, C/Fuencarral 45, Malasaña (91 522 64 03/www.ama-records.com). Metro Tribunal. **Open** 11am-9pm Mon-Sat. **Credit** MC, V. **Map** p323 H10.
Super-friendly staff and a fantastic selection of hip hop, house, nu jazz, reggae, lounge and breakbeat make Ama Records a hub for the city's musical community. It's a great place for flyers.

El Flamenco Vive
C/Conde de Lemos 7, Los Austrias (91 547 39 17/ www.elflamencovive.es). Metro Ópera. **Open** 10am-2pm, 5-9pm Mon-Sat. **Credit** AmEx, DC, MC, V. **Map** p327 F11.
Even if you harbour only a passing interest in flamenco, the brilliant range of CDs, guitars, books and other paraphernalia at this shop will lure you in.

Up Beat Discos
C/Espíritu Santo 6, Malasaña (91 522 76 60/ www.up-beat.com). Metro Noviciado or Tribunal. **Open** 11am-2pm, 5-8.30pm Mon-Sat. **Credit** MC V. **Map** p323 G9.
Soul, jazz and reggae dominate the shelves here, with a hand-picked collection of CDs and vinyl, along with a sideline in donkey jackets, Parkas, Dr Martens, and so on. The shop has a fab '60s feel, with a space dedicated to scooter parts. Staff can track down rareties.

Musical instruments

Garrido Bailén
C/Bailén 19, corner C/Mayor 88, Los Austrias (91 542 45 01). Metro Ópera. **Open** 10am-1.30pm, 4.30-8.15pm Mon-Fri; 10am-1.45pm Sat. **Credit** AmEx, DC, MC, V. **Map** p327 E12.
An impressively wide range of instruments, with everything from traditional Spanish guitars to sitars. A limited range of sheet music is also stocked.

Guitarrería F Manzanero
C/Santa Ana 12, La Latina (91 366 00 47/ www.guitarrasmanzanero.com). Metro La Latina. **Open** *Sept-June* 10am-1.30pm, 5-8pm Mon-Fri. *July* 10am-1.30pm Mon-Fri. Closed Aug. **Credit** AmEx, DC, MC, V. **Map** p327 F14.
For a real taste of Spanish guitar-making, drop by at this master guitar-maker's shop, which also has a great display of old and rare string instruments. Call first to avoid disappointment.

Opticians

Grand Optical
Puerta del Sol 14, Sol (91 701 49 80). Metro Sol. **Open** 10am-9pm Mon-Sat. **Credit** AmEx, DC, MC, V. **Map** p327 H11.

Who's who

Heavies

Pronounced with a guttural, Scottish 'ch' at the beginning, these are the rockers that time forgot. Look for leather and studs, heavy metal T-shirts, big boots and long jackets.
Where to find them: In your nearest park engaging in a *botellón* (*see p241*), and in the suburbs.
Essential accessories: Bottle of Mahou beer, plenty of cigarettes and unruly facial hair.
Seen at: the **Rastro** (*see p196*) for Metallica T-shirts, **Sprint** (*see p182*) for beer and baccy and **Up Beat Discos** (*see p198*) for Dr Martens.

Muscu-locos

The Muscle-Boys. A play on words meaning a mix of 'muscular' and 'crazy about muscles'. Tight tops and vests for this lot, and not just in the summer – biceps as big as your head warrant showing off. These boys are mad about their image and cultivate it in the gym and in the high-fashion boutiques.
Where to find them: The gay quarter of Chueca is the place to marvel at their chiselled features and sculpted torsos. Here they shop, bar-hop and admire each other from afar... and sometimes not so afar.
Essential accessories: Very short shorts, Speedos for the pool, and a roving eye.
Seen at: **Amantis** for toys, **Berkana** for books and **SR** for leather goods (for all, *see p227*).

Fiesteros

The party people. Pierced and tattooed to the hilt, this polysexual crew are the hippest of the hip kids. The requisite uniform is a mixture of purpose-made and improvised clubwear that flaunts the midriffs of the girls and the biceps of the boys.
Where to find them: Their natural habitat is Malasaña and the Mercado Fuencarral where they shop, chat and get even more piercings.
Essential accessories: VIP passes for the next big party, fashionable mullet haircuts from Juan, ¡por Diós! and big Dior sunglasses.
Seen at: **Miss Sixty** (*see p191*) for clubwear, **Lanikai** (*see p191*) for skatewear and **Desigual** (*see p191*) for... well, more clubwear.

Pijos & pijas

The posh kids. Big, floppy '80s-style haircuts – and that's just the boys. Lacoste polo shirts, a jumper tied around the shoulders and white jeans top off the look. For the girls it's espadrilles, pink and white striped rugby shirts and immaculately styled barnets.
Where to find them: Branches of El Corte Inglés in the designer sections, Calle Serrano and any bar or club that *was* cool with the *fiesteros* two months previously.
Essential accessories: Daddy's credit card, a Mini Cooper and a comb to keep that floppy hair in check.
Seen at: **ABC Serrano** (*see p182*) shopping centre, **Adolfo Domínguez** (*see p190*) for sporty sweaters and **Sana Sana** (*see p198*) for a post-shopping massage.

Señores y señoras

The mature couple. For *él* distinguished grey hair will be slicked back and the obligatory moustache neatly trimmed. For *ella* an immaculately coiffed 'do is a must, with the make up erring on the heavy side. A camel-hair jacket for him, a fur coat for the lady. Cigars and cigarettes respectively.
Where to find them: Salamanca, where they'll double park for an hour while *la señora* gets a new bag.
Essential accessories: A small yappy dog, a Mercedes and plenty of bling.
Seen at: **Purificación García** (*see p190*) for something smart, **Mantequerías Bravo** (*see p195*) for some posh nosh and **Loewe** (*see p194*) for indulgent leather accessories.

Fantastically fashionable cuts at **Juan, ¡por Díos!** *See p197.*

This high-street optician is part of the same group as the UK's Vision Express. Frames are by DKNY, D&G, Christian Dior and Cartier, among others, and there's also a wide range of contacts. Prescription glasses or sunglasses take an hour to make up.
Other locations: La Vaguada (*see p182*).

Pharmacies

For general information on pharmacies, *see p300*. The following are open 24 hours a day.

Farmacia Central
Paseo de Santa María de la Cabeza 64, Embajadores (91 473 06 72). Metro Palos de la Frontera. **No credit cards.**

Farmacia Lastra
C/Conde de Peñalver 27, Salamanca (91 402 43 01). Metro Goya. **Credit** AmEx, DC, MC, V. **Map** p325 O9.

Photocopying

Most stationers (*papelerías*) or printers (*imprentas*) also have faxes and photocopiers.

WORKcenter
Plaza Canalejas, Huertas & Santa Ana (91 360 13 95/www.workcenter.es). Metro Sevilla or Sol.

Open 7am-11pm Mon-Sat; 8am-11pm Sun.
Credit AmEx, DC, MC, V. **Map** p328 H11.
For anyone who needs a CV copied in a hurry, posters printed, digital prints produced from any file format or internet access, WORKcenter is the place to go. Staff are helpful and branches centrally located, though net connection isn't cheap at €6 an hour.
Other locations: throughout the city.

Photographic

Foto Sistema
Gran Vía 22 (91 521 20 63/www.fotosistema.es). Metro Gran Vía. **Open** 9.30am-8pm Mon-Fri; 9.30am-2pm Sat. **Credit** AmEx, DC, MC, V. **Map** p324 H11.
Foto Sistema offers a good-quality one-hour developing service for colour, black and white, slides and enlargements.
Other locations: throughout the city.

Fotocasión
C/Ribera de Curtidores 22, Rastro (91 467 64 91). Metro Puerta de Toledo. **Open** 10am-2pm, 4.30-8.30pm Mon-Fri; 10am-2.30pm Sat, Sun. **Credit** MC, V. **Map** p327 F/G15.
A treasure trove for photographers and camera collectors. Owner José Luis Mur is a walking encyclopedia on cameras; he also has great offers on spare parts and new and second-hand cameras.

Image Center

*Plaza Santa Ana 1, Santa Ana (91 532 62 00/
www.imagecenter.es). Metro Antón Martín.* **Open**
9am-9pm Mon-Sat. **Credit** AmEx, DC, MC, V.
Map p328 H12.
A huge branch of a well-run chain, Image Center
offers processing in an hour as well as the usual
range of photographic necessities, video and electronic equipment.
Other locations: throughout the city.

Speciality shops

Almirante 23

*C/Almirante 23, Chueca (91 308 12 02). Metro
Chueca.* **Open** 11am-1.30pm, 5-7.30pm Mon-Fri;
11am-1.30pm Sat. **Credit** MC, V. **Map** p324 J10.
This curiosity shop is packed full with all manner
of old stuff, including toys, tacky postcards, prints,
cameras, watches, bull-fighting programmes and
more. Brilliant for browsing – and buying gifts.

Belloso

*C/Mayor 23, Los Austrias (91 366 42 58/www.
belloso.com). Metro Sol.* **Open** 9.45am-2pm, 4.45-8pm
Mon-Fri; 9.45am-2pm Sat. **Credit** AmEx, DC, MC, V.
Map p327 G11.
This neighbourhood has an abundance of shops
selling Catholic paraphernalia, but Belloso is one
of the best. The gear on offer covers a huge
range, including rosaries, crucifixes and statues of
the Virgin.

La Casa de los Chales

*C/Duque de Sesto 54, Salamanca (91 574 25 73/
www.casadeloschales.com). Metro Goya or O'Donnell.*
Open 8am-1.30pm, 5-8.30pm Mon-Sat. **Credit**
AmEx, MC, V. **Map** p325 O10.
The 'House of Shawls' has a huge range of *mantones
de Manila*, beautifully made fringed and embroidered shawls. Capes, handbags and feather boas
complete the stock.

Casa de Diego

*Puerta del Sol 12, Sol (91 522 66 43/www.casa
dediego.com). Metro Sol.* **Open** 9.30am-8pm Mon-Sat.
Credit AmEx, DC, MC. **Map** p327 H11.
This much-loved shop specialises in hand-painted
fans, umbrellas and classy walking sticks.

Guantes Luque

*C/Espoz y Mina 3, Santa Ana (91 522 32 87).
Metro Sol.* **Open** 10am-1.30pm, 5-8pm Mon-Sat.
Credit MC, V. **Map** p327 H12.
Luque sells gloves in all sizes, colours and materi-
als. If you can't find them here you won't find
them anywhere.

M&M

*C/Cervantes 19, Huertas & Santa Ana (91 429
68 01). Metro Antón Martín or Banco de España.*
Open *July-Sept* 9am-1.30pm, 4.30-8pm Mon-Fri;
10am-1.30pm Sat. *Aug* 9am-1.30pm, 4.30-8pm
Mon-Fri. **Credit** AmEx, DC, MC, V. **Map** p328 I12.

The official art materials supplier to the Círculo de
Bellas Artes, this shop counts Dalí and Picasso
among its former customers. The staff are helpful
and well informed.

Objetos de Arte Toledano

*Paseo del Prado 10, Huertas (91 429 50 00/
www.artetoledano.com). Metro Banco de España.*
Open 9.30am-8pm Mon-Sat. **Credit** AmEx, DC,
MC, V. **Map** p328 J12.
Located across from the Prado, this souvenir shop
par excellence sells traditional *españoladas* such as
fans, flamenco and bullfighting dolls. A great place
to find that gift for your kitsch-loving friends.

Sport

Adidas Stuff

C/Mayor 21, Sol (91 364 45 89). Metro Sol.
Open 10am-9pm Mon-Sat; 11am-9pm 1st Sun in
month. **Credit** AmEx, DC, MC, V. **Map** p327 G11.
This is sportswear as fashion: you can't imagine
customers getting the stuff sweaty or dirty, it's
simply far too cool. Official Real Madrid kits are sold
here too.
Other locations: C/Concha Espina 1, Esquina del
Bernabéu Shopping Centre, Chamartin (91 398 43 00).

Área Real Madrid

C/Carmen 3, Sol (91 521 79 50). Metro Sol.
Open 10am-9pm Mon-Sat; 11am-8pm Sun.
Credit AmEx, MC, V. **Map** p327 G/H11.
A true emporium for the Real Madrid-inclined. On
sale are, naturally, replica shirts and all manner of
other stuff bearing the club's logo, from ashtrays to
mouse mats, bath towels to undies.

Supporters Shop

*C/Goya 50, Salamanca (91 575 88 68). Metro
Goya.* **Open** 10am-2pm, 5-8.30pm Mon-Fri; 10.30am-
2.30pm, 5.30-8.30pm Sat. Closed Aug. **Credit** AmEx,
DC, MC, V. **Map** p325 N9.
Selling shirts and other memorabilia from over 500
clubs worldwide, Supporters Shop can usually kit
out fans of even the most obscure teams.

Tornal Moya Deportes

*Ronda de Valencia 8, Lavapiés (91 527 54 40/
www.tornalmoya.com). Metro Embajadores.*
Open 10am-2pm, 5-9pm Mon-Sat. **Credit** MC, V.
Map p328 H15.
This big, well-laid-out shop stocks the lot: top-name
sportswear, trainers, walking boots, swimwear,
tennis rackets, replica football shirts and bags.

Stamps & coins

Stamp & coin market

Plaza Mayor, Los Austrias. Metro Sol. **Open**
approx 9am-2pm Sun. **Map** p327 G12.
On Sunday mornings, an avid mass of stamp and
coin collectors swarm over the Plaza Mayor, buying,
selling and eyeing up each others' wares. This also
acts as a Sunday-morning attraction for anyone out

on a stroll in town, whether or not they are really bothered about tarnished old pesetas, stamps of all nations and 19th-century share certificates. Other traders sell old magazines, second-hand books, postcards, badges and ex-Soviet bloc military regalia. You can even get phonecards nowadays, along with just about anything else that someone, somewhere, considers collectable.

Ticket agents

There are all manner of ways of avoiding queues to buy tickets (*entradas*) for shows and gigs these days, among them telesales, online purchase and cashpoints. Some of the biggest players in this game are savings banks (Cajas de Ahorro) such as the Caixa de Catalunya and La Caixa, who do advanced sales by phone, as does the all-embracing Corte Inglés.

Each of these services is associated with different venues, so check in a listings magazine such as the *Guía del Ocio* to see which of them handles the telesales for the show you want to attend. The *Guía del Ocio* itself offers online sales for cinemas and other venues via its web-page, www.guiadelocio.com. **Fnac** (*see p182*) is a useful place to pick up concert tickets.

El Corte Inglés

902 400 222/www.elcorteingles.es. **Open** 10am-10pm daily. **Credit** AmEx, DC, MC, V.
El Corte Inglés sells tickets for a huge range of shows and events, either by phone, online or at any of its stores.

Entradas.com

902 488 488/www.entradas.com. **Open** 24hrs daily. **Credit** AmEx (some venues), DC, MC, V.
This 24-hour ticketing service functions both by telephone and online. When dialling, depending on the type of event you wish to buy a ticket for, you get put through to a different number, and it's generally easier to book via the net. Tickets can be collected at the event box office.

Servicaixa/La Caixa

902 33 22 11/ww3.serviticket.com. **Open** 24hrs daily. **Credit** AmEx, DC, MC, V.
Servicaixa has a limited share of the theatre ticket sales market but offers versatility as you have the possibility of purchasing over the telephone, online or from ATM machines.

Tel-entradas/Caixa de Catalunya

902 10 12 12/www.telentradas.com. **Open** 24hrs daily. **Credit** MC, V.
Through the Caixa de Catalunya you can book tickets for theatres, venues and concerts, pay by credit card and pick them up either at a branch of the bank or from the venue's box office itself (depending on the show and the venue). Some staff members speak minimal English, but don't bank on it. Online purchasing, with pages in English, is another option.

Tobacco & smoking

Estancos (tobacco shops; *see p305*) can be found all over town.

La Cava de Magallanes

C/Magallanes 16, Chamberí (91 446 28 17). Metro Quevedo. **Open** *Sept-June* 8.30am-8.30pm Mon-Sat. *July, Aug* 8.30am-2.15pm, 5-8.30pm Mon-Sat. **Credit** MC, V. **Map** p323 G6.
A temple to tobacco, La Cava de Magallanes stocks over 350 different types of cigars, all maintained at optimum temperature in a special humidified room. The knowledgeable owner speaks a little English. There is a good range of accessories too. Note that some credit cards incur a small extra charge.

La Mansión del Fumador

C/Carmen 22, Sol & Gran Vía (91 532 08 17). Metro Sol. **Open** 10.30am-1.30pm, 4.30-8.30pm Mon-Sat. **Credit** AmEx, MC, V. **Map** p327 G11.
Not a place to buy tobacco or cigarettes, La Mansión del Fumador does, however, stock a big range of accessories such as cigar-cutters, lighters, humidors, pipes and ashtrays.

Travel services

Forocio

Carrera de San Jerónimo 18, Santa Ana (91 522 56 77/www.forocio.com). Metro Sevilla or Sol. **Open** 10.30am-7.30pm Mon-Fri. **Credit** DC, MC, V. **Map** p328 H11.
This multi-purpose agency offers services for young foreigners, such as hosting 'International Parties' and providing Interrail and student cards, setting up language exchanges, and organising budget flights, day trips and weekend tours. The 'Tarjeta Forocio' gives a 10% discount on trips. English and other languages are spoken.

Metropolitan Viajes

C/Galileo 25, Chamberí (91 448 54 13/www. viajesmetropolitan.com). Metro Argüelles. **Open** 9.30am-2pm, 4.30-8pm Mon-Fri. **Credit** AmEx, DC, MC, V. **Map** p323 F6.
This small but ultra-friendly agency often has great budget deals on flights to the UK and has also been highly praised by frequent transatlantic flyers.

Viajes Zeppelin

Plaza de Santo Domingo 2, Sol & Gran Vía (91 758 10 40/www.v-zeppelin.es). Metro Santo Domingo. **Open** 9am-8pm Mon-Fri; 10am-1pm Sat. **Credit** AmEx, DC, MC, V. **Map** p327 F11.
This well-established agency with friendly service specialises in cheap European charter flights and long-haul youth fares. You can also book online. **Other locations:** C/Hermosilla 92, Salamanca (91 431 40 36).

Arts & Entertainment

Features

Sala Wind. *See p245*.

Festivals & Events

Europe's greatest party town.

San Isidro, the mother of all *madrileño* knees-ups. *See p205.*

Practically all year round, apart from perhaps during the late winter lull (when everybody is worn out and broke from Christmas, New Year and Reyes) and the end of the summer, anyone coming to Madrid is likely to encounter an arts festival, a music fest, a fiesta or a themed film season. There is something here to suit all tastes, but, to make sure you catch one you like, it's worth doing a little forward planning.

Events and festivals that receive official sponsorship come under the aegis of either the Ayuntamiento (city council) or the Comunidad de Madrid (regional government), and the influence of politics, inevitably, is felt in culture. Municipal events are beginning to look less tawdry and more upbeat with the Mayor Alberto Ruiz-Gallardón at the helm, and Comunidad cultural policy has maintained a consistently high standard in recent years.

Other events are independent and still more are semi-independent, functioning with a mix of public and private money. Visual arts events, like the huge art fair **ARCO** and photographic extravaganza **PHotoEspaña** are organised this way. Alternative music festival **Festimad Sur** has to make do with small grants from the council and a range of private patrons.

Fiestas usually celebrate a religious or historical event, though this is really just a pretext for dressing up, getting out and partying, something for which *madrileños* seem to have an innate talent. **Dos de Mayo, San Isidro**, **San Antonio de la Florida** and **La Paloma** are fiestas that people take part in with great gusto, and all are normally accompanied by good weather. Not that freezing temperatures or a few drops of rain are an impediment for the thousands who step out for **Reyes** (Three Kings' Day) and **Carnaval**.

WHAT'S ON

Advanced festival information is scarce as programming tends to be finalised close to the starting date. For information on Ayuntamiento-backed events try 010 or www.munimadrid.es/ www.esmadrid.com, and for Comunidad-backed events, try 012 or www.madrid.org. See also www.fiestas-de-madrid.com. Otherwise, listings magazines such as the *Guía del Ocio* and *Metrópoli* (a supplement of *El Mundo*), provide pull-out supplements on the Friday preceding big events and festivals. Spanish speakers should also look at www.lanetro.com, a good listings site. Events marked * below incorporate public holidays; for a full list, *see pp308-309.*

Spring

See also p232 **Getting some airs,** for the Música Antigua Aranjuez festival.

Día de la Mujer/Semana de la Mujer

Various venues. Route normally starts at Plaza Jacinto Benavente, Huertas & Santa Ana. Metro Sol or Tirso de Molina. **Information** Dirección General de la Mujer (91 420 85 92) & Centro de la Mujer (91 700 19 10). **Date** 8 Mar & surrounding wk.

International Women's Day is celebrated in Madrid with a march, usually from Plaza Jacinto Benavente to the bottom of C/Atocha. Some of the many other related events taking place over the week include short film seasons and concerts.

Festival de Arte Sacro

Various venues. **Information** Tourist offices & 012/www.madrid.org. **Date** Last 3wks Mar.

This three-week festival of music, dance, theatre, poetry, movies and conferences focuses on the role of religion in art over the centuries. The most recent festival looked at religious traditions throughout the world, from Buddhism to Catholicism and Islam.

Teatralia

Various venues. **Information** Tourist offices & 012/www.madrid.org. **Date** Last 3wks Mar.

A regional jamboree of performing arts, including theatre, puppet shows, circus and cinema as well as workshops and other activities aimed at children and young people. In Madrid itself the main venues are the Teatros Pradillo and Triángulo (for both, *see p263*), the Sala Cuarta Pared (*see p262*), the Círculo de Bellas Artes (*see p100*) and the Carpa de Los Malabaristas (Jugglers' Tent) in the Casa de Campo.

Semana Santa (Holy Week)*

All over Madrid. **Information** Tourist offices & 010/www.esmadrid.com. **Date** wk leading up to Good Friday and Easter weekend (Mar/Apr).

Easter is usually a good time to be in Madrid, as many *madrileños* get out of town for the long weekend, and the weather is usually good. In Madrid and nearby towns, there are many parish processions in which hooded *penitentes* schlep figures of Christ and the Virgin around. Regarded as the most impressive is that of Jesús Nazareno el Pobre from San Pedro El Viejo and around La Latina. All over town there are organ and choral performances in churches.

Klubbers' Day

Madrid Arena (see p238). **Information** www.klubbers.com. **Dates** 6 & 7 April 2007.

This dance festival sets out to be a Madrid equivalent to Andalucía's Creamfields. Despite its name, it's actually a two-day event in Madrid Arena, which, when not being used for sporting events, converts nicely into a giant club. Local and international talent steps up to the decks or does live sets, with names such as Sven Väth, Ellen Allien, DJ Hell, Slam and Cycle on the bill.

Madrid en Danza

Various venues. **Information** Tourist offices & 012/www.madrid.org/www.danza.es. **Dates** 3wks Apr.

Madrid's international dance festival always brings in an impressive range of companies from Spain and abroad. The emphasis is on contemporary dance and there are many parallel activities: symposiums, exhibitions, video showings and workshops. The festival takes place throughout the whole region, but most shows take place in the various theatres around town.

Fiesta del Trabajo* (May Day)

City centre & Casa de Campo. Metro Batán or Lago. **Date** 1 May.

The largest May Day march, attracting upwards of 60,000 people, is called jointly by the communist-led CCOO and the socialist UGT unions, which converge on Sol. Smaller in scale but quite animated is the anarcho-syndicalist CGT's march from Atocha to Plaza Jacinto Benavente. The anarchist purists CNT/AIT, meanwhile, march up C/Bravo Murillo from Cuatro Caminos. Many of the participants then head to the Casa de Campo where the UGT organises a lively party with stalls run by the *casas regionales*, clubs representing Spain's regions.

Dos de Mayo*

District of Malasaña. Metro Bilbao, Noviciado or Tribunal. **Map** p323 G8. *Parque de las Vistillas. Metro Ópera.* **Map** p326 D13. **Information** Tourist offices & 012. **Date** 2 May.

Commemorating the fateful day in 1808 when the people of Madrid rose up against Napoleon's occupying troops and paid for their audacity by being massacred, 2 May is now the region's official holiday and kick-starts a nearly continuous series of fiestas that go on throughout the rest of the spring and summer. Things get going in the Malasaña neighbourhood – named after the uprising's teenage heroine, Manuela Malasaña – in the Plaza Dos de Mayo, where the Monteleón barracks, a main bastion of resistance, then stood. Live gigs are held in the Plaza and in the Las Vistillas park and there are events at a number of other spots around town.

San Isidro*

Plaza Mayor, Los Austrias, & all over Madrid. **Information** Plaza Mayor tourist office & 010/www.munimadrid.es. **Date** 1wk around 15 May.

For six days either side of 15 May, this is the time to see *madrileños* doing what they do best: taking to the streets and having a rollicking good knees-up. The fiestas celebrate San Isidro, Madrid's patron saint, a humble 12th-century labourer and well-digger to whom all manner of miracles are attributed and whose wife, María de la Cabeza, was also canonised, making them the only sainted couple in history. The action centres on the Plaza Mayor, where the fiestas are officially declared open and nightly gigs are held (with the odd classical performance thrown in). There is more music in Las Vistillas park; music, theatre, painting workshops and more are put on for kids in

Arts & Entertainment

the Retiro; classic *zarzuela* arias get an airing in the Conde Duque Cultural Centre; the Auditorium in the Museo de la Ciudad programmes classical music; in the Planetarium there are performances of early, medieval and baroque music, and lovers of Spanish Golden Age theatre are catered for in the Plaza de San Andrés. An associated event is the Feria de la Cacharrería, a ceramics market, held in the Plaza de las Comendadoras, close to Conde Duque. Recent additions to the programming are Documenta, a short season of international documentary films; + Arte, a mixed bag of installations, performances, hip hop, electronic music and sanctioned graffiti, and Universimad, a rock festival at the Complutense.

Throughout the week there are also numerous religious ceremonies in various churches. The 15th itself sees a procession of vintage cars in the Castellana. Possibly most fun of all is the traditional *romería* (pilgrimage) at and around the Ermita de San Isidro, in the park of the same name; families in traditional

Picture this Burial of the Sardine

It doesn't get any weirder than this. On Ash Wednesday, the last day of Carnival, Madrid mourns the death of a sardine. In Pythonesque absurdity, his scaly little corpse, dressed in Sunday best, is somberly paraded through the streets of old Madrid by La Alegre Cofradía de la Sardina (the Happy Brotherhood of the Sardine). They carry his diminutive coffin from bar to bar, enjoying a tongue-in-cheek display of funereal ceremony along with their *cañas*. The route changes annually, but always winds up at the Fuente de los Pajaritos in the Casa de Campo.

The origins of this wacky pageant are sadly unclear. Some say that it derives from the days when abundant sardines were sold on the last day in which eating meat was permitted before Lent began, and that the ripe little fellow came to symbolise the many sacrifices that lay ahead until Easter. The fish may also have phallic implications, and its burial could be a harbinger of sexual abstinence during Lent. Other sources link it to the reign of Carlos III (1759-1788), when a shipload of rotten sardines arrived at his court and he ordered that they be buried immediately.

Despite the ritual's uncertain roots, Goya's masterful and macabre painting suggests that the custom was in full swing by the early 1800s (although the concrete date of the painting is unknown). Goya depicts a frenzied bacchanal of wild cavorting, masks and partner-swapping, overseen by a gruesome death mask. Despite the title of the painting, no sardines are in sight.

The sardine, its burial and all other carnival merriment were temporarily suppressed during the dictatorship. La Alegre Cofradía, then a small group of high-spirited friends, thought they'd chance it anyway. One Ash Wednesday in the early 1950s, they marched the fish to the Casa de Campo, singing and dancing en route. The police were summoned by a humourless priest, who felt this spectacle to be sacrilegious. The police found the entourage to contain so many venerable old lawyers, doctors and journalists, however, that they simply joined the throng.

Nowadays, the Cofradía has more than 90 members and a sister organisation, La Peña del Boquerón (the Anchovy Club), for the widows of the dead sardine. The march usually begins at 6pm, from sardine HQ at C/Rodrigo de Guevara 4 in La Latina (you will know the building by the fish on the door). But be prepared for a mournful moment, as all of the ornately painted miniature coffins from previous years are on display at the Cofradía site, and you will be expected to pay proper respects to the dearly departed fish.

Goya's **Burial of the Sardine** *is found at the Real Academia de Bellas Artes de San Fernando, see p101.*

Arts & Entertainment

castizo garb, looking like something out of a Goya painting, drink from wine skins and stuff themselves with traditional *madrileño* delicacies such as chorizo, morcilla and other offal dishes. **Photo** *p204*.

Feria del Libro Antiguo y de Ocasión
Paseo de Recoletos, Salamanca. Metro Banco de España or Colón. **Information** 91 420 34 21. **Dates** 2wks Apr-May.

An old and second-hand book fair spanning a week either side of the San Isidro weekend, and celebrating its 30th anniversary in 2007. Here you may stumble across rare treasures, out-of-print editions or recent remainders. Don't expect much in English.

Madrid EnCanto
Teatro Albéniz (see p261). **Information** 91 522 02 00/ www.madrid.org. **Date** 3wks May-June.

This short festival of song in the Teatro Albéniz has taken on an increasingly Latin flavour, as singer-songwriters from countries like Spain, Portugal and Latin America feature. Chavela Vargas was back in 2006, and Rodrigo Leão (from Madredeus) did a set with Beth Gibbons. Other artists included Turkish musician Omar Faruk Tekbilek and Argentine Susana Rinaldi.

La Feria del Libro (Book Fair)
Parque del Retiro. Metro Atocha or Ibiza. **Information** 91 533 51 84/www.ferialibro.com. **Date** 2wks end May-June. **Map** p329 L-N, 11-14.

First celebrated in 1933, the Book Fair is now a major international event. Hundreds of publishers are present and well-known writers show up to sign copies of their works.

Summer

Festimad Sur
Estadio Butarque, Leganés. Bus 483/484 or Metro Sur San Nicasio. **Information** 91 522 37 87/www. festimad.es. **Dates** late May 2007.

Despite problems with funding and various other ups and downs in recent years, including changes of venue, Festimad, Madrid's biggest rock festival, is certainly still alive and kicking. In 2007, at least, a range of Spanish indie bands will perform at the Estadio Butarque in Leganés, along with rock in all its variant forms. There will also be dance music, DJ sessions and a few big names. Recent years have seen artists of the calibre of the Pixies, Korn, Ben Harper, Patti Smith and the (International) Noise Conspiracy. Pearl Jam has been confirmed for 2007.

San Antonio de la Florida
Ermita de San Antonio de la Florida (see p124). **Information** 91 547 07 22. **Date** 13 June. **Map** p322 A9.

One of the first of the summer's biggest street parties, the San Antonio celebrations can trace their history back a very long way. June 13 is the feast day of San Antonio, the patron saint of seamstresses. Single girls used to place 13 pins in the baptismal font of the hermitage. If one stuck to her finger she would marry within a year. The main party, including events for kids, takes place across the Paseo de la Florida, in the Parque de la Bombilla.

Metrorock
Parque Juan Carlos I. Metro Campo de las Naciones. **Information** www.metrorock.net. **Dates** 22 & 23 June 2007.

As the name may suggest, this festival started its life as a series of free concerts taking place in Madrid's underground stations. In recent years though, it has grown into a full-sized event, taking place in the well-suited Parque Juan Carlos I. The line-up includes a good mix of international and Spanish acts – Beck, Franz Ferdinand, Paul Weller, The Charlatans and OK Go have all paid a visit.

PHotoEspaña
Various venues. **Information** 91 360 13 20/www. phedigital.com. **Dates** 30 May-22 July 2007.

Every spring/summer since 1998, PHotoEspaña has swept through Madrid's major museums and galleries, redefining the city as an international photography epicentre. Each year has a different theme; the 2006 theme was Nature. In recent years, the retinue of photographic stars, many of whom give workshops and lectures throughout the festival, has included Nan Goldin, Joel Peter Witkin, Philip Lorca di Corcia, and Paul Graham. PHotoEspaña also transforms C/Huertas into an active outdoor exhibition space and puts on slide projections in Plaza Santa Ana and Centro Cultural Conde Duque.

Músicas del Mundo Getafe (World Music Festival)
Various venues in Getafe. Bus 441, 442 from Atocha/train C-4 to Getafe Centro. **Information** 91 208 04 61. **Date** May/June.

The southern industrial satellite town of Getafe organises an annual World Music Festival. For budgeting reasons this festival has had its share of ups and downs but looks set to continue. Past festivals have seen a predominance of African and Spanish fusion performers but in recent years the festival has featured music from the American continent, blues and reggae particularly, and from eastern Europe.

Summercase
Boadilla del Monte. Metro Colonia Jardín, then free shuttle bus. **Information** www.summercase.com. **Dates** 13 & 14 July 2007.

A welcome new addition to the city's music festivals in 2006 (when it had a 1990s feel, with Massive Attack, Fatboy Slim, Happy Mondays, Daft Punk and Primal Scream), Summercase runs simultaneously in Madrid and Barcelona. Acts confirmed for 2007 include !!!, Kaiser Chiefs and the Chemical Brothers. Meticulous organisation and sharp programming make this one a keeper.

Veranos de la Villa
Various venues. **Information** 91 758 92 70/ www.esmadrid.com. **Dates** July/Aug.

Arts & Entertainment

Festival de Otoño.

As part of the 'Summers in the City' festival, a good selection of top names have appeared at the patio of the Centro Cultural Conde Duque, which acts as the festival's main stage. Among them are Brazilians Milton Nascimento, Caetano Veloso and Carlinhos Brown, the fabulous Cape Verdean singer Cesaria Évora, many top flamenco artists, Youssou N'Dour and Femi Kuti, Cubans like Ibrahim Ferrer and some gnarled old rockers. Interspersed among them, however, there has also been a fair amount of dross. Elsewhere, *zarzuelas* are programmed in both the Centro Cultural de la Villa and in the Sabatini Gardens beside the Royal Palace, the 'Titirilandia' puppet season for kids takes place in the Retiro, while Golden Age or more contemporary theatre productions may be seen outdoors beside the Muralla Árabe and in the Centro Cultural Galileo, and fringe venues all over town offer plenty more 'alternative' shows. Also outdoors is a two-screen cinema in the Parque de la Bombilla, down on the Paseo de la Florida.

Verbenas de San Cayetano, San Lorenzo & La Paloma

La Latina & Lavapiés. Metro La Latina or Lavapiés. **Information** Tourist offices & www.munimadrid.es/ 010. **Date** 6-15 Aug. **Map** p327 F/G/H14.

Madrid popular culture at its best – the streets and squares of the old Lavapiés, Rastro and La Latina neighbourhoods are dolled up with flowers and bunting and the locals don their *castizo* gear for some serious street partying. San Cayetano is first, on 7 August, followed by San Lorenzo on the 10th and La Paloma on the 15th. Daytime sees parades and events for kids; by night there are organ grinders, traditional *chotis* dancing, the aroma of grilled chorizo and *churros*, sangria by the bucketful and a lot of good clean fun.

Autumn

Fiestas del Partido Comunista

Recinto Ferial de la Casa de Campo. Metro Lago. **Information** Partido Comunista de España (91 300 49 69/www.pce.es). **Date** mid Sept.

In the political minority nowadays, the Spanish Communist Party still has enough resources and clout to stage a three-day fiesta. There are performances by flamenco and rock bands, theatre shows, stalls run by political groups, debates on many political and social issues and lots of regional cuisine in the *casas regionales*.

La Noche en Blanco

Various venues. **Information** www.esmadrid.com/ lanocheenblanco & 010. **Date** Sept.

To have '*una noche en blanco*' means to spend a sleepless night, and this is insomniac heaven. In Madrid, as in Paris, Rome, Brussels and Riga, for one night only you can wander from exhibition centre to museum, from fashion show to concert all night long and all for free. See the website for a list of participating venues.

Festival de Otoño

Various venues. **Information** Comunidad de Madrid (91 720 81 94/3), tourist offices & 012/www.madrid.org. **Date** 4-5wks Oct-Nov.

The impressive and always enjoyable 'Autumn Festival' offers somewhere in the region of 60-odd theatre, dance and music spectacles and remains one of the city's major performing arts events. The range throughout the festival is quite wide. Acts as diverse as the Brodsky Quartet, Ballets Trockadero de Monaco, musical groups from Rajasthan, La Comédie Française, Eddie Palmieri and the Spanish Orquesta Nacional de Jazz have all popped up in recent years, with *Tartuffe* and *Romeo and Juliet* big theatrical draws in 2006. Events take place both in the capital and surrounding towns, making a trip out quite tempting. Around ten venues in Madrid itself have shows, among them the Teatros Albéniz and Zarzuela, the Círculo de Bellas Artes and fringe spaces such as Teatro Pradillo and Sala Cuarta Pared.

Winter

For **International Fashion Week** and the **ARCO** contemporary art fair (both occur in February), *see p209* **Trade fairs**.

Estampa

Palacio de Cristal, Avda de Portugal s/n, Casa de Campo. Metro Lago. **Information** 91 544 77 27/www.estampa.org. **Dates** late Nov-Dec.
A firm fixture on the arts calendar, Estampa is a well-attended show that brings together galleries and collectors from around the world to exhibit prints and contemporary art editions.

Feria de Artesanía

Plaza de España. Metro Plaza de España, Sol & Gran Vía. **Information** www.agrupacionartesanosmadrid. org & 012. **Date** mid Dec-5 Jan. **Map** p323 E10.
This large and crowded crafts fair is an ideal place to look for original presents and coincides with Christmas, New Year and Reyes.

Navidad* (Christmas)

All over Madrid. **Date** 25 Dec.
Less hyped than in northern climes, Christmas begins, very reasonably, in December, and is traditionally less important than Epiphany (Reyes). Consequently you are not reminded of the number of shopping days left until Christmas at every turn and the absence of piped carols is almost eerie. Father Christmas, tinsel, flashing lights and baubles are far more evident than a few decades ago, however; all these trappings, plus lots of other cheap festive junk, are sold in the Christmas market in Plaza Mayor throughout December. The big family blow-out is usually on Noche Buena (Christmas Eve) with shrimps, red cabbage and either roast lamb, sea bream or both. Some families exchange presents on the otherwise fairly quiet Christmas Day, but the big ones are usually saved for 6 January. Worth checking out at this time are the nativity scenes (*belenes*), displayed in many places, and the many organ recitals, choral performances and chamber music concerts held in churches and other venues.

Noche Vieja (New Year's Eve)

Puerta del Sol, Sol & Gran Vía. Metro Sol. **Date** 31 Dec. **Map** p327 H11.
New Year's Eve is celebrated with gusto, usually *en familia*, and involves another blow-out meal, litres of cava and the curious tradition of eating 12 grapes as the clock chimes midnight. Ever resourceful, many supermarkets now sell seedless grapes pre-packed in dozens for the occasion. The Puerta del Sol is where thousands throng – not recommended with kids or for misanthropes. Clubs and bars organise parties, often starting at 12.30am or later. (Expensive) tickets should be purchased in advance.

Reyes* (Three Kings)

All over Madrid. **Date** 6 Jan.
On the evening of 5 January, Noche de Reyes, thousands of children and their parents line up along C/Alcalá to watch the annual *cabalgata* (parade), which is also televised. Dozens of elaborate floats pass by and the riders hurl sweets to the children. Later, most families have a big dinner, and the following day presents await those who have been good. Those who haven't get a piece of coal.

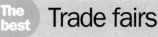 **The best Trade fairs**

Catch all the fun of the *feria* at the Juan Carlos I exhibition centre, out towards the airport (information 91 722 50 00 and www.ifema.es).

ARCO

An international contemporary art fair packed with gallery owners, critics and the general public. Mid February.

International Fashion Week

A biannual showcase for the best of Spanish and international creators. Ostensibly for professionals, but in practice blagging entry is fairly easy. Mid February and mid September.

Science Fair

Wonderful if you have kids in tow, with touchy-feely exhibits to stimulate all the senses. Late March/early April.

Expo-Ocio

Dedicated to hobbies and leisure pursuits, Expo-Ocio always draws huge crowds. November.

SIMO

Computer geeks unite at this huge international data-processing, multimedia and communications show. November.

Feriarte

An international art and antiques fair. Mid December.

Juvenalia

Youth-oriented sports activities, along with magic, juggling, story-telling and so on. Late December.

Festival de Flamenco Caja Madrid

Casa Encendida (see p105) & Teatro Albéniz (see p261). **Information** *Cultyart* 91 553 25 26/ www.cultyart.com. **Dates** 2wks Jan/Feb.
Brings in the top names in flamenco for sessions of *cante jondo*, foot-stomping and guitar playing.

Carnaval

Various venues. **Date** wk of Shrove Tuesday.
Carnival is a very good excuse for dressing up and partying, either in the street or in bars and clubs. It opens in the Plaza Mayor, followed by a parade around old Madrid. On Ash Wednesday, the last day, there is a ribald ceremony during which a fish is carted around to the strains of a marching band, before being interred (*see p206* **Picture this**).

Arts & Entertainment

Children

Major fun with the *madrileños*.

This is a city where children are welcome almost everywhere. *Madrileños* are, in general, a friendly bunch and if you have kids in tow their amiability is sure to go up a notch. The care of children is considered everybody's business. Waitresses will scoop your baby up to show to the kitchen staff and old ladies will happily advise you your child is wearing too few/too many clothes for the season.

Taking children to restaurants or pavement cafés is considered the norm, but be prepared to adapt to Spanish meal times; lunch in Spain is eaten around 2pm and dinner from 10pm. If your kids really can't wait, then the numerous fast-food or pasta and pizza places are your best hope, and high chairs and children's menus can usually be found in these joints.

In summer, afternoon temperatures can hover around a very uncomfortable 40ºC and so outdoor activities are best in the morning. After a late lunch, a siesta is the best option before venturing out into the relatively cool evening air. The city comes alive again in the hour or two before dusk when families come out to stroll, eat ice-cream and watch the world go by.

Be warned that few metro stations have lifts, and buses will only admit pushchairs if they are folded. Baby-changing facilities are limited to shopping centres, the department store El Corte Inglés (*see p182*), and the airport.

Attractions

Kids also enjoy the **Teleférico** cable-car (*see p123*) that runs from the Parque del Oeste deep into the Casa de Campo, and the dizzying **Faro de Madrid** (*see p125*).

Faunia

Avda de las Comunidades 28, Eastern suburbs (91 301 62 10/www.faunia.es). Metro Valdebernardo. **Open** *Feb, Mar* 10am-6pm Wed-Sun. *Apr, May, last 2wks Sept* 10am-8pm daily. *June-mid Sept* 10am-9pm daily. *Oct, Nov* 10am-7pm Wed-Sun. *Dec* 10am-5.30pm Wed-Sun. Closed Jan. **Admission** €22; €16 3-12s, over-60s; free under-3s. **Credit** AmEx, MC, V.
Part zoo, part theme park, Faunia recreates the world's different ecosystems in a series of domes. Best of the bunch is the Amazon jungle house, which echoes with the screech of exotic birds; an intense tropical storm is simulated every half hour. And in summer Penguin World, an impressive reconstruction of a polar zone, where you can see the little fellas zipping about, is wildly popular. Faunia is not a cheap day out and queues can be long.

IMAX Madrid

C/Meneses, Parque Tierno Galván, Legazpi, South of centre (91 467 48 00/www.imaxmadrid.com). Metro Arganzuela-Planetario. **Admission** €10-€7; €9-€5.90 Mon & over-65s; free under-3s. **Credit** AmEx, MC, V.
The hourly wildlife and scientific shows are only in Spanish, but the 3D and Omnimax presentations are awesome enough to be enjoyed by all children.

Palacio de Hielo

C/Silvano 77, Eastern suburbs (91 716 01 59/ www.palaciodehielo.com). Metro Canillas. **Open** *Sept-May* 8.45pm-10pm Wed, Thur; 5pm-11.30pm Fri; noon-3pm, 5-11.30pm Sat; noon-3pm, 5-10pm Sun. Closed June-Aug. **Admission** €4-€10. **No credit cards**.
The Ice Palace is a huge leisure complex dominated by a 1,800-square-metre ice rink. With a curling and skating school, a 24-lane bowling alley and a 15-screen cinema this is good option for a rainy day with teenagers. The site, out towards Barajas Airport, also has a shopping centre and a nursery for kids aged three to 11.

Parque de Atracciones

Casa de Campo (91 463 29 00/91 526 80 30/www.parquedeatracciones.es). Metro Batán. **Open** varies (see website). **Admission** €7; €12 incl 2 rides; Supercalco (all-inclusive ticket) €24.40; €13.90 under-6s. **Credit** MC, V.
A funfair with something for everyone. The wildest ride is El Abismo, The Abyss, which is a 49-metre high roller that follows a 450-metre route of scary drops at 100 kph. There is now a children's version too, so nobody has to miss the terror. Other new features include indoor paintball and a 4D cinema. There are long queues for some rides.

Planetario de Madrid

Parque Tierno Galván, Legazpi, South of centre (91 467 38 98/91 467 34 61/www.planetmad.es). Metro Arganzuela-Planetario. **Shows** vary; phone to check. **Admission** €3.40; €1.50 2-14s, over-65s. **No credit cards**.
Close to the IMAX (*see above*), the Planetarium has seasonal exhibitions on the solar system as well as 45-minute shows. Like the IMAX, the narration here is only in Spanish and may test your kids' interest in the heavens if they are non-Spanish speakers.

Zoo-Aquarium de la Casa de Campo

Casa de Campo (91 512 37 70/www.zoomadrid.com). Metro Batán. **Open** 11am-dusk daily. **Admission** €14.90; €12.20 under-8s, over-65s; free under-3s. **Credit** V.

This attractively landscaped zoo is located slap bang in the heart of the Casa de Campo. The animals look as happy as can be expected of beasts held in captivity, although the big cats could really do with a bit more leg-room. At the Tierra de Gorilas ('Land of Gorillas') a sheet of reassuringly thick glass separates you from the massive, glowering silverbacks that prowl about. Children will enjoy walking through the shark tank and dolphinarium. There is also a petting zoo and a train ride.

Babysitting & childcare

English-speaking babysitters can be found through local English-language publications; for a list of magazines and newspapers in English published in Madrid, *see p303*. Alternatively, parents can leave children aged from four to 12 for short periods at any of the following *ludotecas* (play centres) around town.

Cosmocaixa.
See p213.

The tooth mouse

Ask any Spanish child to name the most famous mouse in the world and few of them will come up with Mickey. By far the most celebrated rodent in Spain and much of South America is Ratoncito Pérez, the mythical mouse who sneaks into children's rooms at night to slip money under the pillow when a tooth falls out. What few people know is that El Ratón (the mouse) Pérez is actually a *madrileño*.

Stroll half a minute from the Puerta del Sol and you can see a plaque marking the house where Pepito Pérez lived in a biscuit tin in the basement of a pastry shop. The ground floor of C/Arenal 8 is now a small arcade of shops. Inside, you'll find a mouse-sized statue (well, hamster-sized, perhaps). There are also illustrated panels telling the story of Pepito and his creator, a Jesuit priest, Father Coloma.

Juan Coloma, who found God after nearly killing himself while cleaning his revolver as a young man, first published the story of Ratoncito Pérez in 1902. He dedicated the book to the young King Alfonso XIII, to whom he had told the story while the monarch was a sickly child.

According to the story the mouse would frequently escape from the basement by means of the sewers. From this labyrinth he could find his way into the bedroom of any child from the boy-king to the poorest *niño* in the land, exchanging a lost tooth for money or a small gift. The tradition continues to this day.

In 2003 the mayor of Madrid finally unveiled the plaque to Ratoncito Pérez, announcing rather grandly that, just as the Americans have Mickey Mouse, Pepito 'deserves recognition as a symbol of the hopes and dreams of all children, and because he is *our* mouse'.

Centro de Recreo Infantil Dinopeppino

C/Mártires de Alcalá 4, Malasaña & Conde Duque (91 559 22 04). Metro Ventura Rodríguez. **Open** 4.30-8.30pm Mon-Fri; 11.30am-2pm, 4.30-8.30pm Sat, Sun. **Admission** €6.20 hr; €50 10hr multi-entry. **No credit cards. Map** p323 E8.
A well-equipped and spacious play centre.

Chiquipark

Estación Chamartín, C/Agustín de Foxá, Charmartín (91 323 19 83/www.chiquipark.com). Metro Chamartín. **Open** 5-9pm Mon-Fri; noon-2.30pm, 4pm-9pm Sat, Sun. Closed Aug-mid Sept. **Admission** (per hr) €7. **Credit** MC, V.
The most central branch of this chain of play centres.

Gorongoro

Avda de Felipe II 34, Salamanca (91 431 06 45). Metro Goya. **Open** *Sept-June* 4.30-9pm Tue-Fri; 11.30am-2.30pm, 4.30-9pm Sat, Sun. *July* 6-9.30pm Mon-Fri; 11.30am-2.30pm, 6-9pm Sat. Closed Aug. **Admission** (per hr) €7.20 over-4s; €6.60 under-4s. **Credit AmEx**, DC, MC, V. **Map** p325 O9/10.
This well-equipped play centre is close to the Retiro and the Goya shopping area.

Entertainment

Events aimed at children are dotted around the year, starting in January with a parade on the eve of **Reyes** (*see p209*), when Spanish children traditionally get their presents. The parade features floats from which the Three Kings throw sweets to children along the route. During **Carnaval** (*see p209*) special kids' activities are organised, and there are also children's events during **San Isidro** (*see p205*) and **Veranos de la Villa** (*see p207*). In April festivities for **El Día del Niño** (Day of the Child) are held in C/Bravo Murillo in Tetuán. The street is taken over by bouncy castles, puppet shows, foam-spraying firemen and candy floss stalls.

Look out, too, for children's theatre. **Teatro San Pol** in the Casa de Campo (C/San Pol de Mar 1, 91 541 90 89, www.teatrosanpol.com, closed July & Aug) puts on occasional shows in English. The **Madrid Players**, an English-language theatre group (91 326 24 39, www.madridplayers.org), puts on a pantomime at Christmas and hosts occasional theatre workshops for kids (check website for details).

In the Retiro park the permanent **Teatro Municipal de Titeres** (91 792 41 12, mobile 670 72 33 60, www.titirilandia.com), near the boating lake, has puppet shows most weekends, albeit in Spanish. **La Casa Encendida** (*see p105*) runs children's workshops on diverse subjects. Storytelling sessions are on Fridays and at weekends there are puppet shows in the patio.

Museums

The **Museo del Ferrocarril** (*see p132*) houses steam, diesel and electric locomotives. Children's activities include theatre at weekends, a mini-train on Saturdays and a monthly market for model train enthusiasts.

Cosmocaixa

C/Pintor Velázquez s/n, Alcobendas (91 484 52 00/ www.fundacio.lacaixa.es). Bus 157 from Plaza Castilla. **Open** 10am-8pm Tue-Sun. **Admission** €3; €1.50 under-16s; €1 over-65s; free under-7s. **Credit** DC, MC, V.

Kids and adults uncover the mysteries of science via hands-on interactive exhibits. The *clik de los*

niños (three- to eight-year-olds), where processes can be tried out, is popular, as is the *toca, toca* (touch, touch) area for small children, where there are animals to stroke. **Photos** *p211*.

Museo de Cera (Wax Museum)

Paseo de Recoletos 41, Salamanca (91 319 26 49/ www.museoceramadrid.com). Metro Colón. **Open** 10am-2.30pm, 4.30-8.30pm Mon-Fri; 10am-8.30pm Sat, Sun. **Admission** €15; €9 4-7s, over-60s. **No credit cards. Map** p324 K9.

Madame Tussaud's it isn't (no queueing for starters), yet this wax museum has a certain tacky charm. Along with the usual rogues, celebs and statesmen – among them the Beatles, Clark Gable and George W Bush – there's a Tren de Terror (ghost train).

Retiro park. *See p214.*

Arts & Entertainment

Parks & playgrounds

Small neighbourhood parks are not Madrid's strong point; play areas have improved in recent years but are still a little tame. One of the better play areas is in the **Plaza de Oriente**, next to the Palacio Real. The **Paseo del Prado** central boulevard has safe wooden climbing frames and slides and **Dos de Mayo** in Malasaña has play areas for toddlers and *terrazas* for adults, as does the nearby **Plaza de las Comendadoras**. **C/Fuencarral** has recently been done up, with widened pavements, and now boasts six small play areas.

The **Retiro** (*see p117*; **photos** *p213*) has a boating lake, cafés around the edge, buskers, artists, puppet shows, sports facilities and a good play area by the Puerta de Alcalá entrance. To the east is the Parque del Oeste, which has great views, decent play areas, ice-cream parlours and the Teleférico. The huge **Casa de Campo** (*see p123*) has the Zoo, the Parque de Atracciones funfair, an even bigger boating lake and the best outdoor pools in Madrid (*see p257*), with a shaded and shallow kids' pool.

Out of town

Most rides in the waterparks around town are suited to older kids, but there are usually areas for small children. For general pools, *see p257*.

Aquópolis-San Fernando

Crta de Barcelona (A-2), km 15.5, San Fernando de Henares (91 673 10 13/www.aquopolis.es/san fernando). Bus (Continental) to Alcalá de Henares or Torrejón from Avda de América/by car A-2. **Open** *June* noon-7pm daily. *July, Aug* noon-8pm Mon-Fri; 11am-8pm Sat, Sun. Closed Sept-mid June. **Admission** €16; €11.50 3-10s, over-65s. **Credit** MC, V.
Madrid's first waterpark, with giant water slides, pools for smaller and larger kids, wave pools and wilder attractions for reckless youths.

Aquópolis-Villanueva

Avda de la Dehesa, Villanueva de la Cañada (91 815 69 11/www.aquopolis.es/villanueva). Bus 627 from Moncloa/by car Ctra de La Coruña (A-6), exit 41, then M503. **Open** *mid June-mid* noon-7.30pm daily. Closed mid Sept-mid June. **Admission** €19; €14 4-9s, over-65s; free under 3s. **Credit** AmEx, MC, V.
One of the largest waterparks in Europe, run by the same company as the Aquópolis-San Fernando and with similar attractions.

De Pino a Pino

Area Recreativa del Chorro, Navafría (mobile 659 45 45 68/www.depinoapino.com). By car A-6/AP-61 to Segovia (100km), then N110 to Navafría (20km). **Open** *June-mid Sept* 10.30am-8pm daily. *Apr, May, Sept, Oct* 11am-7.30pm Sat, Sun. *June* 10.30am-8pm Sat, Sun. Closed Nov-Apr. **Admission** €23; €21 14-18s; €16 9-13s; €12 7-8s. **No credit cards.**

A way from Madrid, but well worth the trip, 'From Pine to Pine' is a forest-based adventure park where logs, hanging bridges and tree platforms are incorporated into routes that criss-cross the pine forests. Courses are designed with varying levels of difficulty according to kids' ages and each takes an hour.

Safari de Madrid

Aldea del Fresno, Ctra de Extremadura (A-5), km 32 (91 862 23 76/www.safarimadrid.com). By car A-5 to Navalcarnero, then M-507 to Aldea del Fresno. **Open** *Nov-Mar* 10.30am-5.30pm daily; *Apr-June* 10.30am-6.30pm daily. *July, Aug* 10.30am-8pm daily; *Sept-Oct* 10.30am-7pm daily. **Admission** €12; €8 3-10s. **Credit** AmEx, DC, MC, V.
A drive-through safari park where giraffes, elephants, big cats and monkeys roam free. In summer there's a swimming pool, a lake with pedalos for rent, a go-kart track, mini-motorbikes and a giant slide.

Tren de la Fresa (Strawberry Train)

Estación de Atocha (902 22 88 22). Metro Atocha Renfe. **Open** depart from Atocha 10am Sat, Sun (return from Aranjuez 6pm). Closed Mid Oct-late Apr, mid July-mid Sept. **Tickets** €23; €15 2-12s. **Credit** MC, V. **Map** p329 L15/16.
A relaxing and enjoyable steam train ride to Aranjuez (*see p284*). The 1920s 'strawberry' train departs from Atocha station and the ticket price includes visits to the palaces and gardens. Aranjuez's famous strawberries are served by hostesses in period costume.

Warnerbros Park

San Martín de la Vega (91 821 12 34/www.warner brospark.com). By car A-4 to km 22, then M-506 to San Martín de la Vega/by train C-3 from Atocha. **Open** varies (see website). Closed Nov-Mar. **Admission** *1 day* €25-€33; €16-€25 5-11s, over-60s. *2 days* €37.50-€49.50; €24-€37.50 5-11s, over-60s. **Credit** AmEx, DC, MC, V.
The park has five themed areas with rides to match: Hollywood Boulevard, Cartoon Village, Old West Territory, DC Super Heroes and Warner Brothers Studios. Popular rides can have long, hot queues, and it's an expensive day out, especially as visitors are not allowed to bring in their own food.

Xanadu

Autovía A-5, km 23.5, Arroyomolinos (91 648 23 65/www.madridsnowzone.com). Bus 496, 498, 524, 528 from Príncipe Pío, or 529H, 531, 531A, 536, N5 from Méndez Álvaro. **Open** 10am-midnight Mon-Sun; 10am-2am Fri, Sat. **Admission** *1hr* €12, €10 under-13s Mon-Thur; €16, €14 under-13s Fri-Sun. *2hrs* €16, €14 under-13s Mon-Thur; €22, €19 under-13s Fri-Sun. **Credit** AmEx, DC, MC, V.
Billed as 'Europe's largest destination for snow, shopping and leisure', Xanadu boasts 24,000sq m of indoor ski slopes. All the necessary equipment can be hired. There are also go-karts, a 15-screen cinema, 200 shops and around 30 restaurants.

Film

Feature comforts.

Golem. See p216.

Madrileños and movies go together like chocolate and *churros*. Indeed, this happy foursome is all that's needed for a perfect night out. Tickets are reasonably cheap even for the plushest screens and the range of film fare is easily a match for Paris or London. Spanish film goes from strength to strength, but it's been a mixed few years for local cinephiles, with several of Madrid's old movie-houses closing down.

Spain has no film censorship and its movie aficionados have long indulged their considered taste for avant-garde cinema, which, in turn, has inspired the works of homegrown masters such as Pedro Almodóvar and Julio Medem. Once the *enfant terrible* of Spanish cinema, the deservedly garlanded Almodóvar now makes mature and richly textured films that are both emotionally and stylistically audacious. The metaphysical Medem, whose thrilling documentary on the Basque conflict, *Basque Ball*, made him a controversial figure in Spain, seems likely to produce his most interesting work in the shape of the eagerly awaited *Chaotic Ana* in 2007. Interestingly, what Almodóvar and Medem have in common is the composer Alberto Iglesias, whose exquisite soundtracks are a prime factor in their pleasure and popularity. Other names to watch for are the social realists

Iciar Bollaín and Fernando León de Aranoa; Catalan director Isabel Coixet; the satirist Álex de la Iglesia, and the precocious maestro that is Alejandro Amenábar – director of Nicole Kidman in *The Others*. Added to this roster are veterans such as Carlos Saura, who is still going strong.

Due to complex funding and distribution policies, an enormous number of films are made in Spain when compared with how many eventually make it into mainstream cinemas. However, a plethora of film festivals of every persuasion provide a springboard for new film-makers and the production of short films is especially booming, with art-house cinemas programming some of the best before their main features.

VENUES

There is no shortage of multiplexes showing Hollywood fodder dubbed into Spanish throughout the city, but for a more refined experience, try the commercially viable art-house cinemas showing Spanish auteurs, documentaries, foreign films in VO (*versión original* – ie, undubbed and with subtitles), and an exhilarating variety of quirky, classic and controversial features. For film seasons and older films, both Spanish and VO, choose the grand **Filmoteca** or the **Enana Marrón**.

TICKETS AND TIMES

Daily newspapers, the weekly *Guia del Ocio* and the www.lanetro.com website have film reviews and full listings. Screenings tend to start promptly with few trailers or ads, though a brisk turnover means that credits are curtailed and latecomers are a constant hazard. Screenings (*pases*) usually start at around 4pm. The 8pm screening is the most popular, though the late screenings (*sesiones de madrugada*) at midnight and 1am can be surprisingly packed if they're showing cult films or current favourites. Read the newspapers for VO listings, and once there check whether your seating is allocated (*numerada*) before paying. Be warned of the rarity of adequately tiered seating – Spaniards are getting taller but the screens are yet to be put any higher. Monday and Wednesday are often *días del espectador* ('spectator days'), offering special discounts, though every cinema has its own policy on price reductions. Internet reservations are available through www.entradas.com and many cinemas will take advance bookings for busy times and popular films.

VO cinemas

Casa de América

Paseo de Recoletos 2, Salamanca (91 595 48 00/www.casamerica.es). Metro Banco de España. **Tickets** €4. **No credit cards. Map** p324 J11.
This cultural centre has its own cinema screening classic and contemporary Spanish and Latin American cinema as themed seasons and special events. Showings at 7.30pm and 9.30pm daily.

Cine Estudio de Bellas Artes

C/Alcalá 42, Huertas & Santa Ana (91 522 50 92/ 91 360 54 00/www.circulobellasartes.com). Metro Banco de España. **Tickets** €4; €2.40 members. **No credit cards. Map** p328 I11.
Originally a theatre, this repertory cinema is part of the grand Circulo de Bellas Artes building. The sound system is excellent, and the programme of themed film seasons goes down well with the trendy audience.

La Enana Marrón

Travesia de San Mateo 8, Chueca (91 308 14 97/ www.laenanamarron.org). Metro Tribunal. **Tickets** €4; €2.60 members. **No credit cards. Map** p324 I9.
A side street in Chueca is the hip and lively location of the strangely named Brown Dwarf microcinema, specialising in experimental films, retrospectives, shorts and repertory classics. A meeting place for movie folk, fans and students with debates and discussions, it also boasts a witty website.

Golem

C/Martín de los Heros 14, Argüelles (91 559 38 36/www.golem.es). Metro Plaza de España. **Tickets** €4.50 Mon; €6 Tue-Fri; €6.20 Sat, Sun. **No credit cards. Map** p323 E9.

This legendary four-screener, until recently known as the Alphaville, was the first of Madrid's art-house cinemas and played a crucial role in the Movida during the '80s. The screens and sound systems are showing their age and tiering is inadequate, but the basement café is still a fashionable meeting place with a bohemian atmosphere. **Photo** *p215*.

Ideal Yelmo Cineplex

C/Doctor Cortezo 6, Lavapiés (91 369 25 18/tickets 902 22 09 22/www.yelmocineplex.es). Metro Tirso de Molina. **Tickets** €6.80; €5.30 Mon. **Credit** MC, V. **Map** p327 H13.
This hugely popular eight-screen multiplex is an efficient if somewhat characterless venue for international mainstream films in *versión original*.

Pequeño Cine Estudio

C/Magallanes 1, Chamberí (91 447 29 20/ www.pcineestudio.com). Metro Quevedo. **Tickets** €6; €4.50 Mon and concessions. **No credit cards. Map** p323 G6.
It's always worth keeping an eye on this peculiar little VO cinema because its rapid turnover means that rarely viewed classics from Hollywood and world cinema often make it on to the programme.

Renoir Plaza de España

C/Martín de los Heros 12, Argüelles (91 541 39 14/ 902 229 122/www.cinesrenoir.com). Metro Plaza de España. **Tickets** €6.20 Mon-Fri; €6.50 Sat, Sun; €4.50 concessions 1st show Mon-Fri except public hols.* **Credit** MC, V. **Map** p323 E9.
The flagship of the enterprising Renoir chain, with screens on the small side and a haphazard queuing system in the cramped foyer, although good sound systems and a keen crowd of film fans ensure enjoyable viewing. The Cuatro Caminos branch is also worth a mention for its larger screens, decent bar and intelligent balance of Spanish and world cinema, while the Princesa also has an eclectic mix of Spanish, European and independent American cinema.
Other locations: Cuatro Caminos Raimundo Fernández Villaverde 10, Chamberí (91 541 41 00). **Princesa** C/Princesa 5, Moncloa (91 559 98 72). **Retiro** C/Narváez 42 (91 541 41 00).

Verdi

C/Bravo Murillo 28, Chamberí (91 447 39 30). Metro Canal or Quevedo. **Tickets** €6.50; €4.80 Mon, 1st show Tue-Fri and concessions; €1 Tue over-60s. **No credit cards.**
This relative newcomer to the ranks of VO cinemas has five screens showing a lively mix of art-house, Spanish, independent and mainstream foreign films.

The Filmoteca

Filmoteca Española (Cine Doré)

C/Santa Isabel 3, Lavapiés (91 369 11 25/bookshop 91 369 46 73). Metro Antón Martín. **Open** *Bar-cafés* 3pm-12.30am Tue-Sun. *Bookshop* 5-10pm Tue-Sun. **Tickets** €2.50, €2 concessions. *10 films* €20, €15 concessions. **No credit cards. Map** p328 I13.

Setting the scene

Cinéfilos will find a mecca of moviedom at Madrid's Ocho y Medio bookshop. Rolling since 1996 and recently relocated to these much larger premises near the Plaza de España, the store's empire is growing quickly.

Stock includes over 15,000 books with titles in Spanish, English, Italian and French, and anything not on the shelves can be ordered. The DVD section is also excellent and visitors will find film posters, T-shirts, calendars and all sorts of filmic gadgets. Not surprisingly, the shop has become something of a living museum for lovers of Spanish cinema – even the carrier bags, re-designed every few months by an actor or director, have become collectors' items.

Framed posters of recent films are scrawled with thanks and blessings from cast and crew and every space on the wall sports a signed doodle or dedication from famous film folk. Frequent guest signings and launch parties have made the store the hub of the Spanish film industry and it now has a thriving series of its own publications, including a celebrated spiral-bound series of scripts.

Given its reputation, it's not surprising that Ocho y Medio's enthusiastic owners, Jesús Robles and María Silveyro, have been awarded several prestigious prizes and are constant recipients of thanks during awards ceremonies from their many friends among the film-making elite. Both of them speak English and are founts of information – if you catch them in, they're always happy to chat. It's worth signing up to the mailing list before you leave, too.

Just across the street are some of the city's best multi-screen art-house and VO cinemas – the Golem, the Renoir Plaza de España and the Renoir Princesa – while a range of tapas bars, *tabernas* and restaurants serves the film-going crowds. So the location is perfect for when the bookshop closes and you're turfed on to the streets... at 8.30pm, of course, hence the Felliniesque name.

Ocho y Medio
C/Martín de los Heros 11, Argüelles (91 559 06 28/www.ochoymedio.com). Metro Plaza de España. **Open** 10am-2pm, 5-8.30pm Mon-Sat. **Credit** AmEx, DC, MC, V. **Map** p323 E9.

Known affectionately as *la filmo* and featured in films by Almodóvar, this chic art nouveau national film theatre was founded more than 50 years ago. The neon-lit foyer/café is a lively meeting place and the tiny bookshop is always full of browsers. A free, expansive, fold-out monthly programme features details of its eclectic seasons of films from the Spanish National Archive and world cinema. The grand auditorium is an especially marvellous place to see silent movies, sometimes accompanied by live music. The outdoor rooftop cinema and bar are open – and unsurprisingly very popular – during the summer months. Note that tickets can't be bought in advance for the Filmoteca, so you will often be required to queue well before the film starts.

Open-air movies

Fescinal (Cine de Verano)
Parque de la Bombilla, Avda de Valladolid, La Florida (91 541 37 21/www.fescinal.info). Metro Príncipe Pío. **Tickets** €4.50; €4 concessions; free under-5s. **No credit cards. Map** p322 B6.

An open-air night-time venue in Parque de la Bombilla for catching double bills of mainstream films during the Veranos de la Villa festival, which takes place between July to September. As well as the massive screen (with wayward sound), Fescinal also offers a smaller one for kids, plus the opportunity to munch on *bocadillos* washed down with *cerveza* for that truly communal experience of movie-watching.

Galleries

Grandes dames, shiny new art centres and an increasingly international flavour.

During the 36 years of Franco, few commercial galleries existed in Spain. As a result, after the demise of the dictatorship, Madrid had a lot of catching up to do – hence the ensuing gallery boom of the 1980s… followed by a disheartening bust in the '90s. Now the climate is stabilising, more collectors are buying, and galleries are more confident of the future.

This is in part due to the growing success of ARCO and PHotoEspaña, combined with a new savvy on the part of the galleries. Some of the best have grouped together as associations: in many galleries you can pick up a brochure featuring a gallery map from either the Asociación de Galerías de Arte de Madrid (www.artemadrid.com) or the association Galerías del 28012/28014 (the postcodes of some of the city's best galleries). Furthermore, provincial Madrid is slowly giving way to worldly Madrid – galleries are refining their skills in promoting Spanish artists abroad while tuning in to the most avant-garde art movements of London, New York and Paris (*see p221* **Ars mundi**).

In a complementary blend of institutional muscle from the big guys and spunk from the smaller galleries, the streets surrounding the Reina Sofía are gradually transforming into the city's art nexus, and major banks are creating plush new art centres in the area. Most notably, La Caixa are due to open a multi-million-euro cultural centre, designed by Herzog & de Meuron, on the Paseo del Prado in summer 2007. Gallery owners are picking up on this creative momentum: twice a year – once at the beginning of autumn and again during ARCO – Galerías del 28012/28014 co-ordinates opening parties on the same night, resulting in something akin to a neighbourhood gallery crawl. Enhancing the artsy vibe, each June PHotoEspaña (*see p207*) adorns C/Huertas with photography in the streets and hosts popular summer slide shows in Plaza Santa Ana.

Madrid's galleries generally exist in clusters, with many lining the same streets. The grandest galleries tend to be around Alonso Martínez and Colón metros, with plenty of interesting places in the environs of C/San Pedro and C/Doctor Fourquet in the Antón Martín and Lavapiés areas. As well as the association brochures, you can pick up the free monthly magazine *Guiarte* in galleries

Ángel Romero.

or tourist offices to see who's exhibiting where. The *Guía del Ocio* and local newspapers also provide up-to-date exhibition information.

Huertas & Santa Ana

Ángel Romero
C/San Pedro 5 (91 429 32 08/www.galeriaangel romero.com). Metro Atocha. **Open** 11am-2pm, 5.30-8.30pm Mon-Sat. Closed July-mid Sept. **No credit cards. Map** p328 J14.
A beautiful gallery with a cavernous basement, which has previously shown some of Spain's most intriguing young artists. In recent years its scope has become more international, with artists from Cuba, France and Germany. Keep an eye out for young German painter Barbara Stammel.

Galería Carmen de la Guerra
C/San Pedro 6 (91 420 03 55/www.carmendela guerra.com). Metro Antón Martín. **Open** 11am-2pm, 5-9pm Tue-Sat. Closed Aug. **No credit cards. Map** p328 J14.
Popular with young artists and collectors, Carmen de la Guerra is innovative, fun and often whimsical (its performance art being a prime example). Spanish actor Jordi Molla exhibits his painting and photography here; other interesting names include Soledad Cordoba and David Trullo. The musty downstairs

cave dates from 1864; it was originally used as a bakery but now exhibits installation and video projects.

Galería La Fábrica
C/Alameda 9 (91 360 13 20/5/www.lafabrica galeria.com). Metro Atocha. **Open** 11am-2pm, 4.30-8.30pm Tue-Sat. Closed Aug. **No credit cards.** **Map** p328 J13.
La Fábrica is a hub of the Madrid art world, heavily involved in exhibitions such as PHotoEspaña. It exhibits major-league as well as up-and-coming artists and is known for its insights into photography. On Mondays in autumn the gallery hosts Los Lunes de la Fábrica – parties and/or book presentations attended by Madrid's arty crowd. It also publishes art books and, in collaboration with website www.notodo.com, organises art competitions.

Lavapiés

Cruce
C/Dr Fourquet 5 (91 528 77 83). Metro Atocha. **Open** 5-9pm Tue-Sat. Closed Aug. **Map** p328 I14.
More than just a gallery, Cruce is a community hub for young Spanish artists, poets and intellectuals. In addition to fun and outlandish exhibitions, it hosts book presentations, concerts and poetry readings. Pick up the monthly schedule to see what's on.

Salvador Díaz
C/Sánchez Bustillo 7 (91 527 40 00/www.salvador diaz.net). Metro Atocha. **Open** 10am-2pm, 4-8pm Mon-Fri; 11am-2pm Sat. Closed Aug. **No credit cards.** **Map** p328 J14.
Located just across the plaza from the Reina Sofía, this is a lovely space to browse. It's open and spacious, and shows new talents in contemporary photography, sculpture and installation work.

Chueca

Antonio Machón
C/Conde de Xiquena 8 (91 532 40 93/www.antonio machon.com). Metro Chueca. **Open** 11am-2pm, 5-9pm Tue-Sat. Closed Aug. **No credit cards.** **Map** p324 I10.
Machón has long dealt with famous older artists like Tàpies, Bonifacio and Jordi Teixidor, but also works with new talents such as Angeles San José, Alberto Requera and Chema Cobo. In particular, the gallery has a real eye for monochromes and abstract art.

Arnés y Röpke
C/Conde Xiquena 14 (91 702 14 92/www.galeria arnesyropke.com). Metro Chueca. **Open** 11am-2pm, 4.30-8.30pm Tue-Fri; 11am-2pm, 5-8.30pm Sat. **No credit cards.** **Map** p324 J10.
The owners of this gallery are a Spanish/German duo who promote abstract and figurative art (photography is a forte). They have been successful in bringing European contemporary art to Spain and Spain's avant-garde to the rest of the world. If you can, try to catch a show by Arnold Odermatt.

Edurne
C/Libertad 22 (91 521 52 52/www.galeriaedurne. com). Metro Chueca. **Open** 11am-2pm, 5.30-8.30pm Mon-Fri; by appointment Sat. Closed Aug. **No credit cards.** **Map** p324 I10.
In 1964, despite the controlling eyes of the dictatorship, Margarita de Lucas and Antonio de Navascues opened Edurne, the first gallery of its kind. This engaging pair is credited with promoting many of Spain's top artists when they were just starting out. Luis Gordillo, Antonio Saura and Gerardo Rueda are among the earlier protégés; recent exhibitions include Enrique Veganzones and Andrés Monteagudo.

Elba Benítez
C/San Lorenzo 11 (91 308 04 68/www.elbabenitez. com). Metro Tribunal. **Open** 11am-2pm, 4.30-8.30pm Tue-Sat. Closed Aug. **No credit cards.** **Map** p324 I9.
Located in the courtyard of a faded old villa, this is a pleasant gallery to wander through. Elba Benítez promotes Spanish art abroad, although her repertoire also includes international artists. The art is very modern, with an emphasis on photography, video and installation pieces. **Photo** *p220.*

Elvira González
C/General Castaños 3 (91 319 59 00/www.galeria elviragonzalez.com). Metro Colón. **Open** 10.30am-2pm, 4.30-8.30pm Mon-Fri; 11am-2pm Sat. Closed Aug. **No credit cards.** **Map** p324 J9.
One of the most distinguished galleries in Madrid, this is an appealing enclave of contemporary art, both Spanish and international. LeWitt, Lichtenstein, Warhol, Judd, Rothko and Picasso have all featured in the past.

Galería La Caja Negra
C/Fernando VI 17, 2º izq (91 310 43 60/ www.lacajanegra.com). Metro Alonso Martínez. **Open** 10am-2pm, 5-9pm Mon-Sat. Closed Aug. **Credit** AmEx, DC, MC, V. **Map** p324 I9.
Something of a leader on the local art scene, representing international mega artists in addition to famous Spanish contemporary artists. La Caja Negra specialises in original graphic works, photography and illustrated books. Chillida, Tàpies, Barceló, Antonio Saura, Richard Serra and even Picasso are all to be found here, while the internationals include Braque, LeWitt, Rauschenberg, Robert Motherwell and Keith Haring.

Galería Juana de Aizpuru
C/Barquillo 44, 1º (91 310 55 61/www.galeriajuana deaizpuru.com). Metro Chueca. **Open** 4.30-8.30pm Mon; 10.30am-2pm, 4.30-8.30pm Tue-Sat. **No credit cards.** **Map** p324 I10.
Madrid's *grande dame* of vanguard photography has been setting the standard since 1983. Juana is known and loved worldwide and represents such local photography luminaries as Alberto García Alex and Cristina García Rodero. Foreign artists who grace the walls include Joel Peter Witkin, William Wegman and Sol Lewitt. Installation work, video and sculpture also feature.

Elba Benítez. *See p219.*

Heinrich Ehrhardt

C/San Lorenzo 11 (91 310 44 15/www.heinrich ehrhardt.com). Metro Chueca. **Open** 11am-2pm, 4.30-8.30pm Tue-Sat. **Credit** AmEx. **Map** p324 I9.

This contemporary gallery originally endeavoured to introduce Madrid to German artists such as Joseph Beuys and Baselitz. In the past few years, however, it has expanded its scope to include several young Spanish artists such as Ángel Borrego and Secundino Hernández.

Moriarty

C/Libertad 22 (91 531 43 65/www.galeriamoriarty. com). Metro Chueca. **Open** 11am-2pm, 5-8.30pm Tue-Sat. Closed July, Aug. **Credit** V. **Map** p324 I10.

Established in 1981, Lola Moriarty's gallery was a prime hangout and showcase for artists on the Movida scene, and today still supports the Spanish avant-garde and contemporary art scene. Some of her current top artists are photographers: the renowned duo Walter Martin and Paloma Muñoz, the surrealist talent Chema Madoz, and Atsuko Arai.

Sen

C/Barquillo 43 (91 319 16 71/www.galeriasen.com). Metro Chueca. **Open** 11am-2pm, 4.30-8.30pm Mon-Fri; 11am-2pm Sat. Closed Aug. **No credit cards.** **Map** p324 I10.

Sen is another Movida-related gallery, and helped fringe artists like Costus and Ceesepe earn the respect of critics. It exhibits established and emerging names in various media – painting, sculpture and photography. Its list of artists includes photographer Carlos García-Alix and cult Movida cartoonist Nazario.

Salamanca

Guillermo de Osma

C/Claudio Coello 4, 1° izq (91 435 59 36/www. guillermodeosma.com). Metro Retiro. **Open** 10am-2pm, 4.30-8.30pm Mon-Fri; noon-2pm Sat. **No credit cards.** **Map** p325 L10.

A classic on the Madrid art scene, Guillermo de Osma specialises in artists from the avant-garde movements of 1910-40 and holds five to six shows a year, always accompanied by a superb catalogue.

In the past it has worked with the crème de la crème of the art world: think Picasso, Braque, Oscar Domínguez and Torres García.

Oliva Arauna

C/Barquillo 29 (91 435 18 08/www.olivarauna.com). Metro Banco de España. **Open** 4.30pm-8.30pm Mon; 11am-2pm, 4.30-8.30pm Tue-Sat. Closed Aug. **No credit cards.** **Map** p324 I10.

Another empress of contemporary art, Oliva Arauna has a taste for large, bold, challenging photographs and slick minimalist sculpture. A small but impressive gallery, this is a good place to get a glimpse of Spain's most inventive photographers. Concha Prada, in particular, is one to watch.

Chamberí

Estiarte

C/Almagro 44 (91 308 15 69/70/www.estiarte.com). Metro Rubén Darío. **Open** 10am-2pm, 4.30-8.30pm Mon-Fri; 10am-2pm, 5-9pm Sat. **Credit** DC, MC, V. **Map** p324 K6.

This gallery has specialised in original graphics for 30 years and represents many big names, past and present – Miquel Barceló, Max Ernst, José Maria Sicilia, Eva Lootz, Calder, Chillida and Picasso.

Galería Javier López

C/Manuel González Longoria 7 (91 593 21 84/ www.galeriajavierlopez.com). Metro Alonso Martínez. **Open** 11am-2pm, 5-9pm Tue-Sat. Closed Aug. **No credit cards.** **Map** p324 I8.

Javier López is a well-known figure on the Madrid art circuit. The gallery originally opened in London, but moved to Madrid in 1996, and shows artists as prestigious – and diverse – as Donald Judd, Andreas Gursky, Edward Ruscha and Hiroshu Sugimoto. The gallery is due to move to a new space in 2007: see website for updated details.

Galería Soledad Lorenzo

C/Orfila 5 (91 308 28 87/www.soledadlorenzo.com). Metro Alonso Martínez. **Open** 4.30-8.30pm Mon; 11am-2pm, 4.30-8.30pm Tue-Sat. Closed Aug. **No credit cards.** **Map** p324 J8.

A forerunner among Madrid's galleries, this large, beautiful space shows highly contemporary installation work, video, painting and photography. Artists are primarily Spanish, and include the likes of Miguel Barceló, Tàpies and Julian Schnabel.

Marlborough

C/Orfila 5 (91 319 14 14/www.galeriamarlborough. com). Metro Alonso Martínez. **Open** 11am-2pm, 4.30-8.30pm Mon-Sat. Closed Aug. **Credit** MC, V. **Map** p324 J8.

This luminary of the Madrid art world represents major Spanish artists (Antonio Saura, Blanca Muñoz, Luis Gordillo), and has branches in London, New York, Monte Carlo and Santiago. The expansive space, designed by US architect Richard Gluckman, is a work of art in itself. Note that the gallery sometimes closes for the afternoon in summer.

ARCO

Feria de Madrid (91 722 50 00/www.arco.ifema.es). Metro Campo de las Naciones. **Dates** 1wk mid Feb. **Open** noon-9pm Mon-Sat. **Admission** €30. Tickets online at www.entradas.com **Credit** varies.

While the Arte Contemporáneo (ARCO) fair has been around since 1982, it has only recently gained major international kudos. Now scores of Spanish and foreign art heavyweights pack into the city each February, seeking out the latest art trends. In 2007 the spotlight country was Korea and Brazil is due to follow in 2008, with hundred of galleries from various different countries setting up stalls at the Parque Ferial Juan Carlos I, transforming the pavilion into a colourful sea of contemporary art.

Ars mundi

Artistically speaking, Madrid has long had a reputation for looking inwards, for not caring for art originating outside Spain – or even outside the city, for that matter. Much of this isolationism can be blamed on the 36-year cross-cultural blockade the country suffered under Franco. Even today, many gallery owners still feel that Madrid lags about four decades behind other European capitals.

But the city is catching up. In the last few years, foreign names have begun to appear regularly in exhibitions, and many more overseas artists have moved here, stimulating a mutual flow of art awareness. There are now many local galleries working in tandem with a foreign branch: cool, contemporary **Marina Miranda** (C/Fúcar 12, 91 420 22 38, www.marinamiranda. com), for example, fosters art *intercambios* with Portugal, and the Argentine-run **Centro de Arte Moderno** (C/Gobernador 25, 91 429 83 63, www.centrodeartemoderno.com; *photo right*) promotes a Spanish/Latin American exchange, especially in the field of photography. The growth of the ARCO and PHotoEspaña art fairs have also given Madrid a strong push into the international limelight.

Helga de Alvear, a feisty, fashionable German gallery owner who has lived in Madrid for over 40 years and runs her eponymous gallery, is a leader in internationalising the city's art climate. Not that this is intentional: as she puts it, 'For me, art doesn't have a nationality. I don't care about nationality as long as I like it.' The artists she selects come from all over: British filmmaker Isaac Julien,

Australian photographer Tracey Moffatt and Canadian artist Christine Davis, for example.

Even so, change has been very slow to manifest itself. Several gallery owners maintain that a good number of local collectors will still only buy what they know and what they have seen before, and there are still those who think that painting is the only respectable art for their homes – not photography or installation work.

Helga de Alvear

C/Dr Fourquet 12 (91 468 05 06/www.helga dealvear.net). Metro Atocha. **Open** Sept-June 11am-2pm, 4.30-8.30pm Tue-Sat. *July* 11am-2pm, 4.30-8.30pm Tue-Fri; 11am-2pm Sat. Closed Aug. **No credit cards. Map** p328 I14.

Gay & Lesbian

Love is all around – and no end of naughtiness too.

Café Acuarela. *See p223.*

The transformation of Chueca from a haven for winos and junkies into a vibrant gay quarter has let Madrid establish itself as one of the world's most gay-friendly cities. What's more, Prime Minister José Luis Rodríguez Zapatero has come good on his pre-election promise to legalise same-sex marriage, making Spain the third country to do so after Belgium and Holland. Further positive legislative changes include the Law of Gender Identity, which gives transsexuals the right to have their change of sex reflected on their ID cards and passports.

The throbbing heart of the scene (*el ambiente*) is the Plaza de Chueca. Tightly packed around what is an otherwise nondescript square in the centre of town, it's home to a dazzling array of bars and services aimed almost exclusively at one of Madrid's most vociferous and dynamic communities. With bars, cafés, hotels, saunas, travel agencies and bookshops, the formerly run-down neighbourhood has emerged as one of the city's most vibrant and trendy areas. But Chueca has become, perhaps, a victim of its own success, its hip hangouts attracting a non-gay crowd in recent years. Now, many want their ghetto back, at least for cruising, and plenty

of shag-and-go gay male-only bars have popped up all over the place. Special events aimed at specific subcultures are a growth industry too: there are camping weekends for bears in the nearby mountains, an action-packed 'Sleazy Madrid' long weekend every spring, plus lesbian raves with dykey darkrooms, body-shaving bashes and sloppy mud parties.

PUBLICATIONS

Some of the best of the free publications lying around in bars are *Shangay Express* newspaper – or its pocket-sized companion *Shanguide* – with listings on the gay and lesbian scene throughout Spain; *Odisea*, which deals more with social and political issues and publishes a handy map, and *Revista Mensual*, sold at news kiosks (its personal ads are riveting). Fetish fans (men only) should look out for *Phetix*, a free quarterly guide to sex clubs and parties.

There are also some good websites, all with guides to the scene plus nifty extra features, such as personals and access to chat. Try www.mensual.com, www.chueca.com, www.vozgay.com or www.naciongay.com and its sister site www.guiagay.com.

Arts & Entertainment

Cafés & restaurants

As well as the places listed below (all of which are in Chueca), other restaurants that are noticeably popular among the gay community include **Suite** (*see p141*), **El Armario** (*see p148*), **La Dame Noire** (*see p151*), **Gula Gula** (*see p141*) and **El 26 de Libertad** (*see p148*). **Ángel Sierra** (*see p174*), while not a gay bar per se, is smack on the Plaza de Chueca and therefore an ideal way to start the evening.

Café Acuarela
C/Gravina 10 (91 522 21 43). Metro Chueca. **Open** 2pm-2am daily. **Credit** MC, V. **Map** p324 I10.
By day a quiet, mixed haven to duck into and catch your breath: curl up with a book and sample one of the teas. After sundown, sip a cocktail, sink into a deep sofa and admire the decor – a mix of kitsch, retro glamour and exuberant baroque. **Photo** *p222*.

Café Figueroa
C/Augusto Figueroa 17 (91 521 16 73). Metro Chueca. **Open** *Oct-May* noon-1am Mon-Thur; noon-2.30am Fri, Sat; 4pm-1am Sun. *June-Sept* 4.30-11.30pm daily. **No credit cards. Map** p324 H10.
Madrid's original gay café is a sedate place where the lace curtains, 19th-century chandeliers and winding wooden staircase lend themselves nicely to a cosy destination for those who want gay in an old Spain way. There's a pool table upstairs. **Photo** *p226*.

Café La Troje
C/Pelayo 26 (91 531 05 35). Metro Chueca. **Open** 5pm-2am Mon-Thur, Sun; 5pm-2.30am Fri, Sat. **No credit cards. Map** p324 I10.
A romantic and popular stop, with friendly service and screens playing chill-out videos. It gets chock-full at weekends with an amiable and mixed crowd, who are generally on their way somewhere else.

Colby Urban
C/Fuencarral 52 (91 521 25 54). Metro Chueca. **Open** 10am-1am Mon-Thur; 10am-2.30am Fri, Sat; noon-1am Sun. **Credit** AmEx, DC, MC, V. **Map** p324 H10.
It's red, it's urban, it's aspirational. Colby Urban is the flagship of a string of cool eateries and chilled-out cafés with a concept. We're not sure what the concept is, but the location is handy, the custom is pretty and the diner-style food hits the spot.

D'Mystic
C/Gravina 5 (91 308 24 60/www.dmystic.net). *Metro Chueca.* **Open** 10am-2am Mon-Sat; 1pm-2am Sun. **Credit** DC, MC, V. **Map** p324 I10.
This den of cool is located at a strategic crossstroads, with bigger-than-average cocktails that make up for the aloof staff. Watch the real world stroll by out-side or gaze at the natural world on the New Agey videos on the screens inside. Relax, listen to the whale songs and the waterfalls. Then get out and head for Eagle (*see p226*).

Diurno
C/San Marcos 37 (91 522 00 09). Metro Chueca. **Open** 10am-midnight Mon-Thur; 10am-1am Fri; 11am-1am Sat; 11am-midnight Sun. **Credit** AmEx, DC, MC, V. **Map** p324 I10.
A minimalist and sexy film-rental café spinning all-day chill-out sounds (and occasional techno). As well as a fabulous selection of movies, there are delicious sandwiches, salads, pasta dishes and cakes. A peace-ful place to start the day, upbeat and lively at night.

Laan Café
C/Pelayo 28 (91 552 68 61). Metro Chueca. **Open** 1pm-2am Mon-Thur; 1pm-3am Fri, Sat. **Credit** MC, V. **Map** p324 I10.
Plonk yourself on the banquettes and you risk being smothered by giant red cushions. This otherwise slick and somewhat stark café is great for people-watching, chatting and getting stuck into the fab chocolate cake. In the mornings breakfast and fresh juices are served, while at night the vibe segues into buzzing New York. New ownership brought a more extensive menu, including a menú del dia for €9.90.

Mama Inés
C/Hortaleza 22 (91 523 23 33). Metro Gran Via. **Open** 10am-2am Mon-Thur, Sun; 10am-3am Fri, Sat. **No credit cards. Map** p324 H10.
Another place to successfully combine a decent breakfast with plenty of eye candy. Chill-out and nu flamenco waft through this modern but surprisingly intimate café during the day, while at night house takes over and the T-shirts get progressively tighter.

XXX Café
C/Clavel, corner C/Reina (91 522 37 77). Metro Gran Via. **Open** 3.30pm-2am Mon-Thur, Sun; 3.30pm-3am Fri, Sat. **No credit cards. Map** p324 I11.
Quiet until the pre-dinner crowd arrives to shake it up, this is a small and popular meeting point where the staff are gorgeous and the regulars friendly. Park yourself by the window for the best view – with any luck, you'll be snapped up in no time.

Clubs & discobares

A *discobar* treads the line between club and regular drinking den. Admission is generally free (exceptions are noted below), and there is normally a diminutive dancefloor to justify the pricier-than-average drinks.

As well as the venues below, **Ohm** (*see p244*) and **Weekend** (*see p245*) also have a big gay following, as does Space of Sound on Sundays at **Macumba** (*see p252*). Unless otherwise stated, all of the following are in Chueca.

Black & White
C/Libertad 34 (91 531 11 41). Metro Chueca. **Open** 10pm-5am daily. **No credit cards. Map** p324 I10.
The grubby upstairs bar is a hit with cocky *latino* rent boys and their older prospective patrons and

Arts & Entertainment

plays host to some of the best cabaret shows in town. Downstairs things really liven up in the heaving *discobar* that is popular with revellers of all ages and orientations. A classic.

Kapital Love

C/Atocha 125, Huertas & Santa Ana (91 420 29 06). Metro Atocha. **Open** midnight-6am Thur, Fri, Sun; midnight-6.30am Sat. **Admission** €16. **Credit** AmEx, DC, MC, V. **Map** p328 J14.

Another palace to brighten up dull Sundays. Keep your bearings as you make your way through Madrid's megaclub, and head for the gay corner of this empire of decadence and dance. *See also p246*.

Liquid

C/Barquillo 8 (91 532 74 28/www.liquid.es). Metro Chueca. **Open** 9pm-3am Tue-Thur, Sun; 9pm-4am Fri, Sat. **Credit** AmEx, DC, MC, V. **Map** p324 I11.

A cool, happening place in which to see and be seen, with a contemporary, minimalist interior, lit up with megascreens showing the latest dance music videos. It can seem a little tame, however, and is inhabited by a slightly older crowd.

Queen Madrid

C/Barbieri 7 (no phone). Metro Chueca. **Open** 10pm-2.30am Mon-Thur, Sun; 10pm-3.30am Fri, Sat. **Admission** (minimum consumption €7). **No credit cards. Map** p324 I11.

Catering for the overflow from nearby Why Not? (*see below*), this big, brash, fun *discobar* gets packed with a young, mixed crowd who dance the night away to an eclectic mix of bouncy hi-NRG and naff Spanish golden oldies. When this pales you can always eye up the gorgeous bar staff.

Rick's

C/Clavel 8 (no phone). Metro Gran Vía. **Open** 11.30pm-6.am Mon-Thur, Sun; midnight-7am Fri, Sat. **Admission** (incl 1 drink) €7. **No credit cards. Map** p324 I11.

Expensive drinks and an expensive, older crowd are the hallmarks of this friendly late-night alternative to the discos. With hi-NRG beats and camp Spanish hits, it's standing-room only at weekends.

Royal Coolture at Cool

C/Isabel la Católica 6, Sol (91 542 34 39). Metro Santo Domingo. **Open** midnight-6am Sat. **Admission** (incl 1 drink) €15. **Credit** MC, V. **Map** p323 F11.

The *número uno* place to be on Friday and Saturday nights. Snarling caged gogos, preening Muscle Marys, serious shirtless studs with sweaty torsos, spaced-out twentysomethings and gorgeous waiters are all part of the coolture at this slick, designerish two-floored club. Join them on the throbbing dancefloor or bop to the handbag music upstairs.

Spank

Sala Wind, C/Montera 25, entrance at Plaza del Carmen s/n (no phone). Metro Gran Vía or Sol. **Open** midnight-6am, Fri. **Admission** (incl 1 drink) €10-€14. **Map** p327 H11.

No female hangers-on here – this is a strictly all-male affair. Sala Wind is the perfect home for this popular gay night, as it's in a basement, is very dark and has an excellent sound system. Tech-house and techno rule the night, shirts are often worn off, and the half-naked go-go dancers look like they spend an unhealthy amount of time at the gym.

Sunrise

C/Barbieri 7 (91 523 28 08). Metro Chueca. **Open** midnight-6am Thur-Sat. **Credit** MC, V. **Map** p324 I11.

If you can make it past the menacing doormen in bad suits, a smart red interior awaits you, filled with a designer-clad young crowd.

Why Not?

C/San Bartolomé 7 (91 521 80 34). Metro Chueca or Gran Vía. **Open** 10.30pm-6.30am daily. **Credit** DC, MC, V. **Map** p324 I10.

It's almost impossible not to make new friends, or indeed to avoid grinding against them, in this packed but charming subterranean dungeon. The music's great, the mixed crowd young, hip and intent on having a good time. The drinks don't come cheap, but with free entrance it's still a good alternative to the clubs.

Exclusively male/hardcore

Bangalá

C/Escuadra 1, Lavapiés (no phone/www.bangala madrid.com). Metro Lavapiés. **Open** 9pm-3am Mon-Thur, Sun; 9pm-3.30am Fri, Sat. **Admission** free. **No credit cards. Map** p328 H14.

It's sleek. It's black. It's red. Bangalá is the latest addition to the Lavapiés scene and promises to outdo its rivals with fetisho-licious nights such as Night of Tongues or Dawn of the Vampires. Behind the bar are cabins and two pristine darkrooms.

Copper

C/San Vicente Ferrer 34, Malasaña (no phone/www.copperbar.net). Metro Tribunal. **Open** 2pm-3am Mon-Thur, Sun; 2pm-3.30am Fri-Sat. **Admission** (incl 1 drink) €7. **No credit cards. Map** p323 G9.

The friendly guys at this sloppy and sweaty club got tired of trying to enforce the dress code so now it's a self-styled 'nudist bar', except on Saturdays when it's Underwear Night. The place can get pretty hardcore, but there's a chatty crowd out front, and a popular large backroom.

Cruising

C/Pérez Galdós 5, Chueca (91 521 51 43). Metro Chueca. **Open** 6pm-3am Mon-Thur, Sun; 6pm-3.30am Fri, Sat. **No credit cards. Map** p324 H10.

A fun, sleazy cruising club that puts the 'laid' into 'laid-back'. Upstairs there's a quieter pub-like area, and a diminutive porn cinema; downstairs there's a dancefloor and a spacious public loo-like darkroom. The place could do with a lick of paint but its faded glory is part of its enduring charm.

Taking Pride

On seizing power in 2004, Spain's Socialist government wasted no time in addressing gay rights, legalising gay marriage and allowing transsexuals to choose whichever gender they wished on their identity cards. Milestone achievements that were celebrated with leather, rubber, bears, tanned toned flesh and non-stop hedonism in that June's Gay Pride (Orgullo Gay) parade. The festivities have continued to grow, and 2006 saw an extended parade, running from the Puerta de Alcalá to Plaza España. It attracted 1.5 million people. For an entire week, the city was invaded by visitors from all over the world, partying hard at night, and sporting an array of ludicrously coloured banana hammocks at the swimming pools by day. As well as the parties and the parades, the week now boasts 300 cultural, artistic and sporting events, as well as off-site parties at the end of the week which attracted the likes of Danny Tenaglia, who stepped up to the decks in 2006.

All the hard work put in by the organisers and the government has not gone unnoticed. In recognition of his efforts for equality, Zapatero was awarded the Civic Courage Prize from Berlin-based gay-rights association Christopher Street Day. Then came the show-

stopping news: from 22 June to 1 July, Madrid is to host the Europride 2007, the gay-pride event for the whole of Europe.

Despite such leaps, bounds and high-heeled trotting towards an equal Spain, there is much still to be done, according to Madrid's numerous gay-rights associations. As a reaction to the passing of the same-sex marriage legislation, 166,000 protesters (1.5 million if you believe the organisers), convened by the 'Family Forum' in June 2006, took to the streets to voice their deep disapproval of same-sex marriage. The protesters, who were made up mostly of right-wing families and their children, members of the clergy and politicians from the opposition Popular Party (PP), carried slogans that claimed that the traditional family unit was at stake, and demanded the resignation of Zapatero. The PP hasn't stopped there, going so far as to bring the legislation before the constitutional courts to contest its legitimacy. Throw in the occasional news story of continuing homophobia, such as the refusal of a popular Madrid restaurant to host a reception for a gay wedding, and it's clear that while, in the words of the major gay associations, Madrid is 'one of the most tolerant cities in the world', there is still plenty to march for.

Stately, old-style gay venue **Café Figueroa**. *See p223*.

Eagle

C/Pelayo 30, Chueca (no phone/www.eaglespain.com).
Metro Chueca. **Open** 2pm-2am Mon-Fri; 5pm-2.30am
Sat; 5pm-2am Sun. **Admission** free. **No credit
cards. Map** p324 I10.

This is the nerve centre of the fetish scene in Madrid.
For a visit to the Eagle, boots, leather chaps and
handcuffs are all that the well-dressed devotee need
worry about packing. The small and cramped downstairs gives way to an even tighter squeeze in the
upstairs play area, which is where the real boys are
to be found. Among the entertainments, you might
chance upon Leather Night, Uniform Night or – if
you really hit the jackpot – Golden Night.

Hell

*C/Buenavista 14, Lavapiés (no phone/www.hell
sexclub.com). Metro Antón Martín.* **Open** 10.30pm-
3am Tue-Thur; 11.30pm-3.30am Fri-Sat. **Admission**
free. **No credit cards. Map** p328 I14.

A tiny and rough fetish club whose denizens get
down to some hard cruising. Tuesday nights are
nude, while Saturdays are given over to kinky
underwear parties. Wednesday is Noche Sport
('sneaker sex' is how they describe it), while
Thursdays are for exhibitionists and those who like
to watch them. Other nights are devoted to private
parties or special events. Log on to the titillating
website for details.

Hot

*C/Infantas 9, Chueca (91 522 84 48/www.bar
hot.com). Metro Chueca.* **Open** 6pm-3am Mon-
Thur, Sun; 6pm-3.30am Fri, Sat. **Admission**
free. **No credit cards. Map** p324 H11.

Hot, hairy, homo heaven at this fun bear den for hir-
sute late thirty- and fortysomethings. Things get
even hotter downstairs in the darkroom. Two drinks
for the price of one, every day until midnight.

Leather Bar

C/Pelayo 42, Chueca (91 308 14 62). Metro Chueca.
Open 8pm-3am daily. **Admission** free. **No credit
cards. Map** p324 I10.

The name of this big, two-floor hangout is a bit misleading as little leather is in evidence, but the crowd
is raunchy, and can be found in the large darkroom
or lurking in anticipation in the cabins. Check out
the individual movie screens over the urinals.

Odarko

*C/Loreto Chicote 7, Malasaña (no phone/www.
odarko.com). Metro Callao.* **Open** 10pm-very late,
Mon-Sat; 6pm-4am Sun. **Admission** (incl 1 drink)
€7-€10. **Credit** DC, MC, V. **Map** p323 G10.

The seedy backstreets off Gran Via make the perfect approach to this lively sex club, where chains
chink, bars rattle and boots scuff the soiled floor.
Dress code is strictly enforced on weekends and
some of the nights are pretty full-on. Check the website in advance, lest you turn up in a crisp Fred Perry
top to find it's the Wild & Wet Piss session.
Improbably, the owners run a little B&B upstairs.

The Paw

*C/Calatrava 29, La Latina (91 366 60 93/www.
thepawmadrid.com). Metro Puerta de Toledo.* **Open**
10pm-6am Wed, Thur, Sun; midnight-8am Fri, Sat.
Admission (incl 1 or 2 drinks) €11-€15. **No credit
cards. Map** p327 E14.

Formerly known as Into The Tank, this louche little joint is off the beaten track but well worth the effort for dress code and fetish fans. If you forgot to pack your cop uniform, don't worry, you can go naked every night. Check out the hot underwear parties: log on to the website for all the lurid details.

Strong Center

C/Trujillos 7, Sol & Gran Vía (91 541 54 15). Metro Ópera. **Open** midnight-7am daily. **Admission** (incl 2 drinks) €8 Mon-Thur, Sun; €10 Fri, Sat. **No credit cards. Map** p327 G11.
The dancefloor at the Strong Center is a forlorn, empty place. Don't dismay, however, as no one comes here for the music, and you're just about to discover Spain's biggest and most labyrinthine darkroom, where you can lose yourself among hundreds of hot, horny men.

Saunas

Men

C/Pelayo 25, Chueca (91 531 25 83). Metro Chueca. **Open** 3.30pm-8am Mon-Fri; uninterrupted 3.30pm Fri to 8am Sun. **Admission** €8; €5 under-25s. **No credit cards. Map** p324 I10.
A small, dowdy sauna with a perplexing door policy (though cute young guys are usually safe). Located right at the heart of the gay scene, Men is always rammed with a cross-section of gay Madrid. There's a bar, darkroom and a few cabins in which to spend a steamy hour or two.

Paraíso Sauna

C/Norte 15, Conde Duque (no phone). Metro Noviciado. **Open** 2pm-midnight daily. **Admission** €12. **No credit cards. Map** p323 F9.
Located in what used to be a popular flamenco club, this extensive, spotlessly clean sauna has maintained its original evocative mosaics. The young, hunky clients often seem more interested in their own well-toned pecs than in you, but there is a small pool, porn cinema, bar, darkroom and cabins as consolation. Massage and sunbeds are also available.

Sauna Príncipe

Travesía Beatas 3, Malasaña (91 548 22 18). Metro Santo Domingo. **Open** 2pm-midnight daily. **Admission** €10. **No credit cards. Map** p323 F10.
This sauna is better equipped than its rivals and caters for a varied crowd, though it's particularly popular with bears, not to mention tourists.

Gay & lesbian shops

A Different Life

C/Pelayo 30, Chueca (91 532 96 52). Metro Chueca. **Open** 10.30am-9.30pm daily. **Credit** AmEx, DC, MC, V. **Map** p324 I10.
A well-stocked bookshop, with some titles in English, plus magazines and a range of cheesy gay gifts. Downstairs you'll find an eye-popping range of porn videos, which can be bought or rented.

Amantis

C/Pelayo 46, Chueca (91 702 05 11). Metro Chueca. **Open** 10.30am-10pm Mon-Sat; 4.30-9pm Sun. **Credit** AmEx, DC, V. **Map** p324 I10.
The most discreet of the city's sex shops in terms of location, Amantis has a sunny feel and seems rather like a small-town shop. Albeit a small-town shop filled with condoms, lube, improbable dildos, porn mags, videos and DVDs.

Berkana

C/Hortaleza 64, Chueca (91 532 13 93). Metro Chueca. **Open** 10.30am-9pm Mon-Fri; 11.30am-9pm Sat; noon-2pm, 5-9pm Sun. **Credit** AmEx, DC, MC, V. **Map** p324 H10.
There are books and videos in English here, and members of staff are friendly and helpful. Browsing is encouraged and you can linger over some of the erotica at the in-store café.

City Sex Store

C/Hortaleza 18, Chueca (91 181 27 23). Metro Chueca. **Open** 11am-10pm Mon-Fri; 11am-11pm Sat; 12.30-9.30pm Sun. **Credit** AmEx, DC, MC, V. **Map** p324 H10.
Bright, shiny and well organised, City Sex Store is a veritable supermarket of porn, with merchandise spread out over two floors.

Lambda Viajes

C/Fuencarral 43, Malasaña (91 532 78 33/www. lambdaviajes.com). Metro Chueca. **Open** 9.30am-2.30pm, 4.30-8pm Mon-Fri; 10am-1.30pm Sat. **Credit** MC, V. **Map** p324 H10.
This travel agency is aimed at a gay clientele, and can book rooms in gay hotels throughout Spain and abroad. It also offers package trips to various destinations. The helpful staff speak English.

SR

C/Pelayo 7, Chueca (91 523 19 64). Metro Chueca. **Open** 5.30-9pm Mon; 11am-2pm, 5-9pm Tue-Sat. **Credit** AmEx, DC, MC, V. **Map** p324 I10.
Everything for the discerning leather and fetish fan. Leatherwear, uniforms, rubber and SM gear, plus indispensable accessories – masks, slings, chains and handcuffs to help you turn that unused boxroom into your very own dungeon. And no, we don't know what the live crocodiles are for, either.

Lesbian Madrid

All those places for the boys, and barely enough bars to make a decent pub crawl for lesbians – what's a girl to do? Keep her eyes peeled, that's what. Madrid's lesbian scene is growing, but it still has a long way to go before catching up with the gay male *ambiente*. There are lots of one-nighters throughout the year, one organised by the Supernenas and another by Diversité – ask around, or look for flyers in the venues on and near Plaza de Chueca. The square is where

Escape.

you should start off, in any case: every bar here seems to be owned by lesbians, even though the clientele is mixed.

Cafés, bars & clubs

As well as the following, other venues popular with lesbians include **Café Acuarela** (*see p223*) and **La Lupe** (*see p247*).

El Barberillo de Lavapiés

C/Salitre 43, Lavapiés (mobile 654 487 598). Metro Antón Martín or Lavapiés. **Open** 10pm-2am Thur-Sat; 1-5pm Sun. **No credit cards.** **Map** p328 H14/15.
A quiet, relaxed café-bar in the heart of Lavapiés. Worth a visit if you're in the area, though it rarely gets busy. There are cards and board games for those with a competitive streak.

Escape

C/Gravina 13, Chueca (91 532 52 06). Metro Chueca. **Open** midnight-6am Tue-Sun. **Admission** (incl 1 drink) €7. **Credit** MC, V. **Map** p324 I10.
This cavernous dancehall draped in bullfighter red is one of the most popular destinations for women and is filled to the brim with the sexiest *chicas* in the city at the weekends. In fact, its popularity has spiralled to the extent that it's now one of the more boisterous clubs around Plaza de Chueca.

Medea

C/Cabeza 33, Lavapiés (91 369 33 02). Metro Antón Martín or Tirso de Molina. **Open** midnight-6am Fri-Sat. **Admission** €8 (incl 1 drink) or €12 (incl 2 drinks). **Credit** AmEx, DC, MC, V. **Map** p327 H13.
Recently given a facelift and redecorated in muted rainbow colours, this welcoming women's disco is one of the clear favourites on the lesbian scene. Men are admitted only in the company of Sapphic sisters.

Muse

C/Pelayo 31 (mobile 600 265 236). Metro Chueca. **Open** 10pm-3.30am Mon-Sat. **Admission** varies. **No credit cards.** **Map** p324 I10.
Britney and Madonna engaging in that famous kiss take pride of place on the wall at Musa, which is a mostly lesbian disco-bar on bustling C/Pelayo. The white walls here are adorned with mirrors shaped like naked ladies and bathed in pink lighting, helping to create a warm setting in which to get your groove on to the vocal house classics that roar out of the sound system. Get there around 1am, when the venue really starts to pack out.

Olivia

C/San Bartolomé 16, Chueca (no phone). Metro Chueca. **Admission** free. **No credit cards.** **Map** p324 I10.
The decor at Olivia is nothing to write home about but this small and chatty den is chock-a-block with lipstick lesbians. Members of staff are approachable and the music is fun.

Smoke

C/San Bartolomé 11, Chueca (no phone). Metro Chueca. **Open** 8pm-2.30am Tue-Sun. **No credit cards.** **Map** p324 I10.
Smoke? More like the whiff of diesel. This is not one for the lipstick lesbian. Nonetheless, it's a really friendly, relaxed crowd, amid the faded glamour of an old Chueca *taberna*.

Truco

C/Gravina 10, Chueca (91 532 89 21). Metro Chueca. **Open** 7pm-3am Mon-Thur; 7.30pm-3.30am Fri-Sat. **Credit** V. **Map** p324 I10.
Truco is often very crowded and usually with an extremely young and loud crowd. No matter: this high-octane corner joint remains *the* place for gals who are looking for gals in the earlier part of the evening. It is also a stone's throw from the very popular girl bar Escape (*see above*).

Arts & Entertainment

Music

The high notes of Madrid's live scene.

Madrid's majestic opera house, the **Teatro Real**. *See p233.*

Classical & Opera

Madrid's cultural clout has steadily increased over recent years and it is gradually shaking off a reputation for producing stuffy composers, ensembles with limited scope and a reactionary public. Credit must go, too, to a city that depends predominantly on public funds to bring in top-class international musicians and ensembles to its worthy concert venues. Madrid has been particularly slated when it comes to contemporary music. But while this has not profited quite as much as contemporary art from the cultural interest shown by banks and businesses in recent times (thanks to the latter's sexier image), things have nevertheless been looking up with ever-increasing accessibility to concerts and recitals.

Traditionally, the scene orbits around three main venues: the modern and austere (and arguably the best-quality classical venue in Europe) **Auditorio Nacional**, the grand **Teatro Real**, hosting opera, and the **Teatro de la Zarzuela** for a decent selection of classical concerts (as well as for *zarzuela*, Madrid's traditional operetta art form).

A word of advice for attending classical concerts in Madrid – get there early. The stereotypical Spanish tardiness is not a trait shared by classical music lovers.

ZARZUELA

Zarzuela is an ineffable part of *madrileño* culture, though tricky for the outsider to get a grip on. It was Spain's early answer to the Italian opera – shorter and funnier and incorporating elements of theatre, slapstick and dance. Golden Age playwrights Félix Lope de Vega and Pedro Calderón de la Barca were early pioneers of the genre, which was later developed by the likes of Ramón de la Cruz and the composer Federico de Chueca and, moving into the 20th century, Amadeo Vives and Jacinto Guerrero. *Zarzuela* is full of local jokes (usually rhyming and rattled off at speed) and traditional songs with which the public will sing

Teatro Real. *See p233*.

along, so be prepared. Catch it in its home ground of the Teatro de la Zarzuela, in the Centro Cultural de la Villa in July or August, or at a summer open-air performance.

INFORMATION AND TICKETS

Check venue websites detailing current and future seasons, as well as any last-minute changes or cancellations. You can pick up leaflets from most of the venues – often quicker than trying to get through by phone – or check the *Guía del Ocio* or daily newspapers. Tickets can usually be bought via phone or internet from the venue itself (check venue listings) or from Tel-entrada or Caixa de Catalunya (902 10 12 12, www.telentradas.com). Tickets for state-run venues such as the Auditorio Nacional and the Teatro de la Zarzuela are sold at one another's box offices as well as ServiCaixa (902 33 22 11, www.serviticket.com).

You can get hold of Spanish classical music magazines in music and specialised record shops and main bookshops. The best are *Scherzo* (see also www.scherzo.es and go to *enlaces* and the month in question); *Ritmo* (or see www.ritmo.es and go to *vamos de concierto*), and *Ópera Actual* for opera, which is based in Barcelona but serves all of Spain.

Orchestras & ensembles

Orquesta y Coro de la Comunidad de Madrid
www.orcam.org
Madrid's state-funded regional orchestra is one of the city's most highly regarded. It provides accompaniment for the shows at the Teatro de la Zarzuela, but also performs at the Auditorio Nacional. The orchestra's artistic director, José Ramón Encinar, provides an occasionally erratic programme of mainly Spanish composers.

Orquesta y Coro de RTVE
www.rtve.es/orquesta
The orchestra and choir of Spain's national state-run television and radio stations (Radio Televisión España), was originally founded for broadcasting. Its home is in the Teatro Monumental and concerts are usually Thursdays and Fridays at 8pm. Season tickets, running from October till late March, are reasonably priced and the programme is consistently good. The artistic director is Adrian Leaper.

Orquesta & Coro Nacional de España (OCNE)
www.ocne.mcu.es
A certain element of instability has hounded Spain's national orchestra and choir over the years, with numerous strikes carried out by the state-employed members when asked to practise at home outside their set paid hours. They take to the stage every

weekend at the Auditorio Nacional, occasionally performing world premières of contemporary pieces. Josep Pons is the current director and is attempting to renovate programme content. He has even displayed an interest in adding jazz, tango and ethnic music to the orchestra's traditionally classical and Romantic repertoire. Mireia Barrera has been director of the choir since 2005.

Orquesta Sinfónica de Madrid
www.osm.es
The *orquesta titular* of the Teatro Real and oldest existing symphonic ensemble in Spain has a reputation within classical music circles for proposing odd, irregular seasonal programmes. Recent years have looked more stable, however, with a proposed series of chamber concerts, *zarzuelas* and symphonic concerts. At the Teatro Real the major operas are also usually complemented by related concerts put on by the orchestra and performed in a new concert space in one of the upstairs rooms.

As well as all the top Spanish conductors, the OSM has also worked with international greats such as Peter Haag, Pinchas Steinberg and Kurt Sanderling. Its artistic director is the esteemed Jesús López Cobos, but his work at the Teatro Real is so demanding that his commitment to orchestral work can sometimes play second fiddle.

Proyecto Guerrero
This is one of the more interesting ensembles covering the much ignored contemporary spectrum. Having said that, professional opinions as to its real competence are mixed. Under the artistic direction of Javier Güell, Proyecto Guerrero is the main component of the Auditorio Nacional's Música de Hoy programme (www.musicadhoy.com).

Venues

The **Círculo de Bellas Artes**' classical and contemporary music programme has broadened immensely over the last few years (*see p100*). The **Teatro Español** (*see p262*) occasionally holds *zarzuelas* and performances by chamber and symphonic orchestras. A handful of cafés and restaurants around town offer an opera-accompanied dining experience. Try the **Café Viena** (C/Luisa Fernanda 23, 91 559 38 28) for its Monday night sessions (dinner followed by a short *zarzuela* or opera performance, all for €30 plus wine). Also, check out the professional singing waiters at **La Favorita** (*see p155*) and **La Castafiore** (C/Marqués de Monasterio 5, 91 319 42 21). Another place to keep an eye on is the **Centro Asturiano** (C/Farmacia 2, 4°, 91 532 82 81), which runs a cycle called Lunes Musicales with concerts performed by small ensembles on Mondays. **La Fídula** (C/Huertas 57, 91 429 29 47, www.lafidula.com) is a cosy café with concerts on Fridays and Saturdays.

Arts & Entertainment

Auditorio Nacional de Música

C/Príncipe de Vergara 146, Prosperidad (91 337 01 40/tickets 91 337 03 07/www.auditorionacional. mcu.es). Metro Cruz del Rayo or Prosperidad. **Open Box office** 4-6pm Mon; 10am-5pm Tue-Fri; 11am-1pm Sat. Closed Aug. **Main season** Oct-June. **Tickets** €6-€28. **Credit** MC, V.

This impressive concert hall has capacity in its main auditorium for over 2,000, and a smaller chamber hall, La Sala de Cámara. As well as the OCNE, the Auditorio hosts the Comunidad de Madrid's orchestra, ORCAM, and is the provisional home of the Joven Orquesta Nacional de España (worth checking out for their youth and enthusiasm – in contrast to the OCNE). In addition, there are ensembles such as that of the Universidad Politécnica de Madrid who invite orchestras to accompany the university's choir, performing selected Friday and Saturday evenings at 10.30pm. But the best concerts are those by invited international orchestras – which are,

happily enough, something the Spanish state likes to invest its music budget in. The best seasons are the Grandes Intérpretes, the Liceo de Cámara, (Fundación Caja Madrid), Ibermúsica, Ciclo de Cámara y Polifonía and the contemporary Música de Hoy programme (*see p231* Proyecto Guerrero). Look out too for organ recitals.

One-off attendees will find themselves joining an ageing audience, the majority of them being serious season-ticket holders, who tend to be particularly expressive. Many make their feelings known when pleased with the odd exultant cheer of '*bravo*', but more save themselves for when they want to voice their disapproval (booings and abuse have been known in reaction to particularly offensive contemporary compositions, especially when the composer is present). Tickets for the Auditorio usually go on sale about a fortnight before the performance, and can be hard to get hold of. Tickets are generally cheaper for Sunday morning concerts.

Getting some airs

Concert programmers in and around Madrid are slowly waking up to the charms of the region, taking music out of the theatres and lighting up monasteries, palaces and gardens. What could be more inviting than a soirée of Rachmaninoff, Fauré, Mozart and Schumann in one of the cool churches of the Sierra when the temperature is in the 40s in Madrid?

The **Clásicos en Verano** concerts may not bring the greatest musicians, but their range is broad. Come July and August, it seems every nook and cranny, every old church and town hall, around Madrid is filled with the sweet sounds of piano concertos, percussion groups, choirs, wind ensembles, string quartets, accompanied poetry and medieval music by local groups. The apparently random programming has led to Bach and Handel arias being performed at the San Andrés church in Rascafría (*see p275*), while, in nearby Alameda del Valle, young men climbed stepladders to read names and numbers from the phone book as if they were poetry.

Not only are these concerts widespread and plentiful (there are nearly 100 of them in 53 different towns), they're also free. Pass by a tourist information office (*see p308*) or the Consejería de Cultura y Deportes on C/Alcalá 31 to pick up a full programme. Some of the more striking venues include the Castillo de los Mendoza in Manzanares el Real (*see p278*); and the Iglesia de San Bernabé and Iglesia de los Arroyos in El Escorial (*see p268*).

There are a couple of other options in historical settings that are more highly respected in classical music circles. Care for a turn about the charming gardens of the Aranjuez Palace (*see p284*) serenaded by *zarambeques*, *folías*, *marionas*, *fandangos* and *pasacalles*? The festival of **Música Antigua Aranjuez** keeps the music live in the place that inspired Joaquín Rodrigo's haunting *Concierto de Aranjuez*, but with sounds from much earlier in the palace's history. At weekends during the months of June and July the palace hosts concerts of medieval, renaissance and baroque music played on original instruments from the period. Many of the composers featured do not enjoy wide exposure today, although they were well known in their day. Concerts are held inside the palace (in the chapel and the Sala de Teatro), as well as in the palace grounds. The much-loved guided 'musical walks' have pauses for concerts along the way. Tickets are around €20 from Tel-entradas (902 10 12 12, www.telentradas.com).

The Fundación Caja Madrid (www.fundacion cajamadrid.es) is behind several impressive classical music cycles throughout the year in places of interest. The **Fiestas Reales** festival puts on very good concerts in El Escorial, Madrid's Real Monasterio de las Descalzas Reales (*see p98*) and San Jerónimo El Real (*see p122*). This foundation is the most active and positively focused in Madrid and these concerts are of an excellent standard.

Real Academia de las Bellas Artes de San Fernando

C/Alcalá 13, Sol & Gran Vía (91 522 48 85/www.insde.es) Metro Sevilla or Sol. **Concerts** *Sept-June* noon Sat. **Admission** free. **Map** p327 H11.

This beautiful building right in the heart of Madrid is a must for a concert experience. It hosts three or four cycles of free concerts a year, usually organised through the Radio Nacional de España for broadcast with musicians from the Escuela Superior de Música Reina Sofia. One well-reputed cycle is the short baroque season, which usually takes place in March.

Teatro Monumental

C/Atocha 65, Lavapiés (91 429 12 81). Metro Antón Martín. **Open** *Box office* Sept-June 11am-2pm, 5-7pm daily; July 9am-2pm Tue-Fri. Closed Aug. **Main season** Oct-March. **Tickets** €6.60-€16. **Credit** AmEx, DC, MC, V. **Map** p328 H13.

Located in slightly seedy Antón Martín, the Monumental has more character than most, but is functional rather than beautiful. Its main purpose is to record broadcast concerts by the RTVE Orchestra and Choir – consequently it may not have the glitz of the Teatro Real, but it does have excellent acoustics and high-quality performances. The principal diet here is generally concerts, with a side order of opera and *zarzuela*. The Monumental opens to the public free of charge for general rehearsals on Thursday mornings and chamber music concerts around midday on Saturdays.

Teatro Real

Plaza de Isabel II, Los Austrias (91 516 06 00/ www.teatro-real.com). Metro Opera. **Open** *Box office* 10am-8pm Mon-Sat, from 2hrs before show Sun. *Visits* 10.30am-1.30pm Mon, Wed-Sun. **Main season** Sept-July. **Tickets** *Ballet* €7-€90. *Opera* €13-€120.*Visits* €4. **Credit** AmEx, DC, MC, V. **Map** p327 F11.

Shaped like a compressed oval, the interior of the city's opera house is breathtakingly ornate compared with its sombre façade, and one of the most technologically advanced in Europe. Productions are impressive, with complicated revolving sets and attention to detail in costume and props, and enjoy funding from some of Spain's biggest companies, as well as the Comunidad de Madrid. Projection screens at either side of the stage show the full-stage action, though this does not quite compensate for the lack of vision at the far ends of the top galleries (the *tribunas* and part of the *anfiteatro*). There is also a screen above the stage showing Spanish surtitles for non-Spanish operas. The acoustics are so good that the quality of the sound is practically the same everywhere in the hall.

The annual Festival de Verano runs alongside the theatre's regular programme in June and July but offers a more orchestra- and dance-orientated programme as well as children's shows (tickets for these events are much cheaper and easier to obtain). Guided tours run every day except Tuesday, and take visitors through the main dressing room and

auditoria. Technical tours can be reserved for Sundays, lasting about an hour and a half (91 516 06 96 for all tour enquiries/booking).

Performances usually begin at 8pm, or 6pm on Sundays, with ballet and family opera matinées at noon. Tickets go on sale approximately ten days before the première, and standby tickets are available on the day. With the cheapest tickets, for rows F and G, vision is seriously reduced; check the website for a detailed plan. **Photos** *p229* and *p230*.

Teatro de la Zarzuela

C/Jovellanos 4, Huertas & Santa Ana (91 524 54 00/http://teatrodelazarzuela.mcu.es). Metro Banco de España. **Open** *Box office* noon-6pm (8pm before shows) daily. **Main season** Sept-July. **Tickets** €6-€36. **Credit** AmEx, DC, V. **Map** p328 I11.

The Teatro de la Zarzuela, which served as an opera house for many years previous to the Teatro Real's renovation, is now principally devoted to its *raison d'être* – staging *zarzuela*, the home-grown Spanish operetta. Despite *zarzuela*'s uncool image and lack of credibility among serious music lovers, it retains considerable popularity, drawing in audiences for daily 8pm performances from October to July. Accompanying the Teatro's packed *zarzuela* programme are performances of dance (often by the Ballet Nacional), music, plays, conferences and special family-orientated shows. The well-reputed annual Ciclo del Lied pays tribute to the lesser-known 19th-century German song form. **Photo** *p234.*

Institutions

Institutions such as the **British Council** (www.britishcouncil.org/es), the **Institut Français** (www.ifmadrid.com), the **Istituto Italiano di Cultura** (www.iicmadrid.com) and the **Goethe Institut** (www.goethe.de/wm/mad) are also worth checking for classical music concerts and related activities. *See also* *p261* Centro Cultural de la Villa.

Centro para la Difusión de la Música Contemporánea

Centro de Arte Reina Sofía, C/Santa Isabel 52, Lavapiés (91 744 10 72/http://cdmc.mcu.es). Metro Atocha. **Main season** Oct-May. **Map** p328 J14/15.

Founded by Luis de Pablo, this pioneering institution boldly goes where few others in Madrid dare to go – into the dangerous world of the contemporary. The Centro gives 30 or so commissions annually to students who debut at the Auditorio Nacional, the Círculo de Bellas Artes or at the Reina Sofía museum itself. The centre also organises an interesting contemporary music festival, La Música Toma el Museo, with free concerts around the museum as well as out on the pleasant patio.

Fundación Canal

C/Mateo Inurria 2, Chamartín (91 545 15 06/ www.fundacioncanal.com). Metro Plaza de Castilla. **Main season** Oct-July.

Take in some home-grown operetta at the **Teatro de la Zarzuela.** *See p233.*

Set up by Madrid's water company, the Canal Isabel II, in recent years this foundation has become active in all areas of the arts, programming various types of occasionally excellent exhibitions and concerts year-round. Music programming has included seasons of chamber music performed by musicians from the Orquesta de la Comunidad de Madrid and several one-off recitals by virtuosos such as the Russian pianist Alexander Moutouzkine. Nonclassical music gets a look-in too; the regular 'conFUSIÓN' series has featured genres as diverse as bossa nova, gospel and jazz.

Fundación Carlos Amberes

C/Claudio Coello 99 (91 435 22 01/www.fcamberes. org). Metro Serrano. **Main season** Sept-June. **Map** p325 L7.
The Carlos Amberes foundation dates back to 1594, when it was founded by a 16th-century Flemish benefactor. Today, as well as exhibitions and conferences, it hosts an average of 15 to 20 concerts per year in three cycles (one at the beginning of the year, another in May and one at the end of the year), both in its rather dingy basement and sometimes upstairs in a converted church, which is pretty but has bad acoustics. The programme tends to nod towards the music of the Low Countries.

Fundación Juan March

C/Castelló 77, Salamanca (91 435 42 40/www. march.es). Metro Núñez de Balboa. **Main season** Oct-June. **Map** p325 N7.

Set up in 1955, this charitable foundation and hive of musical, artistic and scientific activity was one of few such organisations in Spain for a good many years. These days the Fundación Juan March remains a key player in Madrid's classical world, putting on around 150-200 free concerts per year. These usually consist of soloists or chamber ensembles and take place on Mondays at midday and Wednesday evenings from 7pm (the most popular slot, with better-known professional musicians and broadcast on Radio Nacional) as well as some Saturdays at midday with younger musicians. The concert hall seats 300; when it fills up a second hall with a big screen is opened, and then the bar. The programme in general is pretty much free from restrictions as it does not depend on ticket sales; there is a leaning towards Spanish composers, but with a lot of flexibility. Take in some good art exhibitions while you're there – in 2007 these include a look at the work of Roy Lichtenstein.

Festivals

Fiesta season in Madrid kicks off in May with the week of merriment leading up to **San Isidro** on the 15th. The council provides annual free concerts including *zarzuela* in the Centro Cultural Conde Duque (*see p109*) as well as in parks to the west of the city and the Plaza Mayor. Classical concerts, given by ensembles such as the Banda Sinfónica Municipal, are

Noise in the hood

Madrid's villagey nature has led to many neighbourhoods developing their own flavours, and nowhere is this more evident than in the music each *barrio* creates. While the overriding sound is that of commercial radio dedicated to the usual lite Spanish pop fare – like most countries it is dominated by those put through the TV starmaking machinery – the fact remains that the city spits out an impressive array of talent.

You might get the impression that southern Madrid is all rock, rock, rock. It is indeed as hard rocking as you can imagine, with an entire swathe, from Vallecas to Carabanchel, being home to a kind of blue-collar, beer-drinking, dope-smoking form of full-on rock. Stars of this scene include Rosendo, and the lamented Los Enemigos, and countless hardcore bands that play a few shows and then disappear into the ether. But it's not all rock. The southern 'burbs of Madrid proper, as well as southern and eastern satellite towns like Alcorcón, Móstales and Torrejón de Ardoz have seen the emergence of rap and hip hop outfits that are more than passably good. Initially ignored by the media taste-makers, the scene has developed some quality acts over the years including people like DJ Jotamayuscula and Frank T. Recently the scene has started to go international, with records released in Puerto Rico, the US, Mexico, Chile and Argentina.

In central Madrid, Malasaña has always been home to a rockier form of modernity. While its roots lie in La Movida, the creative explosion following Spain's democratisation, these days the music is divided into two different, yet complementary, camps. One

pays homage to the city's love of Spanish-language rock, with testosterone overkill being the rule of thumb. The flipside is the explosion of clubs dedicated to championing Anglo-American alternative rock and dance music. In the best of cases, bands like Femme Fatale manage to add new wrinkles to trends existing in other European capitals with wit and verve.

Northern *barrios* like Salamanca and the area surrounding the Santiago Bernabéu football stadium are rich, yuppified and dearly love their pop. In fact, it's the artists from this scene that put Spain on the musical map. Take the locally adored Iglesias dynasty, for example. Between father Julio and son Enrique, they have shifted umpteen million CDs. Alejandro Sanz was another exponent of the *pijo* scene, and one-time Best Latin Grammy winner. It's interesting to note that as soon as these geezers become big, they abandon the city and their grassroots Ralph Lauren-clad fanbase for Miami's more expensive and clement climes.

Lavapiés, finally yet importantly, continues to be the multicultural melting pot of the city. Most of the successful bands closely identified with the area – La Cabra Mecánica, Amparanoia, El Bicho – specialise in *mestizaje* (cross-breeding). While the root of all continues to be traditional styles such as flamenco or rumba, they mix in rock, Latin jazz, and even electronica to fine effect. In fact, of all the musical cauldrons simmering in Madrid, this is really the one you ought to watch, as it finds itself increasingly in the sights of the international music press.

sometimes held in the Teatro Español. See the council's website www.munimadrid.es or ask at tourist offices for a San Isidro programme.

The international **Día de la Música** on June 21 involves 12 hours of non-stop dance, musical theatre, cinema, photography and, of course, music in an increasing number of museums and other venues across the city, organised by the Círculo de Bellas Artes, and all for free. June also sees classical concerts in **Alcalá de Henares** on some Sundays performed by local orchestras in the Plaza Cervantes bandstand. For the summer festivals **Clásicos en Verano** and **Festival de Música Antigua**, *see p232* **Getting some airs**.

Rock, Roots & Jazz

It's been a difficult few years for live music in Madrid. In the words of one concert promoter: 'On one side there's the musicians and the live music lovers, on the other, the council…' As part of the local authority's continuing crusade against what it apparently deems to be low culture, bar and venue owners continue to fight a sometimes insurmountable battle in order to put on live music. The owners of the much-loved Suristán, Madrid's only true world music venue, simply had to throw in the towel after constant licence checks, a tax on concerts which

Arts & Entertainment

was retroactive for five years and nearly crippled them, and a complete lack of support from any governing body.

The official line given by the authorities for these closures is the noise problem. However, empirical evidence suggests that the moment there is negative press about an area or a street regarding noise pollution or late-night revellers, the council covers its back by finding some licensing anomaly and shutting down at least one venue in that area. To reopen again is a bureaucratic nightmare, because as quickly as a bar may sort out its noise problems, getting the case to the top of the pile either means waiting an eternity or – some allege – handing over a wad of cash in an envelope. In another bizarre twist to the tale, as part of the anti-alcohol drive, the council has also banned under-18s from concerts, something which some lament as the beginning of the end of rock in Spain.

Surprisingly, in the face of such fervent opposition, Madrid's live music scene continues to thrive. CD sales are frighteningly low in Spain, with Spaniards buying an average of only 1.4 CDs a year. Figures suggest that there are as many pirate CDs bought off the street these days as there are in the shops. This doesn't give big acts a huge impetus to tour in Spain, but interestingly, each year seems to attract bigger names to the city, receiving a warm reception from all but the council.

VENUES
In the centre of Madrid there is not one concert venue that holds more than 2,500 spectators. Intimacy is the order of the day then, with many big names coming to play in surprisingly small auditoriums. As well as those listed here, the bullring at Las Ventas (see p44 **Where and how**) sometimes hosts gigs, and being outdoors is perfect for the concerts put on there in July. The Parque de Atracciones (see p210) in the Casa de Campo is another summer venue where you can catch some local rock groups.

Venues listed do not charge admission unless otherwise stated. If there is no charge on the door, there will most likely be a supplement on your first drink, which usually goes straight into the pocket of the band. Few venues will accept credit cards on the door, although we have noted those that do in our listings. To make licensing issues easier, many of these venues stay open as nightclubs after the concerts end, while some clubs in the **Nightlife** chapter (see pp241-252) often host live music.

FESTIVE SOUNDS
With such good weather, music festivals are understandably popular. **San Isidro** is a good place to catch free concerts in Las Vistillas

park. July sees the **Veranos de la Villa** festival, which attracts names such as Erykah Badu and Gilberto Gil. Madrid's indie festival, **Festimad Sur**, is still going strong in its new home in Leganés, and an excellent new music festival has been added in the shape of **Summercase**. The **Carnaval** and **Dos de Mayo** holidays see live acts performing for free, as do the **Fiestas del Partido Comunista** in September and the **May Day** celebrations. For all these festivals and more, see pp204-209 **Festivals & Events**.

LISTINGS
It's good to check out the local newspapers if you want information about upcoming gigs. The listings mags Guía del Ocio, Salir Salir and the Friday supplementsof many Spanish newspapers have details of forthcoming gigs, although they're not always comprehensive. Otherwise, concert information comes on posters, flyers and in free magazines found in bars, and music and fashion shops. Magazines to look for include MondoSonoro, Punto H, Rockdelux, GO and the irregular Undersounds. Concert information is also available on the web if you speak Spanish at: www.lanetro.com, www.madridmusic.com and www.mondosonoro.com.

Rock/world music

La Buena Dicha
C/Santa Hortensia 14, Chamartín (91 413 60 14/ www.labuenadicha.com). Metro Alfonso XIII or Prosperidad. **Open** 10pm-6am Thur-Sat. Closed Aug. **Concerts** 10pm-midnight Fri, Sat. **Admission** (incl 1 drink) €7 for concerts.
A medium-sized venue with a large stage and lots of smoke and light tricksiness, La Buena Dicha programmes little-known local pop and rock outfits, usually of a pretty good standard. Be warned, it can be hard to find, so allow plenty of time.

Búho Real
C/Regueros 5, Chueca (91 308 48 51/www.buhoreal. com). Metro Alonso Martínez or Chueca. **Open** 7pm-3am daily. **Credit** MC, V. **Map** p324 I9.
The lights go down very low in the Búho Real, and the spots come up on a tiny stage. The size limitations here dictate the acts – expect local jazz or acoustic groups, most of them just two- or three-piece bands. The name means the 'Royal Owl', which goes some way towards explaining the large collection of miniature owls on display.

Café la Palma
C/Palma 62 (91 522 50 31/www.cafelapalma.com). Metro Noviciado. **Open** 4pm-3am Mon-Thur, Sun; 4pm-4am Fri, Sat. **Admission** (minimum consumption) €6 for concerts on Thur, Fri, Sat. **No credit cards**. **Map** p323 F8.

Café La Palma. *See p236.*

This is a long-standing favourite amongst the Malasaña crowd. Choose from an area with tables, a chill-out zone where everyone lazes on cushions on the floor or the main room, where from Thursday to Saturday you can catch concerts from local up-and-comers such as Raíces y Puntas. There are plans to introduce food at some point in 2007.

Chesterfield
C/Serrano Jover 5, Conde Duque (91 542 28 17). Metro Argüelles. **Open** 1.30pm-3.30am daily. **Admission** varies **Map** p323 E7.

For a small venue, Chesterfield has an impressive track record, as the signed photos on the wall attest. As well as smaller local acts, Mark Knopfler, Lisa Stansfield and Elvis Costello have all made appearances recently, as well as Spanish megastar Chenoa.

La Coquette
C/Hileras 14, Los Austrias (no phone). Metro Ópera or Sol. **Open** *Sept-Apr* 8pm-3am Mon-Thur, Sun; 8pm-3.30am Fri, Sat; *May-July* 9pm-3am Mon-Thur, Sun; 9pm-3.30am Fri, Sat. Closed Aug. **Admission** €1.20 + cost of drink for concerts. **Map** p327 F11.

This basement bar, going for some 20 years now, was Madrid's first dedicated exclusively to blues. Run by a Swiss-Spanish guy called Albert, who has a large collection of old records that won't disappoint, there are live acts featuring local bluesers from Tuesday to Thursday. Can get very smoky.

La Cubierta de Leganés
C/Maestro s/n, Leganés (91 689 87 15/tickets 91 694 78 46/www.la-cubierta.com). Metro Leganés Central. **Open** varies. **Admission** varies.

La Cubierta is a bullring with retractable roof south of the centre in Leganés. Bullrings often double as concert venues, but sadly the shape of a bullring is not conducive to good acoustics, leaving a crisp kick-drum distorted into a nebulous throb. That said, it's a magnet for rock and heavy metal groups, plus dance acts too: Chemical Brothers, Deep Purple and Tool have all paid a visit.

Garibaldi Café
C/San Felipe Neri 4, Los Austrias (91 559 27 33/ www.salagaribaldi.com). Metro Ópera. **Open** 10pm-6am daily. **Admission** varies. **Map** p327 F12.

A roomy venue with a good sound system and a varied programme. Its staple fare is new bands doing the rounds on the local scene, but in addition there are DJ sessions from Thursday to Sunday. Midweek you'll find stand-ups, storytelling, theatre and dance.

Gruta 77
C/Nicolás Morales s/n, Southern suburbs (91 471 23 70/www.gruta77.com). Metro Oporto. **Open** 8pm-6am daily. **Admission** varies.

A mix of local unsigned groups and touring bands from the States, Australia and Japan pass through this 300-seater *sala*. Punk, rock, ska and *mestizaje* tastes are catered for, with regular rock competitions, the prize being the chance to professionally record an album. An excellent sound system makes it worth the trip out to the 'burbs.

Honky Tonk
C/Covarrubias 24, Chamberí (91 445 61 91). Metro Bilbao. **Open** *Sept-June* 9.30pm-5am daily. *July, Aug* 10.30pm-5am. **Admission** free. **Map** p324 I7.

Honky Tonk programmes local country, blues and rock acts nightly, and its own Gary Moore/Rolling Stones-influenced band performs regularly. Ignore the intimidating-looking doormen and get here early as the large pillars that hold up the building tend to restrict the views of those not at the front.

Madrid Arena

Casa del Campo, Avda de Portugal s/n (91 722 04 00). Metro Alto de Extremadura or Lago. **Open** varies. **Admission** varies.

A behemoth of a venue, refurbished just a few years ago, and well laid out, with good facilities and great acoustics. There are plenty of macro-raves here too – it's not all just about the guitars.

Moby Dick

Avda del Brasil 5 (91 555 76 71/www.mobydick club.com). Metro Cuzco or Santiago Bernabéu. **Open** 10pm-3am Mon-Thur, 10pm-5am Fri, Sat. **Admission** varies. **Credit** (bar only) MC, V.

With two different levels for music, Moby Dick caters for plenty of tastes. Mainly a venue for local groups and touring Spanish bands, it can still pull a few surprises. The Long Blondes, the Libertines and the Feeling have all paid a visit, as have the sublime Fat Freddy's Drop. Warm up next door with a pint of Guinness in its sister bar the Irish Rover first.

Palacio Municipal de Congresos

Avda de la Capital de España Madrid s/n (91 722 04 00). Metro Campos de las Naciones. **Open** varies. **Admission** varies.

This Ricard-Bofill designed auditorium looks to have been purpose-built for a symphony orchestra, but that doesn't mean pop and rock acts can't make use of it. Antony and the Johnsons played here, as did the Woody Allen New Orleans Band. Crosby and Nash defied the security guards to pull the audience on stage. Various awards ceremonies are held here, from the Goyas (the Spanish Oscars) to the annual Canadian Aboriginal Music Awards.

Palacio Vistalegre

C/Utebo 1, Southern suburbs (91 422 07 81/ www.palaciovistalegre.com). Metro Oporto or Vista Alegre. **Open** varies. **Admission** varies.

This stadium is what the Spanish call *multi-usos*, so it serves as a basketball stadium and a conference hall as well as a concert venue. Some of the slightly dubious names to have rocked a crowd here in recent times include Judas Priest, Bryan Adams and Spanish rockers Extremoduro.

Ritmo & Compás

C/Conde de Vilches 22, Salamanca (91 355 28 00/ www.ritmoycompas.com). Metro Cartagena or Diego de León. **Open** Bar 4pm-end of concert programme. **Admission** varies.

A music fanatic's paradise, Ritmo & Compás boasts 160 rehearsal rooms over two sites, recording studios, its own record label and courses and seminars. As a live venue it has a programme as diverse as the facilities, including pop-rock, reggae, northern soul,

metal, blues, funk, techno and breakbeat. The stage and auditorium are well designed, allowing a good view from any angle.

La Riviera

Paseo Bajo de la Virgen del Puerto s/n, Los Austrias (91 365 24 15). Metro Puerto del Ángel. **Open** Gigs varies. **Club** midnight-5am Fri, Sat. **Admission** varies. **Map** p326 B/C12.

This club on the banks of the Manzanares is a major player on the Madrid music scene and is ranked by many as the city's best medium-sized venue. It's certainly popular, and comes equipped with an excellent sound system. All manner of acts have passed through in recent times, among them Missy Elliot, Yo La Tengo, Bloc Party and Jet.

La Sala

Avda Nuestra Señora de Fátima 42, Carabanchel (91 525 54 44). Metro Carabanchel. **Open** 8pm-5am daily. **Admission** varies.

The neon and neo-classical columns in the entrance, the torch-lighting inside – it's all a bit strip joint, but don't let that, or the suburban location, put you off. La Sala's mixed bag of gigs mainly features Spanish pop, but there have also been performances from the likes of Deacon Blue and Ron Wood. There is a concert space with room for 700 on the first floor, while downstairs there are pinball machines, a pool table and a loud but louche atmosphere.

Sala Caracol

C/Bernardino Obregón 18, Embajadores (91 527 35 94/www.salacaracol.com). Metro Embajadores. **Open** 9pm-3am concert nights. **Admission** varies. **Map** p327 H16.

The much-cherished Caracol recently reopened after a couple of years with licensing problems. A cosy venue, it is nevertheless big enough to have hosted the Guillemots and UK Subs in 2007. Once known for flamenco and world music, it is now more likely to feature rock, and has its own competition for up-and-coming bands.

Sala Heineken

C/Princesa 1, Argüelles (91 547 57 11/www.sala rena.com). Metro Plaza de España. **Open** midnight-6am Thur-Sat (concert days opens 10pm). **Admission** varies. **Map** p323 E9.

The venue formerly known as Arena (but not to be confused with Madrid Arena, for which see above), Sala Heineken plays host to several club nights, but is also a fairly hot live music venue. The layout is not especially conducive to everyone getting a good view of the action, but it's an intimate venue, with recent visitors including the likes of !!!, Peaches and the Kaiser Chiefs.

Siroco

C/San Dimas 3, Malasaña (91 593 30 70/www. siroco.es). Metro Noviciado or San Bernardo. **Open** 9.30pm-5am Thur; 9.30pm-6am Fri, Sat. **Admission** (incl 1 drink) €5-€8. **No credit cards. Map** p323 F8.

El Junco. *See p240.*

Regulars at this long-established joint know just what they want, and management are more than happy to provide it, programming a steady schedule of well-established local rock, indie, pop and funk outfits and providing a stage for young hopefuls. In addition, there are late-night DJ sessions covering a broad range of styles. The club has its very own record label and tends to be frequented by A&R types from others.

El Sol
C/Jardines 3, Sol & Gran Vía (91 532 64 90/www. elsolmad.com). Metro Gran Vía. **Open** midnight-5am Tue-Sat, doors open for concerts at 11pm. **Admission** (incl 1 drink) €9. **Credit** (bar only) MC, V. **Map** p327 H11.
A steady flow of top live acts passes through El Sol, another remnant of the Movida. The décor is not up to much, but the vibe and the programme make up for that. A mixture of rock, rhythm and blues, punk, soul, and hip hop from national outfits, complemented by visits from international acts such as the Bellrays, Snow Patrol and Gigolo Aunts.

Jazz

The **Festival de Otoño** (*see p208*) includes a jazz section and many top international names (especially from the field of Latin jazz) appear here. Other venues with occasional live jazz acts include **Marula** (*see p243*), and the otherwise sleepy **Café El Despertar** (C/Torrecilla del Leal 18, 91 530 80 95) in Lavapiés. Fair-trade café **Zanzíbar** (*see p175*) in Chueca has a varied programme of jazz, blues, singer-songwriters and bossa nova.

Café Berlin
C/Jacometrezo 4 (91 521 57 52/www.cafeberlin.net). Metro Callao or Santo Domingo. **Open** noon-4am Tue-Sun. **Admission** varies. **No credit cards**. **Map** p323 G11.
In 2003 the Berlin was another venue to fall foul of enforced closure by the council but has since bounced back impressively, with its own jazz school. While it is mainly a jazz venue showcasing local groups, bigger names such as Eddie Henderson also come to call. These days you can also get a bite to eat – burgers, pasta and desserts with names like Tarta Miles Davis…

Café Central
Plaza del Ángel 10, Huertas & Santa Ana (91 369 41 43/www.cafecentralmadrid.com). Metro Antón Martín or Sol. **Open** 1.30pm-2.30am Mon-Thur, Sun; 1.30pm-3.30am Fri, Sat. **Admission** gigs €6-€12. **Credit** AmEx, DC, MC, V. **Map** p327 H12.
For many years now, this beautiful place with high ceilings and elegant decor has been *the* place to get your jazz fix in Madrid. The artists that come here

Arts & Entertainment

put it among the best of its kind in Europe. George Adams, Don Pullen, Ben Sidran and Bob Sands have all taken the stage, as well as Spanish stalwarts such as Chano Domínguez, Jorge Pardo and the oldest and greatest of them all, Pedro Iturralde.

Café Populart

C/Huertas 22, Huertas (91 429 84 07/www.populart. es). Metro Antón Martín. **Open** 6pm-2.30am Mon-Thur, Sun; 6pm-3.30am Fri, Sat. **Admission** free. **Map** p328 I12.
Escape from the beer-crawl route that is Huertas by slipping into this superb jazz club. There's no cover charge, but the drinks are a bit pricey. A strong backer of Spanish jazz and host to many an international artist, Populart features jazz and blues every night with two shows, one at 11.30pm and the other at 12.30am.

Clamores

C/Alburquerque 14, Chamberí (91 445 79 38/www.salaclamores.com). Metro Bilbao. **Open** 7pm-2am Mon-Thur, Sun; 7pm-4am Fri, Sat. **Admission** (concerts only) varies. **Map** p323 H7.
This emblematic jazz club opened in 1979, and for eight years served as the set for the TV programme *Jazz Entre Amigos*. Stocking what is apparently the widest range of cavas and champagnes in Madrid, it has a very varied programme these days, with tango, pop, rock, bossa, samba and folk all on the bill as well as the jazz that made its name. The live acts sprawl into late-night jam sessions on Friday and Saturday nights.

Colegio Mayor San Juan Evangelista

C/Gregorio del Amo 4, Moncloa (91 534 24 00/www.cmusanjuan.com). Metro Metropolitano. **Open** 10pm Fri-Sun. Closed July-Sept. **Admission** varies.
This auditorium, located in a student residence, and known affectionately as the 'Johnny', is actually much more important than you might think. Contrary to its appearance, it's one of the city's most discerning jazz clubs – hundreds of great names have passed through the doors here in the 30-plus years of its existence. Look out for the annual spring jazz festival and the Flamenco por Tarantos festival in April.

Dizzy Jazz

C/Luz 8, Las Matas (91 635 65 54/www.musica actual.com/dizzyjazz). Trains C-8, C-10 to Las Matas/bus from Moncloa to Las Matas, N-6 Ctra de A Coruña exit Las Matas. **Open** 11pm-4am Fri, Sat. **Admission** concert nights €6.
Las Matas is a bit of a schlep from the city centre, but often worth it for great jazz and Brazilian acts at Dizzy Jazz. There are two shows, the first is at midnight and the second at 1.30am.

El Junco

Plaza Santa Bárbara 10 (91 319 20 81/www.el junco.com). Metro Alonso Martínez. **Open** 11pm-6am daily. **Credit** AmEx, DC, MC, V. **Map** p324 I8.

This is the late-night jazz spot in the city, boasting jam sessions on Sundays and Tuesdays, and gigs on most other weeknights. When there are not live musicians for your listening pleasure, a carefully selected roster of DJs, such as Frenchman Fedi Petit, will be spinning vinyl with just the right amount of off-beats. **Photo** *p239*.

Segundo Jazz

C/Comandante Zorita 8, Cuatro Caminos, Tetúan (91 554 94 37). Metro Cuatro Caminos or Nuevos Ministerios. **Open** 8pm-4am daily. **Admission** (minimum consumption) €5.
Founded many years ago by the owner of the legendary Whisky Jazz Club, this is Madrid's longest standing jazz joint. Nowadays, as well as jazz, the programme takes in Brazilian groups, singer-songwriters and '60s cover bands banging out Beatles and Stones songs. A great atmosphere and friendly staff make it an essential stop, but don't get there too early: concerts start at midnight.

Latin

La Bodeguita de Beny

C/Tres Cruces, 8, Sol & Gran Vía (91 521 34 82). Metro Gran Vía. **Open** 7pm-3am daily. **Admission** free. **Map** p323 H11.
This rather narrow bar, adorned with pictures of Beny Moré, specialises in Cuban cocktails and sounds, and attracts a lively crowd. From Wednesday through to Sunday there are performances on the tiny stage. Expect to find acoustic duos and trios (there's no space for full bands), playing *son*, *guaracha* and Latin jazz.

Galileo Galilei

C/Galileo 100, Chamberí (91 534 75 57/www.sala galileogalilei.com). Metro Islas Filipinas or Quevedo. **Open** 6pm-3am Mon-Sat. **Admission** €6-€15 Mon-Fri; €23 Sat.
A sister club of Clamores, Galileo Galilei presents possibly the widest range of artists to be seen under one roof in all of Madrid. Whatever kind of music you like, you'll likely find it here, since all the bases seem to be covered. There's Latin jazz, flamenco, salsa, singer-songwriters and myriad types of fusion. There are also occasional comedy nights. It's a former cinema, and as such is very spacious, though the mock-Hellenic decor can be a bit over the top. It's non-smoking throughout.

Oba-Oba

C/Jacometrezo 4, Sol & Gran Vía (no phone). Metro Callao. **Open** 7pm-5am Mon-Thur, Sun; 7pm-6am Fri, Sat. **Admission** €8. **Map** p323 G11.
An old favourite, the larger than life Oba-Oba has been serving up ice-cold Caipirinhas and fabulous samba for over 25 years to its good-time clientele. There are live acts jamming here several nights a week, and, given the theme, it's perhaps less than surprising that almost all of them are Brazilian, as are many of its patrons.

Nightlife

Where to find the party in the capital of all-night revels.

The answer to tired old venues: **Sala Wind**. *See p245.*

Sleep is almost a dirty word to this most fun-loving of people: Macbeth didn't murder sleep, Madrid did. The Spanish love to party, and they have always partied harder and later than any other nationality you'd care to mention.

In recent years, however, it seems as if things have changed somewhat. The hedonistic days of La Movida – the libertine backlash against the repression of the Franco era – are gone. Instead, the scene is facing its own backlash, as the local government, and in turn, the police, crack down on the giant night-time playground that is Madrid. This is mainly due to the unwanted by-products of excess: the noise and mess left by the party people, and the political pressure brought on by consistent complaints from the city's residents. Time was when the party kept on going through the morning and into the afternoon, as numerous dodgy after-hours would fling open their doors at a truly ungodly hour to welcome in revelers for whom sleep was not an option. But the police crackdown has put paid to that, and now there are only a few places to go should you want to dance from dawn.

WHAT HAPPENS WHEN

Nightlife here has distinct stages. In the early evening, from 6pm until midnight, teenagers take to the streets. Most of them congregate in parks and squares and engage in what is known as the *botellón*. Thousands of litres of red wine are mixed with Coke, to make a sticky mix known as *calimocho*, the drink that launched a million teen-hangovers. Officially, the *botellón* is now illegal in Madrid; the focal point of a stand-off between the police and wannabe revellers is the Plaza Dos de Mayo, one of the most popular sites for *botellón*. However, 15 squad cars can't be there every night, nor can they cover the hundreds of other squares in Madrid, ensuring that it still goes on every weekend.

At around 11pm a more mature crowd starts to spill out of the restaurants and hit the bars. Generally, bars break down into several distinct categories. *Bares de copas* sell spirit-based drinks with or without a DJ in the corner. Then come the *discobares,* which may require a cover charge and bang out international and Spanish pop, perfect for their alcohol-fuelled clientele. Then there are the funkier pre-club bars, often with

Mondo at **Sala Stella**. *See p246.*

a house DJ warming you up for a night on the town. Thanks to recent legislation, bars must close at around 3am: precisely the moment when the clubs or *discotecas* fill. (*Discoteca* carries no cheesy connotations in Spanish; in fact be careful what you ask for when talking to locals – *club* in Spanish usually means brothel.)

SURVIVAL TIPS

Having changed your body clock around to suit your schedule in Madrid, there are just a few more things you need to bear in mind before you go out seeking *la marcha*, or a good time. Don't get too dolled up; with some notable exceptions, Madrid is not a town where people dress to impress. Creativity is more important than couture. Be careful with the drinks; measures poured here are such that you may, for once, actually ask them to put a little less in. The ticket you are given on the door of a club is almost always valid for a drink, so don't just toss it away. Since the euro came in, Spain has seen a massive hike in prices across the board, and clubs have not escaped. Some of the swankier clubs will charge you as much as €12 for a long drink, and €10 for a beer. Remember though, the measures for long drinks are huge, so if you're looking to penny pinch, stick to the rum and coke.

Finally, before you head out for your night on the town, you might consider checking club websites for printable flyers that will get you in for a discounted fee.

Los Austrias & La Latina

Atenas

C/Segovia & C/Cuesta de la Vega (91 765 12 06/ mobile 650 50 67 93). Metro Ópera or Puerta del Ángel. **Open** noon-4am daily. Closed Nov-Mar. **Admission** free. **No credit cards. Map** p326 D12.

A super-cool *terraza* set in its own small park. The plentiful tables in the front bar are filled by midnight and the overflow swells on to the surrounding gentle slope of grass. With no complaining neighbours to worry about, the crowd can enjoy the easy sounds of Latin house mixed by the DJ long after other *terrazas* have called it a night.

El Nuevo Barbú

C/Santiago 3 (91 542 56 98). Metro Ópera or Sol. **Open** 10.30pm-3.30am Mon-Thur; 10.30pm-4am Fri, Sat. **Admission** free. **Credit** DC, MC, V. **Map** p327 F12.

A sumptuous red velvet curtain separates the chilled front bar from two spacious candlelit chambers at the back where a swirling wash of intensely coloured psychedelic projections bathe the walls and ceilings. The DJ keeps the easy-going, urbane crowd happy with a slick mixture of funk, salsa and African beats. This is more the kind of a place to give you a warm glow than to really light your fire.

Danzoo @ Maxime

Maxime, Ronda de Toledo 1 (902 49 99 94). Metro Puerta de Toledo. **Open** midnight-6am Sat. **Admission** (incl 1 drink) €13; free before 2am. **No credit cards. Map** p327 F15.

Progressive and tech-house with an edge. This is not one for the handbag housers out there, rather this is a hard session; like Spinal Tap's amplifiers, the volume here goes up to 11. The crowd is grungy and tends to be predominantly male. On a Friday, Danzoo is at Macumba (see *p252*).

Deconya

C/Don Pedro 6 (no phone). Metro La Latina. **Open** 9pm-4am Mon-Sat. **Admission** free. **Credit** AmEx, DC, MC, V. **Map** p327 E13.

Known as a hang-out for artists, musicians and the in-crowd. Quieter midweek when the sounds are rock 'n' roll and blues, the weekends see the English resident DJ take the reins and bang out some funky house tracks. Mounted above the dancefloor is a mad professor's representation of the solar system, with a large glitter ball as the sun – proof that in Madrid the world revolves around gettin' groovy.

Kathmandú

C/Señores de Luzón 3 (no phone/www.kathmandu-club. com). Metro Ópera or Sol. **Open** 12.30-5am Thur; 12.30-6am Fri, Sat. **Admission** (incl 1 drink) €7 Fri, Sat; free Thur. **No credit cards. Map** p327 F12.
This basement club is cosy, friendly and nicely chilled. The DJs spin a delicious mix of funk, soul, jazz and hip hop, luring the friendly clientele on to the dancefloor by about 3am. Non-dancers take to ample seating in the cave-like venue and nod along.

Marula

C/Caños Viejos 3 (91 366 15 96/www.marulacafe. com). Metro La Latina. **Open** 11pm-6am Fri, Sat. **Admission** €7 after 1.30am Fri; €9 after 1.30am Sat, otherwise free. **No credit cards. Map** p327 E13.
This small venue serves as bar, club and live music venue. Tuesday nights are concert nights, and there are late-night jams midweek, but the place really hots up at weekends, attracting DJ sessions from local talent such as Señorlobo, Chema Ama and Javi Kalero. The summertime terrace is a big pull, filling up by midnight and staying that way. **Photo** *p251.*

Sol & Gran Vía

Bash

Plaza Callao 4 (91 541 35 00/www.tripfamily.com). Metro Callao. **Open** midnight-6am Wed. **Admission** (incl 1 drink) €10. **No credit cards. Map** p323 G11.
Wednesday is firmly established as hip hop night in Madrid, and judging by the turnout these clubs get, Thursdays must see a massive drop in Madrid's productivity thanks to what must surely be some cracking hangovers. Bash doesn't really get going until after 1am, but once it does there's no room to move. The residents specialise in the latest R&B and hip hop and the guest DJs have featured Funk Master Flex among others.

Cool

C/Isabel la Católica 6 (91 542 34 39). Metro Santo Domingo. **Open** midnight-6am Thur-Sat. **Admission** (incl 1 drink) €15. **No credit cards. Map** p323 F11.
Cool was always too stylish to be dominated by the straight crowd. And so it has come to pass that it now has a mainly gay following. Once you get beyond the stainless steel and the sweeping ramps of the entrance, there are two upstairs lounges, one complete with wall-mounted plasma screens overlooking a large and heaving dancefloor filled with hundreds of muscle-boys. Thursdays see the Sunflowers session, for a smartly dressed mixed crowd, while Fridays and Saturdays see the muscle-boys take over at the gay night Royal.

Joy Eslava

C/Arenal 11 (91 366 54 39/reservations 91 366 37 33/www.joy-eslava.com). Metro Ópera or Sol. **Open** 11.30pm-5.30am Mon-Thur, Sun; 6.30pm-6.30am Fri,

Sat. **Admission** €12 Mon-Thur, Sun; €15 Fri, Sat (incl 1 drink). **Credit** AmEx, DC, MC, V. **Map** p327 G11.
Unusual in that it retains some original trappings of its former incarnation as a 19th-century theatre, in every other respect this is an ordinary high-street club. The vast crammed dancefloor runs the gamut from teenage tribes through housewives, enjoying staple disco house. Also a concert venue these days.

Low

Sala de Nombre Público, Plaza de los Mostenses 11 (no phone). Metro Plaza de España. **Open** 12.30am-6am Fri, Sat. **Admission** (incl 1 drink) €13. **No credit cards. Map** p323 F9.
A nice and grimy basement club, of which the main room is Low – capitalising on the recent mainstream interest in the experimental side of electronica. The DJs – resident and otherwise – spin a varied mix, taking in everything from electro to indie. The large venue doesn't fill up until 3am, so don't rush.

Museo Chicote

Gran Vía 12 (91 532 67 37/www.museo-chicote. com). Metro Gran Vía. **Open** 8am-2am Mon-Sat. **Admission** free. **Credit** AmEx, DC, MC, V. **Map** p324 I11.

The best Clubs

For non-stop dancing
Once it gets going, **El Sol**'s dancefloor is unstoppable. Escape on to the stage when the pace gets too much. *See p245.*

For catching Sesame Street
At **Siroco**, you can watch cartoons and kids' programmes while you get down to a sublime funk and soul selection. *See p250.*

For a budget night out
Live instruments alongside the DJ and no cover charge make **Tempo** a must when the euros are running low. *See p250.*

For objects of desire
Heartbreakingly gorgeous night owls steal the show at **Gold**. *See p252.*

For charming even the snakes
Asian influences, oriental dancers and even the odd snake-charmer are to be found at **Shabay**. *See p252.*

For a cool night out
Arctic-strength air-conditioning or an outdoor terrace are the only things that will get you through the summer months. **Ananda** is the biggest terrace, and the best. *See p250.*

Arts & Entertainment

Independents' day

What's the perfect remedy for a city plagued by a tired and flabby dance-music scene and the closure of several of its best medium-sized concert venues? An indie revival, that's what. And it's not just floppy haircuts and baggy-ness that have exploded all over Madrid; goth has made a major comeback too, with black PVC trenchcoats and safety pins replacing cool clubwear.

If you're pining for the UK, try stepping into the teleportation device that is **Supersonic** (C/Meléndez Valdes 25, www.myspace.com/supersonicmadrid), an always-rammed indie bar where Cool Britannia still rules the airwaves. Here, *Melody Maker* covers from days gone by adorn the walls, while the DJs bang out a cocktail of indie, Beatles tracks and punk – all mixed to imperfection on slightly dodgy CD decks with slightly scratched CDs. This is the after-show venue par excellence when any of the big international bands plays Madrid, often attracting the band members themselves. Kaiser Chiefs put on a legendary display of drunken bar-top dancing here in 2006.

Chugging tech-house has given way to indie, pop and electro at Sala de Nombre Público, with a double helping of nocturnal antics from **Low** and **New Order Club** – the former in the big room, the latter in the back (*see p243*). Low provides an eclectic mix of live acts and DJs, including many record spinners from well-known bands (Placebo's bass player was a recent guest). In New Order, expect the unexpected, as DJs dust off that Rage Against the Machine track everyone used to love in the 1990s and mix it up with some electro-clash and grunge.

For choice of name alone, a visit to **Dark Hole** (C/Mesonero Romanos 13, Sol & Gran Vía, 91 758 04 50, www.tripfamily.com) must be on your gothic agenda when in Madrid. Slap that eyeliner on, make sure your piercings are in place, and leave the handbag behind in favour of one of those coffin backpacks – this is the really dark deal. But if you've satanic leanings, there's **666** (C/Aduana 21, Sol & Gran Vía, no phone, www.gothic666.net), where free entry and slightly cheaper drinks than the big clubs will have you playing devil's advocate.

Kitsch reigns supreme at **Tupperware** (*see p250*), where there are more plastic figures, neon lights and gaudy posters on display than in a 12-year-old's bedroom. One of the staple bars on the Malasaña route, this place is always packed and always banging out top rock and indie tracks. *Star Wars* memorabilia is merely the icing on the cake.

Tucked away in a backstreet parallel to Gran Vía, **Home Bar** (C/Fomento 30, no phone, Los Austrias) is a shrine to Basildon's finest export. Depeche Mode are worshipped in this indie haven, which pulls in the Britophile punters thanks to the singular musical selection and the distinctly Depeche decor.

Museo Chicote was famously a haunt of Ernest Hemingway. It is now a cocktail bar run by Trip Family, the promoters responsible for the best gay nights in town. The crowd is *super-fashion*, and enjoys the sublime soundtrack provided by the city's coolest DJs. On a Thursday night you can catch Spain's answer to Gilles Peterson, DJ Sandro Bianchi, playing electro-soul, funk, hip hop and anything with a groove.

Oba-Oba

C/Jacometrezo 4, Sol & Gran Vía (no phone). Metro Callao. **Open** 7pm-5am Mon-Thur, Sun; 7pm-6am Fri, Sat. **Admission** €5-€12. **No credit cards**. **Map** p323 F11.

The programme at Oba-Oba is well established. The forecast is always for live music early on, giving way later to steady outbreaks of Brazilian beats. The tunes are set on auto-pilot during the week, but at the weekend expect DJ sessions. The crowd is very adept at shaking its booty samba style. Reputed to serve the best caipirinhas in the city.

Ocho y Medio

C/Mesonero Romanos 13 (91 541 35 00/www.trip family.com). Metro Callao or Gran Vía. **Open** 1-6am Fri. **Admission** €10 (incl 1 drink). **No credit cards**. **Map** p323 H11.

Although somewhat anachronistic, Ocho y Medio is the perfect stop on your hedonistic tour of the town if you're looking for an alcohol-fuelled mass of party energy. DJ Smart makes it all sound very '80s and '90s, thrashing out an eclectic mix of indie, electro-clash, electro-pop, new wave and New York rock. It takes a master to meld Blur and Depeche Mode.

Ohm

Bash, Plaza Callao 4 (91 541 35 00/www.tripfamily. com). Metro Callao. **Open** midnight-6am Fri, Sat. **Admission** (incl 1 drink) €10. **No credit cards**. **Map** p323 G11.

While some nights come and go with alarming frequency, Trip Family's Ohm is one that's here for the duration. Strictly speaking it's a gay night, but it's too much fun (and too central) for the straight crowd

Arts & Entertainment

to stay away. The result is a friendly party atmosphere with soulful, vocal-driven house tracks mixed to perfection by residents Kike Boy and Tetsu.

Palacio de Gaviria

C/Arenal 9 (91 526 60 69/www.palaciogaviria.com). Metro Ópera or Sol. **Open** 11pm-3am Mon-Wed; 10.30pm-6am Thur-Sat; 11.30pm-3.30am Sun. **Admission** (incl 1 drink) €10 Mon-Thur; €15 Fri, Sat; €12 Sun. **Credit** AmEx, DC, MC, V. **Map** p327 G11.

Prepare to go large in a stately 19th-century palace. Ascend the splendid sweeping staircase, and enter a multitude of rooms with three dancefloors playing pumping dance tunes, Spanish pop and 1980s favourites. Portraits hang on the walls and frescoes adorn the ceilings… imagine the Ministry of Sound in Kensington Palace and you're halfway there. Thursdays see the International Party attracting foreign students, expats and a smattering of tourists. There are tango and salsa classes too (Mon-Fri, 8pm).

Sala Wind

C/Montera 25, entrance at Plaza del Carmen s/n (no phone). Metro Gran Vía or Sol. **Open** midnight-6am, Thur-Sat. **Admission** (incl 1 drink) €10-€14. **Map** p327 H11.

After the closure of several of the city's finer nighteries, Madrid needed a new club. The answer, my friend, was blowing in the Wind: this old venue got a serious makeover and flung open its doors four nights a week. Wednesdays see drum and bass or hip hop, Thursdays are turned over to tech and electro house, Fridays are gay night Spank (*see p224*), while Saturdays are Elástico, mixing up rock, electro, indie and everything in between. **Photo** *p241.*

El Sol

C/Jardines 3 (91 532 64 90/www.elsolmad.com). Metro Gran Vía or Sol. **Open** 11pm-5am Tue-Thur; 11pm-6am Fri, Sat. **Admission** (incl 1 drink) €9. **Credit** (bar only) MC, V. **Map** p327 H11.

To call this music joint and club 'no-frills' is an understatement – as its faded yellow walls and middle-aged bar staff attest. However, as anyone knows, it's the music and crowd that make a night, and that's where El Sol is a winner. The DJ serves up an eclectic selection of unmixed rock, soul, funk and R&B. Before long you're lured on to the floor and there you will stay, getting down alongside a varied crowd of twenty- and thirtysomethings.

Suite

C/Virgen de los Peligros 4 (91 521 40 31/www.suitecafe.com). Metro Sevilla. **Open** 2-5pm Mon-Fri and 9.30pm-3am Mon-Thur; 9.30pm-4.30am Fri, Sat. **Admission** free. **Credit** AmEx, DC, MC, V. **Map** p327 H11.

This smart pre-club bar, which doubles as a restaurant, owes its look to many a London venue: glass, steel and leather sofas. Packed to the gills at the weekend, there are bouncers but normally no cover charge. The highlight is the upstairs dancefloor, supplying all you need to kick-start the evening.

Weekend

Bash, Plaza Callao 4 (91 541 3500/www.tripfamily.com). Metro Callao. **Open** midnight-5am Sun. **Admission** (incl 1 drink) €10. **No credit cards. Map** p323 G11.

Weekend is one of the longest standing and most successful Sunday club nights, with a funky feel. Resident DJ Roberto Rodriguez downshifts a gear from the harder revolutions of his other appearances and cruises with Latin and nu jazz, taking the mixed gay and straight crowd through to Monday morning.

Huertas & Santa Ana

Alhambra/El Buscón

C/Victoria 5 & 9 (91 521 07 08/91 522 54 12). Metro Sol. **Open** 11pm-3.30am Thur-Sat. **Admission** free. **No credit cards. Map** p327 H12.

Typically Spanish tapas bars by day, these two adjacent eateries assume a whole new identity come the weekend as DJs play a mix of everything from new flamenco and '80s pop to handbag house. Heavily Andaluz, the south of Spain leaps out from every ornately tiled alcove and arch. This place pulls in all sorts, from the international crowd to pony-tailed flamenco aficionados.

Bar de la Comedia

C/Príncipe 16 (91 521 51 64). Metro Sevilla or Sol. **Open** 10pm-3.30am daily. **Admission** free. **No credit cards. Map** p327 H12.

There's nothing funny about Bar de la Comedia. Instead expect a welcome change of pace on this frenzied strip. An international crowd do their thing to a steady soundtrack of hip hop, two step and R&B dance-floor grinders. The door staff are somewhat capricious in their admissions policy.

La Boca del Lobo

C/Echegaray 11 (91 429 70 13/www.labocadellobo.com). Metro Sevilla. **Open** 11pm-3.30am Wed, Thur; 11pm-5am Fri, Sat. **Admission** (incl 1 drink) €8 after 1am Fri, Sat; €5-6 for concerts, otherwise free. **Credit** V. **Map** p327 H12.

Unselfconsciously hip and unremittingly friendly, La Boca del Lobo combines live bands with a heady mix of house, breakbeats and R&B. Emerge from the sweaty downstairs dancefloor to the cramped bar area by the entrance or retire upstairs to find a seat (almost impossible after midnight at weekends) and watch the DJ spin a beguiling cocktail of music.

El Burladero

C/Echegaray 19 (no phone). Metro Sevilla or Sol. **Open** 8pm-4am daily. **Admission** free. **No credit cards. Map** p327 H12.

A cosmopolitan crowd, buzzing to the sound of flamenco and rumba, throngs the Moorish arches, amid Andalucian tiles and a rogues' gallery of bullfighters. Upstairs the rumba rumbles but doesn't dominate. Head up here for a respite and a chat with the languid barman, but the frenzied guitar and pistol-shot hand-clapping will eventually lure you back.

Cardamomo

C/Echegaray 15 (91 369 07 57). Metro Sevilla. **Open** 10pm-4am Mon-Sat. **Admission** free. **No credit cards. Map** p327 H12.

A firm fixture on the scene, this frenetic flamenco bar plays a mixture of flamenco and rumba tunes, often to thundering effect as the crowd dance, stamp and clap both on and off the diminutive dancefloor. On Wednesdays and Sundays there's a great variety of live flamenco and rumba acts.

Las Cuevas de Sésamo

C/Príncipe 7 (91 429 65 24). Metro Sevilla or Sol. **Open** 7pm-2am Mon-Thur, Sun; 7pm-2am Fri, Sat. **Admission** free. **No credit cards. Map** p327 H12.

It's easy to find this basement cavern at weekends – you just have to look for the queue that snakes out of the door. But it's well worth the wait for what's inside: las Cuevas is a sit-down affair, with live piano music from 9pm (except Monday), where punters take advantage of the cheapish drinks and friendly atmosphere. A good choice to start the night rather than a final destination.

La Fontana de Oro

C/Victoria 1 (91 531 04 20/www.fontanadeoro.com). Metro Sol. **Open** 11-6am daily. **Admission** free. **Credit** DC, MC, V. **Map** p327 H12.

As Madrid's oldest bar, this place used to be a real institution. These days, however, it's an Irish theme bar. It's run-of-the-mill during the day, but everything changes when night falls. Then the crowd packs in, fuelling up for the night ahead and losing themselves to a mix of classic beer anthems and a variety of live music.

Kapital

C/Atocha 125 (91 420 29 06/www.grupo-kapital. com). Metro Atocha. **Open** *Night session* midnight-6am Thur-Sat. *Afternoon session* 6.30-10.30pm Fri-Sat. **Admission** *Night session* (incl 1 drink) €15. *Afternoon session* (incl 2 soft drinks) €8. **Credit** AmEx, DC, MC, V. **Map** p328 J14.

The Godzilla of Madrid clubs, with splendid views of the main dancefloor from many of the upper balconies: dance voyeur heaven. Of seven storeys, each has something different to offer: the main dancefloor and bars are at ground level; the first floor has karaoke; the second R&B and hip hop; the third cosy cocktail bars; the fourth is Spanish disco; the fifth has a cinema and more cool sounds, and at the top is a terrace with a retractable roof. No trainers.

Sala Stella

C/Arlabán 7 (91 523 86 54/91 522 88 26/www.web-mondo.com). Metro Sevilla. **Open** 1am-6am Thur; 1am-7am Fri, Sat. **Admission** (incl 1 drink) €12 Thur; €13 Fri, Sat (€11 with flyer). **Credit** AmEx, DC, MC, V. **Map** p328 I11.

If you only go to one club in Madrid, make sure it's this one. Time was when Mondo (Thursdays and Saturdays) and Room (Fridays) played vastly differing styles, but these days you'll most likely hear the same records spun: electro house, verging on

techno. Room relies on a regular stable of guest DJs, while Mondo flies in some of the hottest talent from Europe – particularly Berlin. **Photos** *p242.*

Torero

C/Cruz 26 (91 523 11 29). Metro Sol. **Open** 11.30pm-4.30am Tue, Wed; 11.30pm-6am Thur-Sat. **Admission** (incl 1 drink) free Tue, Wed; €10 Thur-Sat. **No credit cards. Map** p327 H12.

Don't be put off by the forbidding exterior, the only thing not dancing inside Torero is a wall-mounted bull's head that stares down impassively at the mostly local crowd. The ground floor gyrates to a mixture of Spanish and Latin beats, while on the floor below house reverberates off the red-brick walls. No trainers.

Rastro & Lavapiés

If you're interested in some impromptu late-night flamenco, try **Candela** (*see p51*).

Bar San Lorenzo

C/Salitre 38 (no phone). Metro Lavapiés. **Open** 5pm-2.30am daily. **Admission** free. **No credit cards. Map** p328 H14.

Also known as Taurino or, more commonly, 'that bar on Salitre', the San Lorenzo has no sign. Stained-glass windows and furniture that could have been found on the street lend this intimate, smoky and candlelit venue a kooky charm. Dreadlocked and sarong-clad staff alternate tripped-out dub CDs with minimal sounds.

El Juglar

C/Lavapiés 37 (91 528 43 81/www.salajuglar.com). Metro Lavapiés. **Open** 9.30pm-3am Mon-Thur; 9.30pm-3.30am Fri-Sun. *Concerts* usually start at 10pm. **Admission** *Bar* free. *Concerts* average €5. **No credit cards. Map** p327 H14.

Epitomising Lavapiés – a bohemian, cool and laid-back hangout for those who like the tempo of their evening to be energetic but not too frenetic. The bare red brick and chrome front bar provides a chilled background for the broad-based crowd and soundtrack of jazz and soul. After midnight the rhythm speeds up in the back as the resident DJ Señores de Funk spins a mix of souped-up soul, Latin and funk. Sunday nights see flamenco performed by students from the nearby Amor de Dios school.

Kappa

C/Olmo 26 (no phone). Metro Antón Martín. **Open** 8.30pm-3am daily. Closed 10 days mid Aug. **Admission** free. **No credit cards. Map** p328 H13.

An unprepossessing and easily missed little hideaway, Kappa is amiable and intimate and, despite its complete lack of decor, somehow cosy. This chameleon of *locales* has built up quite a cult following among those who feel life should have an unhurried pace, and the DJ plays a bit of everything as long as it's mellow. This is an ideal pre-club launch pad or a haven where you can kick back and chill out when Madrid threatens to overwhelm.

La Lupe

C/Torrecilla del Leal 12 (91 527 50 19). Metro Antón Martín. **Open** 9pm-2.30am Mon-Wed; 9pm-3.30am Thur-Sun. **Admission** free. **No credit cards. Map** p328 H13.

Now with a sister bar in C/Hortaleza, La Lupe is a microcosm of everything that makes Madrid the city it is. The signs on the walls say it all, from the notice that welcomes gays and lesbians to the poster protesting against any law that prohibits bars staying open until whatever ungodly hour they please. A diverse and open-minded crowd enjoys Mojitos mixed to perfection in this alternative nightspot, which also hosts cabaret nights.

La Ventura

C/Olmo 31 (91 521 48 54). Metro Antón Martín. **Open** 10.30pm-2.30am Tue-Thur; 11pm-3am Fri, Sat; 8pm-2.30am Sun. **Admission** free. **No credit cards. Map** p328 H13.

You might not know the place's name, but if you've been in Madrid a while, you're sure to have been here at least once. Lounge on full-length floor cushions while soaking up the measured sounds of trip hop and dub. Later the pace hots up a little with breakbeat, electronica and house thrown in, and the dancefloor is filled by a cosmopolitan crowd of students, ex-students and the casually hip.

Chueca

Areia

C/Hortaleza 92 (91 310 03 07/www.areiachillout. com). Metro Chueca. **Open** 1pm-2.30am Mon-Thur, Sun; 1pm-3am Fri, Sat. **Admission** free. **Credit** AmEx, DC, MC, V. **Map** p324 I9.

Once an Irish bar, Areia has been transformed beyond recognition into a chill-out space that has all the angles covered: by day it's somewhere to get lunch or a snack, in the afternoon it becomes a place to chill, and by the evening the vibe has hotted up enough for a cool crowd that passes through on their nightly tour of the city. The seductive Eastern decor, along with sofas and cushions on which to lounge, can make it difficult to leave.

Mito

C/Augusto Figueroa 3 (91 531 89 96/www.disco mito.com). Metro Chueca. **Open** 11pm-7am daily. **Admission** free before 2am; €8 2-4.30am; €15 4.30-6am. **No credit cards. Map** p324 H10.

One of the few clubs in Madrid that is open every night of the week, this is one to avoid at the weekend. Instead, take advantage of Mito midweek if you really can't wait till Thursday for your all-nighter. A mix of older house tracks and Latin dance grooves await you, along with a crowd that just doesn't know when to stop.

Pachá

C/Barceló 11 (91 447 01 28). Metro Tribunal. **Open** midnight-6am Thur-Sat. **Admission** (incl 1 drink) €12. **Credit** AmEx, DC, MC, V. **Map** p324 H8.

El Perro. *See p250.*

Arts & Entertainment

Hey Mister DJ

Time was when Ibiza was the only place in Spain to turn up any decks talent. Not so these days, with a healthy stable of DJs emerging from a maturing local scene in Madrid, many finding recognition on the national and international circuit. **Wally López** of Weekend Records is Madrid's DJ superstar, having seen Europe-wide success with his instantly recognisable remix of David Guetta's 'A Little More Love'. His own productions and remixes are funky house grooves that sparkle with inventiveness. Signed to the UK label Underwater, he's made guest appearances in Ibiza, Paris, Los Angeles, Tel Aviv, Barcelona and Fabrik in Madrid (*see p252*) and had a residency at Pacha in Ibiza with Pete Tong and another in at The End in London.

Simón García and his partner **Karim Shaker** (*pictured*) are the producers responsible for defining the Madrid sound that's currently garnering support overseas. Under monikers including Sundayprayers, Latin Soul Drivers, Beatfreakers and plain old Simon & Shaker, they have already racked up a back catalogue of dancefloor stormers that have been given plenty of airtime by the BBC's Pete Tong, Roger Sánchez and the king of tribal beats Danny Tenaglia.

Their *Underground Sound of Madrid*, with label collaborator Dimas, showcases not only considerable mixing talents but also the style that characterises the local scene – dark, driving tribal house that hits you with deep grooves and then sets you spinning with its moody instrumental breaks.

On a funkier tip is the **Hi-Top** collective, a record label founded in Madrid by New Yorker David Lapof (aka El Gran Lapofski). It specialises in jazz, funk and Latin beats. As well as David's own sublime selections (see compilations such as *Spain is Different*), label-mate Ruben 'Watch TV' García has dusted off some rarities for his After School Special series. Catch the Hi-Top crew in venues such as Marula (*see p243*).

Look out for **Sandro Bianchi**, the Italian-born (but Madrid-based) DJ and producer. Sandro mixes up a selection of electronica fused with jazz, soul, funk and bossa, and touching on hip hop. As well as his residency in Museo Chicote (*see p243*), Sandro guests all over Spain, particularly at fashion events, and is on contract to mix the sound-tracks for various stores, including the luxury goods vendors Loewe.

Finally, for sheer control of a big room, the resident DJ and promoter of Deep (at Changó, *see p252*), **JL Magoya** is Madrid's Mr House. Not only does he work a crowd to perfection, but José Luis is personally responsible for bringing some of the biggest international names to town. These have included Carl Cox, whose following is so big in Madrid that only the mammoth Fabrik (*see p252*) can host his visits.

In a club scene that ditches the glitz, Pachá is the black sheep. The bouncers may claim it's for royal relatives and the jet set, but it mainly attracts rich kids and posers. Dress up to get in, and expect glamorous go-gos, on-stage dance routines and themed parties, enacted to a soundtrack of soulful house. Wednesdays are hip hop nights, with appearances from the likes of local star Jotamayuscula and Grandmaster Flash. Not on a par with its Ibiza namesake, but fun for those who like a bit of glam.

Stromboli

C/Hortaleza 96 (91 319 46 28). Metro Alonso Martinez. **Open** 6.30pm-3.30am daily. **Credit** MC, V. **Map** p324 I9.

A very cool little lounge that's perfect for a mid-week drink or as a stop on your weekend tour of the town. Very much part of the hip scene around C/Hortaleza and C/Fuencarral, and a place where the club DJs of Madrid drop their big-room style and spin something a little more intimate.

Malasaña & Conde Duque

Binomio

C/Corredera Baja de San Pablo 26, Malasaña (no phone). Metro Tribunal. **Open** 10.30pm-5.30am Mon-Sat. **Admission** free. **No credit cards. Map** p323 H9.

Camper than the Christmas lights with which it's decorated, this cabaret club is quite something. It's also something quite unusual. Drag queens, magicians, bolero singers and more than a few flamenco dancers perform in the most intimate of surroundings, and audience participation is hardly optional. Shows start at 1am, or 2am at weekends.

Café Rock Corto Maltés

Plaza Dos de Mayo 9 (91 531 13 17). Metro Bilbao or Tribunal. **Open** 7pm-2am Mon-Sun; 7pm-3am Fri, Sat. **Admission** free. **Credit** DC, MC, V. **Map** p323 G8.

As well as a sizeable summertime terrace outside, Corto has a great vibe inside, with a troupe of guest DJs spinning a varied selection of deep house, electro and floor-fillers. When summer is over and the terrace is closed, the party doesn't end. Sadly the cavernous basement, the erstwhile haunt of after-hours fun, is no longer open.

Démodé

C/Ballesta 7 (mobile 678 50 52 37). Metro Chueca. **Open** 11pm-3.30am Thur-Sat. **Admission** free. **No credit cards.** Map p323 H10.

The flyers let you know what you're in for – an elegant figure reclines against a backdrop of flock wallpaper in a juxtaposition of the übertrendy and the super-cheesy. This pre-club joint is housed in an old brothel. Faux oil paintings still adorn the walls, but red lighting, sofas and an ample sound system have transformed it into one of the coolest nightspots of the moment. DJs spin both underground house and electro for a mixed gay/straight crowd.

Le Garage

Parking Plaza de los Mostenses (no phone/www.my space.com/legaragemadrid). Metro Plaza España. **Open** 11pm-5.30am Thur, last Sat of the month. **Admission** (incl 1 drink) €10. **Credit** AmEx, MC, V. **Map** p323 F9.

Madrid has a long tradition of putting great clubs in very odd places – disused gyms, train stations, sex shops – but the promoters of Le Garage have surpassed them all by plonking this electro night in a karaoke bar opposite the pay station of an underground car park. Walk down the ramps, locate the exit and look for the bouncers. A mix of local DJs and international names call in, there are regular live acts, and there is that great underground vibe that only a venue as scummy as this one can create.

Morocco

C/Marqués de Leganés 7 (91 531 51 67/www. morocco-madrid.com). Metro Santo Domingo. **Open** midnight-6am Fri, Sat. **Admission** (incl 2 drinks) €10. **No credit cards. Map** p323 F10.

Once owned by Movida legend Alaska, Morocco has two feet firmly planted in the past. From its '80s décor and crowd, everything here smacks of days gone by. The DJ mixes mainly classic Spanish pop with today's nu flamenco. Despite all this throwback action, it's still great fun, being completely free of pretension and brimming with dancefloor energy.

Nasti

C/San Vicente Ferrer 33 (91 521 76 05). Metro Tribunal. **Open** midnight-6am Fri, Sat. **Admission** (incl 1 drink) €7.50. **No credit cards. Map** p323 G9.

The remit here is simple – pack out a small and smoky *sala* with a fiercely loyal crowd, and play anything from the Sex Pistols to Joy Division to make them dance. A riotous, grungy and alternative crowd find their home here, enjoying the live acts such as Fanny Pack or Humbert Humbert and the guest DJs such as 2 Many DJs.

El No.1

C/Minas 1 (no phone). Metro Noviciado. **Open** 7pm-1am Mon-Thur; 7pm-2am Fri, Sat. **Admission** free. **No credit cards. Map** p323 G9.

Spacious, friendly and soothingly decorated, this is an oasis of calm in the desert storm of Madrid's nightlife. With a café-style air, the easygoing crowd partake of whatever exotic tea, coffee or *copa* takes their fancy. Downstairs hosts DJs at weekends who spin a subtle web of jazz and Latin house.

Oui

C/Marqués de Santa Ana 11 (no phone). Metro Noviciado. **Open** 11pm-3am Thur; 11pm-3.30am Fri, Sat. Closed mid Aug. **Admission** free. **No credit cards. Map** p323 G9.

A truly unique bar, Oui is damn difficult to find but worth the search. Its bizarre shape and eclectic music policy – expect anything from early techno to present-day electronica, along with a knowledgeable and loyal clientele, make this a gem among the sometimes mediocre bars of Malasaña.

Arts & Entertainment

El Perro de la Parte Atrás del Coche

C/Puebla 15 (no phone/www.elperroclub.com).
Metro Gran Vía. **Open** 9.30pm-3.30am daily.
Admission (min consumption) €6. **No credit cards.** **Map** p323 H10.

As the unusual name (it means the 'nodding dog') suggests, everything about El Perro is different. The music policy is a mix-up of everything, with hip hop, house, soul and funk from the resident DJs. The live acts take in heavy metal, so you might get Aretha Franklin one night and a Metallica tribute band the next. The crowd comes from all walks of life. A mix that shouldn't work, but really does. **Photos** *p247*.

Radar

C/Amaniel 22 (no phone). *Metro Noviciado or Plaza de España.* **Open** 10pm-2.30am Thur; 10.30pm-3.30am Fri, Sat; 9.30pm-2am Sun. **Admission** free. **No credit cards.** **Map** p323 F9.

For those who get off on experimental electronic music, this is a must-visit venue. Small and dark, the decor – minimalist 1980s computer-game chic – forms the perfect backdrop. When the DJs hit the decks at weekends the electronica, noise and techno enthusiasts flock, and like all good venues it manages to draw you completely into its world.

Sala Dink

C/Amaniel 13 (no phone). *Metro Noviciado.* **Open** midnight-6am Fri, Sat. **Admission** (incl 1 drink) €12. **No credit cards.** **Map** p323 F8.

The star has fallen a bit for this once legendary venue. Despite a refit, Dink is fighting to regain a following. Fridays are Last, with resident DJs from Sala Stella playing electro house and techno. After the long-running Coppelia ran out of venues to get chucked out of, the promoters abandoned the name and started Parabellum on Saturdays in Dink, keeping their industrial-edged house and techno.

Siroco

C/San Dimas 3 (91 593 30 70/www.siroco.es).
Metro Noviciado. **Open** 9.30pm-5am Thur; 9.30pm-6am Fri, Sat. **Admission** (incl 1 drink) €5-€8. **No credit cards.** **Map** p323 F8.

A wonderfully creative crew run Siroco, something that is abundantly clear from their flyers, their programme and the visuals of the club itself. Doubling as a live music venue, it starts to hot up after the concerts finish at around 2am, when a crowd composed mainly of wannabe b-boys, club kids and beardy young students get down to the soul, funk and rare groove seven-inchers deftly woven together by the resident DJs.

Tempo

C/Duque de Osuna 8 (91 547 7518). *Metro Plaza España.* **Open** *Sept-June* 5pm-3am daily. *July* 5pm-3am Mon-Sat. Closed Aug. **Admission** free. **Credit** MC, V. **Map** p323 E9.

A very cool little venue that doubles as a café by day and a venue at night for live acts and DJs. In the pleasant upstairs café you can sit and have a bite,

but as the night wears on, head downstairs, either to the dimly lit chill-out room or the dancefloor bathed with psychedelic projections. The in-house DJ is often accompanied by live percussion.

Tetería No.2

C/Pez 16 (no phone). *Metro Noviciado.* **Open** *Sept-June* 6pm-3.30am Tue-Sun. *July, Aug* 7pm-3.30am Tue-Sun. **No credit cards.** **Map** p323 G10.

The sister venue of El No.1 (*see p249*). Pay careful attention to the names: if you visit them in that suggested order, you'll find yourself nicely warmed up and all ready to dance by the time you arrive at No.2. The split-level venue is narrow but spacious upstairs, the bar by the entrance giving way to a large salon. The downstairs *sala* is a wonderful arched cave, with a higher volume designed to make you dance. Funk and soul music predominate, with occasional live acts.

Tupperware

C/Corredera Alta de San Pablo 26 (no phone). *Metro Tribunal.* **Open** 9pm-3.30am daily. **Admission** free. **No credit cards.** **Map** p323 H9.

Truly postmodern, this place is outrageously kitsch but with a pop art sensibility that saves it from crossing over too far into tackiness. The fake fur, *Star Wars* pictures and the faux-cool 1970s psychedelia hang together surprisingly well, and there's a pleasant anything-goes music policy that brings all kinds of sounds from acid jazz to house to soul. The crowd, slightly older and with less to prove, tend to chill out in the easygoing vibe.

Salamanca & the Retiro

Ananda

Estación de Atocha, Avda Ciudad de Barcelona s/n. *(91 524 11 44/www.ananda.es).* *Metro Atocha.* **Open** midnight-7am Fri, Sat. **Admission** (incl 1 drink) €12. **Credit** AmEx, DC, V. **Map** p328 K15.

This is the mother of all club terraces: the enormous 2,000-square-metre complex comes complete with two dancefloors (one indoors and one out), ten bars and plenty of cushion-strewn sofas and chairs, all of them done up in a bit of an Eastern theme. The regular clientele generally ranges from your usual fresh-faced clubby kids (especially on Sundays for the Sundance parties, where sounds are vocal and tech house) to older guys in suits out sharking for ladies. It isn't cheap, but from June to August you'd pay almost anything to stay cool in the city.

North & west

Argüelles

DU:OM

Sala Heineken, C/Princesa 1 (91 547 57 11/www. salarena.com/www.duomclub.com). *Metro Plaza de España.* **Open** midnight-6am Fri, Sat. **Admission** varies. **Map** p323 E9.

Marula. *See p243.*

A dual-personality club night, with diametrically opposed sounds on each floor. Downstairs Iván Pica and Hugo Serra mix a bang-up-to-date selection of electro house tracks with whooshing high-level sweeps and pounding 4/4 beats that keep the crowd dancing all night long. Upstairs it's an anything-goes policy with Spanish pop (or *pachanga*) thrown together with commercial hip hop, cheesy dance tracks and eurotrance.

Gold

C/Ventura Rodríguez 7 (no phone). Metro Plaza España or Ventura Rodríguez. **Open** 1am-7.30am Fri, Sat. **Admission** (incl 1 drink) €15. **No credit cards. Map** p323 E9.

Where the pretty people go to dance. It was promoted by Spanish actress Paz Vega and, as you would expect from a film star, the emphasis in her club is on glamour. DJs Pablo Sánchez and Sandro Bianchi whack out the sexy house tunes and the crowd enjoy checking themselves out in the mirrors.

Chamberí

Changó

C/Covarrubias 42 (91 446 00 36). Metro Alonso Martínez. **Open** midnight-6am Thur, Fri. **Admission** (incl 1 drink) €10 Thur; €12 Fri. **Map** p324 I7.

One of Madrid's clubs converted from old theatres, Changó plays host to two top nights. First up is Nature, a long-running Thursday night dedicated to breaks, electro and techno. Second is Deep, a night that's suffered a series of venue problems, having passed through three different *salas* in the space of about a year. It's finally downsized to Changó, although giving up a large-capacity venue has meant giving up the big-name DJs; no more Erick Morillo or Roger Sánchez, it's now local talent. Still, the crowd is young, loyal and well up for it, and Deep continues to bring the city one of its best nights out.

Moma 56

C/José Abascal 56 (91 399 09 00/www.moma56.com). Metro Alonso Cano or Gregorio Marañón. **Open** midnight-6am Wed-Sun. **Admission** (incl 1 drink) €10. **No credit cards. Map** p321 J5.

If it's a bit of glamour you're looking for and you actually feel up to the challenge of getting through the door, then you should probably check out Moma 56. Multifunctional in a New York style, the venue is a restaurant, bar and nightclub, with stylish decor and a semi-celebrity crowd.

Shabay

C/Miguel Ángel 3 (91 319 76 92/www.shabay.com). Metro Rubén Darío. **Open** 11.30pm-5am Tue-Thur; 11.30pm-6am Fri, Sat; 9pm-3am Sun. Closed 2wks mid Aug. **Admission** (incl 1 drink) €15. **Credit** AmEx, DC, MC, V. **Map** p324 K6.

Full of Eastern promise, Shabay has lots of intricate decoration and a carefully crafted atmosphere, with oriental and Afrobeat sounds. From Tuesday to

They're getting Deep at **Changó**.

Saturday the place functions as a nightclub, but on Sundays the pace drops a few notches for a chill-out session complete with incense, candles and a selection of treats from Indian and Thai cuisine.

Chamartín

Macumba

Estación de Chamartín (91 733 35 05/902 49 99 94/ www.comunidadspaceofsound.com). Metro Chamartín. **Open** midnight-6am Fri, Sat; 9am-8.30pm Sun. **Admission** (incl 1 drink) €12. **No credit cards.**

Friday night is Danzoo (*see p242*); Saturdays see Sunflowers for an Ibizan vibe and lots of go-go dancers; but the really crowd-puller is Space of Sound on Sundays. It's the city's biggest all-day party, and what a monster it is. The crowd is weirdly territorial, with one area that's mainly gay, another that's predominantly straight and even a group of transsexuals claiming an area by one of the bars. The sound system here is unmatched and, along with the resident DJs – specialists in both tech and progressive house – the promoters bring in the likes of Deep Dish and Steve Lawler.

South of centre

Fabrik

Avda de la Industria 82, Ctra Fuenlabrada-Moralejos de Enmedio (mobile 699 90 96 81/ www.grupo-kapital.com). Metro Fuenlabrada then bus 496, 497. **Open** 11pm-6am Sat; 10am-midnight occasional Sun. **Admission** (incl 1 drink) €18. **Credit** AmEx, DC, MC, V.

Fabrik is a converted warehouse kitted out with a dazzling array of disco surprises: a 60kw sound system; a huge outdoor terrace complete with a fake river and two covered dancefloors; and, in the main arena, a vertical and horizontal megatron to shoot freezing nitrogen into the crowd. The monthly Sunday session Goa is the highlight (see www.trip-family.com for info). It's a bit of a schlep to get here, but well worth the taxi fare.

Sport & Fitness

Preparations for the 2016 bid are already improving Madrid's sport facilities.

Having narrowly lost out to London in the quest to host the 2012 Olympics, Mayor Ruiz-Gallardón, undaunted, announced that Madrid would bid again for the 2016 Games. Quite how wise a decision this is remains to be seen: many pundits believe that a North American city will be chosen next time in the name of diversity. Until the IOC announces the winning candidate in 2009, Madrid continues with its irksome major public works schemes that are deemed as necessary for the bid to get the games as the construction of sports facilities, some 70 per cent of which the authorities claim are already in place or under construction.

Madrid is home to three Primera División clubs (eternal rivals Atlético and Real Madrid, along with plucky upstarts Getafe), and two of Spain's top basketball clubs; what's more, it hosts one of Europe's most prestigious marathons, and is the setting for the finish of the famous Vuelta a España cycling race. Since 2003 the city has also been on the Tennis Masters circuit and hopes to attract Grand Slam tennis as of 2008, when the 'Caja Mágica' ('Magic Box'), a purpose-built arena, opens.

Spectator sports

Athletics/atletismo

Estadio de la Comunidad de Madrid
Avda de Arcentales s/n, Eastern suburbs (91 720 24 00). Metro Las Musas.
This stadium, only partly built, was the centrepiece of Madrid's 2012 Olympic bid and is likely to be a key part of the 2016 project, although it is currently closed. Should the next Olympic bid not prosper, the city council hopes to persuade Atlético de Madrid to move here in some kind of part-exchange deal for the *rojiblancos*' current ground, the Vicente Calderón, which occupies a plot on the banks of the Manzanares river that the council wants to redevelop. Meanwhile, and once the bid is launched, it is likely the council will re-open the stadium for athletics and other events.

Palacio de Deportes de la Comunidad de Madrid
Avda Felipe II s/n, Salamanca (91 258 60 16/www.palaciodedeportes.com). Metro Goya. **Map** p325 O9.
This state-of-the-art 16,000-capacity sports palace was inaugurated in early 2005 and occupies the site where its predecessor stood until it was destroyed by fire four years previously. It is a multi-purpose venue

which can host a wide range of indoor sports thanks to a modern system of retractable stands. As well as sports, you can catch spectacles such as Disney on Ice or any number of rock concerts: Springsteen, Depeche Mode and Coldplay have all performed here.

Maratón Popular de Madrid
Information MAPOMA C/Galileo 74, Chamberí (91 447 96 31/www.maratonmadrid.org). **Open** 9.30am-2pm, 4.30-7.30pm Mon-Fri. **Map** p323 F6.
Madrid's marathon, always held on a Sunday in late April, has grown year after year both in number of participants and prestige and is now considered to be among the world's top ten. In 2007 the event celebrates its 30th year. The halfway mark is in the dead centre of the city; thousands of cheery folk collect in Puerta del Sol to egg on the tiring runners; an estimated million spectators annually take to the city streets to catch the race. A week or two earlier there is a half marathon, a 20km race, organised by Agrupación Deportiva Marathon (91 402 69 62, www.admarathon.es).

Basketball/baloncesto

Basketball is Spain's second most popular sport, and Madrid has two of the country's top teams: **Estudiantes** is the city's best-supported club, while **Real Madrid**, affiliated to the football club of the same name, is traditionally the more successful. Both teams regularly qualify for the all-important league play-offs that run in May to eventually decide the annual champions.

MMT Estudiantes
Telefónica Arena Madrid, Recinto Ferial Casa de Campo, Avda de Portugal s/n, Casa de Campo (91 588 93 93/www.madridespaciosycongresos.com). Metro Alto de Extremadura or Lago. **Map** p326 A11/12.
Since the beginning of the 2005-06 season, 'El Estu' has made the city council-owned Madrid Arena its home. The less successful of Madrid's clubs, Estudiantes nevertheless has passionate supporters. Among them, the most vociferous are a group known as 'La Demencia' who make for a great atmosphere when the team plays at home and even away. You can order tickets (€20-€60) at www.clubestudiantes.com and choose where to pick them up, or simply go in person to one of the sales points listed on the website under 'Entradas' and 'Venta anticipada en tiendas'. Alternatively, call the club on 91 562 40 22.

Real Madrid
Palacio Vistalegre, C/Utebo 1, Southern suburbs (91 398 43 32/91 398 43 81/902 28 17 08/www.realmadrid.com). Metro Oporto or Vista Alegre.

A game of two sides

In the last 50 years Real Madrid have won trophies with clockwork regularity, and in doing so have picked up the support of the floating football voter throughout the country: a recent nationwide survey discovered that 43 per cent of Spaniards admitted to supporting the team they call 'El Real'. In the capital this figure extends to 70 per cent, with only 19 per cent supporting Real's city rivals Atlético de Madrid.

However, the statistics disguise a rather more complex reality. Atlético's 57,000-capacity Vicente Calderón stadium is a mere half-hour walk from Plaza Mayor, in a heavily populated working-class residential area, whereas the Santiago Bernabéu (capacity 75,000) finds itself in the swanky district of Chamartín further uptown. That means the working-class population of south and central Madrid tend to support '*los rojiblancos*' (Atleti, the 'red-and-whites') rather than '*los merengues*' (Real, the 'meringues'). While it's true to say that many Real Madrid match-going fans are from humble, local, working-class *barrios*, a good proportion of the Bernabéu faithful come in from the suburbs, from other cities in Spain, or from even further afield.

Thus the two sets of aficionados tend to behave very differently. Both teams have their nasty right-wing, flag-waving, stand-behind-the-goal-and-sing-throughout-the-match *ultras* (Real's Ultra Sur, Atleti's Frente Atlético). It's the behaviour of the average fan that is more telling. Atleti supporters, known as '*los indios*' (the Indians), sing more, wear their colours more, and get behind the team when they are losing. They pride themselves on their loyalty. In a recent spell in the depths of La Segunda (the second division, otherwise known as '*el infierno*', or hell) their stadium was virtually full every game. Atlético fans are so used to the slings and arrows of outrageous fortune that they have built the expectation of defeat into their collective personality. Their 100th anniversary song, contracted to be written and sung by hard-living singer-songwriter and Atleti fan Joaquín Sabina, rocks to the chorus '*Que manera de sufrir...*' ('What a way to suffer...') '*...que manera de palmar*' ('...what a way to lose a game we should have won').

Meanwhile Real fans ('*los vikingos*'), bloated until recently on a diet of almost constant success, need something really special to get them off their seats. They are quicker to turn against their team when things are going wrong, bringing out their white handkerchiefs to perform '*la pañolada*' (a method of showing dissatisfaction among football crowds) or, indeed, staying away altogether when the team is in a bad patch. Real's 100th-anniversary rendition of their traditional hymn reflects the self-important nature of the club: Plácido Domingo booms '*Hala Madrid... con su bandera limpia y blanca que no empaña*' ('Hail Madrid... with its clean white flag that never gets tarnished').

All this makes for a rather different viewing experience. At the Santiago Bernabéu, there's more likelihood of a spectacular home win, and you even get warmed by vast gas fires in winter. At the Vicente Calderón the warmth is more natural. You're less likely to enjoy the vicarious thrill of victory, it's true, but, whatever the result, you're in for a better atmosphere and a more emotional experience. You might even, if you're that way inclined, end up jumping up and down and joining the Atleti fans in their favourite song and ultimate insult '*¡Quién no bote madridista es, es!*' – 'Whoever doesn't pogo is a Real Madrid fan, oh yes they are.'

Alex Leith is the author of El Becks – A Season in the Sun.

Real Madrid's hoop stars have a trophy record to match that of the football team, and, after a few years in the doldrums look set to return to the top. The team lost its home when former club president Florentino Pérez sold the land to pay off the football team's huge debts and now play in the Palacio Vistalegre, until recently the home of city rivals Estudiantes. Expect exuberant professional cheerleaders.

Cycling/ciclismo

La Vuelta a España (www.lavuelta.com) is an enormous deal in the cycling world, with the best international cyclists competing with a ferocity and determination only surpassed by their efforts in the Tour de France. La Vuelta finishes in Madrid, where a knowledgeable crowd awaits the arrival of the time-triallers.

Football/fútbol

Madrid has three top-flight clubs, the world-famous **Real Madrid** (known as 'El Madrid'), the sometimes-successful **Atlético de Madrid** ('El Atleti') and the modest **Getafe CF** from the southern suburbs. While Real Madrid has historically been Spain's and Europe's most successful club, boasting a dazzling collection of silverware, the last three years have seen the failure of the 'Galácticos' model and the departure of Figo, Owen, Beckham and Ronaldo as well as Zidane retiring. While perennial Champions League qualification is practically certain for El Madrid, El Atleti are currently striving to return to Europe where they last played in 2000. Getafe's struggle is more of a bread-and-butter affair, survival in La Primera being the objective, something they have achieved admirably since promotion in 2004.

League matches are played on a Saturday or a Sunday evening, from September to May or June; at least one of the teams plays in Madrid every weekend. Cup and European matches are held during the week. Tickets can be very hard to come by, especially for Real Madrid games; if you can't get one at the ticket office, you might have to resort to buying a '*reventa*' ('resale') from one of the touts outside the ground. For shirts and various bits of fan-junk, *see p201* **Área Real Madrid**, or try the club shops. Atlético's shop, 1903 Megastore (www.tiendarojiblanca.com) is housed in the stadium.

Good coverage of Spanish football is to be found weekly in Sid Lowe's column at http://football.guardian.co.uk.

Atlético de Madrid

Estadio Vicente Calderón, Paseo Virgen del Puerto 67, South of centre (91 366 47 07/www.clubatletico demadrid.com/shop 91 366 82 37). Metro Pirámides.

Open *Ticket office* 10am-2pm, 5-8pm day before match; from 11am till kick-off on match days. **Tickets** €20-€42. **Credit** MC, V. **No credit cards**. Five years after bouncing back from a humiliating spell in the second division, 'El Atleti' are still chasing that elusive place in Europe. The young squad here is spearheaded by 22-year-old striker Fernando Torres and coached by the wily Mexican Javier Aguirre. The loyal '*rojiblanco*' faithful create a vibrant atmosphere in the 57,000-capacity Calderón stadium and, although the football itself can often leave more than a little to be desired, it is not uncommon for tickets to sell out entirely. When available, tickets can now be bought via the website, or by telephone: 902 530 500. In 2006, a museum was added near Gate 23 (91 365 09 31, closed Mon, admission €8-€3).

Real Madrid

Estadio Santiago Bernabéu, Paseo de la Castellana 144, Chamartín (91 398 43 00/www.realmadrid. com). Metro Santiago Bernabéu. **Open** *(guided tours)* 6-9pm daily, depending on match times. **Tickets** €15-€115. **Credit** AmEx, DC, MC, V. The club has won no titles other than the Spanish equivalent of the Charity Shield in recent seasons. It has suffered all manner of behind-the-scenes shenanigans, including recent presidential elections the results of which are currently being disputed in the law courts. And the era of the 'Galácticos' is surely fading. Yes, Real Madrid's present and future look decidedly iffy. Fans are looking to a new generation of players to bring back glory, something they expect from a club that has won more domestic and European honours than any other. Tickets can only be bought over the phone on 902 324 324.

Getafe CF

Avda Teresa de Calcuta s/n, Getafe (91 695 97 71/ www.getafecf.com). Metro Los Espartales. **Open** 10am-1pm, 5pm-8pm Mon-Fri in weeks before home games, 11.30am-half time match days. **Tickets** €30-€50. **No credit cards**. With the current name dating only from 1983, after the merger of two locally based regional league clubs, Getafe CF reached the top flight for the first time ever in 2004. Against all expectations the '*azulón*' team has not only stayed there but, under the management of Bernd Schuster, is looking ever-more like solid upper mid-table material, able to mix it with the best. Getting tickets for the 14,000-capacity stadium is not usually a problem as the fan base is relatively small, but may be problematic when one of the bigger teams is visiting.

Motor sports

Circuito del Jarama

Ctra de Burgos (A-I), km 27, San Sebastián de los Reyes (91 657 08 75/www.jarama.org). Bus 171 from Plaza de Castilla to Ciudad Santo Domingo. The last time the Jarama track hosted a Formula One race was way back in 1981, but it still has a full calendar of motorbike and truck racing.

Arts & Entertainment

Tennis

Telefónica Arena Madrid

*Recinto Ferial Casa de Campo, Avda de Portugal s/n
(91 588 93 93/www.madridespaciosycongresos.com/
arena). Metro Alto de Extremadura or Lago.*
Since 2002, Madrid has been on the Tennis Masters
circuit, annually hosting tournaments in the Madrid
Arena in the Casa de Campo. Look for information
on www.tennis-masters-madrid.com. A new venue
for top-level tennis, the 'Caja Mágica' ('Magic Box'),
is currently under construction and it is hoped to
bring Grand Slam tennis to the city from 2008.

Participatory sports

Billiards & pool/billares

Shooters Pool Hall & Bar

*Gran Vía 31 (91 522 40 10). Metro Callao or Gran
Vía.* **Open** 3.30pm-2.30am Mon-Thur; 3.30pm-3.30am
Fri; 4.30pm-3.30am Sat; 4.30pm-2.30am Sun. **Credit**
MC, V. **Map** p323 H11.
A fashionable international crowd shoot American
pool (€7-€10.50/hr) in this classy basement bar.

Bowling/boleras

Bowling Chamartín

*Área recreativa, Estación de Chamartín, C/Agustín
de Foxá (91 315 71 19/www.bowlingchamartin.com).*

Shooters, a stylish kind of pool hall.

Metro Chamartín. **Open** 10am-midnight Mon-Thur,
Sun; 10am-2am Fri, Sat. **Admission** (incl shoe hire)
€3.60-€5.10 after 5pm Sat, Sun. **No credit cards**.
A colourful 20-lane alley with a neon-lit bar, now the
oldest and most central in the city. It gets crowded
on Saturdays, when there's lots of whooping.

Football/fútbol

English Football League

Originally made up of British expats, this men's
fútbol sala league (outdoor five-a-side) is now multi-
national, with many Spanish and Latin American
players involved, and each season sees a qualifying
stage after which the league divides into two divisions.
Games are played on Sundays from 2-5pm at the
Colegio del Niño Jesús, just east of the Retiro (Avda
Menéndez Pelayo 65/metro Ibiza or Sainz de Baranda).
Teams are often looking for new talent; if you're in
Madrid for a while and want to get involved, take a
look at the website http://efl-madrid.com/index.htm
where you can place an announcement, or just turn up
and blag your way into a team. The standard varies;
the league is well organised but played in a spirit of
fun, and ages range from 16 to 40-plus.

Golf

Golf clubs around Madrid tend to be quite
exclusive, and expensive, affairs. A full list
of all courses in the Madrid region is available
on the web page of the Federación de Golf de
Madrid, www.fedgolfmadrid.com, click on
'Campos' on the home page and choose from
the many options that appear.

Club de Campo Villa de Madrid

*Ctra de Castilla, km 2 (91 550 08 40/www.clubvilla
demadrid.com). Bus 160 or 161 from Moncloa.*
Open 8am-sunset daily. **Rates** €14-€28.60 club
entry, plus €49.80-€93.70 course fee Mon-Fri.
No credit cards.
Co-designed by Seve Ballesteros, this is considered
the best and most difficult golf course near Madrid.
As well as golf, for members there are squash and
tennis courts, clay pigeon and range shooting, plus
hockey pitches, polo facilities, horse riding and a
swimming pool. It can be very crowded at weekends,
with priority given to members.

Horse riding/hípica

Indiana Parque Recreativo Natural

*Apdo Correos 32, San Martín de Valdeiglesias (91
861 27 99/www.indiana-sl.com). By bus 551 from
Estación Príncipe Pío/by car A-5 then M501
(58.5km).* **No credit cards**.
Trekking here involves crossing rivers and reservoirs, and going up mountains. Beginners can also
take classes in the riding school, or there's climbing, archery and canoeing. It's worth the schlep
out of town.

Splash out

As traffic, work hours and the cost of living grows and the siesta diminishes, Madrid is turning to spas and alternative therapies with increasing frequency.

The shining star of Madrid's current health and relaxation infatuation is the **Medina Mayrit** hammam. An instant hit with *madrileños* from the minute they opened, the baths are still so popular you need to call weeks in advance for a weekend booking. They are an oasis of calm, located just minutes from the bustling Puerta del Sol. A series of pools span out beneath arched ceilings, half lit by flickering lamps. One shallow pool of warm water abuts another of hot water, with a deeper pool of cold water nearby for a chilly plunge.

The company behind the hammam, El Grupo Al Andalus, prioritises historic authenticity. Masons from Andalucía were hired to lay the stone floors, which replicate the streets of Granada's Albaicín (Moorish quarter). The mosaic walls at the entrance are designed in the red, blue and green tiles found in the Alhambra. Upstairs, a tearoom/restaurant, La Colina de Almanzora, specialises in historic Arabic food.

Enthusiasts claim that the hammam provides relief for almost any ailment, from the common cold to arthritis and hangovers. The heat improves circulation, eliminates toxins and keeps the skin clean and supple. After a visit most people feel energised and refreshed, though if it's some deep relaxation you're after, book a 15-minute massage (for an extra fee).

Another good place to sweat out your sins is the **Acquaplaya** bath and spa in the basement of the Hotel Senator España. For €18 you can indulge in 90 minutes of soaking, steaming and swimming (floating oranges in one small pool are a fragrant diversion). Even quirkier is the *sala de relax* in the back, an '80s-style black room that makes your teeth glow. The hotel also provides massage, facials and other treatments, at reasonable prices.

Acquaplaya

Hotel Senator España, Gran Vía 70 (91 524 25 05/www.playasenator.com). Metro Plaza de España. **Open** 10am-10pm Tue-Sun. **Admission** €18 for 90mins. **Credit** AmEx, DC, MC, V. **Map** p323 F10.

Medina Mayrit

C/Atocha 14 (902 333 334/www.medina mayrit.com). Metro Sol or Tirso de Molina. **Open** 10am-2am (last entry midnight) daily. **Admission** *Baths* €23. *Baths & massage* (from 4pm & all day Sat, Sun) €35.50; before 4pm Mon-Fri €25; €23 concessions. **Credit** AmEx, DC, MC, V. **Map** p327 G12.

Las Palomas

Club Hípico, Ctra de Colmenar Viejo km 28.9 (91 803 31 76/mobile 670 972 150/www.telefonica.net /web/chlaspalomas). By bus 721, 724, 725, 726 from Plaza de Castilla. **Open** 10am-2pm, 5-7pm Tue-Sun. **No credit cards**.

Riding courses for all levels (from €145 for 10hrs).

Skiing

Before heading off to the ski resorts out of town, *madrileños* like to practise their turns at the vast Xanadu indoor skiing centre just outside Madrid. *See also p214.*

Squash

Gimnasio Argüelles

C/Andres Mellado 21-23, Moncloa (91 549 0040). Metro Argüelles. **Open** *Sept-July* 8am-11pm Mon-Fri; 9am-3pm Sat, Sun. *Aug* 10am-10pm Mon-Fri. **Rates** *Squash* €18/hr. *Gym* €8. **No credit cards**. **Map** p323 E6/7.

A fully equipped gym open to non-members, with a squash court for dedicated rubber-bashers.

Swimming pools/piscinas

There are many open-air swimming pools in Madrid: see www.munimadrid.es or pick up a leaflet at any municipally run sports centre. The most accessible are listed below. *See also p258* **Estadio Vallehermoso**. There's also a popular rooftop pool at the Hotel Emperador (Gran Vía 53, 91 547 28 00, www.emperador hotel.com). For Madrid' waterparks, *see p214.*

Open-air municipal pools

Piscinas Casa de Campo, Avda del Angel s/n, Casa de Campo (91 463 00 50). Metro Lago. **Open** 11am-9pm daily. Closed Oct-May. **Admission** €4.05. **No credit cards**.

Landlocked Madrid is stiflingly hot in the summer, so at weekends half the city seems to turn up at this beautiful leafy complex with three open-air pools set in green meadows. Topless bathing is tolerated, and there's an informal gay area. Of the other municipal pools, the Francos Rodríguez has a beach volleyball court, and the Barrio del Pilar and La Elipa have nude sunbathing areas; the latter has water chutes. All have the same hours and prices.

Other pools: Barrio del Pilar C/Monforte de Lemos 13-15, Northern suburbs (91 314 79 43); **Concepción** C/José del Hierro, Eastern suburbs (91 403 90 20); **La Elipa** Acceso del Parque de La Elipa, Eastern suburbs (91 459 98 11); **Francos Rodríguez** C/Numancia 1, Tetuán (91 459 98 71); **Moratalaz** C/Valdebernardo s/n, Eastern suburbs (91 772 71 21).

Indoor municipal pools

Piscina La Latina, Plaza de la Cebada 1 (91 365 80 31). Metro La Latina. **Open** 8.15am-7pm Mon-Thur; 8.15am-6pm Fri; 10am-8.30pm Sat, Sun. Closed Aug. **Admission** €4.10. **Credit** V. **Map** p327 F13.

The city has many indoor pools, most of which are open all year except August (hours may vary). La Latina is rather tatty, but convenient, being the only pool in central Madrid. Chamartín, a little further out, is Olympic sized, while the one at the Triángulo de Oro sports centre in Tetuan is easily accessible. **Other pools: Chamartín** Plaza del Perú s/n (91 350 12 23). **Tetuan** C/ Bravo Murillo 376 (91 571 41 17).

Canal de Isabel II

Avda Filipinas 54, Chamberí (91 533 96 42). Metro Canal or Rios Rosas. **Open** *Swimming pool* late May-early Sept 11am-8pm daily. **Admission** *Swimming pool* €3.50-€3.80. **No credit cards.**

Olympic-sized and children's pools, tennis courts, and a bar and restaurant, all with good wheelchair access. Very crowded at weekends.

Tennis

Tennis in Spain is accessible and reasonably priced, with numerous council-run clay and tarmac courts for hire. At municipal *polideportivos*, €5.30 gets you a court for an hour. The best city-run complex is the **Tenis Casa de Campo** in the Casa de Campo, close to the boating lake (91 464 96 17), which boasts 15 floodlit courts. The **Barrio del Pilar, Concepción** and **La Elipa** swimming pools (for all, *see above*) also have tennis courts, as does the **Canal de Isabel II** (*see above*; book in advance).

Arts & Entertainment

Fitness

Gyms/gimnasios

Bodhidharma

C/Moratines 18, South of centre (91 517 28 16/ www.bodhidharma-gym.com). Metro Acacias or Embajadores. **Open** *Sept-July* 8am-11pm Mon-Fri; 9am-2pm, 6-10pm Sat, Sun. 10am-3pm Sun. *Aug* 8am-11pm Mon-Fri; 9am-2pm Sat. **Rates** €51 per mth. **Credit** MC, V.

A well-equipped health club for men and women, with a sauna, free weights, machines and aerobics classes.

Votre Ligne

C/Lagasca 88, 1°, Salamanca (91 576 40 00/www. votre-ligne.com). Metro Nuñez de Balboa or Serrano. **Open** 8am-9.30pm Mon-Fri; 10am-2pm Sat. **Rates** €56 per mth. **Credit** AmEx, MC, V. **Map** p325 L/M7.

This classy, strictly-no-men joint offers classes, a sauna, jacuzzis, a pool and beauticians. There are special rates for non-members in summer.

Sports centres/polideportivos

Madrid has 48 city-owned and run sports centres. For details, see www.munimadrid.es; click on 'English' and then 'Sports'. Otherwise pick up a leaflet at any of them for information about others. Some are more basic than others, though the entrance fees are the same.

Estadio Vallehermoso

Avda de las Islas Filipinas 10, Chamberí (91 534 77 23). Metro Islas Filipinas. **Open** 8.30am-9.30pm Mon-Sat; 8.30am-2.30pm Sun. *Swimming pool* 11am-8pm daily June-Aug. **Admission** *Swimming pool* €3.60-€4. **No credit cards.**

This complex combines an athletics stadium and multi-purpose sports centre with an indoor sports hall, gym, football pitch, open-air pool and facilities for practising golf. It's also a good place for jogging.

Parque de Ocío La Ermita – Paidesport Center

C/Sepúlveda 3-5, Virgen del Puerto, South of centre (91 470 01 11/www.paidesport.com). Metro Puerta del Angel. **Open** *Sept-July* 9am-11pm Mon-Fri; 10am-8pm Sat; 10am-3pm Sun. *Aug* 9am-11pm Mon-Fri; 10am-3pm Sat, Sun. **Admission** *Squash* €14.30/1hr. *Swimming pool* varies. **No credit cards.**

A slick, privately run complex down near the river, open to non-members and generally rammed with earnest hardbodies pumping iron. It has racket courts, an open-air pool, a gym and weights room and an indoor sports hall.

Instalación Deportiva Municipal La Chopera

Calle Alfonso XII s/n, Parque del Retiro (91 420 11 54). Metro Atocha. **Open** 10am-10pm Mon-Sat; 10am-9pm Sun. Closed Aug. **Admission** varies. **Map** p329 L12/13.

Shaded by the trees of the Retiro park and close to the Prado, La Chopera is a fine place to play tennis and 5-a-side football (*fútbol sala*).

Disabled sports facilities

The city sports authorities are slowly adapting their centres to allow full access for disabled users, but this programme is not yet complete. The majority of indoor pools have been adapted, and many outdoor pools have ramps and full-access changing rooms. Those at Casa de Campo (*see p257*) and Concepción (*see above*) have the best disabled facilities.

Theatre & Dance

All Madrid's a stage.

Sala Mirador. *See p261.*

The battle for the hearts and minds of Madrid's increasingly polarised theatre-going public is perhaps best illustrated by the controversy that raged when the Circulo de Bellas Artes put on Iñigo Ramírez de Haro's *Me cago en Dios* ('I Shit on God' – a surprisingly common Spanish exclamation). Cast members were physically attacked, the Church weighed in, and the playwright's sister-in-law, President of the Madrid regional government Esperanza Aguirre, asked the theatre director to cancel the play. Undaunted, Ramírez et al then took the production to the maverick **Teatro Alfil**, where it later opened and ran under a new title: *Me Cago en la Censura* – 'I Shit on Censorship'.

Elsewhere it's a familiar story: Gran Via is littered with Broadway and West End hand-me-downs, while little theatres soldier on in face of local government and city council limits on licences and funds. Spain's fervent passion for the blockbuster musical has not wavered; having closed on Broadway, *Cats, Cabaret, We Will Rock You* and *Mamma Mia* have all been recent big hits in Madrid.

Still, the fighting spirit of the fringe makes up for the mainstream's old-fashioned outlook. The **Triángulo** and **Cuarta Pared** theatres, the oldest of the *salas alternativas*, always offer challenging works, and the beleaguered **TIS** has been a key player too. It has to be said that,

to outsiders, the alternative scene here can seem to be not that alternative, really, but bear in mind that until the late 1980s there was virtually no non-mainstream theatre here at all.

THE DANCE SCENE

As in the theatre world, the best thing going for the dance scene are its festivals, though these are hardly crowd-pullers. Three major companies are based in Madrid: the contemporary, but far from radical, **Compañía Nacional de Danza**, under the direction of Nacho Duato; the state **Ballet Nacional de España**, which specialises in Spanish styles of dance; and the **Ballet de la Comunidad de Madrid**, which is run by choreographer Victor Ullate.

As ever, contemporary dance teeters on an economic knife-edge, but spaces such as the **Pradillo**, **Cuarta Pared**, **El Triángulo**, **El Canto de la Cabra** and the **Centro de Nuevos Creadores** at the Sala Mirador continue to show good work. The two main contemporary dance companies are **10y10**, in residency at the Sala Mirador, and **Provisional Danza**, one of the pioneers of contemporary dance in Spain since 1987, led by the renowned choreographer Carmen Werner. The long-awaited Teatro del Canal is due to open in Chamberi in summer 2007 and will include a space for dance.

SEASONS AND FESTIVALS

The **Festival de Otoño** (*see p208*) is the city's biggest festival for theatre, dance and puppetry, attracting major international names and sometimes putting on shows in English. More alternative theatre and dance is show-cased in January and February in the original **Escena Contemporánea**, the better-funded sibling to the marginally more avant-garde **La Alternativa** festival, while in June there's the

Festival de Teatro Alternativo de Primavera. Also in the spring is **Madrid en Danza**, which offers a variety of dance styles, from flamenco to kathak. The misnamed **Día de la Danza** (actually three days, at the end of April/beginning of May) centres on the Teatro Albéniz and feature top names in dance. The summer **Veranos de la Villa** programme offers even more outdoor performances. The Centro Cultural de la Villa's **Apuesta por la**

Merely Players

Even hardened theatre buffs quail before a show in a language they don't understand and, of course, almost all Madrid theatre is staged in Spanish. English-speaking visitors might get lucky, though, and happen on a touring production in the Festival de Otoño or Escena Contemporánea. In recent years the RSC has visited twice, Cheek By Jowl have brought *The Changeling* and the all-male Propeller Company staged a memorable *Winter's Tale*. But, best of all, English-language shows are available four or five times a year courtesy of local amateur group, the Madrid Players.

It would be easy to dismiss the group as expat ham-drams and frustrated thesps, but they firmly believe there is no such thing as an 'amateur performance' – especially for paying audiences. The Players, with over 60 members of various nationalities, have been going for over 30 years and now regularly perform in some of Madrid's better-known

fringe venues, such as the Teatro Triángulo and the Sala TIS. The staple earner, however, is the colourful, uproarious Christmas panto, which most years attracts total audiences of over 2,000, many of them Spaniards.

Serious drama also has its place: recent seasons have seen performances of Alan Ayckbourn, Samuel Beckett, Thornton Wilder, Michael Christofer, Chekhov and Shakespeare. Some members have worked professionally, others have not, but enthusiasm and sheer hard work ensure high standards. This fact has not been lost on the media; the group has featured several times in major dailies and even made the national news on TV1 last year. It's worth pointing out that the idea of panto doesn't exist in Spain, and what local viewers made of a painted dame and several blokes in tights is anybody's guess.

Anyone interested in catching a show or getting involved can contact the group at www.madridplayers.blogspot.com.

Danza attracts prestigious companies such as Ibérica de Danza and the Companhia Portuguesa de Bailado Contemporâneo. And, for a summer trip out of town, don't miss the **Festival de Teatro Clásico** in the town of Almagro every July. The event pays tribute to Lope de Vega, Molière, Shakespeare and friends with plays, workshops and street performances (get information at C/Príncipe 14, 91 521 07 20). The **Madrid Sur** festival (91 355 58 67, www.iitm.org) takes place in the southern suburbs in the autumn.

TICKETS AND TIMES

Many of the mainstream theatres are closed on Mondays and most fringe venues only open Thursday to Sunday. Cheaper tickets are often available on Wednesdays and Sundays. Most theatres sell through telesales, and we list several in the shopping section, *see p202*. But you can also call the venue to check. The best places to find information are the *Guía del Ocio* and daily newspapers, especially in the Friday listings supplements that most of them publish.

Mainstream theatres

Other theatres to look out for include **Teatro Alcázar** (C/Alcalá 20, 91 532 06 16, www.teatro alcazar.com), the **Calderón** (C/Atocha 18, 91 429 58 90, www.teatrocalderon.com) for *101 Dalmatians* and the like, the **Teatro Lara** (Corredera Baja de San Pablo 15, 91 522 89 04, www.teatrolara.com) for family entertainment, and **Teatro de Cámara** (C/San Cosme y San Damián 3, 91 527 09 54) for heavyweight classics. It's worth noting that the Teatro Real (*see p233*) often stages dance productions, notably with the Ballet Nacional de España and the Compañía Nacional de Danza, as well as small pieces in the informal 'Café Danza'. *See also p233* **Teatro de la Zarzuela**.

Centro Cultural de la Villa

Jardines del Descubrimiento, Plaza de Colón, Salamanca (91 480 03 00/www.munimadrid.es). Metro Serrano. **Open** *Box office* 11am-1.30pm, 5-6pm or until performance Tue-Sun. **Tickets** €5-€25. **Credit** AmEx, DC, MC, V. **Map** p324 K9.
The theatre in the city's purpose-built cultural centre shows an eclectic mix of concerts, opera, *zarzuela*, cinema, drama and dance. There are also jazz performances, workshops and children's puppet shows.

Sala Mirador

C/Doctor Fourquet 31, Lavapiés (91 539 57 67). Metro Atocha or Lavapiés. **Open** *Box office* 1hr before performance Thur-Sun. Closed Aug. **Tickets** €12-€15. **No credit cards**. **Map** p328 I15.
Doubling as theatre/dance school and performance space, this is also the site of the long-running *La Katarsis del Tomatazo*, performed every Friday and

Saturday night at 11pm. The deal is, the audience are given tomatoes as they enter, which they can use to express their feelings on this singing and dancing cabaret. Other less therapeutic productions are a mix of theatre and dance. **Photo** *p259*.

Teatro Albéniz

C/Paz 11, Los Austrias (91 531 83 11). Metro Sol. **Open** *Box office* 11.30am-1pm, 5.30-9pm daily. Closed July-mid Aug. **Tickets** €13-€30. **Credit** V. **Map** p327 G12.
The Albéniz puts on a large amount of dance along with its regular theatre programme: from humorous drag-ballet company Les Ballets Trokadero de Monte Carlo to the stunning Ballet Nacional de Cuba and Spanish two-man company Nuevo Ballet Español. It is also the principal venue for the Festival de Otoño and hosts a series of concerts, Madrid En Canto, from May into June. The venue is under threat of closure and, indeed, demolition, however, unless it can find financial support.

Teatro Alfil

C/Pez 10, Malasaña (91 521 45 41/www.teatro alfil.com). Metro Callao or Noviciado. **Open** *Box office* 1hr before performance daily. **Tickets** €9-€12. **No credit cards**. **Map** p325 G10.
Madrid's renegade theatre, the Alfil has been threatened with closure in previous years, but has battled on, and produces increasingly radical plays – both *The Vagina Monologues* and *Puppetry of the Penis* have been staged here. The Alfil is also one of the few venues to host stand-up comedy, including the Giggling Guiri English comedy nights – see www.comedyinspain.com.

Teatro de la Abadía

C/Fernández de los Ríos 42, Chamberí (91 448 16 27/91 448 11 81/www.teatroabadia.com). Metro Quevedo. **Open** *Box office* 5-9pm Tue-Sat; 5-8pm Sun. Closed Aug. **Tickets** €12-€19; concessions apply Wed. **Credit** V. **Map** p323 F6.
Housed inside an abandoned church, the award-winning Abadía dabbles in music and dance as well as theatre. It participates in the Festival de Otoño and Madrid en Danza festivals, and brings unusual one-offs to the regular programming.

Teatro de Madrid

Avda de la Ilustración s/n, Barrio del Pilar (91 730 17 50/www.teatromadrid.com). Metro Barrio del Pilar. **Open** *Box office* 5.30pm until performance Tue-Thur; 11.30am-1.30pm, 5.30pm until show Fri-Sun. **Tickets** €11-€22. **Credit** MC, V.
The Teatro de Madrid specialises in bringing the highest-calibre Spanish and international dance companies to the city, staging a mixture of ballet, contemporary dance and fusion performances such as flamenco and tango. It is also home to the Nuevo Ballet Español, the company of the fiery duo Ángel Rojas and Carlo Rodríguez, and regularly stages good children's shows around Christmas, as well as a *zarzuela* in the summer. *Swan Lake* will be enjoying a long run in 2007.

Arts & Entertainment

Teatro Español

*C/Príncipe 25, Huertas & Santa Ana (91 360
14 80). Metro Sevilla or Sol.* **Open** *Box office*
11.30am-1.30pm, 5-7.30pm Tue-Sun. **Tickets**
€3-€20. **No credit cards. Map** p328 H12.
This grand theatre on Plaza Santa Ana dates back
to 1745, but that doesn't mean it's old fashioned – in
fact it has enjoyed some fairly radical programming
in recent years. In 2007 it will be showing the politically incisive *Homebody/Kabul* by American writer
Tony Kushner.

Teatro Fernando de Rojas

*C/Alcalá 42, Sol & Gran Vía (91 360 54 00/
www.circulobellasartes.com). Metro Banco de
España or Sevilla.* **Open** *Box office* 1hr before
performance. Closed Aug. **Tickets** varies. **No
credit cards. Map** p328 I11.
Housed in the Círculo de Bellas Artes, and not to be
confused with the unconnected Teatro de Bellas
Artes next door, the Fernando de Rojas stages three
or four works a season, mixing contemporary and
traditional, Spanish and international. It hosts an
annual festival in September showing productions
by a variety of theatre groups from across Spain,
and a dance festival in late November.

Teatro La Latina

*Plaza de la Cebada 2, La Latina (91 365 28 35).
Metro La Latina.* **Open** *Box office* 11am-1pm,
6-8pm daily. **Tickets** €15-€30. **No credit cards.
Map** p327 F13.
Previously known for its homespun comic theatre
(plenty of star names in farcical situations and lots
of banging of doors), this comfortable venue has
undergone a slight shift of image in recent years.
Although it still hosts some comedy acts each season, the programme now mainly consists of quality
drama, most of it 20th century.

Teatro María Guerrero

*C/Tamayo y Baus 4, Chueca (91 310 15 00/91).
Metro Colón.* **Open** *Box office* noon until show
Tue-Sun. Closed Aug. **Tickets** €11-€18; half-
price concessions Wed. **Credit** AmEx, DC, V.
Map p324 J10.
This beautiful late 19th-century theatre is the home
of the state-run Centro Dramático Nacional (CDN).
Having reopened after major renovations, it's
retained its red velvet plushness and is to host
Ibsen's *Enemy of the People* in 2007.

Teatro Nuevo Apolo

*Plaza de Tirso de Molina 1, Rastro & Lavapiés
(91 369 06 37). Metro Tirso de Molina.* **Open**
Box office 11.30am-1.30pm, 5pm until performance
Tue-Sun. Closed mid July-mid Aug. **Tickets** €20-
€30. **No credit cards. Map** p327 G13.
In recent seasons this venue has welcomed such
exciting acts as dancer Joaquín Cortés and the
Mayumana dance-percussion troupe. The big show
of recent years, however, and still running, has been
El Musical de Broadway, incorporating 30 musical
greats in an intense two hours.

Teatro Pavón

*C/Embajadores 9, La Latina (91 528 28 19). Metro
La Latina.* **Open** *Box office* 11.30am-1.30pm, 5-6pm
daily. Closed mid July-early Sept. **Tickets** €8-€16.
Credit MC, V. **Map** p327 G14.
The Compañía Nacional de Teatro Clásico moved
here in 2002 while its real home, the Teatro de la
Comédia, is being restored. An impressive building
that sat semi-derelict for many years, it currently
stages classical productions by the Compañía
Nacional as well as by a number of invited compa-
nies. Here you'll usually get works by Spanish
Golden Age greats along with the occasional
Molière, Shakespeare or the like.

Teatro Valle-Inclán

*Plaza de Lavapiés s/n, Rastro & Lavapiés (91 505
880 01). Metro Lavapiés.* **Open** *Box office* noon
until show Tue-Sun. Closed Aug. **Tickets** €15-€18;
€7.50-€9 concessions. **Credit** AmEx, DC, V. **Map**
p327 H14.
Occupying the space where the popular but tatty
Teatro Olimpia used to stand, the Valle-Inclán
opened its doors in early 2006 and is the Centro
Dramático Nacional's second venue after the María
Guerrero. The main theatre, with 510 seats, is
equipped with the latest technology and offers a programme of contemporary Spanish playwrights as
well as works by authors such as Pirandello, Ibsen
and Jean Genet. In the adjoining Sala Franciso Nieva,
with room for 150 spectators, you are more likely to
find works by newer writers. **Photo** *p263.*

Fringe/alternative

The **Teatro de las Aguas** (C/Aguas 8, 91 366
96 42) occasionally has productions in English.
Small, more alternative spaces include: **DT**
(C/Reina 9, 91 521 71 55) for theatre, cabaret
and dance productions on gay themes; **Nave
de Los Locos** (C/Francisco Guzmán 28, 91
560 14 79, www.lanavedeloslocos.org), which
has an open-air festival in July; and **Lagrada**
(C/Ercilla 20, 91 517 96 98), for kitchen sink
dramas and contemporary plays.

El Canto de la Cabra

*C/San Gregorio 8, Chueca (91 310 42 22/www.
elcantodelacabra.com). Metro Chueca.* **Open** *Box
office* 1hr before performance. **Tickets** €8-€12.
No credit cards. Map p324 I10.
The 'Goat's Bleat' presents 15 to 20 companies a
year, performing contemporary Spanish and international work and some dance. The indoor theatre
seats 70, and popular open-air performances are
given on the patio in the summer.

Cuarta Pared

*C/Ercilla 17, South of centre (91 517 23 17/www.
cuartapared.es). Metro Embajadores.* **Open** *Box
office* 1hr before performance Thur-Sun. Closed
Aug. **Tickets** €10; €5-€7.50 concessions. *Children's
shows* €5. **No credit cards.**

Centro Dramático Nacional

Barcelona
mapa de sombras

Teatro Valle-Inclán. *See p262.*

Cuarta Pared plays a crucial role in training and as a producer. The resident company produces excellent work, it hosts visiting productions, is a major dance venue and stages acclaimed children's theatre.

El Montacargas

C/Antillón 19, Puerta del Ángel, South of centre (91 526 11 73). Metro Puerta del Ángel. **Open** *Box office* 30mins before show Thur-Sun. *Children's shows* €7. **No credit cards.**
Programming favours contemporary Spanish work, but it also hosts the Clown Festival in September.

Sala Triángulo

C/Zurita 20, Lavapiés (91 530 68 91/www.teatro triangulo.com). Metro Antón Martín or Lavapiés. **Open** *Box office* 30mins before show. **Tickets** €8-€10. **No credit cards. Map** p328 I14.
The original and probably the best of Madrid's alternative theatres, Triángulo is fiercely independent. There are always several productions going at once, usually including new writing and cross-art-form collaborations. It works closely with other theatres during festivals (it is the force behind La Alternativa in February, the Festival de Teatro Alternativo de Primavera in June and Al Fresco in July/August).

Teatro Pradillo

C/Pradillo 12, Chamartín (91 416 90 11/www. teatropradillo.com). Metro Concha Espina. **Open** *Box office* 1hr before performance. **Tickets** €12. *Children's shows* €4-8. **Credit** MC, V.

Although principally devoted to Spanish work, the Pradillo sometimes stages work in the original language, especially as part of the Festival de Otoño. Other strengths are children's theatre, particularly puppet shows, and dance. It is one of the principal organisers of the Escena Contemporánea, and runs a festival for European dance companies in December and another for flamenco in August.

TIS (Teatro Independiente Sur)

C/Primavera 11, Lavapiés (91 528 13 59/664 345 789/www.teatrotis.com). Metro Lavapiés. **Open** *Aug, Sept.* 11am-2pm, 5-10pm daily. *Oct-July* 10am-10pm Mon-Thur, Sun; 10am-midnight Fri, Sat. **Tickets** €7-12. **No credit cards. Map** p328 H14.
TIS has only been around a few years, and has yet to secure a licence. Its alternative (and often wacky) performances meet with mixed reviews, but it has put on plays by more than 250 international theatre companies in its short and sometimes precarious lifetime. There's also an interesting gallery with constantly changing exhibitions. Look out for occasional plays in English, such as *The Vagina Monologues* in 2007.

Dance classes

If you take more than a passive interest in flamenco, you might want to try classes. Below are some of the more established dance centres.

Centro de Danza Karen Taft

C/Libertad 15, Chueca (91 522 84 40/www.karentaft. com). Metro Chueca. **Open** *Oct-June* 9am-10pm Mon-Fri. *July-Sept* 10am-10pm Mon-Thur. **Map** p328 I11.
This is one of the foremost dance schools in Spain, and offers classes in classical and modern dance, as well as flamenco.

Clara Ramona

Paseo de las Delicias 35, Atocha (91 530 64 84). Metro Atocha. **Open** varies (call for information). **Map** p328 J15.
Bilingual dancer/choreographer Clara Ramona works internationally but has her *danza española* school in Madrid. She's a great teacher for all levels.

Estudios Amor de Dios

C/Santa Isabel 5, 1°, Lavapiés (91 360 04 34/www. amordedios.com). Metro Antón Martín. **Open** varies (call for details). **Map** p328 I13.
The most famous flamenco school in the world celebrated its 50th anniversary in 2003 by opening at a new location (having been homeless for more than a year). It now sits (or rather stamps) above the Antón Martín indoor market building.

El Horno

C/Esgrima 11, Lavapiés (91 527 57 01/www.centro elhorno.com). Metro Tirso de Molina. **Open** 10am-11pm Mon-Fri; 10am-7pm Sat. **Map** p327 G13.
El Horno has a flamenco and *sevillana* leaning, but also covers African, jazz and capoeira as well as drama, at very reasonable prices.

Arts & Entertainment

Airline flights are one of the biggest producers of the global warming gas CO_2. But with **The CarbonNeutral Company** you can make your travel a little greener.

Go to **www.carbonneutral.com** to calculate your flight emissions then 'neutralise' them through international projects which save exactly the same amount of carbon dioxide.

Contact us at **shop@carbonneutral.com** or call into the office on **0870 199 99 88** for more details.

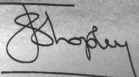

CarbonNeutral®flights

Trips Out of Town

El Valle de los Caídos. *See p271.*

Getting Started

Need some rest and relaxation? Pack your bags and get out of the city.

It's a tough call. Spend the entire long weekend in Madrid in order to fit in all three of the mandatory museums? Or take advantage of one of the city's extraordinary day trips? Three words: change your ticket. Because you'll want to do both. In summer, the cool mountain air of the sierras beckons, along with excellent hiking and some of the best campsites anywhere. In winter, what better than to hole up in a traditional *mesón* in the stately cities of Toledo or Segovia, with red wine, a log fire and some suckling pig? Year round the palaces, monasteries and gardens at Aranjuez, La Granja, Riofrío and El Escorial make for a compelling visit.

The areas to the north and west of Madrid have the most spectacular landscapes, following the three main sierra ranges. The less dramatic country to the south and east – where dry tableland, tufty hillocks and fertile river basins gently intermingle – is full of fascinating towns.

By bus

Within the city, details of bus services are available on 012 (or on 91 580 42 60 from outside Madrid), and you can get information from tourist offices and on the regional transport website, www.ctm-madrid.es. Most buses depart from Estación Sur de Autobuses (C/Méndez Álvaro, 91 468 42 00), but some go from Plaza Castilla (to north-west destinations), the streets around Moncloa, Conde de Casal and Avenida Mediterráneo (heading south), Avenida de America terminus (heading north-east) and Paseo de la Florida 11 (for Segovia and around). Most termini have their own same-name metro station; exceptions are Estación Sur, on the Méndez Álvaro metro and *cercanía* lines, and Paseo de la Florida 11, near Príncipe Pío metro.

By car

In 2004 many major roads changed name, and road map publishers and car-hire agencies were slow to catch up. 'National' roads, such as those formerly known as N-I and N-II, for example, became A-1 and A-2, except on toll-paying roads (*peajes*), where the prefix is now AP. The six notorious major roads, now numbered A-1 to A-6, can all be reached from the M-30 or the outlying M-40 ring road. The A-1 (Carretera de Burgos) leads to the eastern Guadarrama and

Sierra Pobre, the A-2 Barcelona road goes to Alcalá de Henares, and the A-3 Valencia road to Chinchón. The A-42 (formerly the N-401) to Toledo can be reached from either the M-30 or the A-4. The A-6 La Coruña road leads to El Escorial, Segovia, Ávila and Salamanca.

Expect bottlenecks at weekends, especially for the return trip on Sunday evenings: streets can be gridlocked until midnight. Immense traffic jams and a substantial crop of accidents are also depressingly predictable during long holiday weekends (*puentes*). Don't even think about driving at the beginning or end of August, particularly on the A-3 Valencia road. For more on driving and car hire, *see pp295-296*.

By train

The system of local trains (*cercanías*) runs to many interesting towns around Madrid; Alcalá de Henares, Aranjuez, El Escorial, Cercedilla and many more. The ageing but efficient single gauge extension line, the scenic C-9, wends its way up from Cercedilla through mountain pinewoods to Cotos, which adjoins ski slopes and a glacial lake. Services to other destinations leave from main-line stations Chamartín and Atocha, though many trains also stop between them at Nuevos Ministerios and Recoletos stations. It's also worth noting that the high-speed AVE and Talgo trains, from Atocha to Seville and Córdoba respectively, make a weekend or even a day trip to Andalucía a possibility. Depending on when you travel, there are often very good low-price fare deals as well. Several trains a day run to both cities.

RENFE information

91 468 83 32/www.renfe.es. **Open** *Information* 24hrs. *Reservations* 5am-11.40pm daily. **Credit** AmEx, DC, MC, V.
Tickets for long-distance services can be booked by phone with a credit card. Tickets can be delivered to a Madrid address for a small extra charge.

RENFE central sales office

C/Alcalá 44, Huertas & Santa Ana (no phone). Metro Banco de España. **Open** 9.30am-8pm Mon-Fri. **Credit** AmEx, DC, MC, V. **Map** p328 H11.
Information and tickets for the AVE, Talgo and all other RENFE long-distance services are available from this office, which is a short walk from Plaza de Cibeles. It does not handle phone enquiries, which go through the central number above.

North & West

The legacies of mystic saints and reclusive monarchs writ large in stone.

Ávila.

Ávila

It's an impressive sight; a forbidding stronghold encircled by thick 11th-century walls rising out of a boulder-strewn landscape. It is also the highest provincial capital in the country, with bitterly cold winters.

Despite its elegant buildings and well-to-do market town feel, there is something slightly sinister about Ávila's fortressed isolation; plaques around town celebrate Franco's victories and point out that this was the birthplace of Isabel 'la Católica' – the most powerful and merciless woman in the history of Spain. Proverbially a town of *cantos y santos* (stones and saints), it was also home to Spain's greatest mystic, Santa Teresa, the 16th-century spiritualist, reformer and writer who founded 18 convents and revolutionised Catholicism, while living a life of spartan self-denial.

As well as a statue in the town centre, there are countless other reminders of her presence. The baroque **Convento de Santa Teresa** (Plaza de la Santa 2, 920 21 10 30, closed Mon, admission €2) stands on the plot of the house she was born in, while the nearby Convento de San José contains the **Museo Teresiano de Carmelitas Descalzas** (C/Madres 4, 920 22 21 27, admission €1) where you can see her manuscripts and relics. General Franco is said to have kept the saint's mummified arm by his bedside in his final years.

The medieval city is a timewarp of cobbled lanes, sleepy squares, family mansions and stately religious buildings. The highlight is undoubtedly the stark fortified 12th-century **cathedral** (Plaza de la Catedral 8, 920 21 16 41, admission €3), embedded in the walls and rebuilt over the ages in Romanesque, Gothic and Renaissance styles. The **Basilica de San Vicente** (Plaza de San Vicente 1, 920 25 52 30, admission €1.40 Mon-Sat, free Sun), located outside the walls, is a similar hybrid of styles. Built on the spot where St Vincent and his two sisters were martyred in the fourth century, it has gruesome scenes of their torture depicted in relief around Vicente's tomb. Nearby, stand the Romanesque church of **San Andrés** and the palatial but melancholy 15th-century Gothic **Santo Tomás monastery**, containing the alabaster tomb of Ferdinand and Isabella's only son and heir, Don Juan, who died at 19.

The city's wonderfully preserved **walls** (920 25 50 88, closed Mon, admission €3.50), which were built after the knights had rid the city of the Moors, extend for one and a half miles and have nine gates and 88 watchtowers. For the best views go across the River Adaja to **Los Cuatro Postes**, a small Doric-columned monument perched on a knoll west of the city. The walls can be climbed at the Puerta del Alcázar just south of the cathedral and Puerta de San Vicente to the north.

Where to stay & eat

Among the major culinary delights to be found in Ávila are large steaks (*chuletones de Ávila*) from the fighting Iberian strain of black bulls, and delicious haricot beans (*judías* or *alubias*) from Barco de Ávila. Look out too for *cocido morañego*, a local variant on Madrid's famed winter stew; Ávila's own Castilian version of gazpacho, using fresh vegetables from the Tiétar Valley; roast lamb (*cordero asado*) and suckling pig (*lechona*). *Yemas de Santa Teresa* – rich sweets made from egg yolks and said to have been originally created by the saint herself in one of her rare moments of indulgence – are another of Ávila's specialities; you'll see them for sale all over town.

A good place to try them is the charming **Mesón del Rastro** (Plaza del Rastro 1, 920 21 12 19, mains €16, set lunch €15.50), which has all the trimmings of a traditional Castilian tavern (boars' heads, log fires and so on) without the traditionally high prices. **El Rincón** (Plaza de Zurraquín 3-4, 920 35 10 44, restaurant closed Mon & all Feb, mains €10.50-€15, set lunch €9.65-€11.80) is another to serve the same food as everywhere else, but at lower prices. **La Alcazaba** (Plaza Mosén Rubi 3, 920

25 62 90, closed 2wks in Jan, mains €18.75-€20) is more creative – try monkfish tournedor in Pernod sauce, or duck with caramelised apples. On the other side of the river, with a great view of the walls from its terrace, is **Mesón el Puente** (Bajada de la Losa 2, 920 22 50 51, closed Mon & all Jan, mains €10.50).

Many of the town's hotels are located in converted mansions and Renaissance palaces. The delightful **Parador Raimundo de Borgoña** (C/Marqués de Canales de Chozas 2, 920 21 13 40, www.parador.es, doubles €126-€133.75, mains €16.50) serves an exceptional breakfast, available to non-residents as well as guests. **Hospedería de Bracamonte** (C/Bracamonte 6, 920 25 12 80, www.hosp ederiadebracamonte.com, doubles €53.50-€80.25, restaurant closed last 2wks in Oct, mains €16) has a seigneurial air and lots of game dishes. **Palacio de Valderrábanos** (Plaza de la Catedral 9, 920 21 10 23, www. palaciovalderrabanoshotel.com, doubles €117.70) is a grander hotel located on the plaza with splendid views of the cathedral.

Getting there

By bus

Larrea (902 22 22 82, www.lasepulvedana.es) from Estación Sur (91 468 42 00) has eight buses weekdays, 3 buses weekends. Journey time is 1hr 20mins.

By train

There are 20 trains daily from Chamartín or Atocha, 8am-10.30pm. The last return is at 9.30pm. Journey time (Regional Exprés services) is anything between 1hr 15mins-2hrs.

Tourist information

Oficina de Turismo

Pedro de Ávila 4 (920 21 13 87/www.turismocastilla yleon.com). **Open** Oct-June 10am-2pm, 5-8pm daily. July-Sept 9am-8pm daily.

El Escorial

The grand, austere monastery of San Lorenzo de El Escorial never fails to divide opinion, but is indubitably one of the most significant buildings in the history of Spain. Many people see it as the outward manifestation of its founding monarch's mind – Philip II was at once fanatically religious and wildly ambitious, and so his legacy in stone is both spartan and vast. The gloomy building is also symbolic architecturally, and it was the grey slate and spiky turrets of El Escorial that inspired decades of the 'Herreran' style (also known as Castilian baroque).

Construction was completed in record time between 1563 and 1574, initially by Juan Bautista de Toledo – who died shortly after work started – and subsequently by Juan de Herrera. Everything here is on a grand scale: the main façade is 200 metres (700 feet) long, the overhead cupola measures 92 metres (302 feet), and there are 15 cloisters, 16km (10 miles) of corridors, 86 stairways, 88 fountains, 1,200 doors and 2,675 windows.

Philip conceived the palace as a mausoleum and contemplative retreat, built as a final resting place for his father, Charles I, and to celebrate the 1557 Spanish victory over the French at St Quentin on St Lawrence's day (San Lorenzo). It's laid out to resemble the grid-iron on which the saint himself was martyred. The jasper, gold and marble **Panteón de los Reyes**, designed by Gian Battista Crescenzi in the 1620s, contains all but two of the sovereigns who reigned over four centuries (absentees being Philip V, who was buried at La Granja, and Ferdinand VI, whose remains are in Madrid). The Basilica, with its notable *Christ Crucified* in Carrara marble by Benvenuto Cellini, has no fewer than 45 altars.

The main galleries are located on what was the lower floor of Philip's own austere rooms, above the **Basilica**. There is a small jalousie window overlooking the high altar so he could participate in Mass even if he was ill and confined to his surprisingly small bed. His cherished Hieronymous Bosch triptych was just a tiny part of a huge Habsburg art collection that includes celebrated works by Velázquez, Ribera, Alonso Cano and individual masterpieces like El Greco's *Adoration of the Name of Jesus* and Titian's *Last Supper,* concentrated mainly in the museum, church, chapterhouse and the ornate barrel-vaulted library – whose 50,000 volumes rival the Vatican's holdings.

The most refreshing section of El Escorial is the **Palacio de los Borbones**, remodelled by Charles IV in a light airy neo-classical style that contrasts with the general austerity and gloom. Highlights here are the tapestries designed by Goya and his contemporaries. Guided tours can be arranged on Fridays and Saturdays. It is worth noting that it can get very cold inside the building, even on warm days.

Two other small palaces lie in the spacious gardens and parklands surrounding the monastery and can be visited with prior reservation on the palace number: the **Casita de Arriba**, or Upper House (open Easter, July & Aug 10am-6pm Tue-Sun, admission €3.40, €1.70 concessions), and the **Casita del**

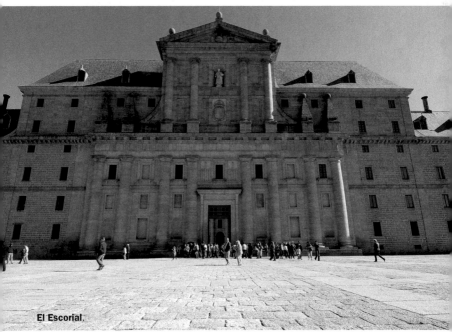

El Escorial.

Franco's vast, overbearing monument **El Valle de los Caídos**. *See p271.*

Príncipe (Prince's House), with paintings by Lucas Jordan, a charming garden with 100-year-old sequoia trees, open at weekends only, from April to September. The park is open year-round from 10am-6pm Tuesday to Sunday.

Outside the monastery El Escorial is really two separate towns. Down below, next to the train station, is **El Escorial de Abajo**, and at the top of the hill, alongside the monastery, is the grander **San Lorenzo**. Look out here for Charles III's 18th-century **Real Coliseo** theatre and the parish church of **San Bartolomé**. A couple of kilometres out on the road towards the Casita de Arriba is the **Silla de Felipe**, 'Philip's Seat', from where he used to watch progress on the building.

Monasterio de San Lorenzo El Real de El Escorial

91 890 59 02/3/4/5/www.patrimonionacional.es. **Open** *Oct-Mar* 10am-5pm Tue-Sun. *Apr-Sept* 10am-6pm Tue-Sun. **Palacio de los Borbones** *Guided tours* 4pm, 5pm, 6pm Fri; 10am, 11am, noon, 4pm, 5pm, 6pm (Apr-Sept only) Sat. **Casita del Príncipe Open** *Apr-Sept* 10.30am-1pm, 3.30pm-6.30pm every Apr-Jun every 30 mins 10.30am-6pm Sat, Sun. July-Sept every 30 mins 10.30am-6pm Tue-Sun. **Admission** *Monastery* (incl tour) €9; €8; €4 concessions; Wed free for EU citizens. *Palacio de los Borbones* €3.60; €2 concessions. *Casita del Príncipe* €3.60; €2 concessions. **No credit cards.** Reservations are essential for the Palacio and Casita tours, at least 24 hours in advance.

Where to eat

Fonda Genara (Plaza San Lorenzo 2, 91 890 16 36, www.restaurantegenara.com, mains €15.50) is a pretty if slightly pricey restaurant with old theatre posters around the walls. **Parrilla Príncipe** (C/Floridablanca 6, 91 890 16 11, www.parillaprincipe.com, doubles €50-€60, restaurant closed Tue and Sun dinner, mains €20-€25) is a small, peaceful 18th-century palace with a hotel on the upper floors and a blend of Castilian and seafood cuisine available in the restaurant below. **Madrid Sevilla** (C/Benavente 1, 91 890 15 19, closed Mon & 2wks Oct, mains €10.50) has simple but reasonably priced food, while **La Chistera** (Plaza Jacinto Benavente 5, 91 890 37 26, closed Mon night, set lunch €8.50, set dinner €14.50) is principally a tapas bar.

One of the nicest places for a drink or snack is the **Babel Café** (C/Juan de Austria 7, 91 896 05 22, www.babelcafe.com), with occasional live music, a small cinema club, exhibitions, internet access and a garden as well as good food. Up above the town in the Monte Abantos district, **Horizontal** (Camino Horizontal, 91 890 38 11, closed Tue-Wed dinner in Nov-Mar, main course €20) offers outdoor eating in summer and a seat by the fire in winter.

Where to stay

Designed by Herrera, the **Hotel Victoria Palace** (C/Juan Toledo 4, 91 896 98 90, www.hotelvictoriapalace.com) is an exquisite hotel with a charming garden just a couple of hundred yards from the monastery. Undergoing renovation at the time of writing, it's due to reopen in summer 2007. Call to confirm prices. **El Botánico** (C/Timoteo Padrós 16, 91 890 78 79, www.valdesimonte.com, doubles €122-€161.60) is a beautifully renovated summer house with a library, gardens and fine views of the monastery. A little cheaper, and right in the heart of San Lorenzo, the **Hotel Miranda Suizo** (C/Floridablanca 20, 91 890 47 11, www.arturocantablanco.com, doubles €78-€85) has reasonably appointed rooms looking out over the monastery and a bustling café, and **Hostal Cristina** (C/Juan de Toledo 6, 91 890 19 61, www.hostalcristina.tk, doubles €44.50-€49.50) is a comfortable, good-value *residencia*.

Getting there

By bus

Herranz (91 896 90 28) buses 661 and 664 from Moncloa (journey time 55mins), every 20mins 7am-11.30pm Mon-Fri, every 30mins 8.30am-10.15pm Sat, 9am-11pm Sun. Last return is at 10.30pm Mon-Fri, 8pm Sat, 10pm Sun.

By train

Cercanías C-8a, 26 trains from Atocha (journey time 1hr 15mins) 5.45am-11.30pm Mon-Fri; every hour 6.30am-11.30pm Sat, Sun. Last return 10.15pm daily. Trains run to El Escorial town, from where it's a 2km (1.25-mile) walk or bus-ride uphill to San Lorenzo and the monastery. The bus (L1) is much more direct.

Tourist information

Oficina de Turismo

C/Grimaldi 2 (91 890 53 13/www.sanlorenzo turismo.org). **Open** 10am-6pm Mon-Fri; 10am-7pm Sat, Sun.

El Valle de los Caídos

Built between 1940 and 1959 by Civil War prisoners of the defeated Republican army, Franco's giant mausoleum, the 'Valley of the Fallen' (the fallen on Franco's side, at least)

stands in a forested valley a few miles from El Escorial. It was the *generalísimo*'s grand project, and its stark, grandiose, authoritarian style is worthy of the likes of Mussolini or Ceaucescu. It is easily spotted from up to 50km (31 miles) away by a huge 150-metre (500-foot) high cross (said to weigh over 180,000 tons) which itself is placed 150 metres above the main esplanade. The monument was completed at great financial and human cost and many Republicans perished while quarrying the dense granite rock needed to build it. Ironically, and to the grief of their families, many of the Republican prisoners' bodies probably now lie side by side with those of their oppressors.

Its cold, atmospherically lit underground chambers, lined with eerie cowled figures, do exert a certain mesmerising aura; like it or loathe it. The mausoleum is basically a huge tunnel, driven 260 metres (867 feet) into the granite rock. At its entrance are 16th-century monoliths, 12 metres (40 feet) high, while deep in the interior you can see bright-coloured tapestries of the *Apocalypse of St John*; a cupola decorated with mosaics showing heaven-bound saints and martyrs of Spain, and an altar-bound polychrome wooden sculpture of Christ crucified. It contains a subterranean church, an ossuary of six chapels bearing the remains of Civil War dead and the tombs of two men – Franco himself and José Antonio Primo de Rivera, the rich young founder of the Falange who died in the early phases of the Civil War, thus conveniently leaving El Caudillo from El Ferrol unchallenged as leader. Both have fresh flowers placed on their graves daily, paid for by the state, to the disgust of most (though by no means all) of the Spanish population.

The views are quite staggering, especially from the base of the cross, reached via a funicular (€2.50 return).

El Valle de los Caídos

91 890 56 11/www.patrimonionacional.es. **Open** *Oct-Mar* 10am-6pm Tue-Sun. *Apr-Sept* 10am-7pm Tue-Sun. **Admission** €5; €2.50 concessions; Wed free for EU citizens. **Credit** MC, V. **Photos** *p270.*

Getting there

By bus

Bus 660 at 3.15pm Tue-Sun from San Lorenzo del Escorial (*see p270*). Return at 5.30pm. Journey time 10mins.

Sierra de Guadarrama

The Guadarrama range runs from El Escorial (*see p270*) in the south-west to Somosierra in the north-east, and separates the two Castilian *mesetas*, or plains: Castile to the north, and La

Trips Out of Town

Out amid the mighty **Sierra de Guadarrama**.

Mancha to the south. For a selection of the many walks possible in the area, the most helpful information centre is that at Valle de la Fuenfría (*see p275*).

Until the 1970s, when a tunnel was built underneath it, the Puerto de Guadarrama pass was the only way out of Madrid to Segovia and Valladolid, and it would often be impassable for days on end in winter. Also known as the Alto de los Leones because of the lion that sits atop a plinth here (the lion is the symbol of the village of Guadarrama), the pass was the scene of bitter fighting during the battle for Madrid during the Civil War, and Hemingway set large parts of *For Whom the Bell Tolls* here. The remains of gun emplacements and bunkers from that era still litter the area.

A dirt road runs from the top of the pass, south-west for 30km (19 miles) to the charming and peaceful village of Peguerinos, from where there are buses and a fully paved road to El Escorial. Along the way there are several opportunities for camping. The track (signposted) veers off to the left from the Guadarrama direction, among a jumble of radio towers and satellite dishes. There is a restaurant called Alto de León on the side of the main road just at the turning. Coming the other way, the track is signposted 'Valle Enmedio'.

Another breathtaking walk, taking around three hours, runs from **Tablada** station. Walk up 2km (1.25 miles) – not all the way to the pass – to a post indicating km 56, and take a forestry track on the right, clearly marked with a stone sign, to the Peña del Arcipreste de Hita (1,527m/5,010ft). The track eventually descends again, to reach the station at Cercedilla.

Cercedilla is not an especially picturesque village, but it has managed to retain its own identity despite its popularity in summer, when the population swells from 5,000 to around 40,000. To find it at its most authentic, visit in winter, especially if you want to try any of the longer walks nearby. Additionally, rooms can be very difficult to find in summer. The village sits at the head of a valley that leads up to the **Puerto de la Fuenfría** (1,796 metres/5,895 feet), a pass that in turn forms a route across the Sierra dating back to at least Roman times. Along the way there is a Calzada Romana (Roman Road), which dates back to the first century AD, with two fine Roman bridges still standing at El Descalzo and Enmedio. The pass is also an important junction of carefully developed modern footpaths.

The most leisurely excursion from Cercedilla is on the old-world narrow-gauge *cercanías* line (C-9) that runs through fine scenery up to the

Cotos ski station, a charming way to get up to and beyond the **Puerto de Navacerrada**, especially when it's snowing. Alternatively, from the *cercanías* station in Cercedilla, a 45-minute walk up the M-966 (the main road in front of you) will bring you to a stretch of open alpine woodland known as **Las Dehesas**, with an information centre that's an essential port of call for visitors to the valley, with good free maps. Las Dehesas is a very popular picnic spot, with natural spring swimming pools, only open in summer, and freezing even then.

The nearby town of **Navacerrada** is a lively place with a mountain village feel, and several decent restaurants serving appropriately Alpine food (expect to be dipping your bread into lots of raclettes and fondues), making it a fun base.

Where to stay & eat

Valle Enmedio (91 898 31 76, www.vallen medio.com, closed Mon-Thur Oct-June, rates €5.30 adults, €4.70 under-10s, €5.50 tent, €5.30 car), 11km (seven miles) along the track to Peguerinos, is an isolated, idyllic and well-equipped campsite with wooden bungalows, set in a forest. In Peguerinos itself, **La Flor** (C/Espinar 7, 91 898 30 40, doubles €42 with shared bathroom, mains €7.50) is a small, basic but friendly *pensión* with a small restaurant downstairs. For food, another good bet is the no-frills **Alto del León** (91 854 12 27, mains €13), on the crest of the pass.

Choices are much greater in Cercedilla. **Casa Gómez** (C/Emilio Serrano 40, 91 852 01 46, mains €12, set lunch €8.50, closed Mon), opposite the railway station, specialises in wild mushrooms and game in season. **El Chivo Loco** (C/Pontezuela 21, 91 852 34 39, closed Tue July-mid Sept, closed Mon-Fri mid Sept-June), meanwhile, does excellent tapas.

As you come out of the station, on the right, is **Hostal Longinos – El Aribel** (C/Emilio Serrano 41, 91 852 15 11, www.hostalaribel.com, doubles €45). Booking is essential in summer and at weekends.

In Navacerrada, one of the better hotels is the **Hotel Nava Real** (C/Huertas 1, 91 853 10 00, www.hotelnavareal.com, doubles €64.20, mains €12), which also has a more imaginative restaurant than most. **Restaurante Paco** (Plaza Doctor Gereda 2, 91 856 05 62, mains €11.50, closed Wed) has tables outside overlooking the town square.

Getting there

By bus
The Larrea (902 22 22 82) bus 684 from Moncloa to Cercedilla leaves every 30mins (journey time 50mins-

Take a hike

As Madrid becomes more and more crowded, so its inhabitants have come to rely on escapes to the Guadarrama and Gredos mountain ranges to maintain their sanity. The mountains are within easy reach: whether by car, bus, or train, one can soon be up in alpine landscapes, 1,000 metres above sea level. Most villages in the sierras now have some kind of information centre, and simple illustrated guides to a varied range of walks (often signposted) are available. The town hall is also a good place to look for information. In summer it is advisable to take plenty of water and clothes offering protection from the sun, and in winter, waterproof, warm gear. Only experienced walkers should try the higher walks in winter. Also, weather in the mountains is notoriously changeable: check forecasts before you go. Buying food and water in Madrid before setting off is also a good idea.

Skiing around the Madrid region is a hit-or-miss affair. Of the resorts near Madrid, Valdesquí (91 570 12 24, www. valdesqui.es) usually has the best (and most) snow. La Pinilla (921 55 03 04, www.lapinilla.es) is directly north of Madrid near Riaza; the others are in the central Guadarrama. The only one with any accommodation is the Puerto de Navacerrada (91 852 14 35, www.puerto navacerrada.com). All-in package trips to these resorts can be booked at any travel agency in Madrid. These ski stations offer limited skiing only and are of little interest to intermediate or advanced skiers, but are great for day trips out of Madrid. Recorded information (in Spanish only) on snow conditions at ski resorts and out-of-season activities can be found on the Atudem phoneline (91 359 15 57, www.esquiespana.org).

1hr) from 6am-10.30pm Mon-Fri, hourly 8am-10pm Sat, Sun. Last return is at 8.45pm. The Larrea bus 691 runs from Madrid to Puerto Navacerrada, leaving Madrid at 9.25am (return 4.25pm) Mon-Fri and at 8am, 8.45am and 9.30am (return 3.45pm, 5pm and 6.45pm) Sat, Sun.

By train
For Tablada, there are two trains daily from Atocha and Chamartin. For Cercedilla, take C-8b to Segovia. Trains run hourly (daily); the last train back from Cercedilla is at about 10.35pm.

Strolling through the ages at **La Granja**. *See p275.*

Tourist information

Centro de Información Valle de la Fuenfría

Carretera de las Dehesas, km 2, Cercedilla (91 852 22 13). **Open** 10am-6pm daily.

Edificio Deporte y Montaña

Puerto de Navacerrada (91 852 33 02/www. puertonavacerrada.com). **Open** *Oct-May* 9am-6pm daily. *June* 10am-6pm Sat, Sun. *July-Sept* 10am-6pm daily.

Valle de Lozoya

The wide, flat Valle de Lozoya runs north-east from below the pass of Puerto de los Cotos (1,830 metres/6,006 feet), to the main A-1 Burgos road. There is little to detain you in the village of **Rascafría** at the western end of the valley. For the most part, it has been drearily overdeveloped, with one exception – the stunning **Monasterio de El Paular** (91 869 14 25, tours noon, 1pm & 5pm Mon-Wed, Fri & Sat, noon, 1pm Thur, 1pm, 4pm, 5pm & 6pm Sun, admission free) nearby. This Benedictine monastery, a short way south of the village, was founded in 1390 but was still being added to 500 years later. It is still partly occupied by monks, even though most of it is now an unobtrusive Sheraton hotel, and it remains a wonderful sight with its stunning backdrop of snow-capped peaks.

One of the many rewarding walks around here is along the GR-10 pathway from the monastery up to the Puerto de los Cotos, which winds its way through pine forests and a picturesque roe deer habitat. Heading in the other direction, the path runs two kilometres to some natural swimming pools at Las Presillas. In summer there is a small kiosk there, selling drinks. From the town itself, it's also possible to walk across the mountains to the palace of La Granja (*see below*).

Where to stay & eat

Casa Briscas (Plaza España 13, 91 869 12 26, mains €10.50, set lunch €9, closed Thur) is the best eating option in Rascafría's main square, and has a terrace that really comes alive in summer. The 44-room **Santa María del Paular** (91 869 10 11, doubles €127.35-€180.90, mains €20, closed Jan) occupies the former monastery cloister and is delightfully peaceful. **Los Calizos** (Carretera Miraflores-Rascafría km 30.5, 91 869 11 12, www.loscalizos.com, doubles €123 incl breakfast & dinner, mains €20) is a stone house by the Lozoya River, located a short distance outside town.

Getting there

By bus

To or from Rascafria, take Continental (902 33 04 00, www.continental-auto.es) bus 194, which leaves Madrid from Plaza Castilla at 8am, 2pm, 6pm Mon-Fri; 8pm, 6pm Sat; 8pm, 3pm Sun. Last bus back is at 5pm Mon-Fri; 8.30pm Sat; 6.30pm Sun.

By train

For Puerto de los Cotos, take C-8b to Cercedilla, then line C-9 to Cotos. There are six trains daily Mon-Fri (9.35am, 11.35am, 1.35pm, 3.35pm, 5.35pm, 7.35pm). Trains run hourly Sat, Sun (9.35am-7.35pm). Last return is 8.43pm.

La Granja

Another palace to start life as a hunting lodge, later to be converted by the Bourbons, is La Granja, about 11km (seven miles) from Segovia back towards Madrid on the N-101. It was built on the site of a former shrine, San Ildefonso, by Philip V, homesick for his youth in Versailles. His wife Isabel Farnese also added some distinctive touches, not least of which are the famous fountains. The result is perhaps the loveliest of all the Bourbon palaces.

Work on the structure was carried out in record time between 1721 and 1723 by Teodoro Ardamans, and the extensive gardens over a longer period under the main supervision of René Carlier. Amid the formal hedgerows, lawns and rows of trees you'll find voluptuous statues, limpid pools and the fountains, some of which spring to life three times a week in the summer and then all of which are turned on for one memorable evening each year, 25 August. Water comes from an artificial lake called El Mar, set in a woodland at the end of the estate and backed by the dramatic sheer wall of the Peñalara, the highest peak in the Guadarrama.

The palace itself, restored after a devastating fire in 1918, is an opulent maze of elegant salons and chambers that abound in classical frescoes, dazzling cut-glass chandeliers (made in the palace's own glass factory, which still functions today) and priceless *objets d'art*. The tapestry selection, though representing only a part of the Spanish and Flemish royal collection, is among the finest you'll see anywhere. Unfortunately visits are only via guided tours of up to 45 people at a time.

The charming village of **San Ildefonso** has long been a favourite resort for escaping the oppressive Madrid summer heat; if you have your own transport it offers a relaxing alternative to staying in Segovia. Among its imposing private houses is the **Casa de Infantes**, built by Carlos III for his sons Gabriel and Antonio.

Segovia

Palacio Real de La Granja de San Ildefonso

921 47 00 19/www.patrimonionacional.es. **Open** *Oct-Mar* 10am-1.30pm, 3-5pm Tue-Sat; 10am-2pm Sun. *Apr-Sept* 10am-6pm Tue-Sun. Fountains operate Easter-June at 5.30pm Wed, Sat & Sun. **Admission** *Palace* €3.50; €2.50 concessions. Wed free EU citizens. *Gardens* free. **No credit cards**. Photos *p274*.

Where to stay & eat

It's essential to reserve ahead at the wildly popular **Casa Zaca** (C/Embajadores 6, 921 47 00 87, closed dinner & Mon, mains €10); it offers home-style cuisine, so instead of the standard roast lamb or *cochinillo* there are gutsy casseroles and braised ox tongue. Alternatively try the tapas, in front of a roaring fire, at the colourful **La Fundición** (Plaza de la Calandria 1, 921 47 00 46, closed lunch Tue-Fri, dinner Sun & all Mon in Jun-Sept; closed lunch Fri, dinner Sun & all Mon-Thur in Oct-May).

Hostal Las Fuentes (C/Padre Claret 6, 921 47 10 24, doubles €96.30-€102.75) is a beautifully restored house with quiet rooms looking down to Segovia or into a flower-filled courtyard. **Hotel Roma** (C/Guardas 2, 921 47 07 52, www.hotelroma.org, doubles €55.65-€62.05, restaurant closed Tue, mains €13.90, closed Nov) is comfortable enough.

Getting there

By bus

La Sepulvedana (91 530 48 00, 902 22 22 82, www.la sepulvedana.es) from Paseo de la Florida 11. Seven to ten buses daily (journey time 1hr15mins-2hrs).

Riofrío

After the death of Philip V, Isabel Farnese could not bear to stay on at La Granja with her stepson Fernando VI, and so had another palace built at

Riofrío. She was to survive Fernando as well, however, and Riofrío was never completely finished. Later Alfonso XII came here to mourn the death of his new bride, Mercedes, and the whole palace still has a melancholy air, despite the warm pinks and greens of its exterior.

It was built in the middle of the best deer-hunting country near Madrid, and later sovereigns also came to this beautiful estate to blast away to their hearts' content. With this in mind, half the palace has been turned into a hunting museum – a mandatory and overlong part of the guided tour. Unless row after row of antlers and stuffed animals really rock your boat, it is probably best admired from outside, particularly with a picnic.

Palacio de Riofrío

921 47 00 19. **Open** *Oct-Mar* 10am-1.30pm, 3-5pm Tue-Sat; 10am-2pm Sun. *Apr-Sept* 10am-6pm Tue-Sun. **Admission** €5; €2.50 concessions. Wed free for EU citizens. **No credit cards**.

Getting there

By train

Segovia trains (*see p265*) stop at La Losa-Navas de Riofrio, about 2km (1.25 miles) from Riofrío.

Segovia

Segovia combines beautiful architecture with visual warmth in a region more associated with austerity. In contrast with the traditional grey chill of Castile it glows, radiant and mellow. Make the approach by road across vast plains and it appears as if by witchcraft, rising on a burnished hillock like an acropolis or ship in full sail. The scene is dominated by the **Alcázar** fortress, with its sharply angled ramparts, spiky towers and high gables; a fantastical fairytale vision.

Impregnably poised on the edge of a hair-raising abyss into which a negligent nurse once accidentally dropped a 14th-century heir to the throne and then flung herself after him to avoid punishment, it was originally built as a modest stone fort 200 years earlier, and underwent radical changes over the centuries. Most of the world-famous fairy castle architecture seen today is a brilliant work of restoration carried out after a disastrous fire in 1862. Though owned by the army, the bastion's purpose is now purely commercial and its chambers are open daily for the public to inspect the weapons, armour, tapestries and artworks on display.

Close by is the huge, airy and very light Gothic **cathedral** (C/Marqués del Arco, 921 46 22 05, admission €3). The current structure was built to replace a predecessor destroyed in a

1521 revolt. Inside there's a tiny museum that holds an interesting collection of tapestries, paintings and a wonderful 16th-century grandfather clock.

Very different, but just as extraordinary as the Alcázar, is the 728-metre-long (2,426-foot) Roman **aqueduct**, made of gleaming Guadarrama granite in rough-hewn blocks that mesh perfectly without mortar, though it no longer brings water from the Riofrío as it first did over 2,000 years ago. The **Plaza del Azoguejo** below, where markets are now held, was a rendezvous for thieves and vagabonds in Cervantes' day. Steps rise up the wall at the place where the aqueduct merges into the rising hill, or you can spiral up the streets channelling traffic up and down. A warren of intricate lanes criss-crosses the old town like a demented spider's web, weaving you past squares, gardens, mansions, palaces and museums. The town is never short of tourists but is still resolutely traditional: in the Plaza Mayor the atmosphere of the past blends with real-life bustle and you can still find plenty of bars and cafés filled only with locals.

Of its dozen or so churches and convents, all built between the 12th and 16th centuries, **San Esteban**, noted for its striking bell tower, and **San Millán**, with its Moorish-influenced decor and elaborately carved wooden ceiling, stand out. Among its secular buildings the **Casa de los Picos**, with waffle-iron studs on its façade, can be found in the shopping streets downhill from the cathedral. Also not to be missed is the **Monastery of El Parral**, founded by Henry VI and now a national monument. One of the best views is from 13th-century **Iglesia de Vera Cruz** built by the Knights Templars with spoils from the Crusades.

Alcázar de Segovia

Plaza de la Reina Maria Cristina (921 46 07 59). **Open** *Oct-Feb* 10am-6pm daily. *Mar-Sept* 10am-7pm daily. **Admission** €3.50; €2.30 concessions. **No credit cards**. **Photo** *p279*.

Where to stay & eat

The **Méson del Duque** (C/Cervantes 12, 921 46 24 87, mains €17) is a long-standing favourite with colourfully decorated dining rooms on several floors serving excellent Castilian fare. **Restaurant José María** (C/Cronista Lecea 11, 921 46 11 11, mains €14.50-€21) is a traditionally styled *mesón* serving first-rate *cochinillo* (suckling pig) and probably the best lamb in town. It also has a good tapas bar. **Cuevas de San Esteban** (C/Valdelaguila 15, 921 46 09 82, mains €14) is another place to avoid the tourist-trap market with reasonably priced Castilian food. For something different, **Narizotas** (Plaza Medina del Campo 1, 921 46 26 79, closed dinner Sun, mains €15) has a selection of risottos and salads, as well as the usual parade of roast meats.

Los Linajes (C/Dr Velasco 9, 921 46 04 75, www.hotelloslinajes.com, doubles €94-€110.20) is an atmospheric 13th-century palace close to San Esteban church with beams, antiques and a lush patio, while the **Acueducto** (C/Padre Claret 10, 921 42 48 00, www.hotelacueducto. com, doubles €100) is a comfortable, established hotel where some of the rooms overlook the Roman aqueduct. Alternatively, try **Las Sirenas** (C/Juan Bravo 30, 921 46 26 63, www.hotelsirenas.com, doubles €64.20-€74.90), a homely hotel in the old town near San Martín church. **Hostal Taray** (Plaza San Facundo 1, 921 46 30 41, doubles €34) is useful for those on a budget, as is the very central **El Hidalgo** (C/José Canalejas 5, 921 46 35 29, doubles €45-€50).

Getting there

By bus
La Sepulvedana (91 530 48 00, 902 22 22 82) buses run from Paseo de la Florida 11, every 30mins (journey time 1hr 15mins). Last return 9.30pm daily.

By train
There are eight trains daily from Atocha or Chamartín, but be warned: it's a slow journey (2hrs).

Tourist information

Oficina de Turismo
Plaza Mayor 10 (921 46 03 34/www.turismo castillayleon.com). **Open** *July, Aug* 9am-8pm Mon-Thur, Sun; 9am-9pm Fri, Sat. *Sept-June* 9am-2pm, 5-8pm daily.

Manzanares el Real & La Pedriza

La Pedriza is a rocky crag crisscrossed with paths. Birthplace of the Manzanares river, it is home to the Sierra's biggest colony of griffon vultures, protected in the Parque Regional de la Cuenca Alta del Manzanares. The area fills up on Sundays, but don't be fooled – many experienced climbers still get lost in La Pedriza, and fatalities have been known. The starting point for a hike is the town of **Manzanares el Real**, dominated by the almost cartoonish vision of a perfect 'Spanish' castle, the 15th-century **Castillo de Manzanares el Real**, once the stronghold of the Mendozas, one of the most powerful aristocratic clans of medieval Castile. Much of its interior is the product of recent restoration work, but the castle retains

a fascinating mix of late Gothic and Mudéjar features, especially in the courtyard and the beautiful upper gallery, which has a spectacular view over the valley.

Castillo de Manzanares el Real
91 853 00 08. **Open** *Oct-June* 10am-5.10pm Tue-Sun. *July-Sept* 10am-5.10pm Tue-Fri; 10am-6.40pm Sat; 10am-5.40pm Sun. **Admission** €1.80; 80¢ concessions. **No credit cards**.

Where to stay & eat

A kilometre or so out of town on the path to El Yelmo is the small but well-appointed **Hostal El Tranco** (C/Tranco 4, 91 853 04 23, doubles €45, mains €11.50). Nearby are a couple of lively bars with terraces. Another option is **La Fresneda** campsite on the Carretera M-608 in Soto el Real (Sept-June open weekends only, rates €6 per person, including tent and car). At the time of writing it was changing hands; call the Ayuntamiento (91 847 60 04) for information.

Getting there

By bus
Colmenarejo 724 from Plaza Castilla, buses approx hourly 7am-11.30pm Mon-Fri, 8am-11.30pm Sat, Sun. The last return is at 10.20pm.

Sierra Norte

In contrast to the majestic alpine landscapes of the Guadarrama, this tract of rolling hills some 60km (37 miles) north-east of Madrid toward Guadalajara at first seems decidedly the poorer relative. Isolated until the 1980s, the Sierra Norte suffered from depopulation, with many villages being abandoned, until it was 'discovered' by *madrileños* looking for a more authentic, and cheaper, weekend retreat. The Sierra Norte is also host to the region's finest deciduous forests. Even at the height of summer the area is never crowded.

The gateway to the area is **Buitrago de Lozoya**, just off the A-1. What remains of its walled medieval centre shows traces of Arab times, and its cool and dignified Gothic 15th-century **Iglesia de Santa María**, recently restored after fire swept through it in 1936, is also worth a visit. The real charm of Buitrago, however, is the quirky little **Museo Picasso** in the basement of its town hall (Plaza Picasso 1, 91 868 00 04, www.sierranorte.com/buitrago, admission free), consisting of some 60 works, especially centred on bullfighting themes, and mostly from his later years. Picasso donated the pictures to his hairdresser and friend Eugenio Arias, a native of the town who met Picasso in

Alcázar de Segovia. *See p277.*

Toulouse, where they were both living in exile. For 26 years Arias cut Picasso's hair in return for his paintings and sketches, and on his return to Spain donated them to the town.

Among the first places of interest after Buitrago is **Montejo de la Sierra**, 16km (10 miles) to the north-east, and a good central point for excursions on foot. It has an interesting Renaissance church, but the jewel in its crown is a magnificent beech forest, 8km (5 miles) away at **El Chaparral**. It can be visited with guided tours, run from the **Centro de Recursos de Alta Montaña** information centre (C/Real 64, 91 869 70 58). It's a good idea to book places well ahead, especially from October to December. This is also popular mountain biking country, and the same centre has information on hiking routes.

An easy-to-follow bike route from Montejo, taking about three and a half hours, but which can also be walked in about twice the time, is along a dirt track that cuts off the road to La Hiruela uphill towards the signposted Puerto de Cardoso and Cardoso de la Sierra, in the province of Guadalajara, before turning back to descend again to Montejo. On the way there are inspiring views north to the Ayllón mountains, and the 2,129-metre (6,985-foot) Peña Cebollera. Further south, at the bottom of a magnificent valley in the very heart of the Sierra Norte, lies **Puebla de la Sierra**. With a population of less than 100, this mountain hamlet has been almost entirely restored, and probably looks better now than it ever has. There are many houses to rent at weekends, and it makes an ideal base for walks to the surrounding reservoirs. Information on walks is available at the Parador de la Puebla – not an official parador – in the centre of the village.

About 25km (16 miles) south-west of Puebla (as the crow flies, not as the road winds) is **El Berrueco**, with a 13th-century church and the huge El Atazar reservoir. **El Atazar** village is the starting point for more walks, and a range of water sports are yours for the asking at the reservoir. The picturesque villages of **Patones de Arriba** and **Patones de Abajo** sit on the southern edge of the Sierra, and are reached via the Torrelaguna road off the A-1 from Madrid. The former is a cluster of slate houses and narrow, cobbled streets, reached by a steep, twisting road, though most live in the latter. A restoration project in recent years has been a mixed blessing, saving many of the villages' ancient houses from decay, but attracting rich second-homers from the city. Patones (as they are collectively known) is thought to have once been a peculiar enclave within Spain, a diminutive Visigothic kingdom which held its independence until the 18th century. A road

north-east from Patones leads 7km (4.5 miles) to the vast **Cueva del Reguerillo**, with prehistoric cave paintings around its underground lakes. The cave is unmarked, so be sure to ask directions before setting off, and a torch is helpful when you get there.

Where to stay & eat

Buitrago has the **Hostal Madrid-Paris** (Avda Madrid 23, 91 868 11 26, doubles €30, closed Sat & dinner Sun, set meal €12-€15), an old stone house with 25 bargain rooms and a great-value restaurant. For old-fashioned food in surroundings to match, try **Asador Jubel** (C/Real 33, 91 868 03 09, mains €10.50). **Mesón del Hayedo** (C/Turco, 91 869 70 23, rates €40, restaurant closed dinner Mon-Thur, Sun & all Mon, mains €15-€20) is small, with a crowded and lively restaurant, not always open to non-guests. **Taberna de Teo** (Plaza de la Constitución 10, 91 868 05 12, closed lunch Tue, dinner Sun, & all Wed) is a beautifully restored wine bar with excellent tapas.

In Puebla de la Sierra, the **Parador de la Puebla** (Plaza Carlos Ruiz 2, 91 869 72 56, rates €48-€54 incl breakfast, closed Tue) only has five rooms, so make sure that you book well in advance. However, staff will recommend other houses in the village that let rooms if you're out of luck. In upmarket Patones the restored five-room country house **Hotel el Tiempo Perdido** (Travesia del Ayuntamiento 7, 91 843 21 52, www.eltiempoperdido.com, weekends only, closed 2wks Aug & 2wks Dec, doubles €191.50) is as good as it gets. And for food, you can't beat the old-world charm of **El Rey de Patones** (C/Asas 13, 91 843 20 37, closed dinner Mon, Thur, Sun, all Tue, Wed & Aug, mains €13).

Getting there

By bus
Continental bus 103 runs from Plaza Castilla to Buitrago (9am or 5pm daily). Last bus from Buitrago back to Madrid is at 6.30pm Mon-Sat, 11pm Sun. Many local microbus services run from Buitrago.

Tourist information

Centro de Turismo de la Sierra Norte
Avda del Cabrera 36, La Cabrera (91 868 86 98/ www.sierranortemadrid.org). **Open** 9am-6pm daily. The tourist office for the whole area is in La Cabrera, 18km (11 miles) south of Buitrago. Buitrago town hall (91 868 00 04, www.buitrago.org) also has a lot of information on activities in the Sierra above the Picasso Museum.

South & East

Visit the birthplace of Cervantes and the city that inspired El Greco.

Alcalá de Henares & around

After the horrific terrorist attacks of March 2004, **Alcalá de Henares** was descended upon by the world's camera crews and catapulted to fame for all the wrong reasons. Centuries before, all eyes were on Alcalá as Spain's centre of learning and culture, with a superb university, founded in 1498, and later as the birthplace of Cervantes. As far back as Roman times, Complutum, as it was known then, was a large and important city.

The university moved to Madrid in the 19th century, but there is still a strong sense of the city's educational history here today. The streets in the old quarter are lined with **Colegios Mayores** – student halls of residence in the 16th and 17th centuries, now converted into hotels and restaurants. One of the most impressive is the **Colegio de San Ildefonso**, famous for its stunning Plateresque façade and its three-tiered patio, which is still the setting for the solemn opening of university terms and for the presentation of the Cervantes Prize for Literature.

The main square, named after the city's most famous literary son, is a great spot to relax over a coffee and admire the buildings that line it, such as the **Casa Consistorial** (town hall) and the **Capilla de Oidor**, a 15th-century chapel now used for exhibitions. If you want to know more about the creator of Don Quixote, head to the author's birthplace, now the **Museo Casa Cervantes** (C/Mayor 48, 91 889 96 54, www.museo-casa-natal-cervantes.org, closed Mon, admission free). On the city's west side are the **Catedral Magistral** and the **Museo de Esculturas al Aire Libre**, an open-air museum with 50 or so sculptures.

One of the most entertaining ways to get to Alcalá is via the Tren de Cervantes (which runs weekends in autumn and spring, leaving Atocha station in Madrid at 11am, and returning at 7pm). Guides in Golden Age costume ply passengers with information about the city, and, on arrival, give them a tour of the town.

From Alcalá you can take a short excursion 17 kilometres (9.5 miles) down the M-204, to **Nuevo Baztán**. A peaceful little place, it was founded by a banker in the early 18th century

The striking façade of the **Colegio de San Ildefonso**.

Garden airs

Inspired by Aranjuez's vast palace gardens, the *Concierto de Aranjuez*, composed in 1939 by Joaquín Rodrigo (1901-1999), is probably the best-known piece of Spanish music. Sneered at by classical snobs, it's nonetheless a 20th-century classic, covered by greats such as flamenco guitarist Paco de Lucía and, famously, Miles Davis, who used its 'Adagio' section as the cornerstone of his *Sketches of Spain* album. The *Concierto* has featured in commercials, World Championship-winning figure-skating routines, and even inspired Jack Black to start his 'School of Rock'.

Blinded after a diphtheria attack aged three, Rodrigo wanted the piece to depict the aural and olfactory pleasures he experienced in the Bourbon monarchs' summer retreat: 'the fragrance of magnolias, the singing of birds and the gushing of fountains'. Rodrigo drew on Spain's musical heritage – the formality of 17th- and 18th-century baroque composers, as well as more passionate folk styles – to conjure up the magical flow of nature, as well as the splendour and darkness of the palace's history.

Unusual for pitting a solo guitar against a full orchestra, the *Concierto* comprises three movements. The first, 'Allegro con spirito', feels like an alfresco jaunt and is built on a series of switching elements – between solos and the orchestra, between the flamenco-tinged strumming of the guitar and the melody. The famous second movement, 'Adagio', is based on an Andalucían lament. Guitar and cor anglais swap the same mournful refrain back and forth, until it's taken up by the whole orchestra to deliver an aching climax. Some say it was inspired by the bombing of Guernica in the Spanish Civil War, others by the death of Rodrigo's baby son. The third movement, 'Allegro gentile', reverts back to the opening jauntiness, a forthright mix of baroque-like counterpoint and folk-dance melody.

'After listening to it for a couple of weeks I couldn't get it out of my mind,' said Miles Davis after hearing the *Concierto* in early 1959. He and collaborator Gil Evans set about reworking that haunting central 'Adagio' section for their third album project together,

Sketches of Spain. Rodrigo, reportedly, wasn't in the end all that impressed, but many other listeners were. In his autobiography, Davis recounts the story a woman had told him of a retired matador, now raising *toros* himself, who after hearing *Sketches of Spain* had got out of his chair, put on his old bullfighting gear, gone outside and fought and killed one of his bulls. 'He said that he had been so moved by the music that he just had to fight the bull,' Davis remembered. 'It was hard for me to believe the story, but she swore that it was true.'

The *Concierto* had its première in 1940 in Barcelona and brought Rodrigo worldwide fame. It is Aranjuez, though, that best commemorates the composer, with a statue just off C/Infantas and, set into the pavement nearby, an inscription that includes musical notation from the *Concierto*. King Juan Carlos awarded Rodrigo the hereditary title of 'Marqués de los Jardines de Aranjuez' ('Marquis of the Gardens of Aranjuez') in 1992. When Rodrigo died in 1999 he was buried in Aranjuez's cemetery.

and the entire village designed by renowned architect José de Churriguera, giving it a wonderfully harmonious feel.

Where to eat

Alcalá's best-known restaurant is the **Hostería del Estudiante** (C/Colegios 3, 91 888 03 30, www.parador.es, closed Aug, mains €22.50, set meal €28.90), which occupies a stunning 16th-century *colegio* and specialises in hearty Castilian food – roast lamb and suckling pig, garlic soup and the Alcalá dessert speciality, *costrada*, which is something like a sweet millefeuille. At the back of the *hostería* and across a garden is the **Cafetería El Restaurado** (Plaza San Diego s/n, 91 885 41 40, closed dinner, all Sat, Sun and Aug, set menu €7.20). It's handy and popular with students for a quick and cheap lunch. **Mesón Don José** (C/Santiago 4, 91 881 86 17, closed Mon dinner & 3wks Aug, mains €9.50, set lunch €9.20) is cheap and quite atmospheric. For good tapas washed down with draught *vermut*, check out the attractive, tiled bar **Cervecería El Hidalgo** (C/El Bedel 3, mobile 627 215 706, closed Wed).

In Nuevo Baztán, the **Mesón El Conde** (Plaza la Iglesia 5, 91 873 53 27, closed 2wks Sep, mains €9.50, set lunch €8) is a reasonably priced, traditional place with balconies over the square and tables outside in summer.

Getting there

By bus

Continental Auto (91 888 16 22) bus 223 leaves from Avda de América every 5-10mins, 6.15am-11pm Mon-Fri, less frequently Sat & Sun. Journey time approx 35 mins.

By car

On the A-2 it's approximately a 25min drive (31km/19miles).

By train

Cercanías C-2; approx every 10mins (15-20mins weekends), 5.20am-11.50pm daily. Journey time 35mins. From the station it's a 10min walk to the centre (go straight down Paseo de la Estación).

Tourist information

Oficinas de Turismo

Callejón Santa María 1 (91 889 26 94/www.turismo alcala.com). **Open** *Oct-May* 10am-2pm, 4-6.30pm daily. *June, Sept* 10am-2pm, 5-7.30pm daily. *July, Aug* 10am-2pm, 5-7.30pm Tue-Sun.
Plaza de los Santos Niños s/n (91 881 06 34). **Open** *Oct-May* 10am-2pm, 4-6.30pm daily. *June, Sept* 10am-2pm, 5-7.30pm daily. *July, Aug* 10am-2pm, 5-7.30pm Mon, Wed-Sun.

Chinchón & around

Out of season Chinchón is a sleepy little town, famous for its *anís* liqueur and pretty, arcaded Plaza Mayor, overlooked by wooden balconies all the way around, and occasionally used for bullfights. This is where you'll find the town hall, tourist office and, most importantly, plenty of balcony restaurants and bars, where the traditional lunch is lamb cooked in a wood-burning oven, washed down with red from the *cuevas* (cellars) and finished off with a glass of the famous local brew.

The neo-classical **Iglesia de la Asunción** overlooking the plaza houses Goya's depiction of the Assumption. Just next door is the **Teatro Lope de Vega,** where the playwright wrote *El Blasón de los Chavos de Villalba* and which now doubles as a cinema. Just outside the town is the 16th-century castle, built on the site of the original 12th-century fortress. Sadly, only the ground floor remains, and it's home to sheep and the local outdoor drinking scene.

Chinchón hosts an open-air folk festival in the plaza at the beginning of June, and during the fiestas in August the bulls run the Avda del Generalísimo (or C/Huertos as some residents prefer), and there are fireworks, a fairground and bands performing near the castle.

It's worth driving to **Colmenar de Oreja**, five kilometres (three miles) away on the M-311. A quiet, untouristy place, it has an unspoilt Plaza Mayor, again ringed with wooden galleries, though on a smaller scale than Chinchón's, and a handsome 13th-century church, the **Iglesia de Santa María**. The tower is by Juan de Herrera.

Where to stay & eat

The balcony restaurants lining the Plaza Mayor all offer similar Chinchón fare – garlic soup and roasted red peppers, roast lamb and suckling pig. **La Casa del Pregonero** (Plaza Mayor 4, 91 894 06 96, www.lacasadelpregonero.com, closed Tue, mains €15) is slightly different – it uses local ingredients with some interesting twists, and has an attractive patio at the back. **Mesón Cuevas del Vino** (C/Benito Hortelano 13, 91 894 02 06, www.cuevasdelvino.com, closed Tue & 2wks Aug, mains €14.50) is an atmospheric place, with an ancient oil press and some old carriages. For accommodation, try the delightful **Parador de Chinchón** (C/Los Huertos 1, 91 894 08 36, www.parador.es, rates €139.10-€149.80), in a 17th-century former Augustinian convent, or the slightly less luxurious, but still very comfortable **Hostal Chinchón** (C/Grande 16, 91 893 53 98, www.hostalchinchon.com, rate €45).

Getting there

By bus

La Veloz (91 409 76 02) runs from Conde de Casal metro station. Buses leave every 30mins, 7am-11pm Mon-Fri; every hour, 8am-midnight Sat, and every 1hr 30mins, 9am-11pm Sun. The last return is at 10pm weekdays and Sun, at 11pm on Sat. Journey time approx 1hr.

Aranjuez

Aranjuez was the official spring residence of the Spanish monarchy and its hangers-on from the 17th to the 19th century. It was probably originally chosen for its setting and lush countryside – it is an oasis in the arid plains of central Spain, situated in a wide valley formed by the Jarama and Tajo (Tagus) rivers. The royals have long gone, but the **Palacio Real** is still the principal tourist attraction, along with the town's famous asparagus and strawberries.

Originally built as a hunting lodge for Charles I of Spain (Charles V of the Holy Roman Empire), the palace took its current shape under Philip II in the 1560s, and was extended in the 1770s by Charles III. It's a charming mix of baroque and classical, and typical of the Bourbon palaces, with a sumptuous **throne room** and a cosy **ballroom**. It is the gardens, however, that provide the real attraction, particularly the 16th-century-designed **Jardín de la Isla** and **Jardín del Príncipe**. The gardens inspired Rodrigo's famous *Concierto de Aranjuez* (see p282 **Garden airs**) and the music continues today with a summer season of mostly open-air concerts and musical promenades, principally featuring baroque music (see p232 **Getting some airs**). It is in the garden that you'll find the delightfully over-the-top **Casita del Labrador**, which was built for Charles IV. Though it was closed at the time of writing, half-hourly tours of this early 19th-century folly – complete with painted ceilings, tapestry-lined walls, and porcelain and marble floors – should be available again from early 2008. Call 91 891 03 05 for information and to book in advance.

In the town itself, **Museo del Toro** (Avenida Plaza de Toros s/n, 91 892 16 43) is also closed for renovation but should also reopen in 2008. The museum aims to re-create the atmosphere of the bullfight and the traditions and entertainments of the court. If you're so inclined you can travel to Aranjuez on the Tren de la Fresa steam train, with hostesses in period costume plying you with cheery historical facts (see p214).

Palacio Real de Aranjuez

91 891 07 40/www.patrimonionacional.es. **Open** *Palaces* Oct-Mar 10am-5.15pm Tue-Sun. Apr-Sept 10am-6.15pm Tue-Sun. *Gardens* Oct-Mar 10am-6pm daily. Apr-Sept 8am-8.30pm daily. **Admission** *Palace* €4.50; €2.25 concessions. *Guided tours* €5-€6; €2.50-€3 concessions. *Casa de Marinos* €3.40; €1.70 concessions. *Gardens* free. Free to EU citizens Wed. **Credit** MC, V.

Where to stay & eat

Casa Pablo (C/Almíbar 42, 91 891 14 51, closed Aug, mains €20) serves up superb seafood, while **La Posta** (C/Postas 23, 91 891 74 23, closed Sun & 2wks July, mains €11.50, set lunch €8.60-€14) is a good cheap and cheerful option.

To stay the night, the sleek **Príncipe de la Paz** (C/San Antonio 22, 91 809 92 22, www.nh-hotels.com, rates €86.70-€124.20) has stylish rooms overlooking the palace, though is often closed to the public during the week, while **Hostal Rusiñol** (C/San Antonio 76, 91 891 01 55, rates €44-€68) is a budget *pensión*.

Getting there

By bus

Buses run from Estación Sur every 30mins, 6.30am-11.30pm Mon-Fri; every hour 7am-11pm Sat; every hour 8am-11pm Sun. Last return 11.30pm Mon-Fri, 11pm Sat & Sun.

By train

Cercanías C-3 from Atocha, trains every 15-30mins 5.40am-11.55pm. Last return 11.30pm. The steam-powered 'Strawberry Train' (Tren de la Fresa) runs on summer weekends and holidays (see p214).

Tourist information

Oficina de Turismo

Plaza de San Antonio (91 891 04 27). **Open** *Oct-Mar* 10am-6.30pm daily. *Apr-Sept* 10am-7.30pm daily.

Toledo

Once the imperial capital of Spain (1087-1561) and still the ecclesiastical heart of the country, 'Holy Toledo' represents two millennia of history and so holds incomparable cultural riches. Its impregnable hilltop position, tremendous fortified walls and the natural moat formed by the River Tagus have made this an important strategic stronghold for everyone from the Romans to the Visigoths, Muslims and Christians.

During the Middle Ages, Toledo was known as 'the city of three cultures' when the Jewish, Muslim and Christian population lived in a

Picture this View of Toledo

Born Domenikos Theotocopoulos in 1541 on the island of Crete, El Greco originally trained as a painter of religious icons. As the island was then a Venetian colony, Venice was the logical place for an ambitious young man to seek his fortune and Il Greco (as he styled himself) spent ten years in Italy adding the influences of Titian, Tintoretto and Michelangelo to his Byzantine roots. The result was a love-it-or-hate-it style that was to influence painters from Picasso to Pollock. Trademark features include figures with elongated limbs and heavy-lidded heroin eyes, psychedelic colours and such distorted perspective that some critics have suggested that El Greco suffered from an ailment that affected his vision.

The painter was attracted to Spain by rumours that Philip II was seeking artists to decorate his El Escorial palace, but the conservative king was horrified by El Greco's freakish, ghostly figures. The artist eventually wound up in Toledo, where he remained until his death in 1614, at the age of 73. Much to the regret of the tourist office, nobody is sure which of the city's numerous churches holds his remains.

In Toledo he found great success and charged such extortionate fees for his work that several clients took him to court, although El Greco claimed that, 'As surely as the rate of payment is inferior to the value of my sublime work, so will my name go down in posterity as one of the greatest geniuses of Spanish painting.' Even so, he died a pauper after blowing all his money on an extravagant home and outlandish whims, such as hiring musicians to play as he dined.

El Greco painted several portraits of his adopted city, the most famous being *View of Toledo*, in New York's Metropolitan Museum of Art. As distorted as his human figures, they are more like spiritual impressions of the city than topographically accurate paintings – for instance, he would move the cathedral and the Alcázar closer together to symbolise the marriage of church and state. Not surprisingly, Toledo became something of a muse for El Greco and, as well as taking centre stage in these landscapes, the city featured in the background of several religious paintings, including *Laocöon*, *Christ in Agony on the Cross* and *The Immaculate Conception*.

uniquely heterogenous society; many religious buildings still bear a strange palimpsest of crucifixes, stars of David and Arab script. Over time, these religions blurred into each other, creating the Mozárabes (Christians who lived under Muslim rule with a semi-Arabic liturgy), and later the Mudejars, Muslims who did the reverse after the Christian conquest. This air of tolerance also attracted many world-class scholars, and Toledo became a famous centre of learning with prominent schools of science, mathematics, theology and mysticism.

Now enjoying a Golden Age of tourism, Toledo is by far the most popular daytrip from Madrid, and the steep, cobbled streets are mobbed with tour groups until the buses depart at sundown. The city is absolutely gridlocked for the duration of the Corpus Christi processions, during which the route is marked by white awnings over the streets and the cobblestones are strewn with rosemary, thyme and rose petals. Incense and chanting give the town an eerie medieval air, as do the period costumes and the priceless Flemish tapestries hung on the cathedral walls.

THE BISAGRA TO THE CATHEDRAL

If you come from Madrid by bus, car or train, the main point of entry to the old walled city is the imposing **Puerta de Bisagra**. This was built at the end of the reign of Emperor Carlos V to replace the original 11th-century Moorish

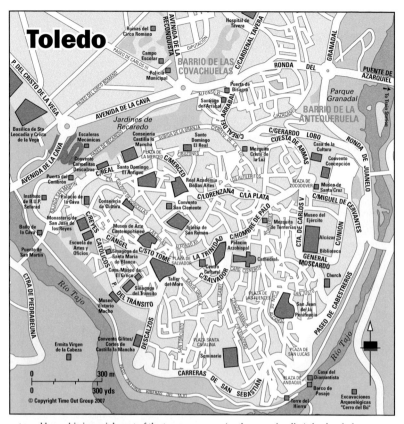

Toledo

© Copyright Time Out Group 2007

gate and bears his imperial crest of the two-headed eagle, the symbol of Toledo. Before going into the old city proper, pick up a map from the tourist office opposite and walk back a little way down the main street to the **Museo de Tavera** (C/Duque de Lerma 2, 925 22 04 51, admission €2.50, guided tour €4). Housed in the 1541 **Hospital de Tavera**, with a fine chapel and Renaissance courtyards, it has works by Tintoretto, Zurbarán and the city's adopted son, El Greco. Part of it may only be visited by guided tour.

To avoid the steep climb from here to the city, take the free escalator (7am-10pm Mon-Fri, 8am-10pm weekends). Alternatively, behind the gate, the superb Mudejar church of **Santiago del Arrabal** stands out, with an impressive brick tower and horseshoe arches. Part of it was once a mosque, but after the Christian conquest it was rebuilt as a church. The maze of streets on either side as you head up C/Real del Arrabal

was (as the name implies) the Arrabal – an area originally outside the Christian city. Off to the right on C/Cristo de la Luz are the gardens and stunning latticed brickwork of the **Mezquita Cristo de la Luz** (925 25 41 91, admission €1.90, €1.40 concessions). Built in 999, this mosque is the oldest surviving building in Toledo. According to legend, its name came from the fact that as Alfonso VI entered Toledo after the reconquest, his horse knelt at the door of the mosque, where, behind a stone in the archway, stood Christ, illuminated by the light of an oil lamp.

Dominating the skyline is the grim, black-turretted **Alcázar**, an enormous fortress built on the highest point of Toledo where Roman, Visigothic and Muslim forts stood before. Its armoury museum is closed until 2008 while it is extended to house the sizeable collection of the Museo del Ejército in Madrid. Using the Alcázar as a landmark, head up C/Real de Arrabal and

Trips Out of Town

C/Cuesta de Armas to the social nerve centre of the city, **Plaza de Zocodover**. Originally known as the *suk-al-dawad,* or animal market, it became the site for *autos-da-fé* after the reconquest, but is now lined with restaurant and café terraces serving everything from partridge to Big Macs. Nearby, the Renaissance **Hospital de Santa Cruz** (C/Miguel de Cervantes 3, 925 22 10 36, admission free) is now a museum housing tapestries, and works by El Greco and Ribera.

C/Comercio, the old town's main street, leads from the Zocodover to the Plaza Mayor, dominated by the **Palacio Arzobispal** (the Archbishop's Palace) and the jaw-dropping **Cathedral** (C/Cardenal Cisneros 1, 925 22 22 41, admission €6).

Spain's second-largest cathedral (after Seville) but for many the more beautiful of the two, Toledo's cathedral was completed in 1493 after 250 years of construction. A Christian church is said to have been founded here in the first century AD by Saint Eugene, the first Bishop of Toledo. Mainly Gothic in style with touches of Mudejar, neo-classical and baroque, the cathedral has 750 stained-glass windows, 70 cupolas and five naves, and is supported by 88 columns with 22 side chapels. You could easily spend a whole day exploring its dark interiors but some of its most extraordinary features include the sacristy's prestigious art collection (including El Greco's *The Disrobing of Christ*) the lavishly carved central choir and, behind the main altar, Narciso Tomé's unique 16th-century *Transparente,* a baroque frenzy of bronze, stucco, coloured marble and painting lit by beams of light via a circular 'sunroof' dripping with alabaster putti.

SANTO TOME AND THE SYNAGOGUES

Just around the corner from the cathedral, the narrow alleys that lead to **Plaza del Salvador** are the most visited parts of Toledo. They are lined with shops selling Toledo's artisan products: Toledan steel has been famous for its strength since Roman times and C/Santo Tomé is packed with shops selling everything from flick-knives to sabres and plumed helmets. Equally ubiquitous is *damasquinado* – the Damascus style of decoration brought by the Moors, in which fine threads of gold and silver are hammered into blackened metal – which covers everything from chess sets to knife handles and jewellery. For the sweet-toothed, Toledan marzipan is sold in all shapes and flavours.

The first major building en route is the **Taller del Moro**, a Mudéjar workshop that used to house exhibitions of Toledo crafts; it remained closed for long-term renovations as we went to press. Behind the Taller, down C/San Juan de Diós, follow the crowds to the Mudéjar church of **Santo Tomé** (Plaza del Conde 4, 925 25 60 98, www.santotome.org, admission €1.90, €1.40 concessions), which holds only one painting: El Greco's masterpiece, *El Entierro del Conde de Orgaz.*

Around the corner lies the **Casa-Museo de El Greco** (C/Samuel Levi s/n, 92 522 40 46), although, despite the fanfare, it has never actually been confirmed that the artist lived here. The house – a reconstructed 16th-century Toledan home – is closed until early 2008 for restoration, but meanwhile its impressive collection of El Greco's later works is in the **Museo Victorio Macho** (Plaza Victorio Macho s/n, 92 525 45 24, www.realfundacion toledo.es, admission €3).

In medieval times this area was Toledo's *judería,* the Jewish quarter, once the world's most important centre of Jewish scholarship. Many of its finest works of Jewish-Mudéjar architecture were restored in 1992 as an act of atonement for the 500th anniversary of the expulsion of Jews from Spain. The most recent beneficiary of the makeover is the **Sinagoga del Tránsito**, a richly decorated multicultural blaze of Hebrew inscriptions, Gothic carvings and Moorish columns. It was built in 1357 and its immense size is a testimony to the huge Jewish population that once lived in Toledo.

Toledo's **Cathedral**.

Today there is not even the minimum number of adult males (ten) to hold a service. After 1492 the synagogue was used as a church, but it now pulls in large crowds with its fascinating museum of Sephardic Jewish culture, the **Museo Sefardí** (C/Samuel Leví s/n, 925 22 36 65, www.museo sefardi.net, admission €2.40, free under-18s and over-65s) where displays include silver and crystal circumcision instruments and a 2,000-year-old ossuary.

The second of the surviving medieval synagogues, the **Sinagoga de Santa María la Blanca** (C/Reyes Católicos 4, 925 22 72 57, admission €1.90, €1.40 concessions) lies at the opposite end of narrow C/Judería. Its small, plain interior, dominated by horseshoe arches, is extremely beautiful, in spite of the gaudy baroque altar that was added later. Behind it, at C/Ángel 15, is a lovely bookshop dedicated to all matters Jewish, the Casa de Jacob.

The main street of the *judería* is now, ironically, called C/Reyes Católicos, and is topped by the very Catholic **Monasterio de San Juan de los Reyes** (C/Reyes Católicos 17, 925 22 38 02, www.sanjuandelosreyes.org, admission €1.90, €1.40 concessions). Built by Ferdinand and Isabella, it was originally intended to be the royal pantheon and has a dramatic Gothic cloister and an exterior garlanded with grim black chains; during the reconquest, these chains were supposedly taken from Christian prisoners and then used to hang Jewish dissidents.

Next to the monastery is a long stone balcony with impossibly romantic views over the River Tagus, the San Martín bridge and the typical *cigarrales* (Toledan country homes) on the hill opposite. For another great view, back over the whole city, head out of town over the River Tagus by the San Martín bridge, and turn right along the Carretera de Piedrabuena.

Where to eat

As Toledo province is the hunting centre of Spain, hearty game dishes dominate. Partridge (*perdiz*) is the most typical dish, and is usually served *a la toledana* – cooked slowly with onion, garlic and bayleaf – or else with *pochas* (succulent white beans) or pickled and eaten cold. Venison and wild boar stews are another speciality, along with roast suckling pig and *cuchifrito* (fricassee of lamb with egg and wine) and *tortilla a la magra* (cured ham omelette).

All these and more are on offer at traditional restaurants such as **La Abadía** (Plaza de San Nicolás 3, 925 25 07 46, mains €15, set lunch €10.70) where a labyrinth of bars and dining rooms fill a 16th-century palace. If a whole pig seems a bit much, try their *pulgas* (bite-sized

rolls). **Restaurante Aurelio** (C/Sinagoga 6, 925 22 20 97, www.casa-aurelio.com, closed Tue lunch, all Wed, mains €18, set meal €33.50) is in the heart of the Jewish quarter and filled with ancient farming tools. Part of a chain, it has three other branches in the city – check the website for details. After more than a century serving food, **Venta de Aires** (Paseo Circo Romano 35, 92 522 52 90, www.ventade aires.com, closed dinner Sun, mains €17.50, set meal €19-€25) must be doing something right. Particularly good at lunchtime when it's packed with locals feasting on excellent cod dishes and, naturally, partridge, is **La Perdiz** (C/Reyes Católicos 7, 92 525 29 19, closed dinner Sun, all Mon & 2wks Aug, mains €16).

For a sophisticated twist on these local staples – quail fried with ginger and lemon or duck breasts with grapefruit sauce – **Los Cuatro Tiempos** (C/Sixto Ramón Parro 5, 925 22 37 82, www.restauranteloscuatro tiempos.com, closed Sun dinner, mains €18, set lunch €19.40) is located in a charming 16th-century National Heritage building. For a real treat, the famous **Asador Adolfo** (C/Granada 6, 925 25 24 72, www.grupoadolfo. com, closed dinner Sun, all Mon & 2wks July, mains €24.60) is worth a visit for its impeccable service, fantastic wine list and light cuisine such as tempura courgette flowers with saffron.

Shamelessly overpriced tourist feeding troughs prevail around the cathedral and Plaza de Zocodover but you can get a good, basic menú del día with the locals in the shady courtyard of **Alex** (C/Amador de los Rios 10, 92 522 39 63, closed Mon, mains €9, set lunch €13.50) or, if you're handy with a map, the bars and restaurants dotted about the **Corral de Don Diego**, a shady patio set back from the street through a narrow archway.

When planning your visit, bear it in mind that most of Toledo's restaurants close for a fortnight in July or August.

Where to stay

Rooms in the old city can be hard to come by at weekends and in the high season, so it's best to book ahead, especially for Corpus Christi. With unbeatable views of the city, the luxury **Parador Conde de Orgaz** (Cerro del Emperador s/n, 925 22 18 50, www.parador.es, rates €135-€210) is about ten minutes' cab ride from the city. The splendid pool and top-notch restaurant make it worth allowing a day just to spend in the hotel. Right next to the Casa El Greco, the charming **Hotel Pintor El Greco** (C/Alamillos del Tránsito 13, 92 528 51 91, www.hotelpintorelgreco.com, doubles €118) occupies a converted 17th-century bakery that

Spires and tyres

You may think you're doing your bit for the environment with that weekly trip to the recycling bins, but the average person's attempts at recycling pale into insignificance compared to the efforts of Justo Gallego, a pensioner in the small town of Mejorada del Campo, to the east of Madrid.

Back in the early 1960s, Justo took it upon himself to start building a cathedral, using stuff other people had thrown away. Neither builder, architect nor engineer, he was a farmer before entering the Convento de Santa María de Huerta, a Trappist monastery in Soria, northern Spain. He stayed there for seven years until he caught TB and the other monks politely if selfishly asked him to leave.

He was at something of a loose end after that, until 12 October 1961 – the feast day of Our Lady of the Pillar – when it suddenly came to him that he had been put on this earth to construct a cathedral in his home town. Justo flogged his belongings and started right away, on a patch of land he had inherited from his parents. Unsurprisingly, the money raised did not go very far, and soon he was using whatever he could scavenge. More than 40 years later, he is still at it. Local firms sometimes donate supplies they no longer need, but otherwise he has recycled the most unlikely of materials, helped along by occasional contributions.

It's a curious sight, but the structure does somehow resemble a cathedral, and mass has even been held there. It is, however, a long way from completion. Now in his 70s, Justo is desperate for more funds and materials to complete his mission while he is still able to do so. Local builders and architects are reluctant to take the project on because it never had planning permission – or, indeed, any kind of official authorisation. In fact, Justo himself readily admits he never drew up any sort of plans and there is no guarantee it won't fall down at any minute.

The structure could be described as neo-Romanesque, and is 40 metres (131 feet) high with 12 towers. It has a large nave, partly covered by a dome with a diameter of almost 12 metres (39 feet). There is also a crypt, cloisters, a library and various other as yet unspecified spaces. Columns are made from oil drums, arches constructed from piles of old tyres and towers built with bits of bricks and piping. Bicycle wheels have been transformed into pulleys to get materials up the structure. The main entrance is approached by mosaic steps and spiral staircases link different levels. The structure has become a symbol of the town and has attracted media attention from all over the world. If and when it will ever be completed, though, only God knows.

Catedral de Nuestra Senora del Pilar

C/Antoni Gaudí, Mejorada del Campo. **By bus**: *from Conde de Casal every 30mins weekdays, every 90mins Sat, Sun.* **By car**: *A-3, then M-203 (21km).*

combines an original façade and patio with mod cons such as satellite TV. More economical is the new and very central **Hostal Santo Tomé** (C/Santo Tomé 13, 925 22 17 12, www.hostalsantotome.com, doubles €52) with ten comfortable rooms in an old Toledan townhouse. **Hostal Descalzos** (C/Descalzos 30, 925 22 28 88, doubles €49-€60) is also great value with en-suite, air-conditioned rooms around a sunny patio with swimming pool and jacuzzi.

Getting there

By bus

Continental Auto (902 330 400, www.continental-auto.es) runs from Estación Sur every 30mins from 6.30am (8am Sun), last return at 11pm (11.59pm Sun). Journey time is around 1hr 15mins.

By train

Trains depart hourly from Atocha station. The first train leaves at 6.50am Mon-Fri, 9.20am Sat, Sun. The last train out leaves at 9.50pm daily; returning, the last train is at 9.25pm daily. The average journey time is 30 minutes.

From Toledo station, take bus 6 to the Puerta de Bisagra, or you'll face a long uphill walk.

Tourist information

Oficina Municipal de Turismo

Plaza del Ayuntamiento (925 25 40 30). **Open** 10.30am-2.30pm Mon; 10.30am-2.30pm, 4.30-7pm Tue-Sun.

Oficina de Turismo

Puerta de Bisagra (925 22 08 43/www.jccm.es). **Open** *Oct-June* 9am-6pm Mon-Fri; 9am-7pm Sat; 9am-3pm Sun. *July-Sept* 9am-7pm Mon-Sat; 9am-3pm Sun.

Trips Out of Town

Directory

Barajas Airport. *See p292.*

Directory

Getting Around

By air

Madrid's **Barajas Airport** is 13km (8 miles) north-east of the city on the A2 motorway. Thanks to the new Richard Rogers-designed terminal T4, the airport capacity is expected to reach 700 million passengers per year. All airlines that are members of the OneWorld network (including BA, Iberia, Aer Lingus and American Airlines) will share T4 for national and international flights.

All other traffic is distributed between three existing terminals: non-Spanish airlines and flights on Spanish airlines from non-Schengen-area countries (such as the UK and USA, *see p308*) use T1; domestic flights and Spanish airline flights from Schengen countries use T2; some local flights and the Madrid-Barcelona air shuttle use T3. In T1 and T2 there are 24-hour exchange facilities, ATM machines and hotel booking desks. There is a tourist office (*see p308*) and rail reservations desk in T1, two tourist offices in T4.

For airport information, call 902 35 35 70 or 91 393 60 00, or check www. aena.es, which has updated flight info. Phone lines are open 24 hours a day.

Aerocity

91 747 75 70/www.aerocity.com.
Provides shuttle services between the airport and city-centre hotels. Handy for small groups and cheaper than taking several taxis. Prices (€17-€38) depend on size of group (from one to seven), the location of the hotel (city centre or outskirts) and the number of pieces of luggage in some cases. The company has two reservation desks at the airport (arrivals at T1 and T2 and T4); phonelines are open 24hrs.

Bus from the airport

Avda de América terminal (information 91 406 88 10).
Line 200 bus service runs between T1, T2 and T3 and Avenida de América, while Line 204 runs to T4. Both take between 30 and 40 minutes, depending on the traffic. There are two stops en route. First buses of the day leave Avda de América and Barajas at 6am; they run every 12mins, 6am-11.30pm. A single ticket costs €1. The airport buses are accessible to wheelchairs.

Metro from the airport

The metro is the cheapest way to get to central Madrid. Bear in mind that the Aeropuerto metro station is between T2 and T3, which means that if, as is very likely, you arrive at T1, you have a 10-15min walk to get there. From T4, take the shuttle to T2 (allow 20mins in total). From the airport it's four stops on metro line 8 (pink) and 12mins to Nuevos Ministerios. On outward journeys, if you are flying with Iberia, Alitalia and some other airlines you can also check in here. From Nuevos Ministerios it's around another 15mins into the centre of Madrid. You can save money by buying a Metrobús ticket at the airport station (*see p294* **Fare deals**).

Taxis from the airport

Taxi fares to central Madrid should be around €19-€22 (depending on the traffic), including a €5 airport supplement (no luggage supplement). There are further supplements after 10pm and on Sundays (for both, 18¢ per km). There are lots of taxis at Barajas, but ignore any drivers who approach you inside the building, just use the ones at the ranks outside the terminal. Check the meter is at the current minimum fare (€1.85) when you begin the journey; it's a good idea to check a map first, and to have a landmark in mind in the area to which you are going. For more on taxis, *see p294*.

Airlines

Aer Lingus
902 50 27 37/www.aerlingus.com.
Air Europa
902 40 15 01/www.air-europa.com.
American Airlines
902 11 55 75/www.aa.com.
British Airways
902 11 13 33/www.british-airways.com.
easyJet
902 29 99 92/www.easyjet.com.
Iberia
902 40 05 00/www.iberia.com.

By bus

Almost all international and long-distance coach services to Madrid terminate at the Estación Sur de Autobuses, C/Méndez Álvaro to the south of central Madrid (information 91 468 42 00, 91 468 45 11 from 6.30am to midnight; bus companies also have their own information lines). It's next to metro (line 6) and *cercanía* (local train lines C5, C7 and C10) stations, both also called Méndez Álvaro. Bus 148 also runs from there to the city centre (Plaza del Callao and Plaza de España). Taxi fares from the bus station carry a €2.50 supplement.

By train

Spanish national railways (RENFE) has two main stations in Madrid. Trains from France, Catalonia and northern Spain arrive at **Chamartín**, on the north side of the city, some distance from the centre. High-speed AVE trains from Andalucía and Valencia, express services from Lisbon and trains from southern and eastern Spain arrive at **Atocha**, at the southern end of the Paseo del Prado. There are exchange facilities at both stations, and a tourist office at Chamartín (*see p307*). Atocha is also the main hub of RENFE's local rail lines (*cercanías*) for the Madrid area (*see p294*).

Metro line 10 is the fastest from Chamartín to the city centre, and Atocha RENFE (the train station; not the same metro as Atocha) is four metro stops from Sol on line 1. A taxi fare to the centre from Chamartín should be around €13, including a €2.50 station supplement. There are extra supplements at night and on Sundays (18¢ per km). The same need for caution with cabs at the airport (*see p292*) applies to drivers touting for fares at main rail stations.

For more information on all Madrid-oriented rail services, *see p266*.

RENFE Information

902 24 02 02/www.renfe.es. **Open** *Information* 24hrs daily. *Reservations* 5am-10.30pm daily.

Estación de Atocha

Glorieta del Emperador Carlos V (Renfe information 914 68 83 32). Metro Atocha Renfe, Salamanca & the Retiro. **Map** p328 J14.

Estación de Chamartín

C/Agustín de Foxá, Chamartín. Metro Chamartín.

Maps

Metro, local train and central area street maps are included at the back of this guide (*see pp320-336*). Metro maps are also available at all metro stations: simply ask for '*un plano del metro*'. The Consorcio de Transportes, the regional transport authority, publishes a range of good-quality free maps, especially the Plano de los Transportes del Centro de Madrid. This map should be available at tourist offices (ask for a transport map, rather than the inferior street map the tourist offices often give out to the unsuspecting). For good shops to buy maps, *see p185* and *p187*.

In addition you can access an interactive map online at: www.munimadrid.es/GuiaUrbanav2/default.htm.

Public transport

To really get to know Madrid, it's best to explore on foot. Most of the main attractions are within walking distance of each other and for orientation purposes think of Puerta del Sol as the centre. Street numbers in Madrid all run outwards from Sol. Public transport is cheap and efficient – both bus and metro will get

you where you want to go within half an hour, although it's best to avoid the buses during rush hour. Note: all transport and taxi fares are subject to revision in January.

For transport outside Madrid, *see p266*. For transport for disabled travellers, *see p298*.

Metro

The metro is the quickest and simplest means of travelling to most parts of the city. Each of its 13 lines (including the new Metrosur and Ramal lines) is identified by a number and a colour on maps and at stations. Metro stations also make essential reference points, and 'metro Sevilla', 'metro Goya' and so on will often be given to you as tags with addresses.

The metro is open 6am-2am daily. Tickets are available at all stations from coin-operated machines and staffed ticket booths. Trains run every three to five minutes during weekdays, and about every 10-15mins after 11pm and on Sundays. The metro can get packed in rush hours (7.30-9.30am, 1-2.30pm, 7.30-9pm).

Night buses (L1 to L11) run along the metro routes. *See below* **Night buses**.

Metro information

C/Cavanilles 58, Salamanca & the Retiro (902 44 44 03/www.metromadrid.es). Metro Conde de Casal. **Open** 6am-1.30am daily.
There are customer service points at the airport, Atocha, Chamartín, Avenida de América, Nuevos Ministerios and Alto de Arenal stations.

Buses

Run by Empresa Municipal de Transportes (EMT; information 902 50 78 50, www.emtmadrid.es). For information about fares and tickets, *see p294* **Fare deals**.

Most run from about 6am-11.30pm daily, with buses every 10-15mins (more often on more popular routes). Night

buses then take over. You board buses at the front, and get off via the middle or rear doors. The fare is the same for each journey (€1), however far you go. Officially, there is a limit to how much luggage you can take on city buses, and trying to board with luggage during rush hours is almost impossible. Drivers are not obliged to give you the change if they don't have it (and if what you give them is more than five times the price of the ticket), nor will they allow you to travel for free. But they must write down your contact details for the bus company to send you the change later on.

For tourist buses, *see p76*.

Useful routes

No.2 From Avda Reina Victoria, above Moncloa, to Plaza de España, then along Gran Vía to Cibeles, the Retiro and Plaza Manuel Becerra.

No.3 From Puerta de Toledo up Gran Vía de San Francisco and C/Mayor to Sol, then up C/Hortaleza to Cuatro Caminos, C/Bravo Murillo; ends close to the Estadio Bernabéu.

No.5 From Puerta del Sol via the Plaza de Cibeles, Plaza de Colón and the Castellana to Chamartín station.

No.14 From Conde de Casal along Paseo Reina Cristina to Atocha, then along Paseo del Prado, Recoletos and the Castellana to Chamartín.

No.27 A frequent service all the way up and down the Castellana from Embajadores via Atocha to Plaza Castilla.

C1 and C2 The 'Circular' route runs in a wide circuit around the city, via Atocha, Embajadores, Plaza de España, Moncloa, Cuatro Caminos, Plaza Manuel Becerra and the Retiro.

Night buses

Between midnight and around 5am there are 24 night routes in operation – N1 to N24 – called Búho (Owl) buses. All begin from Plaza de Cibeles and run out to the suburbs, and are numbered in a clockwise sequence. Although the Metro closes at nights, at the weekends special buses, called Metro Búho, cover the routes of the 11 central metro lines (L1-L11). The buses alight at the bus stop nearest to each metro station. The timetable for each line varies, but generally the buses run from 12.45am until 5.45am. L1-L11 buses run every 15 to 20 minutes. There are three buses that cover the L12 Metrosur route, which connects Alcorcón, Leganés, Getafe,

Directory

Fare deals

Compared to fare structures in many other capital cities, Madrid's is simple – €1 for a single journey on the bus or metro (excluding Metro Sur, which is €1.75) within the capital, no matter how long the journey. On the metro you can change any number of times as long as you don't leave a station. The exceptions are trips to the stations Rivas Urbanizaciones, Rivas Vaciamadrid, La Poveda and Arganda del Rey (all Line 9), and all stations beyond Puerta del Sur on the new Metro Sur line, which circles the southern suburbs.

However, it's easier and more economical to buy a ticket for 10 journeys (*billete de diez/Metrobús*), which can be used on the bus and metro, available at all metro stations and some *estancos* and *kioskos*, but not on the bus. You can share the ticket between two or more people and keep it for as long as you like (or until the prices go up). The current price of a Metrobús is €6.40.

On the metro, you simply insert the ticket into the machine at the gate that leads through to the platform, which cancels one unit for each trip – remember to collect it afterwards – and will reject expired tickets. There is no checking or collection of tickets at station exits. On buses, the Metrobús should be inserted arrow downwards into the blue and yellow machine just behind the driver.

Abonos – season tickets

If you're planning on staying much longer than a fortnight, a monthly season ticket is a good idea. Unlike the Metrobús, it is valid for *cercanías* trains as well as the metro and city buses, allowing you to use it on some trips out of town. Your first *abono* must be obtained with an identity card, available only from *estancos*, for which you will need two passport-size photos and must fill in a brief form. In succeeding months you can buy tickets to revalidate the card from metro stations and EMT kiosks as well as *estancos*. Note, though, that an *abono* is valid for an actual calendar month, not for 30 days from date of purchase, so that if your stay runs across two months, buying one may not be particularly economical unless you qualify for one of the different age discounts. Also, if you can, buy your *abono* before the start of the month to avoid the nightmare queues on the first of the month.

Unless you are planning to travel a lot outside the city, Zone A should cover everywhere you need to go. A standard one-month Zone A *abono* currently costs €40.45, and there are substantial reductions for young people and for over-65s. It can be used on the buses to the airport, for which *see p292*.

Fuenlabrada and Móstoles. The L12 buses run every 30 minutes, from 1.15am to 5.30am.

EMT Information

C/Cerro de la Plata 4, Retiro (902 50 78 50/91 406 88 10/www.emtmadrid. es). Metro Pacífico. **Open** 8am-2pm Mon-Fri.

Cercanías/local trains

The highly efficient *cercanías* or local network of railways for the Madrid area consists of 12 lines converging on Atocha, several of which connect with metro lines along their routes. They are most useful for trips to the suburbs, or to the Guadarrama and towns near Madrid such as Aranjuez or El Escorial. Also, lines C-7a

and C-7b combine (with one change at Príncipe Pío) to form a circle line within Madrid that is quicker than the metro for some journeys, and the RENFE line between Chamartín and Atocha is the fastest link between the two main stations. *Cercanías* lines run from 5-6am to 11pm-midnight daily, with trains on most lines about every 10-30mins. Fares vary with distance, but the lines are included in the monthly season ticket (*see above* **Fare deals**). For a map of the *cercanías* network, *see p335*.

Taxis

Madrid taxis are white, with a diagonal red stripe on the front doors. The city has more than

15,000 taxis, so they are rarely hard to find, except late at night at the weekend or on days when it's raining heavily. When a taxi is free there is a '*Libre*' (free) sign behind the windscreen, and a green light on the roof. If there is also a sign with the name of a district in red, it means the driver is on his way home, and is not obliged to take you anywhere that isn't near that particular route. There are taxi ranks, marked by a blue sign with a white T, throughout the centre of Madrid. At the airport and rail and bus stations, it's always best to take a taxi from the official ranks; within the city, however, those in the know flag cabs down in the street, thereby avoiding the risk both of scams, and of station supplements. To avoid being swindled by a non-official taxi, make sure the driver has their licence number visible on the front and a meter, and always ask for the approximate fare before getting in.

FARES

Official fare rates and supplements are shown inside each cab (in English and Spanish), on the right-hand sun visor and/or the rear windows. The minimum fare is €1.85, which is what the meter should show when you first set off. The minimum fare is the same at all times, but the additional charge increases at a higher rate at night (11pm-6am) and on Sundays and public holidays, and there are extra supplements for trips starting from the bus and train stations (€2.50); to and from the trade fair complex (€2.50), and to and from the airport (€5). Also, the fare rate is higher for journeys to suburban towns in the outer tariff zone (zone B). Drivers are not officially required to carry more than €12 in change, and some accept credit cards.

RECEIPTS AND COMPLAINTS

To get a receipt, ask for *'un recibo, por favor'*. If you think you've been overcharged or have any other complaint, insist the receipt is made out in full, with details of the journey and the driver's signature, NIF number and licence plate, and the date. Make a note of the taxi number, displayed on a plaque on the dashboard. Take or send the receipt, keeping a copy, with a complaints form to the city taxi office at the address below. The form is included

in the Taxi Information leaflet available from tourist offices. You can present the form at any Junta office and they will send it on (information 011, 91 588 10 00); one central office is Plaza Mayor 3, Los Austrias (91 588 23 43).

Sección de Autotaxi y Vehículos de Alquiler
Ayuntamiento de Madrid, C/Albarracín 31, 3º, 28022, Eastern suburbs (91 480 46 27). Metro García Noblejas. **Open** 9am-2pm Mon-Fri.

PHONE CABS

You can call for a cab from any of the companies listed below. Operators will rarely speak much English, so if you aren't at a specific address give the name of the street and a restaurant or bar that makes a suitable place to wait, or position yourself near a street corner and say, for example, 'San Agustín, *esquina* Prado' (San Agustín, corner of Prado). The operator will also ask you your name. Phone cabs start the meter from the point when a call is answered. Very few cabs will take credit cards.
Radio-Taxi Asociación Gremial *91 447 32 32/91 447 51 80.*
Radio-Taxi Independiente *91 405 12 13/91 405 55 00*
Radio Teléfono Taxi/Euro Taxi *91 547 85 00/91 547 82 00.*
Teletaxi *91 371 21 31/91 371 37 11.*

Cycling

Cycling in Madrid is only for the truly experienced (or the utterly insane) in view of the heavy traffic and lack of cycle lanes on any of the city's central streets (there are a few in parks and by the river). However, bike lanes are gradually improving, and bikes are a great idea for trips to the larger city parks (Retiro, Casa de Campo) and especially the Madrid Sierras. Bikes can be taken free of charge on some *cercanías* lines and on the metro at weekends. Cycle hire shops often ask that

you leave proof of identity (take a photocopy to avoid having to leave your passport) as well as a cash deposit. There are an increasing number of companies and associations in Madrid that are dedicated to cycling, including Pedalibre (www.pedalibre.org) and Ciclos Otero (www.oterociclos.es).

Driving

Driving in the city is rarely a quick way of getting anywhere thanks to traffic jams, and finding a parking space is another headache. However, a car is an asset for trips outside the city. If you do decide to drive, bear these points in mind:
● You can drive here with a valid driving licence from most countries, but an international licence, available in Britain from the AA or RAC, is also useful.
● Keep your licence, passport, vehicle documents and insurance papers with you at all times.
● It is compulsory to wear seat belts and carry two warning triangles, spares and tools to fit them, a reflective jacket, spare headlight bulbs and spare glasses if you wear them.
● Children under 12 may not travel in the front seats of a car.
● The speed limit is 50kmph in towns, 90kmph on most highways and 120kmph on motorways – although many drivers ignore this. Speeding fines imposed on motorways (*autopistas*) and highways are paid on the spot.
● Spanish drivers often drink and drive, but the legal alcohol limits are similar to those in most EU countries.
● Do not leave anything of value, including a car radio, in your car, and do not leave bags or coats in view on the seats. Foreign numberplates are particularly tempting.
● In general, drivers go as fast as they can, irrespective of the speed limit. At traffic lights many will follow through on the amber light as it changes between green and red. Do not stop sharply when you see a light begin to change, as you may be hit from behind.
● When oncoming drivers flash lights at you it means they will not slow down (contrary to the usual practice in Britain). On a major highway the flashing of lights is usually a helpful warning there's a speed trap ahead.

Directory

Signs & terms

cede el paso – give way
usted no tiene la prioridad – you don't have the right of way
único sentido – one way
cambio de sentido – indicates a junction that allows you to change direction
recuerde – remember
cinturón de seguridad – seat belt
ronda de circunnavegación – ring road

Car & motorbike hire

Car hire can be pricey, so shop around; there are often good weekend deals. Most companies have a minimum age limit (usually 21) and require you to have had a licence for a year. You will also need a credit card (as opposed to a debit card), or leave a big cash deposit (sometimes up to €500). Check if IVA (VAT), at 16 per cent, and unlimited mileage are included. All the companies listed require you to take out a *seguro franquicia* – a fixed amount you have to pay in the event of an accident or any damage caused to the vehicle, and which is put on your credit card when you take the car (usually around half the hire cost – it is only charged if you return the vehicle damaged).

Avis *C/Agustín de Foxa 25, Chamartín (91 733 32 30). Metro Plaza de Castilla.* **Open** 8am-7pm Mon-Fri; 9am-1pm Sat, Sun. **Credit** AmEx, DC, MC, V.

Easycar *www.easycar.com.* **Credit** AmEx, MC, V.
Booking and payment is done online. Rates can be low, but conditions are pretty complicated.

Econocar *C/Felix Boix 2, Chamartín (91 359 14 03/econocar@econocar. net). Metro Plaza Castilla.* **Open** 9am-2pm, 4-8pm Mon-Fri; 9.30am-1.30pm Sat. **Credit** AmEx, DC, MC, V.
Local company with good rates.

Europcar *Avda del Partenón 16-18, Eastern suburbs (91 722 62 26/ reservations 902 10 50 30). Metro Campo de las Naciones.* **Open** 8.30am-2pm, 4.30-8pm Mon-Fri. **Credit** AmEx, DC, MC, V.
Other locations: (open 8am-9pm Mon-Fri): Barajas airport (91 393 72 35); Atocha station (91 530 01 94); Chamartín station (91 323 17 21); C/San Leonardo 8, Malasaña (91 541 88 92); Tetuán (91 555 99 30); Nuevos Ministerios metro (91 411 80 54).

Motoalquiler
C/Conde Duque 13, Malasaña (91 542 06 57). Metro San Bernardo. **Open** 8am-1.30pm, 5-8pm Mon-Fri. **Credit** AmEx, DC, MC, V. **Map** p323 F8.
Motorcycle specialists.

National-Atesa
Paseo de la Castellana 130, Chamartín (91 782 01 30/902 10 01 01). Metro

Santiago Bernabéu. **Open** *Sept-July* 9am-2.30pm, 3.30-6pm Mon-Thur; 9am-3.30pm Fri. *Aug* 9am-3pm Mon-Fri. **Credit** AmEx, DC, MC, V.
Other locations: Barajas airport (91 393 72 32).

PlanCar *C/Embajadores 216, South of centre (91 530 27 23). Metro Legazpi.* **Open** 9am-2pm, 4.30-8.30pm Mon-Fri; 9am-1.30pm Sat. **Credit** AmEx, V.
PlanCar is a local agency that's convenient for those staying in the south of the city.

Breakdown services

If you are planning to take a car to Spain it's advisable to join a motoring organisation such as the AA or RAC, which have reciprocal arrangements with their Spanish equivalent, RACE.

RACE (Real Automóvil Club de España)

Assistance 902 300 505/information 902 40 45 45/91 592 74 00/www.racc.es.
The RACE has English-speaking staff and will send immediate 24hr breakdown assistance. If you are outside Madrid, call the emergency freephone number, but you will be referred on to a local number. Repairs are carried out on the spot when possible; if not, your vehicle will be towed to the nearest suitable garage. Members of affiliated organisations abroad are not charged for call-outs, but non-members pay around €115 (on-the-spot membership) for the basic breakdown service.

Parking

For car-owning *madrileños* parking is a daily trauma. The city police (Policía Municipal) give out tickets readily (many locals never pay them). Be careful not to park in front of doorways with the sign '*vado permanente*', indicating an entry with 24-hour right of access. The ORA (Operación Regulación Aparcamiento) system now applies (*see below*) to the whole city centre (roughly between Moncloa, C/José Abascal, C/Doctor Esquerdo and Atocha). Residents park for free if they have an annual sticker.

ORA

Non-residents must pay to park in zones painted in blue or green from 9am to 8pm Mon-Fri and 9am to 3pm Sat (9am-3pm Mon-Sat in August). Pay-and-display machines are located on pavements. Maximum validity of tickets is two hours in blue zones and one hour in green, after which a new card must be used, and the car parked in a new spot. Cars parked in the ORA zone without a card can be

towed away (*see below*). In the blue areas, tickets cost up to €2.55 for two hours and in the green areas, €1.80 for one hour. All streets in this zone that have no additional restrictions posted are ORA parking areas.

Car parks

Central car parks *Plaza de las Cortes, Plaza Santa Ana, C/Sevilla, Plaza Jacinto Benavente, Plaza Mayor, Plaza Descalzas, C/Tudescos, Plaza de España.* **Open** 24hrs daily. **Rates** €1 per 30mins, then 15¢-20¢ per min to maximum of €25.60 for 24hrs.
There are some 50 municipal car parks around Madrid, indicated by a white 'P'-on-blue sign. It's especially advisable to use a car park if your car has foreign plates. Car parks have disabled access. See also www.madrid movilidad.es for more details.

Towing away

Information 91 787 72 90/91 787 72 92/www.madridmovilidad.es.
Main pounds *Plaza Colón. Metro Colón.* **Map** p324 K9. *C/Velázquez, 87. Metro Nuñez de Balboa.* **Map** p325 M6. **Open** 24hrs daily.
If your car seems to have been towed away, call the central number and quote your number plate to be told which pound it has gone to. It will cost €135.25 to recover your car. You'll have to pay €1.75 per hour for the first ten hours, timed from the moment it was towed away. For each complete extra day in the pound it's €17.65. You can also locate your car by entering your registration plate number at www.madridmovilidad.es/ madrid_movilidad/bases.aspx. Bring your ID and all car papers when you pick it up.

Fuel stations

Unleaded petrol is *sin plomo*; regular is *súper*, and diesel fuel is *gas-oil*.

24-hour petrol stations
Atocha
Repsol, junction of Paseo de Infanta Isabel & Avda Ciudad de Barcelona, next to Atocha station. **Credit** AmEx, MC, V. **Map** p329 L15.
24hr shop on site.

Campsa
Paseo de Santa María de la Cabeza 18, on southward exit from Glorieta del Emperador Carlos V. **Credit** AmEx, MC, V. **Map** p328 J15.
24hr shop on site.

Avda de América
Repsol C/María de Molina 21. **Credit** AmEx, MC, V.

Salamanca
Repsol C/Goya 24, junction C/Núñez de Balboa. **Credit** AmEx, DC, MC, V. **Map** p325 M9.

Cuatro Caminos
Carba C/Ríos Rosas 1, by C/Bravo Murillo. **Credit** AmEx, MC, V.

Resources A-Z

Addresses

Individual flats in apartment blocks have traditionally been identified by the abbreviations 'izq' (izquierda, left) or 'dcha' (derecha, right) after the floor number (C/Prado 221, 5ª dcha) and occasionally 'int' (interior, inward facing) or 'ext' (exterior); in newer buildings they may be shown more simply (C/Prado 223, 4B). A building with no street number (usually huge places like stations or hospitals) has s/n (sin número) after the street.

Age restrictions

In Spain, you have to be 18 to drive a car, smoke or drink, and get married, but the age of consent is a startling 13.

Business

Administrative services

A gestoría is a very Spanish kind of institution, combining the functions of lawyer, accountant, business adviser and general aid with bureaucracy. They can be very helpful in seeing short cuts that foreigners are often unaware of. English is spoken at these gestorías.

Gestoría Calvo Canga

C/Serrano 27, Salamanca (91 577 07 09). Metro Serrano. Open 9am-2pm, 4.30-8pm Mon-Thur; 9am-3pm Fri. Map p325 L8.
A general gestoría that deals with the areas of labour law, tax and accounts, and residency.

Gestoría Cavanna

C/Hermosilla 4, Salamanca (91 431 86 67/ www.gestoriacavanna.com). Metro Colón. Open Sept-June 9am-1.30pm, 5-7.30pm Mon-Thur; 9am-1.30pm Mon-Fri. July, Aug 9am-1.30pm Mon-Fri. Map p324 K9.
Specialises in taxation and employment law.

Conventions & conferences

IFEMA/Feria de Madrid

Recinto Ferial Juan Carlos I, Northern suburbs (902 22 15 15/www.ifema. es). Metro Campo de las Naciones. Open Office 9am-5pm Mon-Fri.
Madrid's lavish state-of-the-art trade fair centre has ten main pavilions, a 600-seater auditorium, a brand-new 10,000sq m convention centre and many smaller facilities, plus 20 catering outlets and no less than 14,000 parking spaces. By the entrance is the Palacio Municipal de Congresos, a 2,000-capacity conference hall.

Oficina de Congresos de Madrid

C/Mayor 69, Los Austrias (91 588 29 00/www.munimadrid.es). Metro Ópera or Sol. Open Oct-May 8am-3pm, 4-6pm Mon-Thur; 8am-3pm Fri. June-Sept 8.30am-2.30pm Mon-Fri. Map p327 E12.
An office of the city council that assists those planning to hold a conference or similar event in Madrid. The Oficina de Congresos will facilitate contacts with venues and service companies.

Palacio de Exposiciones y Congresos

Paseo de la Castellana 99, Tetuán (91 337 81 00/www.madridconvention centre.com). Metro Santiago Bernabéu. Open 9am-2.30pm, 4.30-7pm Mon-Fri.
This venue is longer established than the Feria de Madrid (see above) and used for several major international conferences. It has conference rooms and galleries of all sizes; the facilities are excellent.

Recintos Feriales de la Casa de Campo

Avda de Portugal s/n, Casa de Campo (91 588 93 93). Metro Lago. Open Sept-July 8am-3pm Mon-Fri. Aug 8am-2pm Mon-Fri.
An attractive site with three halls and open-air space.

Courier services

DHL

Ground services 902 12 30 30/air services 902 12 24 24/www.dhl.com. Open Phoneline 24hrs daily. Pick-ups & deliveries 9am-7pm Mon-Sat. No credit cards.

MFR Distribución Urgente

Avda del Manzanares 202, Southern suburbs (91 476 71 61/www.motorecado.com). Metro Laguna. Open 8am-7pm Mon-Fri. No credit cards.

RUM

C/Galileo 91, Chamberí (91 535 38 16). Metro Quevedo. Open 9am-7pm Mon-Fri. No credit cards. Map p323 F6.

Trébol

C/Buenavista 32, Lavapiés (91 530 32 32). Metro Lavapiés. Open Sept-July 9am-8pm Mon-Fri. Aug 9am-3pm Mon-Fri. No credit cards. Map p328 H14.

Office & computer services

Bitmailer

Avda Ramón y Cajal, Chamartín (91 402 15 51/www.bitmailer.com). Metro Concha Espina. Open 9am-7pm Mon-Fri. No credit cards.
An internet service provider that also offers helpful and efficient back-up services. Bitmailer also sells a range of software.

Travel advice

For current information on travel to a specific country – including the latest news on health issues, safety and security, local laws and customs – contact your home country's government department of foreign affairs. Most have websites with useful advice for would-be travellers.

Australia
www.smartraveller.gov.au

Canada
www.voyage.gc.ca

New Zealand
www.safetravel.govt.nz

Republic of Ireland
http://foreignaffairs.gov.ie

UK
www.fco.gov.uk/travel

USA
http://travel.state.gov

Data Rent

C/Mesena 18, Northern suburbs
(91 759 62 42/www.datarent.es).
Metro Arturo Soria. **Open** Sept-June
9am-2pm, 4-7pm Mon-Fri. July, Aug
8am-3pm Mon-Fri. **Credit** MC, V.
PCs, printers, OHPs etc for rent by
the day, week or month.

Translators

Lionbridge Solutions

C/Orense 69 1º, Tetuán (91 567
54 00/www.lionbridge.com). Metro
Nuevos Ministerios. **Open** 9am-
6.30pm Mon-Fri.
A professional translation service.

Traductora Jurada (Official Translator)

Concepción Pardo de Vera
C/Costa Brava 20, Northern suburbs
(91 734 23 31). Bus 133 from Callao/
Metro Herrera Oria, then 134 bus.
Polidioma
C/Cea Bermudez 6, 6º izq, Chamberí
(91 554 46 20/polidioma@polidioma.
com). Metro Canal.
In Spain, official and other bodies
often demand that foreign documents
be translated by legally certified
translators. Call for an appointment;
rates are higher than for other translators. Some consulates (see p299) also
provide these services or they can put
you in contact with other translators.

Useful organisations

Bolsa de Comercio (Stock Exchange)

Plaza de la Lealtad 1, Retiro (91
709 56 10/902 22 16 62/www.bolsa
madrid.es). Metro Banco de España.
Open 9am-5pm Mon-Thur, 9am-2pm
Fri. **Map** p328 J11.

Cámara de Comercio e Industria de Madrid

C/Ribera del Loira 56, Campo de las
Naciones (91 538 35 00/www.camara
madrid.es). Metro Campo de las
Naciones or Mar de Cristal.
Has a useful information service
for foreign investors in Madrid. You
must make an appointment first.

Instituto Español de Comercio Exterior

Paseo de la Castellana 14-16,
Salamanca (91 349 61 00/902 34 90
00/www.icex.es). Metro Colón. **Open**
Oct-May 9am-2pm, 3-5pm Mon-Thur;
9am-2pm Fri. June-Sept 8.30am-
2.30pm Mon-Fri. **Map** p324 K8.
The state-run ICEX (Spanish Institute
for Foreign Trade) has an excellent
information service to aid small- to
medium-sized businesses.

Complaints

If you have a complaint, ask for
an official complaint form (hoja de
reclamación), which most businesses,
shops, bars and so on are obliged
to have available for customers. Fill
out the form, leaving the colour copy
with the business. Then take this,
and any receipts or other relevant
paperwork, to the official consumer
office, listed below.

Oficina Municipal de Información al Consumidor

C/Gran Via 24, Gran Via (91 211 18
51). Metro Gran Via. **Open** 9am-2pm
Mon-Fri. **Map** p323 H11.
The official centre for consumer
advice and complaint follow-up. You
need to make an appointment first.

Customs

If tax has been paid in the country
of origin then EU residents do not
have to declare goods imported into
Spain from other EU countries for
their personal use. However, customs
officers can question whether large
amounts of any item really are for
your own use, and random checks are
made for drugs. Quantities accepted
as being for personal use include:
● up to 800 cigarettes, 400 small
cigars, 200 cigars or 1kg of loose
tobacco
● 10 litres of spirits (over 22%
alcohol), 20 litres of fortified wine or
alcoholic drinks with under 22% of
alcohol, 90 litres of wine (under 22%)
or 110 litres of beer.
Limits for non-EU residents and
goods brought from outside the EU:
● 200 cigarettes or 100 small cigars
or 50 cigars or 250g (8.82oz) of
tobacco
● 1 litre of spirits (over 22% alcohol)
or 2 litres of any other alcoholic drink
with under 22% alcohol
● 50g (1.76oz) of perfume
● 500g coffee, 100g tea
There are no restrictions on cameras,
watches or electrical goods, within
reasonable limits, and visitors are
also allowed to carry up to €6,000
in cash. Non-EU residents can also
reclaim the Value Added Tax (IVA)
they have paid on certain large
purchases when they leave Spain.
For details, see p182.

Disabled travellers

Madrid is still not a city that disabled
people, especially wheelchair users,
will find it easy to get around.
However, the situation is steadily
improving as new buildings are
constructed with accessibility in mind
and old ones are gradually adapted:
technically all public buildings should
have been made accessible by law,
although in practice a great deal still
remains to be done. Access to public
transport is also patchy.
There is an excellent guide, Guía
de Accesibilidad de Madrid, which
is published by the Ayuntamiento
(city council) in collaboration with
the disabled association FAMMA.
This booklet is available from the
FAMMA office at C/Galileo 69 (91
593 35 50, www.famma.org).

Access to sights

Some of the city's wheelchair-friendly
venues are listed below.
Centro Conde Duque
Centro Cultural de la Villa
Museo de América
Museo de Cera
Museo de la Ciudad
Museo del Libro
Museo Nacional Centro de Arte
Reina Sofía
Museo del Prado
Museo Real Academia de Bellas
Artes de San Fernando
Museo Romántico
Museo Tiflológico
Museo Thyssen-Bornemisza
Palacio Real
Planetario de Madrid
Real Fábrica de Tapices
Santiago Bernabéu stadium

Buses

There are seats reserved for people
with mobility problems behind the
driver on most of the city's buses.
Buses on many routes are now of
the piso bajo (low floor) type, with
low doors and spaces for wheelchairs.
These are identified by the red on
white stripes at the front and back
of the bus and the slogan 'piso bajo
pensado para todos'.

Metro

All new metro stations have been
built with access in mind, which
means that those on newer lines
(Line 8 to the airport, the Gregorio
Marañón interchange, Line 7 to
Pitis, some others) have good lifts.
However, older stations in the city
centre generally have a lot of steps,
and although you may get on at a
station with a lift, it may turn out
to be impossible to get off at your
destination. The metro map on
p336 of this guide and the free
maps available at metro stations
indicate stations with lifts.

RENFE & cercanías

Of the mainline rail stations, Atocha, Chamartín, Nuevos Ministerios and Príncipe Pío all have good access. Cercanías trains have very limited access, but some newer stations such as Méndez Alvaro (by Estación Sur coach station) have lifts connecting metro, train and bus stations. There are also good interchanges at Moncloa and Plaza Castilla.

Taxis

Special taxis adapted for wheelchairs can be called through Euro-Taxi on 91 547 82 00/91 547 86 00 and Tele-Taxi on 91 371 21 31. Make it clear you want an adapted model (ask for a Euro-Taxi). The number of such taxis in Madrid is very limited (although it rose by 100 in 2004) and waiting time can be up to 30mins. Fares are the same as for standard cabs, but the meter is started as soon as a request is received, so the cost can be quite high.

Drugs

Many people openly smoke cannabis, but its possession or consumption in public are illegal. It's theoretically OK to smoke cannabis in private, but not to possess it; this law is rarely enforced. There's been a recent crackdown in bars, however.

Electricity

The standard current in Spain is now 220V, but a few old buildings in Madrid still have 125V circuits, so it's a good idea to check before using electrical equipment in older hotels. Plugs are all of the two-round-pin type. The 220V current works fine with British 240V products, with a plug adaptor. With US 110V appliances you will need a current transformer.

Embassies

For a full list look in the local phone book under *embajadas*.

American Embassy

C/Serrano 75, Salamanca (91 587 22 00/www.embusa.es). Metro Rubén Darío. **Open** *Phoneline* 24hrs daily. *Office* 9am-6pm (8am-1pm passports) Mon-Fri. **Map** p325 L6.
The general switchboard will put you through to the consulate.

Australian Embassy

Plaza del Descubridor Diego de Ordás 3 2º, Chamberí (91 353 66 00/visas

91 353 66 90/emergency phoneline 900 99 61 99/www.spain.embassy. gov.au). Metro Ríos Rosas. **Open** 8am-4pm (visas 10am-noon) Mon-Fri.

British Embassy

Paseo de Recoletos 7-9 4º, Chueca (91 308 06 18/visas 807 429 027/ passports 807 429 026/www.ukin spain.com). Metro Banco de España or Colón. **Open** 8am-1.30pm Mon-Fri. *Visa/passport lines* 9.30am-5.30pm Mon-Fri. **Map** p324 J7.
General commercial, economic and other information about the UK. For information on British passports, call 807 429 026 (9.30am-5.30pm).
British Consulate
Paseo de Recoletos 7-9 4º, Chueca (91 308 52 01). Metro Banco de España or Colón. **Open** 8am-3pm (until 6pm for emergencies) Mon-Fri. For queries relating to passports, visas and legal problems.

Canadian Embassy

C/Núñez de Balboa 35, Salamanca (91 423 32 50/www.canada-es.org). Metro Velázquez. **Open** *Sept-July* 8.30am-2pm, 3pm-5.30pm Mon-Thur; 8.30am-2.30pm Fri. *Aug* 8.30am-2.30pm Mon-Fri. **Map** p325 M9.
Emergency number for citizens (reverse charge calls accepted) is 1 613 996 8885.

Irish Embassy

Paseo de la Castellana 46 4º, Salamanca (91 436 40 93/visas 91 431 97 84). Metro Rubén Darío. **Open** 10am-2pm Mon-Fri. *Visas* 9.30-11am Mon-Fri. **Map** p325 L6.

New Zealand Embassy

Plaza de la Lealtad 2 (91 523 02 26/ www.nzembassy.com). Metro Retiro or Banco de España. **Open** *Sept-June* 9am-2pm, 3-5.30pm Mon-Fri. *July, Aug* 8.30am-1.30pm, 2-4.30pm Mon-Fri. *Visas* 10am-1pm Mon-Fri. **Map** p328 J1.

Emergencies

Madrid has a general number – **112** – to call for the emergency services (you also dial this number from GSM mobiles). Some staff speak English, French and/or German. However, you can be kept on hold for a long time; it's usually quicker to call direct. For more on the police, *see p305*.

Ambulancia (Ambulance) *061/092/ 91 335 45 45.*

Bomberos (Fire service) *Madrid capital 080. Whole comunidad 085.*

Policía Municipal (City Police) *092/91 588 50 00.*

Policía Nacional (National Police) *091.*

Guardia Civil *General 062/ Madrid capital 91 534 02 00.*

Emergency repairs

Electricity

Unión Fenosa *901 38 02 20.*
www.unionfenosa.es
Iberdrola 901 202 020.
www.iberdrola.es
The company you need to call will be indicated on the electricity meter as well as your bill. Both phone lines are open 24hrs.

Gas

Butane gas: Repsol Butano *901 12 12 12/www.repsolypf.com.*
Gas Natural *900 75 07 50/ www.gasnatural.com.*

Water

Canal de Isabel II *901 51 25 12/ www.cyii.es.*

Gay & lesbian

COGAM

C/Puebla 9, Malasaña & Conde Duque (91 522 45 17/91 523 00 70/ www.cogam.org). Metro Gran Vía. **Open** 10am-2pm, 5-9pm Mon-Fri. **Map** p323 H10.
The largest gay and lesbian organisation in Madrid, COGAM is one of the main organisers of Gay Pride and campaigns on various issues. The on-site café is a great place to chill and find out what's new on the scene.

Fundación Triángulo

C/Eloy Gonzalo 25, 1 ext dcha, Chamberí (91 593 05 40/www. fundaciontriangulo.es). Metro Quevedo. **Open** 10am-2pm, 5-9pm Mon-Fri. **Map** p323 H6.
A gay cultural organisation that campaigns on equality issues. It also runs a helpline (91 446 63 94, same schedules as above) and offers legal help and health and AIDS prevention programmes.

Health

EU nationals are entitled to free basic medical attention if they have the European Health Insurance Card (EHIC), which replaced the old E111 form in January 2006. Travellers from the British Isles should apply for one online at www.dh.gov.uk (providing name, date of birth, and NHS or NI number) at least ten days before leaving home. Citizens of certain other countries that have a special agreement with Spain, among them several Latin American states, can also have access to free care. These arrangements won't cover all eventualities, so always take out private health insurance.

Directory

Accidents & emergencies

In a medical emergency go to the casualty department (*urgencias*) of any of the city's major hospitals (*see below*). All are open 24 hours daily; Clínico or Gregorio Marañón are most central. If you have no EHIC or insurance, you can be seen at any casualty department (pay on the spot and get reimbursed back home by presenting the invoices and medical reports). In a non-emergency, pharmacists are very well informed.

For an ambulance call **061**. You can also try the Red Cross (Cruz Roja 91 522 22 22, www.cruzroja.es) or the SAMUR service (reached via the Municipal Police on 092).

AIDS/HIV

Free advice is available on freephone 900 11 10 00 (10am-8pm Mon-Fri)

Centro Sanitario Sandova

C/Sandoval 7, Chamberí (91 445 23 28). Metro Bilbao or San Bernardo. **Open** 8.45am-noon Mon-Fri. **Map** p323 G/H7.
An official clinic that carries out free, confidential HIV tests.

Hospitals

Ciudad Sanitaria La Paz

Paseo de la Castellana 261, Chamartín (91 727 70 00). Metro Begoña.
Near Plaza Castilla to the north.

Hospital Clínico San Carlos

C/Profesor Martín Lagos, Moncloa (91 330 30 00). Metro Moncloa.
Enter Accident and Emergency from C/Isaac Peral, off Plaza de Cristo Rey.

Hospital General Gregorio Marañón

C/Doctor Esquerdo 146, Salamanca (91 586 80 00/www.hggm.es). Metro O'Donnell.

Complementary medicine

Instituto de Medicina Integral

C/Fernández de la Hoz 30, Chamberí (91 576 26 49). Metro Iglesia or Rubén Darío. **Open** 9am-1.30pm, 5-7.30pm Mon-Fri. **No credit cards.** **Map** p324 J6.

There are several English-speaking practitioners at this clinic, which offers treatments including homeopathy and acupuncture.

Contraception & women's health

Condoms (*profilácticos*, *condones* or *preservativos*) are available from most pharmacies, and vending machines and supermarkets.

Asociación de Mujeres para la Salud

Avda Alfonso XIII 118, Chamartín (91 519 56 78/91 519 59 26/http:// web.jet.es/amsalud). Metro Colombia. **Open** 10am-1pm, 4-8pm Mon-Thur; 9am-3pm Fri. Closed Aug.
A feminist medical association offering free advice and counselling.

Clínica Duratón

C/Colegiata 4, Los Austrias (91 429 77 69/www.duraton.info). Metro Tirso de Molina. **Open** Sept-July 9.30am-1.30pm, 4.30-8.30pm Mon-Fri. *Aug* 4.30-8.30pm Mon-Fri. **Map** p327 G13.
Family-planning centre run by women doctors and staff.

Dentists

Dentistry is not covered by EU reciprocal agreements, so private rates apply.

Clínica Dental Cisne

C/Magallanes 18, Chamberí (91 446 32 21/24hr emergencies mobile 661 857 170/www.clinicadentalcisne.com). Metro Quevedo. **Open** Oct-May 10am-1.30pm, 3-8pm Mon, Tue, Thur; 2-8pm Wed; 9am-3pm Fri. *June-Sept* 10am-1.30pm, 3-8pm Mon, Tue, Thur; 9am-3pm Wed, Fri. **Credit** AmEx, DC, MC, V. **Map** p323 G6.
British dentist Dr Ian Daniel is based at this clinic. Hours may vary in summer, and the clinic sometimes closes in August.

Doctors

Centros de salud are local health centres with three or so doctors and various specialised clinics. Waiting times can be long and consultations brief, but if necessary you will be referred to a hospital. Usually open 8am-9pm Mon-Fri and 9am-5pm Sat. These are some of the most central:

Centro de Salud Alameda

C/Alameda 9, Huertas & Santa Ana (91 420 38 02). Metro Atocha. **Map** p328 J13.

Centro de Salud Argüelles

C/Quintana 11, Argüelles (91 559 02 23). Metro Argüelles. **Map** p322 D11.

Centro de Salud Las Cortes

C/San Jerónimo 32, Huertas & Santa Ana (91 369 04 91). Metro Sevilla. **Map** p328 I11.

Opticians

For Grand Optical, a centrally located optician, *see p198*.

Pharmacies

Pharmacies (*farmacias*) are signalled by large, green, usually flashing, crosses. Those within the official system of the College of Pharmacies are normally open 9.30am-2pm, 5-8pm Mon-Sat. At other times a duty rota operates. Every pharmacy has a list of the College's *farmacias de guardia* (duty pharmacies) for that day posted outside the door, with the nearest ones highlighted (many now show them using a computerised, push-button panel). Duty pharmacies are also listed in local newspapers, and information is available on 010 and 098 phonelines (*see p308*) and www.cofm.es. At night, duty pharmacies may look closed; knock on the shutters to be served.

There are two 24-hour pharmacies, open every day of the year; *see p200*.

Private health care

Unidad Médica Anglo-Americana

C/Conde de Aranda 1-1° izq, Salamanca (91 435 18 23/ www.unidadmedica.com). Metro Retiro. **Open** Sept-July 9am-8pm Mon-Fri; 10am-1pm Sat. *Aug* 10am-5pm Mon-Fri. **Credit** AmEx, MC, V. **Map** p325 L10.
Offers full range of services, including dentistry. Will make house/hotel calls.

Helplines

Alcoholics Anonymous

C/Juan Bravo 40 2°, Salamanca (91 309 19 47/www.alcoholicos-anonimos.org). Metro Diego de León. **Map** p325 N6/7.
English-speaking group meets 8pm Mon-Fri; 6pm Sat; 7pm Sun.

Narcotics Anonymous

C/Doctor Piga 4 (902 114 147). Metro Lavapiés. **Map** p328 I14.
English-speaking meeting every Sunday at 5.30pm.

Studying in Madrid

There are plenty of learning opportunities for foreign adults at Madrid's universities and private institutions. Unsurprisingly, many of these are Spanish-language courses.

Language schools offer intensive summer courses in general Spanish (from beginner level to advanced) lasting from one week to four months or more. EleMadrid (www.elemadrid.com), Alba Language Consulting (www.albalanguage.com) or International House (www.ihmadrid.com) also run specialised courses for job-related Spanish (in fields including medicine, law, commerce and hotel management) and for those who plan to become Spanish teachers. Many of the schools, such as Acento Español (www.acentoespanol.com), Academia Contacto (www.academiacontacto.com), Academia InHispania (www.inhispania.com) or Idiomas Plus (www.madridplus.es) balance the tuition programme with leisure activities aimed at allowing students to learn about the city and Spanish culture. Schools can also help with accommodation.

For those who already have a reasonable level of Spanish, there are plenty of other interesting programmes around. Universidad Complutense de Madrid's prestigious summer lecture series have been taking place for the last 17 years in the mountain town of El Escorial. Lecturers have included luminaries such as poet Rafael Albertí, film-makers Pedro Almodóvar and Carlos Saura, and sculptor Eduardo Chillida, along with international artists, politicians, economists and scientists. Subjects are usually related in some way to current events, and have drawn on disciplines as varied as economics, art, politics, literature, psychology, sociology and environmentalism. Places on the lecture series are limited and fees are quite high (for details and fees, see www.ucm.es/info/cv). Students can apply for a scholarship that covers costs of accommodation and meals.

The Madrid Chamber of Commerce offers a good selection of vocational courses. There are classes throughout the year in subjects ranging from business Spanish for foreign executives to Spanish wine-tasting and oenology (you'll need a good level of Spanish for the latter). These courses have a very good reputation, both in Spain and abroad. Tuition fees are reasonable and class sizes are limited, which means there can be some competition for places. Check out www.camaramadrid.es for more information (click on 'formación' and 'monográficos'). Or phone the Chamber of Commerce (91 538 38 38, 8.30am-8.30pm Mon-Fri).

Cooking courses are popular too. Club Cooking (www.club-cooking.com) is a fun and friendly school with classes in cookery for all standards (there are even courses for children). Courses cover topics such as cooking with cod, rice cooking, Moroccan food, and cakes and pastry.

ID

Foreigners should carry national ID or a passport with them at all times, although a photocopy is usually OK. You'll be asked to show the passport itself or a driving licence when paying by credit card in shops.

Insurance

EU nationals are entitled to use the Spanish state health service, provided they have a European Health Insurance Card (see p299), which must be applied for well in advance of travel. This will cover you for emergencies, but for short-term visitors it's often simpler to avoid dealing with the state bureaucracy and take out private travel insurance before departure, particularly as this will also cover you for stolen or lost cash or valuables.

Some non-EU countries have reciprocal healthcare agreements with Spain, but, again, for most travellers it will be best to take out private travel insurance before arriving. For more on health services, see p299. For more on car accidents, see p296.

Internet

Internet access options keep evolving, but the basic choice is between internet service providers (ISPs) that offer free basic access, such as Orange (1414, dial 5 for internet option, www.orange.es) and those that charge a fee for better service, such as Ono (1400, www.ono.com). Gonuts4free (807 51 70 45, www.gonuts4free.com) is an Anglo-Spanish free ISP. In both cases you pay for your internet time in your phone bill.

Madrid has plenty of cybercafés, particularly around Puerta del Sol. For other computer services, see p297.

BBiGG
C/Mayor 1, Sol (91 531 23 64/www.bbigg.com). Metro Sol. **Open** 9am-midnight Mon-Thur, Sun; 9am-2am Fri, Sat. **Credit** V. **Map** p327 G11.
136 PCs, with the latest flat-screen technology and CRT for games.

Cibercafé Alamo
C/Alamo 7, Malasaña (91 542 82 62). Metro Noviciado. **Open** 8am-2am Mon-Fri; noon-2am Sat, Sun. **Map** p323 F9.
A real café with music, friendly staff and a pleasant atmosphere.

WORKcenter
C/Alberto Aguilera 1, Malasaña (91 121 76 00/902 11 50 11/www.workcenter.es). Metro San Bernardo. **Open** 24hrs daily. **Credit** MC, V. **Map** p323 G7.
An office centre where you can send or receive faxes and emails, access the

Directory

net, print from a disk, make copies or get ID photos. Internet access is pricey (from €1/10mins or €3/hour). **Other locations**: Paseo de Castellana 149, Salamanca (91 121 76 30); C/Conde de Peñalver 51, Salamanca (91 121 56 60); C/María de Molina 40, Salamanca (91 121 56 80).

Left luggage

Barajas airport

Terminals T1 & T2 **Open** 24hrs daily. **Rates** €2.65 first 24hrs; €3.30 (small locker) & €4.65 (big locker) per day thereafter.
Terminal T-4 (91 746 60 65) **Open** 24hrs daily. **Rates** €2.85 first 24hrs; €3.58 (small locker) & €5 (big locker) per day thereafter.

Estación Sur (buses)

Open 6.30am-11.30pm daily. **Rates** €1.25 per case per day.
A staffed office.

RENFE train stations

Open *Chamartín* 7am-11pm daily. *Atocha* 6.30am-10.30pm daily. **Rates** €2.40-€4.50 depending on locker size.

Legal help

ARE 2

C/Princesa 3, 12, Moncloa (902 44 77 22/www.are2consulting.com). Metro Plaza de España. **Open** 9am-9pm Mon-Fri (by appointment). **Map** p323 E9.
This Spanish firm can help with residency and work permits, accidents, tax and so on. English is spoken here.

Libraries

Madrid has many municipal public libraries, but few are in the centre of the city and they generally have limited selections of books in English. For a full list of libraries, check '*bibliotecas*' in the local *Páginas Amarillas* (*Yellow Pages*), call 010 or visit www.madrid.org/bpcm.

Ateneo Artístico, Científico y Literario de Madrid

C/Prado 21, Huertas (91 429 74 42/ www.ateneodemadrid.com). Metro Antón Martín. **Open** 9am-12.45am Mon-Sat; 9am-9.45pm Sun. **Map** p328 I12.
A literary and philosophical club founded in 1820, Madrid's Ateneo has often been a focal point in the city's cultural life. It also has the second largest library in Spain, and has the advantage of being open when others are closed. Membership costs €94 to

join, then €40 every three months, and members have access to talks, cultural events and other activities.

Biblioteca Nacional

Paseo de Recoletos 20, Salamanca (91 580 77 19/www.bne.es). Metro Colón. **Open** 9am-9pm Mon-Fri; 9am-2pm Sat. **Map** p324 K10.
Spain's national library has early books and manuscripts on display (in the Museo del Libro), and is also the home of the Hemeroteca Nacional, the national newspaper library (*see below*). To use the library regularly you need accreditation from a university or similar institution, but a one-day pass is quite easy to obtain (you need to take a passport or residency card).

Biblioteca Pedro Salinas

Glorieta de la Puerta de Toledo 1, La Latina (91 366 54 07). Metro Puerta de Toledo. **Open** *Oct-June* 8.30am-8.45pm Mon-Fri; 9am-1.45pm Sat. *July-Sept* 8.30am-8.45pm Mon-Fri. **Map** p327 E15.
The most attractive and convenient of Madrid's public libraries. Books can be taken out on loan.

British Council

Paseo del General Martínez Campos 31, Chamberí (91 337 35 00/www .britishcouncil.es). Metro Iglesia. **Open** *Sept-June* 9.30am-6.45pm Mon-Wed; 9.30am-8.45pm Thur; 9.30am-5.45pm Fri. *July, Aug* 9.30am-2.45pm Mon-Fri. **Membership** €15/mth; €35/3mths; €60/yr. **Map** p324 J6.
The library in the British Council study centre has a massive selection of books and videos in English, as well as CD-Roms, internet access and daily newspapers.

Hemeroteca Municipal

C/Conde Duque 9-11, Conde Duque (91 588 57 71/www.munimadrid.es/ hemeroteca). Metro Noviciado. **Open** *Sept-July* 9am-8.30pm Mon-Fri. *Aug* 9am-2pm Mon-Fri. **Map** p323 F8.
If you just have to track down that essential piece of information, the city newspaper library in the Centro Conde Duque is the place to do it. You need a researcher's card to get in, for which you must provide a copy of your passport and two ID photos.

Lost property

Airport & rail stations

If you lose something before check-in at Barajas Airport, report the loss to the Aviación Civil office (AENA) in the relevant terminal, or call 91 393 61 19 for terminals T1, T2 and T3, or 91 746 64 39 for T4. If you think you've mislaid anything on the RENFE rail

network, look for the Atención al Viajero desk or Jefe de Estación office at the main station nearest to where your property went astray. For phone information on lost property call 91 300 69 69 (Chamartín) or 91 506 69 69 (Atocha) and ask for *objetos perdidos*.

Sección de Taxis del Ayuntamiento

Paseo del Molino 7, South of centre (91 527 95 90/www.emtmadrid.es/ interest/lost.html). Metro Legazpi. **Open** 9am-2pm Mon-Fri.

EMT (city buses)

C/Cerro de la Plata 4, Salamanca (91 406 88 43/www.emtmadrid.es). Metro Pacífico. **Open** 8am-2pm Mon-Fri. *Phone lines* 8am-9pm Mon-Fri.
The lost-property office for items that have been lost on Madrid's city or airport buses.

Negociado de Objetos Perdidos (Madrid City Council)

Plaza de Legazpi 7, South of centre (91 588 43 46/44). Metro Legazpi. **Open** *Oct-June* 9am-2pm Mon-Fri. *July-Sept* 9am-1.30pm Mon-Fri.
This office mainly receives articles found on the metro or in taxis, but if you're lucky, something lost in the street may turn up here.

Media

Newspapers

Spanish newspapers may come in tabloid size, but they are far from light-hearted, preferring heavy political commentary. Sensationalist, celeb-dominated stories are reserved for the *prensa de corazón* (press of the heart), such as *¡Hola!*, *Diez Minutos* or *¡Qué me dices!*. Free daily papers *Metro*, *20 Minutos* and the gossipy *¡Qué!* are handed out outside most central metro stations. The plethora of other free newspapers now on offer includes *Latino*, aimed at the South American market, and *Gol!*, a round-up of the weekend's sport.

ABC

Despite its conservative outlook, *ABC*'s journalists have the highest professional reputation. Read by Madrid's most respectable citizens.

Marca & As

Sports-only (in fact, mostly football-only) papers. *Marca* is usually the country's bestselling daily paper.

El Mundo

This centrist, populist paper made its name by unearthing many corruption scandals under the Socialists during the 1990s. Friday's 'La Luna de Metrópoli' supplement is a good source of listings and information on the cultural agenda.

El País

The liberal *El País* is the established paper of record, and also carries good daily information on Madrid, with Friday's 'Tentaciones' supplement great for music and popular culture.

La Razón

Right-wing and sensationalist daily with much of its editorial coming from ABC.

English-language

Foreign newspapers are on sale in **FNAC** (*see p182*), all **Vip's** stores (*see p182*) and at most kiosks around Sol, Gran Vía, Calle Alcalá and the Castellana.

The Broadsheet

A glossy free monthly with articles on all aspects of life in Madrid and Spain, along with useful classified ads pages.

InMadrid

A free monthly aimed at English-speaking residents – you can pick it up in pubs, bookshops, universities, language schools and tourist offices. Good articles on the Madrid scene, plus listings information, events, reviews and small ads.

Listings & classifieds

Local papers carry daily film and theatre listings, and the Friday supplements of *El Mundo* (Metrópoli) and *El País* (Tentaciones) give fuller information, reviews and so on. For monthly music listings look out for the Barcelona-based magazines *Mondo Sonoro* and *Go* (in bars and music shops).

Segundamano

www.segundamano.es
'Second-hand' comes out three times a week and is the best place for small ads of all kinds.

Guía del Ocio

www.guiadelocio.com
A weekly listings magazine with cinema, arts, entertainment, concerts, nightlife and restaurant listings, and a good galleries section. It's handy, but can be inaccurate.

Music & style mags

Undersounds, *Rockdelux*, the Spanish version of *Rolling Stone* and the new *MTV* magazine are mainly sold in kiosks or music shops and at

festivals. A few free mags to look out for are clubbers' zine *AB*, the smarter monthly *Cartel* and *Mundo Sonoro*.

Radio

The Spanish are avid radio fans; you'll hear radios blaring out in bars, cafés, buses and taxis.
  Radio Nacional de España stations to listen for include RNE-2 (96.5 FM, classical music) and RNE-3 (93.2 FM, an excellent and eclectic mix of rock and world music). There are dozens of other local stations.
  The main commercial broadcaster is **SER** (Sociedad Española de Radiofusión), which controls four networks: SER, a news network, and two music channels.
  One specific English-language programme to look out for is Radio Circulo's Madrid Live on Tuesdays from 8.30pm to 9pm (repeated on Friday at 10pm), which can be found on 100.4FM. Produced and presented by radio journalist Ann Bateson, it focuses on the city's arts, entertainment and social scene.
  The BBC World Service can be found in the evenings on 12095 kHz short wave.

TV

There are seven main channels, which pump out an endless diet of tacky game shows, talk shows, really bad imported *telenovelas* (soaps) from South America and badly dubbed American movies. Just about the only redeeming feature is the news, although **Canal 2** does show some good documentaries and films.
  Non-Spanish films and shows on some channels can be seen in undubbed versions on stereo TVs; look for VO (*versión original*) in listings and a 'Dual' symbol at the top of the screen.

TVE 1 (La Primera)

The flagship channel of state broadcaster RTVE has a reputation for toeing the government line. However, the recent appointment of a committee assigned with restructuring the network comes with the promise from Prime Minister Zapatero that the era of political bias in the broadcaster has come to an end. Time will tell.

TVE 2 (La Dos)

The least commercial of all the TV channels, La 2 is good for documentaries and late-night movies (often in VO).

Antena 3

A private channel with an emphasis on family entertainment mixed with late-night salaciousness.

Tele 5

Another private channel. This celeb-obsessed station is the one to blame for the Spanish Big Brother, *El Gran Hermano*. It is also the Formula 1 channel, which has become a national obsession since the rise and rise of one Fernando Alonso.

Telemadrid

Madrid's own station. Good for live football on Saturday and the Megahit movie on Sunday nights, but bad for political bias. It functions as a mouthpiece for the local PP administration to such an extent that opposition PSOE politicians boycotted the station in early 2007.

digital +

A subscriber channel with a good selection of sport, movies and US hits. Many hotels and bars receive it.

Cuatro

This new channel, which filled the gap left by Canal+, is aiming squarely at people in their twenties with its mixture of American imports, flashy news programmes and chat shows.

La Sexta

La Sexta's launch was plagued by the need to retune everyone's receivers – particularly important given they showed some of the more significant matches in the 2006 World Cup. Now they're up and running, their programming focuses on a mixture of documentaries, films and the obligatory American imports.

Money

Spain is part of the euro zone. One euro is made up of 100 *céntimos*. One thing to remember is that the British/US practice on decimal points and commas is reversed (so 1.000 euros means one thousand euros, while 1,00 euro is one euro). There are banknotes for €5, €10, €20, €50, €100, €200 and €500, in different colours and designs. Then there are three copper coins (five, two and one *céntimo*), three gold-coloured coins (50, 20 and 10 *céntimos*) and large coins for one euro (silver centre, gold rim) and two euros (gold centre, silver rim).

Banks & exchange

Banks and savings banks (*cajas de ahorros*) readily accept cash and travellers' cheques (you must show your passport). Commission rates vary, and it's worth shopping around before changing money (although banks usually give the best rates); also, given the rates charged by Spanish banks, it's often cheaper to get money from an ATM machine

Directory

by credit or debit card rather than with travellers' cheques. It is always quicker to change money at larger bank offices than at local branches.

There are many small bureaux de change (*cambio*), particularly on Gran Vía and Puerta del Sol. Exchange rates are usually worse than in banks.

Bank hours

Banks and savings banks normally open 8am-2pm Monday-Friday. From October to May many branches also open from 9am to 1pm on Saturday. Hours vary a little between different banks, and some have branches that stay open until around 5pm one day a week (usually Thursday). Savings banks often open late on Thursday afternoons, but are less likely to open on Saturdays. Banks are closed on public holidays.

Out-of-hours services

Outside normal hours you can change money at the airport (terminals T-1 and T-2, open 24hrs daily), at main train stations (Atocha, 9am-9pm daily; Chamartín, 8am-10pm daily), in El Corte Inglés (*see p182*), in hotels, at private *cambios* and at the places listed below. At the airport, Chamartín and outside some banks in Gran Vía and Puerta del Sol there are automatic cash exchange machines that accept notes in major currencies, in good condition (be careful if you need to use these at night).

American Express

Plaza de las Cortes 2, Huertas (902 37 56 37). Metro Banco de España. **Open** 9am-7.30pm Mon-Fri; 9am-2pm Sat. **Map** p328 I12.

The usual services, including money transfer worldwide in 24 hours.
Other locations: C/Juan Ignacio Luca de Tena 17 (902 37 56 37).

Western Union Money Transfer

Change Express, Gran Vía 16, Sol & Gran Vía (91 542 81 80 Mon-Fri only/900 63 36 33 daily). Metro Gran Vía. **Open** 9.30am-6.30pm daily. **Map** p324 H11.

The local Western Union agent. It's the quickest if not the cheapest way to have money sent from abroad.
Other locations: Gran Vía 25, 46, 53.

Chequepoint

Plaza de Callao 4, Sol & Gran Vía (91 532 29 22). **Open** 9am-11pm daily. **Map** p323 G11.

An international exchange company.

Mind your queues and peeing

Learning how to be a *madrileño* is all about extremes. While visiting the city it is very likely that within a very short space of time you will encounter a local so kind that you may well want to pack them up in your case and take them home with you. But then you are also likely to meet someone so rude and offhand, that you may be tempted to bash them round the head with said suitcase. Fret not, this is all par for the course and, in a way, part of the charm of the *madrileño* temperament.

Greetings

Rather than awkwardly avoiding everybody else's gaze, as is de rigueur in British and US society, *madrileños* like to greet one another. For example, when you're stuck together in a lift. This extends to any kind of waiting room – a quick 'Hola' to all strangers is essential. And yes, gents, even when you're in that temple of silence, the urinal, you still need to say hello.

Staying in line

British people pride themselves on their ability to queue – but they like to do it silently, forming a line that soon spirals out of control with no one being so bold as to speak up and bring a little organisation to proceedings. Not so with the *madrileño*. Pop by any market stall and the first thing you must say is '*¿Quién es el ultimo?*' Who is last in line? Make a mental note of which four-foot-tall old lady comes before you and be sure not to push in.

Mind the gap

Packed rush-hour metro trains are common, so *madrileños* have a set way of alighting from them. Rather than just push past the people standing in front of the doors, only to find that they are also getting off, it's usual to ask those in front of you: '*¿Va a salir?*' ('Are you getting off?'). If they are not, watch in wonder as a path opens up before you.

Getting the horn

In Madrid, it's more likely you'll get assaulted for not having used your horn, such is the *madrileño*'s affinity with the klaxon. Taxi drivers are the real experts in beeping etiquette, so take your lead from them. The golden rules are: beep at pedestrians, learner drivers, all remaining categories of drivers and anyone who has taken more than a millisecond to notice a light's gone green.

Shouting and hugging

Arguments can start quickly in Madrid, but don't be alarmed – a great big barney will very rarely lead to a fight. So feel free to let rip at a taxi driver should he remonstrate loudly because you slammed his door too hard; tell the grumpy shopkeeper who's turned ignoring customers into an Olympic sport that he's an idiot; and tut loudly at the careless señora who almost poked your eye out with her umbrella. But it's not by any means all yelling and foul moods. Catch a *madrileño* on a good day, and they'll welcome you as if you were one of their own – so be prepared to hug. A lot.

Credit cards

Major credit and charge cards are accepted in most hotels, shops and restaurants. You can withdraw cash with major cards from most bank ATMs, which provide instructions in different languages. Exchange rates and handling fees often work out more economical than exchanging cash or travellers' cheques. Banks will advance cash against credit cards over the counter, but prefer you to use an ATM.

Lost or stolen cards
American Express
freephone 900 99 44 26.
Diners Club *902 40 11 12.*
Mastercard *freephone 900 97 12 31.*
Visa *91 519 60 00/*
freephone 900 99 12 16.

Tax

There are different rates of sales tax (IVA): for hotels and restaurants, the rate is seven per cent; in shops, it's generally 16 per cent, but on some items four to seven per cent. IVA is generally included in listed prices – if not, the expression *'mas IVA'* (plus tax) must be stated after the price. In shops displaying a 'Tax-Free Shopping' sticker, non-EU residents can reclaim tax on large purchases (*see p182*).

Opening times

Eating, drinking and shopping all happen late in Madrid. The siesta has faded to a myth, but *madrileños* do operate to a distinctive schedule. Most shops open from 10am to 2pm, and 5-5.30pm to 8-8.30pm, Monday to Saturday, although many stay closed on Saturday afternoons. Food markets open earlier, around 8am. In July and especially in August most shops and services (such as the Post Office and administrations) close in the afternoon. August is also the time when most shops, bars and restaurants close for their annual holidays (from two weeks up to the whole month). Major stores and malls are open from 10am to 9pm without a break, Monday to Saturday (for the vexed question of Sunday shopping, *see pp181-2*). Big supermarkets (Al Campo, Carrefour) open from 10am to 10pm Mon-Sat and the first Sunday of each month.
  Madrileños still eat, drink, go out and stay out later than their neighbours in virtually every other European country. Most restaurants are open from 1.30-2pm to 4pm, and 9pm to midnight, and many close on Sunday nights and Mondays, and for at least part of August. Many businesses finish at 3pm in the summer. Most museums (state ones) close one day a week, usually Monday.

Police

Spain has several police forces. In Madrid the most important are the local Policía Municipal, in navy and pale blue, and the Policía Nacional, in darker blue and white uniforms (or all-blue combat gear). Each force has its own responsibilities, although they overlap. Municipales are principally concerned with traffic and parking problems and local regulations. The force with primary responsibility for dealing with crime are the Nacionales. The Guardia Civil, in green, are responsible, among other things, for policing inter-city highways, and customs.

Reporting a crime

If you are robbed or attacked, you should report the incident as soon as possible at the nearest Policía Nacional station (*comisaría*), where you will be asked to make an official statement (*denuncia*). It is extremely unlikely anything you have lost will be recovered, but you need the *denuncia* to make an insurance claim. Very few officers speak any English.

Comisaría del Centro
C/Leganitos 19, Sol & Gran Vía (station 91 548 79 85/operator 902 10 21 12). Metro Santo Domingo or Plaza de España. **Map** p323 F10.
The Policía Nacional headquarters for central Madrid, near Plaza de España. Some other police stations in the city centre are listed below; all are open 24hrs daily.

Puerta del Sol
Inside metro Sol, by C/Carretas exit, Sol & Gran Vía (91 521 09 11). Metro Sol. **Map** p327 H11.

Huertas/Retiro
C/Huertas 76-78 (91 322 10 17). Metro Antón Martín. **Map** p328 J13.

Chamberí
C/Rafael Calvo 33 (91 322 32 78). Metro Iglesia. **Map** p324 K6.

Postal services

If you just need normal-rate stamps (*sellos*), it's easier to buy them in an *estanco* (*see below*). Post offices now have automatic stamp dispensing machines (with a weighing system) but they do not always work.

Palacio de Comunicaciones
Plaza de Cibeles, Salamanca & Retiro (91 396 27 33/902 19 71 97/www.correos.es). Metro Banco de España.
Open 8.30am-9.30pm Mon-Fri;

8.30am-2pm Sat (from 2pm to 9.30pm, service is given at Puerta N, in the C/Montalbán). **Map** p324 J/K11.
In the magnificent central post office, all manner of postal services are available at separate windows. Faxes can be sent and received at all post offices, but rates are expensive, so use a private fax bureau. There is an information desk near the main entrance. Not all services are available at all times. Mail sent poste restante should be addressed to Lista de Correos, 28000 Madrid, Spain. To collect, go to windows 17-20 with your passport. For express post, say you want to send a *'carta urgente'*.
  Other city centre post offices are at El Corte Inglés, C/Preciados 1-4, Sol & Gran Via; Carrera de San Francisco 13, La Latina; C/Mejia Lequerica 7, Chueca; C/Jorge Juan 20, Salamanca, and at Terminal 1 in the airport.

Postal rates & postboxes

Letters and postcards up to 20g cost 30¢ within Spain, 58¢ to Europe and North Africa, and 78¢ to the rest of the world. Note that you will pay more for 'irregular' shaped envelopes (basically, not rectangular). Cards and letters to other European countries usually arrive in 3-4 days, those to North America in about a week. Normal postboxes are yellow with two horizontal red stripes. There are also a few special red postboxes for urgent mail, with hourly collections.

Postal Exprés
Available at all post offices, this efficient express mail offers next-day delivery within Spain of packages up to 1kg (2.2lb), for €10-€12, according to distance and dimension.

Estancos

The main role of the tobacco shop or *estanco* (look for a brown and yellow sign with the word *'tabacos'*) is, of course, to supply tobacco-related products. But they also sell stamps, phonecards and Metrobús and monthly *abono* tickets. *Estancos* are the only places to obtain official money vouchers (*papel de estado*), needed for dealings with Spanish bureaucracy. Some have photocopiers/fax facilities.

Queuing

Despite appearances, Spaniards have a highly developed queuing culture. People don't always bother standing in line, but they generally know when it is their turn. Common practice is to ask when you first arrive, to no one in particular, '*¿Quién da la vez?*' or

'Quién es el último/la última?' ('Who's last?'); see who nods, and follow on after them. Say *'yo'* (me) to the next person who asks.

Religion

Anglican

St George's (British Embassy Church)

C/Núñez de Balboa 43, Salamanca (91 576 51 09). Metro Velázquez. **Services** *Sept-June* 7.30pm Wed; 10.30am Fri; 8.30am, 10am, 11.30am Sun. *July, Aug* 8.30am, 11.30am Sun. **Map** p325 M8.

Catholic (in English)

Our Lady of Mercy

Avenida Alfonso XIII 165, Chamartín (91 230 53 36). Metro Pío XII. **English Mass** 11am Sun.

Jewish

Sinagoga de Madrid

C/Balmes 3, Eastern suburbs (91 591 31 31). Metro Iglesia. **Prayers** 8am Mon-Fri; 9.15am Sat; 9am Sun & at dusk daily.

Muslim

Centro Cultural Islámico de Madrid

C/Salvador de Madariaga 4, Eastern suburbs (91 326 26 10). Metro Barrio de la Concepción. **Open** 10am-8pm Mon-Thur, Sat, Sun; noon-4pm Fri.

Renting a flat

The price of flats to rent in Madrid varies wildly, so it pays to shop around. A room in a shared flat costs upwards of €300 a month, while a one-bedroom flat is around €600 or more. Places to look for flat ads are the papers *Segundamano* and *Anuntis* and the English language magazine *InMadrid* (for all, *see p303*). Another option is to look around for *'Se alquila'* (to rent) signs.

Contratos de alquiler (rental agreements) generally cover a five-year period, within which a landlord can only raise the rent each year in line with inflation, set in the official price index (IPC). Landlords usually ask for the equivalent of one month's rent as a *fianza* (deposit) and a month's rent in advance. Details of contracts (especially with regards to responsibility for repairs) vary a lot; don't sign a *contrato* unless you're fully confident of your Spanish and/or a lawyer or *gestor* has looked at it.

Safety

As in most major cities, street crime is a problem in Madrid and tourists are often targeted. One plus point is that pickpocketing and bag-snatching are more likely than any violent crime. Places to be especially on your guard are the Puerta del Sol, Gran Vía, the Plaza Mayor, the Plaza Santa Ana and, above all, the Rastro and Retiro park; watch out, too, on the metro. The area around the junction of Gran Vía and Calle Montera is a centre of street prostitution, and can feel uncomfortable at night. Recently, the Lavapiés district has acquired a reputation for street crime, which has developed alongside growing racial tension in the area, with robberies often attributed to young, homeless North African illegal immigrants, even though most thefts reported by *Time Out* readers and local media seem to involve teenage eastern European or gypsy girls.

Street criminals prey very deliberately on the unwary, and their chances of success can be limited greatly by the following simple precautions.

● When sitting in a café, especially at an outside table, never leave a bag or coat on the ground, on the back of a chair or anywhere you cannot see it clearly. If in doubt, keep it on your lap.

● Give the impression of knowing what's going on around you, and – without getting paranoid – be alert and watch out to see if you are being followed.

● Wear shoulder bags pulled to the front, not at your back, especially in the underground. Keep the bag closed and a hand on top of it.

● Avoid pulling out large notes to pay for things, especially in the street at night; try not to get large notes when changing money.

● Be aware that street thieves often work in pairs or groups; if someone hassles you for money or to buy something, or pulls out a map and asks for directions, keep walking, as this can be a ruse to distract you so that the thief's 'partner' can get at your bag. This is often done pretty crudely, and so is not hard to recognise.

● Be extremely careful when you withdraw money from ATMs. Don't let anyone distract your attention while putting in your PIN code.

● Beware of fake policemen: if someone asks to see your ID, ask to see their identification first.

Smoking

Spaniards smoke – big time. It's not unusual for a bank cashier to serve you while puffing on the first of the day. Likewise, it's unusual to find non-smoking areas in restaurants or bars, although smoking bans in cinemas, theatres, the airport and on mainline trains are generally respected. Smoking is officially banned throughout the metro system, but many people take this to mean on trains only, and not station platforms.

Study

Foreign students from the EU staying more than three months require a residency permit (Tarjeta de Residencia Para la Realización de Estudios); non-EU students may also need a visa. For more details, *see p309*.

Accommodation

RoomMadrid

C/Conde Duque 7, Malasaña (91 548 03 35/91 548 10 21/www. roommadrid.es). Metro Plaza España. **Open** 10am-8pm Mon-Fri. **Map** p323 E9.

This agency specialises in finding rooms in shared flats, with a minimum stay of one month in summer and three months from September to June. Commission starts at €70. At busy times you'll need to make an appointment a few hours in advance.

Madrid Sal y Ven

C/Recoletos 11, 1° B, Salamanca (91 435 22 62/www.salyven.net). Metro Retiro. **Open** 9.30am-2pm, 3.30-7pm Mon-Fri. **Map** p324 K10.

Finds rooms in shared flats with a minimum stay of one week. The agency charges an inscription charge of €60 and commission on top of that.

Language learning

Todo Español

C/General Díaz Porlier 1, Salamanca (91 435 42 38/www.todosp.com). Metro Goya. **Open** 10am-7pm Mon-Fri. **Map** p325 O9.

A very efficient and friendly school, with five students per class. Staff can help students to find accommodation in Madrid.

Carpe Diem

C/Fuencarral 13, 2°, Malasaña (91 522 31 12/www.carpemadrid.com). Metro Gran Vía. **Open** 10am-7pm Mon-Fri. **Map** p323 H11.

A young, funky Spanish-language academy, with small groups and enthusiastic teachers.

Academia Actual Plus

Gran Vía 71, 1° izq, Sol & Gran Vía (91 547 56 08/www.actualmadrid. com). Metro Plaza de España. **Open** 9.30am-2pm, 4-8pm Mon-Fri. **Map** p323 F10.

A central and highly recommended school. There are no more than eight students per class.

Escuela Oficial de Idiomas

Camino del Caño 2, Chamberí (91 636 19 36/www.eoidiomas.com/ eoi/eoi.html). Metro Islas Filipinas. **Open** 10am-1pm, 4-9pm Mon-Fri. Closed July, Aug.

This government-run school offers courses in Spanish through the academic year. The school has several other centres in the Madrid area; call for a full list. Registration is in August/September and April/May; competition for places is extremely stiff.

International House

C/Zurbano 8, Chamberí (91 310 13 14/www.ihmadrid.com). Metro Alonso Martínez. **Open** 9am-8.30pm Mon-Fri. **Map** p324 J8.

Offers Spanish courses at all levels.

Universidad Complutense de Madrid

Secretaría de Cursos para Extranjeros, Facultad de Filosofía y Letras, Ciudad Universitaria, 28040 Madrid (91 394 53 25/www. ucm.es). **Open** *Office* Sept-June 10am-1pm, 3-6pm Mon-Fri. July 10am-1pm Mon-Fri. Closed Aug.

Three-month Spanish courses for foreigners are held during the academic year. Higher-level students can study linguistics, literature and culture; there are also intensive language courses.

Universities

Erasmus, Socrates & Lingua programmes

Information in the UK: UK Socrates-Erasmus Council, Rothford, Giles Lane, Canterbury, Kent CT2 7LR (01227 762712/fax 01227 762711/ www.erasmus.ac.uk).

The Erasmus student-exchange scheme and Lingua project (for language learning) are the main parts of the EU's Socrates programme to help students move freely between member states. To be eligible you must be studying at an exchange institution. Prospective students should contact their college's Erasmus co-ordinator.

Universidad de Alcalá de Henares

C/Escritorios, 4, Alcalá de Henares (91 881 23 78/www.uah.es). **Open** *Office* 9am-2pm, 4-7pm Mon-Fri.

Offers Spanish courses for foreigners.

Universidad Autónoma de Madrid

Ciudad Universitaria de Cantoblanco, Ctra de Colmenar km15, 28049 Madrid (91 497 46 33/www.uam.es). **Open** *Office* 9am-2pm, 4-6pm Mon-Thur; 9am-2pm Fri.

The UAM now competes in prestige with the Complutense.

Universidad Carlos III

C/Madrid 126, Getafe, 28903 Madrid (91 624 95 00/91 624 98 39/www.uc3m.es). **Open** *Office* 9am-2pm, 4-6pm Mon-Fri.

One of Madrid's newest universities, with campuses in Getafe and Leganés.

Universidad Complutense de Madrid

Avda de Séneca 2, Moncloa (91 452 04 00/www.ucm.es). **Open** 9am-2pm, 4-6pm Mon-Thur; 9am-2pm Fri.

The prestigious Complutense is Madrid's main university. The largest and oldest in Spain, it is home to 98,000 students, 3,000 of them from abroad.

Telephones

Since the Spanish national phone company (Telefónica) was privatised, other companies – such as Jazztel and Ono – now compete with it in certain areas. Nevertheless, Telefónica remains the main player in the field as far as infrastructure is concerned, though its prices remain relatively high.

Dialling & codes

It is necessary to dial provincial area codes with all phone numbers in Spain, even when you are calling from within the same area. Hence, all normal phone numbers in the Madrid area are preceded by 91, and you must dial this whether you're calling within Madrid, from elsewhere in Spain or from abroad. Numbers beginning 900 are freephone lines; 901, 902 or 906 numbers are special-rate services and can be very pricey. Spanish mobile phone numbers have six digits and begin with a 6.

International & long-distance calls

To call abroad, dial 00 followed by the country code, then the area code (omitting the first zero in UK numbers) and number. To call Madrid from abroad, dial the international code (00 in the UK, 001 from the USA), then 34 for Spain.

Australia *61.*
Canada *1.*
Irish Republic *353.*
New Zealand *64.*
United Kingdom *44.*
USA *1.*

Mobile phones

The Spanish are mobile (*móvil*) mad and just about everybody has one (or two). You can pay each month or use rechargeable pre-paid cards. Call costs depend on the type of contract you have. Mobile phones from other countries can be used in Spain with a 'roaming' system, which you need to activate before leaving home.

Spain Cell Phone

687 558 529/www.puertademadrid. com/rentacellphone.

Offers short- and long-term mobile phone rental. Call rates are low and incoming calls are free.

Phone centres

For international calls it's often worth using a call centre (*locutorio*). You don't need change (you are charged when you've finished your call), the booths keep out noise, and many offer international call rates cheaper than Telefónica's. There are many phone centres around Lavapiés, Huertas and Malasaña. Often other services – fax, internet, currency exchange, money transfer – are available. There is a directory of *locutorios* at www.ocio latino.com in the 'Guía Latina'.

Eucaris

Plaza Dos de Mayo 22, Malasaña (91 446 10 12). Metro Tribunal. **Open** 9am-midnight daily. **Map** p323 G8.

Money Exchange

C/Infantas 1, Chueca (91 532 75 35). Metro Gran Vía. **Open** 10am-10pm daily. **Map** p324 H10.

Public phones

Payphones are plentiful in the city, although due to the traffic noise, it's often worth using a phone in a bar or café, even though they often cost 50 per cent more than regular booths. Most models of payphone take coins (from five *céntimos* up), phonecards and credit cards, and have a digital display with instructions in English and other languages.

The first minute of a daytime local call costs around 11 *céntimos*; to a mobile phone around 35¢; to a 902 number, around 18¢. You are usually given credit to make more calls without having to insert more money.

Kioskos and *estancos* sell €5 (up to 70 minutes of communication) and €10 (up to 140 minutes) phonecards by various companies. Many of the cards give you a free number to call; an operator or automatic system then connects you with the number you want and can tell you how much is left on your card.

Directory

Operator services

Usually, operators will only speak Spanish, though most international operators speak basic English.

National directory enquiries 11818
International directory enquiries & operator 11825
National operator 11822
National operator for reverse charge calls 1009. After the recorded message, press the asterisk key twice, and then 4.
Telephone faults service 1002
Time 093
Weather 11822
Wake-up calls 096. Key in the time when you want to be woken, using the 24hr clock, eg 0830 for 8.30am.
General information 098. Although less comprehensive than the 010 line, this Telefónica local information service is open 24hrs.

Time

Spain is an hour ahead of UK time, six hours ahead of US EST and nine ahead of PST. Daylight saving time runs concurrently with the UK.

Tipping

There are no rules or percentages for tipping and in general Spaniards tip very little. It is usual to leave five or ten per cent for a restaurant waiter, rarely more than €4, and people often leave a few *céntimos* of small change in a bar. It's also usual to tip hotel porters, toilet and cinema attendants. In taxis the norm is around five per cent; more for longer journeys, or if a driver has been especially helpful.

Toilets

Public toilets are rare, although there are some with an attendant in the Retiro, by the lake; at Chamartín and Atocha stations; and in the Paseo del Prado. However, proprietors usually don't mind if you pop into a bar or café (better, though, if you ask first), and big stores such as El Corte Inglés or fast-food restaurants are a good bet.

Tourist information

City and regional authority (Comunidad de Madrid) tourist offices all provide similar basic information on Madrid and its region, plus free maps (*see also p279*). The city also runs a phone information line for locals, 010, that can be useful to visitors. Tourist offices do not make hotel bookings but can advise on vacancies; for booking agencies, *see pp55-56*.

Full information on what's on is in local papers, listings magazines and local English-language magazines (*see p303*). For useful websites, *see p311*.

Oficina Municipal de Turismo

Plaza Mayor 27, Los Austrias (91 588 16 36). Metro Sol. **Open** 9.30am-8.30pm Mon-Sun. **Map** p327 G12. Also where walking tours begin.

Oficinas de Información Turística

C/Duque de Medinaceli 2, Huertas (91 369 70 70/902 10 00 07). Metro Banco de España. **Open** 8am-8pm Mon-Sat; 9am-2pm Sun. **Map** p328 I12.
Other information offices on the general 902 number are located at: Barajas Airport Terminal 1 & 4 (91 305 86 56); Chamartín Station, near platform 20 (91 315 99 76); and Atocha Station (91 528 46 30). Hours vary slightly between offices.

Summer information officers

During July and August pairs of young information guides, in bright yellow and blue uniforms, are sent to roam the central area ready to answer enquiries in a courageous variety of languages (8am-8pm daily). They also staff information stands at Puerta del Sol, Plaza del Callao, Plaza Mayor, by the Palacio Real and by the Prado.

010 phoneline

Open 8am-9pm Mon-Fri; 9am-2pm Sat.
A city-run information line that will answer enquiries of any and every kind on Madrid, and particularly on events promoted by the city council. Calls are accepted in French and English, but you may have to wait for an English-speaking operator. From outside Madrid, call 91 540 40 10/40. There is also a tourist information line, 901 30 06 00, which usually has more limited information.

Visas & immigration

Spain is one of the EU countries that is party to the Schengen Agreement (which includes all of the EU except the UK, Ireland or the countries that joined in May 2004). These countries share immigration procedures and have reduced border controls between each other. To enter Spain nationals from countries that are party to the agreement need only show their national ID card, but British, Irish, those from the new EU countries and all non-EU citizens must have full passports.

Additional visas are not needed by US, Canadian, Australian, New Zealand or Israeli citizens for stays of up to three months. Citizens of South Africa and some other countries do need a visa to enter Spain. They can be obtained from Spanish consulates in other European countries as well as in your home country.

Water

Madrid's tap water is good and safe to drink, with less of the chlorine taste that you get in some Spanish cities. There are occasional water shortages in summer, and signs posted in hotels urge guests to avoid wasting water.
If you want tap rather than bottled water in a restaurant specify that you want *agua del grifo*.

When to go

The climate of Madrid has justly been described as 'nine months of winter (*invierno*) and three months of hell (*infierno*)'. Many people can't cope with the summer heat, others love it – and the city is great fun during the fiestas. *See also pp204-209.*

Climate

Winter in Madrid can be very cold, although there's often bright, crisp sunshine and most rain falls in autumn and spring. Spring is unpredictable – February can often be freakishly warm, while in April, rain is likely. Summer temperatures range from hot to unbearably hot, although it's a dry heat with little humidity. In July and August it doesn't really cool down at night, making partying in the street great fun, but sleeping less so. Traditionally there's a mass exodus in August. Autumn weather is usually bright and warm and it's often possible to eat and drink outside well into October. *See also p309* **Average monthly climate.**

Holidays

On public holidays (*fiestas*), virtually all shops, banks and offices, and some bars and restaurants, are closed. There is a near-normal public transport service, though, except on Christmas Day and New Year's Day, and many museums are open, with Sunday hours. When a holiday falls on a Tuesday or Thursday many people take the day before or after the weekend off as well, in a long weekend called a *puente* (bridge). Many places are also closed for the whole of Easter Week. For the city's festivals, *see p204-209.* The usual official holidays are:

Average monthly climate

Month	Max temp (C/F)	Min temp (C/F)	Rainfall (mm/in)	Rain (days)
Jan	9/48	2/36	39/1.5	8
Feb	11/52	2/36	34/1.3	7
Mar	15/59	5/41	43/1.7	10
Apr	18/64	7/45	48/1.9	9
May	21/70	10/50	47/1.8	10
June	27/81	15/59	27/1.0	5
July	31/88	17/63	11/0.4	2
Aug	30/86	17/63	15/0.6	3
Sept	25/77	14/57	32/1.2	6
Oct	19/66	10/50	53/2.0	8
Nov	13/55	5/41	47/1.8	9
Dec	9/48	2/36	48/1.9	10

New Year's Day/Año Nuevo 1 Jan; Three Kings/Reyes Magos 6 Jan; Good Friday/Viernes Santo; May (Labour) Day/Fiesta del Trabajo 1 May; Madrid Day/Día de la Comunidad de Madrid 2 May; San Isidro 15 May; Virgen de la Paloma 15 Aug; Discovery of America/Día de la Hispanidad 12 Oct; All Saints' Day/Todos los Santos 1 Nov; Virgen de la Almudena 9 Nov; Constitution Day/Día de la Constitución 6 Dec; Immaculate Conception/La Inmaculada 8 Dec; Christmas Day/Navidad 25 Dec.

Women

Instituto de la Mujer

C/Condesa de Venadito 34, Concepción (91 363 80 00). Metro Barrio de la Concepción. **Open** 9am-2pm Mon-Fri. A government organisation that acts as an umbrella for many other bodies, with a useful information service. The Institute has a legal office at C/Génova 11, Chueca (91 700 19 10, www.mtas.es/mujer).

Working

There is a huge number of foreigners living and working in Madrid. Ninety-five per cent of those from the EU are teaching English. To get a job in one of the academies with better pay and conditions, it's advisable to have a relevant qualification such as TEFL. Private classes are also available, but bear in mind that work often dries up over the summer and holiday periods.

There is a lot of red tape involved in working in Madrid; you can ignore the bureaucracy for a while, but in the long run it's best to sort things out. If you come here contracted from your country of origin, papers should be dealt with by your employer. The quickest way to deal with the state's

love of form-filling is to resort to the agencies called *gestorías* (*see p297*).

A new ruling, made in March 2003, effectively exempts many EU citizens living in Spain from the obligation to apply for and carry a resident's card (tarjeta de residencia). Students, along with contracted workers, freelancers, business owners or retired people who have already made Spanish Social Security contributions, are entitled to live in Spain and use their own country's ID card, or passport, for all dealings or transactions. Not all branches of the administration are aware of the ruling but it is clearly stated both on the British Embassy's website (www.ukinspain.com) and the Ministry of the Interior's (www.mir. es/SGACAVT/extranje).

Everybody in Spain, both nationals and foreigners, is obliged to carry a valid form of ID. In the case of those foreigners who do not have a national ID card, this means carrying your passport, which is risky. Technically not legal, but usually acceptable, is to carry a photocopy of the relevant pages. Alternatively, you can apply for a resident's card voluntarily, at the foreigners' police station, the Comisaría de Extranjería. First you must obtain the NIE (*número de identificación de extranjeros* – foreigners' identity number). The process is simple – go to the Comisaría de Extranjería or a police station that deals with foreigners' affairs with your passport and a photocopy of the important pages, fill out an application form and you will be sent your number by post. The number is used for all financial dealings and is necessary for opening bank accounts, tax declarations and so on. For the residency card, you will then need three passport photos, along with your passport and a photocopy. Proof of income and medical insurance are no longer necessary.

Non-EU citizens have a tougher time. While in Spain on a tourist visa you are technically not allowed to work, though many do. If you are made a job offer while in Spain you must return to your home country and apply for a *visado de residencia* (residence visa). Without this you may not enter Spain to work. The process can take some time and applications aren't always successful. Once the visa has been issued, you can travel to Spain, take up the job and begin the lengthy application process for a resident's card and work permit (*permiso de trabajo*). On making the application, the following documents must be submitted along with the official application form: photocopy of a valid passport; a police certificate from your home city stating that you have no prison record (officially translated into Spanish by a sworn translator); an official medical certificate (obtained upon arrival in Spain); three identical passport photographs; where applicable, documents proving why you are more capable of performing the job than a Spaniard or EU citizen; where necessary, proof that you have the qualifications or training required for the job. Work permits and resident's cards, once issued, are initially valid for one year, the second for two, the third for three. After five years you will be granted a permanent work permit, which, though valid indefinitely, must be renewed every five years. Good legal advice is recommended throughout the process.

Comisaría de Extranjería

C/General Pardiñas 90, Salamanca (general 91 322 68 40/student 91 322 68 13/14/residency 91 322 68 01). Metro Núñez de Balboa. **Open** 9am-2pm, 4-7pm Mon-Thur; 9am-2pm Fri. **Map** p325 M6.

Vocabulary

Like other Latin languages, Spanish has different familiar and polite forms of the second person (you). Many young people now use the familiar *tú* form most of the time; for foreigners, though, it's always advisable to use the more polite *usted* with people you do not know, and certainly with anyone over the age of 50. In the phrases listed here all verbs are given in the *usted* form. For help in making your way through menus, *see p142* and *p162*.

Pronunciation

c, before an **i** or an **e**, and **z** are like **th** in **thin**.
c in all other cases is as in **c**at.
g, before an **i** or an **e**, and **j** are pronounced with a guttural **h**-sound that does not exist in English – like **ch** in Scottish lo**ch**, but much harder.
g in all other cases is pronounced as in **g**et.
h at the beginning of a word is normally silent.
ll is pronounced almost like a **y**.
ñ is like **ny** in ca**ny**on.
A single **r** at the beginning of a word and **rr** elsewhere are heavily rolled.

Basics

hello *hola*; hello (when answering the phone) *hola, diga*
good morning, good day *buenos días*; good afternoon, good evening *buenas tardes*; good evening (after dark), good night *buenas noches*
goodbye/see you later *adiós/hasta luego*
please *por favor*; thank you (very much) *(muchas) gracias*
you're welcome *de nada*
do you speak English? *¿habla inglés?*
I don't speak Spanish *no hablo español*
I don't understand *no entiendo*
what's your name? *¿cómo se llama?*
speak more slowly, please *hable más despacio, por favor*
wait a moment *espere un momento*
Sir/Mr *señor (sr)*; Madam/Mrs *señora (sra)*; Miss *señorita (srta)*
excuse me/sorry *perdón*
excuse me, please *oiga* (the standard way to attract someone's attention, politely; literally 'hear me')

OK/fine/(or to a waiter) that's enough *vale*
where is... *¿dónde está...?*
why? *¿porqué?*; when? *¿cuándo?*; who? *¿quién?*; what? *¿qué?*; where? *¿dónde?*; how? *¿cómo?*
who is it? *¿quién es?*
is/are there any... *¿hay...?*
very *muy*; and *y*; or *o*
with *con*; without *sin*
open *abierto*; closed *cerrado*
what time does it open/close? *¿a qué hora abre/cierra?*
pull (on signs) *tirar*; push *empujar*
I would like... *quiero...* (literally, 'I want...'); how many would you like? *¿cuántos quiere?*
I like *me gusta*
I don't like *no me gusta*
good *bueno/a*; bad *malo/a*; well/badly *bien/mal*; small *pequeño/a*; big *gran, grande*; expensive *caro/a*; cheap *barato/a*; hot (food, drink) *caliente*; cold *frío/a*
something *algo*; nothing *nada*
more/less *más/menos*
more or less *más o menos*
the bill/check, please *la cuenta, por favor*
how much is it? *¿cuánto es?*
do you have any change? *¿tiene cambio?*
price *precio*; free *gratis*
discount *descuento*
bank *banco*; to rent *alquilar*; (for) rent, rental *(en) alquiler*; post office *correos*; stamp *sello*; postcard *postal*; toilet *los servicios*

Getting around

airport *aeropuerto*; railway station *estación de ferrocarril/estación de RENFE* (Spanish Railways); Metro station *estación de Metro*
entrance *entrada*; exit *salida*
car *coche*; bus *autobús*; train *tren*
a ticket *un billete*; return *de ida y vuelta*; bus stop *parada de autobús*; the next stop *la próxima parada*
excuse me, do you know the way to...? *¿oiga, señor/señora/etc, sabe como llegar a...?*
left *izquierda*; right *derecha*
here *aquí*; there *allí*
straight on *recto*; to the end of the street *al final de la calle*
as far as *hasta*; towards *hacia*
near *cerca*; far *lejos*

Accommodation

do you have a double/single room for tonight/one week? *¿tiene una habitación doble/para una persona para esta noche/una semana?*
where is the car park? *¿dónde está el parking?*

we have a reservation *tenemos reserva*
an inside/outside room *una habitación interior/exterior*
with/without bathroom *con/sin baño*; shower *ducha*
double bed *cama de matrimonio*; with twin beds *con dos camas*
breakfast included *desayuno incluido*
air-conditioning *aire acondicionado*
lift *ascensor*
swimming pool *piscina*

Time

morning *la mañana*; midday *mediodía*; afternoon/evening *la tarde*; night *la noche*; late night/early morning (roughly 1-6am) *la madrugada*
now *ahora*; later *más tarde*
yesterday *ayer*; today *hoy*; tomorrow *mañana*; tomorrow morning *mañana por la mañana*
early *temprano*; late *tarde*
delay *retraso*; delayed *retrasado*
at what time...? *¿a qué hora...?*
in an hour *en una hora*
the bus will take 2 hours (to get there) *el autobús tardará dos horas (en llegar)*
at 2 *a las dos*
at 8pm *a las ocho de la tarde*
at 1.30 *a la una y media*
at 5.15 *a las cinco y cuarto*
at 22.30 *a veintidós treinta*

Numbers

0 *cero*; 1 *un, uno, una*; 2 *dos*; 3 *tres*; 4 *cuatro*; 5 *cinco*; 6 *seis*; 7 *siete*; 8 *ocho*; 9 *nueve*; 10 *diez*; 11 *once*; 12 *doce*; 13 *trece*; 14 *catorce*; 15 *quince*; 16 *dieciséis*; 17 *diecisiete*; 18 *dieciocho*; 19 *diecinueve*; 20 *veinte*; 21 *veintiuno*; 22 *veintidós*; 30 *treinta*; 40 *cuarenta*; 50 *cincuenta*; 60 *sesenta*; 70 *setenta*; 80 *ochenta*; 90 *noventa*; 100 *cien*; 1,000 *mil*; 1,000,000 *un millón*

Days, months & seasons

Monday *lunes*; Tuesday *martes*; Wednesday *miércoles*; Thursday *jueves*; Friday *viernes*; Saturday *sábado*; Sunday *domingo*
January *enero*; February *febrero*; March *marzo*; April *abril*; May *mayo*; June *junio*; July *julio*; August *agosto*; September *septiembre*; October *octubre*; November *noviembre*; December *diciembre*
spring *primavera*; summer *verano*; autumn/fall *otoño*; winter *invierno*

Directory

Further Reference

Reading

Art & architecture

Hugh Broughton *Madrid*
The capital's architecture analysed for a lay audience.
Jonathan Brown *Velázquez: Painter and Courtier* The most comprehensive study in English.
JH Elliott & Jonathan Brown *A Palace for a King: The Buen Retiro and the Court of Philip IV* A vivid reconstruction of the life, culture and spectacle of the Habsburg Court, and the grandest of Madrid's palaces.
Francisco de Goya *Disasters of War, Disparates, or the Proverbs*; *Los Caprichos* Dover Books publish these good-value and high-quality reproductions of Goya's three most remarkable series of etchings.
Robert Hughes *Goya*
A dynamic biography of Madrid's favourite son.
Michael Jacobs *Madrid Observed*
A lively survey by one of the best current foreign writers on Spain. A good walking companion.
Angus Mitchell *Spain: Interiors, Gardens, Architecture, Landscape*
Lavishly illustrated.

Food & drink

Alan Davidson *Tio Pepe Guide to the Seafood of Spain and Portugal*
An excellent pocket-sized guide, with illustrations, to Spain's fishy delights.
Sam and Sam Clark *Moro*
The best modern cookbook in English for reproducing the tastes of Spain.

History, politics & culture

Phil Ball *Morbo* A fascinating history of Spanish football, with a good section on Real Madrid.
JH Elliott *Imperial Spain, 1469-1716* The standard history.
RA Fletcher *Moorish Spain* Varied account of a little-known period in European history.
Ronald Fraser *Blood of Spain* An oral history of the Spanish Civil War, the most vivid and human account of Spain's great crisis.
Juan Lalaguna *A Traveller's History of Spain* A handy introduction to the country.
Ian Gibson *Fire in the Blood* Idiosyncratic vision of modern Spain by Lorca's biographer.
David Gilmour *Cities of Spain* With an informative, impressionistic chapter on Madrid.

John Hooper *The New Spaniards* The best survey of post-1975 Spain, updated to cover changes in the 1990s.
Paul Preston *Franco; Comrades!; Doves of War* Exhaustive portraits of the key players on both sides of the Spanish Civil War. The same author's *The Spanish Civil War* is a good concise account of the war.
Rob Stone *Spanish Cinema* A fascinating history of Spanish film through the Franco years and beyond.
Hugh Thomas, ed *Madrid, A Traveller's Companion* A great anthology of writing on Madrid from the Middle Ages to the 1930s, by authors as varied as Casanova, Pérez Galdós and the Duke of Wellington.

Literature

Pedro Almodóvar *Patty Diphusa Stories and Other Writings* Frothy, disposable, but full of the sparky, sexy atmosphere of the Madrid of La Movida.
Camilo José Cela *The Hive* Nobel-prizewinner Cela's sardonic masterpiece on Madrid in the aftermath of the Civil War.
Miguel de Cervantes *Don Quixote* The Golden Age classic, and still an entertaining read. Now available in an excellent and lively new translation by Edith Grossman.
Antonio Múñoz Molina *Prince of Shadows* A psychological thriller based on the legacy of the recent past in modern Madrid.
Benito Pérez Galdós *Fortunata and Jacinta* The masterwork of Spain's great 19th-century novelist, a story of love and class of great depth set amid the political conflicts of 1860s Madrid.
Arturo Pérez Reverte *The Fencing Master*, *The Flanders Road*; *The Club Dumas* (also published as *The Dumas Club*) Elegant, unconventional mystery novels by one of the most lauded of current Spanish writers.
Francisco de Quevedo; anon (Penguin edition) *Two Spanish Picaresque Novels* The anonymous *Lazarillo de Tormes* and Quevedo's 1626 *El Buscón* (translated as 'The Swindler'), an earthy masterpiece and an essential Golden Century text.
Benjamin Prado *Not Only Fire* Examination of post-Civil War intergenerational relationships by one of Spain's bright young hopes.

Music

Plácido Domingo *Romanzas de Zarzuelas* One of his several recordings of lush tunes from the *zarzuelas* that have played a big part in the revival of Madrid's own comic operas.

El Gran Lapofsky *Spain is Different* A fantastic selection of Latin, bossa, nu-jazz and funk-infused tracks – some otherwise unavailable rarities – interspersed with skits from Spaniards telling us just why Spain is different.
Ray Heredia *Quien no corre, vuela* One of the most original new-flamenco performers.
Los Jóvenes Flamencos Several CDs in this series, bringing together all the best *nuevo flamenco* artists of the last 15 years, have been issued by the Nuevos Medios label. One at least is available outside Spain with the title *The Young Flamencos*.
El Lebrijano, con la Orquesta Arábigo Andaluza *Casablanca* Fascinating crossover recording by flamenco *cantaor* El Lebrijano, accompanied by Moroccan musicians and using traditional themes from Muslim Andalusia.
Carmen Linares *Antologia* Classic flamenco themes sung by one of the best younger *cantaoras*. Another CD, *Carmen Linares, Cantaora*, may be more widely available outside Spain.
Corazón Loco *40 Joyas del Pop Español* Excellent intro to the perky, occasionally daft and sometimes pretty cool soundtrack of modern Madrid.
Paco de Lucía *Luzia*, or any of the many recordings by the greatest of modern flamenco guitarists.
José Mercé *Del Amanecer* Fine performances by *cantaor* Mercé, with Vicente Amigo on guitar.
Joaquín Sabina *Pongamos que hablo de Madrid* Sabina is a cool and witty *chanteur* of modern Madrid.
Tomatito *Guitarra Gitana* Exceptional Gypsy flamenco guitarist, former accompanist of Camarón.

Madrid online

www.munimadrid.es The Madrid Ayuntamiento's functional website, with some information in English.
www.madrid.org Equivalent site of the Comunidad: practical information on local services, in Spanish only.
www.ctm-madrid.es Madrid transport information.
www.lanetro.com A useful online listings magazine, with concerts, clubs films and reviews.
www.lecool.com Weekly round-up of the city's quirkiest, coolest events.
www.renfe.es Spanish Railways' site, with online booking.
http://madrid.lanetro.com The hippest and best of local Spanish-language events and listings sites, with news on music, clubs, restaurants, films and more in and around Madrid. It's often hard to access, though.

Directory

Index

Advertisers' Index

Area name	**CHAMBERÍ**
Place of interest and/or entertainment	
Park	
River	
Square	
Highway	
Main road	
Pedestrian road	
Teleférico	
Hospital or college	
Church	
Tourist information	
Metro station	

Maps

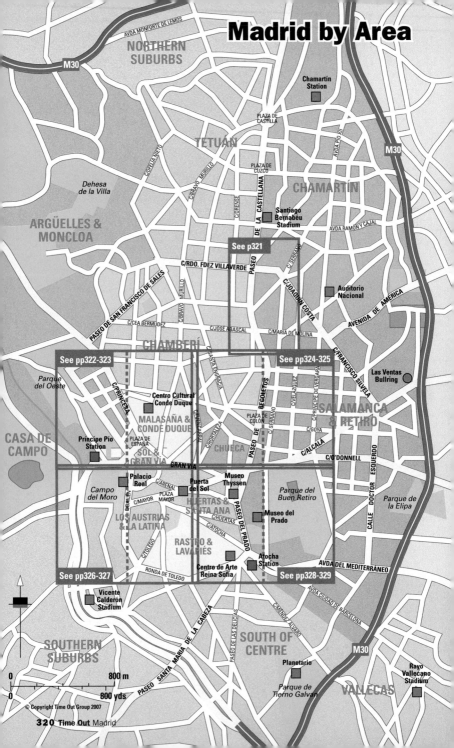

Madrid by Area

AVDA MONFORTE DE LEMOS

M30

NORTHERN SUBURBS

M30

Chamartín Station

PLAZA DE CASTILLA

TETUÁN

PLAZA DE CUZCO

CHAMARTÍN

Dehesa de la Villa

AVDA PIO XII

C/BRAVO MURILLO

CASTELLANA NETO

ORENSE

PASEO DE LA CASTELLANA

Santiago Bernabéu Stadium

ARGÜELLES & MONCLOA

AVDA RAMÓN Y CAJAL

C/RDO. FDEZ VILLAVERDE

See p321

Auditorio Nácional

C/JOAQUIN COSTA

AVENIDA DE AMÉRICA

PASEO DE SAN FRANCISCO DE SALES

C/SERRANO

MURILLO

C/CEA BERMÚDEZ

C/BRAVO

C/JOSÉ ABASCAL

C/MARÍA DE MOLINA

CHAMBERÍ

Las Ventas Bullring

C/FRANCISCO SILVELA

Parque del Oeste

See pp322-323

C/PRINCESA

C/SANTA ENGRACIA

BECQUEROS

C/VELÁZQUEZ

See pp324-325

C/PRINCIPE DE VERGARA

SALAMANCA & RETIRO

Centro Cultural Conde Duque

MALASAÑA & CONDE DUQUE

C/FUENCARRAL

PLAZA DE COLÓN

C/SERRANO

C/GOYA

Príncipe Pío Station

PLAZA DE ESPAÑA

SOL & GRAN VÍA

CHUECA

C/HORTALEZA

PASEO DE RECOLETOS

C/ALCALÁ

C/O'DONNELL

CASA DE CAMPO

GRAN VÍA

Palacio Real

C/ARENAL

Puerta del Sol

Museo Thyssen

Parque del Buen Retiro

CALLE DOCTOR ESQUERDO

Parque de la Elipa

Campo del Moro

C/MAYOR

PLAZA MAYOR

HUERTAS & SANTA ANA

PASEO DEL PRADO

Museo del Prado

LOS AUSTRIAS & LA LATINA

C/HUERTAS

C/ATOCHA

C/TOLEDO

RASTRO & LAVAPIÉS

Atocha Station

AVDA DEL MEDITERRÁNEO

See pp326-327

RONDA DE TOLEDO

Centro de Arte Reina Sofía

See pp328-329

AVDA CIUDAD DE BARCELONA

Vicente Calderón Stadium

PASEO DE LAS DELICIAS

C/ARENE ÁLVARO

M30

SOUTHERN SUBURBS

PASEO SANTA MARÍA DE LA CABEZA

SOUTH OF CENTRE

Planetario

Rayo Vallecano Stadium

0   800 m
0   800 yds

Parque de Tierno Galván

VALLECAS

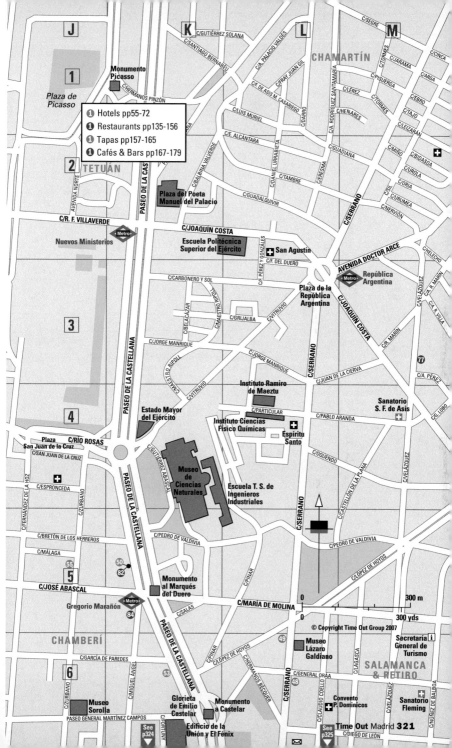

J **K** **L** **M**

1 Monumento Picasso

Plaza de Picasso

❶ Hotels pp55-72
❶ Restaurants pp135-156
❶ Tapas pp157-165
❶ Cafés & Bars pp167-179

C/GUTIÉRREZ SOLANA

C/SANTIAGO BERNABÉU

CHAMARTÍN

C/SEGRE

C/TORMES

C/JARAMA

C/CINCA

C/ARGA

C/PISUERGA

C/LÉREZ

C/EBRO

C/TAJO

C/PALACIO VALDÉS

C/A. RODRÍGUEZ SANTAMARÍA

C/HERMANOS PINZÓN

C/FRAY JUAN GIL

C/F. DE ASIS M. CASARIEGO

C/DARRO

C/HENARES

C/LEIZARÁN

C/MIÑO

C/BIDASOA

C/ORIA

C/URUMEA

C/NERVIÓN

C/LUIS MURIEL

C/E. ALCÁNTARA

C/MANUEL URIBARRIA

C/GUADIANA

C/TAMBRE

C/CERESIA

C/NIL

C/SIL

2 TETUÁN

C/ALBINA VALVERDE

PASEO DE LA CAS

Plaza del Poeta Manuel del Palacio

C/GUADALQUIVIR

C/SERRANO

C/R. F. VILLAVERDE

C/JOAQUÍN COSTA

Metro

Nuevos Ministerios

Escuela Politécnica Superior del Ejército

C/PÉREZ Y GONZÁLEZ

San Agustín

C/F. DEL DUERO

AVENIDA DOCTOR ARCE

C/HELECHO

C/CARBONERO Y SOL

Metro República Argentina

C/VELÁZQUEZ

C/A. R. MARÍN

C/A. VILLA

Plaza de la República Argentina

3

C/BELLIZAR

C/MAESTRO RIPOLL

C/GRIJALBA

C/VITRUVIO

C/JORGE MANRIQUE

C/JOAQUÍN COSTA

C/JORGE MANRIQUE

C/SERRANO

C/R. MARÍN

PASEO DE LA CASTELLANA

C/MAESTRO RIPOLL

C/VITRUVIO

Instituto Ramiro de Maeztu

C/JUAN DE LA CIERVA

C/A. PÉREZ

77

4 Estado Mayor del Ejército

C/PARTICULAR

Sanatorio S. F. de Asis

C/G. LOBO

Instituto Ciencias Físico Químicas

C/PABLO ARANDA

Espíritu Santo

Plaza San Juan de la Cruz

C/RÍO ROSAS

C/SAN JUAN DE LA CRUZ

Museo de Ciencias Naturales

C/OQUENDO

C/VELÁZQUEZ

C/FERNÁNDEZ DE LA HOZ

C/ESPRONCEDA

C/ZURBANO

Escuela T. S. de Ingenieros Industriales

C/SERRANO

C/CASTELLÓN DE LA PLANA

C/BRETÓN DE LOS HERREROS

C/PEDRO DE VALDIVIA

C/PEDRO DE VALDIVIA

C/MÁLAGA

55

50

82

5 C/JOSÉ ABASCAL

Monumento al Marqués del Duero

C/PINAR

C/MARÍA DE MOLINA

C/LÓPEZ DE HOYOS

0   300 m

Metro

Gregorio Marañón

84

C/SALAS

0   300 yds

© Copyright Time Out Group 2007

CHAMBERÍ

C/GARCÍA DE PAREDES

49

Museo Lázaro Galdiano

Secretaría **i** General de Turismo

C/LAGASCA

SALAMANCA & RETIRO

6

C/ZURBANO

Museo Sorolla

53

C/LÓPEZ DE HOYOS

C/HERMANOS BÉCQUER

C/GENERAL ORÁA

48

C/SERRANO

C/CLAUDIO COELLO

C/GENERAL ORÁA

Convento P. Dominicos

C/VELÁZQUEZ

Sanatorio Fleming

C/NÚÑEZ DE BALBOA

Glorieta de Emilio Castelar

Monumento a Castelar

PASEO GENERAL MARTÍNEZ CAMPOS

C/MIGUEL ÁNGEL

Edificio de la Unión y El Fénix

See p324

See p325

Time Out Madrid **321**

C/DIEGO DE LEÓN

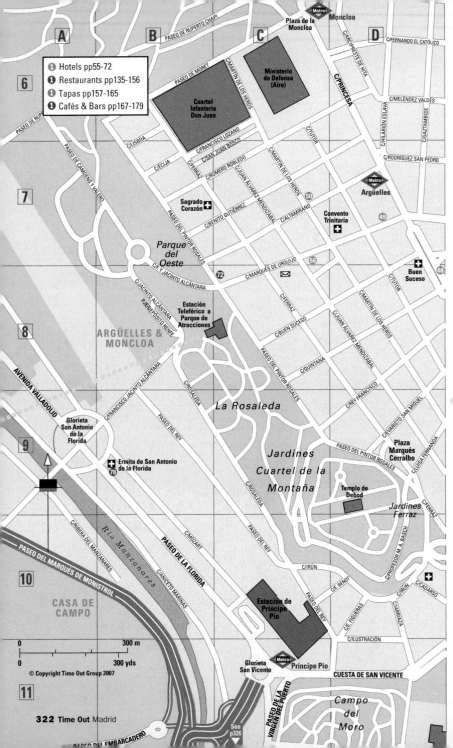

- **A**
- **B**
- **C**
- **D**

6
7
8
9
10
11

❶ Hotels pp55-72
❶ Restaurants pp135-156
❶ Tapas pp157-165
❶ Cafés & Bars pp167-179

Plaza de la Moncloa
Moncloa
Metro

C/FERNANDO EL CATÓLICO
C/MELÉNDEZ VALDÉS
C/HILARIÓN ESLAVA
C/GAZTAMBIDE
C/RODRÍGUEZ SAN PEDRO

PASEO DE RUPERTO CHAPÍ
PASEO DE MORET
C/MARTÍN DE LOS HEROS
C/ARCIPRESTE DE HITA
C/PRINCESA

PASEO DE MORET

Ministerio de Defensa (Aire)

Cuartel Infantería Don Juan

C/LISBOA
C/FRANCISCO LOZANO
C/TUTOR

C/ÉCIJA
C/FERRAZ
C/SAN JUAN BOSCO
C/ROMERO ROBLEDO
C/JUAN ÁLVAREZ MENDIZÁBAL
50
Metro
Argüelles

PASEO DE RUP

PASEO DE CAMOENS Y VALERO

Sagrado Corazón ✚

C/BENITO GUTIÉRREZ
C/ALTAMIRANO
Convento Trinitaria ✚
49

Parque del Oeste

PASEO DEL PINTOR ROSALES

C/F. Y JACINTO ALCÁNTARA
C/MARQUÉS DE URQUIJO
72
56
C/FERRAZ
✉
Buen Suceso ✚
48
C/TUTOR

C/JACINTO ALCÁNTARA
P. HEREDÍA FERRE
C/JACINTO ALCÁNTARA

Estación Teleférico a Parque de Atracciones

C/BUEN SUCESO
C/JUAN ÁLVAREZ MENDIZÁBAL
C/MARTÍN DE LOS HEROS

ARGÜELLES & MONCLOA

C/ROSALEDA

PASEO DEL PINTOR ROSALES

C/QUINTANA
C/REY FRANCISCO
C/EVARISTO SAN MIGUEL

AVENIDA VALLADOLID

C/FRANCISCO JACINTO ALCÁNTARA
PASEO DEL REY

La Rosaleda

Plaza Marqués Cerralbo
C/LUISA FERNANDA

Glorieta San Antonio de la Florida

Ermita de San Antonio de la Florida
78

Jardines Cuartel de la Montaña

Templo de Debod
Jardines Ferraz
C/FERRAZ
C/PROFESOR M. A. BASCH

C/ROSALEDA

C/MOZART
PASEO DEL REY

Río Manzanares
PASEO DE LA FLORIDA

C/RIBERA DEL MANZANARES
C/ANICETO MARINAS
C/IRÚN
C/E. BENOT
C/E. FIGUERAS
✚
C/IRÚN
C/CADARSO

PASEO DEL MARQUÉS DE MONISTROL

CASA DE CAMPO

Estación de Príncipe Pío
C/ARRIAZA
C/ILUSTRACIÓN

| 0 | | 300 m |
| 0 | | 300 yds |

© Copyright Time Out Group 2007

Glorieta San Vicente
Metro
Príncipe Pío
CUESTA DE SAN VICENTE

PASEO DE LA VIRGEN DEL PUERTO

Campo del Moro

PASEO DEL EMBARCADERO

See p326

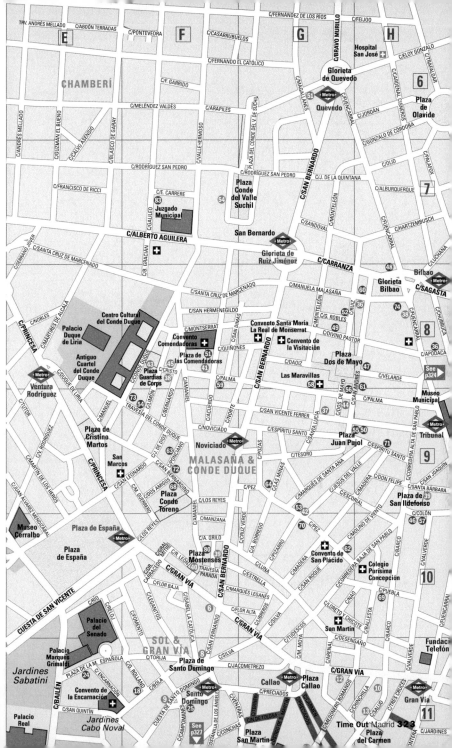

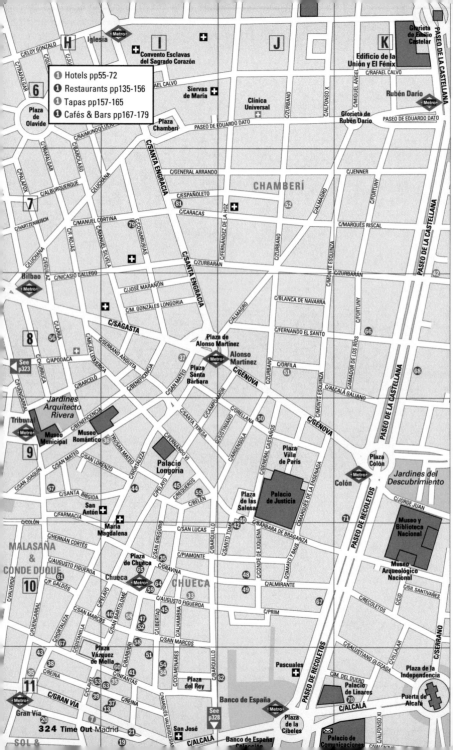

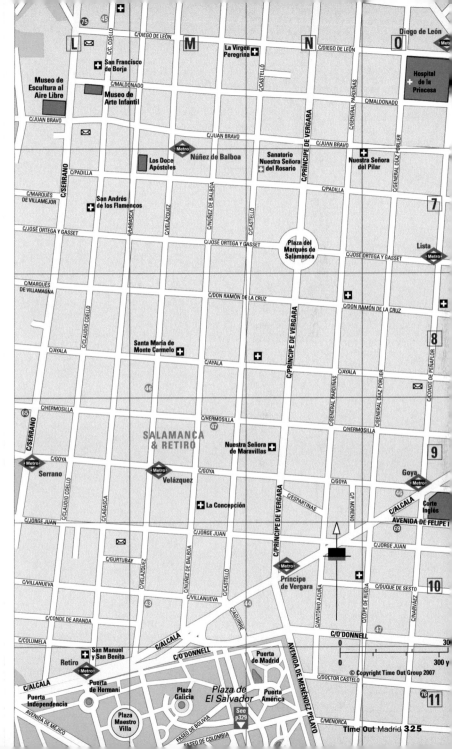

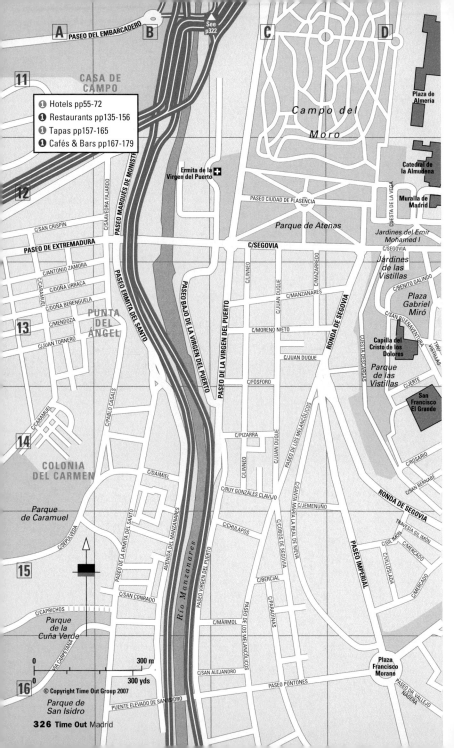

A PASEO DEL EMBARCADERO B

See p322

C

D

11 CASA DE CAMPO

Plaza de Almeria

Campo del Moro

12

Ermita de la Virgen del Puerto ✚

Catedral de la Almudena

PASEO CIUDAD DE PLASENCIA

Muralla de Madrid

Parque de Atenas

Jardines del Emir Mohamed I

C/SEGOVIA

PASEO DE EXTREMADURA

C/SEGOVIA

Jardines de las Vistillas

C/SAN CRISPÍN

C/SAAVEDRA FAJARDO

C/ANTONIO ZAMORA

PASEO MARQUÉS DE MONISTROL

C/LINNEO

C/MAZARREDO

C/BENITO GALINDO

C/CARAMUEL

C/DOÑA URRACA

C/JUAN DUQUE

C/MANZANARES

Plaza Gabriel Miró

C/DOÑA BERENGUELA

PASEO ERMITA DEL SANTO

PASEO BAJO DE LA VIRGEN DEL PUERTO

C/SAN BUENAVENTURA

13 PUNTA DEL ÁNGEL

C/MENDOZA

C/MORENO NIETO

Capilla del Cristo de los Dolores

C/JUAN TORNERO

PASEO DE LA VIRGEN DEL PUERTO

RONDA DE SEGOVIA

CUESTA DESCARGAS

Parque de las Vistillas

C/JUAN DUQUE

C/JERTE

C/FÓSFORO

C/PABLO CASALS

San Francisco El Grande

14 COLONIA DEL CARMEN

C/CARAMUEL

C/PIZARRA

PASEO DE LOS MELANCÓLICOS

C/ROSARIO

C/LINNEO

C/JUAN DUQUE

C/SAN BERNABE

C/DAIMIEL

C/RUY GONZÁLES CLAVIJO

RONDA DE SEGOVIA

Parque de Caramuel

PASEO DE LA ERMITA DEL SANTO

C/SANTA MARÍA LA REAL DE NIEVA

C/JEMENUÑO

TRAVESIA GIL IMÓN

C/CHULAPOS

C/GIL IMÓN

C/MERCADO

AVENIDA DEL MANZANARES

PASEO IMPERIAL

15

C/SEPULVEDA

C/COBOS DE SEGOVIA

C/MERCADO

C/VILLOSLADA

Río Manzanares

PASEO VIRGEN DEL PUERTO

C/BERCIAL

C/SAN CONRADO

C/PARADINAS

C/CAPRICHOS

Parque de la Cuña Verde

C/MÁRMOL

PASEO DE LOS MELANCÓLICOS

0   300 m

VIA CARPETANA

0   300 yds

16 © Copyright Time Out Group 2007

C/SAN ALEJANDRO

Plaza Francisco Morano

PASEO PONTONES

PASEO DR VALLEJO NAGERA

Parque de San Isidro

PUENTE ELEVADO DE SAN ISIDRO

Key box:

❶ Hotels pp55-72
❶ Restaurants pp135-156
❶ Tapas pp157-165
❶ Cafés & Bars pp167-179

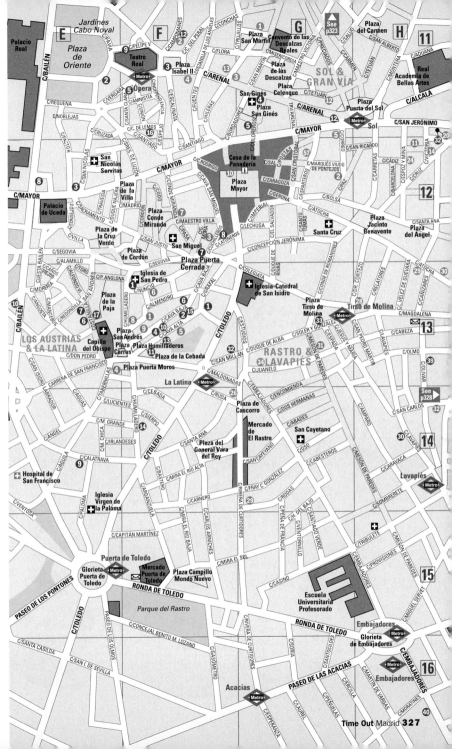

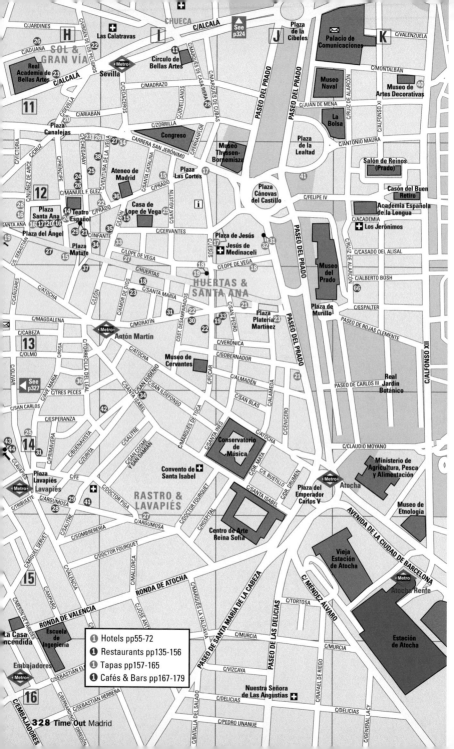

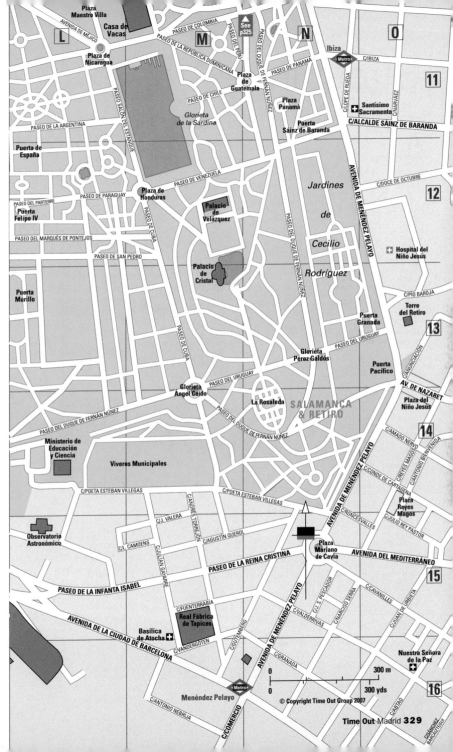

Street Index

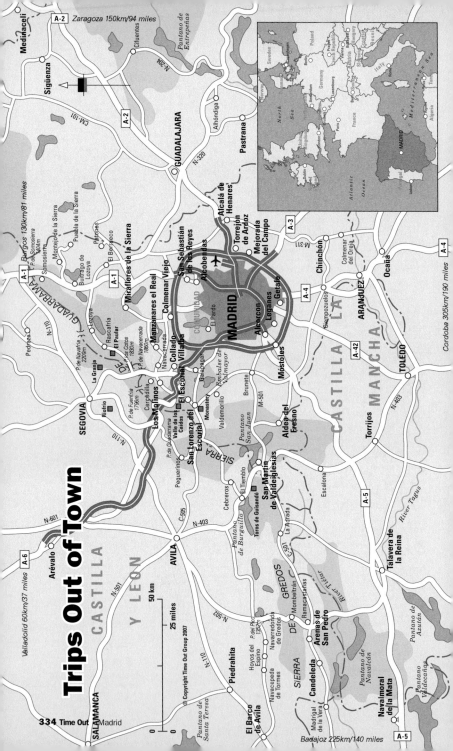

Trips Out of Town

renfe
Cercanías ⊙

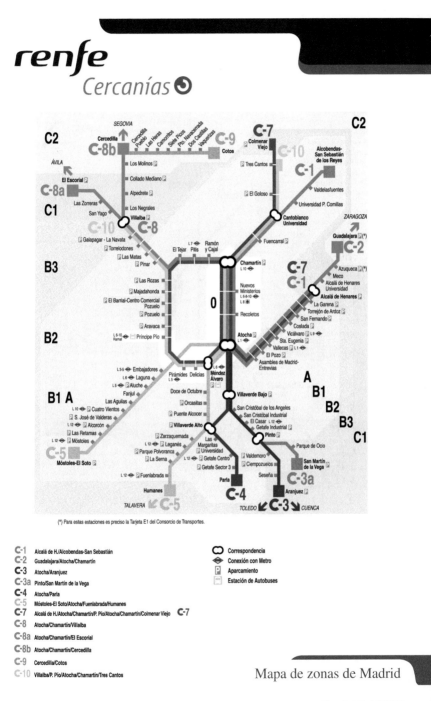

(*) Para estas estaciones es preciso la Tarjeta E1 del Consorcio de Transportes.

C-1 Alcalá de H./Alcobendas-San Sebastián	⬭ Correspondencia
C-2 Guadalajara/Atocha/Chamartín	◆ Conexión con Metro
C-3 Atocha/Aranjuez	P Aparcamiento
C-3a Pinto/San Martín de la Vega	Estación de Autobuses
C-4 Atocha/Parla	
C-5 Móstoles-El Soto/Atocha/Fuenlabrada/Humanes	
C-7 Alcalá de H./Atocha/Chamartín/P. Pío/Atocha/Chamartín/Colmenar Viejo **C-7**	
C-8 Atocha/Chamartín/Villalba	
C-8a Atocha/Chamartín/El Escorial	
C-8b Atocha/Chamartín/Cercedilla	
C-9 Cercedilla/Cotos	
C-10 Villalba/P. Pío/Atocha/Chamartín/Tres Cantos	

Mapa de zonas de Madrid

simbología

- ✚ Estación con horario restringido
- ◯ Transbordo corto entre líneas de Metro
- ⬭ Transbordo largo entre líneas de Metro
- ⓘ Cambio de tren
- ◉ Estación Cercanías-Renfe
- ▣ Estación de ferrocarril de largo recorrido
- ▦ Terminal de autobús interurbano
- ✈ Aeropuerto Madrid-Barajas
- Ⓟ Aparcamiento de disuasión gratuito
- Ⓟ Aparcamiento de disuasión de pago
- ⓘ Centro atención al Cliente
- ▣ Estación con acceso para personas con movilidad reducida / ascensor

B1 B2 B3
Cambio tarifario

◀ Metro ▶

madrid

Ｍ M
La suma de todos

Comunidad de Madrid

líneas de Metro

- **1** Plaza de Castilla / Congosto
- **2** Ventas / Cuatro Caminos
- **3** Legazpi / Moncloa
- **4** Argüelles / Parque de Santa María
- **5** Alameda de Osuna / Casa de Campo
- **6** Circular
- **7** Las Musas / Pitis
- **8** Nuevos Ministerios / Barajas
- **9** Herrera Oria / Arganda del Rey
- **10** Fuencarral / Puerta del Sur
- **11** Plaza Elíptica / La Peseta
- **12** MetroSur
- **R** Ópera / Príncipe Pío

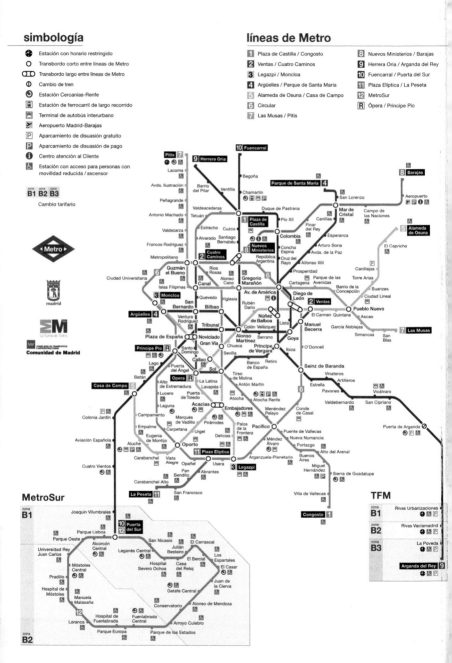

MetroSur

TFM